LON
RES

y to destroy it, an

tto forth in t

forth in t

nating

# THE LONDON DAILY PRESS
## 1772–1792

# The London Daily Press
# 1772–1792

*by*

Lucyle (Thomas) Werkmeister

UNIVERSITY OF NEBRASKA PRESS • LINCOLN

The publication of this book was assisted by a grant from the Ford Foundation.

*To*
*the memory of*
*Reuben Palmer Thomas*
*my father*

# PREFACE

THE PRESENT book has come about by accident, for my interest is Coleridge, not the newspapers per se. But the 1809–1810 *Friend,* of which I am preparing an edition, owes so much to Coleridge's intimacy with the London newspapers and to his association with one of the newspaper titans of his day, Daniel Stuart, that I felt I should take a look at the newspapers before I completed the edition. This feeling was strengthened by the discovery that Stuart first tried to block the appearance of the *Friend,* that he then insisted upon subsidizing it himself, and that, as soon as he was satisfied that the work was, from his point of view, innocuous, he withdrew the subsidy and lost interest in the project. There could, I thought, be only two possible explanations for his behavior: either he was afraid of what the *Friend* would say about himself, or he was afraid of what it would say about a political faction which he represented. In either event I should find the explanation, if I found it at all, not in the *Friend,* but in one of Stuart's newspapers, the *Morning Post* or the *Courier.* With the assistance of a grant-in-aid from the American Philosophical Society, I therefore journeyed to London for the purpose of reading the newspapers. The only newspapers I intended to read were the *Morning Post* and the *Courier,* and I intended to begin my reading with the year 1790, taking a quick glance at the earlier numbers of the *Morning Post* first, in order to familiarize myself with the background. But it was soon evident that a quick glance would not suffice, as it was also evident that I could not restrict my reading to the *Post.* For, just as an eighteenth-century newspaper did not exist in fragments, but as a continuous and developing entity with past, present, and future, so it did not exist in isolation. It was, in a very real sense, a member of a society of newspapers, by each of which it was influenced and each of which it influenced in return. Hence I revised my plans to include the reading of all the newspapers in the Burney collection of the British Museum from the year 1772 on. Although I still thought of the reading as a preliminary chore, I speedily became convinced that it was important in itself: that the founding of the *Morning Post* was, in fact, one of the most significant events in the history of journalism. The studies which follow are the result. More properly, they are the first result, for on some future occasion I shall add to them, extending the survey through the year 1812.

So far as the material is concerned, I can say without much qualification that all I know is what I read in the newspapers. For, although I have attempted to come to terms with histories, memoirs, and extra-newspaper records of various sorts, I have relied insofar as possible on the newspapers themselves and have used the records only to augment or clarify what I have found there. Since my principal interest throughout has been the newspapers, I have been interested in politics only incidentally; but, during the years of the Pitt Administration, the history of newspapers and the history of politics were inseparable, and I have therefore tried to present them as a complex. I do not doubt that political historians and scholars will find my interpretations inadequate in some respects and shocking in others. To them I can only extend my apologies and say by way of extenuation that I have taken my history from the newspapers: the issues with which I am concerned are the issues with which they were concerned, and the interpretations I have presented are, I think, demanded by all the newspaper evidence. My most abject apologies go to the Burke scholars, for them, I fear, I have most grievously offended. My only hope is that they will make the distinction which I have myself made between Burke as a politician and Burke as a political philosopher.

I can promise no new material; or rather the material here presented is new only in the sense that it has previously been buried in the newspapers. To reduce the number of footnotes, I have indicated newspaper sources parenthetically in the text, adhering otherwise to standard practices. For permissions to quote, I am gratefully indebted to Ernest Benn Ltd., successor to Home & Van Thal, publisher of Arthur Aspinall's *Politics and the Press c. 1780–1850* (London, 1949); to Routledge & Kegan Paul Ltd., publisher of Wilfrid Hindle's *The Morning Post 1772–1937: Portrait of a Newspaper* (London, 1937); to Hutchinson & Co., publishers of *The Farington Diary by Joseph Farington, R.A.* (London, 1922); to the Clarendon Press, Oxford, publisher of *The Letters of Robert Burns*, edited by J. De Lancey Ferguson (Oxford, 1931), and James L. Clifford's *Hester Lynch Piozzi* (Oxford, 1941); to the Southern Illinois University Press, publisher of Robert L. Haig's *The Gazetteer 1735–1797* (Carbondale, 1960); and to Yale University and the McGraw-Hill Book Company Inc., holders of the copyright of the *Private Papers of James Boswell from Malahide Castle*, edited by Geoffrey Scott and Frederick Pottle (Mount Vernon, 1928–1934).

For various acts of kindness, I am with equal gratitude indebted to Professor Robert Rea, to Professor Peter Stanlis, to Professor James Clifford, to Professor Earl Leslie Griggs, to the reference staff of Doheny Library of the University of Southern California, to the whole staff of the Henry E. Huntington Library, and in particular to the staff of Section III of the British Museum, without whom the research would not have been possible. Among my major creditors, I must also reckon the American Philosophical Society, which financed the research; Arthur Hudd, Esq., of the British Museum and Arthur Mabbs, Esq., of the Public Records Office, who have guided me through the labyrinths; Miss Amé Parr, who is responsible for the jacket and for the solution of most of my problems; Dr. David Erdman, who, as editor of a forthcoming edition of Coleridge's newspaper essays and therefore an authority on late eighteenth-century newspapers, has been my counselor throughout and has even performed the ultimate service of reading the manuscript; and Professor Paul Zall, whose "knowledge, interest, and articulateness," as well as, I should add, rashness, inasmuch as he has offered to read the galley proof, have been a constant encouragement. Finally, I am indebted to my beloved husband in ways which I cannot adequately express and for the kinds of help which only he could give and which he was himself perhaps unaware of giving.

# CONTENTS

ix

# INTRODUCTION

THE FIRST London daily newspaper made its appearance in 1702. It was entitled the *Daily Courant,* and it consisted of a prospectus and some short paragraphs translated from Continental journals, the whole occupying two columns, one page folio, and selling for 1*d.* The prospectus promised that

[the author] will not, under pretence of having private intelligence, impose any additions of feigned circumstances to an action, but give his extracts fairly and impartially[;] at the beginning of each article he will quote the foreign paper from whence 'tis taken, that the public, seeing from what country a piece of news comes with the allowance of that government, may be better able to judge the credibility and fairness of the relation. Nor will he take upon him to give any comments or conjectures of his own, but will relate only matter of fact, supposing other people to have sense enough to make reflections for themselves.

The *Courant* evidently prospered, for on 22 April it supplemented its translations with some domestic "matter of fact" and a handful of advertisements, which, printed on the reverse side of the sheet, swelled the number of pages to two; and a few years later its sale was estimated at 800 a day. The *Courant* maintained its independence for approximately twelve years.

In 1712 Parliament smuggled into legislation the first of many Stamp Acts. The act stipulated that every newspaper printed on a half-sheet or less would henceforth be taxed ½*d.,* every newspaper printed on a whole sheet 1*d.,* and every newspaper printed on more than one sheet 2*s.* a sheet; in addition it stipulated that every advertisement accepted for publication would henceforth be taxed 1*s.* The effect of this act was to destroy the independent press. The *Courant* capitulated to the Whigs, and, for the next many years, the history of newspapers is only another chronicle of political corruption. The corruption in turn had another effect, which was to overpopulate the country with newspapers. In 1712 the reading public was obviously too small to support more than one daily newspaper, but in 1719 the Tories added a second, the *Daily Post,* and by 1724 they had added a third, the *Daily Journal.* Since the Tories were subsidizing the *Post* and the *Journal* in their entirety, as the Whigs were subsidizing the *Courant,* the three newspapers fared very well until the 1730's, when

1

the subsidies seem to have been abandoned in favor of payments for special services. The *Daily Journal* at once ceased publication; and the other two newspapers, compelled to shift at least in part for themselves, were also in trouble. For, although the number of readers had increased, the increase had not kept pace with the increase in the number of newspapers. With the resignation of the Walpole Ministry in 1742, the situation worsened; even the occasional payments were curtailed. At this point London would have lost a second daily newspaper had it not been for the ingenuity of Matthew Jenour, founder of the *Daily Advertiser*.

Jenour had begun his *Daily Advertiser* in 1730 in the faith that readers would regard advertisements as interesting in themselves and that, by concentrating on long advertisements, he could pay his shilling-an-item tax and still make money. His faith was more than justified. At first the paper consisted of nothing but advertisements and was given away to anyone who wanted it. But it was soon evident that readers were willing to pay for it, and the policy was accordingly revised, a small amount of non-advertising material being added and the paper being sold at the same price as the other daily newspapers. The age of the *Advertisers* had begun. In 1734 there was a second advertiser: the *London Daily Post and General Advertiser,* which in 1744 became the *General Advertiser* and in 1752 the *Public Advertiser.* And in 1735 there was a third, the old *Daily Courant* having become the *Gazetteer and London Daily Advertiser.* Thereafter all daily newspapers were *Advertisers.*

The age of the *Advertisers* lasted until 1772. In 1757 Parliament increased the newspaper tax to 1*d.* for every half-sheet and the advertisement duty to 2*s.;* and the price of newspapers was accordingly increased to 2½*d.,* but there were no casualties. The newspapers even benefited, for, now that the tax for the full sheet was the same as the tax for the half-sheet, the number of pages was increased to four, and in the 1760's the length was further extended by substituting a four-column page for the three-column page, which had been standard since the 1720's. The desideratum was to fill at least three of these pages (pages 1, 2, and 4) with advertisements, and, although the desideratum was rarely realized by any newspaper except the *Daily Advertiser,* it was evidently easy enough to fill two. Moreover, two pages seem to have been adequate; for in 1760 a fourth daily newspaper, the *Public Ledger, or The Daily Register of Commerce and*

*Intelligence,* later renamed the *Public Ledger and Commercial and General Advertiser,* made its appearance, and in 1769 a fifth, the *Morning Chronicle and London Advertiser.* Both papers survived. It would be naive to suppose that, with the possible exception of the *Daily Advertiser,* any one of these newspapers was completely self-sufficient, but the daily press did achieve a degree of political independence it had not known since the early days of the *Courant.* Moreover, it was developing a sense of responsibility. Like the *Courant,* it was convinced that readers wanted and were entitled to the facts, and it was going to considerable trouble and expense to procure them. Although Parliament must have viewed these developments with alarm, it took no real action until the newspapers became involved in its quarrel with the City of London.

The details of the quarrel, which was exceedingly complicated, need not be recited here. To put it in very general terms, the quarrel began in 1763, when Parliament indicted one of its members, John Wilkes, for publishing "a most infamous and seditious" libel on the King and his ministers in No. 45 of the *North Briton,* following the indictment with an order for arrest and an expulsion. The question from the outset was one of Parliamentary privilege, for it was argued by Wilkes and at least one of the courts that Parliament had no right to order the arrest of one of its members. Wilkes solved the problem temporarily by retiring to France in 1764, but the case was reopened upon his return in 1768. The fact that he was thereafter imprisoned for twenty-two months would seem to have settled the matter, but it did nothing of the sort. A number of newspapers, including the *Public Advertiser* and the *Gazetteer* rose to the defense of "Wilkes and Liberty" and in 1769 were indicted ex officio for publishing Junius' famous letter to the King. More important, Wilkes, now an alderman for the City of London, had enlisted the reckless support of another alderman, Richard Oliver, and the Lord Mayor, Brass Crosby; and, since both of them happened also to be Members of Parliament, the ground was laid to test the issue as an issue.

The issue was still Parliament's right to imprison a Member; but Parliament also claimed the right to suppress publication of its debates. In early 1771 there was accordingly a rash of such publications, followed, of course, by a rash of summonses; and, when the printers failed to appear, the summonses were in turn followed by orders for arrest. Oliver and Crosby refused to respect the orders and, when they were called to account by the Commons, refused to explain their behavior. They were immediately consigned to the Tower, and, since the courts subsequently upheld the Commons' action, the result was a triumph for Parliament. The printers had figured in the plot only incidentally, for Parliament's right to suppress publication of its debates had never been questioned, and the right had certainly not been yielded. But it seemed to the people that this was the only matter in dispute, that the printers were the heroes, and that, by submitting to imprisonment, Oliver and Crosby had somehow established the justice of their cause. As it turned out, there was something to be said for this interpretation, for, rather than risk another battle with the City, Parliament delayed further action until it was too late, accounts of the debates being by then the very heart of every newspaper. All it could do thereafter was to hold the press responsible for the contents of the debates. Although the speaker was himself protected by Parliamentary immunity, the newspaper which printed the speech was henceforth subject to prosecution if the speech contained anything of a libelous nature, the argument being that newspapers had no right to print the debates in the first place.

Every newspaper liked to boast that it had a sale of 4,000 or even 5,000 a day. But figures were outrageously exaggerated for the purpose of attracting advertisers, and, even when they were not exaggerated, they were misleading. Wilkes and his friends, for example, must have lavished huge sums on the press, and thousands of copies of the *Public Advertiser,* the *Morning Chronicle,* and the *Gazetteer* were undoubtedly purchased by the City of London for free distribution among its citizens. Sales to individuals would have ranged from perhaps 800 to perhaps 3,000, the *Daily Advertiser* selling somewhat more. Meanwhile the increase in the size of the newspaper, added to the new emphasis on "original intelligence," had resulted in a sharp increase in the cost of production. The fact remains that there had also been a substantial increase in the number of readers and the number of advertisers; and, now that newspapers could publish the debates with a fair degree of impunity, it looked as if a truly independent press might be in the offing. But in the offing was instead the *Morning Post:* by the end of 1772, the age of the *Advertisers* had been succeeded by the age of the scandal sheet, which lasted twenty years and was characterized by such unprecedented corruption that during these two decades the number of daily newspapers increased from five to as many as fifteen.

Although the term *Advertiser* was usually not employed by newspapers commenced after 1780 and was dropped by the *Morning Herald* as early as 1786, it persisted in the titles or subtitles of some newspapers beyond 1792; and all newspapers retained the *Advertiser* format, as, one suspects, the last vestige of respectability. The *Morning Post,* which itself carried an *Advertiser* subtitle until 1792, was founded strictly in the *Advertiser* tradition. It differed from its predecessors in only one respect: whereas they had always assumed that readers wanted to be informed, the *Morning Post* assumed from the outset that they wanted to be entertained. The *Post* therefore extended the scope of its "intelligence" to include everything which might amuse people of fashion, and it presented the material in a way which was itself amusing. Unfortunately a great deal of the material consisted of "anecdotes" and "personalities," that is, gossip and abuse, and, although the conductor, the Rev. Henry Bate (Dudley), was a man of multiple parts, he was nevertheless an adventurer. The *Post* was an extraordinary success, but it had no immediate influence upon the other newspapers, partly because it was circulated chiefly in London's fashionable West End and they were circulated in the City, partly because newspapermen thoroughly disapproved of the Rev. Henry Bate and the kind of journalism he represented, and partly because no one thought the paper could last. But, when, in July, 1773, the *Morning Chronicle* and the *Gazetteer* attempted to hasten its demise by publishing an exposé of Bate's most recent fracas, the *Post* so benefited from the publicity that thereafter it published the exposés itself.

The first newspaper to succumb to the influence of the *Post* was the *Public Ledger,* which in 1775 launched a series of vicious attacks on the actor and playwright Samuel Foote; but, although the influence on the other newspapers was delayed, it was nevertheless inevitable. At the end of 1776, the *Post* became involved in a noisy battle with a spurious *Post,* and, when this battle was over, no one could doubt that the *Post* was a permanent member of the newspaper community. Moreover, since every newspaperman detested forgeries above all things, the Rev. Henry Bate even emerged as a hero. Meanwhile in July, 1776, the newspaper tax was increased from 1*d.* to 1½*d.*, so that the price of newspapers had to be advanced to 3d.; and in November a seventh newspaper was commenced, which, calling itself the *General Advertiser*, at once took its place with the City newspapers, thus increasing competition in that area. Only the *Morning Post* was uninjured by these developments. In 1780 there was more trouble for the old *Advertisers*. This time the advertisement duty was increased from 2s. to 2s.6d., and the City newspapers had two additional newspapers to contend with, the *London Courant*, which had joined their ranks in November, 1779, and the *Noon Gazette*, which was in existence by at least early 1781. While all these newspapers were fighting for their lives, the Rev. Henry Bate performed the incredible feat of setting up a second West End newspaper, the *Morning Herald*, which was modeled on the *Morning Post* and yet soon outdistanced the *Post* and every other newspaper as well. At this point the last resistance to Bate's kind of journalism collapsed.

Although all newspapers were influenced by the *Morning Post*, some of them were more influenced than others. The *Daily Advertiser*, for example, was influenced only slightly; the *Gazetteer* and the *Morning Chronicle* were influenced considerably, and newspapers coming into existence after 1781 tended to be only so many more *Morning Posts*. On the positive side, the influence consisted of a widening in scope of interest to include sports, sciences, travel, fashions, the humanities, and the arts, with special emphasis on literature. Particular attention was paid to poetry. Even the *Daily Advertiser* felt obliged to print an occasional poem, and many newspapers added poets to their regular staffs. There was also an increased concern for style and appearance. The manner of presentation became much more literary, and newspaper boasts of new types became a commonplace. This tendency toward general elegance reached its culmination in 1787 with the founding of "The Paper of Poetry," the very elegant *World*. On the negative side, the influence consisted of a preoccupation with "personalities" and "anecdotes."

The fact that very few ledgers of eighteenth-century newspapers have survived is not as regrettable as it might appear. For, since ledgers were subject to periodic inspections by the Stamp Office, were liable to subpoenas by the courts, and could be used by an unscrupulous employee for purposes of blackmail, a clerk recorded only the legitimate transactions, and even these were in many instances falsified so that the ledgers could be shown to the public. As to the multitude of extra-legitimate transactions, the clerk himself probably knew no more than he could surmise from reading the newspaper. When precisely the "personalities" and "anecdotes" ceased to be simply amusement is therefore conjectural, but it would appear that the *Morning Post* was selling puffs as early as 1772 and that by 1780 there was hardly a "paragraph" in the newspaper that was not paid for by someone. The amount of money the *Post* was realizing on these "paragraphs" is perhaps indicated by the disparity between the £350 at which a share in the *Post* was "valued" and the "near 800*l*." which was required to buy it. By 1785 the practice of selling "paragraphs" had been adopted by other newspapers, and such terms as "puffs," "suppression fees," "insertion fees," and "contradiction fees" had become part of the journalistic language. Since the "paragraphs" were charged for at advertising rates or multiples of advertising rates, the newspapers obviously classified them as advertisements; but, since they did not look like advertisements and no record was kept of the payment, the Stamp Office was never able to collect the advertising duty. Although the Treasury was thereby deprived of a considerable revenue, no one was unhappy, for, in the case of one of its own newspapers, the Government was willing to overlook the evasions, and, in the case of an Opposition newspaper, it was easy enough to plant the evidence of evasion and thereby devise some "trouble at the Stamp Office," which invariably resulted in the elimination of a trouble-maker.

The subjects of the "anecdotes" and "personalities" were people of wealth or prominence. Usually, although not invariably, the subject had something to hide, for which reason one of the favorite subjects after December, 1785, was the Prince of Wales, who had added to his other follies by secretly marrying the Roman Catholic Mrs. Fitzherbert. Until 1788 the subjects were usually alive, but by 1789 they tended to be dead, the practice of abusing the recently deceased having proved particularly remunerative. This practice was temporarily halted when some relations sued the *World* for repeated libels on the memory of the third Earl Cowper; but it was resumed in 1791, when the Court ruled that the laws of libel were not applicable to the dead. The abuse of people connected with the theaters was especially rampant, not only because the managers were willing to pay for silence if the abuse was continued long enough, but because politics and the theaters were inseparable, and by 1788 every newspaper was in the pay of one political faction or another. There was still a good deal of talk about

Liberty of the Press, but the term had been redefined to mean a newspaper's freedom to decide which faction's money it would accept.

Political control of the press varied in kind and degree. On the mildest level a political party or individual politician paid for the insertion of "paragraphs" piecemeal, in which case there was nothing to prevent the newspaper from printing contradictory "paragraphs," although very few newspapers did. Or a political party purchased the newspaper's support on an annual basis, paying a flat subsidy in quarterly installments. Or it leased the political department outright, staffing it with its own writers. Or it leased the entire newspaper. Or it bought into the newspaper through an agent or even set up a newspaper of its own. The Pitt Government exercised control on every level, but control on all but the final level was well established before the Pitt Government came into power.

In 1772 the King of England was George III, and the Government was in the hands of the Tories, Lord North being First Minister. The issue was reform, and the Government had, it is evident from Treasury records, engaged a number of pamphleteers and "paragraph writers" to defend it against the attacks of the Wilkes faction. Since the old *Advertisers* were all on the side of Wilkes, the Government inserted its "paragraphs" in the *Morning Post,* which therefore took its stand with the Tories. In 1774 Wilkes himself lost interest in the cause, having become Member for Middlesex and Lord Mayor of London, but the faction did not; and in 1775 it acquired an additional cause, England having gone to war with the American colonies. The condemnation of the war by almost the entire press was undoubtedly responsible for the increase in the newspaper tax in 1776. Meanwhile the affairs of the Admiralty office had become such a scandal that during 1778 and 1779 demands for the removal of the Earl of Sandwich as First Lord of the Admiralty were even outnumbering demands for peace. The Government replied by filling the columns of the *Post* with "paragraphs" in his defense, so that during these two years the paper was generally known as "L⁰ SANDWICH's Morning Post." But all of this was only a diversion, for the fate of the North Government depended entirely on the outcome of the American war.

There were now four political factions: the Tories, the Shelburne Whigs, the Rockingham Whigs, and the old Wilkes group. Only two of them had been active in the newspapers: the Tories, who published their "paragraphs" in the *Morning Post,* and the Wilkes group, who published their "paragraphs" in the five old *Advertisers* and in the two new *Advertisers*—the *General Advertiser* and the *London Courant*. The object of the Wilkes faction was to oust the North Government; and, having done so, it would join one of the Whig groups, being too weak politically to form a Government of its own. Hence, although it was a nuisance, it was a nuisance only to the Tories. The Rockingham Whigs were a nuisance to the King, for their target was the Crown, their object being to reduce its power by reducing the amount of its patronage. The leader of the Rockingham Whigs was Charles James Fox, but the one who had caused George the most trouble was Edmund Burke, and a good deal of the trouble had concerned the East India Company.

The East India Company had originally (1600) been a trading company, but it had later acquired the functions of a government and, having adopted a policy of conquest, had been responsible for British domination of India. Although its affairs were notoriously corrupt and notoriously confused, there was no indication of concern until the 1760's, and there was no real attempt to deal with the problem until 1773, when the North Government proposed and succeeded in passing the so-called Regulating Act. The act established a Supreme Court of Justice at Calcutta, and it also established a five-member board, headed by a Governor General, for the supervision of the company's civil and military activities. All appointments were to be made on a five-year basis, initial appointments by Parliament, subsequent appointments by the Crown. The first Chief Justice was Sir Elijah Impey, the first Governor General Warren Hastings.

Opposition to this legislation came from the Rockingham Whigs, who maintained that the Government had taken advantage of a genuine need for reform to seize the whole East India patronage for the King. Burke was particularly outspoken both with respect to Hastings, whom he distrusted, and with respect to the power of the Crown, and he became more so during the years which followed. By 1780 he was a pot which clearly needed some Royal watching, and the King watched. But, although George was thereby able to defeat a reform bill which would have deprived him of some domestic patronage, he himself suffered a major defeat on 6 April, 1780, when the Commons resolved that "the influence of the Crown has increased, is increasing, and ought to be diminished." This, the famous Dunning Resolution, made two things clear: the Commons was dominated by the Rockingham Whigs, and the Rockingham Whigs were hostile to George on principle. At this point the Rockingham Whigs became active in the newspapers.

The occasion was a quarrel between the Rev. Henry Bate and the other proprietors of the *Morning Post,* which resulted in Bate's leaving the *Post* and setting up the *Morning Herald* in competition. The *Post* was alarmed, because it could not hope to survive the competition; and the Government was alarmed, because it needed the *Post* to answer the City newspapers, which the increase in the advertisement duty had failed to silence. But no one was so alarmed as George III, for the *Herald* was supporting the Rockingham Whigs. Since the Rockingham Whigs would not have invested money in the *Herald* merely to harass a Government which was already being harassed by seven other newspapers, they were obviously looking out for their own future interests; and nothing was so distasteful to George as the thought of a Rockingham administration. Hence, by the end of 1780, he had arranged for a subsidy of the *Morning Post,* and in 1781 he also acquired the *Morning Herald,* this one by outright lease of the entire newspaper. Both papers savagely supported the North Government and savagely assailed the Rockingham Whigs.

The year 1781 was an active one for George. With the North Government tottering and the Commons already dominated by his enemies, his principal concern was the East India patronage. Since this was also a concern of Hastings, who had been quietly reappointed Governor General, Hastings sent his friend, John Scott, previously a major in the Bengal army, to London to handle matters. Scott arrived in late 1781, introduced himself to George, and promptly commenced his career as pamphleteer, "paragraph" writer, and politician. George provided every assistance. A seat was found for Scott in Parliament, and he was added to the staff of the *Morning Herald,* which thereafter staunchly defended the Regulating Act and the present Indian government and vehemently denounced Edmund Burke. The surrender of Lord Cornwallis on 19 October had meanwhile sounded the death knell for the North Government, and the *Post* and the *Herald* had accordingly shifted their support to Lord Shelburne, while the King tried desperately to avoid negotiations with Fox. By this time there was further trouble with the newspapers.

The manager of the press for the Rockingham Whigs had been Richard Brinsley Sheridan, who had reacted to the loss of the *Morning*

*Herald* by contracting by subsidy for the *London Courant* and the *General Advertiser*. The two newspapers had been transformed from *Advertisers* to scandal sheets, had been staffed with some hard-hitting writers, and had been sent into battle. All rear-guard actions were handled by the other *Advertisers,* the old Wilkes faction having now joined forces with the Rockingham Whigs. By the time the North Government finally resigned, in March, 1782, Sheridan had also succeeded in sabotaging the politics of the *Morning Post,* so that the King was entirely dependent upon the *Morning Herald.* The North Government was succeeded by an uneasy combination of Shelburne and Rockingham Whigs, the First Minister being Lord Rockingham, the Home Secretary Lord Shelburne, and the Foreign Secretary Fox. Since a Fox-Shelburne battle had been raging in the newspapers since the end of 1781, a quarrel between Fox and Shelburne was inevitable, and the quarrel occurred in June. But by this time the King had recovered the *Morning Post* and had also organized the Commons. Hence, when Lord Rockingham died on 1 July, the King immediately appointed Lord Shelburne as his successor with every confidence that his problem was solved. But it was not solved, for in February, 1783, the Tories joined forces with the Rockingham Whigs to censure the Ministry for the peace terms made with the Bourbon powers and the American colonies, and Lord Shelburne accordingly resigned.

George was beside himself. Thirty-seven agonizing days passed before he could bring himself to approach the Fox-North Coalition, which therefore did not take office until April, 1783. The Coalition First Minister was the Duke of Portland, Fox and Lord North being Foreign Secretary and Home Secretary, respectively; and everything was just as bad as George anticipated. Burke submitted exhaustive reports on the affairs of the East India Company, and on 6 July Fox moved for leave to introduce a new East India Bill, which would transfer the East India patronage to Parliament for at least the next several years. The bill was accordingly introduced, but George was able to defeat it in the Lords, and the Coalition Government was summarily dismissed. All it had to show for its eight months in office was the recall of Impey, who was charged with having exceeded his authority as Chief Justice. By the end of 1783, the Government was in the hands of the young Shelburnite William Pitt.

Pitt was hand-picked by a monarch who knew what he was doing, but he did have problems, not the least of which was the newspapers.

Sheridan had also had problems, for he had lost the *London Courant,* which had evidently expired as a result of a stock-jobbing enterprise, and he had had trouble with some of the other newspapers, which were willing to support Fox, but not Lord North and hence not the Coalition. These problems were, however, solved, and in addition Sheridan had again acquired the *Morning Post* and was in the process of acquiring the *Morning Herald,* so that every single newspaper was now on the side of the Opposition. Pitt's first concern, therefore, was to find someone who was a match for Sheridan, and he found or thought he found such a man in George Rose, who was accordingly made Secretary of the Treasury. Rose immediately bought into the *Morning Post.* Since the *Post* was obstinately pro-Fox, some time was required to win over the other proprietors, and more time was required to find a suitable staff. Major Scott had, of course, been moved to the *Post* from the now-Opposition *Herald,* but his target was only Burke; and a newspaper which was to see the Government through the general elections singlehandedly would have to strike at the Opposition in every one of its strongholds, including the whole London press and including by this time Carlton House, the young Prince of Wales having become politically active. The result was that the *Post* was not ready for the elections until late March.

Meanwhile the twenty-four-year-old Pitt was confronted with a Commons already hostile to the King and now doubly hostile to himself because of the "backstairs" manner in which he had come into power. Since he could hardly deny the charge that he had the confidence of neither the Commons nor the people, he contented himself with denying that "secret influence" had had anything to do with his appointment and that he was an "apostate" from the cause of reform. The House listened and on 14 January gave him leave to bring in his own East India Bill. As it turned out, the bill did provide for several much-needed reforms, but, since it left the King's patronage intact, it was unacceptable to the Commons, which rejected it on 23 January. The Opposition at once demanded that Pitt resign, but he did not resign, and he was not dismissed. Moreover the King refused to prorogue Parliament until the *Morning Post* had been brought into line, so that, for the next two months, Pitt was the target of unprecedented abuse both in the House and in the newspapers. Parliament was finally prorogued on 24 March.

Everyone except George was sure that the elections would result in an overwhelming defeat for the Government. Pitt himself evidently thought so, for, after the failure of his East India Bill, he tried hard to make his peace with Fox and the Duke of Portland. The newspapers all thought so, not excepting the *Morning Post,* which had been reluctant to support a cause so obviously hopeless as this one. But everyone had vastly underrated the extent of George's "secret influence"; for, when the elections were over, 160 followers of Fox had been replaced by 160 followers of Pitt, and Pitt had no further worries about the Commons. He also had few further worries about the newspapers.

George had failed in only one instance. Partly because Westminster was the seat of government and partly because the Westminster elections were probably freer from corruption than any in England, there was a unique prestige attached to the two Westminster representations, and this prestige George had reserved for the Shelburne Whigs, Lord Hood and Sir Cecil Wray. But, although he had gone to considerable trouble and expense to elect his candidates, the final count had given Fox 236 more votes than Wray. Since Fox had already been returned for the pocket boroughs of Ross and Kirkwall, only Wray was affected by the upset, and the King was therefore willing to accept it. Not so William Pitt. The "arrogance" which characterized Pitt's conduct for the remainder of his life seems to have been acquired during the course of these elections, for his first speech in the ensuing Parliament was compounded of insults and jeers, almost all of which were directed at Fox. Moreover, when the other high bailiffs submitted their "writs," the "writ" for Westminster was withheld, pending, said Pitt, an investigation of certain "irregularities." Fox protested, and Sir Cecil Wray thereupon requested a "scrutiny," which was duly commenced on 26 July, 1784. Before it was concluded, on 3 March, 1785, it had cost the Treasury thousands of pounds, and it achieved nothing. For, at the end of it, Lord Hood and Charles James Fox were seated for Westminster.

The history of the daily press from 1784 on is largely an account of the cat-and-mouse game played by George Rose and Richard Brinsley Sheridan, in which each was sometimes the cat, sometimes the mouse. Rose played the game with Treasury money and with all the legalistic and legislative machinery of a controlled Parliament: Sheridan played with whatever money he could get from individual Whigs. Rose played for William Pitt, who always supervised and often dictated the moves; Sheridan played for Fox, for one of the Carlton House factions, and for himself: sometimes for all three at once. There were constant intrigues and counter-intrigues, for Rose and Sheridan were masters of intrigue, and neither of them suffered for lack of material.

For one thing there were the general elections. After 1784 the King's affairs were managed by Pitt; but, so far as the elections generally were concerned, very little management was required, for the outcome in almost every instance was settled before the polling began. This was not the case in Westminster, however, and, since this was the election which particularly interested Pitt, a great deal of money was invested in it. During the election of 1788, the Government controlled seven of the ten daily newspapers and had in its employ besides, not only an army of writers, caricaturists, and ballad singers, but also an army of bludgeoners, whose bludgeonings were charged to the Opposition. This time there were two Opposition candidates, Fox and Lord John Townshend, and one Ministerial candidate, Lord Hood. Fox won easily, Townshend coming out somewhat ahead of Hood. The Government was distraught, and, although there was no official "scrutiny," a petition was prepared in Lord Hood's behalf, which alone cost the Treasury £14,000. There was an aftermath. For the Treasury's failure to pay its bills for the election resulted in the publication of some exposés which postponed the elections of 1789 to 1790, and, in fact, the Government's management of the election of 1788 was a Parliamentary issue until 1792, when it become "unconstitutional" to question the Government on any account. The Westminster election of 1790 was supposedly "compromised," Pitt and Fox having agreed to run only one candidate apiece. But the Government nevertheless prepared for this election by increasing (1789) the newspaper tax to 2d. and the advertisement duty to 3s.; and, although all newspaper prices were accordingly advanced to 4d., the Opposition newspapers protested that they were the only ones which were paying the taxes. Moreover, when Parliament was prorogued for the elections, the Treasury controlled nine of the fourteen daily newspapers, and the nine were supporting, not only Lord Hood, but an "independent" candidate, John Horne Tooke, who was purportedly running in order "to save the people from Fox." Tooke's appearance in the contest was never satisfactorily explained, but, since he did not win and since he turned out to be a reformer, the Opposition was willing to forget the matter.

There were also the affairs of Carlton House, which became increasingly involved. That the Prince of Wales should have allied himself with the King's Opposition was a well-established tradition, adherence to which had in this case been inevitable. For the Rockingham Whigs now had no hope of coming into power except through a change of monarch, and, since the Prince of Wales was himself ambitious, they were bound together by a common hostility to the King and his ministers. But the Prince was also unreliable, for, being vain, extravagant, dissolute, and selfish, he was susceptible to influence from any quarter; and, at the end of 1785, he became a real liability by marrying the Roman Catholic Mrs. Fitzherbert. If he had been two years older, this marriage would have barred him from the throne. As it was, it hung around the Whigs' neck like an albatross, for, although it was supposedly a secret, it was a secret only in the sense that it was not publicly announced.

The Government took no advantage of the situation until the spring of 1787, when the Prince applied to Parliament for payment of his debts and increase in his revenue. This application being warmly supported by the Opposition, a spokesman for the Government demanded in return an investigation of the Prince's marital status. In order to prevent such an investigation, Fox stated flatly that the Prince was unmarried. The effect of this statement was to split the Carlton House faction into two parts, for Mrs. Fitzherbert attached considerable value to her reputation, which, it seemed to her, Fox had deliberately tried to destroy. Henceforth Fox had an active enemy and Sheridan a powerful ally in Mrs. Fitzherbert, and the ground was laid for the cabal of 1788.

Although the announcement of the King's illness was withheld by newspapers until 10 November, 1788, the fact that the King was in precarious health had been no secret since early summer, and the cabal seems to have begun at that time. For, during the Westminster election of that year, Sheridan secretly joined Pitt in opposing the interests of Fox, and, by the time the election was over, he had organized the "New Whigs." The "New Whigs," which included in its membership Lord Loughborough, William Windham, and Edmund Burke, was Mrs. Fitzherbert's faction, and it was intended to constitute the personnel of the Prince of Wales's government, Fox and his intimates to be excluded. Fox, who had been traveling on the Continent when the agitation for his exclusion began, returned to establish his authority in the Party, which had never been seriously threatened, but the "New Whigs" continued their activities until 10 March, 1789, when the announcement of the King's recovery put an end to the possibility of a Regency. Their evident confidence that the Prince would finally have yielded to Mrs. Fitzherbert's influence rather than Fox's may well have been justified, although one does not, of course, know. The King's recovery was in any event a disaster for Mrs. Fitzherbert, for she was no longer useful to the "New Whigs," and she was still an embarrassment to the old. To make matters worse, the Prince was soon flirting with the Government. Hence, although the marriage was again an issue in the elections of 1790, it was only an ostensible issue. The real issue was Mrs. Fitzherbert, and she was not even an issue, being by this time *persona non grata* to both parties.

There was also the problem of the East India Company, which soon became more properly the problem of Edmund Burke. On 6 July, 1784, Pitt again presented his East India Bill, which was, of course, speedily passed; and the Opposition, which had generally offered only token resistance, prepared to accept the defeat and turn its attention to something else. But Burke, whose resistance had not been token, had other plans. Burke's connection with the Rockingham Whigs, later known as the Foxite Whigs or "the Whigs" or merely "the Party," as the Shelburne Whigs were later known as "the Tories," was always uncertainly defined. The Opposition newspapers regarded him as an independent, who happened to be a personal friend of the Whig leader, Fox; but Burke regarded himself as a Whig, and, since he was in many respects an ornament to the Party, the Whigs had tried to accommodate him. It had not been an easy task, for, instead of accepting the Whig principles, he had expected the Whigs to accept his, so that he had been for some time the tail which wagged the dog. In 1784 Burke decided that the Whigs would punish Warren Hastings.

On 7 July, 1784, therefore, Burke notified the Commons that he was holding Pitt responsible for the investigation of Impey's conduct, and on 30 July he moved for the first papers relating to the conduct of Hastings. Pitt was silent on both accounts, evidently supposing that, since the investigations aroused no popular interest, they would perish of their own dreariness. But Burke was tenacious, and on 17 February, 1786, he made the first charges against Hastings. By this time Burke was being assailed by all the Ministerial papers, and in perhaps April he filed an action for libel against the *Public Advertiser,* asking £5,000 damages. The jury, which seems to have reflected the public attitude toward the proceedings rather well, reduced the amount of the damages to £100, but Burke's ardor was undiminished; and in April, 1787, his agent, Sir Gilbert Elliot, notified the Commons that he intended to move for the impeachment of Sir Elijah Impey as well, since Pitt was obviously not going to do it. Pitt now had two actions to quash. Although he might easily have quashed both of them himself, he always distributed responsibility whenever he could, and in this instance distribution was possible, Hastings being a Lord and therefore beyond the actual jurisdiction of the Commons. Hence, in what appeared to be a brilliant maneuver, he suddenly supported the impeachment of Hastings, thus sending that case along to the Lords, and five days later (12 Dec., 1787) he permitted Elliot to move for charges of impeachment against Impey. Impey's case was presented to the Commons on 4 February, 1788, and on 9 May Impey was acquitted. The trial of Hastings began on 13 February, 1788, and, although the Lords was prepared to return a similar verdict, seven years elapsed before it had the opportunity to do so.

The trial was an embarrassment to everyone except Burke. Fox, who was one of the "managers," that is, prosecutors, had lost interest in the case before the trial was even begun; and, to make matters worse, the public, which had heretofore regarded the proceedings as merely tedious, now regarded them as ridiculous, and Burke did not accept ridicule philosophically. Torn between a desire to placate Burke and a serious concern for the dignity of the Party, Fox resorted to a policy of temporizing. But he did not thereby hasten the end of the trial, and neither did he placate Burke, for, at the end of 1788, Burke joined two other "managers," Sheridan and Windham, in the plot to turn the Whig leadership over to Sheridan. By late 1789 Burke had lost confidence in Sheridan. The Government was meanwhile embarrassed, for it had never intended to subject Hastings to an ordeal of this sort, and its position became more uncomfortable in 1790.

The French Revolution began in 1789, and the London press was generally sympathetic with it until the beginning of 1790. But on 21 January, 1790, the King's carriage was attacked by a madman; and, with the general elections only a few months away and the clamor for reform increasing, the Government took advantage of the incident to sound an alarm. The attacker was represented as a French agent, the country was represented as a hive of democrats, and, long before the elections began, everyone knew that Burke was defecting. But, although it was commonly supposed that the only issue involved was the French Revolution and the reformers, Pitt knew very well that there was a second issue and that, in accepting Burke, he was expected to support the prosecution of Hastings. Burke, who was no politician, never understood William Pitt. He had already been misled by the maneuver of 1787 into supposing that Pitt actually favored the impeachment of Hastings, and he was now further misled by the Treasury propaganda into supposing that the country actually was teeming with democrats. His service to the Pitt Government as a result can hardly be overrated, for, without the verisimilitude provided by the *Reflections on the Revolution in France,* the Treasury propaganda might well have failed and the plot against the people have failed along with it. As it was, the Government was able to magnify its rumors and finally to invent the alarm of 1 December, 1792, when the King called out the militia to quell a riot which, as Sheridan rightly said, existed only in the "foul imagination" of Mr. Pitt. Pitt was also of service to Burke, for, without all the Treasury propaganda in the newspapers, the *Reflections* would have seemed quite as ridiculous to the public as the trial of Warren Hastings. But Pitt never provided the service which Burke particularly wanted. Although he pretended to approve of the trial, he was, in fact, much more opposed to it than the Opposition had been. Like Fox, he therefore resorted to evasions and extenuations and on a few occasions even to compromises, in which Tories joined forces with Whigs to make Burke the dupe.

The manner in which the daily press contributed to and was affected by these events will be more specifically indicated in the studies of newspapers which follow. It is hardly necessary to say that "matter of fact," which the *Daily Courant* had once regarded as the only rightful province of journalists, will be of negligible concern to these newspapers.

# CHAPTER I

# Henry Bate (Dudley) and the *Morning Post* (1772–1781): Perfidies and Punishments

## SOME WHYS AND WHEREFORES OF THE *MORNING POST*

OF THE several landmarks in the history of newspapers, one is certainly the founding of the *Morning Post,* which, representing, as it did, a new journalistic genre, not only introduced a new kind of newspaper, but altered the whole direction of journalism for perhaps all time to come. The first number of this paper appeared on Monday, 2 November, 1772, and at first it purported to be only a pamphlet. For, although its content seemed to be that of a newspaper, its format and subtitle, *Daily Advertising Pamphlet,* were designed to persuade the authorities that it was not a newspaper and hence not subject to the newspaper tax. The publisher was John Wheble, No. 114, Fleet Street, and, according to the colophon, the printers were Edward Cox and George Bigg, No. 405, Strand. Wheble was well known to the readers as printer and publisher of the *Middlesex Journal* and hence as collusive participant (Febr.–Mar., 1771) in the bitter struggle between the City of London and the House of Commons, which had rocked the country a year earlier.[1] If one can rely upon the Audit-Office records, Wheble was still publishing the *Middlesex Journal* at this time.[2] Cox and Bigg were unknown, and, in fact, Bigg seems to have had little to do with the paper, for the proprietors later (*Post,* 11 Nov., 1776) named Cox as their "first printer" and Bigg as only a "partner to Cox." The Audit Office listed the printers as "D. & E. Cox." [3]

The original proprietors have not been identified. Historians have generally relied upon a list of eleven proprietors printed by the *Morning Post* on 8 November, 1776, but how many of the eleven were proprietors four years earlier is not there indicated, and other newspapers furnish only three of the names. On 11 November, 1776, the spurious *Post,* listing the "outrages" committed by the proprietors of the original *Post* since its beginning, named as "principal" of the

19

original proprietors the Rev. Henry Bate, the Rev. John Trusler, and Mr. John Bell. Of this trio Bate was by far the most prominent member, since he was "the Editor of the Paper at the original setting up of it, and for most of the time afterwards" (*Post,* 24 June, 1780), having once been "discharged" and rehired (*Morning Chronicle,* 19 Nov., 1776). Trusler was perhaps second in importance, since he functioned as Bate's adviser and occasional assistant. Although at one time (9 Nov., 1776) the spurious *Post* spoke of the "Revered [*sic*] editors . . . , Messieurs B[ate] and T[rusler]," Trusler was actually never more than a subeditor. Bell had nothing to do with the literary department, but he played an active role in the business management, as did Bate and Trusler. As to the proprietary in general, one can say only that, from its beginning through at least 1774, the *Morning Post* shared its printers and publishers with the *Middlesex Journal,* so that the two papers were at least closely associated, and they may even have had the same proprietors. In late 1771 the two principal proprietors of the *Middlesex Journal* were Dryden Leach, a printer, and William Palmer David, a bookseller,[4] but the paper may have changed hands before the *Morning Post* was begun.

The hope of evading the stamp duty was blasted in a fortnight; hence on 17 November, 1772, the *Morning Post* appeared as a newspaper, with a new format and a new subtitle, *Cheap Daily Advertiser.* Although it was still, according to the colophon, printed by E. Cox and G. Bigg and published by Wheble, the trio was evidently dismissed shortly thereafter, for, by the beginning of 1773, the Audit Office was holding "Williams & Co." responsible for the publishing of the *Morning Post* and the *Middlesex Journal,*[5] and by 12 February, 1773, the *Post,* now entitled *Morning Post, and Daily Advertiser,* was carrying only the legend, "Sold by J. WILLIAMS, No. 39, Fleet-street . . . and at the Editor's Office, No. 7, Catherine-street, Strand, where the Paper is now printed." Of Cox the proprietors were to hear more in 1776. Wheble was later re-engaged as the publisher of the *English Chronicle,* a triweekly evening newspaper begun by the proprietors of the *Post* at the beginning of 1779.[6] The new publisher of the *Morning Post,* John Williams (not to be confused with John Williams, the writer), was, like Wheble, a one-time popular hero, having on 26 July, 1764, been tried at Guildhall for publishing No. 45 of the *North Briton,* convicted, and on 23 January, 1765, sentenced to spend six months in King's Bench Prison, to stand in the pillory, to pay a fine of £100, and to provide the usual securities for good behavior for a period of seven years. These proceedings had so endeared him to the public that, when he appeared in the pillory, he had been greeted by 10,000 admirers, who presented him with a gift of 200 guineas.[7] When the Court demanded "good behavior" from a printer or a publisher, it meant inactivity, and Williams seems to have been totally inactive for the full seven years. But his period of probation had expired on 23 June, 1772, and he was now free to return to publishing. He continued to publish the *Morning Post* until 1774, during which period the paper established its character as the first West End print.

Almost nothing is known of Bate's staff during this period. Arthur Young later stated [8] that during 1773 he reported the Parliamentary debates for the paper "at a salary, as well as I can recollect, of five guineas a week." But, since, according to Hindle,[9] Bate was receiving only four guineas a week for editing the paper, contributing much of the material, and preparing copy for the printer, Young was at least mistaken about the salary. How much of the paper Bate himself wrote cannot be ascertained, but it was certainly his personality which animated its pages. His interests, which included everything from drama to swordsmanship, from music to pugilism, from art criticism to the breeding of greyhounds,[10] were the interests of the *Post;* and the same spirit which impelled him to settle personal disputes "with sword and fist and pistol" was expressed in his journalism, the violence of which was somehow mitigated by the fact that it seemed to be prompted by a love of fun and adventure. In every respect the *Morning Post* was something utterly new to the London reading public. Heretofore newspapers had concerned themselves almost entirely with politics, and it was still felt that the best newspapers were those which confined themselves to the Parliamentary debates and to information about national and international developments, with perhaps an occasional glance in the direction of the theater. Readers, in short, were to be instructed: they were not to be entertained. But to Henry Bate entertainment was always paramount. Hence, although the *Post* was generally in sympathy with the North Government, it made no attempt to educate or convert its readers. Parliamentary debates were summarized, speeches of popular orators printed in part, sporting intelligence and theatrical news were emphasized, criminal trials, especially those involving people of note, were reported in detail, and gossip, always witty and usually scandalous, was rampant. Even the advertisements were slanted toward a Mayfair clientele: books, theatrical presentations, auctions, domestic servants, and loans on prospective inheritances.

In addition to his professional services for the *Morning Post,* Bate was soon performing services of an extra-professional sort. For the first many months, he kept his own adventures out of the newspaper on the evident assumption that they would damage the paper's reputation. But on 27 July, 1773, William Woodfall published in his *Morning Chronicle* a long account of Bate's most recent fracas. On Friday, 23 July, it appeared, Bate and the elder George Colman had escorted the actress, Mrs. Hartley, to Vauxhall, where Mrs. Hartley was ogled by four or five young men at another table. Bate's attempt to block their view was greeted with jeers, and a noisy quarrel ensued, which lasted much of the night. On the following morning one of the young men, a Captain W. Crofts, challenged Bate to a duel, and Bate accepted. But, before a place could be found for this combat, a second young man, a George Robert Fitz-Gerall, appeared to demand satisfaction for his friend, Captain Miles, first from Crofts, who, Miles charged, had preempted priority in the matter of challenges, and second from Bate. The dispute between Miles and Crofts was settled by Crofts's yielding priority, but Bate insisted on fighting Miles on his own terms, which included boxing "without stopping." This fight had occurred, said the *Chronicle,* and Bate had emerged victorious, Miles being "sent home in a coach, with his face a perfect jelly."

Woodfall, who was one of the most respectable journalists of his time, intended the story as an exposé, which he probably thought would ruin the *Morning Post.* The *Morning Post* evidently thought so, too, for it hastened to extenuate its editor by publishing (30 July) its own version of the affair. The *Post* was answered by the *Gazetteer,* which represented Crofts and Fitz-Gerall, Miles still being in no condition to speak, and by other newspapers, which devoted columns to "The Vauxhall Affray" and "The Rev. Bruiser," including detailed recitals of the events which led up to the fight. But, instead of ruining the *Post,* the publicity actually helped it, so that, from the beginning of August on, Bate's only concern was to keep the quarrel alive. He did not labor in vain, for by mid-August another half-dozen challenges had been issued and another three or four duels fought, all of which were given complete, albeit derisive, coverage by the London press. By the end of August, the newspapers had provided enough material for a thick volume, which the *Morning Post* accordingly published, under the title, *The Vauxhall Affray; or, The Macaronies Defeated; Being a Compilation of all the Letters, Squibs, &c. for Both Sides of that Dispute, with an Introductory Dedication to the Hon. Tho. Lyttelton, Esq.* (London. Sold by J. Williams, No. 39, Fleet-street, 1773). This work having sold at least two editions, the *Post* published *An Appendix to the Vauxhall Affray; or, Macaronies Defeated* (London. Sold by J. Williams . . . 1773), which consisted of "Letters" and "Squibs" previously overlooked. Abuse (or in newspaper terminology "personalities") had already been the *Post's* stock in trade, but from this point on the paper made a practice of deliberately goading someone into challenging its editor to a duel, which Bate thereupon fought to the great delight of readers and the consequent enhancement of the *Post's* circulation. But the other newspapers had also learned a lesson, and hence Bate could look for no further publicity from them.

In 1774 Fox sued the *Morning Post* for a libel. Williams was tried and convicted on 9 July and on 21 November sentenced to a month in King's Bench Prison and fined £100.[11] He was evidently somewhat discouraged by this experience, for on 26 August he resigned as publisher of the *Morning Post* and the *Middlesex Journal*, and he did not undertake the publishing of another newspaper until 1778, when he was connected with the *Whitehall Evening Post*.[12] From 26 August, 1774, through 13 June, 1775, the *Morning Post* was, according to the colophon, "Printed and Sold by WILLIAM GRIFFIN, No. 6, Catherine-street, Strand"; and, until the end of 1774, when the two papers seem to have ended their association, Griffin also printed and published the *Middlesex Journal*.[13] Although he had not previously been named in the colophon of the *Post,* Griffin had probably printed the paper since the beginning of 1773, for the spurious *Post* of 11 November, 1776, stated positively that he was the second printer, and Cox seems to have quit the paper at about that time. The rupture with Cox was evidently violent, for first in the list of outrageous acts charged to Bate, Trusler, and Bell by the same spurious *Post* was that the trio "took advantage of the absence from home of . . . E. Cox, and seized and removed paper and instruments belonging to the paper without notifying him."

Griffin, long a London bookseller and one of the original (1769) proprietors of the *Morning Chronicle*,[14] was no hero. When the House of Lords threatened to prosecute him for publishing *Droit le Roy* [*sic*]; *or, A Digest of the Rights and Prerogatives of the Imperial Crown of Great-Britain* (London, 1764), Griffin unhesitatingly diverted the action to Timothy Brecknock by naming him (23 Febr., 1764) as author of the pamphlet. But, as it turned out, his present position called for no heroism, and he did get along well with the proprietors. Hence these were comparatively halcyon days for the *Morning Post,* but they came to an abrupt end with Griffin's death.

According to the spurious *Post* of 11 November, 1776, Bate and his associates had made a contract with Griffin and his wife whereby the two could print the paper as long as either of them lived; but, with the death of Griffin, the proprietors changed their minds, "[tricked] the *widow* and *orphans* . . . out of the printing . . . , under the assurance of . . . a stipulated annuity for life," and took the printing into their own hands, "engaging R. Haswell, one of the then journeymen of E. Cox, the original printer, to act as their foreman, that they might reap the profits of the *master printer.*" At the same time they "dismissed G. Corral, [who had succeeded Griffin as] their publisher, in order to engross . . . the profits of *publication*" as well. Although the spurious *Post* seems to have been correct, the events to which it referred were spread out over a period of ten weeks. Until 14 June, 1775, the printer and publisher of the *Post* was William Griffin; but on 14 June his name was removed from the colophon, which read simply "Printed at No. 6, in Catherine-street, Strand, where Letters for the editor are received." From 19 June through 26 August the paper was "Printed by E. GRIFFIN at No. 6, Catherine-street, Strand" and on 28 August "Printed by R. HASWELL, Catherine-street, Strand." Except for an alteration in the address by 8 December from "Catherine-street, Strand" to "Blake-court, Catherine-street, Strand," the colophon remained the same through 2 November, 1776. "E. GRIFFIN" was evidently Mrs. Griffin, who immediately succeeded her husband as printer. George Corral succeeded him as publisher and, having no address of his own, moved into Griffin's office. The proprietors probably "tricked" Corral out of the publishing at the same time that they "tricked" Mrs. Griffin out of the printing, but Corral remained at No. 6, Catherine Street, shifting his occupation from publisher to bookseller. For Mrs. Griffin the proprietors, of course, substituted the "foreman," Robert Haswell, and for Corral they seem to have substituted another "foreman," Richard Bell, who may have been one of John Bell's numerous relations. What arrangements they made with

Bell is not indicated, but their contract with Haswell was quite different from their contract with Griffin. Haswell was subject to dismissal at any time, and he also accepted sole responsibility for everything which went into the *Post*, so that, in the event of a prosecution, he could expect no assistance, financial or otherwise, from his employers.

Hindle's statement [15] that so long as "the paper was published from Fleet Street Bate did most of his work at his own house in Surrey Street" is probably accurate so far as it goes. Until this time the *Morning Post* certainly had no address, or, rather, it borrowed its address from its printer and publisher. Hence, with the shift of printer from Cox to Griffin, the editorial office automatically shifted from No. 114, Fleet Street to No. 7, Catherine Street; and, when Griffin found the quarters at No. 7 confined or otherwise inconvenient, printer and editor moved next door to No. 6. But, with the death of Griffin, the subsequent break with Mrs. Griffin, and the engaging of a foreman in lieu of a printing house, the proprietors were compelled to buy a press and find a place to put it, and under these circumstances there was no reason to farm out the publishing. The address on Catherine Street was obviously a makeshift, but by 8 December, 1775, the *Post* had moved to Blake Court, Catherine Street, its first real home. It remained there until 1 July, 1794, when it absorbed the *World* and moved into the *World's* quarters at No. 335, Strand.

## *MORNING POST VS. MORNING POST*

BY THE end of 1775, therefore, the *Morning Post* was firmly established, and everything went well in the house on Catherine Street for about fourteen months. On 2 November, 1776, however, one of the proprietors, offended at something Haswell had printed, demanded his dismissal, and Haswell was summarily dismissed (*Morning Chronicle,* 6 Nov., 1776). But the *Post's* real trouble came from the news-venders, who, having bought their concessions from "their predecessors" at a cost of "from Fifty even to Two and Three hundred Pounds," were suddenly replaced by "a pack of vagabonds, clothed . . . like anticks, and sent . . . blowing horns about the town" (spurious *Post,* 11 Nov., 1776). The news-venders, subsequently (*Post,* 11 Nov., 1776) identified as "GROVER, LUSSAM, Kerbeg, Leage, G. Wall, J. Wall, Lee, Whitaker, Shepherson, Harbach, and G. Riley," reacted to this treatment with a plot to ruin the original *Post* by bringing out an exact imitation. Since they needed assistance to accomplish this end, they appealed to those who held grudges against the proprietors (by this time no inconsiderable number), and most of them responded. Corral joined the conspirators at once as publisher and Mrs. Griffin, of whose promised annuity not "a single shilling" had been paid (spurious *Post*, 11 Nov., 1776), as printer. Cox joined the group somewhat later, Bigg coming in on the opposite side. Bate supposed, although, as it turned out, mistakenly, that Robert Haswell was also won over.

On 4 November, 1776, therefore, two *Morning Posts, and Daily Advertisers* appeared, alike in every detail, except that one was numbered 1257 and signaled the dismissal of Haswell with the altered colophon, "Printed by J. BURD in Blake-court, Catherine-street, Strand," whereas the other was unnumbered and bore the colophon, "LONDON: published by G. CORRAL, (Successor to the late Mr. GRIFFIN) No. 6, Catherine-street." J. Burd had previously operated a printing shop in Fleet Street. In March, 1765, he had been taken into custody by order of the House of Lords for having printed *A Circumstantial and Authentic Account of a Late Unhappy Affair;*[16] but by mid-1769 he had atoned for this transgression and, along with a Mr. "Jacquery," was printing the *Morning Chronicle,* which newspaper the two had themselves "for some time" forged, when the printing was taken out of their hands and "put into [William Woodfall's] hands by the Proprietors" (*Morning Chronicle,* 11 Mar., 1789; spurious *Star,* 1 Apr., 1789). Since forgers were usually *personae non gratae* with proprietors and editors, Burd had not worked for a newspaper since.

The proprietors of the genuine *Post* were not taken by surprise, partly because forgeries of this kind were not unusual, partly because the forgers had no doubt advertised their newspaper by handbill on the previous afternoon. The genuine *Post* of 4 November, 1776, therefore notified its readers that the *"Hawkers who have long envied the success of the public prints, have entered into a combination among themselves to print a New Paper, assisted by R. HASWELL, [the Proprietors'] late Servant, who for his negligence and incapacity has been discharged. Their plan is to . . . have [a paper] printed that shall resemble [this one] in appearance, and to leave it, with their customers, instead of the original one. They have appointed a person at the corner of [this] very Court, to publish it and take in advertise-*

ments." The proprietors admonished the public to be certain to check the serial number and the name of the publisher before accepting the paper and especially certain to leave advertisements "down BLAKE-COURT." The conspicuous lack of a serial number was remedied by the counterfeiters at once: on the second day (5 Nov.) their paper was numbered 2000.

Until they saw the forgery, the proprietors of the *Post* were unaware that Corral had joined the *"combination,"* but they were still convinced that Haswell had, even though he was not named in the colophon. Hence on 9 November they revised their indictment to include both Corral and Haswell, *"their late servants, who for their negligence and incapacity have been discharged from this Office,"* and they again cautioned their "customers" to be sure that the paper they accepted carried the name of "R. BELL," which would henceforth appear above the title as well as at the end of the sheet. Haswell himself had meanwhile fled to Cambridge, from which place he addressed a letter "To the Editor of the *Morning Post,"* assuring Bate that he was no part of the "association formed against you," but insisting that he had nevertheless been unjustly treated, Bate having failed to protest his dismissal. He reminded Bate of various favors he had done for him, such as performing his own and Bate's work many times, once for a period of three weeks, while Bate was visiting his "patron," Lord Lyttelton, and refusing to believe with everyone else that Bate's opera of the preceding year was a mere paraphrase of *Lionel and Clarissa.* He was evidently referring to *The Rival Candidates,* first performed at Drury Lane on 1 February, 1775, Isaac Bickerstaffe's *Lionel and Clarissa* having been performed at Covent Garden on 25 February, 1768.[17] He concluded the letter with a warning that Bate, too, was in danger of dismissal, the other proprietors being by no means satisfied with his work as editor, and sent it to William Woodfall, who had already demonstrated his hostility to the *Morning Post.* Woodfall published it in the *Morning Chronicle* two days later.

The genuine *Post* of 8 November, 1776, carried a long declaration from "The PROPRIETORS of the MORNING POST to the WORLD." Beginning with a statement of their determination to *"lay the Particulars of this infamous transaction before the public, that the few HAWKERS who continue the Insult may be marked and treated as they merit,"* they went on to make six specific charges against the group of *"lawless Banditti."* Four of the charges had to do with the

extent of the fraud, with special reference to numerous acts of violence. The fifth concerned Corral, *"now a bookseller, but formerly
the Proprietors' publisher,"* who had been *"prevailed upon . . . to
become [the hawkers'] publisher, at the very corner of Blake-court in
Catherine-street, and to affix boxes in his shop windows, with* MORN-
ING POST LETTER BOX *inscribed on them"*; and the sixth concerned Haswell, who, they insisted, had been *"likewise artfully spirited
up"* by the hawkers, who sent him *"the day before the publication of
their design, to seduce, if possible by any bribes, the compositors from
their duty."* The declaration was signed

| | |
|---|---|
| JOHN TRUSLER, | THOS. SKINNER, |
| HENRY BATE, | JOS. MERRYMAN, |
| JOHN BELL, | ROB MITCHELL, |
| JAMES CHRISTIE, | JAMES WALSH, |
| RICH. TATTERSALL, | HENRY WATKINS, |
| JER. HARGRAVE. | |

On 9 November the *Morning Chronicle* published a second letter
from Haswell, who again protested that he had nothing to do with the
conspiracy and reminded Bate that he, too, had been "once actually
discharged." On the same day the counterfeit *Post* admitted that it
was a counterfeit. On 7 November it was still printed by Mrs. Griffin
at No. 6, Catherine Street; but by 9 November it was "Printed by
EDWARD COX, No. 73, Great Queen-street, Lincoln's-Inn-Fields [18]
. . . ; and published by G. CORRAL, (Successor to the late Mr.
GRIFFIN) No. 6, Catherine-street." Until this time the war between
the two *Posts* had followed the usual pattern of such wars; but, with
the acquisition of Cox as printer and in light of the damage it had
already done its rival, the spurious *Post* now divorced itself editorially,
at least, from its original. Henceforth, it declared, it would leave
scandal and bickering to the old *Post* and establish itself as an independent and responsible newspaper in the old tradition. That afternoon Cox and Corral underscored the paper's independence by distributing handbills which listed six "outrages" perpetrated by Bate,
Trusler, and that "piratical intruder on the profession of a bookseller," John Bell. The "outrages" included the seizure of paper and
"instruments" from Cox's office, the duping of Mrs. Griffin, the hiring
of Cox's journeyman, Haswell, in lieu of a master printer, the unjusti-
fied dismissal of Corral, the "oppression" and "abuse" of the hawkers,
and the defamation of "the character of everyone." The text of the

handbill was reprinted in their paper of 11 November with the addendum that Haswell had no connection with the newspaper whatever. The same number introduced a column of "EXTRACTS from the LYING POST, or, SCANDALOUS CHRONICLE."

On 11 November the original *Post* named the hawkers who had fomented the conspiracy, but the time for exposures of this sort was past, for by now right seemed to be on the side of the new *Post* rather than the old one, and the proprietors, who had heretofore been able to fight an offensive action, were suddenly forced into a position of defense. Hence the same paper carried two further announcements: first, the proprietors had obtained from the Court of Chancery a restraint on E. Cox and G. Corral from bringing out further copies of their newspaper, and, second, they were printing a handbill, which would be distributed within a few hours, refuting the charges made by Cox and Corral, the refutation to be attested by Cox's one-time partner, Bigg. Bigg's statement, which was reprinted in the *Post* of the following day, was only a blanket denial of all the charges made by Cox and Corral. It was accompanied by a statement from one Robert Cartony, who, describing himself as a "friend" of Mrs. Griffin, attested that she had been fairly treated by the proprietors.

As it turned out, the proprietors were no match for Cox and Corral. The first number of the spurious *Post* (4 Nov.) had had the same title and subtitle as that of the original *Post,* but no serial number; the second number (5 Nov.) had carried the serial number 2000, so that the seventh number (11 Nov.) carried the serial number 2005. On 12 November the paper appeared with a new title, subtitle, and serial number: it was now the *New Morning Post; or General Advertiser,* No. 0008. Cox and Corral explained editorially that they had not been restrained from using the same title as the old *Post,* nor could they be; but, to avoid any semblance of illegality and, more important, to separate their paper completely from its scurrilous original, they had changed the title of their own accord. Instead of suppressing the new *Post,* therefore, the proprietors had strengthened its independence, converting it into a potentially formidable rival. The testimony of Bigg and Cartony also proved more damaging than helpful. On 13 November Edward Cox promised to prove by witnesses the falsity of any specific statement made by George Bigg in behalf of the proprietors. Bigg was silent. At the same time the *New Post* identified Robert Cartony as the executor of Mr. Griffin's estate, but impugned his testimony on the ground that he was also the partner of a proprietor of the *Post*, Rob Mitchell.

The *New Post's* resolve to abstain from further bickering was not, however, put into effect, for until mid-December both *Posts* were choked with charges, denials, and affidavits of one sort or another. The old *Post* continued to pretend that the *New Post* was a forgery, issuing almost daily warnings to its readers to be certain they were getting the authentic paper, and the *New Post* continued to taunt its rival with imitations, which were now meant as mockeries rather than deceptions. Whatever the old *Post* printed was ridiculed with parody by the *New Post*, which was meanwhile cautioning its own readers to be certain they were getting "the *genuine New Post*" and was printing its own publisher's name conspicuously above the title. Until 10 December, when the serial number became simply 31 (instead of 0031), the *New Post* also adhered to a four-digit numbering. Meanwhile the *New Post* had aroused the wrath of the *Gazetteer* by venturing (9 Dec.) to correct some statements made by its law reporter. The *Gazetteer* replied (12 Dec.) with the customary protest of strict neutrality, combined with a battery of countercharges, implying that the conductor of the *New Post* was suffering from "a lack of matter" and a "desperate falling situation," from which he was trying to rescue himself by "writing into *public notice*, a paper verging, perhaps, on the predestined state of eternal oblivion." The law reporter added the information that the conductor was "a pompous solemn blockhead," and the *New Post* accused the *Gazetteer* in return of wanting "decency" and therefore "good sense." [19] Before the *Gazetteer* could respond, the *New Post* was defunct.

The fact that the *New Post* was indeed in a "desperate falling situation" was evident as early as 3 December, 1776, when the old *Post* announced that, despite the "spurious" opposition, its circulation had increased during the preceding fortnight and was now at a peak. The announcement, issued in the form of a notarized statement, signed by Richard Bell, publisher, was repeated almost daily; and on 6 December the *New Post* countered with a declaration that, "on a moderate calculation, [this paper] is daily read by more than Ten Thousand Persons." The declaration, which was, of course, not meant to be taken seriously, was followed by an offer of special rates for short advertisements. The implication that the paper was in difficulty was made explicit on 12 December, when the *Post* announced that all but six of the "desperate, and deluded" hawkers had left "the expiring, *spurious* paper" to return to "the original MORNING POST." The paper was indeed "expiring": it seems to have breathed out its last number on 14 December, 1776, having run through thirty-five issues. There was no indication that it would not reappear, and the proprietors of the *Post* obviously expected it to reappear, for, throughout the remainder of December, all of January, and most of February, they continued to print the legend, "Published by R. BELL, in Blake-court, Catherine-street, Strand," above their title. This precaution was not abandoned until 27 February, 1777, when the proprietors explained in a note to the readers that the *"memento"* was no longer *"necessary," "the con-temptible opposition . . . being now at an end, and the unmanly op-posers sufficiently punished for their folly."* [20]

Although the old *Post* survived, the *New Post* was in some respects a better newspaper. From both an ethical and a literary point of view, its writing was on a higher level, and its mockery of the old *Post* was generally good satire. The fact remains that it had almost no in-formation, and it was also in a precarious financial situation. Both papers probably lost money during this period, but the proprietors of the old *Post,* being numerous and well-to-do, could afford the loss, whereas Cox, Corral, and the news-venders could not. The abrupt end of the paper, added to the *Post's* statement that the conspirators had been *"punished for their folly,"* indicates that the thirty-fifth number was hardly on the street when they were arrested for debt. The debt, which may have included an advertisement duty of £165, still unpaid in 1777,[21] was probably huge; but some adjustment had evidently been made by 1780, for, in 1780 and again in 1784–1786, Ed-ward Cox was publishing the *Courier de l'Europe*.[22] George Corral seems to have had no further connection with newspapers. A third reason for the failure of the *New Post* was that it began as a forgery, and the public evidently disapproved of forgeries, for not one of them ever survived more than a few months.

There was also the old *Post's* "pack of vagabonds," whose employ-ment had been responsible for the forgery in the first place. On 13 November, 1776, Horace Walpole mentioned in a letter to the Countess of Ossory: [23]

Yesterday . . . I heard drums and trumpets in Piccadilly: I looked out of the window and saw a procession with streamers flying. At first I thought it a press-gang, but seeing the corps so well drest, like Hussars, in yellow with blue waistcoats and breeches, and high caps, I concluded it was some new body of our allies, or a regiment newly raised. . . . [As it turned out, however,] this was a procession set forth by Mr. Bate, Lord Lyttelton's chaplain, and author of the old *Morning Post*, and meant as an appeal to the town against his antagonist, the new one. I did not perceive it, but the musicians had masks; on their caps was written *The Morning Post*, and they distributed hand-bills. I am sure there were at least between thirty and forty, and this mummery must have cost a great deal of money. Are we not quite distracted, reprobate, absurd, beyond all people that ever lived? The *new* "Morning Post," I am told, for I never take in either, exceeds all the outrageous Billingsgate that ever was heard of. What a country! Does it signify what happens to it? Is there any sense, integrity, decency, taste, left? Are we not the most despicable nation upon earth in every light? A solemn and expensive masquerade exhibited by a clergyman, in defense of daily scandal against women of the first rank, in the midst of a civil war [the war with the American colonies]! and while the labouring poor are torn from their families by press-gangs! and a foreign war is hanging over our heads! And everybody was diverted by this!—Do you think, Madam, that anything can save such a sottish and stupid nation?

The "solemn and expensive masquerade," which was continued throughout November and early December, was evidently effective, for the *New Post* published several letters, purportedly written by indignant Londoners, who had been awakened early in the morning by drums and bugles, actually written, no doubt, by Corral himself, complaining of it and demanding that the magistrates interfere to stop it. But the magistrates were themselves evidently "diverted."

## THE STRANGE BEHAVIOR OF THE
## DUKE OF RICHMOND

ALTHOUGH every newspaperman must have regarded the war between the two *Posts* with disgust, there was no editorial comment respecting it, and, by the end of February, 1777, everything was again quiet in the house on Catherine Street. On 27 February Richard Bell's name was dropped from the colophon of the *Post* and only the name of the printer, J. Burd, retained. How long Bell continued to publish the paper is not clear. He had certainly been replaced by 1780, since from 1780 through 1783 he was, according to the Audit-Office records,[24] connected with the *General Advertiser*, and he may have been replaced almost at once. On 11 July, 1777, J. Burd was succeeded by Robert Haswell. Haswell had warned Bate that he did not have the support of the proprietors, and nothing could more effectively have established the truth of this statement than Haswell's return. Bate had obviously distrusted him for some time, for, not only had he approved of his dismissal, but he had obstinately maintained, despite all evidence to the contrary, that Haswell was the arch-conspirator against the *Post.* Whatever compunction he may have felt at the subsequent discovery of Haswell's innocence was certainly more than offset by the adverse publicity he had received from Haswell's letters to the *Morning Chronicle.* The rehiring of Haswell was not, therefore, the work of Bate, but of Bate's enemies, who by now, it appeared, constituted a majority of the proprietary. But, faced with the choice of accepting the humiliation or quitting the paper, Bate chose to accept the humiliation, with the result that he continued as editor and Haswell as printer with at least a semblance of harmony for over three years.

By 1780 there had been a considerable change in the proprietary of the *Post.* Of the twenty-five shares, Bate now held five, "being *one fifth of the property,*" and the remaining twenty were divided among seven others: John Bell, Thomas Skinner, James Christie, Henry Watkins, Jeremiah Hargrave, Joseph Richardson, and a Mr. Weatherby (*Post,* 26 Sept., 1780). Tattersall, Trusler, Mitchell, Walsh, and Merryman had sold their shares and retired, Tattersall buying back in perhaps 1786, Mitchell by at least 1793.[25] Trusler's subsequent connection with the paper is in doubt, but he was certainly not a proprietor in September, 1780, as Taylor indicated.[26] Bate was now the largest shareholder (*Gazetteer,* 21 Sept., 1780), and he was still the editor, although all the proprietors, except possibly Christie, Weatherby, and Watkins, were taking an active interest in the management. Politically the *Post* was still supporting the Ministry, and since 1778 it had been so zealous in its support of the First Lord of the Admiralty, the infamous Lord Sandwich, that on 24 April, 1779, the Earl of Bristol referred to it as "L$^\text{D}$ SANDWICH's Morning Post." [27] By this time Lord Sandwich had a second newspaper, for, at the beginning of 1779, the proprietors of the *Post* began a triweekly evening paper, entitled the *English Chronicle, or Universal Evening Post,* which was also Ministerial. The *English Chronicle* was printed at the *Post* office, and, for the first year of its existence, it was published by John Wheble, who may therefore also have been publishing the *Post.* James S. Barr, who had replaced Wheble by 21 March, 1780, was in fact publishing both newspapers. Despite the *Post's* apparent dedication to the Government, there was a schism in the proprietary, for Skinner and Richardson were enthusiastic Foxites, who could be counted on to sabotage the politics of the paper if the opportunity arose.

Even so, it is doubtful that politics had much to do with the first of the events which led to Bate's quitting the *Morning Post*. These events had their beginning in December, 1779, when the *Post* published the first of many paragraphs on the Duke of Richmond, the purport of which was that the Duke was a traitor. Since the Duke was an active member of the Opposition, such paragraphs were in harmony with the paper's political position, but Bate seems also to have been thinking in terms of publicity. Since his last duel had occurred on 13 January, 1777, when Captain Andrew Robinson Stoney, later Bowes, was wounded in the breast and arm and he himself in the thigh,[28] he seems to have felt that the time had come for another; and one might almost have predicted that he would select the Duke as his opponent, the Duke being short-tempered, fond of swordplay, and, of course, a man of consequence. Unfortunately the Duke did not regard the matter as an affair of honor. According to Bate's statement (*Post*, 27 June, 1780), the Duke made no protest to him, but he grumbled about the paragraphs to others, always mentioning Bate as their author. After several months of this, Bate sent the Duke a note of protest, and, when this note was ignored, he sent another, indicating that *he* would like to have satisfaction. The Duke replied on 24 April by moving the Court of King's Bench against the printer of the *Post* for a libel. The paragraph singled out as actionable was a set of "Queries" addressed to him on 25 February, 1780.

Everyone understood that the Duke was prosecuting Haswell only because he had insufficient evidence to prosecute Bate, but Haswell was nevertheless alarmed. He at once applied to the proprietors for indemnification, which Bate strongly advised against granting, since, as he pointed out, Haswell "was under articles to them to be responsible for the publication of any improper matter" (*Post*, 27 June, 1780). The proprietors, who conceded the validity of Bate's argument with some reluctance, refused the application, but gave Haswell permission to call on the Duke and extricate himself if possible. All the Duke wanted was a statement from Haswell implicating Bate, and Haswell supplied it in the form of an affidavit. The *Post* of 24 June, 1780, gives Haswell's version of the affair. On "the 23rd or 24th of February," it appears, Bate,

as [Haswell] had sworn in the affidavit which he had made, . . . delivered
to him the MS. of the Queries, together with other manuscripts, pointing to
them as they lay upon a desk in the editor's office, and saying, "there's the copy
for to-morrow," or words to that effect. [Haswell] recognised the hand writing
. . . of the person from whom it came, who was named [William] Perryman,
and was a journeyman printer at Plymouth. . . . [As] soon as the Duke of
Richmond had moved the Court against [Haswell], . . . [Haswell] waited
on his Grace, by the consent of the proprietors of the Morning Post, and tried
to stop the prosecution, by informing his Grace of all he knew, relative to the
matter. . . . [He] accidentally, and of course mentioned the circumstances
of [Bate's] having delivered the MS. to him for the paper, in his official capacity as Editor. . . . [He] had no idea of the Duke's prosecuting [Bate],
but imagined the author would be the object of his Grace's prosecution.

But the Duke had no interest in Perryman. On the basis of Haswell's
affidavit, he on 28 April applied for permission to file a second information against Bate. Permission was granted on 29 April, and on
22 June, Bate was tried in the Court of King's Bench before Mr. Justice
Buller and a special jury "for being an accessary to the publication of
certain queries addressed to his Grace in the Morning Post of the 25th
of February last."

There was no mention in the newspapers of the actions against Haswell and Bate, and meanwhile the actions evidently had no effect on
the *Morning Post,* for on 1 June, 1780, Walpole observed [29] that "Mr.
Bates [*sic*] had rather lie than speak truth; and for fear he should
even be suspected of veracity, he has chosen the Duke of Richmond
for the hero of his abuse." It is also remarkable that, despite what he
had done, Haswell continued to print the *Post* until 26 June, and he
evidently did so with Bate's consent. There is only one way of accounting for this fact as well as for the nature of Bate's defense at the trial
and his subsequent bitterness: Haswell had promised to retract in his
testimony every statement he had made in his affidavit.

The trial itself was given complete coverage by the *Post,* the first
account, which appeared on 23 June, being only an abridgment of a
second, which appeared the following day. Prior to the passage of Fox's
Libel Act in 1792, verdicts of juries in cases of libel were based strictly
on matters of fact, decisions as to actual guilt or innocence, with their
numerous intermediary gradations, being made by the judges, who supposedly reconsidered the cases later in terms of law. Hence the prosecution, headed by John Dunning, attempted only to establish the

facts that Bate was indeed editor of the *Post* and that he had had prior knowledge of the insertion of the "Queries." Three witnesses were called. One of them, James S. Barr, identified himself as "publisher" of the paper, testified to having received the "Queries" in a "letter . . . from his friend Perryman at Plymouth," but refused to "swear either that the Defendant was the Editor of the Morning Post, or that [the Defendant] delivered the MS. of the Queries to the Printer, knowing nothing of either circumstance." The defense counsel clearly expected the other two witnesses to testify in much the same way. However, the second one, Mr. Skinner, having "deposed, that he was one of the proprietors of the Morning Post," added that he "believed the Defendant was employed as superintendant and conductor of the literary department of the paper." But the real surprise was the third witness, who, in fact, testified first.

Haswell was, it may be supposed, in an awkward position. Not only was he obliged to satisfy the proprietors, one of whom, at least, had indicated that he was no friend of Bate, but there was also the matter of his own interests, for the Duke of Richmond had not dropped the action against him, and it was clear to Haswell that whether it would be dropped or not depended entirely on his present testimony. Whether the testimony he gave was his own impulsive attempt to temporize or whether, as Bate thought, it was dictated by the Duke is a matter of conjecture. One can say only that the Duke was well pleased, and Haswell was not prosecuted. Haswell began by swearing that "he had been employed in the service of the Proprietors of the Morning Post about six or seven years; that he had known the Defendant to be the Editor of the Paper at the original setting up of it, and for most of the time afterwards; that he was the Editor in February last." He then summarized what he had said in his affidavit. However, he went on, although, "when he made his affidavit, he very [*sic*] believed what he swore, viz. that the Defendant had actually delivered the MS. of the Queries to him, as a part of the copy for the next day's paper . . . , a doubt had been started since, whether the Defendant really delivered the MS. of the Queries to him or not, and whether that MS. might not have been taken up by him with other papers, without the Defendant's ever seeing it. . . . He further said, it was no part of the Editor's business to revise the paper," and he did remember that Bate had disapproved of some of the attacks on the Duke of Richmond.

Haswell's apologies succeeded only in establishing his creditability as a witness, for none of them helped Bate. That Mr. Bearcroft, Bate's counsel, was taken aback by the testimony is evident from the fact that he had prepared no defense. He tried to point out that Haswell was "an interested witness, . . . in the situation of a person upon a plank at sea, who had shoved off his companion, for the sake of securing his own safety. The jury would see, that if the Defendant was not convicted, the witness was in the power of the Duke of Richmond, and therefore . . . it was his interest . . . to ensure the Defendant's ruin to preserve himself." Having repeated this statement several times, he said once more that "Haswell . . . had a rope about his neck, with which he was endeavouring to strangle the Defendant in order to save himself," and sat down. It took the jury fifteen minutes to find a verdict against Bate, and on 26 June Haswell was replaced as printer of the *Post* by H. Macleish.

On the following day (27 June, 1780) the *Post* published a letter signed by Bate and addressed to the Duke of Richmond. In this letter Bate reviewed all the events which led up to the trial, showing that each one of them was part of a plot, contrived by the Duke of Richmond, to force him to retire from the *Post*. But, despite the verdict of the jury, said Bate, the plot had failed. As for himself, he had no intention of fleeing the country, as his "friends," the other proprietors, were urging him to do: he would remain in England, serve his sentence, whatever it was, and continue to edit the *Post*. And, as for those other proprietors, he continued, so little were they influenced by the outcome of the trial that they had of their own accord acted to discharge Haswell. "Your agent the Printer, My Lord," Bate concluded, "is [therefore] totally at your service, having been dismissed by the propriety [*sic*] of the paper without a single reproach [of Haswell] on my part. . . . Having thus sacrificed a place of no inconsiderable emolument to your Grace's views, I hope I need not recommend him to your protection." On 3 July the *Post* addressed a second letter "*To* his *Grace the* D– of R–," expressing in two columns of sarcasm its gratitude for the Duke's various services. This letter was signed "Solon." Bate's confidence in the proprietors at this point is hard to understand. As Bate remembered later (*Post,* 26 Sept., 1780), the proprietors had already "proposed to *exonerate* Haswell, . . . though he had *given them an article of indemnity*," they had encouraged Haswell to call on the Duke, two of them were friends of the Duke, one of them had testified against Bate at the trial, and all of them were now urging him to flee to France. But these facts were evidently outweighed by the all-important fact that they had of their own accord dismissed Haswell.

## THE STRANGE BEHAVIOR OF THE PROPRIETORS

THE *Morning Post* of 26 September, 1780, carries a full account of Bate's quarrel with the proprietors. Although the exact dates of some of the events are not specified, the quarrel seems to have begun in July, when Bate attempted to withhold fifty pounds from the paper's profits to apply on the cost of his defense. The proprietors demurred on the ground that they had frequently expressed their disapproval of the paper's vicious attacks on distinguished persons and were therefore under no obligation to indemnify an editor who persisted in admitting them. Bate reacted to this argument by offering to buy out the other proprietors or to sell out himself, and on 7 August the other proprietors decided to purchase. The only question was how much they should pay. According to Bate's account, "our articles stipulated that all shares should be first offered to the Proprietors at the last valuation, viz. 350*l*. each"; but, since he himself "had just given near 800*l*. for one [share], and other Proprietors had subsequently been allowed to sell at that price," it seemed only fair to him that he, too, should receive the "best" price. The proprietors were unwilling to pay £800, "*but at last,*" said Bate, "*offered me* 500 *guineas for each of my* [*five*] *shares, payable in two years and bearing five per cent. Interest. To this proposition I acceded.*"

When the "proposition" was offered, however, the proprietors understood that Bate was leaving London and the newspaper business, having "an expectancy of a Church living at some distance in the country," and his announcement of 22 August that he intended to set up a rival morning paper colored their thinking considerably, especially when, as they charged (*Post*, 26 Sept., 1780), Bate prepared for his new venture by attempting to "seduce" the employees of the *Post*. They therefore sent Bate "a written notice . . . , 'that as it was understood that [he] intended to set up another paper in opposition to them, they retracted from their agreement, and were determined, if [he] would quit the property, it should be at the least valuation.' " The last statement was misleading, for the proprietors were as "determined" that Bate *would* "quit the property" as they were that he would do so "at the least valuation." To be certain that he quit, they recalled Haswell and on 12 September, 1780, gave him complete charge of the *English Chronicle,* of which by this time Bate was no longer a proprietor, having sold his shares to the other proprietors "some time past" (*Post,* 15 Sept., 1780). As Bate recounted this ultimate "insult" (*Post,* 26 Sept., 1780), the proprietors, having already "retracted from" their agreement to pay five hundred guineas a share, "appointed *Haswell* to superintend their Evening Paper, *which they printed at the Morning Post Office without my permission and of which I was not a proprietor.* This I deemed an insult of too violent a nature to be submitted to, and therefore went to the office, where I had the satisfaction to compel the workmen, in presence of most of the proprietors, to take out the name of the said printer from the bottom of the paper, and the next day to remove all their materials out of the house." The *English Chronicle* was thereupon transferred to No. 283, Strand, but Haswell was not discharged.

In the course of ousting the *English Chronicle,* Bate happened to observe that, in rehiring Haswell, the proprietors had demonstrated that they were too "cowardly" to stand out against the Duke of Richmond. Joseph Richardson took exception to this observation, insisting that he was not a coward and demanding that Bate exclude him from the allegation. Several notes passed between them, which were printed and reprinted by the *Post,* the *Chronicle,* and the *Gazetteer—* the *Chronicle* and the *Gazetteer* being unable to contain their joy at the prospect of a fight between two proprietors of the *Post.* Since it seemed to Bate that any qualification of his remark would somehow imply a weakening of his resolve that the "name . . . of *Haswell* shall never appear at the bottom of a paper printed in the Morning Post Office, while I continue possessed of the principal part of that property" (*Gazetteer,* 11 Sept., 1780), he refused to modify it in any respect; and, although he admitted that he might have been "involved in too many contests of a similar nature" already (*Post,* 15 Sept.), he made it clear that he was willing to fight again. His challenge was delivered by Dennis O'Bryen [30] on 13 September, and Bate and Richardson met the following day. An account of the duel, in which Richardson was wounded in the right arm, and of the events which led up to it appears in the *Post* and the *Chronicle* of 15 September, 1780. According to John Taylor,[31] who delivered Richardson's notes to Bate's home "in Surey-street, Strand," although he did not officiate as his second, Richardson had acted throughout in behalf of Thomas Skinner rather than himself. "If I had not a wife and family," Skinner was quoted as saying on 12 September, "I should call [Bate] to account for the stigma which he applied to us." Since Richardson did not have "a wife and family" and since he was much indebted to Skinner, who had "procured for him the situation of a literary contributor to [the *Post*] and afterwards furnished him with the means of becoming one of its proprietors," he felt bound to represent Skinner in the matter.

The proprietors maintained that Bate was dismissed; he himself maintained that he resigned. Both points of view are defensible. By 1780 the *Morning Post* was an extremely lucrative business, and it is certainly true that, once he had declared his intention of leaving, Bate lost interest in leaving, and he would have remained had the proprietors not forced him to go by recalling Haswell. The recall was intended and accepted as an insult. Hence on 13 September, 1780, Bate demanded that the proprietors meet to accept his resignation and decide the terms of the sale. The meeting was set for 19 September at the Rainbow Inn, the "order" being signed by Bate, Bell, Skinner, Hargrave, and Richardson and sent to the "absent proprietors," Christie, Weatherby, and Watkins. The "absent proprietors" seem not to have been involved in the quarrel, for Bate made it clear in his narration (*Post*, 26 Sept.) that they were not included in his "general imputation."

On 19 September, 1780, therefore, Bate sold his shares at £350 each and quit the *Morning Post*. The principal purchaser was probably John Bell, who at least succeeded Bate as the leading shareholder. A few days later Bate published a detailed explanation of his "resignation" in another newspaper, most likely the *Gazetteer*. By this time it seemed to him that a certain radical faction among the proprietors, obviously Skinner and Richardson, had been plotting with the Duke of Richmond to convert the *Post* to "republicanism" and that he had therefore been the victim of political rather than personal intrigue. But it also seemed to him that the proprietors had behaved stupidly and ungratefully, inasmuch as the success of the paper had been due to his "industry and ability" alone. The *Post* acknowledged these opinions on 25 September with the statement: *"The Proprietors of the Morning Post have the pleasure of informing the public, that Mr. Bate is no longer the editor of their paper. Mr. Bate having thought proper to obtrude on the public a case, which he calls a hasty one, respecting his concerns in the Morning Post, the Proprietors propose giving a* faithful state of the facts *in to-morrow's paper which have hitherto been deferred in order to have the deeds of separation finally adjusted and executed. . . ."*

The "faithful state of the facts" appeared on 26 September, headed *"The* PROPRIETORS *of the* MORNING POST *to the* PUBLIC." The proprietors began with the promise that this was "the last word" which they would utter "on the matter" and with the assurance that they would have kept quiet altogether had not Bate himself felt that the quarrel was "a public affair." They went on to reprint in full Bate's letter "TO *the* PUBLIC" of "a few days ago," in which he had set forth the reasons for his "resignation," and then proceeded to answer it. The answer alone filled two columns. Without denying that their conduct had been as Bate represented it, they attempted only to show that it was justified. In particular they took issue with Bate's declaration that his *"industry and ability"* had been responsible for the success of the *Post*. Bate's *"industry,"* they said, was such that for the last two years Haswell had had to edit the paper as well as print it, relying upon "matter furnished by our numerous correspondents, and through those higher channels of information," and Bate's *"ability"* had manifested itself only in vicious and embarrassing attacks on distinguished persons. It was, in fact, Bate's total lack of *"industry and ability"* which had forced the proprietors to "dismiss" him. However, they added, "from a possibility that the publication of his *dismission* may hurt the delicacy of his feelings, we have no objection to his having it understood he *resigned.*" The address concluded with the sentiment: "That the dawnings of grace may in time illuminate all Bishops, Priests, and Deacons; and that Mr. Bate may hereafter live peaceably with all men, stand in awe of the Morning Post and walk in the right way all the rest of his life, is the sincere wish of his old Masters!"

## SOME WHYS AND WHEREFORES OF THE *MORNING HERALD*

BATE subsequently (*Herald*, 1 Jan., 1782) declared that his *"principal object in the institution of [the Morning Herald] was to expose, and punish the unparallelled perfidy of his former Colleagues."* Although he was too wise to attempt another forgery, the idea of using a newspaper as an instrument of "punishment" was undoubtedly suggested to him by his experience with the spurious *Post*. But his situation was vastly different from that of the hawkers, for, whereas the hawkers had been joined by other disgruntled ex-employees of the *Post*, including a printer with press and building, none of the ex-employees was willing to join Bate, and even his attempts to "seduce" the present employees failed, *"one excepted"* (*Post*, 26 Sept., 1780), the *"one"* being, of course, James S. Barr, who had testified in his behalf at the trial. Hence on 19 September Bate was still lacking a staff, a press, a building, and in all likelihood money, for he had lost considerably on the sale of his shares in the *Post*, and even the £1,750 he recovered were probably recovered over a period of two years. Some of the money for the original financing of the *Herald* undoubtedly came from the Rockingham Whigs, since the paper at once undertook their support. It is, in fact, ironic that, having fought "republicanism" for the previous eight years and having supposedly been undone by a "republican" plot, Bate had hardly left the *Morning Post* when he himself became a convert to the "republican" cause. By the time the *Herald* began, he was a personal friend of many of the Rockingham group and an admirer of all of them with the exception, of course, of the Duke of Richmond.

On 28 October, 1780, the proprietors of the *Morning Post*, who had evidently been following the progress of Bate's arrangements with close attention, suggested to their readers *"that in case any other publication should be intruded, or attempted to be imposed upon them in the room of the* MORNING POST, *they will give immediate notice to the* PRINTER. . . . —*The* PROPRIETORS *will take special care . . . to prosecute the offender with the utmost rigour of the law, and to publish his name at length as a proper object of public reprobation."* This suggestion was repeated on 31 October and on 1 and 2 November, and on 1 November the first number of the *Morning Herald, and Daily Advertiser* made its appearance. According to the colophon, it was printed and published by J. S. Barr at No. 18, Catherine Street, Strand, and it did not look at all like the *Post*. It, in fact, specifically stated that it was not the *Post*, but a new newspaper, which would be "conducted upon liberal principles" and upon a high ethical plane, the editor at last having *"power . . . equal to the suppression of* obscene trash, *and* low invective." This sneer, intended as a reply to the proprietors' address of 26 September, elicited no response.

Nothing more was said of the *Post* until 9 November, when Bate struck at the *Post*'s sale, which had, he said, suffered *"an ignominious decline,"* being now far below the *Herald*'s, and, *"[as] to those illiterate men, who to the astonishment of the world have weakly sacrificed so capital a property,—though* disgrace *may not operate upon* them *so sensibly as upon others, yet* . . . *there is no doubt but they have, by this time, made an ample expiation for their* baseness, *and* folly!" On 27 November he referred again to *"our fallen competitors,"* and on 2 December, having boasted that the sale of the *Herald "is now more extensive than that of the* Morning Post *ever was,"* he invited the public to verify the fact by a visit to the Stamp Office. Since a newspaper's ability to attract advertisers depended on its reputed sale, precise figures being rarely mentioned, statements of this kind could usually be counted on to arouse any group of proprietors. But the proprietors of the *Post* noted simply (30 Nov.) that the "simple Editor of a new publication" had been "[employing] incessantly his abuse and scurrility to provoke the attention of the Morning Post, and raise himself to the dignity of our resentment," that "the public" had been demanding that his falsehoods, forgeries, stupidities, dullness, and total lack of wit and learning be publicly denounced, and that they had nevertheless refused and would continue to refuse to degrade themselves and their newspaper to the point of feuding with Bate and his "publication."

At the end of November, Bate tried another tactic, but this time he seems to have had more in mind than "provoking" the proprietors' "attention." According to the colophon, the *Post* was still printed by H. Macleish, but the possibility that Haswell was conducting the paper as well as printing and conducting the *English Chronicle* seems to have troubled Bate a great deal, for one purpose of the new tactic was certainly to identify the present editor of the *Post*. The point of departure for Bate's plot was a paragraph which appeared in the *Post* of 29 November concerning a party given by Mr. Solomons, M.P. In describing the masks worn by the various guests, the *Post* remarked that the "Master Laurences were at home in Captain Flash and Fribble. The youngest was seized with a sciatica, which discomposed the company for a few minutes." It is hard to see how this remark could have been offensive, for Captain Flash and the hypochondriac Fribble, characters in Garrick's popular farce, *Miss in Her Teens,* were frequent visitors at masquerades, and guests were usually described as being "at home" in the characters. But Bate, who evidently knew the younger of the "Master Laurences," a Mr. J. W. Laurence, was able to persuade him that the remark was offensive and that he was bound to demand satisfaction. The *Herald* of 7 December, 1780, published a long letter from J. W. Laurence "TO THE PUBLIC," reporting the consequences.

Laurence had, it appeared, called at the *Post* office several times without being able to find either the printer or the editor of the paper. Having at last learned that the name of the editor was "J. Jackman," but that Mr. Jackman *"had been gone out about half an hour to Buckingham-house,"* Laurence waited for his return, and, when Jackman failed to return, left a letter demanding that Jackman reveal the name of the author of the libel or meet him the following morning in Hyde Park and threatening that, if Jackman failed to appear, he would expose him as "a COWARD, a LIAR, and a SCOUNDRELL." Jackman thereupon challenged Laurence, but he did not, according to Laurence, present himself for the duel, so that he was now being exposed as "a COWARD, a LIAR, and a SCOUNDRELL." On the following day (8 Dec.) Jackman protested in the *Post* that he had appeared and that Mr. J. W. Laurence had not, and, he added, it was his own opinion that the "silly creature" was a "cat's paw" of a "certain Gentleman" who had "had the management of him for some days" in a plot against the *Post.* The *Herald* replied on 9 December with a protestation of Bate's innocence, and on 11 December Jackman published a full account of the affair in the *Post.* He denied that he had ever avoided Laurence; and, as to the duel, he said, he had arrived at Hyde Park in good time, but, instead of finding Laurence, he had found the police, who, he was certain, were sent by Laurence; and he was taken into custody. The whole affair, Jackman declared, had been a plot to identify and ruin the editor of the *Post,* and he, as that editor, intended to sue "the skulking villain who was the great mover of this whole business for libel."

The denunciation of the "Rev. Iago, of Catherine-street" was continued in the *Post* of the following day (12 Dec.), by which time Jackman could report that, according to the "general belief," it was Bate, not Laurence, who "lodged the information . . . , that prevented two Gentlemen from determining an affair of honour in Hyde Park, on Saturday morning last.—The RASCAL it is well known had written the paper himself that occasioned the challenge, and had fomented a dispute between two Gentlemen for the most infernal of all purposes." "The birth, parentage, education, and rogueries, of this unprecedented VILLAIN,—this notorious murderer of private peace and character," would, Jackman promised, "shortly be laid before the public;—nor shall we quit him *'until we put in every hand a whip to lash the Rascal naked through the world.'*" On 14 December the *Herald* published a letter from Laurence, who accepted full and exclusive responsibility for his action. He stated positively that Bate did not write "the paper" which led to the duel, that he saw a copy of it only after it was delivered, and that he then said that he should have advised against its delivery, but added that, once it had been delivered, he did not see how it could honorably be withdrawn. As to the identity of the person who sent the police to Hyde Park, Laurence professed to know nothing.

The identity of the person was, in fact, never ascertained, for on 13 December the *Post* brought the matter to a conclusion with the announcement:

> *The* EDITOR *. . . is obliged to acquaint the* PUBLIC, *that an absolute injunction was laid upon him last night, by those particularly interested in his future endeavours [i.e., the proprietors], never more to trouble the Public with so abandoned a Miscreant as the Rev.* IAGO *. . . ; nor directly or indirectly to reply to any* CHARGE, REFLEXION, *or* INSINUATION, *of* WHAT NATURE OR KIND SOEVER, *the* VILLAIN *may hereafter be induced to invent and impose upon the world.—To promote the sale of a most* contemptible *Publication, he would* sacrifice *the peace and honour of the whole Metropolis. The* EDITOR, *therefore, . . . shall leave him, until by due course of Law, he is delivered into the hands of the common executioner.*

This was strong language. In eighteenth-century journalistic diction, the term *publication* was, for example, itself a term of maximum contempt, as opposed to the term *print,* which was neutral, and the term *paper* or *newspaper,* which was respectful; hence it was almost never preceded by an adjective. But so powerful were Jackman's emotions that he could think of the *Herald* only in double superlatives. He had reason to be angry, for, since newspapers as scurrilous as the *Morning Post* usually preferred to conceal the names of their editors, he could be quite certain that his employment was drawing to a conclusion.

He had been dismissed by at least 1783 and probably much earlier, and he seems to have had no subsequent connection with London newspapers.

This over, Bate returned to the matter of circulation. On 15 December, 1780, the *Herald* declared that its own circulation *"is already increased to the very extensive sale of* 3000 *copies daily, which was the utmost number printed by the* M. POST, *before the late rupture. The proprietors of the last mentioned paper boast, that . . . they are still able to circulate more than* 1000 *papers; but we have . . . reason to doubt the fact . . . and that from the* STAMP OFFICE *records."* This declaration, the proprietors evidently felt, could not be ignored, for on 1 January, 1781, they abandoned their resolve never *"to reply to any* CHARGE, REFLEXION, *or* INSINUATION, *of* WHAT NATURE OR KIND SOEVER" long enough to reply to it. *"Insinuations have been very industriously spread concerning the present state of the* MORNING POST *representing its circulation to have been considerably decreased,"* they noted, whereas, in fact, *"our weekly distribution* at this time amounts to TWENTY-ONE THOUSAND THREE HUNDRED, *and the last six days we had an increase of* SIXTY-TWO: *for the truth of these facts, we refer to the* STAMP OFFICE *receipts now in possession of our Clerk at the* MORNING POST OFFICE." This announcement, which was several times reprinted, concluded with the usual invitation to readers to call at the office and examine the records personally. On 5 January the *Herald* published a letter, signed *"A Clerk in the Stamp-Office,"* which maintained that everything the *Post* had said about its circulation was an "imposition" promulgated by "the proprietors of that once favourite paper, called the *Morning Post."* "I aver," the "Clerk" assured Bate, "that from referring to the books, they have not really worked more than 1000 a day, though formerly under your management, they used to work more than treble that number. I dare the publisher to declare upon oath, that they publish *one half* of the well known sale of the MORNING HERALD." The publisher did not rise to the challenge.

Newspapers' boasts of sales could be taken seriously only if they were supported by affidavits, as not one of these was. Yet the statement that prior to September, 1780, the *Morning Post* was selling "3000 *copies daily"* is probably accurate, for, since the proprietors, to whom the statement was addressed, were as well acquainted with the facts as he, Bate would have had no reason to exaggerate. This figure is of some consequence, for it represents generally the reading public for which the *Post* and the *Herald* were vying. By the late 1770's several news-papers were showing the influence of the *Post* by widening the scope of their interests to include some notice of sports, music, literature, paint-ing, and fashions, and more attention was being paid to "personalities" and "anecdotes." But the *Post* and the *Herald* were still the only news-papers specifically intended for the West End, and hence neither of them had any serious competitor except the other. The trouble was that any competition in such an area was ruinous, for, since in 1780 proprietors paid 1½*d*. stamp duty for every newspaper printed, 2*s*. 6*d*. for every advertisement accepted, and received in return only 3*d*. for every newspaper sold, a sale of even 3,000, although enor-mous by contemporary standards, did not represent a correspondingly enormous profit. Although the *Morning Post* had been a very lucrative business, it had always supplemented its income from sales of news-papers with sales of puffs, having realized a fortune, no doubt, from Lord Sandwich alone. But, now that its income from sales of news-papers had been curtailed, it had to look for supplementation of a more dependable sort. Hence, by 7 December, 1780, Jackman was spending his time at *"Buckingham-house,"* and, by the end of the year, the *Post* was very evidently in the pay of the King's Friends. Until the end of 1781, it supported the North Government, shifting thereafter to the side of the Shelburne Whigs.

Meanwhile Bate, who was still facing a prison sentence for his li-bel on the Duke of Richmond, was apparently unable to make a satis-factory arrangement with the Rockingham Whigs for the period of his incarceration, for, by the beginning of 1781, the *Herald* had also capitulated. On 29 December, 1780, the *Herald* taunted the *Post* for proposing "in almost express terms, to the people of England, to per-mit the influence of the crown (resolved by the representatives of the nation [in the Dunning Resolution of 6 April, 1780,] to have in-creased, to be increasing, and that it ought to be diminished) to pre-vail over the great and . . . *principal* branch of the legislature," and, for a short time thereafter, it continued to defend the Rockingham Whigs; but it soon dropped into a state of political confusion, from which it also emerged as a Ministerial journal. On 21 June, 1781, it published a highly unflattering "Sketch of the Character of [Bate's personal friend,] Mr. CHARLES FOX," and on 22 November it tacitly ad-mitted that it was receiving a "pension" from the Ministry "for ex-posing and vilifying the . . . minority." At the end of the year it shifted to the side of the Shelburne Whigs along with the *Morning Post*. The amount of the "pensions" allotted to the *Herald* and the *Post* is not indicated, but it was probably sizable, for political parties always paid considerably more for scurrilous newspapers than they did for discreet ones with comparable circulations.

## THE *MORNING HERALD* VS. ROBERT HASWELL

ON 25 JUNE, 1781, Bate presented himself in the Court of King's Bench to be judged for the publication of the libel on the Duke of Richmond, this formality having been "delayed . . . because the prison was not . . . sufficiently repaired to admit of prisoners, after the devastation committed by the [Gordon] rioters" in June, 1780.[32] There is a detailed account of the hearing in the *Morning Chronicle* of 26 June. Bate's counsel, Mr. Bearcroft, who had presented no defense at the trial, came prepared with "a variety of arguments for the diminution of punishment." He urged to begin with, that his client was now the editor of a "respectable" newspaper. He observed further that it was "well known, that the verdict [of the jury] had not given the most general satisfaction, and that mens opinions would . . . still . . . persist to entertain *doubts,* at least, of the fairness of that sentence; all he would say . . . was that Mr. Bate could only be considered barely within the pale of legal conviction, and . . . was [therefore] entitled to the most favourable dispensation of punishment." He noted in particular that Bate "had upon oath denied having ever seen the libel, until he saw it tacked to the Duke's affidavit, and it appeared, by Haswell's own evidence, that he had frequently disapproved . . . the insertion of several low and vulgar scurrilities against his Grace."

Mr. Lee, who represented the Duke, insisted that the evidence against Bate had been decisive. He himself was convinced that Bate had written the "Queries" as well as authorized their publication, for the "Queries" were, he said, far too polished to be the work of a journeyman printer. He also insisted that Bate's attitude toward the Duke was unchanged, and he cited as proof the letter published by the *Post* immediately following the trial, in which Bate had indicated that he would continue "the same plan of attack upon opposition as formerly, and of course upon the Duke, as a powerful member of that party." Mr. Peckham added the argument that Bate now owned a "very productive . . . newspaper" and that he also had "two valuable rectories in Essex, of which county he was also a magistrate," so that even a large fine would not tax his resources, and, if it did, "some of his noble friends" would pay it for him. "He then adverted to Mr. Bate's having deviated from the character of a clergyman, and dwelt on the impropriety of his having abused some of the highest and best men of the nation, instead of preaching to his flock." (Bate here objected that "at present, he had not the care of a flock.") But for Judge Edward Willes, himself a strong adherent of the Duke of Richmond, it was enough to know that the *Post* had impugned the Duke at a time when Bate was editing the paper. Hence, "after . . . a strongly coloured eulogium on the Duke . . . , as a disinterested Peer, a man of great abilities, and equal integrity," he sentenced Bate *"to remain for 12 months from this day"* in the *"custody* of the *Marshall of the King's Bench."* Bate, the report concludes, "heard the judgment with the utmost composure."

On 4 July, 1781, J. S. Barr was also called up to receive the judgment of the Court, along with the printer of the *London Courant,* the printer of the *Noon Gazette,* and the printer of the *Gazetteer,* all of whom had been convicted of publishing a libel on the Russian ambassador. Barr fared even worse than Bate, being fined £100 in addition to being imprisoned for twelve months. By mid-1781, therefore, the *Herald* was lacking a printer and publisher as well as an editor. Barr continued to be named in the colophon, but his work was, of course, done by an assistant, possibly by his "friend," William Perryman, the journeyman from Plymouth, who later (20 May, 1786) succeeded him as printer of the paper. Bate retired. Until the end of 1783, when he resumed control and the *Herald* shifted to the side of Fox, the paper was on outright lease to the Government and therefore managed by one of its hirelings, evidently Alexander Chalmers.[33] In any event the lease did not interfere with the punitive function of the newspaper, for, so strong were Bate's feelings about the Duke of Richmond, Haswell, and the proprietors of the *Post,* that he seems to have made a continuation of his war against this group a condition of the lease.

Until Bate was sentenced, the *Herald* ignored the Duke of Richmond, but on 5 July, 1781, it began a series of daily attacks on him, each of which was more violent than the preceding one, so that by 27 July the *Herald* was accusing the Duke, not only of being a traitor himself, but of making "every ignoble . . . attempt to seduce the people into sedition" and of "[traducing] the best and ablest men in the nation." This time the Duke did not prosecute. It also resumed its attacks on the *Morning Post,* the attacks having been suspended for several months in order to justify Bearcroft's plea that the *Herald* was a "respectable" newspaper. It was now ready for Haswell. On 31 July the *Herald* accordingly published the following paragraph:

We are authorized to lay [a certain] transaction before the public as a fact: An *effeminate* Printer, the now *typographer* of an *Evening* Paper, having been in company at a Masquerade with a literary gentleman, concerned in the General Advertiser, on their return from thence, offered him a bed at his house, which the latter readily accepted, conceiving that he should have some difficulty getting into his own lodgings at that unseasonable hour. When they arrived at his house, the Printer, however, made some excuse about disturbing his wife (for the creature is *married*) and therefore begged to partake of the bed he had allotted to his visitor, which the other very unfortunately complied with; for in less than ten minutes after he had laid down, he found himself under the disagreeable necessity of getting up from his bed-fellow, and loading him with the most ignominious terms of reproach for *tender advances,* the bare mention of which puts *real manhood* to the blush!—and from that day to this, has publicly proclaimed the *affectionate* treatment thus offered to him by his *typographical host!*

Further details of the "literary gentleman's" "public proclamation," the *Herald* promised, would follow.

This paragraph concerned an incident which had occurred three months earlier. The "literary gentleman" was James Perry, who later distinguished himself as the originator of the *European Magazine,* the editor of the *Gazetteer,* and the conductor of the *Morning Chronicle.* Perry had joined the staff of the *General Advertiser,* then owned in part by the firm of Richardson and Urquhart, booksellers, in 1777 and had advanced from paragraph writer at a salary of a guinea a week (with an additional half-guinea for assisting with the *London Evening Post*) [34] to conductor at a salary of *"two pounds two"* (*Herald,* 18 Aug., 1781). The *"now typographer* of an *Evening* Paper" was, of course, Haswell.

Since Perry was clearly identified in the paragraph, he could hardly disregard it. His reply was reprinted by the *Herald* of 6 August, 1781, having appeared in the *General Advertiser* a day or two earlier.

The quotation which follows comes from the *Herald,* which is undoubtedly responsible for the italics. "SIR," Perry began,

I am called upon by the duty which I owe to truth, and the character of an acquaintance basely and infamously slandered, to declare my abhorrence of a paragraph, in the Morning Herald, charging Mr. Haswell with attempting the commission of an act dreadful even in thought. . . .—Without having seen . . . Mr. Haswell on the subject, I am induced to . . . say, that I never authorized the insertion of this paragraph in the Morning Herald; nor ever ". . . proclaimed" any thing similar to what is there asserted; but I . . . understand, that the paragraph was manufactured from the following circumstance: About three months ago, at the table of a friend, I mentioned a *ludicrous and whimsical circumstance, that happened to Mr. Haswell and me,* in a moment of *complete intoxication;* without meaning to convey any impression unfavourable to him.

Perry went on to say that he had obviously put no "ill construction . . . upon [Haswell's] behavior," for he and Haswell had "since continued to live in *habits of mutual civility* and *friendly intercourse";* and "Mr. Haswell may assure himself," he concluded, "that he may depend on my anxious assistance in the discovery and punishment of the ruffian that has aspersed him."

The "Editor" of the *Herald* responded on 6 August, making it clear that his "subject" was the "conduct of the accuser," not the nature of the "transaction." He would avoid "animadversions on the *fact itself* of which a certain Printer has been charged by the said *Perry,*" he said, "till the whole affair has undergone a legal investigation." At present he was interested only in why Perry, who had told a group of "gentlemen" three months earlier that he had been "amorously besieged" by Haswell and that "an information [had] already been laid against him and—, the Apothecary, near Bow-street, for similar infamous practices," should now choose to alter his story. It seemed clear to him that either Perry was suffering from guilt for having accused "an *innocent* man" or he was himself *"effeminate":* "So that it may be difficult to decide, whether the approved innocence, or guilt of the Printer will make the conduct of his accuser more completely infamous." The effect of these remarks is evident from the following announcement, which appeared in the *Herald* two days later (8 Aug.): *"We think it incumbent . . . to declare,* that Mr. Newby *is not* the Editor of this Paper, *nor responsible for any matter it contains. This*

*declaration . . . will prevent the public from being* [*misled by*] . . .
*other papers."* "Mr. Newby" was not otherwise identified, and no
"Mr. Newby" is known to have been connected with newspapers during this period.

The *Herald* of 9 August had more to say on the subject of Haswell
and Perry. If Haswell was really *"innocent,"* it asked, why had he not
confronted Perry? Haswell could do "his character strict justice" only
by "[prosecuting] *Perry* as the traducer of his reputation," and the
*Herald* "pledged [itself] to him, . . . that several gentlemen, who are
unwilling to have their names mentioned in the public news-papers,
will come forward in a court of justice, and incontrovertibly prove
upon oath, that, *Perry in their hearing, did in the most positive terms,
charge the said Printer with having been guilty of a* most *unnatural attempt!"* As a token of its pledge, the *Herald* presented a letter from one
of the "gentlemen," for whose signature was substituted the information, " (*My Name is left with the Printer*) ." Similar letters, the *Herald*
promised, would be submitted by other "gentlemen," although Perry
was pleading with them to deny that he had told the story.

The tactic of making Haswell's innocence dependent on his filing
an action against Perry was continued on 11 August, when the *Herald*
devoted an additional three columns to the affair. This time it expressed its astonishment at the suggestion that it was in any way motivated by "personal pique, or resentment": it was motivated only by a
sense of outrage that any man should be so slandered as Haswell had
been, and its sole concern was to see that Haswell obtained justice.
By now it had collected some more information about Perry, namely,
that he had been involved in other affairs of the sort, one of his previous victims being a "baronet," and that this was not the only story he
had told about Haswell. The *Herald* would gladly give Haswell the
details.

The main body of the article, however, was a letter, written by
Dennis O'Bryen and signed by all the "gentlemen" who had heard the
tale. The letter, dated 10 August and now available for public inspection, began with a review of the case from its beginning. According to
this document, the original auditors were *"Mr. Stevens, Mr. M'Carthy,
two or three other gentlemen and* [*O'Bryen*]*,"* *"Mr. Stevens"* being
James Stephen, later (1811) a Master in Chancery and now a student of the law and a reporter and paragraph writer for the *Morning
Post,* and *"Mr. M'Carthy"* being Felix Macarthy, one of the "abun-

dance of low revellers" to be found at "taverns and houses of call," distinguished from the rest by his willingness to do a "political service for his friends." [35] All three "gentlemen" regarded the story as shocking; and, when, several months later, O'Bryen happened to mention it at a dinner table, his host, who was the (unnamed) editor of the *Herald,* remonstrated that it could not be true. O'Bryen cited Perry as his informant, whereupon the editor insisted on making the story public as a matter of journalistic duty. As soon as he did so, O'Bryen, in order to safeguard himself and the newspaper, visited the Court of King's Bench to attest the accuracy of the facts as he had stated them. He revisited the Court after Perry's letters appeared and this time was informed that, since Perry had denied the facts, he (O'Bryen) should perhaps "state the particulars, and the names of the parties to justify the conduct of the paper." O'Bryen was reluctant to do so, inasmuch as he and Macarthy had "lately been engaged in a similar prosecution." The nature of this "prosecution" was not specified. "Mr. Stevens" was also reluctant, since he was "the friend and countryman of *Perry* [Stephen was actually only educated in Scotland; he was born in Dorset], and the attached friend of the Morning Post, by being paid as a writer thereof." O'Bryen then sent for "a Mr. [D.] Coffey" of the First Devonshire Regiment, with whom he was later associated in another quarrel with the *Morning Post* (*Herald,* 16 Sept., 1783) ; and Coffey happily "declared every circumstance that Perry related in charge against the Printer." Their own interests having been looked after, the "gentlemen" were now concerned for Haswell's. But, when one of them visited the Court on Haswell's behalf, he was assured that under the circumstances there was nothing the "gentlemen" could do, for only "by a legal process" could there be "a full and clear investigation of this affair." "If you find [Haswell's] character will bear this scrutiny," the "gentlemen" therefore advised the *Herald,* "you have only to call upon us, and we will produce the amplest evidence that PERRY was his accuser."

By this time the villain of the piece seemed clearly to be Perry, and, whereas Perry had pledged his "anxious assistance" to Haswell, no one offered his "anxious assistance" to Perry. On 14 August the *Herald* noted that "[this] morning, the public are promised to receive the *redoubted* Mr. *Squash Perry*'s account of a late *ludicrous transaction* between him and a certain Printer." Why, it wanted to know, had the account been so long delayed? The only answer it could suggest was that Perry was "not like other men": he "paired off from the masquerade," and, when he "left his bed-fellow," he did not "break the bones of the assailant." No, he, *"gentle* creature, talked only of *wringing [Haswell's] ear, if [Haswell had] not [been] under his own roof!"* Nor did he think of complaining to the authorities. He preferred to conceal the affair "for near *three months"* and then to mention it casually to six gentlemen, one a stranger, in, as he said later, a spirit of "fun."

Perry's "account," which appeared in the *General Advertiser* of 15 August, consisted of "a string of opprobrious appellations" applied to the editor of the *Herald,* along with the following letter. The letter, addressed to Perry, was reprinted by the *Herald* of 16 August:

### (COPY)

On comparing the story published in the Morning Herald, of Tuesday, July the 31st, with that related by you in our company, we find the former greatly aggravated, and that it omits some circumstances connected with the latter, which tend to alter the complexion of the whole. By the one it would appear, that your sleeping with Haswell had resulted from a progressive scheme, and contrivance on the part of that *gentleman;* whereas we clearly recollect, that in the original story, it arose in mere accident, without any premeditation on either side; Haswell offering you a part of his bed, because you could not gain admission to your lodgings, as you were returning in his company from a Masquerade. It is stated too in the paragraph, that you were obliged to leave the bed in *ten minutes,* but we are confident no space of time was mentioned in our company. In addition to those, another aggravation arises from the *general* terms in which the fact is artfully mentioned, for the reader is thereby precluded from the means of forming his own conclusion, by a fair investigation of the premises; he is told that H–'s conduct was indecent, but is not enabled to decide whether it was really so or not, and whether it arose in accident or design.

The most material of the commissions, which we have remarked, are the following: *that Haswell was intoxicated, that you was not certain whether he was asleep or awake, and that you had not, on reflection, thought yourself warranted to retain the hasty impressions of the moment; all which circumstances were annexed by you to the story.*

The account published by Mr. O'Brien, *as far as it goes, is accurate,* and whether the part which appears to have been suppressed corresponds with the above, or otherwise, we doubt not he has spoken the truth impartially to the best of his recollection.

Having acquitted this debt of justice, we shall not think it incumbent on us to appear again before the public, either for the purpose of explanation or reply. The idea of a newspaper controversy on such grounds is disgusting in the extreme, and would be peculiarly improper, as we hear the affair will be decided in a court of law, where our evidence will be required.

We are, Sir,

Your most obedient humble servants,
F. M'CARTHY,
J. STEVEN,
D. COFFEY.

*Mr. Perry, Holyland's Coffee-house.*

The *Herald* had a long comment on this letter. "The reader will recollect," it began, "that *Perry* in his first letter on this subject, *denied* what he had been charged with having asserted; and thus heroically attempted to save the Printer, because he imagined that having concealed the affair so long, their fate would be mutual, and that both must either *sink* or *swim* together; hence arose the *curious* turn he would fain have given the affair, by calling it a *ludicrous transaction,* &c. &c. So stands *Perry's own* defence; it remains therefore only to see how far the few circumstances the gentlemen speak to [*sic*], either *justify* Perry, or corroborate his strange tale." In the *Herald's* opinion, the "circumstances" did not "corroborate" his "tale" in the least. Having argued this point at great length, the *Herald* went on to say:

The gentlemen whose names are annexed to the above paper fairly assert that *"Mr. O'Brien's account, as far as it goes is accurate."*— We require no further justification of our conduct than this, and therefore shall close the present disquisition with two or three observations derived from a review of the whole.

1*st, Perry,* in his letter made the whole a *ludicrous transaction:* the signers of his exculpatory letter, made it a very *serious one,* to be *palliated* only by the innocent suggestions of *sleep* or *intoxication!*

2*dly,* These gentlemen have very carefully confined themselves particularly to what Perry did *not say,* reserving all the aggravating things he *did say,* to a legal investigation, when we trust the *ludicrous transaction* in the *Baronet's carriage* will be amply developed among the rest.

3*dly,* Not one of the gentlemen will assert, that Perry's relation did not leave them impressed with the most unfavourable ideas of the object he had been describing!

4*thly,* Not a tittle of Perry's curious defence appeared in the *Morning Post* of yesterday, to the astonishment of the world; a clear proof how it was received in that *confederate quarter.*

Lastly, not a single word is now offered [by Perry] in defence of the poor, patient Printer. Ungrateful bedfellow! recollect your late professions of *friendly intercourse,* and *"habits of mutual civilities!"* and say, is it honourable, according to your own singular acceptation of the term, to abandon him at such a crisis, to all the horrors of despair?

The *General Advertiser* of 15 August had evidently also included a statement by Dennis O'Bryen, disclaiming responsibility for the *Herald's* paragraph of 31 July. For, having completed its comments on Perry, the *Herald* (16 Aug., 1781) noticed: "We have but one remark to make on the whole of Mr. O'Brien's rhapsody of yesterday: that is to assert, that, he *saw,* attentively *examined,* and *approved* of the article respecting Perry and the *Printer;* suggesting at the same time, the omission of the name of the former. However characteristic it may be with Mr. O'Brien to *tremble* for the consequences of an article he was perusing with *inattention,* he probably forgets, that he further ratified his approbation to a gentleman the succeeding day, in his walk across St. George's Fields!" O'Bryen, who had acted as Bate's second in the duel with Richardson, had probably been connected with the *Herald* since its beginning, and he had undoubtedly approved of the attack on Haswell. But he had obviously disapproved of the attacks on Perry, who was evidently guilty only of having told a story in the wrong company. But his statement may have had an additional purpose, for the *General Advertiser* was in the process of being sold to William Parker, and, since O'Bryen had accepted the post of editor, he was understandably concerned for the reputation of that newspaper. Perry seems to have left the *General Advertiser* on 16 August, for on 18 August the *Herald* celebrated his dismissal with a drama for three characters: "*Squash* Perry," "Master Stephen," and "The Tall Man," who was not identified. A few examples of the verse, taken from "*Squash* Perry's" recurrent laments, are perhaps sufficient:

> Farewell the conduct of the *Advertiser!*
> Farewell my plumed pen—my ink of gall!
>
> —Farewell the *two pounds two,* my weekly pay!
> Farewell the *beefstake* hot, and *porter* cool
> That make a Scotsman happy!—Oh farewell!
>
> The pride, pomp, and circumstance of debate!
> And oh, Charles F–x, whose rude, black *throat,*
> The *infernal* voice of Aetna counterfeits,
> Farewell! *Squash* Perry's occupation is no more!

## L'ENVOI

ON 22 AUGUST, 1781, the *Herald* resumed its war on the proprietors of the *Morning Post*, publishing the first of what was meant to be a series of letters from "The Mouse," who identified himself as the "last fool that stuck by the distrest, ungrateful beings" of the *Post*, until "my fidelity alack! has reduced me to skin and bone." The professed purpose of the letters was to present the final reports of the activities of the proprietors, with special reference to "Dr. *Trusselboard,*" "*Skinflint* the Auctioneer," and "Jerry *Hairgrey,*" before "The Mouse," too, deserted to the *Herald*. The first letter purportedly described a recent "committee meeting," at which it was decided that Haswell must " 'either *persecute* his *accuser,* or fly *into* his own country, in the North!' The Printer replied, 'the former he was not inclined to do, for reasons best known to himself: and the latter, he *could not* conveniently do . . . because, though no proprietor, the principal part of his property was embarked in the *Morning Post.*' " To this the proprietors made no reply, for they could not pay Haswell the money they owed him. At last Tattersall broke the silence by declaring that they had been fools: "he said, for his part, he advised from the first to pay the 50*l. forfeit* [the £50 Bate had tried to withhold to apply on his legal expenses], rather than run the d——d *Richmond sweepstakes,* which would have prevented all this *rig.*" "*Jerry Hairgrey,*" "*Bobby Bohea,*" and "*Mr. Critic*" tended to agree. The proprietors thereupon resolved that (*a*) they did not know what to do and (*b*) "Master Stephen 'be dismissed from the list of *paragraph writers.*' " So ended "The Mouse's" first report, and there was no second.

"The Mouse" seems to have had some acquaintance with Tattersall, who is elsewhere [36] described as coarse and illiterate with little knowledge of anything except horses and horse-racing; but he obviously had no acquaintance with the facts, for Tattersall and Trusler were not connected with the *Post* in the summer of 1780, nor did Bate have any quarrel with them. His quarrel was with Skinner, Richardson, Hargrave, and Bell; and, although Richardson may be the "Mr. *Critic*" of the account, it is unlikely that Bell is the "*Bobby Bohea,*" especially since "*Bohea*" is described as being on the point of emigrating. The joke about Haswell's having a lien on the *Morning Post* is also not very good, since Haswell had not worked for the *Post* since Bate quit the paper. If "The Mouse" was acquainted with the present proprietary of the paper, it had changed considerably in the previous eleven months, but there is no indication that he was. Bell, for example, should certainly have been mentioned, for he succeeded Bate as principal shareholder, remaining so until January, 1786.

The letter from "The Mouse" was the *Herald*'s last personal attack on the proprietors. Thereafter the paper contented itself with sporadic accusations that the *Post* was copying its paragraphs; and on 1 January, 1782, it declared the war at an end and proclaimed itself victor. The announcement was made by *"The Proprietor,"* who, in his New Year's "Address to the Public," explained that, inasmuch as *"His principal object in the institution of this paper,"* which *"was to expose, and punish the unparalleled perfidy of his former Colleagues,"* had now been accomplished, as the *"decisive superiority of the* HERALD *in emolument as well as fame"* proved, he would discontinue hostilities. This was not the declaration of a peace, for Bate continued to harass the *Morning Post* until the last of his enemies, Hargrave and Skinner, finally quit the paper. But it was the declaration of a truce. A truce at this time could not be avoided, for Bate was still in prison and would not be released for another six months, and, now that O'Bryen had deserted to the *General Advertiser,* there was no one who was sufficiently acquainted with the facts to carry on the battle. More important was the fact that the North Government was tottering, and the King was relying heavily upon the combined support of the *Post* and the *Herald* to see him through the ensuing crisis. A war between these two newspapers at such a time would have been unthinkable.

But Bate's statement that, at the beginning of 1782, the *Herald* was *"decisively superior"* to the *Post* *"in emolument as well as fame"* can be taken seriously. Although no precise figures are available, the *Herald*'s circulation seems to have been considerably larger. In fact, if one judges by the advertising duties,[37] the *Herald* outsold every other newspaper in 1781 and bettered its sale in 1782. By late 1783 the sale of the *Post* had dropped from 3,000 (in mid-1780) to approximately 1,650.[38] With respect to *"fame,"* the *Herald,* of course, had no second. Since newspapermen were essentially only businessmen, they were bound to be impressed by Bate's achievements, for, while they had been struggling to keep their own newspapers alive, Bate had founded one successful newspaper and ruined it with another newspaper which was even more successful. Under these circumstances, no newspaper-man could afford to stand out against the influence of Henry Bate: however much he deplored the new emphasis on "anecdotes" and "personalities," he could not do without it.

The means by which Bate had achieved his ends seem mean-while to have shocked no one. They also seem to have injured no one except the owners of the *Post* and perhaps Jackman, of whom nothing is known after 1780. Haswell was not dismissed as conductor of the *English Chronicle,* for he continued to conduct the paper through March, 1783. James Stephen was also not dismissed as "paragraph writer" for the *Post,* as "The Mouse" indicated. By the beginning of 1782, he had inherited some money, with which he was able to pur-chase his admittance to the bar and in 1783 to set sail for the West Indies. The experience did not even leave Stephen with bad memo-ries, for on 23 March, 1810, he told the House of Commons that his work for the *Morning Post* had been one of the most valuable employ-ments of his life. It is perhaps true that the *Herald* cost James Perry the conduct of the *General Advertiser,* for William Parker would probably have retained him had he not been involved in a scandal, but Perry recovered nicely. In January, 1782, he established the successful *European Magazine,* in 1783 he undertook the editing of the *Gazetteer,* and a few years later he became the conductor of the *Morning Chroni-cle,* all of which journals he distinguished by his steady insistence upon "liberty without licentiousness." That his strong feeling on the subject owed something to his ordeal of 1781 is indicated by the fol-lowing statement (*Gazetteer,* 7 Dec., 1789),[39] which, whether it was written by Perry or not, is typical of many he did write:

The abuse of the liberty of the press has of late years become so great, that no character is safe—not even the retirements of domestic felicity remain un-disturbed.

Such was not the case with the papers some years ago; the change took place when some needy adventurers thought that a fashionable Paper, that is, a record of private and public scandal, would suit the taste of the public, and fill *their* pockets better than a periodical detail of political information. . . .

The public *have been* to blame by encouraging such Papers. Many like the tale of scandal, which does not affect themselves—and the man of middling rank chuckled to read the amours and intrigues of Lords and Ladies, little thinking that his turn would one day come, his harmless actions be misrepresented, and his character be blasted in a paragraph.

But the "periodical detail of political information" was now a thing of the past: henceforth newspapers would either trade in "private and public scandal" or succumb.

# CHAPTER II

# The *Morning Post* (1782–1788): The Disreputable Years

### ENTER THE STUARTS

FROM 19 September, 1780, on, the *Morning Post* was in a state of decline. Although it was still being conducted in the Batean tradition, the *esprit* which had been responsible for its original success had disappeared along with the Rev. Henry Bate (after 1784 the Rev. Henry Bate Dudley), and it was now only a scandal sheet with a taste for heavy-handed scurrility. The paper was still subtitled *Daily Advertiser;* it was printed by H. Macleish, Blake Court, Catherine Street, Strand; and the proprietary still included John Bell, who was now the principal shareholder, Joseph Richardson, Thomas Skinner, James Christie, and Jeremiah Hargrave. On 13 December, 1780, the *Post* was being edited by J. Jackman; the identity of his successor is not known.

The support which the *Morning Post* had always given the Ministry was owing to expedience rather than principle, for, not only did the Ministry pay more than the Opposition, the Treasury being more opulent than any individual or group of individuals, but it also provided "priority of intelligence," a very precious commodity to an eighteenth-century newspaper. Insofar as there was any strong political feeling among the proprietors, the feeling was, in fact, liberal rather than conservative, for two of the group, Thomas Skinner and Joseph Richardson, were zealous adherents of the Rockingham Whigs. Thomas Skinner was an early proprietor, being connected with the *Post* by at least 8 November, 1776; Joseph Richardson was a latecomer. Of Richardson one knows only [1] that Skinner first "procured for him the situation of a literary contributor" and "afterwards furnished him with the means of becoming one of [the] proprietors" and that he was a proprietor in 1780. In 1780, too, there was the first indication of political discord, and Bate was probably correct in saying (*Post*, 26 Sept., 1780) that the two took advantage of his quarrels with the other proprietors and the Duke of Richmond to attempt to convert the paper to "republicanism." This attempt, however, failed, and, by the end of the year, the *Post* was in the pay of the King's Friends.

Everyone who valued the responsibility and dignity of the press regarded the kind of journalism represented by the *Morning Post* and the *Morning Herald* with alarm, but not so the politicians, who saw in it the means of dealing with their opponents by ridicule and abuse. Thus, when the King's Friends acquired the *Post* and the *Herald,* the North Government was obviously doomed, and it was of great consequence to the King that it be succeeded by the Shelburne Whigs; but, although most of the other newspapers were supporting the Rockingham Whigs, the King faced the future with every confidence that the issue would be decided by these two newspapers alone. The Rockingham Whigs evidently agreed with him, for, in anticipation of the battle, they acquired and staffed the *London Courant* and the *General Advertiser* for the express purpose of dealing with the *Post* and the *Herald* on their own terms. By the beginning of 1782, the North Government was tottering and the *Post* and the *Herald* were shifting their support to Lord Shelburne; and on 4 January, 1782, the *Courant* announced that henceforth it would dedicate itself to a policy of "attacking" and "exposing" the "political principles of the Morning Post." There was no corresponding declaration of war on the *Herald,* for, if Bate's various scourges achieved nothing else, they struck lasting terror into the hearts of all newspapermen. The *Courant* continued its war for two months, and on 7 March Macleish was replaced as printer of the *Post* by "D. Stuart," who on 16 March was replaced by Charles Stuart.

Since the three Stuart brothers were to be responsible for the destinies of many London newspapers, something should perhaps be said about their background. According to one source,[2] they "were of the Stuarts of Loch Rannoch, in Perthshire [a respectable Scotch family, one of the many that adhered to the unfortunate Stuart princes, and suffered in the cause]. [Their] father's father was 'out' in the rebellion of 1715, as was their father in that of 1745. [Their] mother's father, Patrick Murray, embarked in the same cause, and, having been made prisoner when the young chevalier retreated from England, was one of the ten, among whom were Sir Archibald Primrose and other men of note, who were tried and executed at Carlisle." This information has the disadvantage of being almost entirely unverifiable.

There was, in fact, a "Patrick Murray, the younger," of "Dollair or Doloray" (or Dullany or Dollairs), Clackmannanshire, a goldsmith and/or a "Justice of the Peace and Sheriff Clerk," who was arrested in November, 1745, and, after languishing in four prisons, was executed a year later along with nine others, including Sir Archibald Primrose.[3] But to attempt to discover whether this Patrick Murray was the brothers' maternal grandfather would be as futile as to attempt to ascertain which, if any, of the numerous "Stewarts," "Steuarts," and "Stuarts" embarked in the cause was their father.

By at least 1758 the family was living in Edinburgh, and there in the late 1760's Mr. Stuart, whose occupation is not mentioned by biographers, died, leaving a wife and five children, the youngest an infant. There were two girls, Catherine and Elizabeth, Catherine being the older, and three boys, Charles, Peter, and Daniel. Daniel was born 16 November, 1766.[4] Since Charles was described by Daniel as "the schoolfellow and most intimate companion" of Robert Fergusson,[5] he was probably born about 1750 and Peter, being "eight or ten years younger than . . . Fergusson," [6] about 1758 or 1760. According to Mary Stuart, Daniel's daughter,[7] the two older boys "received their education at the High School, Edinburgh," and it was undoubtedly here that Charles had his short-lived intimacy with Fergusson, who attended the same school from 1758 to 1761. Mary's impression that the school provided its students with "a good classical education" was, however, mistaken, for the Royal High School was not a high school in the ordinary sense. It did not, for example, prepare Fergusson for the university, for he "advanced" from it only to the Grammar School of Dundee, having been graduated from the high school at the age of eleven.

The family remained in Edinburgh until Peter's education was completed, when, again according to Mary,[8] the four oldest children migrated to London, "keeping house together in Charlotte Street, Portland Place," where they were still living in 1782. The migration probably occurred in the early 1770's. They seem to have taken with them whatever savings remained, for it was understood that Daniel's schooling would be postponed until Charles and Peter were financially established, when the family would be united in London and Daniel placed in a school there. As it turned out, Daniel stayed in Edinburgh until 1778, when his mother died and he set off for London willy-nilly, determined at last to get his long-overdue education. By this time the two older brothers were "engaged as Journalists," having also, it appears, learned something about printing.

There are divergent accounts of the events which succeeded. According to one account,[9] more aptly described as a "legend," Daniel was immediately set up as "a tailor" or perhaps apprenticed to a tailor "in the neighbourhood of Covent Garden"; but this account is pure figment. Its source seems to be the *Statesman,* which in 1817 liked to call Daniel "The Poor Tailor of the Courier," without intending any reference to his original profession.[10] According to a second account, this one supplied by Mary Stuart,[11] "instead of placing their youngest brother to a school, [Charles and Peter] apprenticed him on his arrival in London to Sutton, the King's Printer, in St. Martin's Lane, and made him otherwise useful to themselves. [Daniel] in after life much regretted the loss of a good classical education." Although Mary must have got this story from Daniel himself, it is also a figment. No directory of the period lists a printer named Sutton. The "King's Printer" was William Strahan, but Strahan was not located in St. Martin's Lane, and he had no Stuarts among his apprentices. The third account, which is included in Daniel's obituary,[12] is at least plausible:

Daniel . . . was brought up in his brother's house, and to their profession; and at a very early period of his life, and as soon as the progress of his education [probably administered by his sisters] allowed, was employed to assist them in every branch of it in which he could be useful. In this way he acquired a thorough knowledge of business; and being endowed with keen observation and patient industry, and at the same time placed in circumstances which called his attention to the busy world around him, he gradually added to his other acquirements a very considerable acquaintance with the spirit and views of the different parties which then agitated the country. Though necessarily deprived of an academical education, he collected from private study an ample fund of general information, and early acquired the unaffected and forcible style of good sense. . . .

The experience he had gained by his early connection with public journals [later proved advantageous].

The fact remains that there is no actual record of any of the Stuarts until 27 April, 1779, when Charles's *Cobler of Castlebury: A Musical Entertainment in Two Acts* was performed at Covent Garden, the music being supplied in part by William Shield.[13] Although the *Cobler* was not successful enough to be repeated, it was published later in the year. An earlier piece, a farce entitled *The Experiment,* which was performed at Covent Garden on 16 April, 1777, is sometimes "ascribed to Stuart," [14] but on indifferent authority. By 1780 the manager of the Haymarket, George Colman, was looking for petit dramas, which he had found a useful means of "[diverting] the Galleries till the company in the boxes [was] assembled," [15] and in due time Charles tried his hand at this kind of writing. His *Ripe Fruit; or, The Marriage Act* was performed at Colman's theater on 22 August as the "3rd Course" in *The Feast of Thalia. Damnation; or, The Playhouse Hissing Hot* was performed at the same theater one week later. Both performances were benefits. Of the second piece, one critic [16] observed, "Without the play-house being hissing hot, Damnation was *damned." Ripe Fruit* was evidently not damned, but it was also not performed again, and neither piece was published. By the beginning of 1782, Charles was working on a musical afterpiece, entitled *Gretna Green,* also intended for the Haymarket. The combination of playwrighting and journalism was not unusual. In fact, a journalist who had had no connection with the theater, either as playwright or actor, was a somewhat *rara avis.*

The first record of the Stuarts' newspaper activities is the name of "D. Stuart" in the colophon of the *Morning Post* of 7 March, 1782, and the name of "Charles Stewart" in the accounts of the *Gazetteer* of approximately the same date.[17] Against the name of "Charles Stewart" are the initials "M. P.," as if Charles was on loan from the *Morning Post* or perhaps working for the two papers concurrently. "D. Stuart" was probably Daniel Stuart, for, although there was a printer named Duncan Stuart, his career seems not to have commenced until later. Although "D. Stuart" was clearly only an interim printer, holding the position for Charles, who had evidently been engaged as Macleish's successor, he nevertheless left his mark on the *Post.* For the issue of Saturday, 9 March, was numbered 2878, the issue of Monday, 11 March, 2874; and, since this error went unnoticed, all subsequent issues of the paper were similarly misnumbered. Charles, who replaced "D. Stuart" on 16 March, 1782, continued to print the *Post* until the end of 1783; and by mid-September, 1782, Peter Stuart's name was appearing in the colophon of the *London Courant.*

Since the *Morning Post* did not conform with the practice of combining the offices of printer and editor, Charles Stuart was only the printer of the newspaper. But, when Charles Stuart had any connection with a newspaper whatever, one could expect intrigue, and as printer he was in a position to wreak havoc with the *Post*'s politics. All he needed was some financial encouragement from the Rockingham Whigs, and the encouragement was evidently provided. A few days after Charles's name was added to the colophon, the North Government resigned, to be replaced by a government headed by Lord Rockingham, but including as Secretaries of State both Fox and Lord Shelburne. The *Post* responded to this development with a declaration of political neutrality, which was followed by a succession of "letters" expressing uneasiness with respect to Lord Shelburne. By the time the two quarreled, in June, 1782, the *Post* was decidedly on Fox's side. At this point the proprietors changed editors, the new editor being, according to the *Courant* (19 Sept., 1782), an attorney and a personal friend of Lord Shelburne, who, the *Courant* added (20 Sept., 1782), "ought to take care of this man, and confine him in some good *place*, or *other*, for he will never get such another." The change brought this particular intrigue to an end, for the *Post* immediately resumed its support of Lord Shelburne, who to its great delight became First Lord of the Treasury in July. The Shelburne Government lasted until the end of the following February, and there was no further tampering with the politics of the paper during that period. But meanwhile Charles had become involved in an intrigue of another sort.

The plot to sabotage the politics of the *Morning Post* was no doubt contrived by Sheridan, who always handled such matters for the Rockingham Whigs, and it was, of course, supported by Skinner and Richardson. But it was also supported by the *London Courant,* which ceased its abuse of the *Post* as soon as Charles Stuart joined the staff. Although the abuse was resumed in June, 1782, it was directed only at the editor, never at the newspaper itself. The conductor of the *Courant* was John Almon; the printer was Peter Stuart. Although Peter's name was removed from the colophon in November, 1782, there was no indication that he was replaced until March, 1783. By the beginning of 1783, the *Post* was also linked with the *Gazetteer,* for, from 22 January, 1783, through at least 9 April, 1783, a "Mr. Stuart" was debate reporter for that newspaper.[18] This "Mr. Stuart" was evidently the sixteen-year-old Daniel. With one brother printing the *Morning Post,* another printing the *London Courant,* and a third reporting the debates for the *Gazetteer,* the ground was prepared for what seems to have been the first of the Stuarts' stock-jobbing enterprises.

From November, 1782, on, there were recurrent rumors of a peace with the Bourbon powers and the American colonies, each of which had its effect on the stock market. "Yesterday in the forenoon stocks rose nearly five per cent. in less than an hour, in consequence of a report circulated with the greatest confidence, that Mons. de Requeval, Secretary to Mons. de Vergennes, the Prime Minister of France, had arrived with the preliminaries for a general pacification," the *Morning Post* noted, for example, at the beginning of December (quoted by *Whitehall Evening Post,* 30 Nov.—3 Dec., 1782). "—This astonishing increase flattened before two o'clock 1 per cent. at Lloyd's, as another report prevailed very different from the former." With a stock market as sensitive as this one, anyone who had prior knowledge of the precise terms of the peace could realize a handsome return on a very small investment; and the person who would have such knowledge was Lord Shelburne's friend, the editor of the *Post.* The news of the peace was, in fact, placed in his letter box on the evening of 26 January, but he did not have it until late the following morning. The reason was, said the *Courant* (29 Jan., 1783), that the editor had neglected to pick up his mail. The *Courant* spoke with its usual sarcasm:

Whereas sundry persons, in the habit of conveying very great *secrets* to the Morning Post, have lately made it a practice to *drop letters* into the letter box of the said paper, at the top of Blake Court, as was the case with the letter of Lord Grantham [Foreign Secretary] to the Lord Mayor, *concerning the* Peace; the Earl of Shelburne, and his Majesty's other ministers, and the public in general, are requested in future, not to have their letters *dropped in the said letter box,* but sent up Blake Court, and delivered to the Editor himself, in the same manner as the Pepperal Accounts of the Ruin of America, at the very time her independence was offered to her. The particular reason of this caution, is, that a Letter from the Secretary of State [Lord Grantham], announcing the Peace, was lately *dropped in the letter box,* where it continued fast asleep the next morning, while all the world was fully acquainted with the event.

Actually the "world" did not become "acquainted with the event" until 29 January. The newspapers finally heard of it on the afternoon of 27 January, but along with the news they received the following note: "It is the Speaker's Desire, that the Printer of [—] do not Publish in the Paper of To-morrow, any of the Preliminaries of Peace, until the same have been regularly printed according to the Vote of the House this Day./ A Copy shall be sent in due Time." The note was signed by the Speaker himself, "C. W. CORNWALL," and it was dated 27 January. The printers, of course, complied. All of the newspapers remained silent, although the *Post,* the *Courant,* and the *Gazetteer* published the note as evidence that they had received it and were acting in accordance with the Speaker's instructions. The printers heard nothing further, and the forgery would probably never have been discovered had not William Woodfall, conductor of the *Morning Chronicle,* addressed a reply to the Speaker, stressing the wish of newspapermen to cooperate with the Government and offering in effect to act as future intermediary between Government and press. Cornwall, who knew nothing of the note, read Woodfall's reply to the House of Commons on the evening of 28 January, where there was much laughter at Woodfall's expense, he having failed to recognize an obvious piece of stock-jobbing. On the following day (29 Jan.) the news of the peace was in all the papers, and in addition the *Courant* carried a long story, entitled "Forgery Detected," which narrated the events without suggesting any explanation. The forgers were never publicly identified. The *General Advertiser* may have indicated some of its own suspicions, for on 1 March, 1783, the *Courant* announced that it had filed suit against William Parker of *Parker's General Advertiser* for a libel and that the case would be heard in the next session of the Old Bailey. But the case seems not to have been heard, and by mid-April the *Courant* was defunct. The *Gazetteer* and the *Morning Post* evidently escaped mention.

By this time there was another political crisis. Prior to Fox's coalition with Lord North, newspapers were generally divided into two groups: those which supported the Tories and the Shelburne Whigs (the *Morning Post* and the *Morning Herald*) and those which supported the Rockingham Whigs (the remaining newspapers). But the Coalition resulted in a realignment, for the Tory-Shelburne papers were unwilling to accept Fox, and only the most zealous of the Fox papers were willing to accept Lord North. Hence by late 1782 the newspapers were divided into three groups: those which supported the Shelburne Whigs (the *Post* and the *Herald*), those which supported the radical reformers (the *Courant* and the *General Advertiser*), and those which supported the Coalition (the remaining newspapers). At the end of February, 1783, the Shelburne Government resigned, and the country was without a government for thirty-seven days, at the end of which time the King was forced to accept the Coalition. This was a frenzied period for the press. Not only did every newspaper have a selfish interest in seeing its own faction come into power, but all of them had particularly strong feelings about the Coalition. In the case of the *Morning Post,* the feelings were, as usual, divided, for most of the proprietors were determined that the paper would support the young Shelburnite, William Pitt, whereas it was of prime importance to Skinner and Richardson that it support Fox at this crucial moment in his career. The result was another attempt at sabotage. For approximately three weeks, therefore, editorial eulogies of Lord Shelburne and William Pitt were interspersed with enthusiastic "communications" in support of the Coalition. The "communications" came to an end on 17 March with the editor's announcement: *"As several of our Correspondents incautiously direct their Letters to the Printer of this Paper, we find it necessary to request a particular attention in future to the Advertisement (under the head* LONDON*) at the conclusion of the last page. All matter intended for publication in the* MORNING POST *must be addressed to the* EDITOR, *the Printer having no authority to insert a single line without the immediate direction of the Gentleman employed to superintend the Literary Department."* The announcement was reprinted on 19 March. The reference *"to the Advertisement"* was a reference to the colophon, which specifically stated that the paper was "Printed by C. STUART, Blakecourt, Catherine-street, Strand; where Letters . . . for the Editor are received. . . ."

The second plot to subvert the *Morning Post* having failed, Richardson shifted his attention to the *English Chronicle, or Universal Evening Post,* a triweekly newspaper, owned by the proprietors of the *Morning Post* and since 1780 printed and conducted by Robert Haswell. Richardson's first act was to obtain "the conduct" of the *Chronicle* and his second to make "an offer" to Sheridan "to convert his paper into a strong *party* one," provided that, if "this step . . . occasion a breach between him and his partners, and in consequence of it, that either he would be driven out of the partnership or be oblig'd to buy up the shares of the malcontents," he would receive "assistance . . . to enable him to buy the types, etc." Sheridan relayed the offer to Earl Fitzwilliam and Lord Robert Spencer, who provided the "assurance of assistance." The "quarrel" did "take place," but, since they "did afford that assistance at a considerable expence," Richardson retained control.[19] The *Chronicle* was printed by J. Jarvis at No. 283, Strand, Jarvis replacing Haswell when (Apr., 1783) the paper transferred its allegiance to Fox.

## THE *MORNING POST* VS. DENNIS O'BRYEN

RICHARDSON did not sell his shares in the *Morning Post,* and Charles Stuart made his peace with the proprietors of the paper and stayed on as printer. Lord Shelburne's friend evidently also stayed on as editor, for, until the end of April, 1783, the *Post* eulogized Pitt and Lord Shelburne, after which time it abused the Coalition, which had then come into power. But, by the beginning of July, there was evidence of uneasiness among the proprietors, who found themselves in the unwished-for situation of opposing a Government which had already lasted for two months and might last for years. Since the Coalition Government was unwelcome to the King, the proprietors were still unwilling to support it, but they were evidently also reluctant to go on opposing it, for, at the beginning of July, 1783, they dismissed Lord Shelburne's friend and engaged as his successor Carl Francis Badini, who had almost no interest in politics. Badini was not as disreputable as he was sometimes represented.[20] Although he later (20 July, 1789) received £100 from the Treasury "For obtaining Papers respecting the Venetian Lottery and other Services," [21] he was not a hired propagandist, and he was a translator and author of some consequence. From 1767 through 1790 he published heavily in both Italian and English, and, although his original works were confined to the field of opera, his translations ranged from biography to fairly technical works in philosophy.[22] Unfortunately none of his scholarship was reflected in the *Morning Post,* which under his editorship was concerned only with crime, personalities, theatrical quarrels, and literary squabbles. In late July he introduced the first regular gossip column, under the title "Bird of Passage."

Since most journalists had a sometime connection with the stage, the relationship between the theater and the press had always been close. With the new interest in "personalities" and "anecdotes," it became even closer, for the most interesting "personalities" and "anecdotes" were associated with the theaters. The theater and the press were also bound together by politics, for in their way the theaters were quite as political as the newspapers. Drury Lane, one of the proprietors of which was Sheridan, represented the liberals. Its playwrights were followers of Fox, and the plays themselves were sometimes barbed with political commentary, often supplied by the actors extempore. A play produced at Drury Lane or even an actress appearing at Drury Lane could expect shabby treatment from the conservative newspapers. Covent Garden represented the conservatives, and its manager, Thomas Harris, even acted as paymaster for the Treasury in its later relations with the press. Colman's Haymarket constituted a faction of its own, and, since Colman could not, therefore, count on good notices for political reasons, he usually had to pay for them. In the case of Charles Stuart's next production, however, no payment was necessary, for, since Charles's name was still appearing in the colophon of the *Post,* the production would be dealt with on political grounds.

The musical afterpiece on which Charles Stuart had been working for well over a year was finally performed at the Haymarket on 28 and 30 August, 1783; and, as one might have anticipated, it was politely acknowledged by the *Morning Herald* and the *Morning Post* and lambasted by the other newspapers. It seemed to the *Herald* (29 Aug.) that "[*Gretna Green*], although not to be ranked among the first-rate performances of its kind, is far superior to many that have been produced." The *Post* was inclined to reserve judgment: "GRETNA GREEN . . . , being the production of Mr. Charles Stuart, the Printer of this Paper, our opinion may perhaps fall under the suspicion of partiality. We shall therefore content ourselves with observing, that every part of it was received with uncommon and general applause. The music in particular had a most enchanting effect.—It consisted of . . . tunes, selected by Dr. [Samuel] Arnold, and the selection did infinite credit to the Doctor's judgement." Among the liberal newspapers, the *Morning Chronicle* was by far the most vehement, possibly because William Woodfall was still remembering the forgery of Cornwall's note and his own consequent embarrassment. The review, which was almost a column long, began with the statement:

> This little musical Farce is the production of Mr. Stuart, author of the *Cobler of Castlebury, Damnation,* and one or two more theatrical trifles, produced with a view to help the interest of different comedians on their benefit nights. A dramatist, who thus benevolently aids the spittal, deserves at least the candour of the critic, when he writes for his own profit and reputation. In

the *petite* piece before us, we understand he has been lent a helping hand by Mr. [John] O'Keefe, and if this report had not reached us, we should have been prompt to propose such a suggestion, the piece . . . sufficiently evincing from what punnical storehouse, the author drew a great part of his pleasantry.

The aim of Mr. Stuart seems to have been, to connect a few of the most favorite and fashionable Scotch airs, and rather to create a slight fable to hold them together, than to labour at the preperation of a plot.

After some further vituperation, the account concluded with high praise for Dr. Samuel Arnold, who was responsible for the songs, and with an expression of regret that songs of such excellence should be linked with a play of such *"so, so"* quality. The production netted £60, which were divided among Charles, Arnold, and O'Keefe; [23] and, although the piece was many times revived, the libretto was never published. Dr. Arnold's *Songs, Airs, &c. in the Musical Farce Called Gretna Green* appeared later in the year.

Unlike Lord Shelburne's friend, Badini welcomed the assistance of Charles Stuart, so that, although the *Post* was feuding with other newspapers, it was at least at peace with itself. Among the several quarrels in which the paper engaged during this period was one between Colman and Dennis O'Bryen. According to O'Bryen's account (*Herald,* 8 Sept., 1783), this quarrel actually began in May, 1782, when Colman first agreed to produce his play, *A Friend in Need Is a Friend Indeed,* for, although it was clearly understood that the play would go into rehearsal at once, Colman found a variety of excuses for postponement. When O'Bryen at last protested, Colman "positively assured" him that the play "should appear *that* year" and that "friendship . . . was his only motive, for delaying it to the latter part of his season, *that* being always the most productive." In August, his patience exhausted, O'Bryen demanded the immediate "performance of [Colman's] engagement," whereupon, said O'Bryen, "Colman sent Mr. [William] Jewell [the business manager of the Haymarket] to offer me a loan if I would postpone the performance." O'Bryen refused. When Colman repeated the offer, he refused again, and "a rehearsal was held in consequence." Realizing by now the disadvantage of having his play brought out "against the wish of a Manager" and yet being unwilling to forgo "the best part of the season, united to the embarrassment of contracting a large debt," O'Bryen then suggested that Colman buy the play outright. Colman enthusiastically agreed, promising to pay the "highest price" the theater had ever paid for a play. But, when it came to a discussion of terms, Colman remembered that, since the play had only three acts, it was entitled to only a two-nights' run and that this fact would have to be taken into considera-tion in determining the amount. O'Bryen suggested £300, £100 for the copyright and £100 for each night's performance, and after some demur Colman acceded, provided the play was "improved" and ex-panded.

O'Bryen had received the £300 and had begun the revision, when, on 29 August, Mr. Jewell produced a bond, which, he said, Colman had suggested that O'Bryen sign for his "own good," since it entitled the play to a three-nights' run the following season. O'Bryen did sign, for, although there was no "coercion," the bond meant for him, as he understood it, an additional £100. The play was finally brought out on Saturday, 5 July, 1783, but it was brought out for only two nights and then in the middle of the season, so that the production realized only £50 in all. Moreover, Colman now maintained that he had not bought the play, but had only lent O'Bryen £300, which he demanded in return for the £50, which, he said, was the whole of O'Bryen's due. In support of his demand, he pointed to the bond, which, in fact, described the £300 as a loan, not a price of purchase. Having no legal recourse, O'Bryen determined to submit the case to the public, and he did so in the form of two letters. The letters, signed "VARRO," were printed in *Parker's General Advertiser* in late August, 1783. They were answered by Colman, who identified "Varro" as Dennis O'Bryen and denied having mistreated him in any way. Colman's letter was also published by the *General Advertiser*.

The fact that newspapers never buried the past is rather well exemplified by what happened in this particular case, for no news-paper was interested in the facts: it was interested only in Dennis O'Bryen. By 1783 O'Bryen was anathema to almost every newspaper. He had alienated the Shelburne papers a year earlier by *The Sauce-pan* (not identified, but often mentioned by the newspapers) and by the mocking and highly popular (being now in its ninth edition) *Defense of the . . . Earl of Shelburne* and more recently by the *Re-marks upon the Report of a Peace, in Consequence of Mr. Secretary Townshend's Letter to the City,* which had already (1783) been pub-lished in Dublin and would soon be published in London. He had alienated the Coalition newspapers by his connection with the *General Advertiser,* which supported Fox, but steadfastly refused to support his alliance with Lord North. For political reasons alone, therefore, O'Bryen could expect to be trampled on by the entire London press, and in addition he had a host of personal enemies because of his involvement in the old war between the *Post* and the *Herald*. But the fact that he had been involved in this war turned out to be more of an advantage than a disadvantage, for he had been involved on the side of the Rev. Henry Bate, and no newspaper wanted to do battle with Bate. The possibility that Bate might rise to O'Bryen's defense kept many newspapers silent altogether, among them the *Gazetteer*, now edited by James Perry. On assuming the conduct of that newspaper,[24] Perry had declared (*Gazetteer*, 18 July, 1783) : "*We mean to be gay without sinking to licentiousness. . . . We are confined to no party in politics except to the very great party of the people in England, whose servants only we declare ourselves to be.*" But the *Gazetteer*, in fact, supported the Coalition, so that O'Bryen was a political adversary, in addition to being Perry's traducer. Under all these circumstances the *Gazetteer* might have defended Colman "*without sinking to licentiousness,*" but the defense would have been too risky for Perry, for a revival of the scandal of 1781 would certainly have cost him his present position, as it had cost him his previous one.

The *Morning Post* was in a different position altogether, for the other principal in that scandal, Robert Haswell, was no longer connected with the *English Chronicle,* which in any event was now owned by Richardson, not by the proprietary of the *Post*. For the *Post*, therefore, this was the opportunity to get even with O'Bryen and so vicariously with Bate, and it made the most of it. On 1 September, 1783, it published a long comment on the quarrel and along with it a letter, headed "*To Dennis O'Brien; Author of the Friend in need is a Friend indeed.*" "Sir," the letter began, "I have perused your two letters addressed to *George Colman, Esq.* in the General Advertiser, under the signature of VARRO. . . . Your principal complaint is, that Mr. Colman is *sick* of envy. As you have been bred to the profession of a surgeon, I suppose your intention is to *bleed* him." After some extravagant praise of Colman's generosity and some insulting references to O'Bryen's "vanity," the letter went on to inquire: "Did not Mr. Colman lend you three hundred pounds upon the bare ground of your manuscript, even one year before the appearance of your piece? and on its indifferent success, did he not make you a generous present of fifty pounds? Can you, Mr. Dennis O'Brien, think it confident [*sic*] with morality to attack a benefactor in the public prints with groundless and malicious imputations, and to attempt the ruin of a man, who in your need *has been your friend indeed?*" The letter was signed "LANCET," and it was the first of four such letters, all written in the crude "punnical" style of Charles Stuart.

On reading "Lancet's" letter, O'Bryen sent to the *Post,* to be printed as a paid advertisement, a full account of his quarrel with Colman. The *Post* acknowledged its receipt on 3 September with the notation, *"The private anecdotes of* VARRO *are under consideration."* On 4 September the Coalition *Chronicle "[begged] leave to decline"* publication of its own correspondents' comments on "Varro's" letters, on the ground that *"It is a rule of conduct with us* never *to take part in a dispute . . . begun in other papers";* but it made it clear that, were it not for this inflexible rule, it would certainly come to the aid of the injured Colman. On 6 September the *Post* published a second letter from "Lancet," this one concluding, "Believe me, sir, your conduct has already exhausted the contempt and indignation of the public, and nothing can redeem your character but a commission of lunacy."

Until now the *Morning Herald* had defended Colman, for the paper had been leased to the King's Friends since 1781 and was still a staunch supporter of the Shelburne Whigs. Although Bate still owned the newspaper he had had nothing to do with its management. But by this time the Colman-O'Bryen quarrel seemed a continuation of his old quarrel with the proprietors of the *Morning Post,* and, although he could not interfere in the conduct of the *Herald,* the lease to the Shelburne Whigs being effective until the end of the year, he could see to it that the *Herald* published those *"private anecdotes of* VARRO," which the *Post* was evidently not going to publish. Hence, while the *Post* was still supposedly pondering the *"anecdotes,"* they appeared (8 Sept.) in the *Herald* and, of course, simultaneously in O'Bryen's newspaper, the *General Advertiser.* They consisted of a long review and evaluation of the facts, in which O'Bryen took occasion to comment on the enormous influence of Colman: "By the number of scandalous manuscripts which I have received from newspapers, where insertion was refused, I find there are swarms of sycophants and reptiles at work for him." O'Bryen noticed in particular Colman's influence with the *Post,* which had refused to print "a single line" submitted by him, even when it was paid for. But to O'Bryen the most puzzling thing was "Lancet's" letters, which, he said, contained *"information . . .* scarcely known to anyone except Mr. Colman," so that, O'Bryen concluded, the author of those letters was either Colman himself or one of his associates at the Haymarket.

Response to O'Bryen's *"anecdotes"* came from two quarters. Colman promptly released to the *Herald* and the *Chronicle* all of his and Jewell's letters relating to the affair. The letters appeared in both papers on 8, 11, and 12 September. He also released a copy of the bond, which was printed by the *Herald,* the *Post,* and the *Chronicle* on 13 September. Moreover, the whole corps of performers at the Haymarket attested by affidavit their ignorance of "Lancet's" letters, and on 12 September Colman published his own statement in the *Herald:* "Of paragraphs I know nothing, one in *The General Advertiser* only excepted, wherein I signified the writer of *Varro* to be the author of *The Friend in Need.* Of letters . . . I know as little. . . . To Lancet however, I hold myself obliged for entering the lists in my cause, as a *volunteer."* On the same day someone signing himself "QUESTOR," probably O'Bryen, asked Colman through the medium of the *General Advertiser:* "Is Lancet published with your approbation or not? And have you, or have you not furnished the author with some materials for that letter?" But "Questor" already had his answer.

The second response to O'Bryen's communication came from one of O'Bryen's friends. On 10 September the *Morning Post* denied that O'Bryen had ever submitted anything for publication in its columns. However, it added, "Yesterday a person with a cockade, and whose name was unknown, called at the Morning Post Office, and wanted to insert a paragraph in favour of Mr. O'Brien, in a quite despotic and *compulsive manner,* which induced the Editor to refuse it. And as his behaviour was rather troublesome, making use of threatenings and improper expressions, a warrant was obtained against him from Bow-street." Since on the following day the *Post* printed the "paragraph" which the editor had supposedly refused, the report was inaccurate in at least one respect. It was also, as it turned out, inaccurate in other respects, for on the same day (11 Sept.) the *General Advertiser* published "the truth" about the affair, as it was reported by "the person with a cockade." According to this "person," he and a friend had called at the *Post* office, where they finally cornered the editor. The editor accepted the paragraph, but his manner was so abusive that they felt obliged to complain to the proprietors, whereupon they were arrested, taken to Bow Street, and immediately released. They did not learn the identity of "Lancet," although they were given to understand that he was paying for the insertion of his letters. They did learn the identity of the editor, "whose name," said "the person with a cockade," "must *reflect honour* on the cause *he* supports." To this account the "editor" of the *General Advertiser* appended the information: "We hear that Mr. O'Bryen means to prosecute the printer of the Morning Post for some libellous articles which lately appeared in that paper against him."

The *Post* responded by redoubling its attacks on O'Bryen. On 13 September it printed the fourth of "Lancet's" letters, this one concentrating its venom on *A Friend in Need,* which it described as "wretched and despicable": "a nauseous farrago of insupportable dullness." On 15 September the *Herald* presented O'Bryen's commentary. Although the commentary occupied two full columns, O'Bryen added only one fact to those already known, namely, that on 1 September he had been "informed by a man, close in the counsels and dearness of Mr. Colman, that the matter would be settled if I ceased the publications of Varro: that my bond would be cancelled, and my play suffered to take its course in the Theatre." On the following day the "editor" of the *Post* admitted that he had delivered this information to O'Bryen, but he denied knowing anything further of the affair. On the same day (16 Sept.) the *Herald* printed a letter from D. Coffey, 1st Devonshire Regiment, who was a long-time friend of both Bate and O'Bryen, whom he had assisted in the defamation of Perry and Haswell. Having identified himself as the *"Hero in the cockade,"* Coffey went on to speak of "the powerful patronage which supports the Editor of the [*Post*], animating him still to continue his scurilities," and of the editor's distinguished lineage, he being "the grandson of a nobleman, and *Superintendant Général des Finances."* And the "name of this *respectable* Editor," Coffey concluded, "is Signior Carolo Francisco Badini!" On 20 September the *Post* announced that a fifth letter from "Lancet" would appear in the course of a week; otherwise it would *"decline any further publication on this tiresome and hacknied subject."* The fifth letter did not appear, for the obvious reason that the Rev. Henry Bate was becoming much too interested in the affair.

O'Bryen's threat to sue the printer of the *Morning Post* for a libel was not put into action, and there was no further mention of the quarrel between Colman and O'Bryen. But the contingent quarrel between the *Morning Post* and the *General Advertiser* continued for the remainder of 1783 on other grounds, the *Morning Post* being the aggressor and some of the abuse bearing the stylistic mark of Charles Stuart. All the issues were petty, the principal one being the merits of a poem by Dick Yates, which had appeared in the *General Advertiser* of 20 October. This time the *Morning Herald* remained aloof.

## MR. ROSE, MR. BENJAFIELD, AND THE ELECTIONS OF 1784

IN NOVEMBER, 1783, the proprietors of the *Morning Post* made a wrong guess. Evidently concluding, with, no doubt, the assistance of Skinner and Richardson, that a government which had managed to remain in office for seven months in defiance of the King's wishes was not likely to be immediately replaced, they dismissed Badini, who, now that he had been identified was an embarrassment to them anyway, and engaged as his successor John, later (1787) Captain John,[25] Williamson.[26] Since Williamson was a follower of Fox, he at once threw the weight of the *Post* behind Fox's East India Bill. With the defeat of that bill, the Coalition was dismissed, and, by the end of the year, the Government was in the hands of the Shelburnite, William Pitt. By this time all the newspapers were supporting the Coalition, for, encouraged by the political situation and by the *Post*'s recent attacks on O'Bryen, Bate was resuming the conduct of the *Herald*, which was therefore in the process of defecting. Of these newspapers, the only two which politicians regarded as important were still the *Morning Post* and the *Morning Herald*, the others being considered too gentle to be of any force; and, since nothing could be done about the *Herald*, the new Government had to rely upon the *Post*. Hence, while Pitt was forming his cabinet, John Benjafield was being "persuaded" by "an high political friend," specifically by George Rose, the new Secretary of the Treasury, to buy into that newspaper.[27] Benjafield described himself as at this time only a young "ensign of the King's body guard, or yeoman of the guard," but he was also a student of the law, for the Admissions' Register for Lincoln's Inn lists, under the date 5 November, 1783, "John Benjafield, gent., eldest son of Nathaniel B. of Blandford, Dorset, Esq."

When Benjafield made his purchase, the *Morning Post* was as well off as most newspapers, but it was nevertheless in a state of decline, from which it had little hope of recovering. Prior to September, 1780, it was selling 3,000 copies a day. The paper was then divided into twenty-five shares, and, since each share was valued at £350, the property was valued at £8,750; but these figures were misleading, for individual shares were regularly bought and sold at "near 800*l.*" (*Post*, 26 Sept., 1780). By the end of 1780, the *Post* was sharing its West End readers with the *Morning Herald* and suffering a corresponding drop in sales. When Williamson undertook the editorship in late 1783, the sale was estimated at 1650, and Williamson was promised three guineas a week with "an advance of half a Guinea for every five hundred" increase in circulation.[28] But there was evidently no increase, for, by the end of 1783, the property had been redivided, there being now twenty-four shares, and, although under the circumstances Benjafield would have paid the maximum price for his two shares, he paid only "about 400 pounds each," [29] approximately half the amount he would have paid three years earlier." At least part of the cost of purchase was paid by the Treasury, for in 1784 Benjafield collected £200 from Secret Service Funds "to reimburse him for a share in the Morning Post" and an additional £110 "for expenses of various sorts." [30]

Benjafield's first task was to "oppose the politics [of those two zealous friends of the Opposition, Mr. Richardson and Mr. Alderman Skinner]" and so to "[decide] the politics of the Morning Post, in favor of the then Administration" in time for the general elections.[31] More specifically, it was to convince the majority of proprietors that the Pitt Government could win those elections. The task could not have been easy, for all the newspapers were certain the Government would lose. In addition, Benjafield had to replace the present staff with a staff in sympathy with and suitable to his purpose. These labors took time. Some time after 25 December, 1783, and before 3 January, 1784, the name "C. Stuart" was removed from the colophon and the name "D. Stuart" added. "D. Stuart" was again only an interim printer, for, although he was still printing the paper on 17 January, by 22 January he had himself been replaced by "Christopher Etherington." Meanwhile, throughout January, 1784, the *Post* remained militantly Foxite. On 5 February it was willing to admit that Fox might have suffered some "contamination in his first embrace with [Lord North]," but on 23 February it was again expressing alarm at the

King's and Lords' attempts to overawe the Commons and again demanding the resignation of Pitt. By 1 March it had so far wavered as to pledge itself to *"strict impartiality,"* although it went on to caution its readers that Pitt could never win the elections. However, on 5 February it had announced that the *"Editor of this Paper has been indisposed for some time, which has suspended his literary occupations,"* and, so far as the *Post* was concerned, Williamson failed to recover. Before the prorogation of Parliament on 24 March, the editorship was in the hands of the Rev. William Jackson, better known as "Doctor Viper," and the *Morning Post* was securely on the side of the Government. The prorogation of Parliament had, in fact, been delayed until these arrangements were concluded.

In selecting Jackson as the new editor of the *Post,* Benjafield and his Treasury advisers had taken into consideration the fact that the *Post* would probably come into conflict with the *Herald* and hence with the Rev. Henry Bate (now the Rev. Henry Bate Dudley), and they had to have someone who could deal with him on his own terms. Although Charles Stuart had demonstrated talent of Dudley's sort in his letters from "Lancet," his intrigues with the Rockingham Whigs indicated that he could not be trusted. The only other possibility was Jackson. Jackson had had a good deal of experience in abusive writing. From 1766 until late 1777, he had edited the *Public Ledger,* as well as, according to Taylor,[32] the *Whitehall Evening Post,* during which period he had distinguished himself for his "steady and spirited opposition to the measures of [the North Government]." More important for the present purpose, he had distinguished himself for a certain kind of journalism, for, as one biographer, probably Peter Stuart, put it: [33]

No man, perhaps ever went farther in the boldness of his attacks. His great *forte* discovered itself, in that species of writing, known by the name of Paragraphs, which he had the happy knack of giving more *point* to, than any of his cotemporaries. The acrimony of his pen soon rendered him conspicuous to the Public; but the extreme and unexampled virulence of his invectives, though, like the darts of the savage, barbed and poisoned with the most refined art and rankest venom, only served to expose him to the resentment of Government. . . . [People] were at a loss, whether most to admire, the monstruous audacity of his charges, or the astonishing perseverance with which they were followed up.

When it came to personal attacks, Jackson was thought to have no equal. In 1775, for example, he had temporarily "[quitted] the great delinquents of the State" for Samuel Foote, whom he "attacked" and "harassed" in behalf of Elizabeth Chudley, better known as the Duchess of Kingston, who happened to be quarreling with him. Although Jackson did not even know the Duchess at the time, he "fastened upon [Foote], with all the ferocity of a tyger, made fierce and savage by want of food, . . . till poor *Foote,* sinking beneath the weight of obloquy, panted to Dover in [*sic*] his way to Calais, and died of a broken heart!" Jackson had then set out for the Continent to collect his reward from the Duchess and had returned "in his bag and sword, *toute francoise,* having thrown aside his *canonicals,* with a considerable sum of money, as the FINAL reward of his services." He had since been living "at Lyon's Inn, where he had chambers elegantly furnished at the cost of S[amue]l C[la]y H[arve]y, Esq.," who had already "[lavished away a] handsome fortune . . . in his liberal patronage and support of Mr. JACKSON." [34] In addition to writing occasional paragraphs for the Coalition *Public Ledger,* Jackson had in 1783 published a pamphlet, entitled *The Constitutions of the Several Independent States of America,* with a flattering dedication to the head of the Coalition Government, the Duke of Portland. But, since he had no objection to changing his politics, the pamphlet seemed to be of no importance.

Benjafield had also engaged an assistant for Jackson, William Augustus Miles. Although Miles seems to have had no previous newspaper experience, he had some reputation as a composer and a pamphleteer, having already published *A Letter to John Fielding, . . . Occasioned by His Extraordinary Request to Mr. Garrick for the Suppression of the Beggar's Opera* (1773) , *Remarks on an Act of Parliament . . . Intituled "An Act for the Encouragement of the Fisheries"* (1779) , and *The Artifice, a Comic Opera* (1780). The two pamphlets were probably written on assignment. One of his pamphlets, possibly the *Remarks,* had accused a Sir Francis Sykes of being concerned in a monopoly in the East Indies, which resulted in a famine and the consequent loss of 30,000 lives, but Sykes's attempt (19 Nov., 1779) to sue Miles for libel failed because his affidavit had not stated that he was innocent of the charge.[35] Although no one had a high regard for Miles's character,[36] he turned out to be a very effective journalist, remaining with the *Post* until early 1785. Jackson edited the paper until early 1786, and on 26 April, 1784, Peter Stuart replaced "C. Etherington" as printer, to continue as such until 4 February, 1788.

Benjafield's statement [37] that he had "a good deal to do with the conduct of the political and literary part" of the *Post* is true only in part, for he at no time wrote anything for the newspaper, and, with the hiring of Jackson and Miles, he retired from the scene, not to reappear until the end of 1785. He had left everything well organized, however, for the *Post* at once made a two-pronged attack on the strongholds of the Opposition, Carlton House and the press, the attacks on Carlton House being handled by Miles, those on the press by Jackson. Although Miles subsequently [38] admitted authorship only of "several letters . . . , and a long essay, under the signature of 'Neptune,' in the 'Morning Post,' in January, 1785," he, in fact, wrote a great deal of the newspaper. He made his debut on 26 March, 1784, with a long scolding letter, addressed to the Prince of Wales, in which he censured the Prince for his political opposition to his father and for his multiple dissipations and extravagances, all of which were charged to the influence of "the wretched Foxites." "Neptune" warned in particular that, in supporting Fox, the Prince was fostering another Cromwell, whose first act as "PROTECTOR" would be to throw the Royal Family into the Tower. Subsequent letters dealt with Fox's personal conduct, with special and indecent references to his relations with the Duchess of Devonshire. Miles's letters flooded the *Post* during 1784 and early 1785, attracting so much attention that in late 1784 those which had already appeared were reprinted in a pamphlet, entitled *Letters of Neptune and Gracchus Addressed to the P[rince] of W[ales] and Other Distinguished Characters; Now First Collected from Their Original Publication in the Morning Post.* Those addressed specifically to the Prince were included in another collection in 1795, entitled *The Letters of Neptune to the Prince of Wales.* Under the circumstances there were bound to be rampant conjectures as to the identity of "Neptune," and, on at least one occasion, Sheridan concluded a denunciation of the letters in the House of Commons with a demand to know who was writing them. He was answered only by "Neptune" himself, who assured him (*Post*, 27 Sept., 1784) that there would be no answer: "every attempt to discover the author of these papers, will prove abortive. . . . Who I am, or what I am, will remain an eternal secret. . . ."

Jackson opened his own campaign on 17 April, 1784, with the announcement:

> It is necessary to acquaint the public, that the agents of a *certain party*, which has long been aiming, either by violence or corruption, to subvert . . . all that remains of independence and integrity in this kingdom, have either by *threats* or *promises* succeeded in their *attempts* to prostitute the property of the MORNING POST to their purpose. Alarmed at the increasing demand which has lately been made for the Morning Post, in consequence of its SPIRITED and *truly* CONSTITUTIONAL principles, they have insidiously endeavoured to counteract its usual circulation; and have even had recourse to the *pitiful practice* of employing hireling wretches to *steal* the *paper* from several Coffeehouses in London and Westminster, relying on such means to prevent the *dark* and *desperate* manœuvres of the COALITION being exposed to the WORLD.

The exposure of these *"dark* and *desperate* manœuvres" was the burden of subsequent essays, until 26 July unsigned, thereafter signed "SCRUTINEER," with reference to the Westminster Scrutiny then in progress. None of the papers was spared except the *Morning Herald.*

The *Morning Herald,* too, was the only newspaper to come through the elections and the Scrutiny unshaken. On 11 May the *Morning Chronicle* noted in amazement that "The Ministers have had great success in the management of the present General Election," and, although it made it clear that it was still an Opposition paper, its zeal in the cause was obviously weakened. The zeal of the *Gazetteer* was almost completely destroyed, so that, by the time the elections were completed, the *Gazetteer* seemed to be politically neutral. *Parker's General Advertiser* and the *Public Advertiser* remained firm through August, but by September both newspapers were fluctuating, and, by the end of the year, the *Public Advertiser* was supporting Pitt. The *Morning Herald,* on the other hand, became more militantly Foxite as the polling progressed. Through March it purported to be open-minded, and its statement of 10 April that, "[*although*] *the true cause of* WHIGGISM *will always meet with our warmest support, we trust the* MORNING HERALD *will never be conducted upon principles of* DISLOYALTY," indicated that it might support Pitt after all. But, by the beginning of May, it had swung violently to the side of the Opposition, and by June it was by far the most outspoken of the Opposition papers. Its outrage at the manipulation of the elections was by no means confined to attacks on the King's Friends, for several of them were directed at the King himself. John Williams, who later wrote under the name "Anthony Pasquin," may have been responsible for some of these attacks, for, according to one biographer,[39] Williams was associated with Bate Dudley in the conduct of the *Herald* at this time, having previously worked for Irish journals.

Although the *Herald* had a good deal to say of the *Morning Post,* its comments, for the greater part of the year, were confined to the area of general abuse, since until September the identity of "Scrutineer" was as much a mystery as the identity of "Neptune." But, whereas Miles escaped detection because he was a newcomer to the newspapers, Jackson escaped because he was thought to be a staunch friend of the Coalition. Hence the discovery that their supposed friend was, in fact, their worst enemy was a stinging blow to all the newspapers and especially to the *Morning Herald,* which on 9 September, 1784, accordingly re-declared war on the *Morning Post.* "If the *Right* Reverend author of the scrutiny anecdotes, which groan every day from a certain Morning Print, . . . expects to be treated with any other species of language than that which is alone competent to the description of his character, he is much mistaken . . . ," the *Herald* warned: "to an animal, each hour of whose existence is a reproach to the public justice of his country, what delicacy is expected?"

This declaration brought Jackson's effectiveness as editor and essayist to an abrupt end, for, despite his prowess as a newspaper warrior, he was obviously unwilling to pit his wits against Dudley's. For the first two weeks, the *Post* responded to the ferocious attacks of the *Herald* with equally ferocious attacks on the *Morning Chronicle* and the *Gazetteer.* But on 20 September the *Herald* struck a telling blow by publishing a long excerpt from the dedicatory address of the *Constitutions of the Several States of America,* demonstrating that on 8 May, 1783, the author, "WILLIAM JACKSON," had regarded the Duke of Portland as the savior of his country and hoped that he would long remain First Minister. The *Herald* purported to come to Jackson's defense, as it had purported to come to Haswell's defense on a previous occasion:

All the insinuations contained in the public prints, that the Rev. Mr. Jackson is the author of the dull . . . performances entitled the Scrutineer, in one of the Ministerial papers, are . . . a libel on that gentleman's character. To refute this calumny, we need only have recourse to the following extract from his dedication to the Duke of Portland (then first Lord of the Treasury).

. . . We will then submit to the candour of the public, whether the same gentleman can be supposed to be the author of a paper so continually repeating . . . the mischief and abomination of the damnable, monstrous, and accursed coalition.

The *Post* at once apologized. Even if Jackson were its editor, it said (22 Sept., 1784), he would not be inconsistent, for the first part of the dedication had clearly stated that, in the author's opinion, the Duke would never try to change the Constitution, whereas he had since done so, becoming "a *meer machine* in the hands of Mr. Fox."

Such an apology was inevitably damaging to a newspaper, and this one was followed by others, each of which further weakened the political force of the *Post*. It might be said in Jackson's defense that he was not alone in his fear of Dudley, for, when the *Herald* suggested that George Chalmers was supplying some of the material for the *Post*, Chalmers saw to it (1 July, 1785) that the *Post* issued a prompt denial: "It having been asserted in one of the opposition prints of yesterday, that Mr. *Chalmers*, author of a *Comparative Estimate,* &c. [*An Estimate of the Comparative Strength of Great Britain during the Present and Four Preceding Reigns* (London, 1782)] was the writer of what they call the Treasury Pamphlets and paragraphs, the Editor must declare, that to his knowledge, Mr. *Chalmers* has not written any paragraph or other article that has appeared in the *Morning Post,* since the dissolution of the last Parliament."

## SOME WHYS AND WHEREFORES OF THE BENJAFIELD-TATTERSALL LEASE

WHEN the elections began, the Foxite Whigs were very well represented by the press. Although not all of the newspapers were enthusiastic about the Coalition, all of them except the *Morning Post* were enthusiastic about Fox, so that, for the greater part of the year, any shot which the *Post* fired in his direction was answered by a volley from the other newspapers. This was not the case with the Prince of Wales, who until mid-year had no defense against the daily abuse of "Neptune." The first indication that the Prince had found this abuse galling and had taken steps to protect himself was a series of laudatory paragraphs in the *Morning Herald,* beginning in early June, 1784. Arrangements for these paragraphs had evidently been made by the Prince's German maître d'hôtel and confidant, Louis Weltje, for the paragraphs were almost as concerned for him as they were for the Prince. "Mr. Weltje, Stewart [*sic*] to . . . the Prince of Wales, had the misfortune to fall from his horse on Friday, and break a limb," the *Herald* reported, for example, on Tuesday, 8 June. "This is particularly unfortunate for the Prince . . . , for he has introduced a system of such legitimate œconomy in the household, that he enables his Royal Highness to maintain the most Princely munificence by means of the best regulated expence." Weltje was the subject of other paragraphs, most of which stressed his moderating influence; and on 15 November, when he had broken his other arm "and was otherwise very much hurt," the *Herald* took occasion to comment on the beautiful relationship which existed between him and his master, who "was extremely affected" by these accidents to his favorite.

But no defense was adequate against the attacks of "Neptune," and the Prince could not negotiate with "Neptune," since "Neptune" was still known to the world only as a pseudonym. By early September, 1784, however, the Prince at least knew the identity of the editor of the *Post,* and he seems to have opened negotiations with him shortly thereafter, for on 13 January, 1785, the *Herald* announced that Jackson had accepted favors from Carlton House, in return for which he would supposedly stop the abuse of the Prince. The *Morning Post* vehemently denied the charge. "The public may be assured," it said on 15 January, "that the paragraph that appeared in a Morning Paper of Thursday, stating that the Prince of Wales had procured two livings for a certain clergyman, is utterly false. The clergyman alluded to, who has been named among others as author of the letters signed NEPTUNE, . . . never had any connection whatever with the friends of his Royal Highness. The two livings which he got lately, were presented to him by Lord *Thurlow* [Lord Chancellor] and the Duke of *Northumberland* [Lord Lieutenant of Ireland], the former in consequence of the dedication of a volume of sermons, and the latter of old patronage and family connections." But the *Herald* was evidently correct, for, although the Scrutiny did not end until March, "Neptune's" letters ended in late January. There was no further abuse of the Prince until late February.

The purpose of "Neptune's" abuse had never been extortion; the purpose of the new flood of abuse was, although it was apparently extortion of a somewhat disguised sort, the extortionist accepting further favors from Carlton House, in return for which he supposedly silenced someone else. This time the payee was the principal proprietor of the *Morning Post,* John Bell, who, the *Herald* reported on 17 December, 1785, had just been appointed bookseller to the Prince of Wales. But, since the abuse had lasted only from late February to mid-March, this appointment was obviously only a small part of the reward. Although the *Herald* kept a watchful eye on the *Morning Post,* it said nothing of Bell's activities, partly because it was reluctant to embarrass Carlton House, with which it was itself connected, partly because Bell and Dudley were allied in a plot against the Logographic Press. Dudley's interest in this press was inspired by the fact that on 1 January, 1785, it had begun a new newspaper, entitled *Universal Daily Register,* later (1 Jan. 1788) retitled *The Times.* Of this plot one knows only that on 14 February, 1785, the *Herald* observed that the printing of the most recent addition to Bell's British Library, *An Apology for the Life of George Anne Bellamy: Written by Herself,* was below Bell's usual standard. Bell replied to this observation in the *Post* of 15 February, by admitting that the printing was, in fact, inferior, but adding that he did not print the work, the agent responsible for the botching being the Logographic Press, especially the *"censor* and *adviser*-general, *if not the principal* in that office," Dr. John Trusler. Trusler struck back in the *Post* of 19 February. To begin with, he said, he was given insufficient time to print the edition, and now Bell was employing a characteristically devious way of putting the blame on someone else. He was himself personally convinced and could even prove that Bell had contrived the whole incident, even "the oblique reflection on himself in the Herald of [14 February]": "These are the innocent arts of the trade, in which Mr. Bell is an adept."

In December, 1785, the Prince of Wales married the Roman Catholic Mrs. Fitzherbert, and, since the marriage, although supposedly a secret, was soon common knowledge to newspapermen, anyone who controlled a newspaper could henceforth be assured of a very handsome payment from Carlton House. But Bell was unable to reap this harvest, for, at the beginning of 1786, John Benjafield and Richard Tattersall leased the *Morning Post* for a period of seven years.

The Benjafield-Tattersall lease has previously been dated 4 July, 1786, the reason being Benjafield's statement [40] that "in the year 1786" he and Tattersall "obtained a lease of [the *Post*] . . . for seven years, at £1,400 a year" and that "I afterwards, that is, on the 4$^{th}$ of July, 1786, entered into an agreement with Mr. Tattersal [*sic*] . . . that Mr. Tattersal should exclusively have the management of the money concerns; and that I should have the exclusive controul of the literary department . . . for the term of our lease." But Benjafield did not say that the lease immediately preceded the agreement with Tattersall, and it would be strange if it did, for, except in very extraordinary cases, changes involving the proprietary of a newspaper, such as leasings and transfers of shares, were made at the end of a calendar year. Benjafield's further statement [41] that, "Thus possessed of the Morning Post, I devoted it to the object, with a view to which I originally became a proprietor, namely the support of the administration of that day," is at least misleading. For, since the *Post* had been "devoted" to "the support of the administration" all along, this "object" obviously had nothing to do with the lease. The sole purpose of the lease was to monopolize the blackmailing activities of the newspaper for the next seven years.

That the proprietors regarded the Benjafield-Tattersall offer as too attractive to be refused is proof that, at the end of 1785, the *Morning Post* was not in a flourishing state. According to Hindle,[42] the circulation had risen from 1,650 in late 1783 to "2,100 clear daily" in late 1784, at which time "a dividend was 'declared and made of Fifteen hundred pounds, from the profit.' " But Hindle is mistaken in concluding that this "meant interest at 18⅓ per cent." He is also mistaken in implying that the "2,100 clear daily" represented a sale to individuals, for, while the elections and the Scrutiny were in progress, the Government would have bought hundreds of copies of the newspaper for free distribution to taverns and coffeehouses and other public places. On 20 April, 1785, the proprietors fixed the "declared" value of the *Post* at £8,400, "as before," that is, at £350 per share. But by this time the margin between "declared" and market value had evidently narrowed considerably, for, by the end of 1785, the proprietors were happy to accept £1,400 a year for their paper for the next seven years, which, as Benjafield pointed out,[43] "produced an annual dividend upwards of £58 to each holder of a 24$^{th}$" or approximately 16⅔ per cent of the "declared" value. There was only one condition, namely, that "the lessees *indemnified* the other proprietors against any depreciation of shares below £350, for each 24$^{th}$." [44]

Bell, who had probably opposed the leasing of the *Post*, at once applied for permission to sell his shares, and permission was granted. The purchaser was probably Richard Tattersall, who seems to have succeeded him as principal proprietor and who may have returned to the paper at this time. Bell's separation from the other proprietors was evidently achieved without a battle, for advertisements for the British Library lingered in the *Post* until 28 January, when they were transferred to the *English Chronicle, or Universal Evening Post,* which thereafter carried the insignia of the Prince of Wales in its masthead, along with the legend, "JOHN BELL, BOOKSELLER TO HIS ROYAL HIGHNESS THE PRINCE OF WALES." The *Chronicle*'s announcement of a change of conductor (28 Jan., 1786) was accompanied by an altered colophon, John Wheble's name being substituted for that of "J. Jarvis," although the paper was still printed at No. 283, Strand. Wheble, who had been the first publisher of the *English Chronicle,* as well as the first publisher of the *Morning Post,* was at this time also publishing the (Suffolk) *County Chronicle, and Weekly Advertiser,* and he continued to do so through at least 1812.[45]

Since very few copies of the *English Chronicle* are extant for this period, much of its history remains in doubt. Until April, 1783, it was supposedly owned by a majority of the proprietors of the *Morning Post,* but, when Richardson converted the paper "into a strong *party* one," he was "oblig'd to buy up the shares of the malcontents." How many of the proprietors were "malcontents" was not indicated, but it would appear that almost all of them were, for the *Post*'s statement of 25 February, 1785, that "The English Chronicle . . . avowedly speaks the language of the Coalition, and is certainly carried on by the friends of Mr. Fox" indicates that the proprietors knew very little about the newspaper. One has Earl Fitzwilliam's word for it [46] that, "in consequence of the line the paper had adopted, it lost all its sale, and [Richardson] was oblig'd to abandon it" and that, as a reward for his services, he was subsequently granted an annuity of £200, payable "out of the general subscription to newspapers, etc.," which was paid until 1793. But Fitzwilliam failed to say when Richardson "abandoned" it. On 28 January, 1786, he did relinquish the conduct to John Bell, who transformed the paper into an organ of Carlton House; and he may at this time have intended to quit newspapers altogether, for, according to the Admissions' Records for the Middle Temple, "Joseph Richardson, only son of Joseph R., late of Hexham, Northumberland, gent., decd.," was "Called 5 May, 1786," having been admitted on 24 March, 1781. But, as Boaden said,[47] Richardson was a tool in the hands of Sheridan, who "ruined" him both as to character and talents; and the reappearance of J. Jarvis's name in the Audit-Office records [48] indicates that Richardson resumed the conduct of the *Chronicle* in mid-1786. Before the end of 1787, however, the paper was being printed by John Vint,[49] and it may have been repossessed by the proprietors of the *Morning Post* when Vint undertook the printing. One knows only that the issue of 30 April—2 May, 1789, was printed at the *Post*'s address in Blake Court, Catherine Street, Strand. The paper continued to be printed by Vint at this address until 1794.

In addition to its other several distinctions, the *Morning Post* had the distinction of being the first newspaper to make a business of extortion. The practice of selling puffs and demanding payment for the suppression of a story or the contradiction of a story already published was already well established, but it remained for John Benjafield to systematize and expand these practices so that they became the principal source of revenue. Unlike his predecessors Benjafield was not interested in single fees. He settled only for annuities; and, since he achieved his ends by simple harassment, a list of his victims and the date of their first payment can be read from the newspaper itself. One of the most obstinate of the group seems to have been the wealthy potter Sir Joshua Wedgwood, who was subjected to daily and increasingly vicious attacks throughout almost the whole of January. The Prince of Wales was considerably more malleable, only two paragraphs being required in his case. The first one, which appeared on 8 February, 1786, relied on innuendo: "Mrs. *Fitzherbert* pays a hundred guineas for her box at the Opera House, from which it may be presumed, that the connections and suite of that Lady have increased, are increasing, and [are] not likely to be diminished." The second paragraph, which appeared on 18 February, was more pointed: "It is confidently reported, that a certain marriage has been solemnized by a *Romish Priest,* who immediately quitted the kingdom." This paragraph accomplished its purpose, and nothing further was said of the Prince's affairs until 1788.

It seems to have been understood from the outset that "Mr. Tattersal should exclusively have the management of the money concerns; and that [Mr. Benjafield] should have the exclusive controul of the literary department . . . for the term of [the] lease." But Tattersall had a penchant for "interfering" (see, e.g., *Post,* 9 Dec., 1793) , and, since his "interfering" confused the activities of the newspaper and exasperated the personnel, he was persuaded to sign the collateral agreement of 4 July, 1786, which made further "interfering" on his part punishable by law. Unfortunately this agreement came too late for the Rev. William Jackson. According to John Taylor,[50] then drama critic for the *Morning Post,* Jackson survived the leasing, but some time therafter Tattersall "interfered" to "recommend" his dismissal because of "the vast quantity of paper which he consumed in writing his political articles." Benjafield probably welcomed the opportunity to get rid of him, for he had certainly not proved to be another Henry Bate Dudley, and Jackson may have welcomed the opportunity to quit, for in 1787 he and John Palmer were "partners" in the Royalty Theatre.[51] Benjafield himself being a man of "no literary talents," [52] the editorship was handed over to the printer, Peter Stuart, so that, for the first time in the *Post's* history, the offices of printer and editor were combined. Peter Stuart continued to print and edit the *Post* until 4 February, 1788, with only one mishap. In 1787 a Mr. W. J'Anson sued the newspaper for having named him as ringleader of a group of "divers swindlers and common informers," who preyed on innocent people. Peter was tried and acquitted in the Court of Common Pleas, but on 15 May, 1787, the case was transferred to the Court of King's Bench, where the judgment was reversed.[53] Although Peter's sentence is not recorded, it seems to have been too slight to interfere with his work for the *Post.*

If Benjafield had had any interest in the legitimate operation of the newspaper, the year 1786 would have been a good one for the *Morning Post,* for by this time the *Morning Herald,* still its only rival in the West End, was having difficulties. In 1785 or 1786 Dudley quarreled with his assistant, John Williams, who, according to Williams's biographer,[54] retaliated with "an intemperate satire on his antagonist." Dudley thereupon filed an information against Williams, but the matter was "terminated by the interference of some friends," and in 1787 Williams supposedly departed for France. Far more serious was Dudley's trouble with William Pitt. In October, 1785, the *Herald* had copied from the *General Advertiser* two paragraphs accusing Pitt of having "cleared above 150,000*l.*" by "jobbing in the alley on the Dutch peace." Pitt had sued for £150,000 damages, and in early 1786 J. S. Barr, the printer of the paper, was tried for the offense, but, although the jury convicted, it valued the damage to Pitt's reputation at only £250. This verdict, which was regarded as a great triumph for the Opposition, was no triumph for the *Morning Herald,* which had to expect systematic persecution from this point on. In anticipation, perhaps, of what was ahead, J. S. Barr quit the paper on 20 May, 1786, and is not caught sight of again until 26 December, 1790, when he was printing *Ayre's Sunday London Gazette, and Weekly Monitor.* He was replaced as printer of the *Herald* by his "friend," William Perryman, whose "Queries" to the Duke of Richmond, published by the *Morning Post* on 25 February, 1780, had been cited in the Duke's action against Dudley. The *Herald* also tried to retire into obscurity in the evident hope of appeasing Pitt by sheer inconspicuousness. Although it continued to support the Opposition, the support had none of its former vigor, and even its "personalities" and "anecdotes" were restrained.

The year 1787 was quite another matter, for on 1 January the *Morning Post* acquired a formidable competitor in the *World, and Fashionable Advertiser,* a new West End newspaper, printed by John Bell and conducted by Major Edward Topham. The *World* was an immediate success, and by 19 October it was selling 2,600 copies.[55] Although some of the success was owing to the paper's prose writers, more of it was owing to the paper's poets. So popular were "Della Crusca" (Robert Merry) and his "tuneful disciples" that on 27 November the *World* dropped its subtitle and described itself editorially as henceforth "The Paper of Poetry." A newspaper thus dedicated to poetry was something new, and none of the other newspapers was prepared to compete with it, least of all the *Morning Post,* whose present interest in literature was limited to a steady abuse of James Boswell. Throughout 1787 the *Post* attempted to solve the problem by invective, but on 1 January, 1788, it announced a complete change in editorial policy. *"News-papers have long enough estranged themselves . . . totally from the elegancies of Literature, and dealt only in malice, or at least, in the prattle of the day . . . ,"* it observed. *"But it is a blame out of which the* MORNING-POST *is resolved to struggle; and for that end plans are now settling with a number of Literary Gentlemen, and particularly with* one, *whose name would do our Paper the highest honour, were we at liberty to announce it."* From now on, the *Post* promised, it would be *"sought after . . . [by] the lovers of literature and taste."* The author of this announcement was Peter Stuart, who obviously supposed that he had been given a free hand to remake the policy of the paper. He was mistaken. For the next month the *Post* did take some interest in painting and music and sufficient interest in *"the elegancies of Literature"* to supplement its abuse of Boswell with some excerpts from Mrs. Piozzi's *Anecdotes of Dr. Johnson;* but nothing further was said of the *"plans"* with *"Literary Gentlemen,"* and by the beginning of February the paper had sunk back into the slough of scurrility. On 4 February Peter Stuart turned the printing and editing over to his brother Daniel and left, having saved £1,000 toward the establishing of the first daily evening newspaper, the *Star.*

Daniel Stuart's name continued to appear in the colophon of the *Post* until 1 May, 1789: until 11 August, 1788, as printer and thereafter as publisher. Until January, 1789, he was also the editor. His first act was to resume abuse of the *World,* his second to resume abuse of the Prince of Wales, for the *Morning Post* had been seriously affected by certain developments relating to his marriage.

Although nothing had been said of the Prince's marriage since February, 1786, Benjafield's two paragraphs in the *Morning Post* had not been forgotten, for, when in the spring of 1787, Alderman Newnham announced his intention of applying to Parliament for the payment of the Prince's debts and some addition to his revenue, John Rolle, the member for Devonshire, threatened that, if such application were made, he would demand an inquiry into "matter by which the Constitution, both in Church and State, might be essentially affected." On the authority of the Prince, Fox thereupon categorically denied that the marriage existed: it could not, he said, exist legally, and it did not exist in any way whatever. Mrs. Fitzherbert was outraged. She forgave the Prince, who persuaded her that Fox had greatly exceeded his instructions, but she never forgave Fox for having "rolled her in the kennel like a street-walker, [when] he knew that every word he said was a lie." [56] At the Prince's request, Sheridan then undertook her defense in Parliament; and, since his instructions were to salvage her reputation without admitting the marriage, he dwelt at length on her status as a woman of impeccable virtue and said nothing about her status as a wife. Horne Tooke supplied the deficiency. His *Letter to a Friend, on the Reported Marriage of His Royal Highness the Prince of Wales* (London, 1787) was such an impassioned presentation of the whole case for Mrs. Fitzherbert that she was supposed, although perhaps mistakenly, to have been a collaborator. The *Letter*

frankly admitted the fact of the marriage, proof of which Tooke
seemed either to possess or to have examined, and went on to urge
that it was an honorable marriage and should be approved as such by
Court and Parliament. In the postscript Tooke angrily denounced
Fox in that, "be the marriage true or false," he should "get up and
make this avowal; and thus give it the appearance of sacrificing, on
compulsion, a defenceless woman's character . . . for so mean a consideration as a paltry sum of money." [57]

Tooke's *Letter* was a blow to John Benjafield, who had been relying upon threats to expose a marriage which was now publicly admitted, on the evident authority of the bride herself. Carlton House
seems to have continued its payments to the *Morning Post* through
1787, but to have discontinued them at the beginning of 1788, for on
27 February, 1788, the *Post* published a reminder. Since it evidently
had nothing to add to what Tooke had already said about the marriage, it fell back on the matter of the Prince's dissipations, with
special reference to his gambling, which had by now become a "matter
of notoriety in . . . political circles," the Prince reputedly losing two
or three thousand pounds in an evening.[58] The reminder, which consisted of the observation, "The Club at *Weltje's* under the PRINCE
and the three ROYAL DUKES, is established on the most familiar and
accommodating footing with respect to conversation and play," was
intended to jog Weltje's memory as well as the Prince's. Before the
*Post* could publish a second reminder, the *World* had also become
interested in the Prince's affairs, and Benjafield was well enough
versed in the techniques of his trade to recognize a competitor. "A
*minor* print is daily dealing out abuse against the PRINCE of WALES,
and the DUKE of YORK," the *Post* proclaimed on 6 March, 1788: "—the
reasons for this conduct are well understood at CARLTON-HOUSE, and
will shortly be as well understood by the public." The *World* reacted
to this proclamation with some derogatory remarks about "a certain
*low* print," but the abuse was discontinued. On 18 June the *Morning
Post* published its second reminder, this one returning to the matter
of the Prince's marriage, and on 21 June it published a third, which
had to do with the Prince's extravagance. "In addition to the PRINCE
of WALES's beautiful PAVILION at BRIGHTON," it observed, "is a new
and elegant house adjoining, the property of Mr. WELTJIE [*sic*]." But
the Prince was more sophisticated with respect to the press than he
had been two years earlier. He refused to be blackmailed any further

with respect to his marriage, and his dissipations and extravagances, including his lavish support of Weltje, were not at this time a Parliamentary issue.

Benjafield was in a predicament. From every point of view, the *Morning Post* was a failure. As a legitimate business, it was worthless, its sale under his management having dropped to less than 500 a day [59] and its advertisements having dwindled accordingly. It was evidently not even profitable as a vehicle for general extortion, for it seems to have been depending for its support mainly on the subsidy from Carlton House. The worst of it was that Benjafield could not abandon it, for he and Tattersall were bound by the terms of the lease to keep the paper alive until 1 January, 1793, and then to "[*indemnify*] the other proprietors against any depreciation of shares below £350, for each 24th." Since the only solution was to sell it, Benjafield began to look around for a purchaser.

## SOME WHYS AND WHEREFORES OF THE WELTJE-TATTERSALL LEASE

THE FIRST person upon whom Benjafield's eye fell was the younger George Colman. The Colmans were known to be very much interested in newspapers. On 7 February, 1785, the *Morning Post* had itself stated flatly that the elder George Colman was a proprietor of both the *Public Advertiser* and the *St. James's Chronicle;* "and," it added, "Mr. *Colman* is violently suspected, to say no more, of writing frequently in them. Indeed, the extravagant panegyric that appears often in the *St. James's Chronicle* and the *Public Advertiser* on Mr. *Colman*'s productions, and his operations as a manager, as the printers of both [newspapers] are known to be men of sense, can be supposed to be the manufacture of Mr. *Colman* alone, or of some scribe in his interest."

The possibility of selling the *Morning Post* to the Colmans was suggested to Benjafield by the controversy over the younger Colman's *Ways and Means,* which was performed at the Haymarket on 10 July, 1788. None of the newspapers understood this play. The *World* (11 July), for example, found the characters only "thinly disguised portraits" of certain "personalities of the day," all of which "have meanings they should not have had," and the whole work, therefore, somewhat "indelicate." The *Morning Chronicle* (14 July) suggested that the play might be "[leveling] a very pleasant shaft at private theatricals," perhaps "the Dramatis Personae at Richmond House." The *Public Advertiser* (14 July) admitted that it did not know what the play meant, but it was willing to trust Colman, who was a man of "genius," even though his "taste" seemed in this instance to be somewhat warped by the modern conception of comedy. The triweekly *St. James's Chronicle,* now evidently edited by Nathaniel Thomas,[60] was ecstatic (12 July); although it also did not know what the play meant precisely, it was enthusiastic to the point of hysteria. The review in the *Morning Post* (14 July) consisted of an excerpt from the review in the *St. James's Chronicle* with the introductory comment: "It is worthy of note what the *modest* Mr. Colman jun. says of himself and his last new production: the following quotation being part of the criticism which appeared in an evening paper of Saturday, of which the *elder Colman* is a Proprietor, and by that means the *younger Colman* has unlimited power to *puff* himself. . . ." This comment inspired a comment from the *World,* which on 15 July observed that "Young COLMAN seems to have given most mortal offence to the *Lower Prints.* Having abused them somewhat severely, they are now retaliating with all the fury they can command." This was the first reference to the epilogue, which was the real issue, for the epilogue had described newspaper writers as nothing but hired character assassins; and the *Morning Post* at once took up the cudgel. On 17 July it advised its readers: "Some of the daily prints have been mean and absurd enough to attempt a defence of young COLMAN in his attack upon newspapers, to the lenity of which, and the aid of good acting, and not to any merits in his miserable writings, he owes the little portion of fame he has acquired."

At this point the *Post* had to interrupt its attacks on the Colmans to deal with the general elections, which had begun on 8 July, 1788. Although the paper was still obligated by the terms of Benjafield's purchase of shares to support the Ministerial candidates, the Government no longer regarded the *Morning Post* as of any particular consequence. Not only was the *Post* too mean in character and too paltry in circulation to be influential, but the Treasury had revised its thinking about newspapers generally, with a new emphasis upon quantity as well as quality. Hence, although the Government had relied upon one newspaper to see it through the critical elections of 1784, the Treasury now liked to "boast" that it controlled every morning newspaper except the *Herald,* the *Gazetteer,* and the *General Advertiser:* "exactly *seven* to *three"* (spurious *Star,* 29 May, 13 June, 1789). That the Treasury placed slight value on the *Morning Post* even as a statistic is evident from the fact that it was the only one of the seven newspapers which was not paid for its loyalty. On 9 August, 1788, Benjafield collected 156 guineas (tabulated as £163 16s. 0d.) [61] "for the person who writes for the Morning Post," possibly Horne Tooke, whose devastating "Portraits" of Fox and his friends appeared in that paper from 21 July through 27 August and in the *World* beginning 22 August, possibly for someone whose name he himself did not know; but for the paper itself he received nothing.

In early August the *Post* returned to the matter of the epilogue. The fact that the *World*'s opinion of *Ways and Means* had suddenly shifted from condemnation to approval was sufficient evidence that the Colmans had come to terms with that newspaper. They may also have tried to come to terms with the *Post,* but Benjafield was now looking for a purchaser, not a subsidizer. The point of what the *Post* had to say was that Colman, who had always got better treatment from the press than he deserved, was an ingrate and an arrogant coxcomb, and by mid-August it was supplementing these remarks with the suggestion that the London newspapers organize in a boycott of the Colmans and the Haymarket. This suggestion was many times repeated, and on 1 September the *Post* noted jubilantly that, in the preface to the published version of the play, Colman had in fact admitted that he was indicting all but three of the London newspapers, whereas, said the *Post,* every one of those newspapers had "protected" him "till he wantonly forfeited all pretensions to [protection]." "The newspapers have indeed acted properly with regard to young COLMAN," the *Post* continued on 4 September, "for talents, such as his, hardly deserved their notice, and the resentment they display, though certainly well-founded, only tends to keep him and his works from the obscurity in which they would otherwise repose." On 5 September the *Post* struck out at the *World,* which, by coming to Colman's defense, had demonstrated, it said, that it would sacrifice the very soul of the British press "for a paltry sum of money." The *World* evidently replied to this observation, for on 9 September the *Post* announced that the *"flimsy* print, which, with such affected impudence, calls the several morning papers the *lower* prints, is, by its common-place nonsense and frivolous malignity, so well entitled to the appellation of the LOWEST print, that we trust . . . the public will hereafter distinguish it only by that appellation."

The paragraph of 5 September was the *Post*'s last comment on the Colmans. For the remainder of the month, the paper carried only the usual Treasury propaganda, while Benjafield awaited developments in another quarter. In dealing with Carlton House, the *World* had the advantage of having among its advisers Richard Brinsley Sheridan, who was an intimate of the Prince of Wales and Mrs. Fitzherbert and who was himself a master at intrigue. As Sheridan well knew, the result of the events of 1786–1787 had been, not only to split the Opposition into a Whig, or Foxite, faction and a Carlton House, or Sheridanite, faction, but to split the Carlton House faction itself into two cliques: the first headed by the Prince, whose politics were, as Fitzgerald says,[62] "chiefly . . . regulated by his own interests," and the second headed by Mrs. Fitzherbert, who was intent on safeguarding her reputation and who, it appeared, had a will of her own. Since Mrs. Fitzherbert refused to tolerate any aspersions on her character as an honest woman, she also refused to tolerate any question as to the status of her marriage, so that she was moved, not by the suggestion that she might be properly married, but by the suggestion that she might not be. On 6 September, 1788, the *World* accordingly published a long "epitaph," which began: "To the Remembrance of one/ Who was—, Wife and no Wife, Princess/ and no Princess. . . ." Mrs. Fitzherbert immediately responded, and by early October the *World* was very evidently in the pay of Carlton House. Carlton House had, in fact, offered Topham £4,000 cash and a lifetime annuity of £400 for outright purchase of the newspaper,[63] as Benjafield might have learned from his drama critic, John Taylor, who was not only associated with all the principals of the *World* in the "Beef-steak Club," [64] but was also "upon the most intimate footing with Sheridan, Richardson, and their political associates." [65] On 10 October Benjafield made his own overture, which was essentially only a prose version of the *World*'s "epitaph": "A *Question*.—What is the reason that Mrs. FITZHERBERT, who is a lady of fortune and fashion, never appears at Court? She is visited by *some* ladies of high rank—has been in public with them— and yet never goes to the Drawing-Room at St. James's. This question is sent for publication by a person who pays no regard to the idle reports of the day, and wishes to have this mystery cleared up." By the end of the year, Benjafield had sold his interests in the *Morning Post* to Louis Weltje.

Since Carlton House's investment in the *Morning Post* has been a matter of great interest to historians, a detailed consideration of how the sale was effected may not be amiss. There are four pieces of evidence, the first of which is, of course, the *Morning Post* itself. The paragraph of 10 October, 1788, was directed at Mrs. Fitzherbert, and negotiations were apparently commenced at once, for the *Post* said nothing further about anyone at Carlton House for over a month. But, although Mrs. Fitzherbert could be counted on to exert a powerful influence, the money for the purchase would have to come from the Prince of Wales, so that the decision to buy or not to buy was ultimately his. Here events were working in Benjafield's favor, for on 10 November all the newspapers admitted that the King was seriously ill. The *Morning Post* went a step further. On 13 November it stated that "[the] malady with which HIS MAJESTY is afflicted is of such a nature—that the MEDICAL Gentlemen have their doubts as to future consequences, and if the KING continues a few days longer in his present situation a REGENCY will BE APPOINTED; at the head of which will be HIS ROYAL HIGHNESS THE PRINCE OF WALES." This statement was followed by a long discussion of the probable nature of the "REGENCY," taking into consideration the Prince's qualifications and reputation, and, since this was a question which greatly agitated the Prince, the purpose of the discussion was to persuade him that he needed newspaper support and therefore the *Morning Post* immediately and desperately.

The third paragraph, which appeared on the following day (14 Nov.), was directed at Sheridan as well as the Prince of Wales, who were accused of conspiring to suppress the news of the King's illness. Sheridan was evidently also involved in the negotiations between Carlton House and the *Morning Post:*

> The Opposition prints daily teem with abuse, because it has been mentioned, that the leaders of the ex-party have taken pains to conceal the real dangerous state of the KING's illness;—and they also deny the fact.—We, however, . . . assert it to be true, that one of the leaders of the Opposition [Sheridan] made use of all his influence, to induce the Conductors of the Public Prints not to mention the illness of the KING. This being in some measure disregarded, a circular was sent to the same persons, stating, that it

was the *Command* of [the PRINCE of WALES], that nothing should appear on the subject of his MAJESTY's indisposition. . . . The motive for this conduct, on the part of Opposition, is obviously to make good some ground, and to extend their connections in case a certain melancholy event should happen.

The newspaper which had "in some measure disregarded" Sheridan's instructions was the *Post* itself, which on 20 October had noted that "[the] KING was taken ill on Friday [17 Oct.], as he was stepping into his Chaise to come to Town. His MAJESTY continues much indisposed."

On 9 December the *Post* expressed its satisfaction that it was called "Mr. Pitt's GAZETTE." The "appellation" did not "in the least," it said, "weaken our zeal in defence of so excellent a Minister. We even rejoice that this paper should have drawn upon itself such an appellation." And, on the following day (10 Dec.), it published the fourth and last paragraph in the series. Although this paragraph struck primarily at Mrs. Fitzherbert, it managed to include in the scope of its remarks the whole Carlton House coterie. The italicizing of *intended* in the two instances was meant to imply that the Prince might be compelled to retain the Pitt Government:

A very extraordinary circumstance has recently occurred, which will probably be the means of delaying for some time, the final and complete arrangement of the *intended Blue and Buff* Administration. This impediment originates with Mr. Fox. . . .

The memorable declaration of Mr. Fox in the House of Commons, on the subject of a *marriage* between a certain GREAT CHARACTER, and a LADY well known in the higher circles, cannot but be fresh on the memory of almost every individual in this kingdom.

That connection, on account of the difference in *religious* principles, appears to Mr. Fox fraught with possible mischiefs to his measures:—he has therefore declared his POSITIVE RESOLUTION, not to take any part in the *intended* new Ministry, until the EXACT LIMITS of that connection are SATISFACTORILY DEFINED, as he has now reason to believe that it is of a more COERCIVE and PERMANENT nature than he was induced to *imagine,* and ANNOUNCE.

To annul the ground of Mr. Fox's objection, no less a sum than the *annual* allowance of TWENTY THOUSAND POUNDS have been offered to the LADY, on condition of her retiring to the Continent—this the Lady has *positively refused,* expressing a firm determination to abide by an authority that she is said to hold forth as UNANSWERABLE and INALIENABLE.

A Character who has lately started into oratorical consequence [possibly

Grey], is the NEGOCIATOR of this important business; who, finding the Lady obstinate, has offered, in addition to the enormous income above mentioned, THE RANK OF AN ENGLISH DUCHESS.

The Lady, however, firmly resists all these alluring temptations, urging, that she was in circumstances entirely independent previous to her being induced to coincide with that condition from which she is resolute not to recede, as character is to her of much more importance than affluence, however abundant, if attended with the deprivation of that rank to which she HOLDS HERSELF ENTITLED.

There was only one comment on this paragraph. On 11 December the *General Advertiser,* then in the pay of the Whigs, remarked that the "ridiculous nonsense which appeared in the *Morning Post* of yesterday, respecting the PRINCE of WALES, we should have thought was too contemptible even for Mr. *Rose* to have written." George Rose was still Secretary of the Treasury.

In addition to the evidence furnished by the *Post,* there are three firsthand accounts of the transaction, all of which are evasive and both intentionally and unintentionally misleading and yet each one of which is in its own way illuminating. The first account is supplied by John Taylor,[66] who, at the commencement of the negotiations, was the drama critic for the paper and at their conclusion its editor:

During the agitation of the first Regency bill, . . . I became, by a circumstance of some importance in the political world at that time, the conductor of "The Morning Post." It appeared that a lady, supposed to be in great favour with a high personage, and not merely connected by the *ties of mutual affection,* had determined to assert claims not sanctioned by law, but which if openly . . . promulgated, would, perhaps, have been attended by a national agitation. It was stated in "The Morning Post," rather as rumour than assertion, that the lady in question had demanded a peerage and 6000*l.* a year, as a requital for her suppression of a fact which might have excited alarm over the empire, and have put an effectual stop to all farther proceedings on the subject of the pending regency.

I was engaged merely as the dramatic critic for "The Morning Post" at that time, and was on intimate terms with a confidential servant of the high personage alluded to. This confidential servant sent to me, and when I went to him he assured me that there was not the least foundation for the paragraph in question, and requested that I would convey this assurance to the person who had *farmed* the paper [Benjafield] from the chief proprietor [Tattersall]. I told him I was convinced that such a communication would have no effect, or rather a contrary effect, for that, finding the subject had made an impression, it would certainly be followed by articles of the same nature and tendency, and that silence was the best policy. The person alluded to did not seem to be convinced by my reasoning, and determined to consult people more likely to form a better judgment; yet he desired me in the mean time to convey the assurance which he had given. I did so, and, as I expected, there was next day a stronger allusion to the same mysterious event. The same confidential agent then satisfied of the propriety of the advice which I had given, asked me if I thought that the *farmer* of the paper, who was also a proprietor, would dispose of the period for which he was authorized to conduct it [i.e., would sell the lease], and of his share in the paper; and I was desired to make the requisite enquiry. I did so, and as the *farmer* possessed no literary talents, and "The Morning Post" had sunk under his management into a very different state from its [later] fashionable interest and political importance, he was glad of the opportunity of relieving himself from a weight which he had not strength enough to carry. He, therefore, struck the iron while it was hot, received a large sum for his share in the paper, another for the time that he was to hold a control over it, and an annuity for life. Such was the importance attached to this mysterious secret: "The Morning Post" was purchased for the allotted period, and I was vested with the editorship.

Since Taylor was writing forty-four years after these events, some error is to be expected, and many of his facts are in error. Of the two paragraphs relating to Mrs. Fitzherbert, for example, the first made no mention of a settlement, and the second indicated, not that she "had demanded a peerage and 6000*l*. a year," but that she had refused "THE RANK OF AN ENGLISH DUCHESS" and "TWENTY THOUSAND POUNDS" a year. Moreover, although the first paragraph did base its query on "idle reports of the day," the information regarding the settlement was presented as "assertion," not "as rumour"; and the paragraphs did not appear on successive days: they were separated by a period of two months. The remainder of the account also requires editing, but it nevertheless sheds considerable light on the early stages of the negotiations.

Since the beginning of 1786, Carlton House had been dealing directly with John Benjafield through the agency of Louis Weltje; but this time Carlton House approached Benjafield's "dramatic critic" rather than Benjafield himself. The reason is, of course, that the "confidential servant" in this case was Sheridan, not Weltje, and he was representing Mrs. Fitzherbert, not the Prince of Wales, who was not only not involved in these early negotiations, but was probably not even aware of them. Since Taylor and Sheridan were "on intimate terms" and Taylor was certainly not stupid, he undoubtedly stated at once what Benjafield had in mind and the amount he was likely to demand for his interest in the newspaper; and, having verified these statements by consultations with Tattersall and others, Sheridan thereupon presented the case to Mrs. Fitzherbert, who in turn presented it to the Prince. But, since the Prince was reluctant to invest a large sum of money in a newspaper as wretched as this one, negotiations dragged on for two months without making any progress. The *Post*'s paragraph of 13 November was intended to add weight to Mrs. Fitzherbert's arguments, but by this time Benjafield was losing patience, for the paragraph of 14 November was directed at Sheridan, who had thus far represented Carlton House in the matter, as well as at the Prince. Sheridan evidently assured Benjafield through Taylor that a decision was in the offing, for the *Post* remained silent for another month. But Benjafield could not wait indefinitely, for he was determined to rid himself of the newspaper at the end of the calendar year; and the paragraph of 10 December was therefore meant to bring negotiations to a speedy conclusion by needling everyone concerned. It succeeded only because political developments had worked in its favor. It would certainly not have alarmed the Prince two months earlier, but he could afford no publicity respecting his marriage, now that the Regency Bill was finally in the making.

The second account, which is submitted by Benjafield, deals with the final stages of the negotiations. Benjafield, in fact, left two accounts. The first one [67] stated only that he had been approached by Charles Bicknell, the Prince's solicitor, who asked him to retract some statement regarding an "imaginary impediment to the formation . . . of a *'blue and buff'* administration," that he had refused, and that during the same month Weltje had made him an offer for his interest in the newspaper, which he thereupon sold. He saw no connection between the two events, he said, supposing only that Louis Weltje wanted to invest in a newspaper. The second account [68] went into greater detail. "[Upon] *the great question relating to the Regency,* in 1788," Benjafield began, "the Morning Post took a decided and possibly a most violent part—it maintained the *constitutional measures* proposed by Mr. Pitt in opposition to the *speculative opinions* advanced by Mr. Fox. . . . About the middle of December, 1788, I was applied to, by Mr. Weltje, then maître-d'hôtel to . . . the Prince of Wales, on the subject of the disposal of the Morning Post,"

Mr. Weltje offering "500 guineas for each of my two 24ths, and 300 pounds a year, for my interest in the lease and controul over the paper." This offer was refused, and some time later Weltje advanced the amount of the annuity to "a clear £350 per annum." Benjafield then agreed to consider the offer, and, as he put it (the brackets are his), upon "my consulting my political friends, I was advised [the great business of the Regency being then considered as settled] to avail myself of the offer . . . , and . . . with the consent of Mr. Richard Tattersal, . . . on the 2d of January, 1789, I entered into an agreement with Mr. Weltje, by which, in the consideration of 1000 guineas for my two 24ths, and of an annuity [for life] of £350 for my interest in the lease and controul over the Morning Post, and my property in the debts and utensils due and belonging to it,—I transferred all my stated property and interest in that paper to him," he agreeing that "real security should be given by him for the annuity" and that "obligations" specified in the lease should be "performed." Benjafield again stressed the fact that he never *"possessed any information, or entertained any suspicion* whatever" that Weltje was acting for the Prince of Wales, and he purported to be outraged at the suggestion that he should have forced anyone to buy the lease by threatening "to publish certain papers or intelligence . . . reflecting upon a person of considerable rank or note." He had simply succeeded "in carrying forth the objects and views of the administration of that period (. . . I speak of the prospective regency in 1788)," so that his work was done, and, having an opportunity to dispose of his interest in the paper, he did so.

Two comments should be added to this account. The first has to do with the "political friends" who advised Benjafield to sell the newspaper. Chief among these was the Secretary of the Treasury, George Rose, whom the *Morning Post* had been extolling since 1784. "There have been few Secretaries to the Treasury, who have, like Mr. Rose, discharged the duties of their office with that strict attention to business, sound sense, and unimpeached integrity, and who have also like him, escaped censure, and obliquy," the paper observed typically on 24 September, 1785. Since the Treasury had paid for his shares in the *Post,* at least in part, Benjafield could, of course, not sell them without Mr. Rose's consent, and the consent must have been given with alacrity, for the chance to saddle Carlton House with a newspaper as disreputable as this one would have impressed the personnel of the

Treasury as capital sport. But the real joke was Rose's statement that the Government no longer needed the *Post,* "the great business of the Regency being then considered as settled." One cannot believe that Rose could have made this statement or that Benjafield could have listened to it without laughing; for, as they both knew, the Prince of Wales was being coerced into buying the *Post* only because "the great business" was completely unsettled, and, so little did Rose himself think that it was "settled" that, not only did he continue subsidies to the other newspapers and increase the subsidy of *The Times* to £300 a year,[69] but he promptly offered Topham £600 a year for political control of the *World:* [70] the highest amount the Treasury had ever offered for a newspaper.

The second comment has to do with the price which Carlton House finally paid for Benjafield's interests, namely, "1000 guineas for [his] two 24[ths], and . . . an annuity of £350 for [his] interest in the lease and controul over the Morning Post." Although these amounts do not represent separate purchases, one might note that the price of the shares was alone exorbitant. Although Benjafield had himself paid an inflated price, he had paid only "about 400 pounds each," and, since he had bought them, the shares had sharply decreased in value, the sale of the *Post* having dropped from 2,100 to less than 500 copies daily. Moreover, the Treasury had just offered John Walter only £4,000 for a half-interest in *The Times,*[71] or approximately £333 a share for a newspaper which was selling perhaps 1,750 copies a day. The price indicated for the lease is even more exorbitant. Since the lease had cost Benjafield nothing, the £350 a year was pure gain for him, whereas until 1 January, 1793, Carlton House was obligating itself to pay half the rental of the newspaper, that is £700 a year, in addition to the £350 annuity, and on 1 January, 1793, to reimburse the other proprietors if the value of the shares was then "declared" below £350 each. But even this was not all, for the annuity was guaranteed to Benjafield, not for the period of the lease, but for life. Hence the annuity actually had nothing to do with the lease. It also seems to have had nothing to do with the suppression of any secret information, for there is no evidence that Benjafield had such information. Its sole purpose was to guarantee his silence about the present transaction and to absent him from the London newspapers in perpetuity.

The final account of the negotiations is supplied by the editor and publisher of the *Morning Post,* Daniel Stuart.[72] Since Daniel was writing (3 Aug., 1811) at the request of Benjafield, who was then involved in a lawsuit on account of his annuity, he was trying in part to excuse Benjafield; but he was trying most of all to excuse himself, for he was very much afraid of being called as a material witness:

About this time, say 1784 or 5, the proprietors agreed to farm the paper for seven years to Messrs. Benjafield and Tattersal [*sic*] at a given sum, I believe £1400. . . . Mr. Tattersal had, I believe, the management of the money affairs, and Mr. B. the direction of the literary department. But I do not believe Mr. Benjafield ever was the editor . . . ; nor can I suppose he received any thing as a managing proprietor, he having such a direct interest as lessee. The Morning Post had generally been, and certainly was, during Mr. Benjafield's management, a ministerial paper. When the question of the Regency arose in 1788, the Morning Post took a very violent part against the party of the Prince of Wales, in consequence of which Mr. Benjafield was bought out, and the paper changed sides. It was said he received £2000 for his two twenty-fourth shares, and an annuity of £350 for his interest as lessee, a sum which probably his profits as managing proprietor produced. This transaction made a great noise at the time, and perhaps the circumstances were much exaggerated. . . . The apostacy of the Morning Post at the time of the Regency, [also] made much noise . . . ; but no part of Mr. Benjafield's conduct in that sale was blameable—he had a right to get as high a price as he could, and I make no doubt he got more than the value, much more, but the precise value I know not. With the change of politics in the newspaper he had nothing to do: he did not change; and the persons who purchased of him were entitled to make of the property what they pleased. . . .

This statement as fully answers . . . all . . . queries, as it is in my power to answer them; but how far you can rely on its accuracy you must judge, when I inform you, I know no one of these circumstances of my own knowledge, except that Mr. Benjafield was the conductor of the Morning Post. I never had any connection with Mr. Benjafield, and but very little intercourse, never having spoken to him above three or four times in my life. Most of the circumstances occurred long before I was engaged in any newspapers, my first engagement being only four or five months before Mr. B. left the Morning Post: they occurred when I was a very young man, and I had the account of them by hearsay. . . .

At the time the *Morning Post* was sold, Daniel Stuart had been printing and editing the newspaper for eleven months, and it is hard to believe that during that period he had not "spoken to [the conductor] above three or four times." It is also hard to believe that he was not the author of those four paragraphs which effected the sale and that he was not rewarded by Benjafield accordingly. But the ability to affect a childlike innocence under the most incriminating circumstances was one of Daniel's principal talents. His statement that the "apostacy of the Morning Post . . . made much noise" is an exaggeration, for the *Morning Post* was too obscure for its politics to be a matter of consequence. Only *The Times* commented on the "apostacy," and on 30 January, 1789, it addressed

*A Few* QUERIES *to Mr.* WELTJIE.

Pray, are you not both Cook, Counsellor, and Major Domo, to the P– of W–?

Would it not therefore perfectly become you to confine your studies to your stew-pans, and your influence to your patron's closet?

Are you a fit person to influence the press, or to assist its prostitution in favour of a factious party?

Have you not within these few days, purchased a leading share of a morning Print, with the express view of making it subservient to the P–'s friend [Mrs. Fitzherbert]?

There were a few more such gibes at Weltje, and then *The Times,* too, lost interest.

Not everyone profited from these transactions. Daniel Stuart, for example, lost the editorship of the *Post,* although he continued as publisher, and Richard Tattersall later became involved in considerable litigation on Benjafield's account. Sheridan paid for the political control of the *Post* with the political control of the *World,* and Mrs. Fitzherbert never got the support of the *Post* which she might have expected. Yet some of the participants did profit. Benjafield, of course, reaped the largest harvest, and he did so without forfeiting the respect of his contemporaries, for in October, 1791, he joined Topham, Miles Peter Andrews, Robert Merry, Frederick Reynolds, and other literary and journalistic notables of his day in the formation of a club, called "Keep the Line," which met weekly at the Turk's Head Coffeehouse in the Strand.[73] John Taylor was rewarded for his services by being made editor of the newspaper at a salary of two guineas a week [74] and by being appointed Oculist to the Prince of Wales,[75] and Weltje emerged with at least a financial interest in a newspaper. Even those who did not profit expected to profit, so that what began as Benjafield's plot ended as a complex of plots of which the Prince of Wales was ultimately the victim. Since everyone had a reason for urging the purchase and no one was concerned with the price, everyone was in his way a co-conspirator with Benjafield. One cannot say positively that Benjafield was even the arch-conspirator. Since, in dealing with late eighteenth-century newspapers, one can hardly be too suspicious, it is safe to wonder if the plot did originate with him or if it perhaps originated with his "high political friend," George Rose. There is a shrewdness about the strategy which is not otherwise evident in Benjafield's behavior, and, although Benjafield certainly fared very well as a result of the sale, he may not have fared quite so well at that as the Government, which rid itself of the disreputable *Morning Post* and acquired in its stead the very elegant *World*.

# CHAPTER III

## The *London Courant* (1779–1783) and the *General Advertiser* (1781–1790): Some Newspaper Adventures of "That Rogue Almon"

### THE WAYS OF A BOOKSELLER

A LATE eighteenth-century newspaperman, whether he was a proprietor, a conductor, an editor, a paragraph writer, or only a printer, was primarily a businessman, and he might resort to any manner of chicanery, provided the chicanery did not violate a certain ethical code. The fundamental principle of this code was adherence to a contract. Every newspaperman was accorded the right to make whatever contract he pleased and to terminate it whenever he pleased, but, so long as the contract was in force, he was expected to conform with it in letter and spirit. The code demanded, therefore, that a newspaperman would be loyal to his newspaper. If he was named in an indictment for libel, he would accept responsibility without implicating anyone else; if one of his superiors was in trouble, he would purport to know nothing about it and even to be unaware of the superior's identity; and he would, of course, support the policy of the newspaper at all times. If he did not like the policy or did not like his associates, he could quit, and he might even begin a rival newspaper, but he could not engage in forgeries or piracies. Similarly the code demanded that a newspaperman would be loyal to the political party which was paying him. The code recognized his right to sell his services to the highest bidder and to shift political allegiance whenever it served his interests to do so, but, while he was in the pay of one political party, he was bound to serve that party unswervingly. If he was going to engage in extortionary or blackmailing practices, he would select his victims from the opposition party, and, if he was going to sell puffs, he would sell them to members of his own party.

Any newspaperman who violated this code was *persona non grata* with the London daily press.

Newspapermen, therefore, always regarded Henry Bate Dudley as a hero. According to their code, he invariably fought on the side of right, and his punishment of the forgers of the *Morning Post,* of the proprietors of the *Morning Post,* and of Robert Haswell was considered a glorious victory for the ethics of the press. Even his scourge of James Perry was approved on the ground that Perry should not have interfered in the administration of justice. According to the same code, John Benjafield had behaved honorably. Daniel Stuart was speaking for newspapermen in general when he said that "no part of Mr. Benjafield's conduct in . . . the sale [of the *Morning Post*] was blameable." Had Benjafield been an agent of Carlton House, it would have been wrong for him to coerce Carlton House into buying the newspaper, but he was an agent of the Government, he had served the Government well, his services were no longer needed, and he therefore "had a right to get as high a price [for the paper] as he could" and to get it by any means he wished. The offender in the transaction was Carlton House, for the code strongly disapproved of political factions buying into newspapers, whatever the provocation. Subsidizings of newspapers were accepted as a legitimate source of income, but purchases of shares constituted a threat to "Liberty of the Press," that is, to a newspaperman's God-given right to make contracts without coercion of any sort.

There was no such code among the booksellers, who employed contracts only as ruses. Hence a reputable newspaperman always regarded a bookseller with a certain amount of contempt, and a bookseller never quite understood the ways of newspapermen. John Almon was both a bookseller and a newspaperman.

Almon's career, the early part of which is here only briefly reviewed, began in 1760, when he migrated to London from Liverpool and there worked for various booksellers as editor and nondescript pamphleteer. By the beginning of 1761, he had joined the staff of the *Gazetteer* as assistant conductor and, since the *Gazetteer* was liberal in its point of view, had become a staunch defender of the elder William Pitt, whose virtues he extolled in numerous articles and in the pamphlet *A Review of Mr. Pitt's Administration* (London, 1762). Although his writings attracted some attention, Pitt was unmoved; but not so his brother-in-law, Richard Grenville, Earl Temple, who by

1763 had added the young Almon to his own coterie. Through Temple, therefore, Almon became acquainted with most of the Whig leaders and with at least one budding radical, John Wilkes; and with Temple's encouragement he supported the group in a series of articles, signed "An Independent Whig," and in a number of pamphlets, among them *A Letter to the Right Hon. George Grenville [Temple's Brother]: By an Independent Whig* and *a Letter to J. Kidgell, Containing a Full Answer to His Narrative [Attacking John Wilkes]* (both London, 1763). With Temple's encouragement, too, he resigned as assistant conductor of the *Gazetteer* and, in the autumn of 1763, opened his own bookselling shop in Piccadilly.[1]

Although the shop in Piccadilly soon became the official publishing house for the Whig Club, Almon was until 1768 little more than the creature of Earl Temple, for, of the flood of pamphlets which emanated from his shop, almost all reflected the interests of his patron, who in many instances had also had a hand in their compilation. The most important of these pamphlets were *An Enquiry into the Doctrine Lately Propagated Concerning Libels* (1764), which procured for Almon the enmity of Chief Justice Mansfield and the threat of a prison sentence, from which he was saved only by a lucky change of ministers, and the *History of a Late Minority* (1765), of which Almon was himself the author. Even the eleven-volume *Political Register* (1767–72) was at least begun in Temple's behalf. The intimate working relationship between Almon and Temple during this period was given some publicity by the anonymous author of *A Letter to the Right Honourable E[arl] T[emple]* (London, 1766), who introduced his epistle with a preface, entitled "A Curious Dialogue between a Certain Rt. Hon. Author and His Bookseller," the "Bookseller" being designated as "Little Vamp." [2] Although the work was narrowly circulated, it left its imprint on the newspapers, which thereafter referred to journalists as "vamps" and to John Almon as "John Vamp."

At the beginning of 1768, Almon's political position shifted from liberalism to radicalism. The reason for the shift was that John Wilkes, who had been living on the Continent since 1764, returned to England to face the old charges of having published "An Essay on Women" and No. 45 of the *North Briton*. Almon, who had always admired Wilkes, welcomed him back by bringing out (1768) the introduction to his *History of England,* by visiting him during the twenty-two months he was in King's Bench Prison, by angrily defend-

ing his interests in the pamphlet (1769) *A Letter to the Right Honourable George Grenville Occasioned by His Publication of a Speech
He Made in the House of Commons on the Motion for Expelling Mr.
Wilkes [as Member for Middlesex]*, and by otherwise dedicating himself and his shop to Wilkes's service for the next six years. Since
Wilkes was a good deal more adept at the game of politics and publishing than Temple had been, the relationship was no doubt mutually
profitable. It was probably owing to Wilkes's influence, for example,
that, by the beginning of 1770, the shop in Piccadilly was ceasing to be
simply a pamphlet factory and was becoming the *locus operandi* for
political activities generally.

In 1770 Almon had his second encounter with the Attorney General. There is some reason to suppose [3] that he was still writing for
Charles Say's *Gazetteer* as late as 1767, and from 1767 to 1772 he was,
of course, publishing the *Political Register*. At the beginning of 1770,
he also began the *London Museum of Politics, Miscellanies, and
Literature*, a monthly journal, which lasted until December of the
following year, and, at approximately the same time, he acquired a
managing interest in the triweekly *London Evening Post*. Both papers
were printed by Charles Say's son-in-law, John Miller, and, since
Miller was also printing the *British Monitor*,[4] Almon may have had a
connection with that paper as well. On 19 December, 1769, at any
rate, the *Public Advertiser* published Junius' letter to the King, and,
although the letter was copied by almost every journal in London, only
six of the offenders were indicted: Henry Woodfall of the *Public
Advertiser*, George Robinson of the *Independent Chronicle*, Henry
Baldwin of the *St. James's Chronicle*, Charles Say of the *Gazetteer*,
Miller of the *London Evening Post*, and Almon of the *London Museum*. Of the six Almon, whose *Museum* was the last paper to publish
the letter (1 Jan., 1770), was tried first, and on 2 June, 1770, he was
found guilty in the Court of King's Bench of disseminating a libel on
the King. Miller was tried at Guildhall on 13 July and acquitted, and
Woodfall and Baldwin were subsequently also tried and acquitted, the
charges against Robinson and Say being dropped. On the basis of these
developments, Almon's counsel petitioned (13 July) for a new trial,
but the petition was denied, and on 28 November Almon was fined
ten marks (£6 13s. 4d.) plus costs (£139 0s. 11d.) and ordered to
furnish securities for good behavior for a period of two years, £400 to
be provided by himself and £200 apiece by two sureties.[5] These events,

which may have owed something to Judge Mansfield, whom Almon had antagonized several years earlier, were brought to public notice in a pamphlet, printed, according to the colophon, by John Miller and entitled *The Trial of John Almon, Bookseller, upon an Information, Filed ex officio . . . for Selling Junius's Letter to the King* (London, 1770).

The actual printer of *The Trial of John Almon* had, of course, been Almon himself. It was a common practice for newspapers to have "an article" with their printers, who thereby accepted exclusive responsibility for the publication in the event of an action for libel. But the printer was handsomely paid for the "article," and he was also completely indemnified. Almon had no such "article" with Miller, but, for the next many years, Miller incurred all the risks and suffered all the penalties for enterprises from which Almon alone reaped the reward. The extent to which John Miller was the dupe of John Almon is exemplified by the events (1771) relating to the publication of the Parliamentary debates,[6] for, although Almon was the real principal in the drama,[7] his role was played throughout by Miller. Since from 1770 to 1774 Almon was hiding behind Miller, his newspaper activities are traceable only through Miller. At the beginning of 1771, according to Morison,[8] Almon and William Woodfall established the *London Packet, or New Evening Post;* but Morison cites no authority, and, since the newspaper was not printed by Miller, Almon was probably not concerned in it either. After 1770 Miller also did not print the *British Monitor* or the *London Museum,* although he did print the *London Evening Post* from 1769 through 1773 and the *London Mercury* from 1771 through 1773,[9] and in late 1771 and early 1772 he was very much involved in a struggle between Charles Say and Roger Thompson for control of the *Gazetteer,*[10] perhaps, again, in Almon's behalf. During 1774 and 1775 Miller seems to have been in prison.

On 2 February, 1773, the *London Evening Post* accused the Earl of Sandwich, then First Lord of the Admiralty and one of Wilkes's principal foes, of having sold a position in the Admiralty Commission for £2,000. The accusation was made in the form of a letter, signed "ALFRED" and written, of course, by Almon. Sandwich immediately instituted an action of *scandalum magnatum* against the newspaper, asking £10,000 damages, and Miller accepted sole responsibility for the publication. The case was tried before Judge Mansfield on 8 July, 1773, and the jury found for the plaintiff, awarding Sandwich

£2,000.[11] Miller was unable to pay such a sum, and he evidently received no assistance from Almon, for on 9 March, 1774, he "was taken in execution, at the suit of Lord Sandwich, for the whole damages given him by a late verdict, and [was] confined in Fleet-prison." [12] Since his name is lacking from the colophons of 1774–1775, he apparently remained in Fleet Prison until the beginning of 1776, when he resumed the printing of the *London Mercury* and the *London Evening Post;* [13] and, although in February, 1777, he was fined another £100 for publishing the announcements of the Constitutional Society,[14] he continued to print both newspapers until 1781.

## THE *"PATRIOTIC LABOURS"* OF MR. ALMON

ON 14 JANUARY, 1774, Walpole stated [15] that he had "found [John Almon] to be a rogue." By this time Almon was a thoroughgoing rogue. So long as John Wilkes needed his assistance, he was at least loyal to the political faction which Wilkes represented, but in 1774 Wilkes became Member for Middlesex and Lord Mayor of London, leaving Almon with no patron and no cause except the cause of financial expedience. From this point on Almon worked for all political factions. One of his techniques, according to William Jackson (*Morning Post,* 16 Oct., 1784) , was to write pairs of pamphlets, the second taking issue with the first; or, as Jackson put it, speaking in behalf of Almon:

My pamphlets were generally my own, and I never answered one which I compiled myself, but the answer had the greatest sale. My letter to Lord George Germaine on his being appointed Secretary to the American Department, only ran to three hundred copies, whereas the answer which I had prepared before the letter was published, went off so well, that a thousand were sold in three days. But what, I ask again, have the public to do with all this? I have had nothing to do with writers since I paid twenty pounds to the *Reverend Mr. O'Beirne,* for his Defence of Lord Howe, and a guinea and half [sic] for his Monody on the Death of Lord Northampton, which did not pay for advertising.

Not all of these pamphlets have been identified. Lord George Sackville-Germaine became Secretary of State for the American Colonies in November, 1775, and in 1776 Almon did publish *A Letter to Lord George Germaine, Giving an Account of the Origin of the Dispute between Great Britain and Her Colonies;* but the pamphlet to which this is an answer and from which Almon would, of course, have with-held his own name is not listed in the catalogues of the principal libraries. He also published several pamphlets which are currently attributed to the Rev. Thomas Lewis O'Beirne, later Bishop of Meath, one of which is entitled *Candid and Impartial Narrative of the Trans-actions of the Fleet under the Command of Lord Howe, from the Arrival of the Toulon Squadron, on the Coast of America, to the Time of His Lordship's Departure for England; With Observations: By an Officer Serving in the Fleet* (1779). The reference to a "Monody on the Death of Lord Northampton" is puzzling, for, since the seventh Earl of Northampton had died in 1763 and the eighth Earl did not die until 1796, a "Monody" appearing during the period 1774–1784 would have been, to say the least, ill-timed.

At the same time, according to Jackson (*Morning Post,* 16 Oct., 1784), Almon was pretending to be sympathetic with the American colonies in order to obtain information from other American sym-pathizers, which he thereupon sold to the newspapers. None of the information had cost him a penny, and for some of it he was in-debted only to American newspapers in coffeehouses. Almon was rep-resented as denying the charge that he had got this information for nothing:

> The public charge you bring against me, is false and infamous. You say, that the extracts from the American papers only cost me the price of a dish of coffee, and the trouble of a walk from Piccadilly to the Royal Exchange. Now the fact is, That I frequently was observed to take a coach, and that I paid *George* the waiter at the New-York, and *Bob* the waiter at the Carolina coffee-house, each a two and threepenny piece a quarter for selecting matter for the London Evening. This was all money out of pocket; and taking that and my loss of time into account; surely two guineas and a half a column, was no great profit. I have received three guineas, as you have asserted; and even the articles of the Saratoga Convention [the surrender of General Burgoyne, 17 Oct., 1777], which were *given* me by a gentleman, I only *sold* for five guineas to the paper in which they appeared, although I could have made three times the sum, if I had printed them in a pamphlet.

Jackson answered this supposed denial (*Morning Post,* 20 Oct., 1784) with an elaboration of the charge:

> It was your boast when in business, *Mr. Vamp,* that you supplied the pub-lic with the most authentic American intelligence during the unfortunate war

with the Colonies. You knew the consequence of good information, and you endeavoured to procure it. So far, *Mr. Vamp,* you were in the right. Your industry was commendable. But, here lies the misfortune: you talked of the public, and you meant yourself. . . . Permit me to refresh your memory with an instance, which, like a case in point, will confirm what I have allowed. Mr. Samuel Wharton, who formerly lived in Craven-street, but who is now at Philadelphia, having received some American papers which he was desirous of communicating to the public, sent for you, and requested that you would carry them to a printer of one of the newspapers. You very readily agreed, expressing a great desire that such important articles should appear. Now comes the sequel, *Mr. Vamp;* and a precious sequel it is. The papers which Mr. Wharton entrusted you to carry to a Printer, was SOLD to the *General Advertiser* FOR SEVEN GUINEAS! I need not call to your recollection the indignant scorn with which Mr. Wharton treated you, on the transaction being revealed to him; nor, as he was a man of honor, is it necessary to observe, that he never would exchange a syllable with you afterwards. Doth this fact stand in need of a comment? I fancy it is sufficiently explanatory of the nature of your *patriotic labours;*—they were all for the good of your country.

Wharton, an American land speculator and later a delegate to Congress (1782–83), Justice of the Peace (1784–86), and Judge of the Court of Common Pleas (1790–91), had been living in London for ten years, trying to obtain the King's approval of the Indiana Grant. He left England early in 1779. He and Almon may well have quarreled prior to that time, but Jackson was mistaken in thinking that the rift was permanent, for on 20 March, 1779, Wharton sent Almon the following letter [16] from Paris, where he had gone to join Benjamin Franklin:

Dear Sir
. . . . I wish to give you some American papers for your Remembrancer, and if I thought you would not lose them, Through the Infidelity of the Post Office, I would immediately send them;—perhaps, I may venture in forwarding Them notwithstanding the Expence of the Postage, by this Conveyance. You may depend upon my forwarding the American Newspapers, as soon as I can get Them, and always upon my Friendship. I have done you ample Justice, where you would wish to stand well, and you may fully rely upon my [word illegible] I ordered in your Behalf in America;—for I am very sensible of y$^r$ obliging recommendation in several Instances. I shall take proper Care of your Son's Interest in Indiana. . . .

S. Wharton.

It is certainly true that not everything which issued from the shop in Piccadilly carried Almon's name, but everything which did carry his name was strongly opposed to the policies and personnel of the North Government. Since, in addition to the more outspoken pamphlets, there were numerous volumes purportedly devoted to information and/or entertainment, such as *The Fugitive Miscellany* (1774), *A Collection of . . . Papers, Relative to the Dispute between Great Britain and America; Shewing the Causes and Progress of That Misunderstanding, from 1764 to 1775* (1777), the *Parliamentary Register* (1774–80), and *The Remembrancer, or An Impartial Repository of Public Events* (1774–84), it is not surprising that Almon should have become acquainted with a number of people who disapproved of the war with the American Colonies or with Lord Sandwich's management of the Navy. And, since many of these people had access to information, it is also not surprising that his shop should have become a kind of collecting and distributing agency for news: in particular, for American news. Some of Almon's sources are evident from his private papers.[17] In addition to the letter from Samuel Wharton, there are, for example, several notes from Thomas ("Governor") Pownall, politician and long-time friend of the Colonies, arranging for meetings. There is a letter "with Packet" from Admiral John Blankett, undated, but evidently written in mid-July, 1778:

M$^r$ Almon—

The french fleet of 32 Sail of the line sailed the 3$^{rd}$ July from Brest & were off the 3 days [word illegible] last Friday—They took the Folkston Cutter— Expresses were dispatched to Government immediately. Inclosed is Admiral Keppel's line of Battle.

The Vengeance and Defiance, are so ill manned as not to be a match for Ships of equal force. You may expect the News of a [general?] Action hourly.

You will receive by another Conveyance two Papers which are both Authentick. I would advise you to print them first in French, as that seems to stamp their Authenticity better with the Publick.

The Minister [Lord Sandwich], who has so shamefully neglected our fleet & admitted so great a superiority to France deserves all an enraged country can do to him

From Admiral Blanket [*sic*]

NB. In the inclosed list are the Terrible & Shrewsbury. The former by sickness & desertion has only 320 men; the latter upwards of 200 sick.

The "Packet" consisted of a lengthy and highly detailed description of every ship in Admiral Keppel's fleet.

There is also a letter from John Augustus Hervey, Earl of Bristol. This letter, although similarly undated, was probably written on 24 April, 1779, for it evidently refers to Lord Bristol's speech in defense of his motion for the removal of Lord Sandwich:

M$^r$ Almon, as yesterday night's debate was a very special one, and one I sld. not wish L$^d$ SANDWICH's Morning Post, to misrepresent me in to the Public: *I beg of you to publish this in* y$^r$ *Paper tomorrow*—& to put it in any of the Ev'ning Papers you please; with$^t$ saying you had it from me—I have set [sic] down this Morning & recollect all that passed as [well?] as I can, & I believe is really almost word for word what I said—as my memory seldom fails me;—I send you also the motion least [sic] yourslf. not have an Authentick Copy, & will soon be glad to Contribute to y$^r$ usefull paper, by any thing I have that may be proper to convey to the Public—I shall be in Town Friday Morning & glad to see you—as I may have something worth y$^r$ having.

*This* will Serve you also for y$^r$ Monthly Reg.

Almon published the speech as a pamphlet. Since Lord Bristol died before the year was over, Almon received little additional information from him, but there were many other sources. Hence, if, as Jackson maintained (*Morning Post,* 16 Oct., 1784), Almon did not give the information away, but "levied [a tax] on the printers" of newspapers for its use, the "tax" being as high as seven guineas an item, then he certainly had a very comfortable income from this project alone.

By the beginning of 1776, someone had paid Miller's debt, and Miller was free to resume the printing of the *London Evening Post,* and in November, 1776, William Cooke began the *General Advertiser,* which Miller also printed, the two newspapers probably having a common proprietary. "One of the principal proprietors" of the *General Advertiser* was Urquhart of the firm of Richardson and Urquhart, booksellers, the others being unknown. James Perry joined the staffs of both newspapers in 1777.[18] Although Almon's precise connection with these newspapers during this period is in doubt, it is clear from Jackson's statements that he was selling most of his information to them; and on 24 April, 1779, Lord Bristol was under the impression that Almon had a daily morning newspaper and easy access to several triweekly evening newspapers. In any event Almon had quit the *General Advertiser* by the end of the year, for in November, 1779, he began the *London Courant.*

THE STRAND IN THE EIGHTEENTH CENTURY

## THE CASE OF THE *LONDON COURANT*

THE PROSPECTUS of the *Courant* [19] was issued in the form of a letter, dated 6 November, 1779:

Sir

I beg leave to inform you that on Thursday the 25th instant, being the first day of the meeting of Parliament, a new morning Newspaper is intended to be published, entitled The London Courant and Westminster Chronicle.

The principal design of this Undertaking is, to furnish the Public with early and authentic Intelligence of every public Transaction, both at home & abroad; for which every known channel of communication has been opened, nor will any pains or expence be spared to discover others, as well as to preserve every source of Information. At the same time no attention will be wanting, to prevent the insertion of any articles of falsehood, malignancy & private scandal. In the conduct of this publication, it shall be a fixed principle to meddle with no private character of either sex. But public characters in public stations will be treated with freedom yet always with liberality.

On this plan, it is hoped the London Courant will be worthy of your Notice. However, by ordering it of your Newsman for a short time you will best discover whether these promises are fulfilled, & whether the Paper is worthy of your future encouragement; for which the best endeavours shall not be wanting, of

Sir

Your

most obedient &
most humble servant

J ALMON.

Almon was not the only proprietor of the *Courant,* for Jackson referred (*Morning Post,* 16 Oct., 1784) to "some [other] gentlemen who were concerned in the [enterprise]." Although Jackson did not identify these "gentlemen," it seems clear from the advertisements that flooded the paper that they were all booksellers and that the *Courant* was instituted primarily as a vehicle for advertising. Among the proprietors were evidently Samuel Bladon, Benjamin White, George Kearsley, J. Walker, [John] Fielding, Robert Faulder, and James Barker. At least three of the group had had a previous connection with newspapers. Benjamin White had been a proprietor of the *Gazetteer* since 1775; [20] S. Bladon had published the *General Evening Post* in 1771; and George Kearsley was one of the founders of the *Morning Chronicle.*[21] Kearsley had also distinguished himself in other respects. The original publisher of the *North Briton*, No. 45, he had been involved with Wilkes in the prosecutions and counter-prosecutions of 1763, and he had played a minor role in the farce of 1771. He had received further notoriety in 1775, when he had incurred the wrath of the elder William Pitt by publishing his speech of 20 January and had been obliged to make public retraction.[22] Kearsley was an old associate of Almon, having published his *Review of Mr. Pitt's Administration* in 1762.

The printer of the *London Courant* was Joseph Cooper, who had printed the *General Evening Post* in 1771, while the paper was being published by Bladon; and the publisher was James Barker, who seems previously to have published mainly plays. The conductor was Almon, but Almon was assisted in the editorial work by the Irish political writer, Hugh Boyd, who in 1775 was a debate reporter [23] and who, Almon insisted to the last (see, for example, *Morning Post*, 9 Sept., 1800), had been the author of Junius' letters. Almon may also have received some help from the Rev. Thomas Lewis O'Beirne and some of his other pamphleteers. According to J. Hamilton Trumbell of Hartford, Connecticut, a "corresponding Member" of the Massachusetts Historical Society,[24] there was another member of the staff: George Greive, an attorney from Northumberland, who had gone to London for the specific purpose of supervising the printing of the *Courant*. But Greive's labors supposedly came to an abrupt end in 1780, when, having been "detected" in "the most detestable of all crimes," he spent a year in prison, escaping *"from the pillory"* to Holland and later to America. Trumbell's source was a letter in the Philadelphia *Gazetteer*, but since there is no evidence to support these assertions and since much information in the letter is patently false, one is inclined to question the whole account.

The *London Courant, and Westminster Chronicle* began, as Almon had promised, on 25 November, 1779. The colophon read: "Advertisements, Letters, and Intelligence for this Paper are taken in by the Publisher, J. BARKER, opposite the Pit-door, Russel-Court, Drury-Lane . . . [and by] J. COOPER, PRINTER [in] DRURY-LANE"; but the colophon was contradicted by a legend in the heading: "All Information, Letters, Orders and Advertisements for this Paper, are desired to be sent to J. ALMON, Bookseller, opposite Burlington-House in Piccadilly, LONDON." The *Courant* was in many respects an anachronism, reminiscent of the old (1771) struggle between Parliament and the City of London. Insignia of Guilds, crudely reproduced, flanked the title, and the point of view of the paper was militantly radical. In addition to the numerous booksellers' advertisements, the first number consisted of only two items: a three-column list of holders of Government pensions in Ireland and a six-column letter from "THE OBSERVER./[To be continued occasionally]." On this occasion "THE OBSERVER" was speaking *"To* EDWARD GIBSON, *Esq. one of the Lords of Trade,"* a recent addition to the "group of placemen and pensioners" and a "zealous," although "very late ministerial convert," censuring him in particular for his writings for the Treasury. Subsequent numbers concerned themselves with social and political problems, taking a strong stand on the side of the American colonies, the radical reformers, and the wool-growers. There was no real change in the paper until mid-1781.

But, at the beginning of 1781, the *Courant* published some disparaging remarks on the Russian ambassador, Ivan Simolin, whom it accused, in effect, of stock-jobbing. The paragraph was copied by at least eight other newspapers, and actions for libel were filed against the printers and publishers of seven: the *London Courant,* the *Noon Gazette,* the *Morning Herald,* the *Gazetteer,* the *Whitehall Evening Post,* the *Middlesex Journal,* and the *St. James's Chronicle.* The offenders were tried, convicted, and on 4–5 July sentenced. Although the standard sentence was a year in prison and a £100 fine, there were exceptions. Cooper, for example, was also ordered to be *"set on the Pillory"* for one hour for having originated the libel, Vincent Trehearn, Jr., of the *Noon Gazette* was sentenced to eighteen months and a session in the pillory for having attempted to justify the libel in a subsequent paragraph, and Mary Say of the *Gazetteer,* being "a female," was sentenced to only six months and fined only £50 (*Morning Post,* 8 Aug., 1796).[25] But by this time Almon had retired, Hugh Boyd had gone to India, and the *Courant* was directing correspondents to send "Advertisements, Letters, and Articles of Intelligence" to "J[OHN] STOCKDALE, Bookseller, in Piccadilly."

According to the *Memoirs of a Late Eminent Bookseller,*[26] purportedly written by a friend, but actually written by Almon himself, Almon retired because of ill health, and he remained in retirement for three years. Or, in Almon's words:

At length, ill health obliged him to seek for peace and recovery in retirement. . . . With this view he quitted his [bookselling] business, in favour of a very worthy . . . young man (Mr. [John] *Debrett*) and went into the country. But he was scarcely settled there, when he had the misfortune to lose his wife. He left London in June, 1781, and Mrs. *Almon* died [on 31] August following. . . . He remained in the country until 1784, occasionally employing his pen on temporary subjects. The names of the pieces he wrote are not exactly known. . . . In the month of September 1784 he married the widow of *W. Parker,* printer of the General Advertiser, and returned once more to London, and to business, taking up his residence in Fleet-street. He left ease and affluence, to encounter fatigue and rescue indigence.

Although one has Almon's word for the accuracy of these facts, his word is not very good, for he was writing the *Memoirs* in 1790, when it was of desperate consequence to him to placate both Fox and Pitt. To admit that he had been politically active during the years 1781–1784 would have defeated the very purpose of the *Memoirs.*

It is true that in June, 1781, Almon announced his retirement and moved to Box Moor in Hertfordshire, where he was still living on 31 August, 1781, when his wife died. But not one of his correspondents referred to his being in ill health, nor did he himself refer to it in any of his letters. The real reason for his retirement is evident from the fact that Joseph Cooper rather than John Almon was indicted for the libel on the Russian ambassador. The Government never settled for a printer if it could identify an editor or conductor, and the *Courant* carried the name of its conductor in its masthead. But the Government also never settled for a prosecution if it could make a bargain. For its only purpose in prosecuting was to rid itself of a troublemaker, and, if the troublemaker chose to change his politics or to retire rather than spend twelve months in prison and an hour in the pillory, the Government was always willing to forget the matter. Since Almon could not change his politics without sacrificing all his sources of information, his choice lay between prison, with the added bonus of the pillory, and retirement. He chose retirement.

But, although Almon left London in June, 1781, and was inactive until the following September, his retirement was at best, according to Jackson (*Morning Post,* 15 Oct., 1784) , incomplete, for he did not sell his interests in either the bookselling shop or the *Courant.* He certainly did not sell his interests to John Debrett, for by 1780 Debrett had a bookselling shop of his own. It had been Almon's practice to issue some of his pamphlets in collaboration with other booksellers. In 1779, for example, he brought out *A Short History of the Administration* in collaboration with Fielding and Walker. But the Rev. O'Beirne's two pamphlets, *A Short History of the Last Session of Parliament, with Remarks* (1780) and *Considerations on the Principles of Naval Discipline and Naval Court-Martials* (1781), were brought out in collaboration with Debrett. If Almon sold to anyone, he sold to Stockdale, for after June, 1781, "John Almon, Bookseller in Piccadilly," became "John Stockdale, Bookseller in Piccadilly," and Stockdale's name was substituted for Almon's in the masthead of the *Courant*. But it was Jackson's opinion that Stockdale was only a partner in these enterprises, if he was even that. In mid-September, 1781, Almon resumed the conduct of the *Courant*.

While Almon had been leading his life of "ease and affluence," the Rockingham Whigs had been preparing for battle, for the North Government was at last crumbling, and it was no secret that the King preferred the Shelburne Whigs to the Rockingham Whigs as its successor. Moreover, the Shelburne Whigs would have the support of the *Morning Post* and the *Morning Herald,* and, although the Rockingham Whigs could count on the support of the other newspapers, the other newspapers were too mild to be of consequence. What the Rockingham Whigs needed was a brace of newspapers as vehement in their own defense as the *Post* and the *Herald* would be in defense of their opponents. In mid-August, 1781, they had accordingly acquired the *General Advertiser, and Morning Intelligencer.* The purchaser was William Parker, known to the Government only as the printer of such obscure and innocuous papers as the *London Intelligencer,* the *Morning Intelligencer,* and *Owens's Chronicle,* all of which Parker continued to print through 1783; [27] the publisher from 1780 to 1783 was Richard Bell, No. 183, Fleet Street,[28] who had previously (1776–77) published the *Morning Post.* The arrangements which the Rockingham Whigs had made with Parker are indicated by Almon's comment of 1794: [29] "The short state of the Fact is this—The newspaper called the General Advertiser was allowed 300ˡ· per an. for certain services. Mʳ Sheridan made the bargain. The money was paid to the end of the year 1784." But, although Parker was the ostensible conductor, the actual conductor was Dennis O'Bryen. O'Bryen had been lured away from the *Morning Herald,* where he had been trained by one of the all-time masters of newspaper abuse, the Rev. Henry Bate.

It is evident from the following letter [30] that no "bargain" was made with Almon until after he returned to London. The author of the letter is Almon's friend and physician, Richard Brocklesby, and the letter is dated 4 September, 1781:

Dear S$^r$.

I wrote to you a letter by Saturdays [1 Sept.] post w$^{ch}$ I believe you had not received when your last letter came away. I really feel for your melancholy condition at present. My advice is after the funeral [of your wife] is over, come to town for a few days, shift the Scene & do nothing important, yet for some time. In conversation I will give you my reasons for your again coming into some business or other. But I advise none particular, till you have time to look about you, but leave your Children in the Country w$^{th}$ their Aunt & you may have a bed made up for you at my house & you will insensibly interest your mind in farther engagements to alleviate your too anxious concern for one who is irrecoverable. I sympathise for you as a Man though I would have you bear misfortunes as a Man. . . .

Since Almon would not have "come to town" immediately, arrangements for the *Courant* were evidently made somewhat hastily. The terms which "M$^r$ Sheridan" offered Almon were probably identical with those he had offered Parker, namely "300$^{l.}$ per an." But, in view of the risk he was taking, Almon was in a position to ask something more. What he asked, according to Jackson (*Morning Post,* 16 Oct., 1784), was a Commissionership in the Stamp Office in the event that the Rockingham Whigs came into power. Meanwhile, in order to reduce the amount of the risk as much as possible, he engaged as printer the one man he could be certain would not betray him under any circumstances, John Miller.

The *London Courant* of 18 September, 1781, was quite a different newspaper from the *London Courant* of only a few days earlier. All the promises made in the prospectus regarding "the insertion of any articles of falsehood, malignancy & private scandal" were shelved, and the *Courant* was now prepared to meet the *Morning Post* on its own terms. The colophon was also changed, for, although the legend in the masthead still instructed correspondents to send "Advertisements, Letters, and Articles of Intelligence" to "J[OHN] STOCKDALE, Bookseller, in Piccadilly," the paper now had a new printer. There had evidently been numerous changes in the colophon since Cooper's departure on 4 July, 1781, for, although the issues are lacking during this period, the Audit Office had held James Barker, James Fleming, John Fielding, and Thomas Thirlwind successively responsible for the paper; [31] and, by the beginning of September, the colophon was, in fact, naming Thomas Thirlwind, "opposite Somerset-house, near Catherine-street, Strand," as printer. On 18 September John Miller's name replaced that of Thomas Thirlwind. The Government at once pounced.

The first lot of indictments for the libel on the Russian ambassador had not included the names of John Bew of the *General Evening Post* and John Miller of the *London Evening Post,* but, in the case of Bew, the error had been rectified, Bew being tried and convicted on 28 July, 1781 (*Morning Herald* and *Morning Chronicle,* 30 July, 1781), and subsequently, no doubt, fined the usual £100 and imprisoned for the usual year. Miller had continued to print the *London Evening Post* unmolested. But the *Courant* of 18 September was hardly on the street when he was taken into custody and confined at "Mr. [John] Armstrong's in Carey-street," where he was held until 28 November. On 28 November he was delivered to the Court of King's Bench on a writ of habeas corpus. There he was charged with having on 20 January copied "a paragraph respecting the Russian Ambassador, from a Morning Paper into the London Evening Post, of which he was then Printer," and summarily fined £100 and dispatched to King's Bench Prison to remain a twelve-month. Although he protested all the while that he had not pleaded guilty, that he had been denied counsel, and that he had been unlawfully refused a trial by jury, his protests were heard by no one.

The reason for the long confinement at "Mr. Armstrong's" is evident. For, since the Government was interested in Almon, not in Miller, all it wanted from Miller was an affidavit, stating that John Almon was again conducting the *Courant.* If Miller had supplied the affidavit, he would have been released and an action brought against Almon on the same ground. The Government's reaction to Miller's refusal is apparent from the fact that, during the two decades covered by the present work, this is the only instance of a newspaperman's being denied counsel and/or trial by jury, as it is also the only instance of a newspaperman's being indicted, tried, and sentenced on the same day. The *Courant* indicated a gratitude of sorts. Although it itself said nothing in Miller's defense, it accorded him certain favors. On 29 November, 1781, it published a letter in which he described and protested the manner in which he had been treated. On 15 December it published another letter in which he said that, although he "chear-fully submitted" to "the confinement allotted [him] by the Court of

King's Bench," he still did have "A WIFE and NUMEROUS OFF-SPRING OF SEVEN CHILDREN" to support. He also pointed out that he had always served the cause of "The People" and that he had spent "the last Seven Years in descrying, and exposing the Wickedness and Folly of the American War." He hoped to continue the service, he said, but he must have financial assistance in this moment of crisis. Readers were asked to deliver their contributions to Stockdale's shop in Piccadilly. This letter, headed "THE PRINTER'S ADDRESS TO THE PUBLIC ON HIS PRESENT SITUATION," was reprinted by the *Courant* on 17, 19, and 20 December.

The *Courant* itself contributed nothing to Miller's fund, and response was generally slow. Six weeks later only £42 15s. had been pledged and only part of that amount collected. By this time Miller was redirecting his appeals: "Mr. MILLER . . . humbly presumes to hope, after a service of fourteen years in the Public cause, that he shall not under his present expensive confinement, and Fine of One Hundred Pounds, be totally forgotten, with a Wife and Seven Children, by those generous and distinguished persons, to whom men, sinking under the weight of oppression and misfortune, have been accustomed to approach with the most confident expectation," the *Courant* announced in his behalf on 1 February, 1782. This appeal was probably addressed to Wilkes, but there was no response to it either. Reports on the progress of the fund and on the condition of Miller's health, which was much impaired, continued to appear for a while and then ceased. Some time between 16 April and 10 May, 1782, the printing office of the *Courant* was moved from "opposite Somerset-house, near Catherine-street, Strand" to "opposite Exeter-change, in the Strand"; and some time between 11 May and 6 September, 1782, Miller's name was dropped from the colophon. Since Miller was to be released from prison at the end of November, the dropping of his name at this time seems odd. But there is no reliable reference to his activities after this period,[32] and so one of the missing numbers of the newspaper may have carried a notice of his death.

Almon exercised every caution to escape detection. Although he celebrated his conversion to the cause of the Rockingham Whigs by writing *A Letter to the Right Honourable Charles Jenkinson* (Nov., 1781), which he signed "An Independent Whig" (a signature he had not used since 1763), and by following it with two more pamphlets similarly signed, *An Address to the Interior Cabinet* (Febr., 1782) and *The Revolution in MDCCLXXXII Impartially Considered* (Mar., 1782), every one of these pamphlets was published by Debrett, whereas O'Bryen's two pamphlets, *The Saucepan* and the sarcastic *A Defence of the . . . Earl of Shelburne* (both 1782), were printed by Almon's successor, Stockdale. In addition, the *Courant* withheld the name of its printer, in the sense that it held Miller responsible for the printing for much or most of the time he was in prison. There was also a constant fluctuation in the paper's subtitle.

Included perhaps in the new plan for the *Courant* was an amalgamation with the *Noon Gazette, and Daily Spy.* A precursor of the daily evening newspapers, the *Noon Gazette* was "Published at Twelve o'Clock" in order to bring the public "all the actual News of the Nine Morning Papers" (*Daily Advertiser, Gazetteer, General Advertiser, London Courant, Morning Chronicle, Morning Herald, Morning Post, Public Advertiser,* and *Public Ledger*). But the *Noon Gazette* had never been a success, and, now that its publisher and evident conductor, Vincent Trehearn, Jr., was serving an eighteen-month sentence for publishing the libel on the Russian ambassador, the paper was probably purchased at little cost. Originally the *London Courant, and Westminster Chronicle,* the *Courant* had by 1 January, 1782, already changed its title to the *London Courant, Westminster Chronicle, and Daily Advertiser;* and on 21 January, 1782, it signaled the purchase with a new title, the *London Courant, Noon Gazette, and Daily Advertiser,* and with the announcement that it would adhere to the *Noon Gazette's* policy of reprinting the "best" from other newspapers. On 11 March it again altered its title, substituting *Morning Gazette* for *Noon Gazette,* in order, as it explained editorially, to stress the fact that it was still published before eight A.M., and on 11 April it dropped all reference to the *Gazette,* calling itself simply *London Courant, and Daily Advertiser.* On 15 April it returned to its earlier title, *London Courant, Westminster Chronicle, and Daily Advertiser,* but by 10 May it was again the *London Courant, and Daily Advertiser,* and it continued to fluctuate in this manner until it expired. The reason for these changes is puzzling, but Almon may have hoped that the fact that the paper seemed to have no continuous existence might be of some help in the event of an indictment for libel.

From 18 September, 1781, on, the *Courant* gave unstinting support to Fox, Burke, Sheridan, and the Duke of Richmond, as so did the *General Advertiser,* and the support increased in vigor when, at the end of 1781, the *Morning Post* and the *Morning Herald,* which had heretofore supported Lord North, shifted their support to Lord Shelburne. On 4 January, 1782, the *Courant* declared war on "the political principles of the Morning Post," which it viciously assailed for approximately two months, and in late March the North Government was succeeded by a government headed by Lord Rockingham. Almon, who was spending a weekend in the country when the news reached him, at once, said Jackson (*Morning Post,* 16 Oct., 1784), "posted to town [to collect his reward], and solicited [Fox, one of the new Secretaries of State] to be made one of the commissioners of the Stamp Office. [But the] party knew [him] too well; and a flat refusal was the consequence."

Although "the party" could have had no possible quarrel with Almon, whose behavior during the preceding six months had been exemplary, the fact remains that he did not get the Commissionership in the Stamp Office. But he evidently did continue to collect his £300 subsidy, for the "flat refusal" had no effect on the politics of the *Courant.* On 23 March, 1782, the paper had rejoiced over the resignation of the North Government and predicted that the Marquis of Rockingham, the Duke of Richmond, Burke, Sheridan, and Fox would be "the salvation of this country," and it had even spoken well of Lord Shelburne, now that he was to be one of the Secretaries of State. Since the war with the Colonies was over, "the salvation" it had in mind was Parliamentary reform, to which it gave impassioned support in the months which followed. In June it sided with Fox in his quarrel with Lord Shelburne, and it purported to be a bitter foe of the Shelburne Government, which took office in July. Although, by the end of the year, it was more radical than liberal, giving the burden of its support to drastic reform and the cause of the Constitutional Society, the Duke of Richmond, John Wilkes, Horne Tooke, and Major Cartwright, it still included among its heroes Fox, Burke, and Sheridan; and, since the *General Advertiser* was behaving in much the same manner, one cannot interpret the shift as a break with the Foxite wing of the party.

But, according to Jackson, the *Courant* was now only a medium for rogueries of various sorts. Jackson did not specify the nature of these rogueries, for he had got his information from Peter Stuart, who, since he was involved in some of the rogueries himself, was understandably reluctant to enumerate them; and the only one which is evident from the newspaper is the stock-jobbing enterprise of January, 1783, contrived by Almon and the three Stuarts. But the newspaper itself would have aroused anyone's suspicions, for, not only did it have no settled title, but it also had no settled printer, publisher, or address. From September, 1782, on, almost every one of the subsequent (and sporadic) extant numbers of the *Courant* has a different colophon. For example, on 6 September, 1782, the paper was printed by J. Acton, on 19 September by Peter Stuart. Stuart's name persisted through 1 November, but by 3 December it was dropped and only a publisher's name, James Ridgway, mentioned. Ridgway continued through 1 March, 1783, although, some time between 3 December, 1782, and 14 January, 1783, the address of the printing office shifted to "No. 116, near Exeter-change, in the Strand." On 10 March the paper was printed by R. Gardiner, no publisher being named, and on 15 March it was published by A. Simpson, no printer being named. Simpson continued as publisher, and on 10 April the name of R. Heydon was added as printer. But, when the paper expired a few days later, it was evidently again published by James Barker.[33] Since the "publishers" seem to have been proprietors of the newspaper and the "printers" were possibly members of the staff, the fluctuating colophon may have been a device to distribute responsibility.

The stock-jobbing coup of late January, 1783, may or may not have brought about the demise of the *Courant*. On 1 March, 1783, the *Courant* announced that it had brought suit against its old friend and political ally, William Parker, proprietor of the *General Advertiser,* for a libel and that the hearing was scheduled for the next session of the Old Bailey, but there was no indication of the nature of the libel. William Jackson indicated (*Morning Post*, 16 Oct., 1784) that Almon's businesses failed, or, as he put it, Almon "left trade, because trade had left [him]." But in another context Jackson indicated that Almon had been forced out of his businesses by *"Stockdale,* [who,] with his nonsense about honesty, [was threatening to] *overset* [him]." There does seem to have been a quarrel between Almon and Stockdale and, in fact, a disagreement among the proprietors generally, for the affairs of the *Courant* were finally referred to the Stamp Office. All one knows of the results of this referral is contained in Jackson's reminder (*Morning Post*, 16 Oct., 1784):

> You inform me, *Mr. Vamp*, that you *paid* the Rev. Mr. O'Beirne twenty pounds [for his *Candid and Impartial Narrative* (1779)]. You have made a small mistake: you *advanced* him that sum on account, for which he gave you his note; and when all pecuniary matters were adjusted between you, he asked for his note, and you told him it was burnt. There again, *Mr. Vamp*, your memory failed you, for when the accounts of the *Courant* were submitted to the arbitrations of Mr. Crawford, some how or other this very note which you assured O'Beirne had been destroyed, was produced by you as a voucher for money paid, and for which you wanted to have credit given you. Although *Parson O'Beirne* and myself are not on good terms, yet I dare say he will vouch what I have related to be a fact, but if he should refuse me that favour, I have better proof at hand.

Jackson continued the reminder on 20 October:

> I have another fact of a public nature at your service, *Mr. Vamp;* and it is a very curious one. Long before the *Courant* was in existence, you were informed that Mr. WILKES was much distressed for cash. In the favor of public spirit you declared, that you had gotten hundreds by him, and he never should want ten pounds so long as you were worth that sum. Conformably to this declaration, you dispatched a messenger to Mr. Wilkes, with a ten pound bank note, which you requested him to accept. This would have been a generous act of public spirit, *Mr. Vamp*, were it not for the unfortunate sequel which I am now going to relate. When the accounts of the *Courant* were submitted to the arbitration of Mr. Crawford, of the Stamp-Office, you charged the very ten pounds which you had presented to Mr. Wilkes, long before the paper was in existence, to the partners, as *cash paid to Mr. Wilkes* for some essays *which he had written in the Courant.* You must recollect with what disdain and acrimony Mr. Crawford resisted the attempt. . . .

Almon's reply to these charges, as devised by Jackson (*Morning Post*, 16 Oct., 1784), was: "As to the stamp-office business, I was foolish enough to let Mr. Crawford be the arbitrator between me and some gentlemen who were concerned in the *Courant.* I did not know at that time that Mr. Crawford understood so much of accounts, or I should have seen him at the Devil before he should have been the arbitrator. But this again is a private affair."

The last available number of the *London Courant* is dated 10 April, 1783, at which time the paper was still defending Fox, Burke, and Sheridan, along with the radical reformers. The fact that his rogueries had never interfered with the paper's defense of the Rockingham Whigs probably saved Almon a prison sentence for the old libel on the Russian ambassador. For, by the time his political activities became known to the Stamp Office and hence to Lord North, the Government was in the hands of the Coalition, and Almon had a mediator in Fox. He had not been quite so loyal as Fox supposed, for in January, 1783, he had assailed him in a pamphlet, entitled *Free Parliaments: or, A Vindication of the Parliamentary Constitution of England, in Answer to Certain Visionary Plans of Modern Reformers,* the pamphlet being published by John Debrett and signed only "— *Hall,/* 20 *January,* 1783." But this pamphlet was immediately followed by another pamphlet, entitled *A Letter to the Author of a Pamphlet, Entitled Free Parliaments,* etc., which was lacking the names of both author and publisher; and Fox was, of course, told only of Almon's authorship of the second. John Stockdale seems to have found his experience with John Almon, the *London Courant,* and the Rockingham Whigs completely disheartening, for he immediately shifted to the side of the Shelburne Whigs, collecting £288 from the Pitt Government in 1784 for publishing pamphlets and various other propagandistic tracts in its behalf,[34] and he had no further connection with newspapers.

## THE CASE OF THE *GENERAL ADVERTISER*

IN ADDITION to losing the *Courant,* Almon also lost the shop in Piccadilly, which passed into the hands of John Stockdale, and there is no record of his further activities until September, 1784. Meanwhile the *General Advertiser, and Morning Intelligencer,* some time during the week of 5–11 May, 1782, renamed *Parker's General Advertiser, and Morning Intelligencer,* tried to carry on the work for both newspapers against somewhat desperate odds. Its bickerings with the *Morning Post,* which ripened into a real quarrel in August, 1783, when O'Bryen charged that he had been mistreated by Colman respecting his play, *A Friend in Need Is a Friend Indeed,* did not help the prestige of the newspaper, and there was also a political problem. For, although O'Bryen was a sincere admirer of Charles Fox, he could not conscientiously support his union with Lord North. While the Coalition was in office, the *General Advertiser* was therefore almost non-political. But, as soon as the Pitt Government took office, it re-sumed its defense of Fox and reform, widening the scope of its de-mands to include penal and prison reforms; and, during the West-minster election of 1784, it gave vehement support to Fox, as opposed to the Ministerial candidate, Sir Cecil Wray. On approximately 12 May, 1784, the proprietor of the newspaper, William Parker, died. On 8 May, 1784, the *General Advertiser* was still "Printed and Published by W. PARKER, No. 183, Fleet-street," on 12 May it was "Printed by AUGUSTUS KEPPEL PARKER," William Parker's brother, at the same address, and in September John Almon married Mrs. Parker.

Almon's opinion that, in marrying Mrs. Parker, he had left "ease and affluence, to encounter fatigue and rescue indigence" was not shared by William Jackson, who provided a detailed account (*Morn-ing Post,* 16 and 20 Oct., 1784) of the circumstances of the marriage. When the marriage occurred, said Jackson, Almon had been for many months a writer for the Treasury. During the Westminster election of 1784, he had supported Sir Cecil Wray, to whom he was "under great obligations" for various favors; and, by the time the election was over, he had so ingratiated himself with the Ministers generally that, had Lord Salisbury, the Lord Chamberlain, not "prevented" the "appoint-ment," Almon's name would then have "[honoured] the Commission of the peace." Since Almon "only thought of matrimony to better his fortune" and since Mrs. Parker, although "a very worthy woman," knew nothing about business, there was no mention of a marriage settlement until her brother-in-law interfered in behalf of her son, then evidently still a minor. Specifically he demanded, first, that the newspaper would never be entitled *Almon's General Advertiser* and, second, that it would be deeded to William Parker's son at Almon's death. The first demand was honored. The marriage settlement stipu-lated that, although Almon had "the right of devoting the paper occasionally to any and to every side of the question which promised fairest for the most advantage," he could not attach his name to it and that, in addition, he was to pay Mrs. Parker £100 annually for the property, evidently as a kind of rental. The second demand was not honored; for, "as you have thought proper to boast about settle-ments," Jackson asked Almon, "how came you, after promising your wife's brother-in-law to make a settlement on her son, to get married in such a confounded hurry while the instrument was preparing, and afterwards hint that it was too late to execute the deed? You may perceive, *Mr. Vamp,* that I know something about your private generosity."

If Jackson was correct in asserting that Almon had been an agent of the Treasury, then Almon would have been writing for the *Morning Post,* since the *Morning Post* was the only newspaper to support the Pitt Government during the Westminster election. And, if Almon had, in fact, been writing for the *Morning Post,* then two other puzzles are immediately solved. The first has to do with the source of Jackson's information. Information respecting Almon's activities prior to the demise of the *Courant* would, of course, have been provided by Peter Stuart, who had been associated with Almon on that newspaper and, from 26 April, 1784, on, was associated with Jackson on the *Morning Post.* But Jackson would have known nothing about Almon's activities since unless Almon had himself been on the staff of the *Post.* The second puzzle is Jackson's preoccupation with the politics of the *General Advertiser* after Almon acquired the paper. Not only did he know precisely when Almon acquired it, but he was certain that it would at once undertake the support of the Government, and he regarded it as a kind of personal outrage that it failed to do so. What he did not know was that Almon had not broken his ties with the Opposition, which knew nothing about his work for the Government, and that he was bound to react to the present situation like a bookseller, not a newspaperman.

When Almon assumed the conduct of the *General Advertiser,* the Westminster election had been resolved in Fox's favor, and the Scrutiny, which was to contest the results of that election, had begun. Sir Cecil Wray's interests were being represented by the *Morning Post* in a series of essays, signed "SCRUTINEER" and written by William Jackson; and Fox's interests were being represented by the *General Advertiser* in a series of counter-essays, entitled "THE GARRAT-SCRUTINY" and written in all likelihood by Dennis O'Bryen. Almon had evidently promised to discontinue "THE GARRAT-SCRUTINY" and to dismiss O'Bryen, and by late September "THE GARRAT-SCRUTINY" was no longer appearing. The *Morning Post* was jubilant. "If the Ghost of a *certain Printer* of a *certain Paper* should . . . arise and walk," it mused on 28 September, 1784, "what would he think of *certain changes;* think! why *poor soul* he'd go distracted. What (would the ghost say) my paper . . . *come to be ministerial!* What, my paper! that stuck by Charles Fox *like his creditors attornies!* . . . My paper, that was more abusive, more rancorous, more licentious at one time, than any other paper in the world." But several weeks passed with no announcement of a change in policy or management and with little further change in the newspaper itself. By mid-October Jackson had lost patience, and on 13, 16, and 20 October "Scrutineer" devoted his columns to an exposé of "Mr. JOHN VAMP."

Since it was now obvious to Jackson that the *General Advertiser* was wooing both political parties, the purpose of his first essay (13 Oct., 1784) was to notify everyone concerned that John Almon had exclusive charge of the newspaper. Although the essay also referred darkly to Almon's past and obscenely to his marriage, the references were threatening rather than illuminating. The second essay (16 Oct.) was more specific. This one began with a letter, signed "JOHN VAMP./ *Fleet-street, Oct.* 15," which had purportedly been "delivered 'to the office of the Morning Post' by one of the 'Devils' in the printing shop." Addressed to "Mr. SCRUTINEER" and, of course, written by Jackson himself, the letter was mainly a series of confessions and apologies respecting Almon's double-dealings as bookseller and pamphleteer. As to the politics of the *General Advertiser,* said "Vamp," he himself had no "sentiments about the matter," and, since he also regarded *"conscience"* as "downright nonsense," "until I see which is the most advantageous side of the Scrutiny, I will take none." "I defy your malice," the letter concluded; "and whatever your vanity may prompt you to think of the Scrutineer, I know that you [i.e., Jackson] are not entitled to any merit, for the best papers are written by other persons, and you are merely entrusted to send them to press. But I shall find out more; and when I do you shall hear again from/ Yours,/ JOHN VAMP." The implication that Almon himself might have supplied some of "Scrutineer's" "papers" was not pursued, for the Treasury did not welcome this kind of publicity.

The letter was followed by Jackson's reply, which began: *"Mr. Vamp,/* I am very sorry that you should have been so exceedingly hurt at the trivial notice I condescended to take of you. All I meant was to convey a gentle admonition, that in case you should be so impudent as to permit any aspersions to be thrown out in your new-modelled miscellany against the cause of Sir Cecil Wray, I would deal with you in the manner such ingratitude merited. You must be sensible, *Mr. Vamp,* that you are under very great obligations to Sir Cecil.

. . ." Jackson went on to comment on the present character of the *General Advertiser*. He noticed that it was now printing some Treasury material and that it had discontinued "THE GARRAT-SCRUTINY," contenting itself with "no more than a daily catalogue of the names of the voters who are disallowed or admitted," but he noticed also that it had not dismissed Dennis O'Bryen, who was still wearing his Blue and Buff in the office, attending meetings of the Whig Club at the Shakespeare, and eulogizing the proceedings in the newspaper. Having added some remarks on the terms of Almon's marriage, Jackson then returned to the matter at hand:

As to your public line, you profess . . . not to be of any party. But, *Mr. Vamp*, do you not want some party to lean a little to your side of the question? If the sudden transformation of your daily farrago of vulgarity, be not occasioned by principle, it must have been caused by [self-]interest. As you do not seem inclined to let the world into the secret of your motives, I will do it for you. This then is the fact. On the ascension of Mr. Fox, and the Rockingham party to power, you posted to town, and solicited to be made one of the commissioners of the Stamp Office. The party knew you too well; and a flat refusal was the consequence. I take it for granted, that you will prefer a similar request to the present ministers; and, if I augur right, you will experience the same non-success.

The letter concluded with an invitation and a threat: "I shall be always ready to receive *Mr. Vamp*, and to whisper this in his ear, that he had better not intermeddle with politics, for the less his public character is known the less will it be despised."

The third essay (20 Oct., 1784), which was dated *"St. Martin's Vestry, Tuesday, Oct.* 19," began with the explanation:

As I do not possess a relish for altercation, it was my intention not to have taken any further notice of Mr. VAMP. . . . I actually should not have known, that he had issued general orders to the scavengers of his office, to throw dirt at a gentleman supposed to be concerned in these Papers [Jackson himself, who had by now been publicly identified as "the *Right* Reverend author of the scrutiny anecdotes" (*Morning Herald,* 9 Sept., 1784)], were it not for the information of some friends. Thus circumstanced, I am compelled to recommence a correspondence; and it will entirely depend on the future good behaviour of *Mr. Vamp,* whether the following epistle shall not be the last he ever will receive from me.

After two paragraphs of remarks on the outrage, Jackson continued:

Thus much for your scribes.—And now, *Mr. Vamp,* let me have a little conversation with you. Previous to which, I desire you to take notice, that the facts which I am about to mention, are combined with political circumstances, which render them of a *public nature.* In private life I have not any thing to do with you. It is . . . your political transactions, which are the objects of my animadversions; and even those I should not have noticed, had you not been so weak as to permit the Scrutiny, and Sir Cecil Wray, to have been traduced in your *Miscellany.* . . .

There was more of this "little conversation" at the conclusion:

There are a few more facts, *Mr. Vamp,* which I could bring forward; but I realy am disposed to treat you with lenity. You are half a convert to the right, and I should be sorry to obstruct your progressive motion in the paths of truth. There is a little of the old leaven which still clings to your nature, for, in one column of your farrago, you represent Mr. Fox in very odious colours, and in the next you lament the ill-usage he hath experienced by the institution of the Scrutiny. Which of these contradictions do you mean seriously to adopt? To maintain both can never answer your purposes; and, as much merit as you may claim on account of the sudden change of your political creed, I have a better opinion of the discernment of the present Ministers than to believe that they will be easily induced to appoint *honest Master Vamp* a Commissioner of the Stamp Office. If Lord Salisbury were consulted on the subject, I am very confident that the appointment would not take place, for he prevented your name, *Mr. Vamp,* from honouring the Commission of the peace.

THE SCRUTINEER.

This "epistle" was the last, for Jackson had said everything he could say without embarrassing the Government.

In part, Jackson was censuring Almon in behalf of newspapermen generally, for services to both political parties at the same time constituted a violation of the newspaper code. In part he was censuring him in behalf of the Government, for the *Morning Post* spoke for the Government. Since one of the proprietors of the newspaper was an agent of the Treasury and a personal friend of the Secretary of the Treasury, George Rose, Jackson's statements regarding Almon's negotiations with William Pitt were facts, not assumptions, and his advice was the advice of Pitt himself.

But Almon's problem was more complicated than even Jackson realized. When Almon assumed the conduct of the *General Advertiser,* he was undoubtedly receiving some emolument from the Treasury;

but meanwhile the *General Advertiser* was still receiving its £300 annual subsidy from the Opposition, so that he was being paid by both political parties. Although he was willing to relinquish the £300 subsidy, he was willing to relinquish it only for the Commissionership in the Stamp Office. For this reason he had not dismissed Dennis O'Bryen, and for a similar reason he had not informed the Opposition of his connection with the newspaper and hence of his responsibility for its indecisiveness. But, with the appearance of Jackson's exposés, any further dissimulation on Almon's part would have been only additionally prejudicial, and hence, after the usual discreet delay, *Parker's General Advertiser* made its long-overdue announcement. On 27 October, 1784, the paper was still, according to the colophon, "Printed by AUGUSTUS KEPPEL PARKER, No. 183, Fleet-street"; but the next extant number (11 Nov., 1784) was "Printed by J. ALMON, No. 183, Fleet-street," and it was carrying the following notice: *"The Printer of this Paper begs leave to acquaint . . . the Public, that he has commenced the Printing Business at the Office, No. 183, Fleet-street, where he executes all kinds of Printing: such as Books, Pamphlets, Cases in Law and Parliament, Hand-bills of every sort, &c. . . . And . . . farther . . . that on Monday next* [15 *Nov.*] *the title of this Paper will be changed from* Parker's General Advertiser, and Morning Intelligencer, *to that of* THE GENERAL ADVERTISER, *only. . . .* [*The Printer invites*] *every fair political argument . . . on both sides of every public question."* The remainder of this number was a long apology to Fox. On the evident assumption that he had lost the Commissionership in the Stamp Office anyway, Almon explained that he had never meant to disparage him, but had opposed only his partner in the Coalition, Lord North, and that, although the *General Advertiser* was purporting to be neutral, it would inevitably find itself in sympathy with him.

Fox was not persuaded, for, by the end of the year, the *General Advertiser* had lost its £300 subsidy, the reason given for the cancellation by "M^r Sheridan" being "the Westminster Scrutiny, at that time, and other great expences happening." [35] Since by late November the *General Advertiser* was tending to support Pitt rather than Fox, Almon probably received the news shortly after the publication of his apology, by which time the subsidy for 1784 had already been paid. It was not paid for 1785 or 1786. The attempt to woo Pitt also proved unavailing, so that, for the next two years, Almon was out of favor with both parties, although he continued to serve both in the hope of getting back into the favor of one. He himself said that "the letters and all other papers sent [by the Foxite Opposition], which were known by a private mark settled between M$^r$ Sheridan & me, were all of them constantly inserted." [36] He might have added that "the letters and all other papers" sent by the Treasury were also "constantly inserted," and, for much of the time, the "papers" sent by the Treasury predominated. Even so, he was evidently afraid to publish O'Beirne's *A Gleam of Comfort to This Distracted Empire, in Despite of Faction, Violence and Cunning, Demonstrating the Fairness and Reasonableness of National Confidence in the Present Ministry* (London, 1785) , for the work was brought out by Debrett.

Almon never got back into the favor of the Government, but in 1786 he made his peace with the Opposition. The occasion was the publication of two libels on William Pitt. The first one, which appeared on 20 October, 1785, noted that "His Majesty's ministers have made more by jobbing in the alley on the Dutch peace than any cabinet junto we ever had. Mr. *Pitt* has cleared above 150,000*l*. This is the gentleman that lamented so much the mischiefs of lottery-gambling,— *Credat Judeas!*" The second one, which appeared on 27 October, added to this: "Mr. *Pitt*, it is said, in order to make himself popular, means to bring in a bill to prevent the false sale of stocks, commonly called stock-jobbing; but when it is so well known how much the minister and his friends have made by jobbing on the Dutch peace, it is not to be imagined that they will put an end to so lucrative an evil." [37] Since these paragraphs also appeared in the *Morning Herald,* now a strongly Opposition newspaper, Pitt brought suit against the printers of both papers for "contriving and maliciously intending to injure and ruin [him] in his good name, character and reputation, and to bring him into utter disgrace, contempt, and infamy with his said Majesty and his subjects." On 20 February, 1786, Almon, represented by Erskine, was accordingly tried at Westminster Hall before Lord Mansfield and a special jury. Almon entered the usual plea, namely, that he "was totally ignorant and innocent of the two publications: he was in the country at the time the libels were printed, he had no knowledge of them at the time, and the first moment he knew that Mr. *Pitt* was offended, he instantly contradicted the paper." Edward Bearcroft meanwhile urged in behalf of Pitt that the publication of the libels was no small matter, inasmuch as the *General Ad-*

*vertiser* was "a paper in great request, and generally published to the number of 2000 every day." The jury decided in favor of Pitt, to whom it awarded £150. In the case of James S. Barr, who was tried separately for the libel in the *Morning Herald,* Pitt was awarded £250.

Since Pitt had demanded £150,000 from each newspaper, these verdicts were regarded as glorious triumphs for the Opposition, which responded by forgiving all of Almon's transgressions. Almon probably deserved some remission, for the paragraphs in question had probably been sent to the *General Advertiser* bearing "[M$^r$ Sheridan's] private mark"; but he was nevertheless grateful, especially since the result of the reconciliation was far better than he could have hoped. The Foxites did not pay Almon's expenses, but "M$^r$ Sheridan" did assure him that the annuity was still in effect: "that . . . the money [for the years 1785–1786] should certainly be paid, and should continue to be a claim until discharged: [but,] he added, that it was the wish of his friends, for a little time, to pay . . . 200$^1$ per an. and that the other 100$^1$ per an. should be added to the former arrear, and continue in like manner to be a claim until punctually discharged. This 200$^1$ per an. was paid by M$^r$ Geo. Reid (who received the money from lord Robert Spencer) to the year 1790, when the paper ceased, owing to the prosecution." [38] From 1787 through 1789, therefore, the *General Advertiser* received £200 annually from the Foxite Whigs, and, when the paper ceased, Almon had a claim against them for £900.

The *General Advertiser* had never been "a paper in great request, and generally published to the number of 2000 every day," as Bearcroft asserted, and, although the file of the *General Advertiser* for the years 1787–1790 is highly incomplete, there is no indication that it became one later. But there is also no indication that Almon engaged in any extra-party intrigues during this period, for he seems to have been inactive as a pamphleteer, and the other Whig newspapers regarded his newspaper with respect. During the elections of 1788, the *General Advertiser* was one of the three daily morning newspapers not controlled by the Treasury; and, during the fight over the Regency, which followed the elections, it joined the *Morning Herald* and the *Gazetteer* in supporting the claims of the Prince of Wales and the claims of the Foxites in his behalf. In addition, Almon is thought [39] to have begun the *Sunday Chronicle,* which lasted from 30 March,

1788, to 20 June, 1790, conducting it also in the Whig interest. Although the Register of Admissions for Lincoln's Inn lists, under the date 17 June, 1786, "Dennis O'Brien, gen., eldest son of Dennis O'B. of Dublin Esq.," O'Bryen continued his journalistic activities; and, at the end of 1788, Almon published a collection of his essays under the title, *The Prospect before Us: Being a Series of Papers, upon the Great Question Which Now Agitates the Public Mind.* The essays, all of which urged the Prince's right to an immediate and unfettered Regency, had, according to the "Advertisement," previously appeared *"in three of the daily prints"* during the period 28 November to 8 December, 1788, the three *"prints"* being, of course, the *General Advertiser,* the *Morning Herald,* and the *Gazetteer.* The Whigs' faith that even a bookseller could learn a lesson seemed for the moment to be justified.

## A TRIAL AND SOME TRIBULATIONS

ALTHOUGH Pitt was a patient man, he was not a forgetful one, and by 1790 he had wreaked his revenge on both the *Morning Herald* and the *General Advertiser.* In the case of the *Herald,* according to the *Gazetteer* (18 Oct., 1790), he employed *"treachery* of the worst kind"; in the case of the *General Advertiser,* he employed "Treasury *finesse."* The manner in which "Treasury *finesse"* effected the ruin of the *General Advertiser* is described in detail by Almon himself,[40] who in this instance had no reason to prevaricate. On 18 November, 1788, according to Almon's account, the *General Advertiser* printed "a short paragraph, which might have escaped almost any observation, sent to him in a hand-writing that had made itself familiar for some weeks past, affecting to be that of a friend, but as it . . . seems with the sole view of *ensnaring* him." The paragraph was promptly denounced as a libel on the King, and Almon was "immediately prosecuted by the King's Attorney General. As soon as the paragraph was printed, the writer ceased his correspondence, and although the paragraph appeared in other papers, yet Mr. *Almon alone* was prosecuted." Moreover, "the ministers took more care and caution in the institution of this prosecution than they usually observe in the preparation of more important measures, [for] *before* the defendant was served with any notice, they retained the flower of the bar against him. No less than six of the most eminent council were retained to support this prosecution." Almon finally found a lawyer to defend him, but the lawyer "deceived" him at every step of the proceedings. To begin with, he "repeatedly assured" him "that the trial would not come on. Whether it was sheer ignorance, or neglect, or any other cause . . . , [it] is certain, that when the trial came on, it was discovered that even the ordinary attention had not been paid. . . . Had Mr. *Almon* put his cause into other hands, . . . there can be no doubt, but that an impartial jury would have acquitted him."

The jury, of course, convicted, and, as soon as the trial was over, it "was suggested" to Almon that he write a letter to the Prince of Wales, asking him "to lay his distressed situation before the King." The Prince responded by "[commanding] Lord *Southampton* [since 23 May, 1787, a member of the Prince's council] to write to the Lord Chancellor [Lord Thurlow], to solicit his lordship to put a stop to any farther proceedings." But Lord Thurlow refused to intervene; and meanwhile Almon was being assured by "one of the principal law officers of the crown" that he intended to "press for the severest punishment, and in particular, for the pillory." "In this circumstance" Almon "was obliged to dispose of his paper, and printing materials, with all possible expedition. Unfortunately for him, the person who contracted for them, and who got possession, proved insolvent, and he [Almon] did not receive for his property, which had cost him [or, more properly, William Parker] several thousand pounds, an eighth part of the value. Under the advice of many of his friends, and even some of the learned gentlemen who had been retained against him, he [therefore] went to France" and was shortly thereafter declared an outlaw.

Since the newspapers were not greatly interested in Almon's affairs, most of his account can be neither proved nor disproved, but it is generally plausible. One may, for example, accept the statement that the circumstances under which Almon was indicted, tried, and outlawed were contrived. It is not necessarily true, however, that the offensive paragraph was sent to him "with the sole view of *ensnaring* him"; for, since, from 10 November, 1788, on, many of the London newspapers were outspoken about the nature and extent of the King's illness, Almon would have printed a paragraph on the subject on 18 November even if he had been totally unfamiliar with the handwriting of the author. There is no mention of the indictment or the trial in the newspapers, but there is a mention of a subsequent hearing, from which it appears that the lawyer who defended Almon and was, in his opinion, responsible for his conviction was William Garrow. The mention occurs in the spurious *Star*, then conducted in part by Almon's former printer, Peter Stuart, on 28 May, 1789, under the heading "KING'S BENCH": "Monday [25 May] the Attorney General prayed judgment against Mr. *Almon* of the General Advertiser, for printing and publishing a libellous paragraph./ Mr. Garrow applied to the Court to postpone the sentence till next Term. His Client, he said, did not receive notice of his being to be [*sic*] brought up for judgment till ten o'clock on Saturday night./ The Attorney General said, he should not oppose the judgment being postponed; upon which the Court ordered it to stand over till next Term."

Almon's failure to appear for sentencing on 25 May, 1789, was probably owing to the fact that he was awaiting the result of his appeal to the Prince of Wales. The letter of appeal is itself lacking, but the following letter,[41] addressed to his son Charles, then living at No. 10, Piccadilly, contains instructions for its delivery and indicates its content. Almon was approaching the Prince through one of his intimates, Captain Jack Payne, and was asking the Prince to approach Sir Archibald Macdonald, the Attorney General, through another of his intimates and a member of his household, Lord Southampton. Almon's letter is undated:

My dear Charles

Enclosed is a letter for Capt$^n$ Payne, but as the Prince's establishment is altered, he may not now be at Carleton [*sic*] House. However you will find him out, & deliver it as soon as possible. I have not sealed it, that you may know its contents, & give an answer if any question concerning it should be ask'd you. You will endeavour to get an answer from him.—My plain request is, (but I am afraid to be so very particular as fully to express it) that he would give you a letter to L$^d$ Southampton, for L$^d$ Southampton to write to the Attorney General. Therefore you will politely beg for an answer when you carry the enclosed, or endeavour to get an answer as soon as possible. God bless you & most affectionately yours

J Almon

Put a wafer or seal to the enclosed before you carry it.

Almon's statement that Southampton appealed to the Lord Chancellor rather than the Attorney General is plausible, for Sir Archibald Macdonald had had no connection with Carlton House, whereas Lord

Thurlow had been very much involved in the Carlton House intrigues of late 1788.

Lord Thurlow's refusal to act would have "obliged" Almon to abscond before the next session of the Court, but it would not have "obliged" him to sell "the paper and printing materials"; and the fact that the Whigs paid him for the *General Advertiser* for the whole of 1789 would indicate that he did not sell them until the end of the year. According to the records of the Audit Office,[42] Almon was succeeded as publisher of the *General Advertiser* by a Mr. Downes, who was in turn succeeded by a Mr. Yardley; and, although there is no proof that Downes and Yardley were also proprietors of the newspaper, there is reason to suppose that they represented two successive and distinct proprietaries. Almon was clearly referring to the first one when he said that the purchaser "proved insolvent," so that he did not realize "an eighth part of the value" of the property. But the *Gazetteer* was clearly referring to another one altogether when it announced on 18 October, 1790: "A Treasury Printer, who lately made a purchase of the Whig paper with [the name of the *General Advertiser*], on Saturday [16 Oct.] stifled its independent voice. With what motive he did this, we leave the Public to judge." The paper had evidently been resold only a few days before it perished.

The fact that the *General Advertiser* remained a "Whig paper" to the end is indicated by the *Gazetteer's* invitation to the staff of the *General Advertiser* to join its own staff, for "the people," it promised (18 Oct., 1790) , "shall [still] hear their voice through the GAZETTEER—that from its outset in the cause of Whiggism no power has been able either to *silence or corrupt.*" Although the Treasury certainly had much to do with the disasters of the *General Advertiser,* the *Gazetteer* seems to have been mistaken in supposing that it was responsible for the ultimate disaster. For, twelve days before the paper expired, John Bell, then a proprietor of the *Oracle,* was trying to persuade Major Edward Topham, a proprietor of the *World,* and Thomas Y. Hurlstone, the conductor of the *Morning Herald,*[43] to join him in buying and suppressing the newspaper in order to rid themselves of a competitor. Although by this time the *General Advertiser* could probably have been acquired for a few hundred pounds, Almon having absconded and the first purchaser having "proved insolvent," Topham and Hurlstone refused. "In the answer to Mr. Bell, which need not be given immediately," Topham instructed Mary

Wells on 4 October, 1790,[44] "I am of opinion, with Mr. Hurlstone, that to the WORLD and HERALD it does not signify a sixpence whether there is such a paper as the General Advertiser or not. They can receive no benefit from its being abolished."

But, although Almon's account seems otherwise generally accurate, the statement that he fled to France in 1789, where he remained until 1792, can certainly be regarded with suspicion. Everything points to the fact that he fled only to Box Moor in Hertfordshire, where he set about the task of trying to placate the Government, from which he hoped to obtain leniency, without unduly antagonizing the Opposition, from which he hoped to obtain the £900 still owing him. The first fruit of this desperate labor was the *Memoirs of a Late Eminent Bookseller*, renamed on the second title page *Memoirs of John Almon: Bookseller of Piccadilly* (London, 1790). Since this work was intended as a vindication of Almon's political conduct during the last many years, it was forthright and extenuative with respect to those facts which were already public knowledge and evasive and deceptive with respect to the rest. Although the purpose of the *Memoirs* was to appease Pitt, not to offend him further, everyone regarded the work as dangerous. Almon wrote in the third person, attributing authorship to "A Friend," the publisher withheld his name, and it is evident from the following letter [45] that even William Woodfall, who was presently a favorite of the Treasury, was afraid to print extracts at random:

August 12, 1790

Sir:

My father [William Woodfall, conductor of the *Diary, or Woodfall's Register*] is vexed that your advertisement was inserted two days together, but it escaped his observance. He has given directions that the terms of your note of yesterday shall be complied with.

He particularly desired me to write to you on Saturday [7 Aug.] and state, that if you would send him a copy of the book in boards, with a written letter of reference to such extracts as you wish to have taken, they shall occasionally appear in the Diary; he at the same time, wished me to request you not to point out any extracts inconsonant with his principles as a friend to Government and a moderate man in politics. . . .

W Woodfall jun.

Almon's publisher through 1792 and occasionally thereafter was J. S. Jordan, No. 166, Fleet Street, for, although Almon evidently still owned the building at No. 183, Fleet Street, he had quit the bookselling business when he quit the *General Advertiser*. Jordan seems also to have been Almon's employer, for the following note [46] refers to a work which was clearly written on assignment. Almon addressed the note to his son, and the note is undated:

D[r] Charles

   I did intend being in town at this time but am prevented for a few days longer. In about a week or ten days at farthest I shall be up. Send me down by the [Trig?] Coach on Saturday the Hist[y] of France you had out of the library. I am particularly in want of it Jordan having requested me to take up the Hist[y] of France on a sudden, Beckford having disappointed him. Tell M[r] B. the Inst rent is all paid, M[r] Hayton, M[r] Ginger's executors, &c all included. I am sorry he has not been able to get the rent for the [back?] House in Fleetstreet, the matter must be urged with spirit. . . .

JA

The four-volume *History of France, from the Most Early Records, to the Death of Louis XVI: The Ancient Part by William Beckford, Esq.* . . . *the Modern Part by an English Gentleman, Who Has Been Some Time Resident in Paris* was published by Jordan in 1794.

On 1 January, 1792, Almon meanwhile completed his two-volume *Anecdotes of the Life of the Right Hon. William Pitt, Earl of Chatham,* and the work was published by Jordan shortly thereafter. Originally entitled *Memoirs of . . . Lord Chatham,* the work had first been advertised in February, 1782, in Almon's pamphlet, *An Address to the Interior Cabinet,* which described it as then being "IN THE PRESS." Its failure to come out of the press may have prompted "Governor" Pownall's query: [47] "How goes on the Memoires of L[d] Chatham —." At that time Almon would have explained the delay on the ground of expedience, for, since Lord Chatham's son, the younger William Pitt, was associated with the Shelburne Whigs, the publication of the work would have seemed an act of disloyalty to the Rockingham Whigs, from whom Almon was then expecting a Commissionership in the Stamp Office. He would have explained the delay on similar grounds during the years which followed, for, even when he was courting the Pitt Government, he was concealing the courtship from the Opposition. The publication of the *Anecdotes* in 1792 was still prejudicial to Almon's interests, for, although it was brought out anonymously, the Opposition would not have forgotten that it was originally advertised as his. But Almon seems to have felt that the gratitude of the First Minister for this fine tribute to his father might prove more valuable to him in the present situation than the payment of a debt of £900.

In mid-December, 1791, Almon notified Pitt's mother, Hester Grenville, the Dowager Countess of Chatham, of his esteem for her husband and of his literary labors in his behalf and received her assurance that she would await the appearance of the *Anecdotes* with confidence that "the abilities and virtues of my late dear Lord" would be "painted in those colours that suit [his] dignity and wisdom." [48] Having seen the work through the press, given Pitt sufficient time to read it, and engaged Alan Chambre to represent him in lieu of William Garrow, Almon thereupon surrendered. He was consigned to King's Bench Prison early in March, 1792, and there he remained for the next eight months, forgotten. On 20 November, 1792, several newspapers reported that on the previous day "John Almon, convicted some years ago of a libel on the King, and who afterwards disappeared and was outlawed, was [at last] brought into Court to assign errors to his outlawry. Errors were assigned in writing, which were ordered to be recorded, that they may hereafter be argued. Mr. Almon was then remanded to the King's Bench Prison, there to remain until he be discharged in due course of law." Almon was again forgotten, and on 11 January, 1793, the *Oracle,* then edited by his long-ago associate, Peter Stuart, protested that certainly "Mr. Almon's patient Sufferings claim some Relief from the hand of Power. We forbear any opinion on the Merits or Demerits of his Case: suffice it to say, that he has already amply atoned for the Trespass alluded to; and that his Enlargement would reflect honour on the Feelings of those whom his Imprisonment may have concerned."

This protest evidently proved unavailing, for there was no further mention of Almon's case until 29 April, 1793, when it was the subject of two paragraphs. The paragraph in the *Oracle* stated merely: "On Friday [26 Apr.], the Court of King's Bench, in the case of the KING v. Mr. ALMON, Proprietor of a *ci-devant* Morning Paper, . . . ordered the outlawry against the Defendant to be reversed./ Mr. ALMON is expected to be brought up on Wednesday next [1 May], to receive judgment for a Libel inserted in the *General Advertiser* four years ago, and for which he has already suffered near eighteen [actually near fourteen] months imprisonment." The paragraph in the *Morn-*

*ing Chronicle* stated that the "Writ of Error to reverse the Outlawry against Mr. Almon, who had been tried and convicted for a Libel, and afterwards outlawed for not appearing to receive the Judgment of the Court," "came on to be argued" on "Saturday [27 Apr.]." Mr. Chambre, Almon's counsel, "had pointed out several objections to the form of the proceedings of the outlawry," it said, which "he contended sustained the Writ of Error," and he urged "that therefore the judgment of Outlawry against his client ought to be reversed. The Court opined that technical accuracy was a matter of great importance" in procedures in outlawry, "for which reason it reversed the outlawry, as being subject to an error in proceedings. The defendant will now be brought into court to receive sentence for the libel."

Almon was brought into court for this purpose on 8 May. The *Oracle* (9 May, 1793) accorded the hearing special notice:

Court of King's Bench.
Wednesday.
The King, v. Almon.

The Defendant was brought up by his own order for Judgment, for a Libel published in the year 1788: the ATTORNEY-GENERAL [since 13 Febr., 1793, Sir John Scott], however, opened the case in the most polite and gentlemanlike manner; and after admitting many circumstances in Mr. ALMON's favour, which he acknowledged to have been acquainted with, Mr. Justice BULLER interrupted him, by asking, *Why Mr.* ALMON *had not been pardoned?* —The ATTORNEY-GENERAL replied, that he thought it was the most honourable, as well as the most respectable for Mr. ALMON's character, that he should have a public acquittal by the most public testimony of his innocence. The Court immediately ordered Mr. ALMON to be discharged upon his own recognizance of 100*l. sine die.*

*The Times* (9 May, 1793) carried a somewhat less farcical version of this hearing. It stated that the Attorney General had expressed the hope that, since Almon had already been imprisoned fourteen months without cause, the Court would see fit to mitigate his punishment for the publication of the libel. Lord Kenyon, the Chief Justice, had promised to consider the suggestion and had meanwhile ordered that Almon's recognizance be taken for £100 and that Almon himself be released until such time as he was again called to receive the judgment of the Court.

Although *The Times* was mistaken respecting the publication of the libel, which it dated 7 March, 1789, its version seems otherwise to have been the more accurate of the two. If Almon had actually been pardoned, he would not have been required to post a £100 bond, and, more important, he would have been free to make his peace with the Opposition and so to collect the money which was owing him. But his first act on emerging from prison was to write a pamphlet denouncing the reformers and giving vigorous support to the Government's "Constitutionalism." The pamphlet was entitled *The Causes of the Present Complaints Fairly Stated and Fully Refuted* (London, 1793), and it was published by John Sewell of Cornhill, Jordan being generally a Whig publisher. Although the work was unsigned, a copy was, of course, delivered to Pitt along with a letter identifying Almon as author. Since Almon had been imprisoned fourteen months without cause, he would hardly have performed this service out of gratitude. This was an act of simple expedience, and there were evidently several other such acts during the anxious years which followed, for the Attorney General, whose memory in such instances depended entirely on the conduct of the offender, finally forgot to move for sentencing altogether.

"Mʳ Sheridan" seems to have paid the initial cost of Almon's defense, but nothing thereafter; and by 1792 it seemed to Almon that the Opposition owed him £100 for his "last Attorney's bill," some recompense for the "heavy expence of an imprisonment of fourteen months," and £900 "Arrear" for the years 1785–1789. Although he undoubtedly made numerous attempts to collect, only one attempt is recorded. On 21 July, 1794, he addressed a long letter [49] to "My Lord Duke" from "Box Moor near Hemel Hempstead, Herts." The letter, which began with an apology "for presuming to solicit your Grace's attention only for a moment," continued:

The last time I had the honour to apply to Your Grace You were pleased to refer me to Mʳ [William] Adam, but the transaction having happened before he came into the department, he said he could say nothing to it, upon which I applied to Lord Robert Spencer, to whom I had the honour of stating the several circumstances. His Lordship candidly avowed that it was a hard case, and added, that he thought something ought to be done. But subsequent occurrences have undoubtedly been too interesting to permit this trifle to affect any memory but my own. . . . The long train of misfortunes & losses, which a lengthened & severe prosecution brought with it, have so essentially injured my circumstances, that necessity obliges me to trouble Your Grace once more.

In the light of Almon's conduct since his release from prison, one is hardly surprised to find this letter endorsed: "To be referred to Mr [Baldwin?]/ advised no notice to be taken of it."

Every newspaperman would have felt that the Whigs acted honorably, for, although no newspaperman was expected to be honest, he was expected to adhere to a certain code of ethics and, if need be, to become a martyr to the code. But John Almon had been a bookseller too long even to understand the code. He handled the *London Courant* as if it were only a series of pamphlets and therefore only a means of plundering everyone connected with it, and he tried to handle the *General Advertiser* in the same way. That this attempt failed was owing mainly to the efforts of the Rev. William Jackson, who, by putting an end to his flirtations with the Ministry, delivered him from evil during the years 1787–1789. But, although Almon behaved like a newspaperman during these three years, his instincts were still those of a bookseller, and, with the first hint of trouble, he reverted to type. The result was that, instead of serving twelve months in prison, he served fourteen, and, instead of emerging from the ordeal with all expenses paid and £900 in his pocket, he emerged heavily in debt and without one single friend upon whom he could rely. To a newspaperman this would have seemed retributive justice on a rather high level.

# CHAPTER IV

# The *World* (1787–1792):
# *Sic Transit Gloria Mundi*

## THE JOURNAL OF ELEGANCE

WHEN Bell sold his shares in the *Morning Post*, as he did in January, 1786, he "declared" his "resolution" of "publishing a NEW PAPER on the first of January following" (*Oracle*, 1 June, 1789) ; [1] and the newspaper he had in mind was the *World*. Like John Almon, John Bell was a bookseller, not a newspaperman, but it seemed to him that a newspaper was a necessary adjunct of his trade. As proprietor of the *Morning Post*, he had enjoyed the privilege of inserting advertisements for the British Library in the paper whenever and wherever he pleased and backing them up with occasional paragraphs praising himself and his work; and his business had prospered accordingly. But meanwhile it seemed to him that he had learned something about newspapers themselves. Specifically it seemed to him that, if the "innocent arts of the [bookselling] trade" were applied to newspapers, newspapers could be made to yield a very handsome profit; and he was encouraged in this opinion by his experience with Carlton House. He was perhaps too encouraged. For on 28 January, 1786, he undertook the management of the already-established *English Chronicle, or Universal Evening Post* and fared so badly that on 5 May he was compelled to move his advertisements back to the *Morning Post*, where they remained until the beginning of 1787. But the venture was not a complete loss, for, although he was still convinced that the idea was sound, he was no longer willing to invest any of his own money in it. At this point he had the good fortune to meet Major Edward Topham.

For the events which ensued, historians are indebted to Bell himself, who left the following account in the *Oracle* of 1 June, 1789. The first plans for the *World*, said Bell, were made in June, 1786, when he happened to mention to Major Topham his "resolution" to begin "a NEW NEWSPAPER on the first of January following." Topham, who

DUKE OF SULLY'S HOUSE IN THE STRAND

DENHAM HOUSE, STRAND, IN 1790

was immediately interested, "proposed himself as a Partner in the undertaking," provided the two could agree on terms. Bell replied that his "terms were concise"; for, since he regarded his "experience," his "judgment," and "the time and fatigue which [he] must necessarily devote to the establishment, as equal to any sum of money that can be required," he would "not risque one shilling of [his] own property." He would therefore "propose to reserve *one fourth* of the property, whatever it may be, and to admit *Partners* for the rest, who will advance to the extent of two thousand pounds, if required, to be appropriated, *at [his] discretion,* but solely to the establishment of the paper: if the property should not succeed at the end of twelve months, or if the two thousand pounds should be sooner expended, then every party should be at liberty to relinquish any further concern in the property." Topham considered the proposal for a few days and then not only agreed to these terms, but "reserved *three fourth* parts to himself." But a few weeks later Bell revised the terms. As he explained:

I perceived that the *fatigue* of the establishment would principally rest on myself; I thought *one fourth* part of any *possible* success, would be very inadequate to my deserts, considering that the money to be advanced would be merely a loan, if the property succeeded, as it was to be returned out of the first profits. I therefore proposed to make my share one *third* of the *whole,* by taking an additional twelfth, subject to a proportionable pecuniary risque. Captain TOPHAM acquiesced. The agreement was concluded. The plan, as suggested and conducted by myself, was carried into execution. [The *World*] was continued under our joint management until the 31st of December [1788], when I sold my property therein.

As marvelous as this account is, the facts are even more marvelous. When Topham subsequently (*World,* 14 May, 1789) observed that he was finally compelled to pay "the said J. BELL the sum of Four Thousand Pounds, for the share given by him in the first instance to the above J. BELL, in the origin of the Paper," Bell angrily declared (*Oracle,* 1 June, 1789) that,

if there was any *giving* of Shares of the old WORLD, in the first instance, in the origin of the Paper, *I was the giver,* and *not* the person *given to.*—I invited Captain TOPHAM to the enterprize; I dictated the terms; I suggested the plan; carried it into execution; was principally instrumental in establishing and supporting it:—my services were more than equal to the stipulated loan, the extent of which however, was only 600*l.* and which was refunded to him, according to agreement, out of the profits of the Property;—and therefore *if any gift* was in the question, *I was the generous donor.*

Yet, even according to the first "proposal," Bell would have received a fourth share, which was then valued at £2,000, whereas, according to the revised "proposal," he received a third share, which was supposedly valued at £2,667. But, in fact, a third share was now valued at 4,000 guineas; for Bell neglected to mention that, in increasing his holding from a fourth to a third, he had also increased the price of the other two shares to 4,000 guineas each, so that Topham finally paid 8,000 guineas for a two-thirds interest instead of 6,000 pounds for a three-fourths interest (*Gazetteer*, 21 Sept., 1790). In addition, Bell assumed "a proportionable pecuniary risque" only to the extent that, if the paper succeeded, he could not sell his third until Topham had realized 4,000 guineas from his share of the profits and, if the paper failed, he could collect only one-third of the final value of the property. But meanwhile he would have been paid for the printing, have had "the privilege of writing what [he] chose in [the paper]," and have been able to use it generally "to answer the purposes of [his bookselling] business" (*Oracle*, 1 June, 1789). In return for these considerations, Bell was to provide his "experience" and "judgment": obviously not respecting the mechanics of getting out a newspaper, of which he knew little more than Topham, but respecting all those extra-ethical "arts of the trade," at which he was acknowledged to be "an adept."

"Thank fortune," said Frederick Reynolds,[2] "it was my fate to write comedies, during a period when the town was replete with original characters of every description. . . . My profits on Topham alone, in different comedies, must have amounted to upwards of one thousand pounds":

He drove a curricle, (constructed after a plan of his own,) with *four* black horses splendidly caparisoned, and followed by two grooms in conspicuous liveries.

His dress consisted of a short scarlet coat, with large steel buttons; a very short white waistcoat, top-boots, and leather breeches, so long in their upper quarters, as almost to reach his chin. . . . [It] must be remembered that, at that time, every other person wore very long coats, and very long waistcoats; and breeches so very *short*, that *half* the day, and one *whole* hand were entirely employed in raising them *en derriere,* to avoid any awkward declension, *en avant.* . . .

In spite of all his oddities, however, few men had either purer taste, or clearer judgment, than Topham; and he possessed also, in a high degree, those lighter talents that enable a man to shine in society and conversation.[3]

According to one biographer,[4] Topham had had some previous experience with a newspaper, having been an "original proprietor of the Morning Post." But there is no evidence to support this assertion, for his name is not mentioned in connection with any of the paper's quarrels, nor is it included in the list of proprietors printed by the *Post* on 8 November, 1776. There is also the fact that, when the *Post* was begun, he was only twenty-one years old, and he had not yet come into his inheritance. In 1786 he was thirty-five with an Eton-Cambridge education, an adjutancy in the Horse Guards, a handsome property, a wide acquaintance in fashionable and theatrical circles, and considerable literary talent. His chief interest at the moment was the theater. One of his farces, *The Fool,* had been produced at Drury Lane on 15 April, 1785, another, *Small Talk,* had been produced at Covent Garden on 11 May, 1786, and he was completing still another, *Bonds without Judgment,* for production at the same theater the following year.

Since Topham had a liking for domesticity and no corresponding liking for marriage, he had had a succession of mistresses, the most recent of whom was Mary Wells. The two had been living together since perhaps early 1784, and, since she was already married to an actor, their relationship could not be legitimatized in England, although she had been given to understand that it would be legitimatized in Italy as soon as "circumstances enabled [Topham] to perform his engagement." By late 1786 they had "resided in Bryanstone-street for three years," where she "[had become] the mother of two lovely children," and they were in the process of moving to "Beaufort-buildings, where he [would establish] the World."[5] Mrs. Wells, who was evidently little more than half Topham's age, was at the height of her career as an actress, but her success was owing less to her dramatic ability than to her beauty and flair for "imitations" and even to these, it was suspected, less than to Topham's assistance. She was also an "original character." According to George Bernard,[6]

[She] loved to oppose all the tastes and customs of the world; to wear furs in the summer, and muslins in the winter; to improve her health by riding down to Oxford or Cambridge in Hackney coaches, and to relieve the ferment of town society, by incurring premeditated debts, and getting into sponging houses, where she might enjoy her reflections undisturbed;—of all of which vagaries the gallant editor supplied the means with his purse, and defended the propriety with his pen. . . .

Of all [her] peculiarities, perhaps the greatest was her imagining that every man she saw or spoke to, fell in love with her. As she visited the public places, . . . she set down all his Majesty's ministers, and half the nobility of the land, as her dying inamoratos. But she went farther, and wanted to make Topham call them all out (six at a time . . .) to revenge the insulted dignity of her feelings.

Although Topham did not always comply with her wishes, he found them generally charming.

It was currently "understood" that Topham's interest in a newspaper was inspired by his interest in Mrs. Wells's career,[7] but it was Mrs. Wells's opinion that Topham intended to exploit her talents rather than eulogize them. Although the paper did undertake her defense and although it also became in some degree her responsibility, the truth seems to be that she did not figure in his original plans at all. For on 18 September, 1786, she was considering leaving London for a year, and, although Topham protested, the protest included no mention of the newspaper: "[Follow] your own inclinations, [but] you know my partiality to a regular London engagement; and it is on this principle, that, if after going one year into the country you could then resume your situation [at the Haymarket], all would be well; but in that time [Colman] has made his arrangements, and you are thrown out there for ever. But let nothing of this sort bias, without you can make a profitable *article*."[8] There is no indication that Topham thought of the *World* as other than a business, to which he and his friends would contribute, from which he would profit, and the responsibility for which would be chiefly Bell's. But, as it turned out, he had trouble with Bell before the newspaper was even begun, so that the responsibility turned out to be his, Bell functioning only as printer and publisher.

The *World, and Fashionable Advertiser* made its appearance on 1 January, 1787. "PRINTED under the direction of J. BELL, at the British Library, in the Strand" and "SOLD by V[incent] DOWLING, Corner of Exeter 'Change, in the Strand," the *World* was as different from the *Morning Post* as the *Morning Post* had been from the *Morning Chronicle;* for this was a newspaper of elegance. Not only was it elegant in appearance, but it was elegant in style and content, and it obviously regarded itself as an authority in matters of taste. Since not everyone agreed with its judgments, not everyone liked it; but no one was indifferent to it, and the reactions of William Gifford and James Boaden are therefore typical. The *World* was begun by "a knot of fantastic coxcombs," said Gifford.[9] "It was perfectly unintelligible, and therefore much read: it was equally lavish of praise and abuse . . . , and as its conductors were at once ignorant and conceited, they took upon themselves to direct the taste of the town, by prefixing a short panegyric to every trifle which came before them." The *World* was distinguished, said Boaden,[10]

by a more marked reflexion of literary and fashionable existence, than had been displayed by other papers of the day. . . . [It] assumed a style utterly unknown in English literature. It seemed always to hint rather than discuss, and to lighten rather than shine. [It was] at all times entertaining, and often instructive. [Its] taste, whether we look to morals or intellect, was generally good. Genius, in particular, was followed with a veneration certainly not affected, and the public attention was called, with an authoritative voice, to the claims of conspicuous virtue or conspicuous talent. The eccentricity of style at first perplexed its readers, at last diverted them. . . .

Much of the paper was written by Topham himself, who, when he was in town, seems to have supplied most of the miscellany and theatrical commentary. When he was out of town, the "theatrical criticism" was supplied by Mrs. Wells,[11] who remained in London to appear at Covent Garden during the 1786–1787 season. In addition, Topham drew heavily on his friends. "Whilst *The World* was in being," said Mrs. Wells,[12] "the house in which Mr. Topham and I resided, in Beaufort-buildings, was the constant resort of men of high literary character." One of the habitués was Sheridan, who was quietly furnishing the political commentary, which Topham redirected to the printer. "Some time since I sent you *original letters*—an article," Topham mentioned to Mrs. Wells on 18 November, 1787:[13] "it contained one from a *Chinese Philosopher* to *Charles Fox,* and another from *Nobbi Wortz* at Operto to the *Duke of Norfolk;* but I have seen nothing of them: perhaps they may be in [the printer's] hands./ Enclosed I send various articles which may appear as soon as wanted." There were also Edward Jerningham, Joseph Jekyll, and Topham's intimate, Miles Peter Andrews,[13] all of whom were, like Topham, "original characters" for Reynolds' comedies.

There were several additions to the staff during the first year. There was, for example, Emanuel Samuel, who was employed to report the Parliamentary debates. Samuel, whom Mrs. Wells described [15] as "an apostate Jew, overwhelmed with debt, and supporting himself merely by writing a few paragraphs for the Morning Post at a salary of one guinea per week," had recently married her sister; and, in order to save her sister from "starvation," Mrs. Wells had not only guaranteed the payment of some of his debts, but had "prevailed upon" Topham "to give him the more lucrative situation of a reporter" at a salary of two guineas a week. Samuel joined the staff in the fall, possibly replacing "Captain [John] Williamson," who left the World at about this time, "being otherwise engaged." [16] Williamson, too, had once (1783–84) been connected with the Morning Post. But the most important addition was Robert Merry.

When the World made its appearance, Merry was, according to Reynolds,[17] living in Florence, where for seven years he had been associated with the Della Cruscan Academy, an English coterie dedicated to the appreciation and cultivation of poetry, and with "a beautiful married woman [Lady Cowper]," whose husband had "entirely surrendered" the "domestic arrangements of the 'Home Department'" to him. While he was thus writing his poetry and enjoying a life of "ease and splendour" at no cost to himself, "some lines . . . appeared, in the 'World' newspaper, tributary to his genius," written, Reynolds "believed," by Topham. A copy of the newspaper was "sent to him abroad," and Merry responded by "transmitting some poetry to England," which Topham accordingly printed, "[giving] it the signature of DELLA CRUSCA." The "poetry" seems to have been the "Adieu and Recall to Love," which appeared in the World of 29 June, 1787. As it happened, Merry was in England almost as soon as his poetry, for, owing to the objections of her family, he was at last being separated from the "lady he sincerely loved" and to whom, of course, the "poetry" was addressed; and, forced by this development to live "upon the remnants of his small property," he had had no choice but to go home. Back in England, he "renewed his intimacy with Topham; with whom he had been brother officer in the Horse Guards, and fellow commoner at Cambridge," and, since he proved to be "a most entertaining character," he was promptly taken into "the Beef-steak Club," which numbered among its members Sheridan, Topham, Miles Peter Andrews, Henry Bate Dudley, William Woodfall, John Taylor, and some thirty-five others, "one-third of whom were noblemen." [18]

Meanwhile Merry's "poetry" had found numerous admirers, one of whom, Mrs. Hannah Cowley, writing "under the assumed appellation of ANNA MATILDA," had replied with some "poetry" of her own, which the *World* had printed on 12 July. Since Merry needed money and since he was, in fact, languishing with love, although not for Mrs. Cowley, whom he did not meet until 1789, he was easily persuaded to continue this lovesick correspondence. The correspondence aroused immediate and widespread interest. "The verses of *Della Crusca* are the most beautiful things I ever saw or read in my life," Topham said on 18 November, 1787.[19] "I would give all that I am worth to be the author of them." Most readers shared his opinion, and their interest was enhanced by the fact that the identity of the correspondents was concealed. According to Boaden,[20] the verses were "ascribed, and never formally denied by them, to the brightest geniuses of the age. I remember Sheridan did not discourage the attribution of Merry's share to himself, and Mrs. Piozzi was usually asserted to be his correspondent."

Merry attracted two other members of the Florentine Academy: the "[weak], unstable, inordinately conceited" William Parsons and the "much more balanced" Bertie Greatheed,[21] who were soon writing for the *World* under similar signatures and in a similar mood. This group in turn attracted a host of other poets. Most of the habitués of Beaufort Buildings became Della Cruscans, Miles Peter Andrews, who signed himself "Arley," being the most prominent of Merry's Beaufort Buildings disciples; and there were numerous others, only a few of whom have been identified. Gifford [22] named some of them: for example, Thomas Adney, who reversed the spelling of his name for the pseudonym "Mot Yenda," and Thomas Vaughn, who, Gifford thought, was writing "under the alluring signature of Edwin," although Vaughn denied the fact. But, although the *World* was choked with mawkish verse, there was never enough to satisfy the readers. Gifford was not overstating the case in saying [23] that "not a day passed without an amatory epistle fraught with thunder and lightning, et quicquid habent telorum armamentaria coeli.—The fever turned to a frenzy: Laura Maria, Carlos, Orlando, Adelaide, and a thousand nameless names caught the infection; and from one end of the kingdom to the other, all was nonsense and Della Crusca." The interest in poetry was as old as the *Morning Post,* and by the late 1770's most newspapers were printing occasional poems, several of them having even introduced a "Poet's Corner." But the *World* was the first and probably the only newspaper to trade in poetry as the *Morning Chronicle* had once traded in Parliamentary debates; and to each poem was affixed a laudatory headnote.

The immediacy and extent of the *World's* success has no precedent in the history of newspapers. On 19 October, 1787, Topham noted [24] that the daily sale of the *World* had risen to 2,600 and that "the receipt on advertisements" was "growing very considerable." On 27 November the paper dropped its subtitle, to be known henceforth as simply the *World,* announcing meanwhile that, although it would remain broadly fashionable in its interests, it now regarded itself as more specifically "The Paper of Poetry." On 1 January, 1788, it apologized for the tardiness of its appearance by explaining that its sale had increased from an original 2,000 to a figure which fluctuated between 3,000 and 4,000, which number could not be printed by eight A.M.; and on 26 June, 1788, it reissued some of its verse in a two-volume collection, entitled *Poetry of the World; Containing Poems by Della Crusca, Anna Matilda, and Arley,* which itself went through three editions.

All of the newspapers were affected by the *World's* success, but the newspapers most affected were, of course, the other West End papers, the *Morning Herald* and the *Morning Post.* The *Herald* responded with silence, partly perhaps because its conductor, Henry Bate Dudley, was associated with Topham in "the Beef-steak Club," partly because the two papers were in political accord, and partly because it was characteristic of the *Herald* to reserve its animosity for the *Post.* The *Post* reacted with invective until 1 January, 1788, when it suddenly announced a revision of its own editorial policy with subsequent emphasis on *"the elegancies of Literature."* But its *"plans . . . with a number of Literary Gentlemen"* failed to *"settle,"* and on 4 February its editor, Peter Stuart, left the paper to found the evening *Star,* and the *Post,* now edited by Daniel Stuart, resumed its invective.

## THE FLESH AND THE DEVIL

THE *World's* success also had an effect upon the *World* itself, for the success was as surprising to Topham as it was to everyone else.

The fact that Topham had lost confidence in Bell even before the newspaper appeared had not altered his respect for Bell's plan in the least; and the disappearance of Bell's name from the colophon on 16 January, 1787, the colophon thereafter reading simply "SOLD by V[incent] Dowling, Corner of Exeter 'Change, in the Strand" or a few months later "SOLD by J[ohn] Wilkie, Corner of Exeter 'Change, in the Strand," indicates that he intended to put the plan into effect as soon as the newspaper was fairly established. But, in order to do so, he had to find a substitute for Bell, and meanwhile the *World* was doing so well as a legitimate enterprise that he did not even begin the search until perhaps July. At least, the Rev. Charles Este was not approached until August.

Este himself said only (*Gazetteer,* 21 Sept., 1790) that Topham first tried to manage the *World* alone, failed, and then applied to him for assistance, having obtained an introduction through the Archdeacon of Surrey. But Este was probably recommended to Topham by Sheridan, who was as well acquainted with newspapermen as anyone in London and who would also have been acquainted with the kind of newspaperman Topham wanted. Este, who was "one of the readers of the royal chapel at Whitehall," was described by a contemporary [25] as "the most extraordinary character . . . of his time." Educated for the Church, he was "more attached to the stage" and had once even been an actor. He was also "more attached" to the press, and here, too, he was not without experience, although he had gone to considerable trouble to conceal the fact. Some time earlier he had worked for the *Public Advertiser* as an "established correspondent," and more recently, in perhaps 1784 or 1785, he and the actor John Kemble had begun their own newspaper, the failure of which had cost each of them £300. This newspaper has not been identified. The terms which Topham offered Este were approximately those demanded by Bell: Este was to receive the usual salary of an editor and in addition a gift of one-fourth of the property. Since the fourth came from Topham's two-thirds (*Oracle,* 18 Jan., 1793), this meant that, by the end of 1787, the *World* was divided into twelve shares, of which Topham held five, Bell four, and Este three. But, whereas Bell had promised in return only "experience," "judgment," and "time," Este brought with him "some MS." which was guaranteed to "make the fortune of a Paper" (*Gazetteer,* 21 Sept., 1790).

Este prepared for his new assignment by publishing his autobiography, the purpose of which was to disavow his connection with newspapers for all time. On the pretext that he had been subjected to some recent "newspaper abuse" and had even been accused of writing for "several newspapers" himself, Este made what purported to be a full confession. It was true, he said, that he had sown a few wild oats. As a young man, he had been attracted to the stage and somewhat later to medicine. But he had never been attracted to the press, and, since his ordination in 1777, he had devoted all his thoughts to his calling. His only regret was that God had not seen fit to place him in the country. "The Press with 500l. a year," he assured the public, "is less desirable to me than a Pulpit with half the money./ I pant for the country, [where] I have lived . . . these four months" and for the life of "a simple country clergyman, doing good on an humble scale": "The Press, though a powerful engine for *taste and morals*, I should, under a sense of obligation to superior service, leave to others."[26] A month after Este enunciated these sentiments, he was on the staff of the *World*.

Although Este's services were scheduled to begin on 1 January, 1788, they actually did begin in October, 1787. The reason was that Topham needed someone to manage the paper during the hunting season, which he invariably spent in Suffolk, and Mrs. Wells was incapable of doing it. Not only had she renewed her contract with Covent Garden, but her third child, a boy, was born at about this time. The child evidently died shortly after birth, for she later[27] referred only to three daughters, and Reynolds also indicated[28] that there were only three girls: Juliet, Harriet, and Maria. Este's services to the newspaper and Mrs. Wells during October and November were regarded by Topham as a personal favor, for on 18 November he wrote to Mrs. Wells:[29] "Pray give my compliments to Este, and a thousand times thank him for all his attentions: as they are out of number, they are out of all return; but my remembrance of them, which will be perpetual."

That Topham's feeling about Este was by no means shared by Bell is evident from an incident which occurred shortly after Este assumed his responsibilities. The *World* had published an account of Dr. Edward Kentish, Physician to the Bristol Dispensary and author of numerous medical works; and, since the account reflected unfavorably on the Veterinary College, the Veterinary College threatened to sue the newspaper, evidently delivering the threat to "J. Wilkie," who

transmitted it to Bell. Bell responded by sending Topham a long letter filled with abuse of Este, but the letter was so incoherent that
Topham had to find out what was the matter before he could reply.
"I hope *Este* knows nothing of Bell's absurd letter," he told Mrs.
Wells on 22 October, 1787. "I cannot make out what it is he alludes
to. Has *Este* written anything *out of the House* that is not right [i.e.,
violated any privilege of the Commons]?" Mrs. Wells assured him
that Este knew nothing of the matter, but she was apparently too ill
to call on Bell, and Bell refused to talk to Este. He also declined to
answer letters, so that, by the time Topham learned the facts, almost
four weeks had elapsed, and the matter was urgent. "A THOUSAND
thanks for your concern," he told Mrs. Wells on 18 November:

I have [at last] heard from Bell: he understands that all legal proceedings will
drop if they could but know the auther [*sic*] of Dr. Kentish's case. I have
written to him, to tell him it is *Doctor Kentish* himself, who, having set his
name to it, can have no wish or idea to shrink from it: lest the letter I wrote
by this post . . . should not reach him, communicate this to him yourself, and
*immediately;*—as the proceedings will go on, if not stopped, on Tuesday.

   I . . . can do no further good than this, and hope all will end properly;
for the attempt of the college is very nonsensical, and I should laugh at it were
it not at one's own expence.

Since the college had never wanted anything except the name of the
author, "the matter about Doctor Kentish" was accordingly settled.[30]
But "the matter" about Este was not settled. Bell later (*Oracle,*
1 June, 1789) complained that only once or twice, during the whole
course of their association on the *World,* did Este see fit to visit him,
and, since Bell never visited Este, the only links between the editorial
office in Beaufort Buildings and the printing office at the British Library were Topham and Mrs. Wells.

   Throughout 1787 the *World* was conducted as a legitimate enterprise, but by late February, 1788, arrangements had been made for
the conversion, Este having obtained an "article" from a printer, who
thereby consented to be the scapegoat in the event of an action for
libel. On 25 February the colophon was accordingly adjusted to read
"Printed by B[UCHANAN] MILLAN," and on the same day the
*World* made the first of several attacks on the Prince of Wales and
the Duke of York, much to the alarm of the *Morning Post* (6 Mar.,
1788), which had heretofore had a monopoly on the blackmailing of
Carlton House. Although these attacks were discontinued, they were

followed by attacks on other people of note and by a battery of attacks on the *Post* itself, the existence of which the *World* had previously ignored, the *Post* being only a blackmailing sheet and hence a threat only to other blackmailing sheets. There was also sporadic abuse of productions at the Haymarket, and on 11 July the *World* joined most of the London newspapers in condemning the younger Colman's *Ways and Means,* which had been performed at that theater on the previous day. But by 15 July it had shifted to the side of the *St. James's Chronicle,* a newspaper in which the elder Colman was thought to have a financial interest, and was defending the play against all "the *Lower Prints.*" The price which the *World* asked for this shift was evidently enormous, for the paper was henceforth assured of a £300 annual subsidy "for Theatricals" as long as it existed (*Public Advertiser,* 1 June, 1792; *Oracle,* 18 Jan., 1793). That the elder Colman should have contracted to pay £300 a year for what turned out to be only silence is perhaps explained by Reynolds' statement [31] that, as "chief conductor and proprietor of 'The World,' [Topham] was then, almost the manager's manager [of theaters]" and by the fact that this particular money was always assigned to Topham's side of the ledger rather than Este's.

In mid-July the *World* turned its attention to politics, and, during the elections of 1788, it was by far the most violent of the seven Treasury newspapers. All of its violence was directed at Fox, whom it accused of innumerable physical outrages, supporting the accusations with long lists of casualties, one of which (4 Aug., 1788) alone consisted of two hundred names. Although Sheridan's Drury Lane was several times denounced as a vehicle for propaganda, Sheridan and his "friends" were themselves absolved from any wrongdoing, being represented as anguished protestants, whose protests were powerless to stop the carnage. On 4 August the *World* admitted the defeat of the Ministerial candidate, demonstrating the poignancy of its grief by the thickness of its black frame. But the admission was accompanied by another condemnation of Fox and further praise of Sheridan and his "friends," who were now identified as Burke, Lord Loughborough, and "the Norfolk [William] Wyndham." Nor did the matter end here, for the *World* continued its abuse of Fox throughout August and well into September, reprinting from the *Morning Post* Horne Tooke's insulting "Portraits" and other material which had little present relevancy.

Since the political position of the *World* had always been controlled by Sheridan and since Sheridan was certainly not defended by
any other Treasury newspaper, one cannot escape the conclusion that
there was a plot, headed by Sheridan and supported by Burke, Lord
Loughborough, and William Windham, to remove Fox as leader of
the Opposition Party and that Topham had given the plotters carte
blanche use of the newspaper for the remainder of the year. By the
summer of 1788, there was much more at stake than an election, for,
although nothing was being said of it in the press, it was common
knowledge that the King was ill, that he had gone to Cheltenham for
reasons of health, and that he was not recovering. It was also no secret that the Prince of Wales had no liking for Pitt and that, if he
succeeded his father even on an interim basis, he would ask for a
change of government. The expectation was, of course, that the new
government would be headed by Fox, but Sheridan evidently had
other plans. Since he was still not ready to announce these plans, the
*World*'s alliance with the Pitt Government had served everyone's purpose admirably. The paper's attacks on Fox and its defense of Sheridan and his "friends" had been charged to Pitt, and meanwhile Topham had been rewarded by the Treasury for what were, in fact, only
favors for an old friend. But, once the elections were over, Sheridan's
purposes were better served by an alliance with Carlton House, and
one might almost have predicted that the *World* would shift its allegiance accordingly.

By August, 1788, the King's health had worsened. Although it was
still too early to talk about it, everyone was thinking of the possibility
of a regency, and intrigues were already in the making. With respect
to the elections, Sheridan and Pitt had had a common enemy in Fox,
but it was inevitable that, with respect to the matter of a regency,
Sheridan and Fox would have a common enemy in Pitt, who would,
of course, oppose the Regency Bill as long as possible, and, when opposition was no longer possible, would resort to his usual attenuative
tactics. For this reason alone, therefore, the *World* had to divorce
itself from the Treasury, and, since it could not ally itself with the
Foxites, it had necessarily to ally itself with Carlton House. There
were also real advantages in such an alliance, owing to Mrs. Fitzherbert. For, whereas the Prince had no quarrel with Fox, Mrs. Fitzherbert had not forgiven him for denying her marriage in the spring
of 1787; and, whereas the Prince paid little attention to the newspa-

pers, she paid a great deal. Hence, not only would she aid the conspirators in every way she could, but, if she were properly approached,
she would see to it that the Prince subsidized the newspaper.

The approach, although perhaps not proper, was at least direct,
for on 6 September, 1788, the *World* published without comment the
following "epitaph":

MRS. F–TZH–RB–T.
To the Remembrance of one
Who was —, Wife and no Wife, Princess
and no Princess, sought, yet shunned,
courted, yet disclaimed; the Queen of all
Parties, yet the Grace of none; the
Theme of Wonder, Curiosity, and
submissive respect; yet
the constant Subject of Doubt, Reserve, and
Apprehension.
Mrs. F—
was fond of Sovereignty, and obtained it; fond
of the World's Friendship, and secured it;
fond of that best Courage, the Courage of being unabash'd, and contrived
to exercise it safely.

The author of this "epitaph" could have been only Sheridan. For,
even if Sheridan was not otherwise aware of Mrs. Fitzherbert's pas-
sionate concern for her reputation, he could not have forgotten the
domestic storm which followed Fox's denial of her marriage the previous year, when he was hastily dispatched to Parliament to testify to
her character as a virtuous woman. The agent who opened negotiations in behalf of Carlton House was probably also Sheridan, for
Sheridan represented Mrs. Fitzherbert (and the Prince) in other such
transactions. Supposing that he would have to buy the newspaper in
order to silence it, the Prince offered Topham £4,000 cash and a lifetime annuity of £400 for outright purchase,[32] but Topham refused to
sell, and the matter was finally settled in terms of a subsidy.

Since the Prince of Wales took no personal interest in the *World*,
Mrs. Fitzherbert and Sheridan were free to manage the political department of the paper as they pleased; and, since they saw eye to eye
on the matter of Fox, the *World* was soon lamenting the quality of
Fox's leadership and observing sadly (10 Oct., 1788) that the "personal worth [of Mr. SHERIDAN, Mr. BURKE, and an other Gentleman

or two] alone can uphold a drooping Party from decay." Such lamentations continued throughout November and December, accompanied by periodic pleadings that Fox and his "close friends" retire, so that Sheridan could organize the "new Whigs" into a "respectable Opposition." These pleadings did not, of course, originate with the Prince of Wales, but, since the *World* was clearly marked as a Carlton House newspaper, it was generally supposed that they did. Hence, when the King's illness was finally admitted, several newspapers predicted that Sheridan would head the Regency Government. There were also mentions of additions and possible additions to the roster of "new Whigs," among them the Duke of Norfolk, who was meanwhile, the *Morning Post* confided (21 Oct., 1788), "the *friend* behind the curtain who advances eighteen thousand pounds to Mr. SHERIDAN, to purchase DOCTOR FORD's share of Drury-lane." But the situation was abruptly altered by Fox's declaration of 10 December that "the Prince of Wales had as clear, as express a right to exercise the power of sovereignty" as he would have "in the event of his Majesty's demise." Since Sheridan and Burke and, in fact, everyone who valued the Prince's friendship felt obliged to subscribe to this declaration, the declaration had the effect of reuniting the Whigs and confirming the leadership of Fox, so far as the press was concerned. From its point of view, the "new Whigs" had ceased to exist, and the struggle was again only a struggle between Whigs and Tories. The "new Whigs" had not given up, however, for the *World* continued to demand Fox's resignation until the end of the year, when it became a Treasury print and the "new Whigs" transferred their activities to the *Morning Post.*

Although Sheridan had something to do with the transfer, the transfer was not part of his plan, for the "new Whigs" would not willingly have left a newspaper like the *World* for a newspaper like the *Morning Post.* But in January, 1789, controlling interest in the *Morning Post* was sold to Carlton House, and the Secretary of the Treasury, George Rose, had hardly authorized the sale when he opened negotiations with Topham for political control of the *World.* In view of the fact that the "new Whigs" would now have the *Post,* Topham felt free to dispose of the *World* as he saw fit, and he therefore signified his willingness to come to terms, provided the terms were sufficiently attractive, mentioning, however, that he had or had had an opportunity to sell the paper to "the [Prince of Wales's] Opposition" for £4,000 cash and a lifetime annuity of £400. Rose responded by offering an annual subsidy of £600, the paper to remain in Topham's possession. Since this was the largest sum the Treasury had offered for a newspaper and much more than the *World* had been receiving from Carlton House, Topham accepted; and the subsidy was paid in four annual installments through mid-1793.[33] The result was that Sheridan left the *World* altogether, but not without some rancorous feelings toward both Este and Topham.

While Topham was coming to terms with Rose, he was also coming to terms with Bell and Este. According to the spurious *Star* (29 Apr., 1789), Bell sold out because he was *"obliged . . . to sell out"* by Topham's *"ungentlemanly"* conduct." But Bell himself indicated (*Oracle*, 1 June, 1789) that he wanted to sell, and one might suppose that this was the case, for, since he had had nothing to do with the management of the paper, he would probably have seized the first opportunity to collect his 4,000 guineas and retire as proprietor. The sale was effected in the usual manner: in mid-December, 1788, Bell stated that he would like either to sell his shares or buy Topham's, and, since Topham preferred to purchase at the price Bell was willing to sell rather than to sell at the price Bell was willing to buy, the sale was fixed for 31 December. Most of this was a formality, for the original partnership contract had stipulated that Bell would receive 4,000 guineas for his third. But, as a condition of the sale, Bell demanded the right to print the paper forever, "the Printing of it . . . being materially necessary to [his] own pursuits in business, and therefore a consideration with [him] not to be departed from." Topham or, more properly, his adviser, Charles Edward Wilsonn, demurred, so that the contract finally stipulated that Topham could withdraw the printing at any time, provided he bought Bell's "Printing Materials at a fair valuation"; that, if he did withdraw it, Bell was free to begin another newspaper; and that Bell was meanwhile to post a bond of £1,000 as guarantee that he would not "cause, or suffer any injury whatever to the property, that could be in the power of any Printer to prevent." Although Bell later (*Oracle*, 1 June, 1789) maintained that Topham privately assured him that he had no intention of withdrawing the printing, this assurance was not part of the contract.

Although Bell had fared very well, having, in the course of two years, realized a return of 4,000 guineas on no investment whatever, Topham had fared even better, for, by the end of 1788, a third share in the *World* was worth much more than the 4,000 guineas Bell was compelled to accept. Topham expected to fare equally well in his dealings with Este, even though the contract in this instance seemed to be ruinous. For on 21 December, 1788 (*Oracle,* 18 Jan., 1793), Topham and Este signed an extraordinary document, the following part of which was printed by the *Gazetteer* on 30 September, 1790:

### EDWARD TOPHAM's DEED.

The said E. Topham at this time being the sole owner and proprietor of a Daily Paper, published under the title of THE WORLD, in which till this day, the said C. ESTE had a FOURTH SHARE—but which he has surrender'd to the said E. TOPHAM, and the advantages therefrom, as a certain fourth, the said E. TOPHAM *having* AGREED DURING THE JOINT LIVES of the said E. TOPHAM and C. ESTE, TO PAY to the said C. ESTE, the ANNUAL SUM OF FOUR HUNDRED POUNDS, by quarterly payments commencing from Dec. 25, 1788 &c. &c. &c.

The said C. ESTE shall have FREE LIBERTY TO INSPECT ALL AC-COUNTS and papers relative to the said Daily Paper.

Lastly it is agreed, that if the said C. ESTE SHALL SURVIVE the said E. TOPHAM, that the SOLE RIGHT AND OWNERSHIP of the said paper shall belong to, and be the SOLE PROPERTY of the said C. ESTE, clear of all deductions and incumbrances whatever, but the annual payment of five hundred pounds, during the life of one nominee.

The precise nature of the provision for that "one nominee," obviously Mrs. Wells, is actually in doubt, for on another occasion (*Gazetteer,* 10 Sept., 1790) Este indicated that the paper would revert to him only "if Mr. Edward Topham dies before [the] Nominee." The "&c. &c. &c." included at least three other stipulations: if Topham defaulted on the payment of the annuity, Este was to receive one-fourth of the profits up to £2,000 and half the profits in excess of £2,000, "the 300*l.* that was paid for Theatricals" not being included in the profits (*Public Advertiser,* 1 June, 1792; *Oracle,* 18 Jan., 1793); Este was to remain a member of the staff (*Oracle,* 18 Jan., 1793); and he was to retain possession of "copyrights" and "some valuable MS. so materially necessary to the due *controul* of the concern, and which [Mr. Topham] knows would make the fortune of a Paper" (*Gazetteer,* 21 Sept., 1790).

But there was another stipulation not mentioned in the contract: Este was to put his "copyrights" and "valuable MS." to the most lucrative use and to devote his talents generally to the enhancement of the income of the newspaper by any means possible, the money to be turned over to Topham. For this reason Este was also to be given a free hand to manage the newspaper as he pleased, Topham assisting, but not interfering except in the case of the drama department, which he would continue to manage himself. Moreover, since Este would need to keep a watchful eye on the printer and since his relations with Bell were already uncomfortable, it seems to have been further understood that the connection with Bell would be severed as soon as possible. At least, on 3 January, 1789, Topham and "an intimate friend" stopped off at Chelmsford on their way to Suffolk to visit Bell, who was spending the day there, in order to notify him that a severance was in prospect.

According to Bell's account of the interview (*Oracle*, 1 June, 1789), Topham stated that he had "given directions for a house to be found and taken" for the purpose of consolidating the two offices of the *World*, that he would be withdrawing the printing shortly, and that he was therefore ready to buy the printing materials, "according to the *Bond* of Obligation," as well as "a new Type." Bell replied that he would not require Topham to buy the materials, but he would insist upon his right to begin a new newspaper, whereupon, said Bell, Topham changed his mind and said that, since "Printing the Paper was . . . of serious consequences in reference to [Bell's] general business," then, of course, "the Printing *ought to remain*, and *should remain with [Bell]*." Este repeated this statement in Topham's behalf a few days later, Bell added, and, since Topham himself repeated it a month later, he "[thought] no more of what had passed" until 9 May. But the truth was that Bell came away from the interview knowing very well that the printing would be withdrawn as soon as "a house" could be found and that he would have to find himself another newspaper shortly.

Topham's domestic affairs at this time were somewhat tangled, inasmuch as Mrs. Wells was dividing her favors between Topham, with whom she was still living, and the dramatist, Frederick Reynolds. Her intimacy with Reynolds seems to have begun in mid-1788, for Reynolds himself stated [34] that it lasted four years and expressed his astonishment at Mrs. Wells's comment: "I am, and have been, during the last *four* years, the most unhappy woman living.—Calais, April 1st, 1792." The prime mover had been "the lady herself," for, again according to Reynolds,[35] the affair had begun with a message, delivered to him in the country, "that a love entanglement, of no ordinary nature was preparing for me—that a certain handsome, celebrated actress, had fixed her mark upon me—and there [was] no chance of escape." Reynolds hurried to town and there discovered "that the lady did not 'protest too much,' " for, "in point of beauty, [she] was certainly, the leading theatrical star" and "had rejected the overtures of half the rank and fashion in London." Moreover, she "had no mercenary feeling," and, "as an actress, she possessed considerable comic talent, and in some parts, shone unrivalled," whereas "she displayed even more humour in real, than in fictitious, life." But, Topham, too, was not without "humour." Hence, although he was undoubtedly aware of this "entanglement," it did not alter his admiration for Mrs. Wells, and, when he met Reynolds, as he did in March or April, 1789,[36] he and Reynolds at once became intimate friends. At the beginning of 1789, therefore, the future of the *World* and everyone connected with it looked very bright, and Topham went off to Suffolk, free from responsibilities and with no anxieties of any sort. But at this very point the fortunes of the *World* suddenly shifted, and the remainder of its history is a chronicle of disasters.

## THE FIRST HARASSMENTS

SINCE a newspaper changing political sides liked to pretend that it was undergoing a thoughtful conversion, the change was usually undertaken as a process, requiring at least a month for its completion. There was, therefore, no real difference between the *World* and the *Morning Post* until early February. Both papers condemned Fox, both of them approved of Sheridan and Burke, both of them admired Pitt, but were uneasy about his "friends," and both of them were fond of the Prince of Wales. But some divergence was evident by 20 January, for, whereas the *World* was insisting that the King's health was actually much better than it was represented, the *Post* was hinting that it might be much worse; and, whereas the *World* was suggesting that a thorough investigation of "a supposed marriage" ought to be undertaken, if only as an act of precaution, the *Post* was regretting that this "very unpleasant and generally scouted topic" should be mentioned at all. Although the *Morning Post* was now edited by John Taylor, the political department was regulated by Sheridan, who had previously pinned his political hopes on the advocacy of Mrs. Fitzherbert, but who now evidently felt that he would be better off without her or was, at least, ready to sacrifice her if need be.

In early February Topham returned to London. By this time there had been drastic alterations in both newspapers, which were taking vigorous stands with respect to the Regency Bill, introduced on 5 February, and with respect to each other. The *Post* had exposed Este as editor of the *World* and was referring to him daily as "the *Reverend* Editor of the *booby* print." Since Este did not know the identity of the *Post*'s editor, he was retaliating by calling the *Post* "a certain *low* print." Meanwhile Este was making use of his "copyrights" and "valuable MS." by inserting "libels" in the newspaper "with a view to extort money; and . . . if he could obtain a sum of money, he would desist from such abuse" (*Oracle*, 18 Jan., 1793) ; and in addition he had joined forces with Burke's old enemy, Major John Scott.

Scott, who returned to England from India in late 1781, had been active in a succession of Ministerial papers in behalf of Warren Hastings. From late 1781 through 1783, his fulminations had been concentrated in the *Morning Herald;* when the *Herald* defected to the Opposition, Scott had moved to the *Morning Post;* and, now that the *Morning Post* was supporting the Opposition, he had moved to the *World,* taking with him a writer of political doggerel, who signed himself "Simkin" and was tentatively identified (*World,* 25 Febr., 1790) as "Ralph Broome, Esq. of Rumfort, in Essex." "Simkin's" penchant was the trial of Warren Hastings, which he ridiculed with such effect that, as the *World* said later (23 Febr., 1790) , he singlehandedly *"kept the* TRIAL *alive,"* so far as the public was concerned, for almost three years. Scott's penchant was Edmund Burke. It was no accident that Scott had always been allied with Ministerial newspapers, for, since his purpose had been to prevent any inquiries into the affairs of the East India Company, his activities had always had the blessing of the Treasury.

Whatever satisfaction Topham may have felt at the way things were going was, however, short-lived. The first problem was John Bell. Bell now had the 4,000 guineas he had realized from the sale of his third share in the *World,* plus "above 500*l.*," out of which the "rascal" had "cheated" Walpole,[37] and he was quietly making plans for a rival newspaper, as Topham must have realized. But meanwhile, on 13 February, 1789, his friend, Peter Stuart, having quarreled with the other proprietors of the original *Star,* set up a spurious *Star,* which was dedicated to the interests of the Prince of Wales; and, although Bell did not print this paper, he acquired a great deal of influence over it. He may even have been an early proprietor, for, from 13 February through 9 March, the spurious *Star* carried advertisements for the British Library, and it also accorded Bell special textual consideration. For example, although it conformed with the usual newspaper practice of relegating births and deaths to an inconspicuous column on the last page, it presented as a news item, set off by margins and special type, the information: "Yesterday morning [2 Mar.] died at Writtle, in Essex, Miss BELL, only child of Mr. BELL of the British Library, Strand." More important, however, it published in his behalf a long essay, entitled "WORKS OF ART AND OF LITERATURE COMBINED," the point of departure being the two-volume *Poetry of the World,* which he and Topham had brought out the previous year. The essay appeared in the spurious *Star* of 16 February, 1789:

> The productions of DELLA CRUSCA and ANNA MATILDA, which have displayed the charms of Fancy, and the true spirit of Poetry, in the most bewitching colours, have also been the means of attracting superlative praise, by an evident improvement in the ART of PRINTING. The admirers of typographical excellence, have considered these elegant volumes as the *ne plus ultra* of perfection; but the world should be told, that the Art of Printing has evidently not yet attained, in this country, the glory of pre-eminence.
>
> Many courts in Europe are now contending for the honours of the Press; whilst the Printers in England, for nearly a century past, have been carelessly sacrificing their reputations to the sordid consequences of dispatch. However, to his credit be it spoken, Mr. BELL is now endeavouring to awaken emulation in the Arts, and has given a recent proof of his laudable pretensions to support and encouragement. The classical arrangement of Fugitive Poetry, may be fairly offered as an instance in support of this opinion; for surely a more chaste and beautiful specimen of Poetry and Printing never has been seen.
>
> DIDOT has long reigned the Prince of Printers in France, and unequalled throughout Europe; but England may hope, from the efforts of Mr. BELL, soon to dispute, and even bear away the laurels.

Another long paragraph followed to the same effect. This kind of essay appeared in all newspapers with which Bell was involved, but, although Bell still "[retained] the privilege of writing what [he] chose" in the *World (Oracle,* 1 June, 1789), this particular essay did not appear in that newspaper for the reason that he was under a £1,000 bond to refrain from injuring Topham's property and the essay was not what it purported to be. The essay was not intended to extol the *Poetry of the World*, for, although Topham had edited the work, his name was not mentioned, and neither was "Arley's," although "Arley's" name had appeared even in the title. The essay was also not intended merely to extol Bell's printing, for it meticulously included in the scope of its praise "DELLA CRUSCA" and "ANNA MATILDA." Topham could not have escaped the conclusion that, when Bell left the *World*, he expected to take Robert Merry and Mrs. Cowley with him. Thus alerted, he was able to frustrate this expectation, but he could expect further trouble from the spurious *Star*, for, in addition to Bell, that newspaper had among its proprietors the elder George Colman, who was still reluctantly paying Topham £300 a year "for Theatricals." In March the spurious *Star* added to its board of directors another of Topham's ill-wishers, Sheridan.

By the end of February, 1789, the tumult over the Regency Bill was at its height. But, while the English Parliament dallied, the Irish Parliament not only passed the bill, but on 26 February sent a committee to the Prince of Wales to invite him to assume the Government of Ireland independently. The Opposition newspapers were delighted, the Ministerial newspapers dismayed, and there was some noisy exchange. The spurious *Star*, being an evening newspaper, was properly concerned only with the other evening newspaper, the genuine *Star*, but it nevertheless took advantage of the situation to remark (5 Mar., 1789) that the "illiberal and unmanly *balderdash* of a *Renegade* CAPTAIN, and a *prating* PRIEST against the HIBERNIAN COMMISSIONERS—the MAJESTY of IRELAND—has induced many of her sons to the determination of giving them the most public marks of their *detestation*, the first time they are seen at the Theatre." By this time Topham had sold his commission in the Horse Guards. The *World* was also, of course, constantly beset by the *Morning Post*, the *Post* threatening exposés, which were invariably deferred on the ground that the threats were effective enough in themselves. "The *quaint nonsense* of a certain *Reverend slanderer*, like the cloven-foot of SATAN will always betray him," the *Post* observed typically on 6 March. "That this paper should be the object of his impudent scurrility is not surprising, since it was this paper that first pulled *off his mask*, and therefore made his FEAR operate as a restraint upon his MALIGNITY. . . ."

The King's recovery, officially announced on 10 March, 1789, brought an end to the present Regency Bill, but to nothing else. For, since his recovery was incomplete and conditional, supposedly depending on a long rest and freedom from responsibilities, there was now the matter of an interim regency. There was also the matter of the next general elections, which were assumed to be imminent. But, inasmuch as the issue in those elections would be the conduct of the Pitt Government (and hence by indirection the conduct of the Opposition) during the King's illness, the matters were inseparable. The result was that the announcement was only an incentive to increased journalistic violence. By way of preparing for what was ahead, Sheridan arranged for a subsidy of the spurious *Star,* with the understanding that the paper would first be strengthened by "communications" from the "ingenious and intelligent of every denomination" (spurious *Star,* 24 Mar., 1789) and then brought out as a morning newspaper. The spurious *Star* reacted to these arrangements by declaring war on the *World,* which it described (21 Mar.) as "a *coarse, desperate* PA-PER." "We perfectly coincide in opinion . . . ," it added editorially, "that Captain DASH and his man the CURATE, ought not escape with impunity. They who condemn, according to interest or caprice, many worthy members of society, should certainly suffer the lash of criticism. Their diurnal Conundrum contains so much illiberality against the IRISH NATION, that we are astonished the lusty SONS of HIBERNIA have not given them a gentle application of their SHILELAH."

Two of the "lusty SONS" had already come forward in answer to the appeal of 5 March. For on 19 March the spurious *Star* had included among its notes "TO CORRESPONDENTS" the items: "Account of a spirited young Nobleman's forcing the most redoubted HERO of the WORLD to swallow a CAT, is rather TOO ROUGH for our DIGESTION. It shall, however, be preserved and may serve to SCRATCH the DELINQUENT at a fit opportunity./ POETICAL DIALOGUE between CAPTAIN TOPHAM and PARSON ESTE, is received." The "Account" was permanently withheld, but the "POETICAL DIALOGUE" appeared on 23 March, entitled *"The* CAPTAIN *and the* CURATE./ AN OCCI-DENTAL ECLOGUE,/ TRANSLATED FROM THE CHERO-KEE." The poem was in the main only generally abusive, but it is evident from the following passage that Topham had had some unpleasant experiences on Este's account:

CAPTAIN.—I too, by wearing once the King's cockade,
Speak in the Ton—ah! ah!—to pick up trade.
Tho' now the brave shun me as [Rose]'s pander,
And say, BLUFF deals in nought but fibs and slander.
CURATE.—Oft am I sorry for the words you eat.
CAP.—What! from O'–N? I'd have else been beat.
CUR.—I don't mean those—I mean from B–YM–RE.
CAP.—Ah, ah, ah, ah!—His Lordship threatened sore,
Because I said, in jest—ah, ah! he'd strive
To eat a cat—ah, ah! a cat alive,
His Lordship's horsewhip—ah!—did so prevail—
CUR.—He made you swallow PUSS, both head and tail!
CAP.—Ah, ah!—I think—ah, ah!—that these disorders—
CUR.—May be prevented by your taking Orders:
Your sacred function, then, will check all blows—
CAP.—True—ah, ah!—then none dare to touch my NOSE.
CUR.—See, how I stalk, protected by my cloth.

"O'–N" was Dennis O'Bryen, who had vigorously supported the Prince's right to succeed his father without an intervening act of Parliament. "B–YM–RE" was the Prince's intimate, Richard, Earl of Barrymore, Viscount Buttevant, and Baron Barry of Ireland, who was noted for rowdyism of various sorts. For the next several weeks the spurious *Star* had too many problems of its own to concern itself at any length with the *World,* although on 21 March it indicated that it was doing some research on Topham's past, with special reference to a mysterious seduction in Edinburgh.

The *World* itself prepared for what was ahead by undertaking the support of Philip Withers. The possibility of a regency had inevitably revived interest in the Prince of Wales's marriage and hence in Horne Tooke's *Letter to a Friend, on the Reported Marriage of His Royal Highness the Prince of Wales* (1787), which had seemed to establish the fact that there had been a marriage. On 2 February, 1789, Philip Withers, who was "Chaplain to Lady Dowager Hereford" and had already published "several polemical Tracts of Divinity, a few Remarks on the Commerce and Civil Policy of [his] Country (in approbation of the conduct of Government), and prepared some criticism of Aristarchus," [38] was inspired by Tooke's *Letter* to try to publish a letter of his own, this one addressed to Mrs. Fitzherbert. The letter was entitled *Strictures in the Declaration of Horne Tooke, Esq.,* it was signed "ALFRED," and it informed Mrs. Fitzherbert that, since it was evident from Tooke's *Letter* that she was married, she would do better to admit the fact rather than to give the impression that she was a harlot and that she ought to admit it so that the matter could be acted on by Parliament, as it should have been long ago. According to Withers,[39] printed copies of the *Strictures* were delivered to James Ridgway, bookseller in York Street, on 2 January, but Ridgway declined to publish the work because of "interference by Carlton House," and he also refused to return the copies, since he had been told by Lord Sydney and others that the pamphlet constituted high treason, contending, as it did, that the Prince of Wales had married a Roman Catholic. The truth was, however, that Ridgway used the pamphlet for purposes of extortion and declined publication only after he had come to terms with Sheridan, who was then handling such matters for Mrs. Fitzherbert. For the diary of the Duchess of Devonshire records,[40] under date 2 January, 1789: "A hand bill was sent to Mrs. Fitzherbert telling her y$^t$ tomorrow 500 libels w$^d$ be published declaring the P had forfeited his right to the Crown by marrying her—Sheridan call'd here at 2 in his way to the Booksellers to suppress it"; and, under date 12 January, 1789: "Sheridan shew'd us to night the hand bill announcing the Libel ag$^{st}$ Mrs. Fitz—it is to be deliver'd in Sloane St Tomorrow. It is sad stuff."

The handbill of 12 January announced another pamphlet, entitled *History of the Royal Malady, with Variety of Entertaining Anecdotes, to Which Are Added Strictures in the Declaration of Horne Tooke, Esq. respecting "Her Royal Highness the Princess of Wales," Commonly Called (The Hon.) Mrs. Fitzherbert; With Interesting Remarks on a Regency: By a Page of the Presence.* No attempt was made to suppress this one, probably because Sheridan could not learn the name of the author, printer, or publisher. The author, who identified himself as a "senior Page of the Presence," whose "apartment" was "situated between the grand Anti-chamber, and the Closet of Private Audience," devoted much of the text to "anecdotes" of the King's behavior, many of which were obscene. But he also devoted much to Mrs. Fitzherbert, who, he said, was still brooding over the paragraph in the *Morning Post* of 10 December, 1788, stating that she had been offered £20,000 a year and "a ducal coronet" if she would retire to the Continent.[41] Although the abuse was directed at various members of the Royal Family and most leaders of the Opposition, no one was named, the King being designated, for example, as Henry IV of

France, the Prince of Wales as Prince Henry, Mrs. Fitzherbert as Lady Herbert, Fox as Falstaff, Burke as Edmund. But the letter to Mrs. Fitzherbert, which Ridgway had refused to publish and which was here included, was addressed "To Mrs. Fitzherbert," and on the fourth page of the pamphlet was the announcement: *"In a few Days will be Published,/* A Circumstantial Narrative of the violent and illegal Measures by which the Pamphlet was suppressed of which this is a literal Copy./ PHILIP WITHERS/ SLOAN SQUARE./ *Jan. 9th,* 1789."

The next pamphlet was accordingly entitled *Alfred, or a Narrative of the Daring and Illegal Measures to Suppress a Pamphlet, Intituled, Strictures in the Declaration of Horne Tooke Esq.,* and the preface was signed "PHILIP WITHERS/ SLOAN SQUARE./ *Jan. 19th,* 1789." This time Withers recounted his experience with Ridgway and explained that, "when Mr. Ridgway declined the sale" of the *Strictures,* "the Author was reduced to the alternative of publishing his own name, or of exposing honest men to the resentments of the [Whig] PARTY." In admitting authorship of the *Strictures,* Withers did "not deny" that his "supreme design" had been "to serve [his] country, by supporting Mr. PITT," nor did he deny that he had "written in Pitt's defense before, but never for money," and he insisted that one of the King's pages had been his "authority" for the "anecdotes" in the *History of the Royal Malady,* even though he himself had been the actual author of that work.[42] Otherwise the pamphlet was a vituperative treatise on the subject of Mrs. Fitzherbert, with the promise that *Another Letter from Alfred to the Prince of Wales* would appear shortly.

The *Letter . . . to the Prince of Wales* seems to have been abandoned in favor of *Nemesis, or a Letter to Alfred: From* —. Although this work was lacking the name of author, printer, publisher and even the date of publication, the preface was dated 13 February, 1789, and, since it dealt principally with the enormous sale of the *History* and *Alfred,* it was reasonable to suppose that Withers had at least published the work. The *Letter* itself concerned Mrs. Fitzherbert's intimacies with the Marquis de Bellois in Paris, who was supposedly trying to recover £2,000 he had lent her during the course of their intimacy and was holding her letters until the sum was repaid. Mrs. Fitzherbert was represented as having sent him £200 and he as refusing to surrender the letters until he received the full amount. Shortly after this pamphlet appeared, Mrs. Fitzherbert filed an information for libel against Philip Withers as publisher, and Withers was consigned to prison, where he remained until 28 February, 1789, when someone provided bail.[43]

While he was in prison, Withers busied himself with another pamphlet, entitled *Alfred to the Bishop of London,* which he probably published early in March, since the last postscript was dated 3 March, 1789. The burden of this one was that, in calling Mrs. Fitzherbert "either a WIFE or a WHORE" and more specifically "a CATHOLIC WHORE," Withers had been motivated by a sense of duty to Church and State. Although the pamphlet had something to say about the persecution Withers had suffered as a result, it seemed to regard Mrs. Fitzherbert's action as of less consequence than attacks which had been made on Withers by certain pamphleteers, the most recent one being "ALFRED UNMASKED; or the NEW CATALINE," of which "Mr. Sheridan, it is said, is the Author." [44] While Withers was penning his last postscript, Mrs. Fitzherbert sent word that she would drop the action provided he apologize. He replied that "an *Apology* was in the press" and a few days later sent her a copy of *Alfred to the Bishop of London.* Even then she indicated her willingness to forget the matter provided only that he denied being or knowing the author of *Nemesis.* Withers submitted no denial.[45]

Although Withers was a fanatic, there can be no doubt that he was abetted by the Treasury, which must have financed his publications, provided the bail to liberate him from prison, and guided his actions generally, for he had put the Opposition in a desperate position. To begin with, he had raised a question which the Opposition could not afford to discuss, for which reason it had moved for no ex officio action, despite the fact that every one of Withers' pamphlets had constituted a gross libel on some member of the Royal Family; and he was now seeing to it that the discussion would occur by refusing to allow Mrs. Fitzherbert to withdraw a private action which she had evidently filed impulsively and was now trying to drop at the behest of her advisers. The Opposition could console itself only with the fact that Withers had confined his activities to pamphlets. But even this consolation was short-lived, for, although Withers was not himself interested in newspapers, the Treasury was greatly interested in newspapers on his account. Hence, at the beginning of April, 1789, the *World* presented the Withers-Fitzherbert case to the newspaper-reading public, taking a firm stand on the side of Withers. Since the

Opposition could not defend Mrs. Fitzherbert, it retaliated with personal attacks on the personnel of the *World*, concentrating its abuse in the spurious *Star*.

On 11 April, 1789, the spurious *Star* accordingly addressed the following letter to

TOPHAM *and* ESTE.

*To the renowned Captain* TOPHAM, *and the Rev. Parson* ESTE, *Conductors of what* THEY *call, a* SUPERIOR *Print*.

*Par nobile fratrum!*

*Manly, delicate, and holy Sirs,*

As a consequence of your advertisement in the WORLD of this date, I beg the *particulars* of the *agreeable* and *accomplished* lady who wants a *friend* in a *single gentleman,* to take the *place* of *one* who, by *some means or other,* it seems is lately *dead;* if it is either of your sisters, cousins, nieces, or daughters, shall have no objection to an *engagement.*

You have *promised* an *immediate* answer from your *Office,* and it is therefore expected, by *Lyon's Inn,* No. 31                          A BACHELOR.

.    .    .    .    .    .    .    .    .    .    .    .    .    .    .    .

P.S. As you have opened an *Office* of this sort, shall apply *occasionally* for several of my *friends* who may be in *want* of such *assistance*—I have several *cast-off* mistresses, which, as damaged goods, you may advertise for your *Office* of *Accommodation.* I am glad to hear you have a *respectable* connection with *King's Place,* and that the refuse will be advertised for *exhibition* or *engagement* at your office, which is now more useful than either the *Magdalen* or *Locke* Hospitals.

Another two such letters followed on 14 April. The first one read:

MR. PTINER,

Though yours is one of the Low Prints, if you will recommend me to your friends, the *Captain* or the *Parson,* at the *Office* of that SUPERIOR Print, the *World,* as I think myself *qualified* to *answer* their late advertisement for an *engagement,* will be grateful, and glad to see you, as under, being as soon your's or their's, or any body's,

*King's Place.*                                                SALLY BLY.

The second letter, similar in content, was signed "BETT BLASSUM./ *Edge Lain, up tu pare of stares.*" The *World* said nothing further about Withers until the end of April, and until that time the spurious *Star* also said nothing further about the *World*.

But on 23 April, 1789, the spurious *Star* revealed a secret which the *World* had guarded for almost two years, namely, that "Della Crusca" was Robert Merry. The spurious *Star* made this revelation with the casual notice that an "Ode on the Restoration of His Majesty," which it had reprinted from another newspaper, was the work of "Mr. MERRY, Author of the DELLA CRUSCA POEMS." This information it had, of course, got from Bell, who was fortunately too remote from the editorial office of the *World* to know much more. For by this time Topham was having trouble with the Della Cruscans generally. According to Clifford,[46] the group had never been harmonious: "Merry and Greatheed refused to speak to each other," and "Parsons was always at odds with either one or the other." But Merry and Mrs. Cowley, at least, had remained attuned, carrying on their lovesick correspondence in the same old blissful vacuum, for, having never met, they had nothing to quarrel about. The meeting which disrupted their harmony seems to have occurred in early April, 1789, although the details are somewhat in doubt. Boaden, who probably had the story from Merry a year or two later, stated [47] that "the two parties became known personally by an accidental rencontre at an inn," and, since "Merry was an enthusiast in beauty as well as verse" and since "the proportion of the former to the latter in the lady was less than might be desired," he bid Mrs. Cowley "a rhapsodical farewell" and turned his thoughts to other matters. The "rhapsodical farewell" was supposedly "The Interview," which was supposedly followed by a few regrets on Mrs. Cowley's part and then silence. But Reynolds,[48] who was much better acquainted with Merry than Boaden ever was, "[could never] forget Merry's ecstatic feelings, on the day he discovered where his adored Anna Matilda was to be seen." Although, according to Reynolds, Merry subsequently tried to conceal the fact that his beloved was a "plain respectable matronly lady," the world soon discovered the truth, and the correspondence had to be discontinued. Reynolds's account seems to be accurate except in one particular, for the world did not discover the truth until November, so that the correspondence survived the meeting by seven months, although on a far less enthusiastic basis. But by this time "Della Crusca" had acquired a second "disciple" in Mrs. Mary Robinson, a discarded mistress of the Prince of Wales, who wrote under the pseudonyms "Laura" and "Laura Maria." [49]

## "DELENDA EST CARTHAGO"

ON 24 APRIL the *World* resumed its interest in the case of Philip Withers, and on 27 April the spurious *Star*, now making its debut as a morning newspaper, concluded its address "TO THE PUBLIC" with the promise: "We shall not war with the *dead* [i.e., with the proprietors of the original *Star*], but aim at more noble exploits, and endeavour to hold a competition with the INDUSTRIOUS and INTELLIGENT CONDUCTORS of the MORNING PRINTS." But it was evident even from this number that the only "MORNING PRINT" which it had in mind was the *World* and that it was thinking in terms of annihilation. The Opposition's plans for the spurious *Star* had always included a war with the *World*, not only because the *World* was the leading Treasury newspaper, but because the spurious *Star* represented three of Topham's personal enemies, Sheridan, Colman, and Bell. But the plans had evidently been revised, so that the war was no longer one of simple harassment, but one of total destruction, for the remainder of the paper was nothing but a collection of jeers. Since the spurious *Star* never dealt with issues when it could deal with personalities and since in any event it could not deal with the issue of the Prince's marriage, it directed its jeers at the personnel of the *World*, most of them at Topham. "The ensuing exhibition of the Royal Academy, will be abused by that stupid paper the *World*," it predicted, for example. "This prognostication is founded on two reasons.—Captain TOPHAM is totally ignorant of painting—and he was refused admission to the Anniversary Dinner of the Academicians, with marks of derision and contempt." But the paper also had something to say of "Della Crusca" and "Anna Matilda," whose verse it had previously (16 Febr., 1789) described as embodying "the charms of Fancy, and the true spirit of Poetry, in the most bewitching colours." In this case it resorted to parody:

DELLA CRUSCA sat on [*sic*] the World office, with ANNA MATILDA in his lap.—A better mode of sitting is impossible.—Their feelings were congenial, their strains reciprocal—and better congeniality and reciprocity are not extant.

The man in the great fur coat, who shews the outlandish beasts [evidently a zoo-keeper in the neighborhood of Beaufort Buildings], overheard some of their effusions, to this effect:

DELLA CRUSCA.
Sweet as the breath of balmy morn,
When DIAN's waning veil is worn,
And each mountain, as in scorn,
Glows with orient beams unborn,
Is the charm my burning bosom feels
To hear the rattling of the Royal wheels.
Topham, haste thee from below!
Quick thy tiny tin-ball throw!
With homage meet,
The pious Pilgrims greet,
And lay thy matchless world beneath their feet!

The Bard's voice here became so energetic, that it roused (such is the sympathy of sounds) the great African lion, whose growl put in motion the . . . wires of Mr. PRESTON's [Mr. Preston was a proprietor of the original *Star*] harpsichords. They "brayed horrible discord," and the cream-coloured horses of the Royal carriage were observed to shudder all over. ANNA MATILDA then responded thus:

BOREAS, from the Surry *Hills,*
I invoke thine icy puff!
Rapture through my breast so thrills,
'Twill scorch my midriff to a snuff!

The eclogue was here interrupted by an antiphone from Parson ESTE and Mrs. WELLS, which they chanted as well as they were able. . . .

The "antiphone" expressed, of course, their great relief at the King's recovery and hence the end of the Regency Bill.

This time the *World* refused to be silenced, for the general elections were expected at the end of the present session of Parliament, and the Government expected to win those elections on the basis of two issues: Mrs. Fitzherbert and Edmund Burke, one of which was almost as embarrassing to the Opposition as the other. Since the beginning of the year, the *World* had spared no effort to make Burke look as ridiculous as possible, and it had taken an especial delight in Burke's reaction to the ridicule and his inability to do anything about it, for Burke was afraid, it taunted, to sue on his own account, and he could not persuade the Commons to sue for him. It reminded its readers that in 1786 he had filed a private suit against the *Public Advertiser* and that, although the jury admitted that he had been gravely libeled, it valued his reputation at only £100, instead of the £5,000 at which he had rated it. The present value of his reputation, said the *World,* was considerably less. The possibility of an ex officio action the *World* regarded as too preposterous to consider, for even the Whigs, it said, would not be so foolish as to defend the proceedings against Hastings.

It looked very much as if the *World* was right, for not one of the Opposition newspapers had spoken up in Burke's behalf, and one or two of them had even suggested that Burke might be more of a liability to the Party than an asset. But on 27 April, 1789, Burke said something in his own behalf. In support of one of his charges against Hastings, he submitted a copy of the *"Morning Herald* of last year," which included a bill against Major Scott, still, said the *Herald,* unpaid, and he called particular attention to one item in the bill, which read, "attacking Mr. Burke's veracity, 5s. 6d." Scott promptly admitted that, from April, 1782, to December, 1783, he had, in fact, engaged the *Herald* to support the interests of the East India Company, but he insisted that he had paid the bill, and he implied that he had had nothing to do with any newspaper since. Although the incident ended in laughter, the spurious *Star* was emboldened to conclude its report (28 Apr., 1789) with an apology for Burke:

> There is so much unlike a gentleman in Capt. ATLAS's abuse of BURKE, that he was hissed by some men of fashion in coming out of [Westminster] hall. Mr. BURKE, although not faultless, and too full of flights of imagination, is a scholar and a man of great genius. He is as superior to the Horse-guards deserter, as [the Horse-guards deserter] is to one of his devils.
>
> Some Irish gentlemen intend to toss Captain ATLAS in a carpet, for his illiberal abuse of BURKE, that ornament to his country.
>
> Captain TOPHAM, by the law of Scotland, was actually married to Miss AITKEN, sister to JOHN the PAINTER. No wonder, therefore, the Captain is so fond of blowing up private characters.

The last paragraph was another reference to the Edinburgh seduction.

On 29 April the *World,* which had meanwhile indicated increasing anxiety for the plight of Philip Withers, announced that it was driven by considerations of justice and simple humanity to publish all the correspondence between Withers and Horne Tooke; and it was evident from the first installment, therewith included, that the correspondence was lengthy and that its subject was the marriage of Mrs. Fitzherbert and the Prince of Wales. In the first letter Withers maintained that he had said no more in his pamphlets than Mr. Tooke had said in his *Letter to a Friend,* that Mrs. Fitzherbert was afraid to sue Tooke, that he himself had relied for his information upon

Tooke's statements, that Tooke was therefore responsible for his predicament, and that it was consequently Tooke's duty to produce the proof. What Withers wanted specifically was the name of the clergyman who officiated, the names of the witnesses, the date and place of the ceremony, and any other data respecting the marriage which Tooke was able to provide.

None of the newspapers was prepared for this particular tactic, and, in fact, none of them quite understood it. For not only had Withers shown no previous concern, but, since Mrs. Fitzherbert was suing because she had been accused of an intimacy with the Count de Bellois, the proof that she was married to the Prince of Wales was, to say the least, irrelevant. The *Morning Post* responded (30 Apr.) with the equally irrelevant explanation that Withers was "Uncle to the Reverend Mr. Este, one of the Conductors of the World." The spurious *Star* was flippant. Topham, it said, "meant to set *dull* TOOKE and *mad* WITHERS by the ears—TOOKE swears that the marriage was incog. on the PEAK of TENERIFFE—they went in an open boat from BRIGHTON one evening to tea, and returned to supper." But the correspondence nevertheless continued to appear throughout May and well into June, Withers' letters consisting of appeals for proof of the marriage, Tooke's letters consisting of evasions and half-promises.

Since the spurious *Star* could offer no apology for Mrs. Fitzherbert, it retaliated with further ridicule of the personnel of the *World*. On 30 April it published what purported to be a letter of instructions *"From* MAJOR SCOTT *to* NED TOPHAM":

DEAR NED,

Abuse BURKE, ridicule GREY, and lengthen the oratory of Sir JAMES ERSKINE. Mr. H[ASTINGS] says, that your wit is without point, and your humour without laugh. But never mind that, while I have HIM at a *dead lock!*—let you and I laugh—*who wins!*

I know . . . that you do not stick at *trifles* in your *designs*—the failure is only in your EXECUTION [another reference to "John the Painter"]!

But that may be *amended,* for every DOG will have his day, as [John] MURRAY, my Bookseller [and a proprietor of the original *Star*] says,—who, by the bye, was once swabber in a man of war. . . .

They say that you are brother-in-law to JOHN *the* PAINTER. . . .

Does BECKY [WELLS] still *soap your nose?*

Yours,

J. S.

P.S. BARRYMORE the Lord, swore by the Lord, that it slipt through his fingers. That was, as it should be.

This letter was followed by a letter from "NED TOPHAM *to* MAJOR SCOTT," written in the same vein. On 1 May the spurious *Star* presented another of its imitations, this one an account of the Royal Procession in the style of Topham, which it signed "WHISKERANDOS," and it again referred to the "strange story going about town respecting JOHN the PAINTER," who was now supposed to have been "driven" "up the hill" by Topham "after he had set fire to the dock yard." By this time the spurious *Star* had also discovered Mrs. Wells's intimacy with Reynolds, of which it promised more details later. It concluded its remarks with the announcement: *"We are proud to acknowledge the receipt of a* POEM *from the charming pen of* DELLA CRUSCA. *The* WORLD *must now be at an end, when the Prince of Lyrics plucks himself away, to brighten the radiance of the* MORNING STAR. *His inimitable* ODE *shall appear to-morrow, or next day at farthest."* An "ODE TO THE MORNING STAR," supposedly written by "DELLA CRUSCA," did appear on 4 May. It began with the announcement that Merry had left the *World* forever:

> . . . . O mighty MORNING STAR!
> The WORLD, and all its works, be damn'd!
> Like a good Christian, I renounce them;
> Its paltry pages, nonsense cramm'd,
> I with the Hangman's torch may trounce them!

The announcement was followed by a volley of ridicule of Topham, Mrs. Wells, "John the Painter," and even "Della Crusca" himself; and the "Ode" was in turn followed by an enraptured comment by the spurious *Star*, which concluded with the opinion that the *"defection"* of "DELLA CRUSCA" *from the* WORLD *to the* MORNING STAR, *is the highest compliment we have yet received."* More such burlesques were to come, for elsewhere in the paper was the announcement: *"As we had reason to hope, the charming* ANNA MATILDA *has followed her beloved* DELLA CRUSCA. *Her admirable* Ode on May-Day, *with the delectable* Episode *of the* Dancing Chimney-Sweeps, *shall have the earliest preference."*

Except for some derogatory remarks about Major Scott, which appeared on 7 May, the spurious *Star* said nothing further about the *World's* affairs until 11 May; and, on the morning of Saturday, 9 May, Bell was informed by Miles Peter Andrews and Edward Wilsonn that the printing materials for the *World* were to be removed from his shop that afternoon. He was supposedly dumbfounded: "I never had the least knowledge, directly or indirectly, of any such intention." He, of course, demanded to see Topham, but Topham refused to see him, and he was therefore compelled to deal with Andrews and Wilsonn, who stated only that Topham intended to print the paper himself the following day, that he was "ready to take [the] printing Materials at a fair valuation," although he did not need them, having procured his own from the Caslon Foundry, and that he recognized Bell's right to begin his own newspaper. Bell replied that he would not require Topham to purchase the materials and that he would permit him to print the paper in his shop until it was convenient to move it. Topham accepted these favors and on the same day gave a dinner for Bell's workmen in order to invite them "into his service," not knowing that it "is a rule of law in the Trade, that no Printer shall leave his employer without giving a fortnight's notice." Despite this act of perfidy, Bell "suffered [his] men to serve [Topham], and actually assisted him by the loan of many articles," for which he "never had even his Thanks." This was Bell's account of the affair, as it appeared in the *Oracle* of 1 June, 1789. Topham left no account.

Bell's account was accurate to the extent that Bell was surprised by the announcement, that he succeeded in delaying the removal of the printing a fortnight, and that Topham was represented throughout by Andrews and Wilsonn. But Bell was surprised only because he had intended to quit Topham before Topham quit him. He had been planning his own newspaper since at least February, and, by the end of April, the plan had evidently been expanded to include a coup, for on 29 April the spurious *Star* announced in his behalf: "Captain TOP-HAM, knowing that the *sale* of the *World* has *rapidly decreased* since his *ungentlemanly* conduct *obliged* BELL to *sell out,* is now running about every where—*where he is admitted,* puffing this *absurd print,* which has no other recommendation than *impudence,* and BELL *singularity.*" The public would have been astonished to hear that Bell had had anything "to *sell out.*" So far as it knew, he had been only a publisher of the *World,* and, since his name was dropped from the colophon on 16 January, 1787, it would have supposed that he had not even published the paper since that time. This was, of course, what Bell had wanted the public to believe; but now the situation was altered, for his quitting the *World* to begin a newspaper of his own might lead to a quarrel between him and Topham, which had to be prepared for in advance. That he had still not begun the paper by 9 May was owing in part to the fact that he was lacking a staff, although he may also have been looking for another Topham to finance the enterprise.

The anecdote about the clandestine dinner can be disregarded altogether, for it assumes that Topham had overlooked the matter of a printer until the paper was ready to go to press. Yet the printer of an eighteenth-century newspaper was one of the two most important members of the staff, not only because he was in a position to sabotage the work of the editor, but because the entire staff had to depend on him to accept responsibility for whatever the newspaper printed. The selection of Robert Bostock to replace Bell's Buchanan Millan had certainly, therefore, been made with care and arrangements completed well in advance; and, since there is no indication that Bostock was a previous employee of Bell, Bell probably demanded the fortnight's notice in behalf of Millan, who was the printer Topham was technically dismissing.

So long as Bell was connected with the *World,* he was under a £1,000 bond to refrain from injuring it, but the bond did not prevent his being active in other areas. Hence on Sunday, 10 May, 1789, he distributed copies of a handbill announcing that he would bring out a new newspaper on 1 June. The text of the handbill (for which see *Oracle,* 1 June, 1789), now somewhat altered, appeared as a box advertisement in the spurious *Star* of the following day:

A NEW NEWSPAPER.

J. BELL, of the BRITISH LIBRARY, *Strand,* RESPECTFULLY informs the Public, that he is no longer interested, directly or indirectly, in the Newspaper which he originally instituted and established under the title of
THE WORLD,
as even the printing thereof has been rashly and unhandsomely withdrawn from him by Captain TOPHAM.—J. BELL is at present a free, and, he hopes, an irreproachable agent; he therefore means to submit
A NEW DAILY PAPER
to the patronage of the Public.
The time and Title will be announced shortly.
His plan will be novel, interesting, and useful.
If long experience—extensive literary connections—the most immediate and unbounded sources of intelligence, and a proper style of communication, can warrant a hope of attraction—all these qualifications the publisher has to

offer in his favour. Every exertion shall be made to gratify public taste, and completely to answer the best purposes of a Daily Print.

It may not be in our power to command success,

But we will do more—WE WILL DESERVE IT.

On the same day (11 May) the spurious *Star* resumed its abuse of the *World* with the pronouncement: "If any thing can add to the CON-DEMNATION of HASTING's character, it was fully *exemplified* on Thursday. The CULPRIT came to the bar, ARM IN ARM with JOHN the PAINTER's *brother-in-law*, Captain TOPHAM.—God *send* them a *good deliverance!*" On the same day, too, the *World* altered its colophon from "Printed by B. MILLAN, and Sold at the Corner of Exeter 'Change, Strand," to "Printed by B. MILLAN, and Sold at No. 335, Strand, Opposite Somerset-house."

On 12 May the spurious *Star* printed a long poem with the head-note: "ANNA MATILDA./ It were superfluous to introduce the following delightful poetic composition with an encomiastic preface. We cannot forbear, however, congratulating the public and ourselves, on the acquisition THE MORNING STAR receives by the correspondence of this Lady and her beloved DELLA CRUSCA; between whom, we hope, many replies and rejoinders will pass, for the entertainment and admiration of our Readers." Although the poem was entitled "TO DELLA CRUSCA," it was mainly a condemnation of Topham for his treatment of Bell, with incidental gibes at Este and Mrs. Wells. On the same day, not on 11 May, as Bell indicated (*Oracle*, 1 June, 1789), the *World* notified its readers of a forthcoming consolidation of offices:

### TO THE PUBLIC.

*The* GREAT INCREASE *of the* Commercial Business *of this* Paper, *has of late made it* inconvenient *to have the* Advertising Office *and the* Printing and Publishing Offices *detached. On these accounts, for the* accommodation *of the* Public, *the following arrangements have taken place:*

*The* GREAT WHITE HOUSE, *No. 335, opposite Somerset-house in the Strand, is now the* WORLD *office.*

*Till* Monday next, Advertisements *will be received at the* Old Office, *the Corner of Exeter Change; and all Orders and Letters may be sent there till that day.*

*After that day, the* GREAT NEW HOUSE *before mentioned, which will then be the only Office, will alone receive Advertisements, etc.*

*The* WORLD *of this day, is printed, as its Readers will see, on an entire*

*New Letter. The beauty of it has to boast Mr. CASLON as its Founder. It has been some months preparing with the utmost care.*

On 13 May Bell moved the advertisements for the British Library from the *World* to the spurious *Star*, which was now busily censuring "that despicable creature, Captain TOPHAM, and that irreverend scandal-monger, Parson ESTE," for "dastardly paragraphing [the Prince of Wales's friend] Lord MALMESBURY"; and on 14 May the *World* commented on Bell's handbill:

An Hand-Bill having been distributed through the Town, with the name of J. BELL at the bottom of it, in which were these words—"That the Printing of this Paper has been *unhandsomely* withdrawn from him by CAPTAIN TOPHAM;"—we can . . . say, that the express conditions of the legal agreement were complied with, by which CAPTAIN TOPHAM had a right to order the Printing of his Paper to be where he chose, and to be taken when he chose, away.

That such was the agreement, signed by each Party, when CAPTAIN TOPHAM paid the said J. BELL the sum of Four Thousand Pounds, for the share *given* by Him in the first instance to the above J. BELL, in the origin of the Paper.

And we for ourselves say, that on the part of CAPTAIN TOPHAM, we made, as the legal agreement specified, a tender of purchasing the Letter, Presses, and Materials formerly used in the Printing of this Paper, with which offer Mr. BELL declared he was satisfied, but declined accepting it.

We have further to add, that we have not, nor never had, any interest or concern whatever in this Paper.

MILES PETER ANDREWS,
CHARLES EDW. WILSONN.

*London, May* 13, 1789.

The PROPRIETOR of THIS PAPER would have held the above in his own mind perfectly needless; but as some people, from want of due information, might judge wrong, it was held proper to publish it. In removing *his* PROPERTY to *his own Premises,* he intended to take care of it: if he has been mistaken, he alone is to blame.

The spurious *Star* responded (15 May, 1789) with some abuse of Andrews. Andrews, who owned the huge powder magazine at Dartford, was also a playwright, his comic opera, *The Baron Kinkvervankots-dorsprakingatchdern,* having been performed at Colman's Haymarket on 9 July, 1781, and damned by the audience, supposedly because of its vulgarity.[50] As to the author of this piece of abuse, it may be worth noting that the figure upon which the first letter is based was used by the younger Colman in a similar context later. Not only was Andrews, he said,[51] "a pest," but he "was in truth so wretched a writer, that his new plays in London, like his powder-mills at Dartford, were particularly hazardous affairs, and in great danger of going off with a sudden and violent explosion":

DOODLE *and* NOODLE.

DOODLE.

*From* CAPTAIN TOPHAM *to* MILES PETER ANDREWS.

DEAR NOODLE,

You know that by *blowing up* MINISTRY, through my *bore,* in the WORLD, *You* obtained a good GUN-POWDER *contract.*

Besides, you likewise know that I was not backward in admitting *your own* PUFFS upon your own ARLEY. Will you sign your name to the inclosed CRACKER [a lie, as well as a kind of fireworks: a reference to Andrews's and Wilsonn's statement in the *World* of the preceding day]?—Deny our *worldly* connexion. —This will be delivered to you, by a *chubby child* in a *muslin frock.*

I have looked the parish books [*sic*] for her age, and I am happy to hint, that she will be *fourteen* next MIDSUMMER, that very day on which your Play of the BARON was damned, and your POWDER-MILL *blown up!*

E. T.

*The Answer.*

NOODLE.

*Dearest* DOODLE,

I'll do as you desire—but why touch upon any other subject than the MESSENGER? which, by the bye, I hope you have not touched.

Are you sure she is no OLDER?

M. P. A.

Andrews was again the target in the spurious *Star* of 16 May:

ARLEY.

As one sheep followeth another, the inimitable Poets of the WORLD have leapt in a string to the MORNING STAR. ARLEY, though last not least, we are proud to announce. Of his friends DELLA CRUSCA and ANNA MATILDA, we are already secure, and we safely defy the WORLD to produce such a TRIO.

Ye nymphs of *Catherine-street,* begin the song;

This weary WORLD, . . . soon must *fall.*

BECK, NED, and ESTE, I see are in the wrong—

The DEVIL and DOCTOR LEAKE may take them all!

O charming Mrs. WELLS!
   Still, spite of TOPHAM's puffs so slender,
Thy cheeks are ruddier far than lobster shells,
   And soft as butter is thy beef so tender.

I hate things fat      ⎫
Thick and squat,       ⎬
Like DELLA CRUSCA and his cat! ⎭
He and his ANNA MATILDA clapt together

May melt away, like lard in sunny weather;
While I, among the rural rills,        ⎫
And little, mighty, monstrous hills,   ⎬
Improve my *poetry* and *powder-mills.* ⎭

I jump and caper like a top,
   To recollect that night of *damn'd* despair,
When both at once blew up,
   And left me like a forked radish bare.
My bold German BARON,
The critics made war on;
   While inflammation seiz'd my smutty bags,
   And rent the MILLS to rags.

Yet still to me remains,
Secur'd by patent, the unrivall'd skill,
To grind and mingle, as I will,
   Gun-powder grains,
   And eke poetic strains!

                                             ARLEY.

Since the spurious *Star* had now wreaked its revenge on Andrews for his statement in the *World* of 12 May, it was free to return to other members of the staff. The paper of 18 May, therefore, included a column-long letter from "ANNA MATILDA," who charged that she had been "seduced" into writing for the *World* by her "passion for that fine little *merry* fellow DELLA CRUSCA," whose poetry she thereupon ridiculed at length. The editorial comment on this letter was another reference to the seduction in Edinburgh. By 22 May the spurious *Star* had readied one more of its burlesques:

## DELLA CRUSCA.

We have anxiously expected to hear from this matchless LYRICIST; and the public we hope will join with us in rejoicing at his safe return to the earth.

But as he is still in an awkward situation, and moreover has promised some account of his celestial adventures, our curiosity still remains upon the stretch without abatement. The following ODE can only be considered as the first effusion of his fancy, crammed and running over with a surfeit of novel ideas.

---

### ARGUMENT.

The Bard abuseth Capt. TOPHAM, and sheweth the cause—describeth a new SIGN in the *Zodiac*—speaketh of Mr. PITT and the Rev. Mr. ESTE—invoketh ANNA MATILDA—and depicteth his descent to the earth.

Although the "Ode" was very long, it had nothing to add to what had been said many, many times before.

At this point Topham fled to his villa in Suffolk, turning over the conduct even of the drama department to Este. In April Reynolds had marveled [52] that Topham had only to "commend" his play, *The Dramatist,* and Thomas Harris accepted it, and he had only to remark that Mrs. Wells might like it for her benefit, and Harris reserved it for her benefit. But, although Reynolds' *The Dramatist* was, in fact, performed at Covent Garden on 15 May, 1789, as a benefit for Mrs. Wells, Reynolds failed to notice that this time Harris had not yielded to "commendation" alone, for behind the "commendation" was a series of abusive paragraphs, which persisted until the play was actually produced. Topham was no longer "almost the manager's manager" of theaters because the *World* was no longer the authority on elegance. The spurious *Star's* war on the *World* had been quite different in kind from the *Herald's* war on the *Morning Post* of 1780–1781. For, whereas the *Herald* had set out to ruin the proprietors of the *Post* by ruining the *Post,* the spurious *Star* had set out to ruin the *World* by ruining everyone connected with the *World.* Hence, whereas the *Herald* had dealt in general abuse having to do with the circulation and conduct of the newspaper, the spurious *Star* had dealt entirely in "personalities," and, since it had made no specific charges against any of the persons it had attacked, relying solely on the persuasiveness of ridicule and derision, no defense was possible. Moreover, whereas the *Morning Post* was something other than its proprietors, the *World* was in a real sense Topham, Este, Mrs. Wells, Andrews, Merry, and Mrs. Cowley. If these people were not themselves "virtuous" and "talented," then the *World's* judgment as to what constituted "virtue" and "talent" was farcical, and it is evident from Topham's flight that he, at least, was now regarded as neither.

Topham remained in exile until the following year, and, during the summer of 1789, his villa "near Clare, in Suffolk," afforded a haven for Andrews, Merry, and on occasion Reynolds as well.[53] Mrs. Wells stayed in London to help Este with the *World,* and on 23 May the spurious *Star* inquired: "What thought you of BECKY WELLS's industry yesterday, in taking one of Topham's *shirts* to ripple in WESTMINSTER-HALL?" The question was answered at indignant length by someone who signed himself "DECENCY" and promised that, if Mrs. Wells "displays her *work-bag* in the Hall, on Wednesday next, she will be taken into custody, not by his Grace of QUEENSBURY or Lord SANDWICH, but by the HIGH CONSTABLE." "DECENCY's" letter was published on Monday, 25 May, 1789, and on the same day Este removed the printing of the *World* from Bell's shop to the "GREAT WHITE HOUSE" at No. 335, Strand. Since the move was made without editorial notice, it was indicated only by the altered colophon, which substituted the name of "R. BOSTOCK" for that of "B. MILLAN." Buchanan Millan subsequently became the first printer of the *Oracle;* Robert Bostock was the last printer of the *World,* as the "GREAT WHITE HOUSE" was its last home. The spurious *Star's* comment on the move consisted of some verses and of the following letter, which was published on 27 May:

*From Captain* TOPHAM *to Parson* ESTE.

DEAR PARSON,

One thing shocks me much respecting my new house.

Do you know that I saw last night the GHOST of the NOON GAZETTE, which expired years since within these walls. Can you afford consolation?

E. T.

*The* ANSWER.

DEAR NED,

I'll offer up prayers every night to cast out the hated phantom. . . .

C. E.

The *Noon Gazette,* which was absorbed by the *London Courant* on 21 January, 1782, had given as its address only "Near Catherine-street, Strand"; but the house may have been unnumbered at that time, and the fact that No. 335, Strand was "Near Catherine-street" is indicated by "Arley's" invocation (spurious *Star,* 16 May, 1789) , "Ye nymphs of *Catherine-street.*"

The spurious *Star* kept a close watch on Mrs. Wells's activities, and, since it had nothing new to report, it made the most of what it had. On 26 May it dropped to a new level of coarseness with some verses which it attributed to "ANNA MATILDA" and addressed to "DELLA CRUSCA." The following passage is typical:

> Hast thou not heard how BECKY WELLS,
>   Whose fame the *World* so frequent tells,
> Went to the Hall to hear BURKE's speeches,
> And took with her a pair of TOPHAM's breeches,
>   Made of Buck-skin,
>   Greas'd without, and soil'd within;
> There to the view of many a blushing maid,
> Her sampler sweet display'd,
> And while the vulgar with amazement stared,
> Each tag and rag with cunning hand repair'd?
>
> Now what she did for him, I'll do for thee,
> Thou God of my idolatry!
> Each tatter I will stick so smooth and even,
>   Each seam I'll draw so close, and bite so toughly,
> I will not suffer the rude winds of Heav'n
> To visit thy poetic bum too roughly.

But Mrs. Wells continued her sewing with no evident concern, and on 30 May the spurious *Star* observed almost with resignation: "Mrs. WELLS summers it in Westminster-hall, *mending,* on the Woolsack, in the character of *Britannia."*

Bell finally brought out his own newspaper on 1 June, 1789. Although he had been obliged to finance it himself, he obviously hoped to recover his money during the elections, now expected to begin within a few weeks. The paper was "Printed by B. MILLAN, and Sold at Bell's British Library, in the Strand," and its title, the *Oracle, or Bell's New World,* indicated that it was intended to be an imitation of the old *World.* But it had none of the old *World's* elegance in either appearance or content, and it was evident from the address "TO THE PUBLIC" that it was also lacking a staff and a political sponsor:

The practice of Newspaper Editors is to commence their career with professions of Principles, and with plans of Propriety, to which, from observation, it will be found out that they but seldom adhere.—THE ORACLE means to be an exception to this general rule:—nothing shall be promised, either with respect to Principle or Propriety;—but experience in the present concern shall prove the test of truth—Neither Liberality to encourage Genius and Information—neither Candour, Secrecy, nor Assiduity shall be found wanting by those who are pleased to sanction this Paper.—Ye MORALISTS, ye POETS, HISTORIANS, PHILOSOPHERS, and POLITICIANS! Ye ARTISTS and MEN of COMMERCE, send therefore your Communications hither—APOLLO is the Standard, and he directeth THE ORACLE OF TRUTH!

In short, Bell could not say what "Principles" "THE ORACLE OF TRUTH" would represent until he heard from some "POLITICIANS." The "POLITICIANS" he preferred to hear from were obviously the Ministers, for several paragraphs in the paper were intended for the eye of the Secretary of the Treasury, George Rose:

THE KING'S Health and Spirits improve daily, and therefore the Nation has every probable hope of enjoying his happy government for many years to come.

Nothing can be a more convincing proof of the merits of the present Administration, than the flourishing state of the Funds. . . .

The introducing an *unauthorised* advertisement to the Public, by the *Conductor* of the *World,* is an additional proof of the great care necessary in the management of a Paper, and at the same time shews the influence of *Daily Prints.* For in the late instance, the FRENCH AMBASSADOR'S GALA, given to THE QUEEN in honour of HIS MAJESTY'S recovery, was completely deranged [i.e., misreported] by the *inattention* of an individual.

The last paragraph was meant to suggest that perhaps Topham was not the proper person to be managing a Treasury newspaper. Further than this, Bell was unable to go, for the conductor of a would-be Treasury print did not assail the conductor of an established Treasury print. Most of the newspaper was taken up with a recital of Bell's grievances against Topham, Wilsonn, and Andrews, but the recital was cautiously restricted to the "rashness" and "unhandsomeness" of their conduct to him; and, even so, much of it was presented apologetically. Since under the circumstances the *Oracle* could not belabor Topham or the *World,* the real abuse had to come from the spurious *Star,* and so it did.

On 2 June, 1789, the spurious *Star* introduced a daily column of coarse anecdotes, relating mainly to Topham, and it resumed its interest in Mrs. Wells:

### *From* BECKY WELLS *to* CAPTAIN TOPHAM.

NEDDY,

By the living *Jingo,* if you don't couple me in my summer tour, where I am to be *hawked* about with REYNOLDS, I'll play *hell.* Dare you, ye dog, say no.

### ANSWER.

*My dearest Beck,*

You know I am your slave. I have sent you ENTICK's dictionary; and as you are in fact EDITOR of the paper, write what you please.

Send me *my* NEXT PUFF about yourself.

Mrs. Wells was again mentioned on 4 June: "BECKY WELLS, with her new *enamorate* REYNOLDS, attended Sadler's Wells on Saturday last. BECKY went alone, to prevent the jealousy of the Captain. She was met there by REYNOLDS, who was keeping a place for her. They retired together, like CHARLOTTE and WERTER, to enjoy 'The first intercourse 'tween soul and soul.'" The first English translation of Goethe's story of Werther's love for his friend's wife had appeared in 1779 and had been adapted for the stage by Reynolds in 1785, having its first performance in Bath. On 5 June the spurious *Star* implied that Este had been promised a *"living"* by George Rose and that he ought to have "a MITRE"; and it added some verses *"On the* EDITOR *of the* WORLD, *announcing to the Public his Removal from* THE LITTLE OLD OFFICE, *to the* GREAT WHITE HOUSE." On 12 June it observed that "Mrs. WELLS still attends at the trial of Mr. HASTINGS, but not with her *needle.* Mother WINDSOR, with her *tits* [i.e., harlots], has not yet procured admission." On 13 June it announced:

TOPHAM—the *Ministerial Scavenger*—has taken so much liberty with the *side curls* of the DUKE of YORK, that several *drill* SERJEANTS have threatened to give him a *dressing.*

BECKY WELLS, *Mother* JOHNSON and several LADIES of *King's Place,* have promised this summer to visit *Margate.* It is thought *Capt.* TOPHAM, *Capt.* HUBBARD, *Capt.* WENTWORTH, and many other *public* characters, will be present.

On 15 June the spurious *Star* was at last ready to present an account of the often-referred-to seduction in Edinburgh. Since the account was dated 1 June, the editors had held it for some time, perhaps in the hope of completing certain aspects of the research, perhaps with the intention of publishing it on the day the elections began.

That the editors of the spurious *Star* regarded the following story as a coup is evident from the prominence it accorded it:

### JOHN THE PAINTER'S BROTHER-IN-LAW.

Mr. TOPHAM, about twenty years ago, was a Student in the University of Edinburgh.

He there became enamoured of a Miss AITKEN, the daughter of a blacksmith, who was father to Mr. JAMES AITKEN, the celebrated JOHN THE PAINTER.

Miss A. was seduced by Mr. T. under promise of marriage, at the death of a rich Yorkshire relation.

They consequently cohabited together, as man and wife, for near two years.

The mother of Miss A. finding out the connection, compelled her daughter to raise a prosecution against Mr. T. for a *maintenance* to HIS WIFE!

The LAW of SCOTLAND, much to its credit, is particularly careful of guarding the *honour* of the FAIR SEX.

By that *law*, if a man cohabits with a woman for a *year and a day*, it is MARRIAGE.

If he acknowledges her before witnesses, though only in jest, as *his wife*, it constitutes *marriage*.

Now Mr. T.'s case came under every one of these heads.

He offered *five hundred* pounds to be *off* the bargain; but it would not do.

Foiled in every attempt to evade, or compromise, he fell upon an *honourable plan*, by which he got entirely rid of his wife, without any damages.

The poor, artless, worthy girl was decoyed by some of his *friends* into an OYSTER-SHOP, or cellar (as they are styled here), a sort of tavern, where everything may be had, but where oysters are the predominant commodity.

They there, as the scheme was laid, got her quite intoxicated. Next morning, each being ready, as in the case of Lady WORSLEY, to swear against her CONSTANCY, the unfortunate creature, shunned by her parents, and country, and losing all claim then, by the Scotch law, upon Mr. T. as his wife, came up to London, and went afterwards to New York, with a Clergyman and his lady, as their servant.

What was not more shocking than true, she was actually in PORTSMOUTH, about embarking, when her brother, *John the Painter,* was hanged there!

She was totally ignorant of his identity, until she heard it on the beach, when she was viewing the body, as an unconcerned spectator.

Miss A. upon the discovery, went into hysterics, crying out "Her dear Brother!" and was carried almost lifeless into a tavern. . . .

Had not the oyster-cellar affair taken place, she might have now been a worthy wife to Mr. T. and have *mended* his *shirts* in WESTMINSTER HALL, with more credit to himself than any other.

I should be glad if any of your correspondents would inform me where Mr. T. resided, when his brother JOHN suffered?

I should think the accident must have somewhat afflicted him, as I am told he has great feeling for

*Edinburgh,* June 1.                                                HIMSELF!

The "case of Lady WORSLEY," often cited by the newspapers, dated back to 21 February, 1782, when Sir Richard Worsley brought suit against George M. Bissett, an officer in the Hampshire militia, asking £20,000 damages for "criminal conversation" with his wife, Lady Seymour Dorothy Worsley, later Lady Fleming. The jury found for the complainant, but reduced the damages to 1s. because of his connivance.

Although "HIMSELF" was five years amiss as to dates, his story is otherwise plausible. Topham's *Letters from Edinburgh, Written in the Years 1774 and 1775: Containing Observations on the Diversions, Customs, Manners and Laws of the Scotch Nation* (Dublin, 1776) fixes the period of his sojourn there as 1774–1775, not 1768–1769 or 1769–1770. James Aitken, otherwise known as James Hill, James Hinde, James Actzen, and so forth, stated in his confession,[54] which was dated 7 March, 1777, that he had been born in Edinburgh on 28 September, 1752, and that his mother was still residing there, but that she had been in America from 1773 to March, 1775. Her absence during the "near two years" of his daughter's intimacy with Topham would explain why her discovery of the intimacy was so long delayed. Aitken, who was endeavoring to burn up all the docks and shipyards in England, was tried at the Winchester Assizes on 6 March, 1777, and was hanged on Portsmouth Common four days later. In answer to the query as to "where Mr. T. resided, when his brother JOHN suffered," one can say that he resided in London.

## "THE DRUDGERY OF ENDEAVOURING TO REDEEM A FALLING JOURNAL"

WITH the exposé of Topham's Edinburgh adventure, the spurious *Star* expired. Although the *World* was a shambles, the worst of the carnage was over, and the paper was free to recover whatever dignity it could. The fact that the elections had now been postponed until 1790 added another problem to those which it already faced, for the already-tired issues of the Prince's marriage and Hastings' trial had to be kept alive for another year.

The correspondence between Philip Withers and Horne Tooke, which the *World* had promised in late April, appeared in daily installments until mid-June, when Withers was finally tried. Although the newspapers are not specific about the date, the trial seems to have occurred on 15 June, 1789, Mrs. Fitzherbert being represented by Erskine, Withers representing himself. While Erskine was presenting her case, Withers scribbled out the denial which she had demanded and sent it to the "Clerk in Court," [55] but he indicated no anxiety when the trial proceeded and no great anxiety when he was convicted. In fact, his first act thereafter was to write and publish *Alfred's Apology, Second Part . . . with a Summary of the Trial of the Editor of Nemesis, on the Prosecution of Mrs. Fitzherbert, for a Libel.* The "First Part" of the "Apology" had been *Alfred to the Bishop of London. Alfred's Apology* was a fresh attack on Mrs. Fitzherbert, who had shown herself, said Withers, to be an indecent woman, rightly shunned by all except the most disreputable society. The *World* responded with long impassioned appeals to Tooke in its own behalf, the gist of which was that Tooke could still save Withers if only he would turn over the information about the marriage. The appeals continued throughout the remainder of 1789 and until mid-1790, along with Tooke's replies, which remained indecisive. Although no other newspaper was interested in Withers, the Opposition newspapers were very much interested in the *World's* interest in Withers, which none of them understood. By 6 August, 1789, the *Morning Post* had reached the conclusion that there was something odd about Tooke's communications, and it was ready to believe that Tooke might be in league with Withers and perhaps working for the *World* himself. But it saw no reason to question Withers's communications, and its discovery (17 Aug.) that Este was now the "sole Conductor" of the *World* tended to exonerate the *World* as well, Este being, as it still believed, Withers's nephew.

On 21 November, 1789, Withers was summoned for judgment. On this occasion Erskine submitted his latest pamphlet, which, he said, was even more libelous than the publication for which he had been tried; and Withers was accordingly sentenced to serve twelve months in Newgate Prison, to pay a fine of £50, and to find securities for good behavior for a period of three years. Withers promptly wrote another pamphlet, this one entitled *Alfred's Appeal, Containing His Address to the Court of King's Bench, on the Subject of the Marriage of Mary Anne Fitzherbert, and Her Intrigue with Count Bellois.* The preface was dated December, 1789. Much of the pamphlet was taken up with Withers' complaint that the law was hostile to discovery of truth and freedom of the press and that it was persecuting a man only because he had done his duty as a "good Citizen and a PROTESTANT Minister." [56] The pamphlet concluded with another volley of abuse of Mrs. Fitzherbert. But, in the course of his remarks, Withers disavowed any relationship with Este. "This gentleman I have never seen," he said; [57] "but in Point of Age, is he old enough to be my GRANDFATHER." As to the *World's* interest in his case, Withers added, he was as puzzled as everyone else, for, not only did he have no friends on the staff of that newspaper, but he had never written any of the letters which had been attributed to him. The fact that all of them had therefore been manufactured in the office of the *World* was not, however, mentioned by any newspaper, and the *World* continued its own appeals as if *Alfred's Appeal* had never appeared.

The second issue had also not been neglected, for, while the spurious *Star* had been ridiculing Topham's and Mrs. Wells's conduct at the trial of Warren Hastings, the *World* had been ridiculing the trial itself, with special attention to Edmund Burke. By June its repeated taunts that the trial had driven a wedge between Burke and his party, which refused to support him in any action in its defense, had compelled the Whigs to support some such action or admit that the *World* was right. Hence on 16 June, 1789, Charles Marsham called attention to a paragraph in the *World* of that date, which stated that "Mr. Hastings's Trial is to be put off to another session, unless the Lords have *spirit* enough to put an end to so SHAMEFUL a business"; and, on a motion introduced by Marsham and vigorously urged by Burke, the House ruled that the paragraph reflected on the Commons in its inquisitorial capacity and that the Attorney General should be instructed to prosecute the printer and publisher of that paper, Robert Bostock. The *Morning Post* was jubilant, not because it liked Burke, but because it particularly disliked the *World*. On 17 June it observed triumphantly that a newspaper which, "to the disgrace of our Church, [is] conducted by a CLERGYMAN" was at last getting its just due. The *World* was not correspondingly depressed. It said nothing of the action of the Commons, mentioning only (17 June) that

Burke had again been trying to organize his friends in defense of the trial and that as usual his motive had been personal animosity and not, as he liked to pretend, concern for the dignity of the House; and a few days later it was assailing him more viciously than before. There was actually no reason for depression, for, as Grey said on 18 June, the Attorney General often forgot to move against a Treasury newspaper. He could himself, he added, remember several prosecutions ordered by the House which had "never been brought to an issue," and he could therefore only hope that this time the Attorney General would remember to act. Pitt did not reply, having already, no doubt, assured Bostock that the Attorney General would not act.

Although Este saw to it that the *World* earned its £600 subsidy from the Treasury and that it realized as much as possible from his "valuable MS.," he was not interested in matters of prestige and circulation, and until the following year he had sole responsibility for the newspaper. Topham remained in Suffolk, from which place he addressed occasional letters to Este, expressing his satisfaction with the way things were going, and at the end of June, 1789, Mrs. Wells went to Cheltenham for her health. Although by this time the spurious *Star* was defunct, its influence lingered in other newspapers, and on 2 July, 1789, even *The* Ministerial *Times* joined the sport by publishing [58] what purported to be "A GENUINE LETTER" from *"Mrs.* Topham at her *tiny, little wee-bit of lodgings,* at Cheltenham, to Mr. Topham at the *great, big, large, monstruous white house,* in the Strand." The first part of the letter was devoted to *"Mrs.* Topham's" complaints about her husband's *"whiskers,"* his *"manly* strut," and "that ugly fashion you have of putting up the frill of your shirt every moment," the second part to her illness: "By the advice of *Doctor Ditto-repeated,* I am to drink one *gallon of water* per day: I wish to God it had been *punch.* . . . He took me kindly by the hand, not knowing our marriage, and said, 'Mrs. Wells, be assured that no power in existence can make you *lose your reason,* for *ex nihilo, nihilo fit.'* I begged him to write down this Latin prescription . . . , because you know, lovey, if it be proper for me it must be proper for you. . . ." Topham himself seems to have been bewildered by Mrs. Wells's condition, for on 24 July, 1789, he wrote [59] to her from Chelmsford in Essex: "By a letter which I had this day from Mr. Samuel, I am informed you are only 'indifferently well.' Let me beg, if you find your illness continue, that you will come to town. I shall never be happy till your illness is

ascertained, and you have some advice to determine what it may be."
Mrs. Wells had returned to town by late August; but, according to
"her own print," she was still "very ill" and under the constant care
of Este (*Morning Post,* 31 Aug., 1789). The *Morning Post,* which on
17 August had expressed its astonishment "that the *Reverend* Mr.
ESTE . . . did not succeed as an Actor . . . ; as he appears to be so
devout when he reads prayers at St. Martin's," was now (31 Aug.)
concerned that a "Parson eternally affecting morality" should be "in
reality the servile puffer and constant associate of a *kept actress."*

On 20 November, 1789, the *Morning Post* noticed that Mrs. Wells
was again under contract to Covent Garden and that the *World* was
at last treating poor Harris "civilly." But by this time the newspapers
had lost interest in her affairs, and even the *Post's* abuse of Este was on
a political rather than a personal level. "Mr. PITT, to reward the services of a *reverend* Editor, is making out an appointment to him for an
office, in which he is qualified to be of great service to the Public," the
*Post* observed, for example, on 31 October. "The appointment is that
of GEOGRAPHER [i.e., writer about earthy matters] to his Majesty."
Of Merry, too, little was said. Although by late November it was generally known that "Anna Matilda" was Mrs. Cowley, the papers made
nothing of the discovery, for by this time Merry had gone to France,
leaving his harem with Bell. "THE WORLD being now abandoned by
its original choir of minstrels, the poetic DELLA CRUSCA and his tuneful
disciples ANNA MATILDA and LAURA, the Captain and the Curate have
engaged a new set, who are soon to make their appearance," the
*Post* announced on 9 December. But there was no "new set," and the
*World* made do with "Simkin," "Arley," and a few minor hangers-on
until 1 January, 1790, when it introduced the Poet Laureate's New
Year's ode with the customary eulogy, only to discover that it had been
the victim of a hoax. "We are authorized by Mr. WHARTON [*sic*], to
say," it apologized on 4 January, "that the Ode sent *in his name,* as
usual, to all the papers [actually only to the *World*], was a forgery
—which, from its total *dullness, ignorance,* and *vulgarity,* every body
who respects a scholar and a poet, will be glad to find."

A few months before the elections began, the *World* lost Este.
Este said later (*Oracle,* 18 Jan., 1793) that he left the *World* because
Topham "had informed him that he should have no further assistance." Topham said (*World,* 15 Sept., 1790) that Este left because
of his "CONTEMPTIBLE LUCUBRATIONS" or more specifically (*Oracle,*

18 Jan., 1793) because it had been his practice to insert "libels" in the paper "with a view to extort money; and . . . , if he could obtain a sum of money, he would desist from such abuse," but that one of the "libels" had "unfortunately" resulted in "a prosecution for a Libel, which had obliged him (Mr. ESTE) to abscond, and [he] was of course incapable of being Editor, and therefore he (Mr. TOPHAM) ceased to employ him." John Taylor said [60] that Este left because he was "suspected of having introduced in . . . 'The World,' some defamatory articles on the memory of Lord Cowper." Every one seems to have been correct. During early February, 1790, the *World* published several paragraphs derogatory to the memory of the third Earl Cowper, who had died the previous December; but, instead of responding with money, the heirs of Lord Cowper responded with an indictment. Their action was based on a paragraph published on 17 February, and it was directed against Topham as proprietor, Este as conductor, and Bostock as printer and publisher. Este chose to "abscond," Bostock chose to plead guilty, and Topham chose to stand trial. He retained James Mingay as counsel, the heirs of Lord Cowper being represented by Erskine.

Topham returned to London immediately, and, since Mrs. Wells was now expecting a fourth child and "conceiving Beaufort-buildings too confined for the children," he first of all "removed [his family] to Weymouth-street, Portland-place." [61] He then set about the Gargantuan labor of reclaiming the *World* and, if possible, doing so within the next three months, the elections being scheduled for June. By this time the circulation of the paper had dropped markedly. On 1 January, 1788, the *World* had estimated its sale at between 3,000 and 4,000; in December, 1789, Topham had estimated it at approximately 2,000 (*Gazetteer*, 5 Oct., 1790); Este's last estimate was "above 1400" (*Gazetteer*, 10 Sept., 1790). Since the character of the paper had also greatly deteriorated, Este having no interest in "elegance," Topham at once tried to recapture the readers by remaking the *World* in its original image. His own last contribution had been a serialized biography of the miser, John Elwes, who had died on 26 November, 1789, the biography having been republished (20 Jan., 1790) by Ridgway, under the title, *The Life of the Late John Elwes, Esq'.;* and there is no indication that he contributed anything further. But he went to considerable lengths to reassemble the former staff.

The one person upon whom he had particularly depended, Mrs. Wells, turned out to be of no assistance whatever. For the family was hardly settled in its new quarters when, as she herself explained,[62] "I was delivered of my fourth child two months before my time, in consequence of a fright I received, occasioned by a duel being fought between two gentlemen on my account, from some expressions dropped respecting me. Mr. Reynolds, the dramatist, was one of the seconds. But Mr. Topham, having sold his *commission* in the Guards, . . . looked upon the quarrel of the gentlemen with that *sagacity* which his time of life warranted." At the same time she discovered (or imagined that she discovered) an intimacy between Topham and her closest friend, with the result that she was "seized with a milk fever" and was generally supposed to be mad. There was evidently some warranty for this supposition, for, according to Bernard,[63] "Among the number of pleasure-yachts that sailed into Plymouth this summer, (1790,) was one bearing that dramatic Cleopatra—Becky Wells; who, in the flying finery of her dress and the buoyancy of her person, was no bad emblem of the boat itself. She was attended by a female friend tolerably old and ugly, as an object of contrast, and whom she never permitted to say more than monosyllables, in order to prove agreeable company."

But, although Topham was also unable to lure Mrs. Cowley and Mrs. Robinson back from the *Oracle,* he still had Miles Peter Andrews, and he re-engaged Robert Merry, who had returned from France. He also solicited contributions from new poets, and on 23 March, 1790, he published a long statement about the *World*'s past and future, in which he reminded the readers that the *World* "[had] been *honoured with* the *appellation* of 'The Paper of Poetry' " and that it had been the first newspaper to publish the verses of "Della Crusca" and "Anna Matilda." He went on to promise that the paper would continue to stress the literary arts and concluded with the announcement that a third volume was now being added to the two-volume *Poetry of the World,* published in 1788. Although nothing further was said of this third volume, which, in fact, never appeared, the remainder of the statement was many times repeated, and it did attract some new Della Cruscans, among them the seventeen-year-old Samuel Taylor Coleridge, whose first known publication, "The Abode of Love," appeared on 26 July, 1790.[64] But the circulation continued to drop, so

that by the following October it had fallen to "MUCH LESS than
*fourteen hundred*" and possibly "*not* much *more* than ONE THOU-
SAND . . ." (*Gazetteer,* 5 Oct., 1790) .

Whatever the *World* wanted in influence it made up for, however,
in zeal, so that the Treasury had no reason to complain on that account. It fought the battle of the elections with proper ferocity and
adhered strictly to the two issues which had been assigned to it: the
Prince's marriage and Hastings' trial. Philip Withers, who had already performed so many services for the Government, performed a
final service by sickening and dying while the elections were in progress, his death occurring on 24 July, 1790. The *World* was thus enabled
to represent him as a martyr to the cause of truth and freedom and
Mrs. Fitzherbert as his jailer and murderer. For such crimes as hers,
it said flatly (29 July, 1790) , there was no retribution, although she
could at least support Withers' wife and four children for the remainder of their lives. With respect to the second issue, the *World*
fared less well.

Burke's break with Sheridan of 9 February, 1790, laid the ground
for a number of Ministerial intrigues, of which, it would appear from
the newspapers, Burke and the *World* were the principal victims. As a
reward for his defection, which was now clearly imminent, Burke had
a right to expect relief from further abuse, and the Treasury saw to it
that he obtained such relief from every newspaper except the *World*.
But the defection of Burke had not altered the Government's thinking
about the proceedings against Hastings; and, since, as Burke already
knew, the *World* was the stronghold of his enemy, Major Scott, he
would inevitably blame Scott for whatever appeared in that newspaper. With the blessing of the Treasury, therefore, the *World* continued to ridicule the trial and hence Burke as its prime mover. So far
as the quarrel was concerned, its sympathies were entirely with Sheridan, and on 23 February, 1790, it purported to rejoice that Sheridan
had at last organized his own "pack," "instead of toiling on amongst
the PORTLAND PACK subservient and at a distance." "All the remedy
which *poor* BURKE has against this manoeuvre," it added, "is, with his
head in the clouds, to write a Pamphlet *'on the affairs of France,'*
—which, as we understand, is nearly copied from THIS PAPER—and
which will be proved by those who will compare it with the *Authentic
French Intelligence* we have published from time to time, and the
comments we have hazarded upon that Intelligence."

But, since Burke was now in a position of some influence with both parties, the *World* had already (25 Febr., 1790) taken the precaution of naming Ralph Broome as "reputed author of the celebrated Letters of SIMKIN," with the obvious intention of diverting any action on "Simkin's" account from its printer, Robert Bostock, who was already under one indictment. Burke was not, however, interested in "Simkin." On 21 May, 1790, General Burgoyne complained to the House of a letter condemning the proceedings against Hastings, which, he said, had been published by the *World* of that date over the signature of Major Scott. Pitt agreed that the letter seemed libelous, but, in matters involving its own privileges, he said, the House ought to proceed with particular caution. On his motion the debate was therefore postponed until 27 May. By the time the debate was resumed, there had been a compromise, the nature of which is evident from the fact that on 26 May, 1790, Robert Bostock was suddenly brought into the Court of King's Bench and tried for the libel of 16 June, 1789, which had also involved the proceedings against Hastings. Bostock was convicted. On 27 May General Burgoyne accordingly limited his motion so that it applied only to Major Scott, who was reprimanded "in his place" and the incident concluded. In the course of the discussion, however, Fox stated [65] rather pointedly that he had himself always deplored libels on the House respecting the proceedings against Hastings, and he called especial attention to the fact that "the printer of the World had been prosecuted . . . by order of the House, and convicted recently, within this day or two." This statement, obviously intended for the ears of Burke, indicates, not only that Burke knew nothing about the compromise, but that one ground of his quarrel with the Whigs had been their reluctance to defend the trial of Hastings against the press, either by demanding new prosecutions or seeing that the old ones were "brought to an issue." As it happened, the prosecution of Bostock was never "brought to an issue" either, for on 9 June, 1790, Bostock's counsel, Mr. Fielding, moved for a new trial on the ground that there had been some irregularities in the previous one, and there the matter ended.

In November the *World* swung to the side of Burke, but meanwhile it was sinking under new weights of woe. Before the elections were over, Emanuel Samuel, who had been reporting the Parliamentary debates, was "thrown into the Fleet-prison by his creditors." Mrs. Wells effected his release by signing numerous vouchers on his account, and in early 1791 he went to India, where, with Topham's assistance, he had secured the position of auditor to the Nawab of Oudh.[66] Nothing further is heard of him until 1807, when he was the proprietor and editor of a new London newspaper, the *Pilot*.[67] On 4 October, 1790, Topham mentioned [68] that he had "arranged with Mr. Bourne about the national debates" and could only hope that "Smith" had "settled with Mr. Cooper." "Mr. Bourne" was possibly Frederick Bourne, who in March, 1792, was editor of the *Observer, and Sunday Advertiser;* he may also have been the same "Mr. Bourne" who in January, 1793, was editing the *Gazetteer*.[69] The only "Cooper" previously active in newspapers was Joseph Cooper, last heard of in July, 1781, when, as printer of the *London Courant,* he was sentenced to one year in prison for libeling the Russian ambassador. "Smith," who was mentioned frequently in Topham's letters, was perhaps Colquhoun Smith, who later printed the *Telegraph* and still later the *Morning Post*. "Smith's" position on the *World* seems to have been that of general reporter and subeditor, for Topham went on to inform Mrs. Wells: [70]

> You must . . . tell Smith we are very deficient in official intelligence; such as parliament being prorogued, which was at full in the Oracle, and indeed in every other paper: besides all business that might be learned at the offices— of arrivals of naval captains—what news they bring—what ministry are about; all of which he might get by a blank to clerks at the offices, and which should be the leading paragraphs of a paper.
>
> He is well enough known to get this, full as well as old Walsh.—This is very material, as it is what the old dons call NEWS. [Major] Scott, when in town, could give you a great deal of intelligence of this sort.

"Old Walsh" may have quit the *World* to work for the *Gazetteer;* at least, he was working for that newspaper in February, 1792.[71] He was also employed by the Opposition to "[send] out written notices of business in the H[ouse] of C[ommons]," although, when he later (1793) applied to William Adam and through him to Earl Fitzwilliam for a pension, he was advised to return to his "profession" as "a writer." [72]

By 12 September, 1790, Topham had also added a "Mr. Simon" to the staff.[73] "Mr. Simon," not otherwise identified, may have had something to do with the discovery and exposure of a scandal involving the families of General Gunning, the Duke of Argyle, and the Duke of Marlborough, which engrossed all the London newspapers during early 1791,[74] for on 27 October, 1790, Topham was telling Mrs. Wells: [75] "Simon can be of use, I see, and seems to have a knack of writing *fashionable fiddle-faddle;* in regard to which you may promise him, if he does well he shall have the special privilege of mentioning himself." By 4 October, 1790, Topham had in addition employed Isaac Swan and John Fuller, a lawyer and a student of the law, respectively, Fuller, identified in the records as the "eldest son of William F., late of Warrenbrook, Cork, Ireland esq., decd.," having been admitted to the Middle Temple on 13 June, 1789. Swan and Fuller were still connected with the *World* in September, 1791, although it is not clear in what capacity.

Topham's principal assistant during the elections was Robert Merry, who contributed much of the *World's* political commentary over his own signature. But, since Merry remained with the *World* because of his affection for Topham and not because of his affection for the Ministry, his services could not be relied upon. On 28 June, 1790, the *World* vehemently denied a report that "Mr. Merry has undertaken the conduct of [another] daily print"; and on 4 October Topham advised Mrs. Wells: [76]

> In regard to public business, you must see Merry, for he appears to me now to be doing nothing (though Smith can tell you), and if he does not, he then certainly means to do no more; in which case I must look out for a proper person.
>
> At all events, this must be determined. If you send to him, at Osborne's hotel, Adelphi, a note that you wish to see him, . . . he will naturally wait on you. . . .
>
> At every event see and resolve about Merry, for this can be trifled with no longer.

Merry was again writing for the *World* in November, but, by the beginning of 1791, he had moved to the *Morning Post.* Although on 4 September, 1791, Topham observed [77] that "Merry talks of coming to town on Saturday," he seems to have had no hope that Merry would rejoin his staff.

The identity of the "proper person" selected as Merry's replacement is in doubt. According to one biographer,[78] it was the Treasury writer, John Heriot, who, having had "a difference with [Bell], . . . left 'The Oracle' [in mid-1790] and joined 'The World,' of which he became the sole and responsible editor; but in a short time, tired of the drudgery of endeavouring to redeem a falling journal [and] quitted it." Although the biography purports to be based on a journal in Heriot's own handwriting, there is no evidence in Topham's correspondence to support this statement. Of the three references to Heriot, two of them [79] indicate that he was only a drama critic, employed as a kind of substitute for Mrs. Wells. "Let Mr. Heriott [sic], if it come out shortly, write the account of NOTORIETY," Topham instructed Mrs. Wells on 27 October, 1791; and on 17 September, 1792, he "[supposed] Mr. Herriot will take care of the GRAND OPENING of the NEW DRURY." Frederick Reynolds' Notoriety was performed at Covent Garden on 5 November, 1791, Mrs. Wells playing the role of Sophia Strangeways. On the third occasion,[80] Topham referred to Heriot as only "a man [in his] office." It would seem more likely that Merry was replaced by "Smith" or perhaps by "Smith," Swan, and Fuller.

Mrs. Wells was even less dependable than Merry. She was back at Covent Garden for the 1790–1791 season, but she evidently did little writing for the newspaper, for Topham concluded his letter of 4 September, 1790, with the suggestion, "As soon as you are able, give all the information and variety you can to the World"; and on 27 October he again entreated her to "Think of the World." [81] Mrs. Wells thought instead of the King, whom she now imagined to be "among the number of her victims," and, during the summer of 1791, she "hired a yacht at a guinea a-day (for which Topham paid), and attended him in all his excursions." The King was not amused.[82] Although she returned to London for the 1791–1792 season at Covent Garden, she was soon arrested for debts incurred in Samuel's behalf and was in prison until mid-January, 1792, when Topham procured her release and she and Reynolds fled to a "solitary farm-house, close to Netley Abbey." They remained there until mid-March and then proceeded to Calais, where she had "the romantic idea of settling in a convent." By late June they were back in England, Topham having notified them that "pecuniary matters had been arranged," and a few months later Mrs. Wells "at length discovered her real complaint; and that was —madness!" [83] On 17 September, 1792, Topham commented [84] on what seems to have been her last contribution to the World: "Your OLD KENT was good. Any private intelligence you can give at any time, do not neglect on any account; and theatricals, with apt quotations, under the signature of Old Kent, will always have good [sic]. . . ./

How goes on all at the office? Attentively and well?/ Be particular on this subject, and on the World."

## FINIS AND AN OBITUARY

THE PRESTIGE of the *World* had meanwhile suffered another stinging blow. On 1 July, 1790, Topham was tried in the Court of King's Bench for the libel on the memory of Earl Cowper and was convicted, while Este continued to live "entirely in the Country" (*Gazetteer*, 18 Sept., 1790) until this matter was settled. But Este had not forgotten the £400 annuity, of which he had thus far collected only about £200 in all (*Oracle,* 18 Jan., 1793), and in July he applied for payment of the arrears. He continued to apply until 10 September, 1790, when he inserted the following advertisement in the *Gazetteer:*

THE WORLD NEWSPAPER.
To be SOLD by Auction,
If not dispos'd of by private Contract, A RENT CHARGE of 400*l.* or the clear Fourth Part of the profits of the World, with other valuable contingencies; a right to inspect all papers, accounts, &c. relative to the said Newspaper of the World; and the Reversion in Fee of the said entire Paper, if Mr. Edward Topham dies before another Nominee. The sale is above 1400. Printed particulars of the whole establishment will be ready forthwith, and will be distributed through London, and through every chief town in Great-Britain and Ireland. At the same time some valuable Copyright will be sold, consisting of unpublished M.S. materially accessory to the due controul of the concern.
Apply, post paid, to F. Booth, Esq. Craven-street, Strand, London.

When this advertisement appeared, Topham was again in Suffolk for the hunting, so that he did not receive the news for two days. On Sunday, 12 September, 1790, he wrote to Mrs. Wells: [85] "Perhaps you may have heard of Parson E.'s attempt, which is as ludicrous as it is contemptible.—I have written to Smith, to tell him Mr. [Francis] Const's advice is always ready, and who, being retained for The World annually [as legal counsel], will give either you or him any advice." At Const's suggestion, therefore, Smith formulated the following reply, which appeared in the *World* of 15 September:

NOTICE.
A RIDICULOUS ADVERTISEMENT having been inserted in several daily prints [actually only in the *Gazetteer*], that a Rent Charge and Reversionary Inter-

est in this PAPER were to be sold; we think it necessary to inform the public, that such an INVENTION can only be attributed to the artful desire of some EVIL-MINDED person, to injure the World in its sale, by representing its circulation to be much inferior to what it really is; or perhaps to the enormity of a man whose CONTEMPTIBLE LUCUBRATIONS would really have REDUCED it, had they any longer been suffered to appear.

Este responded with a second advertisement, which was printed by the *Gazetteer* on 16 September:

### THE WORLD NEWSPAPER

THE SALE of the RENT CHARGE, and the Reversion of the entire Paper in Fee, will be advertised in due time, through Great-Britain and Ireland.

The FALSEHOOD of FOLLY cannot make much mischief long.

It is needless to bandy about ill manners with any INCAPABLE VULGAR IN DESPERATE CIRCUMSTANCES.

The SELLER of the Rent-charge on the WORLD, and the Reversion of the WHOLE PAPER in FEE, does not condescend to answer the writer in a paper of yesterday—Because EDWARD TOPHAM's WRITTEN DEED will do it for him.

The *Gazetteer,* which was described by one correspondent (*Gazetteer,* 21 Sept., 1790) as "the regular COCKPIT for all such battles," was ecstatic. On 17 September it published a long article, headed "A LOW PRINT./ THE RETORT COURTEOUS," in which it called attention to what was going on. "OUR readers will not be displeased to see the curious *paper war* that is now raging between the present CONDUCTOR of the WORLD [Este] and its original CREATOR [Topham]," the article began. "These two gentlemen, who used to treat their contemporaries with modest respect, and who even spoke of their own merits with the diffidence of genius, have now discovered the true quality of their talents, and exercise them in the proper direction." To be certain that its readers savored every juicy morsel, the *Gazetteer* reprinted Este's first advertisement and the *World*'s reply. "Now the public are fairly seated in the gallery, and the *cocks* are *pitted,*" it concluded excitedly. "We are only the feeders. The odds are 4 to 1— the *black cock* [Este] against the *red.* There will be no murder, however, but of the King's English; for

'—— They have no SPUR
To *prick* the sides of their intent but only
Vaulting Vanity, which o'ercaps *itself,*
And falls on the other.' "

The *World* was silent. Este's answer appeared in the *Gazetteer* of the following day:

LOW PRINT.

THE

RETORT COURTEOUS.

Under this head, your pleasantry, Mr. Editor [nominally James Perry], in yesterday's *Gazetteer,* happens in two or three places to have erred. To talk of errors is, with a man of proper temper to advance to their sure correction. . . . . Mr. EDWARD TOPHAM cannot be thought the ignorant, who wrote the ruffian falsehoods in question.—It must be some other man, who is *not* a MAGISTRATE FOR SUFFOLK! because . . . it is not possible for a man, however profligate, to *deny* a STAMP'D DEED he has signed—and to *dis*-BELIEVE *all* the words that he has uttered!

The STAMP'D DEED, signed by Edward Topham, has been shewn to you, Sir, and among hundreds of other people, to all the persons at the office of the TIMES.

The words EDWARD TOPHAM has uttered and which I copy from his letters, merely for his exculpation, to prove at once he could not be the poor mistaken man who has so falsely scandalized any little marketable fame that . . . I may be supposed to have—will, all, be, in the close, authenticated by an OATH before a Magistrate, that they are precise, verbal, literal TRANSCRIPTS FROM THE LETTERS of Mr. E. Topham to Mr. Este.

The purport of the letters, which were dated 19 October and 1 December, 1789, was that Topham was delighted with Este's management of the newspaper.

Este did not correct another error in the *Gazetteer's* article, namely, that he was "the present CONDUCTOR of the WORLD," because his continued connection with that newspaper was one of the terms of the "STAMP'D DEED." Not only did he maintain that he was still associated with the newspaper, albeit *in absentia,* but on 21 September, 1790, he stated (*Gazetteer*) that he had been continuously associated with it for "above four years," although the *World* was not even begun until 1 January, 1787. On 20 September the *Gazetteer* published an additional communication from Este, characterized by the same mock-humility and the same pseudo-naive refusal to believe that Topham *"would have traduced my Character* and *injured* also *my Property,* in the WORLD" and including three more letters to the same effect as before, one undated, the other two dated 14 and 28 October, 1789, respectively. This communication concluded with the stipulation that Este would *"answer nothing* originally printed in the WORLD./ To

ANY OTHER PAPER, authenticated . . . with the WRITER'S NAME, attestation that he has written *without* help, &c. &c. and sent me Post Paid (for I live entirely in the Country,) to such . . . I will answer with my name.—/ C. ESTE." The *Gazetteer,* which was now in a state of frenzy, called upon Topham for a reply, entreating him to use as much of its space as he wished; but Topham was silent.

On 21 September, 1790, the *Gazetteer* printed a "Public Notice" from C. Este to E. Topham, regarding Este's property in the *World,* namely, "an ANNUITY of 400*l.* &c. &c./ And the Reversion of the ENTIRE PAPER IN FEE." The notice made two proposals: first, that "the whole affair" be referred "to ARBITRATION" and, second, that Topham buy Este's interest for 3,000 guineas. "This price, for the mere annuity, or fourth, is precisely tantamount to what Mr. Topham gave (viz. 4000 guineas) for a third./ The Reversion in Fee, and some valuable MS. so materially necessary to the due *controul* of the concern, and which he knows would make the fortune of a Paper, shall be included." If both these proposals were rejected, Este would demand "INSTANT SATISFACTION, **BEFORE THE PUBLIC.**" Topham had denied him the right to inspect the accounts in private: Este would demand the right to inspect them in public. If the paper had so fallen that a fourth interest was no longer worth 3,000 guineas, it was up to Topham to prove it. These demands did not alarm Topham, but they greatly alarmed George Rose and Major John Scott, so that, for the next several days, the *Gazetteer* was concerned with the question of whom precisely Este was threatening.

On 30 September, having waited, as he said, one week for a reply from Topham, Este announced (*Gazetteer*) that he would now prove that he owned the property and proceed to the sale of it. He began by publishing in part his copy of the deed and giving Topham two days to find his own copy and make a collation. On 5 October he stated (*Gazetteer*) that, since he had heard nothing from Topham, he was arranging for the sale. As to the circulation of the *World,* he said, he had greatly overestimated it when he stated in his advertisement of 10 September that it was "above 1400," for he had since learned from "the printing office" that it was then "MUCH LESS than *fourteen hundred.* All I can say, is, it is now *not* much *more* than ONE THOUSAND!!!" There was no auction, and there was no public inspection. On 7 October Este warned (*Gazetteer*) that he had sent the "LEGAL INSTRUMENT" to Erskine for examination and that meanwhile, if Topham told the public anything about him, he would reveal everything he knew about Topham. He also corrected his statement that he had got his information from the printing office: he had got it from the Stamp Office. So far as the newspapers were concerned, the quarrel was now over, except for the banter, which continued another two weeks. An "Epigram," printed by the *Gazetteer* on 14 October, is typical:

> HARD is ESTE's case, in nature's despite,
> Whom cruel fortune dooms to write;
> But harder still is TOPHAM's lot,
> Condemn'd to read what ESTE has wrote.

Topham was "condemn'd to read" a good deal of unpleasant material during this period. Este's threat to open the ledgers of the *World* to public inspection seems, for example, to have inspired a Mr. Brydges to try some blackmailing on his own account, for on 4 October, 1790, Topham mentioned to Mrs. Wells [86] that he had "found on my return home . . . a letter from him I did not well understand, but should I ever receive such another, I will, without one moment's delay, give instructions to proceed legally against him for the note I have of his: that as to his publishing any accounts of mine, I don't care one farthing if they were published to all the world: that when Mr. Woodman [evidently a clerk] and Mr. Smith have looked over his accounts and settled them, he shall pay or receive what may be his due: that his salary, as he knows, is a kindness of mine, and which shall only be paid on his good behaviour."

On 10 November, 1790, Mingay moved for a new trial in the case of the heirs of Earl Cowper versus Topham, and "the Court granted a Rule *nisi* for a new trial, and another in arrest of judgment" (*Diary,* 11 Nov., 1790). Const, who represented Bostock, said that he had no instructions to move for an arrest of judgment in Bostock's case, but Bostock's sentence was also deferred. On 22 November Erskine appeared in behalf of the plaintiffs to argue against a new trial, whereupon the Court announced that it would take the whole matter under deliberation. It deliberated until 29 January, 1791, when it ruled against the retrial, but granted Topham and Bostock arrest of judgment on a technicality, the laws of libel being deemed inapplicable to the dead. Since the same ruling applied to Este, who was still under indictment, he was free to return to London; and, although he had never got along with John Bell before, there was now a bond between them, both of them being at odds with Topham. Hence Bell at once offered Este the conduct of the *Oracle* (*Oracle,* 18 Jan., 1793), and, according to John Taylor,[87] Este at once set about collecting his "200*l.* annuity": "Without resorting to law . . . , Mr. Este opened a literary battery against Topham in . . . 'The Oracle.' . . . Este persevered in his attacks, to which he added his name; and Topham . . . agreed to grant the annuity which Este secured by an insurance on the life of his quondam friend and admiring coadjutor." But Taylor was either misinformed or forgetful. The annuity was £400, not £200, there was no "literary battery," and Este certainly did "resort to law."

Topham's reaction to the news that Este had submitted his claims to the Court of Chancery is indicated by his letter of 4 September, 1791: [88]

As to the letter you enclosed, it is too contemptible for notice.

You may send, however, for Smith, who may give this *verbal* answer, *not written*—"That when the accounts are settled, Mr. Este's bill shall be sent in, as well as the expences of the law-suit in which he involved the paper [i.e., the suit brought by the heirs of Earl Cowper]; and then whatever may be due to him for salary, if any such thing shall be due to him, shall be deducted." As to any other notice, it is not worth thinking about. Let him bring his action whenever he pleases.

If any application be made at the office, Mr. Swann [*sic*] or Mr. Fuller are to return for answer that no accounts are ever shewn to strangers: but that, when the expence of the law-suit in which Mr. Este involved the paper are ascertained, they shall be sent in to him with his bill, and if any thing is due to him for salary, it will be deducted.

Until Este brought his action, Topham denied that the deed existed. In court he admitted that it did exist and that the annuity had not been paid; but he contended that, in leaving the paper, Este had violated a condition of the contract, thereby forfeiting his claim to a share of the paper's profits, the profits being in any event trifling. Este contended that Topham had compelled him to leave and that the profits were considerable. On 1 June, 1792, the *Public Advertiser* included in its reports of legal proceedings the latest ruling on the

claim of Mr. Este on Mr. Topham . . . for a *fourth* part of the profits of the paper called the WORLD, and for a moiety of the profits, when they exceed 2000*l.* a year, with the *entire Paper in fee,* on the death of Topham.

The answer from Mr. Topham to the Bill, must be in the course of next month, and it may be expected to make more noise than any trial, since that of Lady Worsley; for the answer from Topham must be on oath, and it must *circumstantially detail the daily sale* of the World, and all persons whatever, "within liberties or without," from whom "*These presents* shall have come, GREETING."

But Topham's "answer," when it was finally submitted, was too evasive to attract any attention whatever. On 16 January, 1793 (*Oracle,* 18 Jan., 1793), the case was further argued in Lincoln's Inn Hall, the argument covering the same ground as before and terminating with Este's declaration that Topham's "answer to the Bill" had been "scandalous and impertinent." The Court, which had obviously never expected, much less wanted, a forthright answer, was evasive. Since the newspapers do not record the conclusion of this litigation, Taylor may or may not be right in saying that Este finally won his case. On 28 January, 1801, Este sued a Mr. Broomhead to recover £150, which, he contended, he had paid Broomhead "in consideration of an annuity"; [89] but this seems to have been another annuity altogether.

Topham said later (*World,* 21 Apr., 1794) that he leased the *World* at the beginning of 1792 and had nothing to do with it thereafter. But this statement is contradicted by his letter of 17 September, 1792, urging Mrs. Wells "not [to] neglect on any account" her various contributions and making anxious inquiries about how "all" was going "at the office." There is a possibility that the paper was leased at the beginning of 1793, and on 8 March, 1793, *The Times* even announced that it had been sold: "A certain Morning Print has again changed Masters. The Chief Governor is changed from the Stable [a reference to Topham's former commission in the Horse Guards] to a Lawyer's study. A Barrister now gives it proprietorship—one of the *Wig Club.*" But *The Times*'s authority was the Court records, which were in this instance misleading. The paper was certainly not sold until 1794, and the possibility that it was even leased seems remote in view of the fact that Topham continued to collect the £600 subsidy from the Treasury until June, 1793.

It is nevertheless true that Topham had very little to do with the *World* during the last months of its existence; for the spectacular success he had had with the newspaper at the beginning had been followed by a series of such equally spectacular failures that he finally despaired of doing anything about the situation himself and turned the problem over to Isaac Swan. By this time the circulation could hardly have exceeded a few hundred a day, and the extra income the paper had enjoyed as a result of Este's "valuable MS." had disappeared with Este. Swan had no "valuable MS.," but he did have a close connection with Thomas Harris, the manager of Covent Garden, who had certain personal grievances and was evidently willing to pay for satisfaction. Foremost among these grievances was one involving Charles Dibdin. Swan had already been harassing Dibdin in another newspaper, and the only noticeable result of his assuming the conduct of the *World* was that the harassings and the resulting litigations were transferred to that newspaper.

Swan had been associated with the *World* since at least October, 1790, but on 4 December, 1791, Frederick Bourne had begun the *Observer, or Sunday Advertiser,* which he himself edited and which was printed and published by William Locke at No. 283, Strand; and Swan had thereafter written for the *Observer* as well as the *World.* By this time Dibdin had quit Covent Garden to open "a place of entertainment" in the Strand, called "Sans Souci," where he was singing ballads and chanteys which he had supposedly written himself. According to his version of what happened,[90] which is certainly not very accurate, he immediately received "letters from all the understrappers of the newspapers, requiring free-tickets, and accommodations, in so peremptory a style, as if they [were demanded] by some tributary convention," and, when he refused these "requirements," "whole cargoes of ignorant ribaldry" were "levelled at [him] every morning," the point of which was that he had stolen the songs from Isaac Bickerstaffe. On Sunday, 18 March, 1792, Dibdin wrote a letter to the *Diary,* promising to sue the very next person who made such a statement, and on the same day the *Observer* published "an unqualified libel . . . upon the old infamous subject." Dibdin thereupon sued the printer, from whom he was awarded £200 damages, and he had the ultimate satisfaction of knowing that he had been personally responsible for the demise of the *World.* For, said Dibdin, "though the libel appeared in *The Observer,* it originated from some of the understrappers concerned in a paper, called *The World.* I had prophesied . . . that this same *World* would soon be at an end, but little thought at that time it would be through my means." But Dibdin was mistaken on almost every account.

On 18 March, 1792, the *Observer* did, in fact, publish a paragraph denouncing Dibdin as a plagiarist, and Dibdin did file an action of trespass against William Locke, the printer, and Isaac Swan, who was identified by the editor, Frederick Bourne, as author of the paragraph. But on 17 October the *World* published a similar paragraph, and this time Dibdin filed an information for libel against Swan as "sole proprietor" and Robert Bostock as printer. The actions for trespass were tried in the Court of Common Pleas. Locke was convicted on 26 February, 1793 (*Oracle,* 28 Febr., 1793), and Swan on 18 May, the juries awarding Dibdin £100 damages from each of them (*Diary,* 20 May, 1793). The actions for libel, however, were tried in the Court of King's Bench, where on 25 June, Swan and Bostock were found guilty of damaging Dibdin's character to the amount of one shilling (*The Times,* 26 June, 1793). Swan was encouraged by this hilarious verdict to continue his abuse, which, until the end of the year, was the only animated writing in the *World.*

But the income from services of this sort was evidently not in itself enough to support the newspaper. For, with the cancellation of the Treasury subsidy on 20 June, 1793, Topham began to look for a purchaser, and on 1 July, 1794, the *World,* renamed *Fashionable World* with obvious reference to its long-lost elegance, became a subtitle of the *Morning Post.* On 2 October, 1797, it ended its existence even as a subtitle, the *Morning Post, and Fashionable World* becoming the *Morning Post, and Gazetteer.* Only the *True Briton* commented on its demise. "We hope to hear no more reflections on the manners of the higher circles," it remarked on 4 October, 1797, "for the *Fashionable World* is no more—*Sic transit gloria mundi!* This Captain Topham can best explain." But "Captain Topham" was probably more puzzled than anyone else. A newspaper subsidized by the Treasury almost invariably deteriorated, and the *World* had deteriorated further under the management of Charles Este. Yet, when Topham resumed the management in early 1790, he exerted every effort to improve the quality, and, despite the fact that he worked against ponderous odds, the quality did improve. But the improvement had no effect whatever on the circulation, which continued to drop, for from mid-1789 on it was not the *World* which was at fault so much as the reputation of its personnel: and "this" the spurious *Star* could "best explain." There was another factor, however, which only the readers could "explain."

Although the *World* had been modeled on the *Morning Post,* it had transformed the model from a mirror of fashion to an arbiter of taste. As Boaden said, it did not purport to reflect the opinions of its readers: it told them with "an authoritative voice" what their opinions should be. Moreover, readers respected its authority, so that, for a period of over two years, the *World* was the sole judge of what was good in the fields of manners and the arts. Under these circumstances its influence was much greater than even its sale indicated, and it was correspondingly obstinate. In 1789 the spurious *Star* impugned its authority once and for all by persuading the public that its principals were themselves lacking in "virtue" and "talent," and, for the next five years, the *World* was the butt of general ridicule. Yet during this period it furnished the model for the spurious *Star* which destroyed it, the *Oracle* which tried to replace it, and the *Morning Post* which absorbed it; and every single one of the newspapers which ridiculed it had adopted the device of the laudatory headnote and in its own way was also purporting to be an arbiter of taste. The influence of the *World* also persisted in another way, for, although after 1789 the *World*'s pronouncements were regarded as generally laughable, the pronouncements it had made prior to that time continued to carry weight. This was especially true in the case of poetry. The Della Cruscans would have attracted no notice had their work not been constantly acclaimed in encomiastic headnotes, and, although the spurious *Star*'s derision of "Della Crusca," "Anna Matilda," and "Arley" diminished the rage for these particular poets, the enthusiasm for their kind of poetry continued until the end of the century. Every newspaper felt obliged to have at least one Della Cruscan among its contributors, and few poets, even poets of stature, were able to resist the influence of Della Cruscan verse. Hence the influence of the *World* far outlived the *World* itself, leaving an indelible mark on the history of literature as well as the history of journalism.

# CHAPTER V

# The Two *Stars* (May, 1788–April, 1789): Conflict in the Afternoon

## THE CASE FOR AND AGAINST PETER STUART

THE QUESTION of who actually began the *Star* was one of the hotly debated issues of February, 1789, for Peter Stuart maintained that he had begun it, and the other proprietors maintained that they had begun it. Since the claims were made categorically and since they were backed by the usual exaggerations and half-truths, they seemed to be irreconcilable, but, in fact, they were reconcilable, and together they provided a pretty good indication as to what probably happened.

The "idea of establishing an EVERY EVENING NEWSPAPER" first occurred to him, said Peter Stuart (spurious *Star*, 13 Febr., 1789),[1] when he left the *Morning Post*. He left that paper on 4 February, 1788, having printed it since 26 April, 1784, and printed and edited it since early 1786. He did not leave the *Post* because of the "idea," but rather, it appears, in consequence of a quarrel with the conductor, John Benjafield. For, by the beginning of 1788, the *Morning Post* was hard pressed by the ultra-literary *World,* and it seems to have been Peter's feeling that the *Post* could meet the competition only by stressing *"the elegancies of Literature"* itself (*Post,* 1 Jan., 1788). But Benjafield, who "possessed no literary talents"[2] and who had thus far used the newspaper as a vehicle for Treasury propaganda and general abuse, felt otherwise. Peter therefore turned the printing and editing of the *Post* over to his brother Daniel and departed; and at three P.M. on 3 May, 1788, the first number of the *Star, and Evening Advertiser* made its appearance. The colophon noted that the paper was "Printed by P. STUART, No. 31, Exeter-street, Catherine-street, Strand," and no one ever denied that "P. STUART" was also the conductor and one of the proprietors.

Peter Stuart had himself invested £1,000 in the newspaper (spurious *Star*, 16 Febr., 1789),[3] and on 5 February, 1789, there were twelve other proprietors (*Star*, 16 Febr., 1789),[4] at least four of whom had invested another £1,000 each. Since there is no indication of a change in the proprietary prior to that time, all of the twelve were probably proprietors when the paper was begun. The four leading shareholders were, in addition to Peter Stuart, the two booksellers, the elder John Murray and William Lane, the engraver, John Hall, and a Mr. T. Preston, who may have manufactured musical instruments (spurious *Star*, 27 Apr., 1789). Most of the remaining proprietors were evidently connected with the bookselling trade, for, not only was the paper filled with booksellers' advertisements, but a prospectus, included in the first number, stated that the *Star* had been begun by *"several Gentlemen of property and character, who having large commerce with the World, are unavoidably engaged in giving and receiving intelligence."* Their purpose in beginning it, the prospectus went on, was to have a medium for advertising, for they had suffered *"many abuses and inconveniences . . . by the neglect and inattention of other Papers— Many of their advertisements were not inserted properly, others not at all, and others not until the procrastination rendered them of no use."* This was a common complaint of booksellers, and it was evidently justified, for the average conductor of a newspaper did not like booksellers, whom he regarded as arrogant and demanding. According to Daniel Stuart,[5] every bookseller insisted on "having his cloud of advertisements inserted at once in the front page"; he refused to settle for "a few new and pressing advertisements at a time . . . ; he would have the cloud," and he was "affronted, indignant" at the suggestion that the "cloud" occupy the last page. Since in addition booksellers' advertisements were regarded as of almost no interest to readers, several newspapers refused to carry them at all.

Daniel Stuart said [6] that Peter had conceived the "idea" of a daily evening newspaper "in consequence of the increased facilities of communication by Palmer's mail-coach plan, then just begun"; and this was perhaps the case. For Palmer's "plan," expanded in 1785 to include the distribution of newspapers, did speed delivery somewhat. Still it did not speed it sufficiently to encourage a daily evening press. Readers in Bath, for example, saw the evening newspapers late the following afternoon, whereas the morning papers reached Bath "at about TEN or ELEVEN o'clock" at night and "SUBSCRIBERS [were] served with [them] on the very same evening" (spurious *Star*, 27 Apr., 1789). Hence, although the "plan" may have entered into Peter's thinking, he would have been unable to sell his "idea" to investors on the basis of it. But a group of booksellers, looking for a vehicle for advertising, would have been attracted for another reason. For, whereas a morning daily had to offer original information and "entertainment" in order to compete with the other morning dailies, no one expected an evening newspaper to be other than a digest, and this meant that it could be brought out at a minimal cost. There had been such a newspaper before: the *Noon Gazette, and Daily Spy,* which was absorbed by the *London Courant* at the beginning of 1782. The *Noon Gazette* was an innovation. It differed from the morning dailies in that it presented only "the actual News of the . . . Morning Papers"; it differed from the evening papers in that it was a daily; and it differed from both groups in that it was "Published at Twelve o'Clock" and was circulated in both the City and the country. The *Star* was a *Noon Gazette* published three hours later.

The *Star* was probably, therefore, a combination of two "ideas": Peter Stuart's "idea" of "an EVERY EVENING NEWSPAPER" and the booksellers' "idea" of an inexpensive vehicle for advertising, and, since neither one necessarily implied the other, the two "ideas" were probably conceived independently. Hence in one respect Peter Stuart and the booksellers could, with equal justification or lack of justification, claim credit for having begun the newspaper, the only question being who was the prime mover in the enterprise. The prospectus indicated that the booksellers were, and one would be inclined to trust the prospectus were it not for the booksellers' later (*Star,* 16 Febr., 1789) declaration that they had "embarked in" the enterprise as "friends" of Peter Stuart and "with a view purely to give him employment." If they had concluded their remarks with the statement that Peter "had been recommended, countenanced, and employed [by them], chiefly from the opinion entertained of his integrity," one might believe them, but the declaration that they "embarked in" the newspaper "purely" to give him employment is too much. Although eighteenth-century booksellers must have had some virtues, altruism of this high order was not among them. The very ludicrousness of the declaration therefore drives one to the conclusion that the booksellers had "countenanced" Peter because he had approached them with an "idea" which suggested to them an economical means of realizing their own "idea."

The leader of the booksellers was the elder John Murray, who specialized in the publication of histories. Peter Stuart seems to have known Murray very well and for quite a long time. He was acquainted, for example, with Gilbert Stuart, whose *History of Scotland from the Establishment of the Reformation till the Death of Queen Mary* Murray had published in 1782, and he knew something about Gilbert Stuart's subsequent quarrel with Murray. Gilbert Stuart died in 1786. Peter was also acquainted with other historians whose works Murray had published, and he was "in the habits of friendship, or at least intimacy" with Murray himself (spurious *Star,* 13 Febr., 1789). Since Murray had been an original proprietor of the *Morning Chronicle,*[7] the two may have been associated on that newspaper after Peter left the *London Courant* in early 1783 and before he joined the *Morning Post* on 26 April, 1784. By 1788 Murray had suffered a paralytic stroke, but he was still active,[8] and it seems probable that he was the first of the booksellers to be approached. Although "P. STUART" later said only (spurious *Star,* 13 Febr., 1789) that he "communicated" his "plan" to Murray and that Murray "approved of it" and "requested [him] to add his name to the list of proprietors," the "list" could not at that time have been very long. For "P. STUART" went on to describe Murray as "the BEACON of my HOPES," the reason evidently being that Murray had promised to bring a number of other booksellers with him.

Although the *Star* was totally lacking in originality, it was a very respectable newspaper. Four months earlier (*Morning Post,* 1 Jan., 1788) Peter Stuart had deplored the fact that newspapers *"dealt only in malice, or at least, in the prattle of the day,"* and he was still deploring it, for the first number of the *Star* (3 May, 1788) promised that it would avoid all "abuse," all "malignancy," and all "invidiousness," and the promise was kept in subsequent numbers. Although politically the *Star* professed a devotion to the Prince of Wales and even carried the Prince's insignia in its masthead, its devotion was inconspicuous, and it managed even to maintain a neutrality with respect to the elections, then in the offing. There was some early difficulty with a Mrs. Elizabeth Johnson, but this was speedily settled. Mrs. Johnson, who had been publishing the *British Gazette, and Sunday Monitor* for a number of years, added another newspaper on 1 April, 1788, which she called the *Evening Star, and Grand Weekly Avertiser,* changing the title, when the *Star, and Evening Advertiser* appeared, to the *Original Star.* Although Peter Stuart maintained that she had never thought of her *Star* until she saw the prospectus for his, the competition was short-lived, for Mrs. Johnson's *Star* lasted only a few weeks.[9] As Peter recalled later (spurious *Star*, 13 Febr., 1789), there was also some early intra-proprietary difficulty, but this was also speedily settled. For "the undertaking" had hardly begun, said Peter, when Murray attempted to interfere in the management, but, "finding that I would not sacrifice the interest of a general concern to his particular views, and that his attempts at overbearing were treated by others, as well as myself, with contempt, he absented himself for several months from all meetings, which caused harmony to become fixed." Since Murray was represented as a staunch friend of the Pitt Government, one was given to understand that the nature of his interference was political.

Peter Stuart seems to have had very little interest in politics and a great deal of interest in literature, which he regarded almost with veneration, for, whenever he had a free hand with a newspaper, it invariably stressed *"the elegancies of Literature"* and paid only cursory attention to politics. He seems also to have been unenterprising to the point of downright honesty, for, whenever he was left alone, he managed his newspaper as a legitimate and therefore totally unprofitable business. But he was almost never left alone. For, although he was able to resist every sort of monetary temptation, he could not resist his friends, in whose behalf he would deviate from the straight and narrow at any time; and, since his friends were perpetually in need of assistance, he was perpetually crossing the line to provide it. In addition, he was dominated by his older brother, Charles, who, one could predict, would usurp the management of the *Star* as soon as he saw any advantage in doing so.

In 1788 the five Stuarts were still living in Charlotte Street, Portland Place, where they had been "keeping house together" since they migrated to London from Edinburgh.[10] Charles, Peter, and Daniel were now aged approximately thirty-eight, twenty-eight or thirty, and twenty-two, respectively, Catherine being in her late thirties and Elizabeth somewhat younger. The brothers had heretofore functioned pretty much as a team. Charles, who had dominated Peter and Daniel by virtue of his age, had seen to it, for example, that work remained in the family, so that, except for a three-month interval at the beginning of 1784, the *Morning Post* was printed by one Stuart or another from 7 March, 1782, to 1 May, 1789. There had also been a great deal of silent collaboration, so that no Stuart was idle so long as one Stuart was working. But Daniel, who had never been fond of either of his brothers, was now old enough to act on his resentments, and from this point on he was no longer necessarily involved in their enterprises. The household was meanwhile being held together only by the practical wisdom and homely virtues of Catherine.[11] None of this, however, affected Peter, who was as much under the influence of Charles as he had been before.

Charles's activities from the time he left the *Morning Post* in late 1783 or early 1784 until the summer of 1788 are only partly traceable, but enough can be learned of them to indicate their direction. From late 1786 or early 1787 until late 1790, when Pitt subverted the paper through "*treachery* of the worst kind" (*Gazetteer*, 18 Oct., 1790), Charles furnished the weekly column, "Abridgment of Politics," for the Foxite *Morning Herald,* by arrangement with Sheridan, although he was not paid for his labors until July, 1791.[12] His theatrical pieces, too, were performed at Sheridan's Drury Lane. In 1785 he wrote the farewell address for Mrs. Bellamy, which was recited on 24 May after a production of *Braganza*, the role of the Duchess being played by Mrs. Yates, then in retirement herself;[13] in 1787 he wrote the one-act farce, *Box-Lobby Loungers,* which was licensed on 12 May and produced on 16 June;[14] and in 1788 he wrote *The Stone Eater: An Interlude,* which was licensed on 10 May, produced on 14 May, and published later in the year.[15] The last play has been rated by one critic[16] as "one of the most contemptible pieces ever produced." Despite the fact that these plays were produced at a theater which was usually regarded as propagandistic, not one of them was political. This was not the case with *The Distress'd Baronet.*

In the spring of 1787, the chief Parliamentary issue was the matter of the Prince of Wales's debts, and, since "The Distress'd Baronet" was an innocent young man in the act of being victimized by dishonest lawyers and unscrupulous tradesmen, Charles's purpose in writing the play, as well as Sheridan's purpose in producing it, was obvious, but the purpose was underscored by many sympathetic references to the Prince and sarcastic references to his enemies in Parliament. The play, "which [Boswell] liked very well, tho' some ill-natured creatures hissed,"[17] was first performed on 3 May, 1787, and again on 11 May, having meanwhile undergone some revisions. The revised version was enthusiastically reviewed (12 May) by the Opposition newspapers. "Mr. *Stuart,* . . . by adopting a few necessary alterations, and by changing the Attorney from a reproachable character to that of an honest man, has rendered his production unexceptionable," said the *Morning Chronicle.* "[The farce] is enriched with great knowledge of the world, and the various ingenious sarcasms were deservedly applauded." "The farce of the *Distress'd Baronet* . . . seems to have been greatly altered since its last representation," observed the *Morning Herald.* "The Attorney Quirk is not now a marauder on society; but satirises a great part of the profession in another manner, by acting with disinterested probity. The few objectionable parts have been entirely done away with, and the farce is received throughout with unvaried approbation." The *World* was equally laudatory: "The *New Farce,* THE DISTRESS'D BARONET, was in distress no longer.—There was much applause, and nothing else.— except in one short sentence,—and there surely, the disapprobation, small as it was, must be unmerited—for the words were these, the pawnbroker's utterance—'Oh! my Lord always redeems his property, in my hands, after the meeting of Parliament.' "

By the time *The Distress'd Baronet* was published (London, 1787, 1787; Dublin, 1788),[18] the matter of the Prince's debts was settled, so that the publication was somewhat anticlimactic. In order to prevent an investigation of his relationship with Mrs. Fitzherbert, the Prince had, however, agreed to certain concessions, and Charles made these concessions the occasion for a fulsome dedicatory epistle, addressed "TO HIS ROYAL HIGHNESS GEORGE PRINCE OF WALES." "SIR," the epistle began,[19]

You are the phenomenon of your rank. Even the Courtier must admire your honour, while every good citizen reveres your most unparalleled princely probity. For when did the heroism of any Prince, besides your Royal Highness, ever condescend to sink into the level of a commoner, in order to be *just?* This was true magnanimity! Such a glorious degradation has exalted you in the eyes of all mankind. . . .

Before your Royal Highness reached maturity, Britain stood in small estimation among nations, as a polished state. . . .

The taste, however, the hospitality, the affability, and the elegant accomplishments of your Royal Highness, burst at once upon the nation, and soon were blazoned throughout the Continent. Even the French nobility themselves, those arbiters of fashion, were among the first to subscribe to the general opinion. Your Royal Highness was admired and imitated by every foreigner of rank and taste. Whatever dress you wore, whatever carriage or caparison your fancy approved of, was sure to become the reigning fashion in France as well as in Britain. Your entertainments were splendid. Your guests were learned, noble, and accomplished. Your amusements were polished and manly. You were the only Prince throughout Europe, whose manners commanded universal imitation; and your Royal Highness stamped a character on the English nation, for their taste and refinement, heretofore unacknowledged.

In this career of your splendour, that reflected such honour on the empire, your Royal Highness was unfortunately stopped. But every good citizen now hopes to see you soon resume the lustre of your rank. Thus once more elevated to your proper sphere, accomplished natives, and intelligent foreigners will again be honoured by your society, Your Royal Highness's taste will reillumine the circles of fashion both in Britain and on the Continent. Trade will be promoted; all the branches of your illustrious family be made happy; and your Royal Highness's princely conduct become the theme of every tongue, because you are the *magnificent patron of every British art.* . . .

Since the Whigs had supported payment of the Prince's debts and an increase in his allowance, *The Distress'd Baronet* was only a service to the Party. But the dedicatory epistle was an application to the Prince of Wales. In effect, Charles was offering to help the Prince get enough money to "resume the lustre of [his] rank" in return, of course, for the Prince's giving him some money. The dedicatory epistle was a sample of the kind of help Charles intended to give. Although the offer was not accepted, Charles must have received an encouraging response, for one cannot otherwise account for the Prince's insignia and the motto, *Vespero surgento,* in the masthead of the *Star.* None of the proprietors of the newspaper was a devotee of the Prince, and neither obviously was Peter, since, for the first several months, the paper remained generally neutral.

Whatever plans Charles may have had for the *Star* at the beginning never came to fruition, for, when the paper was begun (3 May, 1788), he was busy with *The Stone Eater;* and, from 17 July, 1788, through 1 August, 1788, he was an agent of the Treasury. Since one of his duties was to handle the newspapers in behalf of the Ministerial candidate in the Westminster election, it was inevitable that he would make use of the *Star,* as, it is evident from the following letter,[20] he did. The letter was addressed to George Rose, a Secretary of the Treasury: "Sir, I'll do myself the honour of waiting on you in an hour.—The poem [as it appeared in the morning papers] is incorrect, from its lateness—but it will be correct in the Star—The papers of this day only cost about 20£.—Yours, &c./ C. Stuart./ Wed. [30 July, 1788]." But the paper managed to preserve its political neutrality despite Charles, and Charles himself quit the Treasury even before the elections were concluded. One next catches sight of him on 17 August, when his "Farewell Address" to the Royal Family was recited at the Theater Royal in Cheltenham. The address, which extolled the King for his stern dislike of reformers and innovators and saluted the Prince of Wales as "our CONSTITUTION's sacred Shield," was printed in the Ministerial *World,* the political department of which was controlled by Sheridan, on 18 August and in the *Morning Post,* still edited by Daniel Stuart, on 18 and 22 August, the second printing being justified on the ground that the first was "[done] in an incorrect manner." One may safely assume that it also appeared in the *Star.*

The fact that the King had gone to Cheltenham for reasons of health had a good deal to do with what subsequently happened, but by this time someone else had come within the sphere of Charles's influence. James Mackintosh had migrated to London from Scotland in the spring of 1788; and, although he had been a student of medicine at the University of Edinburgh, his interests were actually law, the study of which he had foregone because his father's fortune "was thought too small for [him] to venture on so uncertain a pursuit," and politics, in which he was an idolator of Edmund Burke. Having settled himself as "a boarder in the house of Mr. Fraser, . . . a maternal relation, who was then carrying on the business of a wine merchant in Clipstone Street," he joined the Constitutional Society, a middle-class Whig club, founded in 1780 and now the most active of the Whig organizations, and during the Westminster election he probably lent his support to the Opposition candidate, John Townshend. But meanwhile his landlord had introduced him to Catherine Stuart, and he was soon "a frequent visitor" at the house in Charlotte Street.[21] Since his interest in Catherine was something more than fraternal, he was for all practical purposes a member of the family and hence inevitably to be included in any of Charles's schemes.

Charles had, of course, been keeping a watchful eye on the King's health, which continued to worsen. On 20 October, 1788, the *Morning Post* reported that "His MAJESTY" was "much indisposed," and on 10 November this fact was admitted by all the newspapers. At, one suspects, the urging of Charles, Mackintosh at once advertised a pamphlet on the nature of insanity, the purpose of which was to demonstrate the necessity for a pro tempore ruler, but this work was abandoned in favor of the more urgent *Arguments concerning the Constitutional Right of Parliament to Appoint a Regency*, which was published (London) at the end of the year.[22] Since the *Arguments* supported Lord Loughborough's contention that Parliament had no right to interfere in the matter of succession, Lord Loughborough was grateful, and in 1799 he repaid the favor by exerting "some influence and even authority, in his capacity as chancellor," to induce the benchers of Lincoln's Inn to lend Mackintosh their hall for his lectures.[23] But the pamphlet was intended as a service to the Prince of Wales, who, it concluded, in the mood of Charles's dedicatory epistle, "has not been every where idolized, [only] because he could not be universally known"; and the Prince was also grateful. Although the *Arguments* "dropped *still-born* from the press," [24] it was said [25] that the Prince "always professed a kindly recollection of the service thus done to his cause." By this time he had additional reason for gratitude.

Until mid-November, 1788, Peter Stuart and the other proprietors of the *Star* got along very well. Although the paper did not flourish, the proprietors professed their satisfaction with Peter's conduct of it, and they regarded him as a man of "integrity." Peter in turn seems to have respected them. But in mid-November, according to the proprietors (*Star*, 16 Febr., 1789), Peter suffered a "sudden and total corruption of . . . heart." In connivance with "a few desperate associates" and, the proprietors had "reason . . . to believe," "for *certain considerations*," he, "upon his own authority, agreed to change the [neutral] Line of their Paper and carry the Influence of the STAR to support [the Prince of Wales's] faction. . . . The Complexion of the Paper from day to day justified their Suspicions." There was, however, a great deal the proprietors did not know, for Peter was acting, not "upon his own authority," but upon the authority of his brother, Charles, and it was Charles and James Mackintosh who were changing "the Line" of the newspaper, not Peter. Upon the basis of present evidence, the proprietors seem also to have been mistaken in supposing that the subversion was prompted by "*certain considerations*" from Carlton House. By this time the Prince, who was already having financial difficulties, knew that he would be obliged to buy the *Morning Post* at approximately Benjafield's price, and it does not seem very likely that under such circumstances he would have contracted for a second newspaper. Under any circumstances one cannot believe that he would have contracted for the *Star,* for the paper was selling only 400 copies a day and was selling those 400 mainly in the country. All Charles and Mackintosh had, therefore, was probably the oral equivalent of a promissory note, payable when and if the Prince became Regent.

## CRIMINATIONS AND RECRIMINATIONS

THERE are two accounts of the quarrel between Peter Stuart and the other proprietors, the first of which is the account of "P. STUART." But this account is confusing, for, although it purports to have been written by Peter Stuart, the author was actually Charles Stuart, who was speaking for Peter and was employing the same argumentation he had already employed with him.

It was "P. STUART's" contention, to begin with (spurious *Star,* 16 Febr., 1789), that he had altered "the Line" of the *Star* only "for the *good of the Proprietors at large."* He had always, he said (spurious *Star,* 13 Febr., 1789), been "actuated by principles of impartiality," and his support of "the PRINCE of WALES, and every friend to the BRITISH CONSTITUTION" had in no respect violated those "principles." The *Star* had continued to "[censure] and [praise] Mr. Fox and Mr. PITT for particular measures"; and the paper had meanwhile flourished. Because of its support of the Prince, the *Star* had had access to certain secret information about the King's behavior which no other newspaper had, and, among the "LITERARY GENTLEMEN" it had added to its staff had been a medical man, who was an authority on insanity. By February, 1789, the sale of the *Star* had accordingly increased to "ABOVE TWO THOUSAND daily," the information "respecting the KING's health" having alone "raised the property from [a sale of] *four hundred to fifteen hundred"* (spurious *Star,* 16 Febr., 1789) .

There would have been no trouble whatever, said "P. STUART" (spurious *Star,* 13 Febr., 1789) , had it not been for John Murray, who, having previously "absented himself" from the proprietors' meetings, suddenly returned and "appeared so contrite" regarding his early attempt to interfere with the newspaper that Peter, his "heart at rest wrapped up in its own integrity," forgave him. But there was a sinister reason for Murray's return, for the *Star* was now "in the *city phrase* A GOOD THING" and therefore a "THING" which interested the

Treasury. Hence, as soon as he had, "as he thought," "lulled" Peter's suspicions, Murray "duped [William Lane], to lead by EPICUREAN INTRIGUE, the rest of the PROPRIETORS into his own INTERESTED views. The BAIT took," and Peter was thereupon ordered to "support Mr. PITT, through THICK and THIN" and to *"assassinate"* the character of the Prince of Wales. "P. STUART" admitted that, as editor of the *Morning Post,* he (Peter) had "occasionally exercised" his "feeble aid" in Pitt's support: "But then it [had] been with the freedom of a MAN—not by compulsion—but by conviction." This time his "nature" supposedly "revolted at these *literary scavengers."* Still, Murray had the backing of a majority, and so Peter "apparently acquiesced, that [he] might, at a future period, be prepared to do [himself] justice." With hope, but little expectation, that "the rest of the Proprietors would open their eyes to the arts of these men," Peter "prepared for the worst."

"The worst" happened, for, not only did the eyes of "the rest of the Proprietors" remain sealed, but, according to "P. STUART" (spurious *Star,* 16 Febr., 1789), these

certain ACTING PROPRIETORS . . . , very often, when every operation of the day was completed for the press, WOULD NOT ADVANCE ONE FARTHING FOR STAMP-PAPER, TO SAVE THE PROPERTY FROM DESTRUCTION. By these unfortunate circumstances, the existence of the concern was for sometime in a very doubtful state, the Printer not receiving *one sheet* of stamped paper, *till nearly the hour appointed for publication.* About [16 December, 1788], it was with the utmost difficulty *The Star* made its appearance. The principal Clerk applied to the ACTING PROPRIETORS for cash to purchase the necessary number of stamps for the Day. His earnest solicitations were treated with contempt, and these CONFIDENTIAL GENTLEMEN peremptorily *refused to give the least pecuniary assistance for the* SALVATION of the PROPERTY . . . ; and had not a very worthy friend granted a loan for IMMEDIATE RELIEF, the existence of the Paper must have that day terminated. That amiable and spiritual gentleman has made several applications to be refunded the sum lent, and has not yet been able to obtain his money.

Having labored to keep the newspaper alive under such impossible conditions, Peter was at last rewarded by being "DISMISSED AT A MOMENT'S WARNING." So said "P. STUART."

It may well be true that Charles Stuart's subversion of the *Star* animated John Murray, who persuaded a majority of the proprietors that the newspaper should support Pitt. For, although the paper had

previously taken no stand respecting the Regency, the proprietors
were thereafter determined that it would support the Government, the
cause of the Prince of Wales being deemed "inimical to the Interests
and Prosperity of this Country." But, of the reason for this determination, the proprietors said nothing. According to their account (*Star,*
16 Febr., 1789), the trouble began when they noticed the altered
"Complexion of the Paper," for, assuming that Peter Stuart was responsible for it, they at once called a meeting and "came to various
Resolutions," intended "to prevent his design, and to preserve Public
Virtue and Consistence of Character." The meeting seems to have
occurred in early December. But, although Peter willingly "acceded"
to the "Resolutions," the "Resolutions" had no effect upon "the Line"
of the newspaper. They protested, Peter apologized and promised to
mend his ways, and still the result was the same. By this time it should
have been evident to them that Peter had no "design" and that the
only question was whether he would ultimately be dominated by them
or by his brother. Even this was not much of a question, for, although
he was bound to them by considerations of "integrity," he was bound
to Charles by the much stronger ties of emotion, habit, and the
agonizing fact of his own weakness. The miracle is that he vacillated
as long as he did. But, because Peter accepted responsibility for his
conduct, the proprietors assumed that he was responsible, and in mid-
December they resorted to the somewhat desperate tactic of with-
holding funds. This tactic they wisely abandoned before "[that]
amiable and spiritual gentleman," who could hardly have been other
than Peter Stuart's "very worthy friend," John Bell, got control of the
newspaper altogether; and they seem to have taken no further action
until early February.

At the beginning of February, however, said the proprietors (*Star,*
16 Febr., 1789), it was "reported" to them "that in order to insure
success to [his] virtuous scheme, [Peter] had conceived a Design
hostile to the whole concern, by a New Print: to the destruction of the
present Property of his friends. . . . A Design so treacherous and unprincipled, it was imagined could not be harboured in the breast of a
man, who had been . . . employed, chiefly from the opinion entertained of his integrity." When they questioned him about the report,
they were "pleased to find, that . . . he totally and unequivocally,
disclaimed all such profligate intentions. And in testimony of his
abhorrence of the design imputed to him, . . . he agreed to, and

[on 5 February, 1789,] signed the following Resolutions with twelve other Proprietors." The "Resolutions" specified that Peter would henceforth keep "the line of the Paper PALPABLY in favour of Administration," that he would "in future draw cordially with the majority of Proprietors./ And further, the Printer has declared that he has at present given up every idea of an interest in any other Newspaper, and never will be concerned in any adventure of that kind, the execution of which will impeach his character for dishonour with the present Proprietors." But the *Star* continued to support the Prince of Wales, and meanwhile the "reports" of that "New Print" persisted. Hence on 12 February the proprietors again questioned Peter, and "Mr. Stuart once more disclaimed all engagements with any other Paper." But the *Star* of that day was hardly printed when "the Pressmen and Compositors struck working, and retired from the office, by the arts of this very honest man; who practiced this manœuvre, in order if possible to make it impracticable for the Proprietors to publish the STAR [on the following day]." At this point the proprietors delayed no longer, and "Mr. Stuart" was summarily dismissed "for repeated acts of Disobedience, Contumacy, and Breach of Promise." If they had any doubt as to the necessity for this action, the doubt was short-lived, for on 13 February, 1789, said the proprietors, Peter Stuart "PRINTED a new Paper in EXACT IMITATION OF THIS; which from undoubted proofs had been long in preparation; in order to usurp, or to grasp the whole property for the emolument of himself, and a few desperate associates."

Except for the fact that they had attributed to Peter Stuart crimes which should have been attributed to Charles Stuart, the proprietors' account seems to have been remarkably accurate, erring, insofar as it erred at all, on the side of understatement. The last number of the *Star* to be printed by Peter Stuart (12 Febr., 1789) was almost entirely given over to eulogies of the Prince of Wales, intimate details of the King's behavior, and abuse of William Pitt; and, when "Mr. Stuart" left that newspaper, he took with him, not only "the Pressmen and Compositors," but "ALL THE LITERARY TALENTS and CONNECTIONS" and evidently even the clerks: *"sixteen* or *eighteen* persons" in all (spurious *Star,* 16 Febr., 1789) . He robbed the paper of everything except its address, and this, too, he seemed to have taken. For on the morning of Friday, 13 February, the *Morning Herald,* for which Charles was still writing a weekly column, announced what seemed to be a change of location: "The STAR, printed by P. Stuart, is removed from Exeter-street and Temple-bar, to No. 9, Feather's Buildings, Drury-lane; and at No. 262, Strand, opposite Essex-street: it can be had only, in future, at the above places, where it will continue to be published this and every afternoon as usual." It is notable that this announcement did not appear in the *Morning Post,* although the controlling interest of the *Post* was now owned by Carlton House and the paper was published, even though no longer edited, by Daniel Stuart. But the plot to block publication of the original *Star* at least failed, and so, at three o'clock on the afternoon of 13 February, two *Stars, and Evening Advertisers* made their appearance. The first was "printed" by John Mayne at No. 31, Exeter Street, Catherine Street, Strand, the second by "P. STUART, No. 9, Feather's-court, Drury-lane, where advertisements, Articles of Intelligence, &c. addressed to the Printer, are received. Also at the Receiving and Publishing Office, No. 262, opposite Essex-street, Strand." The two papers were identical except that the second *Star* repeated the legend, "Printed by P. STUART," above the title, and it was lacking a serial number.

The original *Star* had nothing to say about the quarrel; the spurious *Star* had a great deal to say, for almost the whole of the first number was taken up with an address, entitled "P. STUART'S REASONS FOR ABANDONING THE EXETER-STREET STAR," the address being reprinted on the following day. It began, of course, with the usual apology: "Although it be an irksome task for an humble individual to obtrude himself upon the public attention, yet when my professional character and rectitude of conduct are attacked and abused, I have too great confidence in the liberality of an unbiassed people, to hesitate in appealing to that justice and impartiality. Conscious that by the decision of my fellow-citizens I shall stand or fall, a plain statement of unquestionable facts is best calculated for a refutation of my insidious enemies." This was dissimulation, for the people were never "unbiassed" with respect to spurious newspapers, every one of which had failed. What "P. STUART" actually meant was that in this instance there was no justification for bias, as he would attempt to demonstrate.

The demonstration was obviously not going to be easy, for, since the proprietors had not publicly attacked him, his attacks on them would only bias the already-biased tribunal further. But

"P. STUART" solved this problem by generously refusing to name the proprietors unless they "sport [their names] as a sanction for their proceedings" and, more important, by representing them as dupes of John Murray. Murray, too, was not named, but he was clearly enough identified, and readers could be counted on to remember the numerous quarrels he had had with his authors. "P. STUART" depicted himself as only another victim of Murray's wiles, Murray supposedly being very old (he was actually only forty-three) and cunning and he himself very young (he was at least twenty-eight) and innocent. "It is natural for youth to place a confidence in age," "P. STUART" reminded his readers; "especially when such age seduce by trivial attentions, well-timed and consequently properly applied. Notwithstanding, therefore all the strong hints from a late celebrated Historian of an unfortunate Queen [Gilbert Stuart]—notwithstanding living Historians [who had had dealings with Murray] fully confirmed his declarations—Still was I so infatuated by the blandishments of this man, that my ears were shut against all advice and reproof." "P. STUART" proceeded to review Murray's conduct from his first ineffectual attempt to win over the proprietors to "his particular views" to his final "duping" of William Lane and so of the proprietors in general. The fact that the proprietors themselves had succumbed to "EPICUREAN INTRIGUE" seemed to him a sufficient extenuation of his own gullibility; or, as he put it: "If *conviviality* sometimes overcomes the understanding of the SKIL-FUL, it is no wonder that the unsuspected [*sic*] heart, unhackneyed in the ways of men, should be MISLED."

At this point "P. STUART" interrupted his narrative to speak of "POLITICS." He felt very strongly, it appeared, that "the PRESS" was the "MODERN MAGNA CHARTA of BRITISH LIBERTY" and that "the CON-DUCTOR of a paper" should therefore remain aloof "from the rancorous Bias of PARTY." Hence, when the proprietors ordered him to "support Mr. PITT, *through* THICK and THIN" and even sent along "a number of paragraphs, some of which were . . . *wretchedly spelt,* against His ROYAL HIGHNESS the PRINCE of WALES," he rebelled. He respected "several parts" of Pitt's "conduct," of course, but why, he asked, "must the PRINCE of WALE's [*sic*] *reputation* be wounded, in order to support the Minister 'through thick and thin?' " If Pitt himself did not "spurn this base act of such *hostile* flatterers, he ought to forfeit all claim to the support of society." "P. STUART" went on to promise that his *Star* would "never be pledged to any man or set of men," except, of course, the Prince of Wales, and to repeat that his only sin had been to "censure and praise" both political parties according to their deserts, to refuse "to *stab* through the medium of [*his*] *name,* every person whom [the proprietors'] dastardly minds chose to assail," and to support, "as far as [his] feeble talents could effect, the PRINCE of WALES, and every friend to the BRITISH CONSTITUTION." This part of the address was intended for the eye of the Prince rather than the eye of the "people," for, since the Prince was no popular idol, the "people" would have been unmoved by the tale of "P. STUART's" sufferings on his account. But the Prince, it was hoped, would feel otherwise.

Thus far "P. STUART" had dealt entirely in irrelevancies, for, since it would have seemed to his tribunal that the proprietors of a newspaper had a legal and therefore a moral right to decide what political "Line" their own newspaper would take, the only question was whether they had or had not surrendered this right. To this question "P. STUART" replied that he "thought" so: that he was under the impression that he "always possessed a discretionary power to act for [their] general benefit," and, since "the Paper increased daily in sale," he "[apprehended] that there was no reason for complaint." But this answer would not have satisfied the readers, and it obviously did not satisfy Peter Stuart, who was evidently still beset with qualms, for the concluding paragraph of the address can be explained only as "P. STUART's" final concession to the uneasy Peter:

> To prove to the PUBLIC the purity of my intentions, I declare, that should ALL MY FRIENDS wish for a reconciliation, I shall be very happy to re-unite with them on amicable terms; and whoever shall express himself to that effect before TOMORROW EVENING, shall be accepted with every testimony of cordiality.—But I can never consent to relinquish the power and controul to TWO VERY HONOURABLE MEN [Murray and Lane], whose measures, I am well informed, have within these few days sunk the sale of the Paper between *two and three hundred a day.*

"P. STUART" had evidently forgotten that, up to and including the previous day, he had himself been responsible for those "measures."

There was an irony in the charge that the proprietors planned "to *stab* through the medium of [Peter Stuart's] *name,* every person whom their dastardly minds chose to assail." If they had done such a thing, they would have done no more than John Benjafield had done a year earlier and much less than Peter's "desperate associates" were planning to do now, for at least a thousand people would be "assailed" in the name of "P. STUART" before the spurious *Star* finished its work. By way of preparing for what was ahead, the paper was already making a great deal of the fact that its conductor was Peter Stuart. His name appeared in every masthead, and readers were frequently reminded editorially that "P. STUART" was the sole conductor of "this Paper." Yet he was the least important of a trio of conductors, one of whom, Charles Stuart, could not afford to identify himself with an anti-Pitt newspaper until he collected a debt owed him by the Treasury, another of whom, James Mackintosh, felt that a known connection with the daily press would jeopardize his future career in politics and the law.

On Saturday, 14 February, the proprietors replied to the spurious *Star*'s address of 13 February, the reply being reprinted on 16 February. Having presented their version of the affair, they made it clear in a concluding paragraph that there would be no reconciliation: "It would be folly in the extreme, to waste time in loading a man of this Complexion with the epithets he deserves. He excites greater pity in the breasts of the Proprietors than indignation; they lament the sudden and total corruption of a heart they once placed confidence in; and . . . they take leave of the friendship and services of Mr. Peter Stuart for ever." "P. STUART" published a rebuttal on 16 February. Although he had previously said that he would not identify any of the proprietors unless they identified themselves "as a sanction for their proceedings," this promise was forgotten, and Murray and Lane were named. Of all the "low ribbaldry and unfounded assertions" included in the proprietors' declaration, the most galling to "P. STUART" was the statement that the "idea" for the *Star* had been theirs and that he had "[acted] in the sole capacity of their SERVANT." Since, if this had been the case, there would have been no shadow of justification for his behavior, he devoted at least half of the rebuttal to establishing the fact that he "WAS THE ORIGINAL and PRINCIPAL PROPRIETOR, and made them PARTNERS in the PROFITS of an INVENTION ENTIRELY [HIS] OWN."

In answer to a charge that he had bribed the newsmen to substitute the spurious *Star* for the original *Star*, "P. STUART" made a countercharge. It was "an incontrovertible truth," he said, "that the ACTING

PROPRIETORS invited [the newsmen] to a FEAST, and, after supper, when the President had complimented them with all the oratorical flowers of *Leadenhall Market,* those very ACTING PROPRIETORS, thinking themselves in their Star-Chamber Committee, *abused, assaulted,* and *wounded* many respectable NEWSMEN, their WIVES, and CHILDREN!—This was verifying the old adage—*inviting them to a feast, and sticking the visitants with the spit!"* This was one of "P. STUART's" very few blunders. Since, in battles of this sort, one of the protagonists always accused the other of bribing the newsmen, no one took the accusation seriously, and the conventional response was either silence or a similar accusation. But in this instance the readers would have asked themselves why the proprietors should have given the newsmen "a FEAST" and followed the compliments with abuse, if the newsmen had not, in fact, accepted bribes from "P. STUART."

While the opportunity was at hand, "P. STUART" again reminded the Prince of Wales that he had set up the spurious *Star* solely on his account, for his "BROTHER PROPRIETORS," he said,

could never force me to commit a suicide on my reputation, by tamely publishing the scandalous and miserably-written libels which were sent to me against the PRINCE of WALES, whose character is an honour to humanity, and whom every good subject of HIS MAJESTY looks to with respect and admiration.

To support Mr. PITT or any other MINISTER, through THICK and THIN, would be an infamous prostitution of that confidence which the Public has given me. I shall never be dragged into the degrading trammels of a party, and tamely become the despicable tool of the unprincipled attempts of its most abandoned and dastardly retainers. Through the medium of my name, they wished to stab the most distinguished and respectable characters in the kingdom. . . .

But there was another passage which the Prince would have found far less gratifying. For, having stated that the proprietors had ordered him to " 'SUPPORT *Mr.* PITT THROUGH THICK AND THIN—*reprobate and condemn Mr.* FOX *and Mr.* SHERIDAN, *as enemies to their country—and asperse and vilify the* PRINCE *of* WALES *and a certain amiable Lady* [Mrs. Fitzherbert], *as foes to Mr.* PITT *and* HIS ADMINISTRATION,'* " "P. STUART" went on to say: "If any person entertains the most distant shadow of a doubt with regard to these bitter truths, my instructions, with PARAGRAPHS and LETTERS in the HANDWRITING of these MISERABLE SCRIBBLERS, are in my custody, for the inspection of

the curious. I have it in contemplation to print the articles alluded
to. . . ." If the "articles" had actually existed, they would already, of
course, have been printed by the original *Star*. But they did not exist,
and "P. STUART's" threat to print them was only an attempt to get
immediate financial assistance from Carlton House. Since by this time
the Regency Bill had already passed the Commons, had been read
twice without opposition in the House of Lords, and was scheduled
to go into committee on the following day, "P. STUART" could
hardly have selected a less opportune time to make the attempt, and
the fact that he nevertheless did make it indicates how desperate was
the financial state of the spurious *Star*.

## SOME WAYS AND MEANS OF THE SPURIOUS *STAR*

THE question of who did finance the spurious *Star* for the first several weeks is one of the real puzzles relating to the newspaper. Although many of the paper's creditors may have been willing to gam-
ble, as "P. STUART" was himself gambling, on the Prince's becoming Regent within a few days, still it was impossible to begin a
newspaper with no capital whatever, and the capital could not have
been provided by the Stuarts. Peter's £1,000 would still have been invested in the original *Star*, Charles was already in semi-hiding to avoid
arrest for various debts he had contracted in behalf of George Rose,
and Daniel would not have invested his money in one of
Charles's enterprises. Mackintosh may have contributed the remainder
of his "small fortune," for, on the morning of 18 February, 1789, he
left "the house of Mr. Fraser," paused at Marylebone Church long
enough to marry Catherine, and, on the evident assumption that six
could live as cheaply as five, moved into the house in Charlotte
Street.[26] "The relations of both parties" are supposed to have been
"offended at the rash proceeding": hers because Mackintosh was a
young man of twenty-three "with no prospect of any immediate professional settlement" and with the "little fortune" which he had inherited "rapidly diminishing"[27] and his because Catherine represented "neither much beauty nor fortune."[28] But there is no
indication of disapproval on the part of the Stuarts, and there was no
reason for disapproval on the part of the Mackintoshes, for, although
the bride was lacking youth as well as "beauty" and "fortune," she had

numerous domestic virtues, and her insistence upon "industry" and "economy" [29] should alone have endeared her to Mackintosh's relations.

It should be added that, according to one of Mackintosh's biographers,[30] Catherine Stuart was living in Gerard Street, Soho, at the time of her marriage, but Daniel Stuart's daughter stated positively [31] that the Stuarts had always lived in Charlotte Street. However, she added, the marriage "broke up the home, and on the younger sister Elizabeth joining Mr. and Mrs. Mackintosh, the brothers were left each to his own course." According to another biographer,[32] the Mackintoshes later moved to Buckingham Street and, in the summer of 1790, removed "to a small house in the village of Little Ealing, in Middlesex"; but they were soon back in the house in Charlotte Street, and they did not again leave until 1795. For the present purpose it is sufficient to know that the Stuarts and Mackintoshes constituted one household until the autumn of 1789.

But Mackintosh's "small fortune" would not have launched the spurious *Star*, and the only clue to other investors is the spurious *Star* itself, which circumstantially furnishes the names of three. The first one is John Bell, with whom Peter Stuart had been associated on the *Morning Post* and with whom he was still "in the habits of friendship" as well as "intimacy." By this time Bell had sold his shares in the *World* and was connected with that newspaper only as printer. The evidence that Bell was financially interested in the spurious *Star* is rather strong, for, from 13 February through 9 March, the paper carried advertisements for his British Library and performed certain textual services in his behalf, and Bell always exerted a powerful influence on the paper's policy. But the evidence that he was not financially interested is even stronger, for throughout this period he was planning the *Oracle*, as he would not have been, one would suppose, if his money was already tied up in the spurious *Star*. More important, Bell was too cautious to invest money in a venture as risky as this one. It was one thing to lend the Stuarts a small sum to purchase a one-day's supply of stamps for the original *Star*, for he could always get the money back in advertising; but it would have been quite another thing to give them a thousand pounds or more for this particular enterprise, and one cannot quite see Bell doing it. He would more likely have dealt with them as he had dealt with Topham, trading his "experience," "judgment," and "time" for a share in the newspaper, with the understanding that he would assume no financial risk of any kind.

A second name circumstantially furnished by the spurious *Star* is that of the elder George Colman, manager of the Haymarket. Colman's tampering with newspapers had been a matter of notoriety for years. In 1785 he was identified (*Morning Post,* 7 Febr., 1785) as a proprietor of the *Public Advertiser* and the *St. James's Chronicle,* and he was often enough accused (see, e.g., *Morning Herald* and *General Advertiser,* 8 Sept., 1783) of having "swarms of [journalistic] sycophants and reptiles at work for him." By 1788 he was evidently no longer a proprietor of the *Public Advertiser,* but he was still, according to the *Morning Post* (14 July, 1788), a proprietor of the *St. James's Chronicle,* "by [which] means," the *Post* added, "the *younger Colman* has unlimited power to *puff* himself." Charles Stuart's acquaintance with Colman had begun in 1781, when Colman accepted two of his pieces for performance at the Haymarket, one of which, *Ripe Fruit; or, The Marriage Act,* was performed on 22 August, the other, *Damnation; or, The Play-house Hissing Hot,* being performed on 29 August. On 28 August, 1783, Colman had brought out a third piece, *Gretna Green,* which Charles wrote in collaboration with John O'Keefe and Dr. Samuel Arnold; and he was more than repaid for his trouble. For a few days later Charles, then printer of the *Morning Post,* had given Colman vigorous support in his battle with Dennis O'Bryen. Colman had been so moved by this unsolicited assistance that he felt "obliged" (*Herald,* 12 Sept., 1783) to express his gratitude publicly. That Colman was an investor in the spurious *Star* there can be no doubt, for almost every number of the newspaper extolled the virtues of the Colmans.

There is one further name, for, just as Topham was using the *World* to further the career of his mistress, the actress Mary Wells, someone was using the spurious *Star* to further the career of the actress Charlotte Goodall. Many, if not most, of the reviews of productions at Drury Lane concluded with the complaint that the public was not seeing enough of Mrs. Goodall, and her genius was proclaimed several times weekly in separate paragraphs. Previously connected with the Bath theater, Mrs. Goodall had made her debut at Drury Lane in October, 1788, but had quarreled with the manager, John Kemble, when she refused to play the role of Lady Anne in *King*

*Richard the Third.* The quarrel had reached the newspapers in late 1788, when her husband, Thomas Goodall, a merchant captain in Bristol, employed the *Morning Post* to defend her interests against Kemble's.[33] Although this quarrel was now settled, Goodall seems to have been dissatisfied with the progress of his wife's career. Since Charles was himself connected with Drury Lane, he would have known both the Goodalls, and, since the puffs of Mrs. Goodall continued for the life of the spurious *Star,* Thomas Goodall can be safely included among the list of proprietors. There are numerous other puffs in the newspaper, but there are not enough of any one person to be of significance, and there are no advertisements of consequence.

The cost of setting up a newspaper was estimated at £6,000 at the very least, of which Colman and Goodall had evidently provided a modicum, for the spurious *Star* at once looked about for supplemental revenue. Since it could not appeal to the Government, it appealed to the Opposition or, more specifically, to Sheridan, who handled such matters for the Opposition. The very first number of the newspaper (13 Febr., 1789) disclaimed forever "the rancorous Bias of PARTY"; however, it added separately, it must commend "Mr. SHERIDAN" for the "moderation with which [he] supports an unremitting abuse in the public prints": "The shafts of malignity fall harmless from the object they are designed to wound. Compared with such feeble assailants, we regard him as the great GULLIVER with the Pigmies of *Lilliput.* . . . Our professed respect for justice demands this tribute from our hands in favour of Mr. SHERIDAN." There was no response, and on 16 February the paper threatened the Prince of Wales. Although it was persuaded not to repeat the threat, the persuasion was apparently not in the form of cash, for on 18 February the spurious *Star* resumed its courtship of the Opposition with the hope that, "when the opposition come into power, they will, by their actions, give the lie to all the illiberal abuse that has been thrown against them by their adversaries. . . . [Whatever] his Grace of PORTLAND does, or his connections at large undertake, we are certain will be intended for the good of the country."

On 24 February and 4 March, Sheridan was the subject of some poetic eulogies, signed "MARIA FALCONER" and "MRS. BOYS," respectively; and on 27 February the spurious *Star* replied to a correspondent, who expressed his gratification at its refusal to support "Mr. FOX or Mr. PITT, or any other POLITICAL METEOR, through

'THICK and THIN,'" with a declaration of its devotion only to the "PARTY of the PUBLIC," which declaration it repeated on 3 March. In effect, the paper was divorcing itself from the Foxite Opposition, otherwise known as the "Party of the People," and was restricting its support to the Sheridan faction, previously known as "The New Whigs" and now evidently renamed the "PARTY of the PUBLIC." But Sheridan, like the Prince of Wales, seems to have responded for the present only with expressions of gratitude and with the assurance, no doubt, that he had the paper's interests at heart. For there is no indication that the spurious *Star* received any money from the Whigs during this period, and, although on 27 February it supported their demands for repeal of the shop tax, payment for this service would have been provided by the shopkeepers, not by the Whigs.

Had it not been for its extraordinary success in another area, the spurious *Star* would probably not have survived more than a week. The plan "to *stab* through the medium of [Peter Stuart's] *name*, every person whom [the conductors'] dastardly minds chose to assail" seems to have been as old as the newspaper, for the first number of the spurious *Star* (13 Febr., 1789) suggested that "Mr. B–n and Miss J–s should not shew their affection so much in public" and that "Mr. V–s should ogle less from the boxes, and think more of the world of which he must soon be an inhabitant." These two paragraphs, which were surprisingly crude in view of the fact that the paper could draw on the "experience," "judgment," and "time" of John Bell, were, however, only harbingers. On the following day (14 Febr.) the spurious *Star* discharged a volley of scurrility at the residents of Bath, of which the following is an example:

> The Bath hounds are in excellent condition; but the gentlemen of the Hunt keep them confined, as there is a Fox in town whom all wish to preserve rather than destroy.
>
> The dangler continues his impertinent gallantries with his usual vanity. He is particular [*sic*] fond of married women, and at present pays his devoirs to one of the most elegant in Bath. At card parties his figure is truly ridiculous; he seats himself opposite this lady with his knees almost touching his chin, his face reclining between his hands, and his elbow resting upon his knees. In this attitude he sits, like an old sun-burnt frog just ready to leap, admiring the fair, and imagining the eyes of the whole room are noticing him. From this delightful reverie nothing can rouze him but the news of supper being ready.
>
> This Adonis is short, thick and bow legged; with a tawny complection, and bald head.

Paragraphs of the same clumsy kind, still directed at the residents of Bath, appeared in subsequent numbers of the spurious *Star*, and on 20 February the paper added some abusive verse. On the same day it experimented with a list of "SHAKESPEAREAN PORTRAITS," submitted by a Bath correspondent, who signed himself "A STARGAZER," the "PORTRAITS" consisting of brief quotations from Shakespeare set against the names of various prominent people.

The experiment was evidently very successful, for the lists soon became a regular feature of the paper, and in a short time the spurious *Star* was publishing two such lists, one relating to the residents of Bath, another relating to the residents of Bristol. The lists coming from Bristol were signed "PETER PEPPER" or "PETER PICKLE." "P. STUART" was delighted with the lists and repeatedly urged correspondents to send in more of them, promising in return the strictest anonymity. "Many dastardly attempts have been made to discover several Correspondences," he observed on 2 March; "but we are too grateful for the testimonies of their partiality to be in any degree instrumental in the operations of treachery." He should have been grateful, for, since anyone could, of course, buy himself out of the lists for a small sum, the "Correspondences" were enabling the spurious *Star* to practice extortion on a wholesale basis and to do so with a minimum expenditure of space. In addition the market was entirely new. For, whereas other extortionary sheets confined their activities to London and Middlesex and concentrated on politicians, the spurious *Star* was active only in Bath and Bristol and was interested only in people of fashion. As time went on, titles of plays were sometimes substituted for quotations from Shakespeare in order to relieve the monotony, but the effect was the same.

The numbering of the spurious *Star* began on 16 February, 1789, with the serial number "3," and on 23 or 24 February the title was changed from *Star, and Evening Advertiser* to *Stuart's Star, and Evening Advertiser*. The two *Stars* were always identical in format and, except for the altered title and the legend, "Printed by P. STUART," which the spurious *Star* continued to carry above its title, in masthead. They were also similar in kind, for both of them had been modeled on the *World,* and, although the original *Star* was now conducted by John Mayne, Mayne had introduced no innovations. The spurious *Star* was, to begin with, conducted by Charles Stuart, the medical and political editor being James Mackintosh and the miscellaneous editor Peter Stuart. But on 25 February, Charles Stuart was finally arrested for some of the debts he had incurred in behalf of George Rose (spurious *Star,* 29 Apr., 1789), and from then until mid-March the general conduct was in the hands of Mackintosh.

Although the original *Star* for the year 1789 is almost entirely lacking, the paper seems to have remained generally silent after its declaration of 14 February; but not so the spurious *Star,* which continued to reply to the declaration in every number which followed. On 21 February it responded to the charge that it had bribed the newsmen with the announcement: "Complaints being made by several of our friends, that the *Dog Star* has been foisted upon them instead of STUART's STAR, it is requested that every person who is imposed upon by the spurious print, will send to the Office . . . , and they may depend on being served regularly with STUART's STAR in future." By 24 February this announcement had been altered to read: *"Many complaints having been made, that a wretched imitation has been imposed upon our Friends instead of* THIS PAPER, *it has been judged expedient to make the distinguishing alteration in the* TITLE [*to*] STUART's STAR." The last announcement was repeated daily through 3 March and, in an expanded and modified form, on 1 April:

We cannot help acknowledging the *obligations* we feel for the *last* efforts of the *dying Dogs,* who, finding that they could not impose upon the PUBLIC by their wretched imitation of STUART's STAR, and being convinced that the SPIRIT, ENTERTAINMENT, and ORIGINAL INFORMATION OF THIS PAPER, are unimpeachable, and much superior to their *paltry fabrication,* have kindly added to the distinction of the two papers, by dressing their *horn-boys* in *Merry-Andrew cloaths;* but what right *one* LANE, or any other city *horn-boy,* has to assume the *crest* of the PRINCE of WALES, we cannot divine, unless it be the right which they have arrogated, of endeavouring to libel and defame his ROYAL HIGHNESS.

As many complaints have been made, that the *Dogs* have been impudently forced upon our friends instead of THIS PAPER, we request that they will always ask for STUART's STAR.

As to the stupid and feeble menace against the NEWSMEN, for serving *"any other* print," we can only say, that the *last speech* of the *dying Dogs,* is inconsistent, absurd, and contemptible. . . .

Before we conclude, we are induced by principles of humanity to *pity* the poor *credulous taylor* who furnished *one* LANE and the other *horn-boys* with *party-coloured jackets!*

To anyone who remembered the battle between the two *Posts,* this must have sounded very familiar.

Since the quarrel which resulted in the spurious *Star* was, in fact, political and since "P. STUART" wanted also, no doubt, to keep reminding the Prince of Wales that the battle was being waged on his account, much of the paper's ridicule and resentment had to do with his interests. For example, on 16 February the spurious *Star* burlesqued the bulletins of the King's physicians with some bulletins of its own, one of which related to Lane, the other to Murray:

FLEET-STREET, Feb. 15.
*Mr.* MURRAY *had a very restless night—has been much disturbed—and is irritable . . . this morning.*

W. LANE,
T. PRESTON.
(A True Copy.)
J. HALL in waiting in Exeter-street.

Another such bulletin followed on 18 February: "Dr. LANE yesterday *walked* JOHN MURRAY round St. Dunstan's. The MANIAC knocked down a *dustman*, bit the finger of a *sweep*, and overturned some mad oxen in *Fleet-market*. Dr. LANE was obliged to put on the *strait-jacket* as soon as he became more tame, his friends being very apprehensive of their *personal safety*." There were no further burlesques, but the campaign continued to a high degree political. Several letters from such correspondents as "CANDIDUS" (18 Febr.), "JOHN BULL" (27 Febr.), and "AN UNPREJUDICED SUBJECT" (7 Mar.) testified that, because of the spurious *Star*, their authors had seen the errors of their political ways; and on 24 March the paper boasted that "ALL the LITERARY ASSISTANTS, and indeed every person—MEN and BOY—with whom [P. STUART] was connected in the direction of the *dying* DOGS, immediately, and *of their own free will*, united with the Printer to crush the engines of despotism and corruption."

On 26 March the spurious *Star* summarized and augmented what it had been saying in a long address:

TO THE PUBLIC.

The Printer returns to the *dying Dogs* his sincere thanks for corroborating every assertion which he advanced relative to the principles on which he differed from them. To vilify the PRINCE of WALES, and the FRIENDS of the CONSTITUTION, has been their uniform practice since the Printer left them. Every publication has teemed with some wretched LIBEL against COMMON SENSE and VIRTUE; but that of yesterday, about his ROYAL HIGHNESS, contains such infamous insinuations and assertions that the Printer is glad to hear a prosecution is to be commenced and the abandoned *dog* who devised it will perhaps receive his reward by the *pillory* or a *gibbet*. [No prosecution was commenced.]

From these indisputable facts, every candid person must admit, that the Printer and Conductor of THIS PAPER has, by refusing to act as a mean creature and assassin to the *abandoned* DOGS, been actuated by manly and honourable principles. The Printer and Conductor, who was the ORIGINAL INVENTOR and PROPRIETOR, and responsible for every thing which appeared, received his dismission from his late employment, merely because he refused to assassinate the characters of the PRINCE of WALES and his FRIENDS. The opposition to such a measure he considers as the most honourable act of his life; and he is happy to acknowledge, that a generous public—ever willing to protect the injured—perfectly coincide with him in opinion, by whose uncommon encouragement the extensive circulation of STUART'S STAR has already exceeded his most sanguine expectations.

Although the spurious *Star* repeatedly boasted that it was more "spirited" than the original *Star,* it said little about its "entertainment," possibly because it had no one to compete with "Sylvester Otway [John Oswald], and the other favourites of the Muses," the "lustre of [whose] genius" was now evidently "illuminating" that newspaper.[34] The *Star* had never before printed original poetry, but the proprietors evidently felt that under the present circumstances some originality was demanded. The spurious *Star* had no poet whose pseudonym would have been recognizable to readers except Dr. John Wolcot ("Peter Pindar"), whose "SONG" (5 Mar.) was followed by "ODE" (12 Mar.), and, since Dr. Wolcot was writing for the *Morning Post,* these pieces may have appeared in the *Post* some time earlier. Whatever was original among the early poems was probably provided largely by Charles Stuart. Charles seems, for example, to have been "CADWALLADER," whose verses *"To Mr. PITT,/ On the Prospect before Him"* were published on 13 February. Although readers were promised (14 Febr.) more of "our good adherent CADWALLADER's" work on 16 February, nothing appeared until 19 March. But on 25 February there was an "ADDRESS *to* STUART'*s* STAR," signed "HERSCHEL" and introduced with the headnote: "Among other steady adherents, it is with particular pleasure the *Printer* communicates to his readers the following poetical effusion of his firm friend HERSCHEL. When he declares, that ALL THE LITERARY GENTLEMEN who produced the rapid and uncommon circulation of

the other paper [the original *Star*], voluntarily offered their immediate assistance, he may, without the inspiration of prophecy, flatter
himself that STUART's STAR will rise superior to the shafts of malignity." The "firm friend HERSCHEL" was probably also Charles Stuart,
who, in addition, would have provided many of the *jeux d'esprit*
and epigrams, as well as the abusive verse in general, until he was
removed by the authorities. There was another poet, however, who
was certainly not Charles Stuart, although he seems to have been attached to the paper, too. This one, who signed himself "CALIDORE,"
was author of the lines, *"On a Lady Sleeping,"* which appeared on
25 February, author of some verses, entitled "THE HERMIT,"
which appeared on 11 March, and author of a long letter, part verse
and part prose, entitled "COMPARISON *of the* ROMANCE *and*
NOVEL," which appeared on 25 March. In addition, there was
"W. J.," who wrote the "ANACROSTIC,/ BY A RECLAIMED
LIBERTINE" (21 Febr.) and perhaps some unsigned trifles. "W. J."
seems to have been Peter Stuart's former associate on the *Morning
Post,* the Rev. William Jackson.[35]

But what the spurious *Star* lacked in quality it compensated for
in quantity. By 21 February it could boast a full column of verse, even
though much of it was abusive, much of it political, and anything
which purported to be poetry came in the main from plays or other
newspapers. It also compensated by a catholicity of interests. Like the
*World,* the spurious *Star* was interested in only one sport, boxing, but
it was interested in all the arts, as well as in history, biography, and
philosophy, as the following list of some of its "entertainments" indicates: *"The Second Ode of Anacreon./ Translated in the Scottish
Dialect"* (16 Febr.), a letter from Dr. Priestley on the subject of the
Trinity, dated 14 December, 1788 (21 Febr.), *"Verses [in Latin]
Written at Eton College./ By Sir Gregory Page Turner, Bart."*
(7 Mar.; a translation followed on 26 Mar.), verses *"To the Prosaic
and Metrical* CRITIC, *on Dr.* PARR's WARBURTONIAN
TRACTS," signed "CACAFAGO" (10 Mar.), "ADDRESS [*from
Benjamin Franklin*] *to the United States of* AMERICA, *on the dis-
affection that has prevailed towards the System of Government intro-
duced in that Country"* (10 Mar.), "LITERARY INTELLIGENCE/
Proceedings of the ACADEMY of TROULOUSE [*sic*]" (12 Mar.),
"THE ARTS" (14 Mar.), and "LITERARY INTELLIGENCE/
*Programme of the Academy of Arts, Science, and Belles Lettres of
Lyons"* (19 Mar.).

But the spurious *Star*'s real claim to distinction was, as "P. STUART" often enough said, "the . . . ORIGINAL INFORMATION OF THIS PAPER." Since the newspaper had correspondents in Bath, Bristol, Edinburgh, and Dublin, it was exceptionally well informed respecting activities in those centers; and, although the information from Bath and Bristol was generally limited to gossip, the information from Edinburgh and Dublin was extensive and important. Partly because of the Prince's popularity with the Irish Parliament, of which it made much, it published the Irish debates at greater length than any other newspaper and, according to its own statement (e.g., 7 Mar., 15 Apr.) , at least one day in advance of any other newspaper. It does seem to be true that even the morning press depended on the spurious *Star* for the Irish debates. It also provided the most detailed accounts of Lady Strathmore's action for divorce and recovery of her estates against Andrew Robinson Bowes, once Stoney. Lady Strathmore and Captain Stoney had last been mentioned by the newspapers in 1777, when he and the Rev. Henry Bate Dudley had fought a duel because of some libelous paragraphs respecting her in the *Morning Post*. They had married the same year, had separated a few years later, and, after his attempt to win her back by abduction failed, were finally divorced on 3 March, 1789. In addition, the spurious *Star* obtained an early priority on lottery drawings, so that by 19 February it could predict that *"two thirds of* STUART'*s* STAR *Prize-list of* YESTERDAY *[will appear in]* the expiring DOG-STAR *of* THIS EVENING." On 21 February it announced that henceforth a *"correct* LIST *of* BLANKS *and* PRIZES *in the* LOTTERY *will be published in* STUART'*s* STAR *every day,* TWO HOURS AFTER THE DRAWING, *which must render* THIS PAPER *very valuable to all* TAVERNS, COFFEE-HOUSES, *and* PUBLIC-HOUSES, *in* LONDON *and* WESTMINSTER—*The* Dog-Star, *as a desperate effort to save a ruined reputation, is attempting in this, as in every other respect, to follow* STUART'*s* plans at an humble distance." When one remembers that evening newspapers had heretofore offered no "ORIGINAL INFORMATION," these were important steps toward the building of a solid evening press.


## PROBLEMS OF A REGENCY NEWSPAPER

THE CENTRAL interest of the spurious *Star* was, however, the complex matter of the Regency; and the second number of the newspaper

(14 Febr.) was devoted almost entirely to the King's illness, the Prince of Wales's popularity, and the machinations of the villainous William Pitt. With respect to the King's illness, readers were given to understand that physicians' bulletins could not be trusted, the physicians being in league with the Government, and that only its own reports were reliable. "It is very remarkable," it noticed "that during the whole of his Majesty's illness, whenever any *great point* was to be discussed in Parliament, [the King] was always declared BETTER. As POLONIUS says, 'although it be *madness,* yet there is *method* in it.' " However, "this—the *real* STAR," would provide "a true statement . . . of the KING's health," correcting and interpreting the statement submitted by the physicians. The first such "true statement" followed:

> Reports of a ROYAL CONVALESCENCE, are more the effect of good wishes, and loyal hopes, than having any real foundation in truth. It is true that His MAJESTY has been more *calm* and *tranquil* for these few days, than he has been before, but the derangement is as *lamentable* as ever!
>
> His assuming the habit and manner of a QUAKER, and many other *singularities* of late, which were rumoured at Kew, confirm this. . . .
>
> Extreme calmness, gentleness, and timid docility, in insane disorders, are more often the effects of confirmed mental imbecility than convalescence.
>
> His conversation now, unless occasionally about some mere trifling objects of vegetation, is as incoherent as ever; and, sorry are we to record it, that he dwindles much into a harmless and passive state.
>
> At the same time we cannot but applaud [the physicians'] loyalty, in affording to every good subject a gleam of hope, although on the most trivial change in the health of his Majesty. But let not this loyal zeal go too far, else it can only tend to mislead and distract the country.

The same number carried several flattering "ADDRESSES" from various Boroughs "TO HIS ROYAL HIGHNESS," along with the gratified announcement: "We have reason to conclude . . . that . . . the PRINCE of WALES was, on Wednesday last [11 Febr.], by the voice of an independent Parliament, called upon to assume the Regency of [Ireland], unfettered by any disgraceful restrictions."

From this point on, the leading article in every number of the spurious *Star* was a column, headed "THE KING," which detailed the King's behavior, provided information on the subject of insanity, lauded the Prince and his English and Irish friends, and stressed the necessity for an immediate Regency. The Regency Bill, which had already passed the Commons, was scheduled for committee considera-

tion by the House of Lords on 19 February, but on 19 February the
Lord Chamberlain (Lord Salisbury) reported an improvement in the
King's health, and the House adjourned to 24 February. The spurious
*Star* (20 Febr.) was suspicious:

In the midst of unbounded joy at the favourable medical report, we are
sorry to find that neither the PRINCE of WALES nor the DUKE of YORK were admitted into the Royal presence on Tuesday [17 Febr.].

There is something so *mysterious* in this behaviour of the *Keepers* of the
KING'S PERSON, that PARLIAMENT ought immediately to develope it.

If HIS MAJESTY be so far recovered as is reported, why not permit his children to be witnesses of the pleasing change?

. . . Why preclude the HEIR-APPARENT and his BROTHER from the pleasure of an audience? Are the Keepers afraid, that the PRINCE of WALES may so
far ingratiate himself into the good graces of his SOVEREIGN, as to procure the
Royal signet to the Regency, during will and pleasure?

Whatever be the reason, it is certain, that the nation will murmur at such
treatment of the KING'S sons.

*It is hoped that the* POLITICAL GAME *which was played in the reign of the*
SIXTH HENRY *is not to be followed now.*

On 24 February the spurious *Star* admitted that the King was better.
But, it went on, even his physicians regarded the "rapidity in his
amendment" as not necessarily a good sign, and they were privately
"hinting" that he ought to be relieved of all "public business" for
"two or three months after every deranged symptom has ceased." The
paper's own medical editor regarded it as a very bad sign, obviously "a seeming recovery" rather than "a real recovery," and it was
his opinion that there must be a Regency for at least six months. Although on 21 February the paper had reported that the Prince and
the Duke had "applied again yesterday for permission to see their
Royal Father, but had the mortification to experience a second refusal," it was now (24 Febr.) able to announce that they had seen
their father on 23 February: that the "scene was very affecting; and it
is rumoured about Kew Palace, that the KING has made some remarks
disagreeable to those concerned about the treatment of his Sons and
Brothers."

But the King had also made some remarks which were "disagreeable" to the Prince. In the interview of 23 February, said the spurious
*Star* (25 Febr.), the King had suggested "that a COUNCIL should be
formed with all possible speed, in which it was proposed that [the

Prince of Wales] should preside, in conjunction with her MAJESTY [the Queen] and the present Administration, if agreeable to the ideas of the Prince," the council to function "for at least SIX MONTHS." But by 26 February the spurious *Star* had discovered that the King had meanwhile sent for his brother, the Duke of Gloucester, who, the paper pointed out, was a personal friend of Pitt, "to have his . . . opinion, respecting the late PARLIAMENTARY CONDUCT of [the Prince] and the two other ROYAL DUKES." The spurious *Star* was greatly agitated. Its first reaction (26 Febr.) was to defend the Prince and his friends, impugn the Opposition, and admit that it might have been mistaken with respect to Pitt:

> The confirmed SANITY of HIS MAJESTY will be attended with many blessed effects; the greatest . . . of which will be, restoring the CONSTITUTION to its *pristine* SANITY.
>
> It has been so convulsed, since the KING's illness, by the ambitious views of [the Whig] PARTY, that nothing but his immediate renovation of health, or a most lamentable event, could restore it to its former . . . equilibrium.
>
> . . . His MAJESTY has a great reliance on the integrity of the Duke of GLOUCESTER. And it is said, that His Highness vindicated the behaviour of all, by supporting the cause of the HEIR APPARENT, in such a manner as was highly satisfactory to HIS MAJESTY.
>
> In the mean time, . . . if Mr. PITT has egregiously erred in his conduct to the PRINCE, let us hope that it proceeded from the best, though the most mistaken motives.

The spurious *Star* actually did not know what the Duke of Gloucester had said, and it was not cheered by the rumor, which it reported on 27 February, that the King was now proposing a "plan of government" which would make "the PRINCE and QUEEN *joint Regents,* assisted with a COUNCIL, [the] present Ministry to remain." But, instead of defending the Prince, the spurious *Star* defended his friends, the implication being that, if anyone was ambitious, it was they:

> A very unjust and most disloyal rumour is attempted to be circulated as a truth: Namely, that all those who supported the cause of the PRINCE, during His MAJESTY's indisposition, had DESERTED their SOVEREIGN in the hour of infirmity. Now the contrary, however, is the fact. The supporters of a much-injured PRINCE, displayed more true loyalty to their SOVEREIGN, by endeavouring to invest him with FULL CONSTITUTIONAL POWERS during his FATHER's malady. . . . There is no doubt . . . that his Grace of QUEENSBERRY, the Marquis of LOTHIAN, Lord MALMSBURY, and others, will be most cordially

thanked by HIS MAJESTY, for supporting the DIGNITY of the House of BRUNS-
WICK, free from any other fetters than those already laid on it by the CONSTI-
TUTION.

The same number of the spurious *Star* reaffirmed its own strict "IM-
PARTIALITY" respecting political parties, but ventured some further
gibes at Pitt, who, it was "now whispered," would marry the Countess
of Albany during her visit to England in May. Should the marriage
occur, said the spurious *Star*,

the successful PREMIER of this country, whose AUTHORITY lately has been *most*
PRINCELY, would be the son-in-law to the late PRETENDER, who, in 1744, was
created by his father PRINCE REGENT of BRITAIN!

The MINISTER, by such a marriage, would instantly gain the affections of
all the JACOBITES, which would add considerably to the support of his upright
administration.

In that case, the irony of the Opposition gentry, who lately styled the
Premier, PRINCE PITT, would lose much of its point. Nothing would more
chagrin the enemies of our excellent Minister, than such a fortunate marriage.

By 28 February the spurious *Star* had recovered sufficient aplomb
to suggest that the King himself had never favored a restricted Regency and that at present he wanted the Prince to assume full monarchical powers while he went to Hanover for a long convalescence,
having even "expressed himself somewhat to that effect." It was Pitt
who proposed the restricted Regency, it said, and "[what] the Minister [now] wants, is TWELVE LORD JUSTICES, and the PRINCE to be OF-
FERED the PRESIDENT's CHAIR." On 2 March it again reported that
"HIS MAJESTY, it is certain, has dropped some hints, that he is not
altogether pleased at the conduct of his MINISTER respecting the treatment of his SONS and BROTHERS. A few days will, perhaps, bring forward an event that will astonish the empire./ He is minutely informed of every transaction that happened during his malady. The
QUEEN was his faithful reporter." No "event" was "brought forward,"
but on 2 March the spurious *Star* restated its thesis that Pitt had been
playing a "POLITICAL GAME." "Who is there in the kingdom, unless
the blind and mercenary retainers of his administration, that can ap-
plaud his late conduct to the PRINCE of WALES?" it asked. "For our
part," it said (3 Mar.) in answer to its question, "we cannot but highly
censure this *contradictory, capricious,* and *unbecoming* conduct to the

PRINCE of WALES./ Were the PRINCE a *private gentleman,* we scruple not to assert that he would have *resented* the Minister's conduct by that mode which is the result of the feelings of an injured man of honour." On 4 March it returned to praise of the Prince, whose "manly, yet forbearing conduct . . . , from the first appearance of his ROYAL FATHER's complaint to the present hour, has been such, that there is not a more popular man at present in Europe"; and on 5 March it demanded an investigation of Pitt's conduct: "There is such a mystery, and, we doubt [*sic*], foul play, respecting the situation of our AMIABLE MONARCH, that for PARLIAMENT to be longer *delicate* must be *destructive.* It ought to be sifted to the bottom." By this time it was the spurious *Star's* opinion that the King's recovery was a piece of fiction, devised by Pitt and Dr. Francis Willis, who must, said the paper (7 Mar.), "bring the KING forward to his people, before a thorough credit can be given to their assertions. He must be seen at the Theatres, at the Levees, upon Windsor Terrace, at all public places, *unconstrained.*"

The spurious *Star* had not previously relied upon conjectures in such matters, but its "ORIGINAL INFORMATION" concerning the conduct of the King had come to an abrupt end with the dismissal of the King's pages. The paper was very much disturbed by this dismissal. What, it asked on 6 March, had the pages done except to "speak the truth, during the [King's] malady?" "The PAGES have been dismissed because they were *prying!*" it proclaimed on 7 March. "—If the KING be in all respects recovered, what mischief could attend such curiosity?" It was especially distressed at the dismissal of a "Mr. [Lewis] RAMUS," whose misfortunes it recounted at length until, failing to find other employment, he went to the East Indies. "Poor RAMUS," it observed on 24 March. "Like a poor wounded deer, he was deserted by the herd that formerly carressed [*sic*] him." But the Prince of Wales had not "deserted." For "His ROYAL HIGHNESS," whose "eye never wanted a tear for distress, and whose heart is for ever ready to relieve the unfortunate," had provided money right along and, now that "poor RAMUS" had "sought exile," had helped him with "every recommendation in his power." There was one final mention of the pages. On 9 April the spurious *Star* announced that, "[in] addition to the DISMISSION of the PAGES, we are extremely sorry to learn, that the FEMALE ATTENDANTS who kept the PRINCE of WALES's apartment at Windsor, have been *likewise dismissed.* There is such a malignant rancour *somewhere* against every one who *dare* shew an attachment to an *amiable* PRINCE, as cannot be justified on any principle of virtue or patriotism." The "FEMALE ATTENDANTS" were dismissed before the spurious *Star* had had time to profit from their informations, so that the paper never found a substitute for the pages.

Although the King's recovery was officially announced on 10 March and the spurious *Star* liked to think that it was "the first paper that proposed the ILLUMINATIONS" and "a GENERAL THANKSGIVING on a *particular day,*" it continued to question the fact of the recovery until 12 March, when, as it explained, "We are desired to mention by way of caution, that the Judges have declared it as their opinion to be TREASON to assert, either *orally* or *in print,* that the KING's mind is *deranged,* or that he is not in a capacity to act as SOVEREIGN of the BRITISH EMPIRE." Thereafter it raised no questions on its own account, but alongside the "caution" was a full-column extract from a work on insanity, supposedly translated from the French, the point of which was that questions should be raised in such cases. Also, while it was devoting columns to the various "ILLUMINATIONS" celebrating the recovery, it was pointing out (18 Mar.) "that many scandalous doubts are still in circulation respecting the health of our gracious MONARCH. Why then do not Ministry, to remove any such ill-founded suspicions, advise his Majesty to meet the eyes of his people?"

This obsession with the conduct and activities of the King continued, and, although the spurious *Star* never found another "Mr. RAMUS," it steadfastly maintained that it had more "ORIGINAL INFORMATION" about the Royal Family than any other newspaper. On 14 March it announced with "much satisfaction" the receipt of a long communication from Windsor: "an additional instance of our WINDSOR CORRESPONDENT's friendship. Not having lately an opportunity of transmitting any article of importance, his valuable exertions—during HIS MAJESTY's unfortunate malady—remained dormant; but that event which has diffused universal joy, has likewise revived the spirits of the Printer's worthy well-wisher. . . ." The communication was a description of the celebrations in Windsor. Under the circumstances the spurious *Star* was bound to react violently to the discovery (23 Apr.) that it had been anticipated by the genuine *Star* in the case of the General Thanksgiving: "MATCHLESS IMPUDENCE,/ AND/ PUBLIC ROBBERY!/ *The* DYING DOGS, *wishing rather to gratify themselves than the* PUBLIC, *by the view of the* PROCESSION, *sent their wretched Print to Press this morning at* FIVE O'CLOCK, *and actually had the* PROPHETIC IMPUDENCE *to mention the Procession as if it had passed, some hours before the Military were under arms!/ We hope the* SWINDLING SOCIETY *will take this act into consideration."* But on 2 April the spurious *Star* had itself got out a special edition. For on 3 April it informed its readers that "SEVERAL THOUSAND *copies of an abridged account of the* REPEAL *of the* SHOP TAX, *were last night distributed* gratis *throughout the* CITIES *of* LONDON *and* WEST-MINSTER, *as a* SUPPLEMENT *to* STUART's STAR. . . . *We do not mean to arrogate to ourselves any particular merit for this act of attention to our friends, it being a duty upon us to evince our gratitude for their extraordinary encouragement."* The edition of 2 April was the first special edition to be brought out by an evening newspaper.

## PROBLEMS OF AN EXTORTIONARY SHEET

THE SPURIOUS *Star* seemed to be far ahead in its battle with the original *Star,* and it is perhaps safe to say that in general no newspaper had ever achieved so much in so short a time as it had. Not only had it been the first evening newspaper to offer "ORIGINAL INFORMATION," but it had compelled the original *Star* and, in fact, all daily evening newspapers henceforth to do so too. In addition, it had been the first newspaper to present a well-developed editorial. Heretofore newspapers had confined their opinions to short paragraphs or had disguised them as letters from "Correspondents"; but the spurious *Star* had carried a daily commentary on the subject which most interested the readers, "THE KING," had located it in the central column of the third page, where it would attract the most attention, and had taken credit for it itself. That the political opinions expressed were at times almost verbatim transcripts from Mackintosh's *Arguments,* the medical opinions being taken most likely from his unfinished work on insanity, did not alter the fact that the opinions had constituted an editorial. But the spurious *Star* had also been the first newspaper to outrage and consolidate public opinion, and because of this achievement the ultimate victory went to the original *Star.*

For the first several weeks the spurious *Star* could not have survived without the "SHAKESPEAREAN PORTRAITS." The circulation of the paper was inevitably low, and the advertisements consisted of theater notices, a very few Government announcements, listings for Bell's British Library, and a half-dozen statements regarding perfumes and patent medicines. But by 27 February the spurious *Star* had some financial assistance from the shopkeepers, which was continued until early April, and by mid-March it was being lavishly supported by the Whigs, so that the "SHAKESPEAREAN POR-TRAITS" were no longer necessary. They were continued nevertheless; and, although the first lists had come from Bath, later lists came almost equally from Bath and Bristol, and by late March two thirds of them were coming from Bristol. They were published over such signatures as "PETER PICKLE," "PETER PEPPER," "QUIZ OD-BODY," "TOBY TICKLE," "TOBY SQUIB," "PETER POUNCE," "QUINBUS FLESTRIN," and "RODERICK RANDOM." Also the lists were longer, every number of the newspaper carrying almost a column of these two-or-three–line "PORTRAITS," and they were considerably more vicious.

The spurious *Star* had always boasted that it was the favored *Star* in *"all* TAVERNS, COFFEE-HOUSES, *and* PUBLIC-HOUSES." "It is now fashionable in the few COFFEE-HOUSES where the *Dog-Star* is taken in, to say, 'D—n the *Dog-Star*—give me STUART's STAR, which is both impartial, and satirical, without low scurrility,' " the paper observed on 18 February; and letters from supposed readers solemnly affirmed that this was the case. On 21 March "A FRIEND TO MERIT" reported that he had been personally present "at one of our first coffee-houses [in Edinburgh], where upwards of *forty* gentlemen stood forward, and insisted upon the proprietor's immediately giving up the *Dog-Star,* and continuing STUART's: which request was accordingly complied with at the expiration of last month, to the entire satisfaction of the whole frequents of the room." To encourage such incidents, the spurious *Star* sometimes noticed a popular coffeehouse editorially, and, since Jack's Coffeehouse in Bristol promised to be very popular, it celebrated its opening by publishing (9 Mar.) some verses of rollicking welcome, entitled "JACK's COFFEE-HOUSE, BRISTOL," which had been submitted by an anonymous correspondent. There was no further mention of "Jack's" until 8 April, but it was evident by 4 April that all was not well, for on that day the spurious *Star* addressed the following notice *"To our* READERS *in* BATH *and* BRISTOL": "The Nobility and Gentry in BATH [and BRISTOL?] are respectfully informed, that W. DARLING, the late Distributor of

STUART's STAR, having abused his craft, and neglected the publication of the Paper—the Proprietors have changed the place of sale . . . to Mr. LATHAM's News-office, next door to the Pelican Inn, in Walcot-street; where T. DAVIS, his agent, will serve the Public in the most punctual and expeditious manner."

A few days later the original *Star* published a very strange adver-tisement. Although the conductors of the spurious *Star* were clearly bewildered by it, they nevertheless reprinted it on 8 April, along with their own headnote and footnote:

#### To our READERS in BRISTOL.

The Printer and Conductor of STUART's STAR, not having yet received any authentic information concerning the subsequent Advertisement, he must at present consider it as an ingenious mode adopted yesterday by a very *Low Print* to advertise THIS PAPER. To the *Dogs* he returns his warmest acknowl-edgments for their unintentional friendship, and is now convinced, that they can at times inadvertently stumble upon a good action.

---

BRISTOL, *6th April*, 1789.
*At a numerous and respectable* MEETING, *this day, of the* SUBSCRIBERS *to* JACK's COFFEE-HOUSE,
*Sir* JOHN DURBIN *in the Chair,*
*It was Resolved, that they unanimously consider the* EDITOR *and* PUB-LISHER *of the Paper, called*
#### STUART's STAR,
*As deserving of the most exemplary Punishment; and the* AUTHOR *or* AUTHORS *of the late very scandalous and* malignant REFLECTIONS *on some* respectable CHARACTERS *in this City, of the severest Chastisement.*
*That the* Waiter *do immediately* (*being 'Change time*) , *in the most* con-temptuous *and ignominious* manner, KICK THE FILE, *containing the whole of the* PAPERS *called* STUART's STAR, *out of this Coffee-Room, into the Public street, and there* BURN *them: Which being done accordingly, it was further Resolved,*
*That Mr.* WEEKS *be ordered not, on any account, in future to admit* STUART's STAR *into this* Coffee-Room, *until the Editor shall think proper to make some* Public Apology *for his conduct, and*
*That Mr.* WEEKS *be further ordered not to purchase* ANY NEWSPAPER WHATEVER *of the Person who shall vend* STUART's STAR *in this City.*
*And it was at the same time Resolved,*
*That the* SUBSCRIBERS *do engage, individually to each other, not to buy any*

*Paper sold by the Distributors of* STUART's STAR: *and that an engagement be immediately drawn up to that effect, for their signatures.*

> Signed by the Chairman,
> On behalf of the Meeting,
> JOHN DURBIN.

.    .    .    .    .    .    .    .    .    .    .    .    .    .    .    .    .    .    .    .

*Resolved, That the above Resolution be printed in all the Bristol Papers, in the* DOG STAR, *in Woodfall's Diary, and Morning Herald.*

---

The Printer and Conductor of STUART's STAR—not having yet received any authentic intimation to the above effect—is at present of opinion, that the whole is a *fabrication,* calculated to throw Sir JOHN DURBIN, a gentleman who is in every respect an honour to BRISTOL, into a ridiculous point of view.

But the possibility that the advertisement was not "a *fabrication,*" added to the fact that Jack's Coffeehouse had 292 "subscribers," gave the spurious *Star* pause. There were no "PORTRAITS" on 8, 9, and 10 April, and on 10 April "The PRINTER" tucked a half-apology into his notes *"To Correspondents"*: *"Many Bristol Characters are received.—The laudable Spirit and Entertainment of this Paper can only offend those who are conscious of deserving censure.—We mean none. . . ."* By 11 April the paper had recovered some of its poise: "However absurd and unaccountable a few individuals may have behaved, we mean not to take an advantage of their infirmities," it said generously. "The innocent raillery, and attractive entertainment of STUART's STAR, cannot be extinguished, either by the terror of the great, or by the malversation of the envious.—We are sensible of the uncommon patronage of the Public, and shall make every exertion to merit a continuance of their partiality." In the same paper there was a communication from Bristol, signed "ALPHA & OMEGA" and entitled "A FRAGMENT." The "FRAGMENT" read in part:

9. When lo! as if by Providence, a Star, a goodly Star, rose in the East, whose countenance was like that of an Angel's, and its aspect diffused general joy unto all men. . . .

11. But because of its exceeding brightness and truth, a murmur ran through all the land, and the wicked ones were sorely vexed, and in their wrath swore vengeance against THIS STAR, saying, one with another, this is not the true Star.

12. And they bribed Judas with large gifts and promises to write against it; but fearing the indignation of the chosen, they called him LEONIDAS. . . .

The remainder of the "FRAGMENT" treated with coarse ridicule everyone who frequented "the shop which JACK built." There were still no "SHAKESPEAREAN PORTRAITS" from Bristol, but there was a half-column of them from Bath. By the following Monday (13 Apr.) there was trouble in Bath.

The spurious *Stars* of 13 and 14 April were devoted in large part to explanations and denials. "The PRINTER" began (13 Apr.) with the trouble in Bath:

BATH, *April* 12.

A hand-bill has been given away here for these two days, which in very impotent, and filthy language endeavours to depreciate STUART's STAR; but we well know that its style is disgusting to our numerous and fashionable readers. —And extraordinary as the operations of such stuff may appear, it has served to increase instead of diminishing the sale of the Paper.

Nevertheless, we think our friends should be informed that it was drawn up by a *Bookseller*, notorious for writing characters and defamatory paragraphs for the service of our opponents, and as notorious for denying the infamy of such an action. This man's heart naturally prompts him to malignity and detraction. . . . —The insidious smile on his cheek declares how well he can play the hypocrite.

*There never was any meeting at Guildhall;* the CORPORATION know better the dignity due to the characters of men. The whole was fabricated by the *learned* CAMP, and the *enlightened* PRINTER, who advertises his stupidity every Wednesday night, to delude the public, and serve our *expiring* opponents, on whose pay they both are; yet dull as the Printer is, he had sufficient sense of shame to prevent his name being affixed to the bottom of the bill, a custom invariably observed in Bath, excepting on *such* dishonourable occasions.

On the following day (14 Apr.) the spurious *Star* advised "the insidious Gentleman who called last night at the Office, and begged the insertion of a paragraph injurious to many worthy inhabitants of BATH" to apply to "the *dying* print": he could not, it said, "commit forth his spleen and ill-founded aspersions through the medium of THIS PAPER." The same issue included a few Bath "PORTRAITS," entitled "VELUTI IN SPECULUM" and signed "VERITAS." They were all very inoffensive, the worst perhaps being "Ladies, I love you dearly—Sir JOHN DURBIN." Another half-dozen portraits, equally inoffensive, appeared on 16 April.

The boycott of the spurious *Star* and its Bristol representative was evidently quite effective, for in its clumsy manner the paper tried hard to placate the "subscribers" to Jack's Coffeehouse. It began on 13 April:

### The PRINTER's ADDRESS
### TO THE
### INHABITANTS OF BRISTOL.

The very generous support and approbation given to STUART's STAR in BRISTOL, demands the most serious attention of the Printer to whatever is conducive to the satisfaction of his readers, and a continuance of their patronage. He confesses that on first reading the Resolutions of the Meeting at JACK's COFFEE-HOUSE, he looked upon the whole as an invention calculated to throw Sir JOHN DURBIN into a ridiculous point of view; as he could not believe a gentleman so universally esteemed as a husband, a father, and a citizen, could be weak enough to come ostensibly forward in a transaction which is laughed at, even by those who, in some degree, approve of the intentions of the Meeting. In consideration of his amiable character, to Sir JOHN DURBIN the Printer will say no more, unless it be to return thanks for the honour done him by Sir JOHN's uncommon anxiety about the influence of the paper.

Had the numerous SUBSCRIBERS TO JACK's COFFEE-HOUSE, *unanimously* signed the Resolution, the Printer would have revered the mandate of so very respectable a body; but when *nineteen* Gentlemen arrogate the authority of *two hundred and ninety-two,* he must treat them as an insignificant minority —more especially when the MAYOR and CORPORATION, men of great worth and estimation, thought such proceedings beneath their notice.

To the numerous FRIENDS of THIS PAPER in BRISTOL the Printer declares, that a wish to hurt the peace of mind of any individual never existed in his breast. At the distance of a hundred and twenty miles he cannot be supposed capable of distinguishing truth from falsehood; therefore the blame should be thrown on his correspondents.—He is extremely pleased to hear that the principal complaint of the Gentlemen is—"why hurt the feelings of the Ladies?—Let the paper joke with us—but let the LADIES, whose honour is more tender, remain unmolested"—a sentiment that must give delight to every MAN, and a sentiment which always has, and now shall be observed with redoubled care.

The Printer, therefore, declares, that his only motive for inserting the greatest part of the letters sent to him from BRISTOL, was a conviction of the eagerness with which they were read; that it was with an idea of pleasing rather than of incurring resentment; that he will still insert the favours of his correspondents; but that he will be more cautious in molifying [*sic*] them, particularly those which notice the FAIR SEX.

This, he conceives, is all the PRINTER's FRIEND's [*sic*] require; but after the violence of the *nineteen* subscribers to JACK's COFFEE-HOUSE, he thinks any acknowledgment to them would be dastardly meanness. Had they applied to him, they should have had every species of redress which could have been wished.

The Printer returns thanks to his correspondent who has favoured him with the DEBATES at JACK's COFFEE-HOUSE on Monday April 6. They shall appear to-morrow.

The "DEBATES" did appear on 14 April, occupying a column and a half, but they turned out to be only a burlesque of the proceedings. "This day, pursuant to notice," they began,

the Subscribers met to take into consideration the state of STUART's STAR. The house was but thinly attended, only nineteen members out of two hundred and ninety-two being present.

Sir JOHN DURBIN being called to the chair, Sir STEPHEN NASH took the oaths and his seat as representative for the borough of Intrepidity.

Mr. HALL then rose, and in a very animated, and brilliant speech declared, that the same STUART's STAR was not as it should be—that it was not liked by commonality or genteelality [*sic*] that it was a nuisance to every man of learning as he was. . . . He therefore moved, that as STUART's STAR was obsequious to the people, it be burnt, and turned out of the Coffee-room.

Mr. CROPPER rose to second the motion, he began with observing that as he was a man, and a—a—a—a— that was all.

Sir STEPHEN NASH said, that if he had any doubts of the calamities in STUART's STAR, the last honourable speaker cleared them in such an explicit manner, as left him perfectly satisfied. . . .

The debates finally concluded with the editorial statement:

*The Printer is happy to find that the above wise transaction has increased the sale of* STUART's STAR *in* BRISTOL *to a degree unknown before to any London newspaper. As to his Correspondents, to whom he is much obliged, they multiply so wonderfully, that he is under the necessity of employing a gentleman to inspect their favours.*

*The particulars of the Conflagration* [i.e., the burning of the spurious *Star*] *shall appear to-morrow, when many ludicrous incidents shall be related.*

Along with the *"particulars of the Conflagration,"* which occupied (15 Apr.) another half-column, were some derisive verses, unsigned, on the action of the "subscribers" and *"The* PRINTER's ADDRESS/ TO THE/ INHABITANTS OF BRISTOL," reprinted from the paper of 13 April.

Nothing further was said of either Bristol or Bath until 24 April, when the spurious *Star* published a strictly factual report from Bath and among its poetry some verses submitted by "M.," dateline "Bristol," concerning a Bristol flirt and including some derogatory references to Dr. Plomer, Mr. Hall, and other "subscribers" to Jack's Coffeehouse. On 29 April the "SHAKESPEAREAN PORTRAITS" from Bristol reappeared, occupying three-fourths of a column. The attacks were comparatively mild, but they were not mild enough for the Bristolians. On 30 April there was an agonized letter from a Kerkpatrick [*sic*] Estcot, entreating the *"Printer"* to assure the residents of Bristol that he had never written a single line for the paper, and by 4 May the Bristol Post Office had taken action on its own account. The spurious *Star* of that date was indignant:

> *Having received intimations that the Letters of many of our* BRISTOL FRIENDS *have been rejected at the* POST-OFFICE, *we shall in the course of a few days, suggest another mode of conveyance; but we cannot comprehend the reason of the* POST-MASTER, *or his Assistants, refusing any letter addressed to this Paper. If any set of men attempt to injure this property, by insulting our* CORRESPONDENTS, *we shall deem it a duty incumbent upon us to bring them to a sense of candour and propriety by commencing hostilities against them.*

To prove that it was undaunted, the spurious *Star* published more Bristol "PORTRAITS" on 6 and 7 May, these far less mild than the preceding ones. The "PORTRAITS" were again discontinued until 25 May, when a full column of "BRISTOL POETICAL PORTRAITS" appeared over the signature of "JEREMY NETTLETOP." Another third-column appeared on 28 May. These were the last from Bristol, and the "PORTRAITS" from Bath were not resumed after 16 April.

The war between the two *Stars* had meanwhile come to an end on 27 April, when *Stuart's Star, and Evening Advertiser* became the *Morning Star*. Reasons for the change were set forth in the usual address "TO THE PUBLIC," which concluded with the statement: "To talk of a competition with the former feeble opponents of THIS PAPER, would be absurd and ridiculous. We shall not war with the *dead,* but aim at more noble exploits, and endeavour to hold a competition with the INDUSTRIOUS and INTELLIGENT CONDUCTORS of the MORNING PRINTS." But the truth was that the spurious *Star* had not been warring with the dead, but with something which was very much alive—public opinion.

# CHAPTER VI

# The Spurious *Star* (March–June, 1789):
# A Never-Never Election and
# "An Injured Man"

## THE FORMATION OF THE ANTI-ROSE COALITION

FROM late 1783 or early 1784 on, Charles Stuart had been in the pay of the Whigs, and, from late 1786 or early 1787 until 1790, he was writing the weekly column "Abridgment of Politics" for the Foxite *Morning Herald,* by arrangement with Sheridan.[1] But Charles always had more energy than principle; hence since 1787 he had also been wooing the Prince of Wales, and, from 17 July to 1 August, 1788, he was employed by the Treasury.

This employment had begun when, according to Charles (spurious *Star,* 29 Apr., 2 May, 29 May, 13 June, 1789),[2] George Rose, one of the Secretaries of the Treasury, "voluntarily [*sent*] for [him] to become [his] AGENT in the Westminster election," then in progress. The interview took place at Pitt's house "at DOWNING-STREET" on 17 July, 1788, and Charles and Rose were alone. Having "confessed" that the Treasury now "commanded every MORNING PAPER" except the *Morning Herald,* the *Gazetteer,* and the *General Advertiser,* Rose went on to say that he needed "a person" of Charles's initiative to supervise the manufacture and distribution of "HAND-bills, HAT-bills, [and] POSTING-bills," the texts for which would be furnished by "Mr. ROSE and his friends," to see to the insertion of propaganda in certain newspapers, and apparently to manage the "BALLAD-SINGERS, &c." Charles accepted the assignment. It was then agreed that he would receive an immediate £200 to cover his initial expenses and that he would call upon Rose for additional advances when this money was exhausted. How much he was to be paid for his own services is not indicated, but he evidently included in his demands £83 to cover his personal debts and was authorized to withhold this amount from the

£200. When it came to the actual payment of the £200, however, Charles discovered that Rose was himself only an agent for Pitt: "The GREAT MAN was the SOLE EMPLOYER." And, since Pitt was "*out a-riding*" at the time, Charles was obliged to wait for, as he said, "an hour and a half, until Mr. PITT came in, by the *garden-stairs,* into the ROOM where *I was;* and . . . in *two* MINUTES, [Rose came] out to me *with the* MONEY." Charles accordingly departed with his £200, "A FLASH SONG," and an "ode," entitled "Choice Spirits at the Shakespeare," which he supposed (spurious *Star,* 6 June, 1789) was written either by Rose or by "the Marquis of GRAHAM, or HARRY DUNDAS," it being obviously "the *production* of a SCOTCH-MAN."

Charles had many other interviews with Rose, one of them "at the Archbishop of CANTERBURY's, in *Lambeth*" (spurious *Star,* 2 May, 1789), and meanwhile he spent a great deal of money. The first £200 was paid on Thursday, 17 July, 1788, and on Tuesday, 22 July, he submitted the following statement: [3]

Disbursement

| | | | |
|---|---:|---:|---:|
| Mr. Stewardine | 30″ | 0″ | 0 |
| Mr. Gilwray, engraver | 20″ | 0″ | 0 |
| Saturday's papers | 6″ | 0″ | 0 |
| Sunday's D° | 1″ | 10″ | 0 |
| Monday's D° | 5″ | 3″ | 6 |
| Tuesday's (to-day) | 15″ | 0″ | 0 |
| Doucers [sic] to leaders of papers | 13″ | 13″ | 0 |
| Bill-stickers, & others, coaches, clerks and incidents in a table [sic] and salary to them | 16″ | 0″ | 0 |
| Cockades | 2″ | 10″ | 0 |
| Private debts | 83″ | 0″ | 0 |
| Remains | 7″ | 3″ | 6 |
| | 200″ | 0″ | 0 |

"Mr. Stewardine" was probably William Stewardine, who by 1 May, 1790, was directly in the pay of the Treasury;[4] "Mr. Gilwray" was possibly the caricaturist James Gillray. On the day he submitted this statement (22 July), Charles received an additional £50,[5] which, added to the 7/3/6 remaining from the £200, came to 57/3/6. Possibly mistaking the *3* for a *7,* he submitted a second statement for

Expend. of 57£.7

| | | | |
|---|---|---|---|
| Wed. papers | 9″ | 7″ | 0 |
| Thurs d° | 13″ | 11″ | 6 |
| Frid d° | 12″ | 5″ | 0 |
| Sat | 8″ | 1″ | 0 |
| Contingencies | 9″ | 4″ | 0 |
| On Hand | 4″ | 19″ | 0 |
| | 57″ | 7″ | 6 |

On Monday, 28 July, Charles received £100,[7] which was more than exhausted by Friday, 1 August: [8]

| | | | |
|---|---|---|---|
| Recd—100 | | | |
| Run out on Saturday. | | | |
| Sunday's papers | 4″ | 7″ | 0 |
| Monday's D° | 12″ | 13″ | 6 |
| To pay out of the 100£ | 17″ | 0″ | 6 |
| On *account* for paper to engraver | | | |
| & printer, 15£ each | 30″ | 0″ | 0 |
| Tuesday's papers | 9″ | 18″ | 0 |
| Wednes D° | 18″ | 12″ | 6 |
| Thurs D° | 16″ | 5″ | 0 |
| Frid D° | 9″ | 14″ | 6 |
| | 101″ | 10″ | 6 |

The reason for these advance payments is indicated by Charles's statement (spurious *Star,* 29 May, 1789) that "[even] some of [Rose's] own PRINTS . . . would not obey the *gratis nod* of [his] PRIVATE SIGNATURE, but insisted on *double price* [in advance], as it was ELECTION TIME," so that Rose "liquidated" these bills *"daily, from POLITICAL NECESSITY."* The £350 which Charles had himself collected was evidently earmarked for the "liquidation" of some of these bills, and in addition Charles seems to have collected and expended the sum of "about 600*l.*" for "BALLAD-SINGERS, *cum multis aliis,"* who also "could not, or would not, go on without *daily* pay." But, whenever Rose could defer payment, he did, so that, by the time the election was over, he was in debt to a number of people. Although Charles had paid little or nothing out of his own pocket, he had contracted some debts in Rose's behalf, which were still unpaid on 1 August, when his employment was terminated. For example, the "15£ each," which he paid "On *account* for paper to engraver & printer" sometime between

28 July and 1 August, was evidently only part of a bill, for the whole of which he had made himself personally responsible, whereas, in an addendum to the statement of 1 August, he noted, "I have bill-stickers, hand-bill distributors, &c. to pay besides since Saturday." Moreover, he owed 147/8/6 for the printing of handbills, hatbills, and posters, for the payment of which he was also personally responsible (spurious *Star*, 19 May, 1789) .

Charles's attempts to collect from the Treasury were only partly successful. On 2 August, 1788, Charles received from George Rose "a *draught* on COUTT's, Bankers in the Strand, for *fifty pounds*" "in *part payment*" of the bill for 147/8/6 (spurious *Star*, 6 May, 1789) ; [9] and on 9 August Rose gave him £70, noting in his ledger that "other Accompts. are not settled of M^r Stewart's." [10] That the "other Accompts." remained unsettled is evident from the accusations which Charles subsequently (spurious *Star*, 6 May, 1789) addressed to Rose:

> Did you not, at your house *near* LYNDHURST, *New Forest*, HAMP-SHIRE, declare to me, that you had given orders to Mr. [John] FROST [a solicitor in the Stamp Office], through Mr. ESTCOURT, to merge *your* account in the *general business?*
>
> Did you not, before the CHRISTMAS Holidays, promise, upon your *word of honour,* that you would give me ALL, or PART?
>
> Did you not go out of town, in VIOLATION of your word of honour, without giving me all, or part?
>
> . . . . Did you not order Mr. [Thomas] STEELE [the other Secretary of the Treasury] to send me an *apology* for your *breach* of PROMISE?
>
> Did he not, in consequence, send Mr. [William] CHENNERY to me, your *private* SECRETARY, with an assurance of my bill being discharged, or the greatest part of it, when you came to town?
>
> Were those repeated promises ever performed?

Since William Chennery functioned as one of Rose's paymasters, his name appears often in the Treasury records of 1788. The name of John Frost does not, for, although Frost was also paid out of Treasury funds, he was paid by Lord Hood, being Lord Hood's "Solicitor and Agent." Mr. Estcourt is perhaps the same "Mr. Estcourt" who "in the summer of 1803 . . . came to [Daniel Stuart, then conductor of the *Morning Post*] with a message of thanks from the prime minister Mr. Addington, offering any thing [Stuart] wished." [11]

Having concluded his work for the Treasury, Charles had turned his attention to the Royal Family; but by this time the King's illness had introduced the possibility of a Regency, and, since the Prince of Wales was already well disposed toward him for previous services, this was too good an opportunity to be overlooked. Hence in November, 1788, he had moved over to the *Star, and Evening Advertiser,* then conducted by his brother, Peter, and, with the assistance of James Mackintosh, had shifted the political "Line" of that newspaper to the side of the Prince. When the shift resulted in a quarrel between Peter Stuart and the other proprietors, he, Peter, and Mackintosh had founded the spurious *Star* in the Prince's interests. But, despite the fact that Charles was the prime mover in the enterprise, his name had not been attached to the paper. For, so long as the Treasury was still in his debt, he could not afford to identify himself with a newspaper which was bitterly opposed to the Government in the crucial matter of the Regency; and, so long as his own creditors were looking for him, he could not afford to identify himself with any newspaper at all. But the creditors were not to be eluded. Hence, less than two weeks after the spurious *Star* was begun, Charles was, in fact, not connected with it. His statement of 29 April, 1789 (spurious *Star*), that *"nine weeks"* had then elapsed since his arrest would indicate that the arrest occurred about 25 February. The charge was "supposed embezzlement."

Charles may first have tried to get the money from his friends or from his brother Daniel, who was still publishing the *Morning Post,* for it was not until a week after his arrest that he "sent a very polite letter to [George Rose], *informing* him of his SITUATION, and requesting that *debt* and *costs* should be immediately discharged." From Rose he "received no answer." (Spurious *Star,* 29 Apr., 1789.) He also, no doubt, applied to the Prince of Wales, from whom, too, he evidently "received no answer," for on 14 March the spurious *Star* appealed to the King, expressing a "hope" that, "as the debtors in the several prisons of the kingdom were disappointed of an act of insolvency when the PRINCE of WALES came of age [1787], which was generally expected, . . . HIS MAJESTY will consent to such a measure at this period. All acts of lenity and grace will be peculiarly proper [in celebration of the King's recovery]." The King did not respond. By this time Charles's situation was desperate on two accounts, for, in addition to the fact that he had no hope of freeing himself, he had no hope of saving the spurious *Star,* its expectation of Princely reward having been officially blasted by the announcement of the King's recovery on 10 March. Except for the possibility that the announcement

57/7/6, which covered his expenses through Saturday, 26 July: [6] was one of Pitt's tricks, the paper would have ceased to exist before now.

Fortunately for Charles, the situation of the Whigs was equally desperate, for, not only had they no hope of coming into power, but they were facing (or seemed to be facing) the next general elections with no ammunition whatever. Although the issue in the elections would be the conduct of the Government during the King's illness, the conduct of the Whigs was itself so suspect that this issue could not be mentioned, and meanwhile the Government had chosen as its own weapons the Prince's marriage and Hastings' trial, against which no defense was possible. What the Whigs needed was a similar weapon, and Charles provided it.

The Westminster election of 1788 had been the most scandalous election in English history. By the time it began, the Treasury had controlled seven of the ten morning daily papers and most of the tri-weekly evening papers, and it could count on the assistance of a host of printers, caricaturists, and journalists. Although only a few of Rose's accounts are extant, it is evident that much of his work was done by agents, of whom Charles Stuart and William Chennery were but two. In addition, there was Thomas Harris, probably the same Thomas Harris who managed Covent Garden, who on 17 July, 1788, collected £200 for the *Morning Chronicle*, £100 for the *St. James's Chronicle*, £100 for the *London Evening Post*, and £50 for the *Public Ledger*.[12] There was also Lord Hood, the Ministerial candidate himself, who on 20 July collected £500, on 29 July £1,500, and on 7 August £1,000.[13] By no means all of the money had been spent on newspapers, handbills, hatbills, posters, and ballad-singers, for the Treasury had also had in its employ an army of ruffians, whose acts of violence were denounced by the Ministerial newspapers as outrages committed by the Whigs. The fact that the election had finally been resolved in favor of the Whig candidate, John Townshend, was over-shadowed by the more-important fact that the Commons had condoned the Treasury's conduct by categorically refusing to consider any motion for an investigation of Rose's activities. The result was that Rose had continued to manage the press in Pitt's interest during the agitation over the Regency Bill, and by mid-March, 1789, he still controlled most of the evening newspapers and six of the ten morning newspapers, the *Morning Post* having defected. Under these circum-

stances a conference between Sheridan and Charles Stuart was bound
to result in more than mutual commiserations.

Some time during the period of his incarceration, Charles would,
of course, have applied to Sheridan for the money which the Whigs
owed him for writing the column for the *Morning Herald* for the
past two years, and the application was evidently ignored, for the bill
was not paid until July, 1791.[14] But, although the Whigs were not
interested in Charles's account with them, they were very much interested in his account with George Rose. The result was that by 19
March, 1789, Charles was out of prison and had rejoined the staff of
the spurious *Star* as "our good adherent CADWALLADER," author
of some verses *"To his Grace The* DUKE *of* LEINSTER, *and the
other* COMMISSIONERS *from* IRELAND," and by 24 March the
paper was able to announce lavish "FUTURE ARRANGEMENTS."

Since Charles's confessions were to be the Whigs' answer to the
Prince's marriage and Hastings' trial, a great deal of consideration
had been given to the mode of their presentation and hence to the
spurious *Star* generally. It was evidently decided, first of all, to build
the spurious *Star* into a paper of some consequence, comparable in
stature to the *World,* and to publish the confessions in the morning,
when they would attract more attention than they would in the
evening. It was evidently also decided to defer publication until just
before the election. Since the element of surprise was crucial to the
success of the plan, it was evidently further decided to conceal the
preparations as far as possible and especially to conceal the Whigs'
connection with the paper, which would therefore purport to represent only Carlton House as before. But there was an additional reason
for this last piece of deception, for both the Whigs and the spurious
*Star* would need to hide behind the Prince of Wales. The Whigs were
already pleading loyalty to the Prince as an excuse for their machinations during the King's illness, and the spurious *Star* could have no
better insurance against an ex officio prosecution than the presump-
tion that the Heir Apparent had an interest in the newspaper.

The spurious *Star, and Evening Advertiser*—after 23 or 24 February, 1789, retitled *Stuart's Star, and Evening Advertiser*—was in some
respects the worst newspaper the Whigs could have selected. According to the colophon, it was still printed by "P. STUART," and the
paper insisted that "P. STUART" was also its conductor. But, while
Charles was in prison, the real conductor had been James Mackintosh,

Peter Stuart handling only the "entertainment," and even Mackintosh's conduct had been limited to the political department, for the paper was cursed with an overactive proprietary. When Charles resumed the conduct, the paper was extremely scurrilous, and, although much of the scurrility was directed at the Ministerial original *Star,* much of it was not. Prominent citizens in Bristol and Bath were being assailed in daily lists of literary "PORTRAITS," which for financial reasons the proprietors were unwilling to discontinue, and, in addition, the proprietors had their own personal jealousies and resentments, the satisfaction of which took up a great deal of the newspaper's space and dissipated a great deal of its energy. Thomas Goodall was dedicated to his wife's career and was contentious whenever it was threatened; and John Bell was currently quarreling with the proprietor and conductor of the *World,* of which he was now only the printer. The spurious *Star* had already (5 Mar.) lashed out at Major Topham and Charles Este on Bell's account. George Colman was a man of multiple wraths. Since late 1785 he had been suffering from a mysterious malady, the symptoms of which were morbidity, overactivity, and periodic confusion, and the illness was to "[blaze] forth unequivocally in June, 1789," bringing his career to a close.[15] The approaching climax of the disease may account for his exaggerated concern for himself, his son, and the Haymarket.

If all this rancor could have been put into political harness, the situation would have been different, but the Whigs had to reconcile themselves to the fact that the spurious *Star* would inevitably become involved in the proprietors' personal quarrels. They also had to reconcile themselves to the fact that neither of the Stuarts had any real notion of newspaper ethics. Peter, whose interests were literature, not politics, would help a friend at any time, without regard to the political confusion which such help entailed; and, although Charles could be counted on to do what he was paid to do, he was inclined to use a newspaper as an instrument of retributive justice, rewarding those who had been kind to him and punishing those who had not. In addition, Charles was completely lacking in taste. To him coarseness was synonymous with humor, abuse synonymous with spirit. Under all these circumstances, there was little possibility that the spurious *Star* would adhere to the proper political line, and there was no possibility whatever that it would become a journal of elegance or even of simple respectability.

## PREPARATIONS FOR THE ELECTIONS OF 1789

BUT THE paper was not without merit, for it had excellent correspondents in Edinburgh and Dublin, it was presenting the first lists of lottery drawings, and it was offering well-developed editorials. Its principal lack was in the field of "entertainment," and what it needed more than anything else was a brace of poets, comparable in popularity with "Della Crusca" and "Anna Matilda." On 24 March, 1789, the spurious *Star* accordingly advertised for help, the advertisement appearing in the form of an announcement:

> An excellent House is now fitting up in an elegible situation for the printing and conducting of STUART's STAR, which, as soon as ready for its reception, will be announced and occupied by the Printer and his Connections. The ingenious and intelligent of every denomination are solicited for their communications, who will be liberally rewarded—SEVERAL THOUSAND POUNDS—if wanted—being deposited at a Banker's for the establishment of THIS PAPER.
>
> The PRINTER'S FRIENDS might justly deem it pardonable were he to delay returning them his warmest thanks for their uncommon attachment. His success has already exceeded his most flattering expectations. Hence he is confident, that the machinations of his enemies [the proprietors of the original *Star*] will very soon be totally overturned.

The response was evidently immediate, for on 28 March the spurious *Star* promised its readers that the space heretofore assigned to the lottery drawings, now concluded, would henceforth be occupied by "articles of original INFORMATION and ENTERTAINMENT."

Included in the additions to the editorial staff were probably James Boaden, Theophilus Swift, John Williams ("Anthony Pasquin"), and the Rev. William Jackson. There is some question about Jackson, for one knows only that he left for the Continent in late April and that by 11 May he was employed by the paper as foreign correspondent.[16] James Boaden, who seems to have had no previous newspaper experience, had contributed an "EPITHALAMIUM," signed "J. B–n," which was published by the spurious *Star* on 20 March, and he evidently joined the staff then or shortly thereafter, for on 6 April the paper celebrated his marriage to "Miss C. D–y" ("Newport-pond, Essex, 31 March") with another epithalamium, signed "AMICUS." Theophilus Swift had been called to the bar of the Middle Temple in 1767, but had abandoned law for literature and in 1777 had published

*The Female Parliament.* Since then he had been working for Irish newspapers. When the spurious *Star* was begun, he was living in Dublin, and he may therefore have functioned as the paper's Irish correspondent during the first months of its existence; but he was in London by at least May, for he was undoubtedly responsible for the abuse of Colonel Lennox, which began at that time. Although one suspects that he was the author of the many poems and paragraphs relating to Irish politics and Irish politicians, only two poems, both non-political, were attributed to him by the newspaper: some verses *"To the* DUCHESS *of* RUTLAND" from *The Female Parliament* (29 May) and *"On* IMPRISONMENT FOR DEBT./ By Theophilus Swift, Esq." (3 June).

Of John Williams' newspaper experience, little is known. According to his biographer,[17] Williams had worked for the *Morning Herald* during the elections of 1784, but had quit the newspaper in 1785 or 1786 as the result of a quarrel with the conductor, Henry Bate Dudley. He then supposedly wrote "an intemperate satire on his antagonist" and, being saved from a prosecution by the intervention of some of Dudley's friends, went to France. Returning to England, he supposedly set up "The Brighton Guide," acted as drama critic for "one of our newspapers," and took up residence in Bath, "from which place he was . . . under the necessity of withdrawing precipitately." But to the extent that these facts are accurate, they are, to say the least, disorderly. If there was "an intemperate satire" on Dudley, it was not included in Williams' collected writings. In fact, the only reference to Dudley in any of his writings seems to be a pun, which occurs in *A Serio-Comic and Admonitory Epistle, Addressed to a Certain Priest . . . Respecting Some Late Conduct of the Rev. C– B–, Curate of W–: By Anthony Pasquin, Esquire* (London, n.d.) : "Here then with your leave we will *bate;* and, like sociable travellers, talk over the next stage." [18] But the *Epistle* was published long after 1786, for a letter included in the text is dated 15 July, 1793. Of Williams' sojourn in France, nothing is known; but "The Brighton Guide," which is evidently *The New Brighton Guide, Involving a Complete, Authentic, and Honourable Solution of the Recent Mysteries of Carlton House,* seems not to have appeared until 1795 or 1796, for the fourth edition is dated 1796. However, Williams does seem to have been living in Bath in 1789, for in 1789 he published *The New Bath Guide* and in 1790 *A Postscript to The New Bath Guide,* both over the signature of

"Anthony Pasquin." These two works may account for his "precipitate withdrawal" from that city.

Williams had previously published *The Children of Thespis*, the dedicatory epistle of which was dated 1 March, 1786; *Shrove Tuesday*, which had originally appeared in several parts, the second dated 20 February, 1787, the third 22 February, 1788; and *Poems*, the preface of which was dated 7 April, 1789. All of these works were successful. By 1792 *Children of Thespis*, a collection of laudatory poems addressed to various actors and actresses, was in its thirteenth edition, by which time the preface included "An Apologetic Distich," signed by Peter Stuart. *Shrove Tuesday*, a group of poems satirizing Sheridan and other Parliamentary orators, was many times reprinted, "notwithstanding every corrupt act to suppress it"; [19] and the volume of *Poems*, which included Charles Stuart's name among the subscribers, went through several editions in 1789 alone. Two poems from this volume, *"The* SERGEANT *and* DRUMMER./ A TALE" and *"The* PRIEST *and the* PLAYER./ A TALE," were reprinted by the spurious *Star* on 13 and 22 April, 1789, respectively, and on 4 June the paper also printed Williams' "VERSES/ To the WITTY and BEAUTIFUL *Miss* ANNE FULLER." But Williams had probably joined the editorial staff much earlier, and one even suspects that he was the original Bath-and-Bristol correspondent and that he was at all times responsible for the paragraphs and poems relating to that area, some of which may have been included in his *New Bath Guide*. It may be of additional consequence that he was an intimate of an intimate of the Prince of Wales, Lord Barrymore, of whom he was later also the biographer.[20]

All of the editorial assistants seem to have contributed verses, and there were many poets besides, at least three of whom were regular contributors: "R. F.," Dr. Wolcot, and Andrew MacDonald. "R. F.," never further identified, contributed songs and epigrams, and Dr. Wolcot contributed his usual variety of poems, many of them introduced with headnotes. For the name of Andrew MacDonald, historians are indebted to Daniel Stuart. "At the time of the Star in the years 1789 and 1790," Daniel said in 1838,[21] "my brother Peter engaged Mr. Macdonald, a Scotch poet, author of the play of 'Vimonda,' an accomplished literary gentleman, with a large family, in very distressed circumstances. My brother rendered him important pecuniary services. But his poems attracted so much notice, that the Morning Post tempted him, after a time, by a large salary, to leave my brother." Although in context these remarks seem to pertain to the original *Star*, Peter Stuart left that newspaper in mid-February, 1789, to found the spurious *Star*, with which he was associated until the following June; he was then connected with no newspaper until perhaps the beginning of 1790, when he joined the staff of the *Oracle*. The possibility that Daniel was thinking of the spurious *Star* and perhaps the *Oracle* rather than the original *Star* is strengthened by the fact that no poetry in the original *Star* has been traced to MacDonald, whereas on 12 June the spurious *Star* "rendered" MacDonald the kind of "service" it reserved for its regular contributors. "The tragedy of *Vimonda,* which was so much admired [when it was first performed in 1788], is now getting up at COLMAN's, and will soon be welcomed by the town," it announced. "VIMONDA is the only tragedy, since DOUGLAS, that has deserved praise by the critics, as true dramatic poetry, devoid of turpidity and bombast." *Douglas,* first performed in 1757, was written by the Scotch minister John Home, who was obliged to quit the ministry because of it. There is still the question of when MacDonald was engaged and what poems he contributed. He may, of course, have been responsible for the several imitations of Burns (27 and 31 Mar.; 4 Apr.) and even for the poems signed "R. F.," but he may also have had nothing to do with the spurious *Star* until shortly before its demise. On 10 June the paper introduced a poem, signed "PHILANDER" and entitled "TO HER WHOM I SAW WEEP," with the headnote: *"The sweet Verse which follows, is from a new Correspondent—as such, we shall greet him as he merits."* Since by this time *Vimonda* was in rehearsal at the Haymarket, the *"new Correspondent"* may have been MacDonald, whom the Stuarts had just met through Colman. In any event MacDonald was still connected with the spurious *Star* on 12 June, and, since the spurious *Star* expired on 16 June, the *Morning Post* probably lured him away from the *Oracle*. MacDonald died in 1790.

Peter Stuart offered salaries to two other poets, who declined them: Ann Yearsley and Robert Burns. Mrs. Yearsley, who posed as a pure nature poet, signing herself either "The Milk-woman of Bristol" or "Lactilia," was one of the celebrities of her day; and, since the spurious *Star* was much read in Bristol, Peter was especially eager to publish her work regularly. She seemed eager to have it published, for, without waiting for an invitation, she submitted a poem, addressed *"To the Incredulous Mr. Collins."* Supposing that the poem was for sale and having at that time no money to pay for it, Peter adopted the customary expedient of losing it. "The VERSES OF ANN YEARSLEY have been unfortunately mislaid," he announced on 17 March. "As soon as they can be found, they shall be published. We shall esteem that Author's future correspondence a favour." The poem was, of course, found as soon as the spurious *Star* came into its fortune, and Peter at once opened or attempted to open negotiations with Mrs. Yearsley, but weeks elapsed, and the negotiations were still in a state of confusion. By 25 April he was completely befuddled, for on that day he announced the receipt of "ODES on the PROCESSION of ST. GEORGE's DAY, from Mrs. YEARSLEY, and Miss [Anna] SEWARD, which shall appear as soon as possible. The preference given to our paper by these Ladies, so deservedly famed in the Poetical world, is," he added, "highly flattering." But Miss Seward's verses *"On* HIS MAJESTY's HAPPY RECOVERY *and* APPEARANCE *in* PUBLIC *at* ST. PAUL's *this Day"* had already been published on 23 April over the signature, "A.S.," and Mrs. Yearsley's did not appear. On 27 April he promised "VERSES from ANN YEARSLEY, the Bristol Milk-woman, to the Incredulous Mr. COLLINS" for "to-morrow," and again the verses were lacking.

The difficulty was that Peter Stuart was thinking in terms of money, and Mrs. Yearsley's thoughts moved on another level altogether. Although he was willing to pay well for her poems, especially for poems in praise of the Royal Family, he was reluctant to publish even the verses to Mr. Collins until he knew how much she expected. But Mrs. Yearsley was thinking of her character as a nature poet, which "Mr. Collins" had impugned and which would therefore remain blackened until the spurious *Star* published the verses which proved him wrong. On 1 May she lost patience. Having, as she said, "[perused] your second apology respecting the 'non-publication of my lines in your STAR,'" she informed "The Printer" that she did not write for money: she wrote only "to soothe the calamities of mankind." "Lactilia," she said simply, "is a philanthropist, without a purse!" She would also not send the "Ode." She had once, it was true, "attempted to reach" the "exaltation" of "MAJESTY" by celebrating "the King on his arrival at Cheltenham"; but her "daring was early checked by the well-timed neglect of the Right Hon. Lord COURTOWN," to whom she had sent the poem. Although it did seem to her that "Politeness should have whispered, that a line was in answer due, even from Lord

COURTOWN to a *milk-woman*," still she was bound to thank him for thus reminding her of her unworthiness. If the spurious *Star* wanted "the poem in question," she would send it, along with her "grateful acknowledgment to the Right Hon. Lord COURTOWN," it being the only poem she had ever written "in which royalty has the least share." But she did ask that her verses *"To the Incredulous Mr. Collins"* be printed without further delay. The verses were printed on 6 May, with the author's note that they had been written "in less than ten minutes, (without alteration or correction)" in the presence of four witnesses, including "the Incredulous Mr. COLLINS," who had "doubted the truth of her being the author of those poems published in her name." Her letter of 1 May was printed on 7 May and the poem *"To the KING/ On HIS MAJESTY's Arrival at CHELTENHAM"* on 15 May. The burden of the "grateful acknowledgment" to Lord Courtown "of His MAJESTY's Household, Cheltenham" was that the author had had "NATURE only for her TUTORESS." Although these pieces were perhaps not what Peter Stuart had in mind, they were all Mrs. Yearsley was willing to provide, and he paid nothing for them.

He also paid nothing for Burns's poems. Burns's connection with the spurious *Star* was the result of several accidents and a few deceptions.[22] Two days after the spurious *Star* published its advertisement, it published (27 Mar.) some doggerel ridiculing the Duchess of Gordon, which it attributed to Burns. More of such doggerel followed on 31 March and 4 April, also attributed to Burns. The first verses were sufficiently Burnsian to mislead the editor of the *Gazetteer* (possibly J. Beauchamp),[23] who silently reprinted them on 28 March; but, with the appearance of the second set, it was evident even to him that these were crudely devised imitations. Burns knew nothing of the doggerel, not having access to the spurious *Star;* but he had heard of the appeal for contributions, and on 7 April he submitted his "Ode to the Departed Regency Bill," to be published anonymously. Peter Stuart, who was, of course, overjoyed, replied at once, opening negotiations, not only for the "Ode," but for other poems, to be submitted at regular intervals. While he was addressing this letter to Burns, Burns was addressing a letter to the editor of the *Gazetteer,* having by ironic chance come across the number of 28 March. Supposing that the verses had originated with the *Gazetteer,* he was demanding that the editor publish a retraction, stating that Robert Burns was not "the author of those verses." This letter was dated 10 April, and on 12 April Burns learned from a friend that some more "silly verses on the Duchess of GORDON" had appeared in the spurious *Star*.

But on 13 April Burns received Peter's letter, and the warmth of the response persuaded him that the spurious *Star* was innocent of any wrongdoing. Hence, although his second letter to Peter requested that the spurious *Star* "undeceive the Public, by letting them know . . . that I am guiltless of . . . the . . . miserable pieces of rhyme," the tone of the request was respectful, and Burns even sent along a song "as a bribe." This letter, dated 13 April, was published in the spurious *Star* of 16 April, and on 17 April the *Gazetteer* published Burns's letter to its own editor. The letter was followed by a sarcastic commentary, in which the editor suggested that "Mr. Burns [would] do right in addressing his petulance to the proper delinquent, the Printer of the [spurious] *Star,* from which Paper the Stanza was literally copied into the *Gazetteer*." *"The Printer"* of the spurious *Star* responded to the suggestion that afternoon with a *"[regret] that the* CONDUCTOR *of the* GAZETTEER, *of whose candour and politeness he [had] formed a high opinion, has not, in the* note *to* Mr. BURNS's *Letter, which appears this day, acted with his usual urbanity of character."*

Since Burns was applying to the Government for a post in the Excise, he could not afford to ally himself with an anti-Ministerial newspaper on any basis, and he certainly could not afford to have his name attached to any one of his contributions. But he was indiscreet and unacquainted with the ways of London newspapermen, and he was also very grateful to the spurious *Star* for "[clearing him] from the foul aspersions respecting the D[uchess] of G[ordon]." Hence, although he refused to become a regular contributor, he gave Peter Stuart permission to publish the song over his signature and agreed to send other poems, provided they were published anonymously, asking in return for these favors only a subscription to the newspaper.

On 17 April the spurious *Star* accordingly published the "Ode to the Departed Regency Bill." The ode was signed only "AGRICOLA./ EDINBURGH/ April 7," but the headnote identified the author as *"a* GENIUS *who ranks very high in the* REPUBLIC *of* LETTERS." The text had been altered to conform with the paper's political policy, so that it was now a strong indictment of Pitt. "SONG./ *By* R. BURNS" ("ANNA, thy charms my bosom fire") appeared on 18 April and was copied by the *Gazetteer* on 20 April. Copies of the newspaper containing these two poems were not sent to Burns. On 7 May the spurious *Star* published the "ODE./ *Sacred to the Memory of the late Mrs. [Oswald], of [Auchencruive]*," with a letter stating that the author of the poem was unknown. The letter, which was signed "TIM NETTLE," was, of course, devised by Burns. But immediately following this letter was a letter from Robert Burns to Peter Stuart, which identified Burns, not only as author of the "ODE./ *Sacred to the Memory of the late Mrs. —, of —*," but also as author of the "Ode to the Departed Regency Bill." One can be certain that this copy of the newspaper was also not sent to Burns. By 4 May Burns had mailed the lines, beginning "O sing a *new song* to the L–." They were published on 14 May along with Burns's preface and were signed only "DUNCAN M'LEERIE./ *Kilmarnock, April* 30." This poem was Burns's last contribution to the spurious *Star,* for, although Burns forgave Peter Stuart, he did not forgive the newspaper.

In addition to its other "entertainment," the spurious *Star* often carried a full column of verse, which, after 24 March, may be regarded as entirely original. It was therefore buying a great deal of poetry, much of it on a piecemeal basis. The problem of identifying these occasional poets is insoluble. Almost every poet sometimes wrote for the newspapers, but, since any type of journalistic employment was regarded as disreputable, he usually signed his work with a pseudonym or with initials or omitted the signature altogether. To complicate the problem further, the pseudonyms and initials were constantly varied, for no self-respecting poet would risk exposure by using the same signature twice. Editors, on the other hand, were more interested in poets than in poetry, so that an editor who had a distinguished poet as contributor could rarely resist the temptation to eulogize him and even to supply some hint as to his identity. The fact that there were very few eulogies in the spurious *Star* would therefore indicate that the paper had very few distinguished poets. But this is not necessarily the case, for it had at least one whom it did not eulogize: William Cowper. Although Cowper may have contributed many poems to the newspaper, only one has been identified,[24] "*The* NEGRO*'s* COMPLAINT," which was published on 2 April with neither signature nor headnote. The fact that the paper respected Cowper's confidence when it did not respect Burns's may be owing to Cowper's friendship with George Colman.[25] Except for Cowper, the only occasional poet who is at present identifiable is John Agg. Agg, formerly a linen-draper in the Strand, was writing for several newspapers over the signature, "Peter

Pindar, Jr." [26] His first poem in the spurious *Star*, "SONG./ *To* J[ames] B[oade]n," was published on 16 May.

The spurious *Star* celebrated Charles's liberation by reprinting (19 Mar.) from an earlier number, but "in a more correct state," a "POLITICAL INCANTATION," subtitled "INCANTATION/ *For raising a* PHANTOM, *imitated from* MACBETH, *and lately performed by* HIS MAJESTY's SERVANTS *in* WESTMINSTER." The parody had to do with the King's illness and the Regency and was unsigned. There was also some praise of the character and military knowledge of the Duke of York and more praise of the courage and loyalty of the Prince's friends in Ireland, especially of the Duke of Leinster. But on 20 March the paper digressed to sing the praises of the Duke of Norfolk, who had perhaps just "deposited [the SEVERAL THOUSAND POUNDS] at a Banker's for the establishment of THIS PAPER," as he had also, according to the *Morning Post* (21 Oct., 1788), been "the *friend* behind the curtain who [advanced] eighteen thousand pounds to Mr. SHERIDAN, to purchase DOCTOR FORD's share of Drury-lane"; and it had several kind words to say for Sheridan, who had made the arrangements. The Stuarts were obviously grateful. On 21 March it returned to the matter at hand by declaring war on the *World* or more specifically on Topham and Este, supposedly because of their "illiberality against the IRISH NATION." "There is so much low scurrility against the PRINCE and his FRIENDS, in those papers devoted, through *thick* and *thin*, to the Minister, that we forbear to take notice of them in general," it observed. "We cannot, however, pass over an article in a *coarse, desperate* PAPER of *this day*, which directly accuses Mr. GRATTAN of TREASON and asserts that Dr. WARREN and Mr. SHERIDAN were parties in endeavouring to DETHRONE his MAJESTY!" There was another attack on Topham and Este on similar grounds on 23 March.

For the next several days the spurious *Star* was too concerned with French fashions, its war with the genuine *Star*, the dismissal of the King's pages, the repeal of the shop tax, and the "SHAKESPEAREAN PORTRAITS" to interest itself in politics. But on 28 March it found time to state editorially that it was a "supporter of the PRINCE of WALES." "[By] committing ourselves as the supporter of the PRINCE of WALES," it added, "we mean no more than to espouse the *cause* of the HOUSE of HANOVER, in the person of HIS ROYAL HIGHNESS. The glare of political trickery that at present deludes many, will soon pass away—and the time . . . is not very distant, when it will be the general opinion, that, in supporting the *rights* of the PRINCE, we are doing no more than *maintaining* the BALANCE of the CONSTITUTION." Readers would have supposed that the spurious *Star* was strictly non-factional, and, except for notices of the Whig Club, which were appearing regularly among the advertisements, there was now nothing in the paper to correct this supposition. Having thus committed itself, the spurious *Star* concentrated its attention on the Prince, who, it earnestly declared, was "the most accomplished of any of the blood-royal of Europe," until 1 April, when the Prince yielded priority to his enemy, but Peter Stuart's friend, William Woodfall.

## DIGRESSIONS AND PRETENSES

VERY LITTLE is known of the political and journalistic activities of William Woodfall. On 11 March, 1789, he stated (*Morning Chronicle*) that his "connexion" with the *Morning Chronicle* had then "subsisted for twenty years (a few months only excepted)," but on 30 March, 1789, he added (*Diary*) that, although he had printed the *Chronicle* for almost twenty years, he had edited and conducted it for only "over eighteen." He was an original proprietor of that newspaper, along with John Murray, William Griffin, James Christie, George Kearsley, and others,[27] but he was not the original printer, for, according to his own statement (spurious *Star,* 1 Apr., 1789), the paper was pirated by the previous printers, Jacquery and Burd, "for some time" after the printing was taken out of their hands and "put into [his] hands by the Proprietors." He was also not the first reporter of the debates, for he had nothing to do with the content of the *Chronicle* until perhaps the beginning of 1771, whereas the paper was printing the debates in 1769 and 1770. In March, 1770, he was the only one of a number of printers, summoned by the Commons to answer for the publication of its proceedings, who was able to plead innocent, being already in Newgate Prison on a similar charge. He did, however, distinguish himself as reporter of the debates during his long tenure as conductor.

The identity of the other proprietors during this period was never revealed, but among them was evidently Andrew Strahan, for Woodfall felt obliged to consult him on all matters relating to the newspaper. At the beginning of 1783, for example, he could not even comply with a request to suppress the news of the peace until he had conferred with Strahan, although he did not doubt that the request was made by the Speaker of the Commons (*London Courant,* 29 Jan., 1783). The proprietors were, at any rate, always sympathetic with the Opposition, and until mid-1788 Woodfall conducted the *Chronicle* in accordance with their instructions. But the elections had hardly begun when he shifted the paper to the side of the Ministry, and, despite the protests of the proprietors, he continued to support the Ministry during the elections, during the fight over the Regency Bill, and even thereafter. The shift resulted in a long and bitter quarrel between Woodfall and the other proprietors, and on 11 March, 1789, the *Morning Chronicle* announced that, owing to "a difference arising between a Newspaper Printer and his Employers," "after the 28th Instant, [William Woodfall would] no longer continue Printer, Publisher, and Editor of the [paper]," but that "on Monday, the 30th of the present Month, he [would] publish a new Daily Paper, for the benefit of himself and his family."

Andrew Strahan may or may not have been involved in this piece of chicanery, but he was very much involved in another, which by 1789 was causing Woodfall considerable anxiety. When Woodfall first undertook the conduct of the *Chronicle,* he along with John Almon had, according to Morison,[28] founded a triweekly paper, called the *London Packet; or New Evening Post.* But, if Morison is correct, they had soon lost control of that newspaper, for by the early 1780's, it was printed and apparently owned by Francis Blythe, printer and proprietor of the *Public Ledger.* Blythe had continued to print both newspapers until his death in 1788, when the *Ledger* had been inherited by John Crowder.[29] The *London Packet* is next heard of on 20 March, 1789, when Woodfall wrote Strahan a desperate letter [30] respecting some manipulations of the *Packet* in which, as he reminded Strahan, the two had been involved "without authority" "now more than a twelvemonth." Woodfall's fear was that his partners in the *Chronicle,* who "would leave no stone unturned" to ruin him, might discover what had been going on: "They are men in *our* business, are likely to discover, and would rejoice to hit the blot, and divulge, or rather proclaim the predicament in which you and I stand," he warned. He went on to entreat Strahan to enlist the aid of George Rose at once, so that "the value of the P[acket] if we should get it hereafter" would not be "destroyed." Woodfall and Strahan evidently did not "get" the

*Packet,* for on 11 December, 1792, "the partners of the *London packet"* were, according to Boswell,[31] "[Charles] Dilly [the bookseller], little Davies (the son of Lockyer), Lowndes (Bookseller), [and John] Crowder (printer)*."* Alexander Chalmers was identified as "their former Editor," and by 3 October, 1793, he was editing the *Public Ledger.*[32] But Strahan did handle the matter so that Woodfall was able to quit the *Morning Chronicle* without a scandal.

Since by 1789 Peter Stuart could "recollect" many instances of [Woodfall's] partiality and friendship" (spurious *Star,* 1 Apr., 1789), he was probably connected with the *Chronicle* at some time or other: most likely in late 1783 or early 1784. Although his activities from late 1782 or early 1783 until 26 April, 1784, are not accounted for, the devastating review of Charles's *Gretna Green,* which appeared in the *Chronicle* of 29 August, 1783, would indicate that Woodfall was not acquainted with either of the Stuarts at that time. From April, 1784, through March, 1789, Peter could have seen Woodfall only occasionally, but he was greatly interested in his quarrel with the proprietors of the *Chronicle,* partly, no doubt, because it seemed to parallel his own quarrel with the proprietors of the original *Star.* The fact that Woodfall's politics were diametrically opposed to those of the spurious *Star* did not diminish his admiration for Woodfall in the least, and he was therefore very upset when, in his address "TO THE PUBLIC" of 11 March, 1789, Woodfall referred disparagingly to the pirating of newspapers. Assuming that Woodfall was referring to the spurious *Star,* Peter at once sent off a letter of protest, to which Woodfall replied on 12 March:

DEAR SIR,

I do assure you I by no means allude to your separation from the Proprietors of THE STAR in my Address. The fairness of a Printer's conduct who dissolves partnership with Proprietors, or is dismissed by them from the office of Printer, depends always on the circumstances of the case. I have no doubt but you acted fairly and honourably in your separation from the Proprietors of THE STAR; and beg you to be satisfied, that the argument in my Address to the Public alludes to the case of the Morning Chronicle itself, which, when put into my hands by the Proprietors, was pirated for some time by Mess. *Jacquery* and *Burd.* I am,
     Dear Sir,

                                        Your's sincerely,
                                        W. WOODFALL.

This letter should have brought the matter to a close, but Woodfall was Peter's friend, and Peter was therefore bound to help him in his hour of need.

On 24 March, 1789, "The Proprietors of the MORNING CHRONICLE [took] the liberty of informing the Publick, that on Monday next, the 30ᵗʰ inst. and in future, their Paper [would] be published at No. 79, Fleet-street, three doors west of Salisbury Court; where [their] friends . . . are requested to direct their advertisements and letters to the Editor." To this notice Woodfall appended the information that after 28 March he would no longer be connected with the *Morning Chronicle* and that on 30 March he would begin a new newspaper, to be entitled the *Diary, or Woodfall's Register* and to be published at the former address of the *Chronicle,* namely, No. 62, Dorset Street, Salisbury Square. His successor as conductor of the *Chronicle* was not named, but the probability is that it was James Perry. Although Haig has recently discovered [33] that Perry did not resign as conductor of the *Gazetteer* until 27 November, 1790, Collier stated positively [34] that Perry succeeded Woodfall as conductor of the *Chronicle,* "subsequently [obtaining] the proprietorship [of that paper]," and his statement is supported by the newspaper evidence. For after March, 1789, the *Gazetteer* underwent a marked deterioration, as if it was being managed by an underling, whereas there is no change in the character of the *Chronicle* after April of that year.

The first number of the *Diary, or Woodfall's Register* (30 Mar., 1789) carried another address *"To the* PUBLICK," in which Woodfall identified himself as the sole proprietor of the paper, admitted that his attitude toward the Regency Bill had been Ministerial, and indicated that his sympathies were still very much with the Government. On the same day the *Chronicle* made it clear that its sympathies were decidedly with the Opposition. The spurious *Star* ignored the *Chronicle,* but went out of its way (1 Apr.) to wish the *Diary* Godspeed:

### TO THE PUBLIC.

Many of the Printer's *good-natured* friends having *absurdly* imagined that a passage in Mr. WOODFALL's Address, announcing his intention of publishing a new paper called THE DIARY, alluded to the Printer of this paper's conduct in his separation from the *Dying Dogs* [the proprietors of the original *Star*], P. STUART, in contradiction to such report, has Mr. WOODFALL's permission to publish his letter to him on the subject:—

[The letter follows.]

From the date of the foregoing [12 Mar.], it must be obvious that the Printer of THIS PAPER, notwithstanding his possession of such respectable authority in his favour, has not been very anxious to take any advantage of it; and, had he not been particularly advised, would not have troubled his readers on the subject.

The case of Mess. JACQUERY and BURD has no resemblance to the present: *Neither* of them was, like P. STUART, the ORIGINAL PROPRIETOR and INVENTOR of the Paper in question, and received the others into partnership with him. Neither were they, like P. STUART, dismissed from their office, *at a moment's warning,* for refusing to become the contemptible tool of a party, and to assassinate the characters of the PRINCE of WALES and his FRIENDS.

The Printer of this Paper has always entertained too high an opinion of Mr. W. WOODFALL's candour to have believed, for one moment, that he meant any prejudicial allusion to his conduct, especially as he recollects with pleasure many instances of that Gentleman's partiality and friendship;—to whom, without offense to any person, he cordially wishes every success which his uncommon abilities merit.

This address was reprinted on 2 April. But the real irony was a set of verses, which appeared in the spurious *Star* of 10 April, written, of course, by Peter Stuart, but signed simply "S."

To Mr. W. WOODFALL,
*On Publishing his* DIARY.

After quitting his connection with the MORNING CHRONICLE, wherein the PARLIAMENTARY DEBATES were many years well detailed.

BEGIN thy new career! be TRUTH thy guide!
Still bend thy faithful pen on FREEDOM's side!
Then Britain shall again thy genius crown,
Again decree the palm of fair renown!

Each SPEAKER thanks thee for thy candid page;
Each Reader sees, in this enlighten'd age,
New colours in fair Freedom's picture shine,
And this new art of printing first was thine!

As Peter very well knew, Woodfall's "faithful pen" was now being "bent" on the "side" of the Treasury, which paid £400 a year for this newspaper through 1793.[35] The *Diary* was discontinued on 30 August, 1793.

By this time the spurious *Star* seemed to have lost sight of its purpose altogether, for nothing was said of the Prince of Wales, and a great deal was said of the Whigs. On 4 April the paper described Sheridan as a truly "great orator" and commended Sir Joshua Reynolds for using both "his *eyes*" and "his *Ear-trumpet*" when he painted his portrait; and on 18 April it exulted that "Mr. SHERIDAN is recovered [from his illness]— . . . *Genius* smiles at the event—he is one of her favourite sons." It meanwhile gave Fox and Alderman Skinner sole credit for the repeal of the shop tax, although Pitt had also supported the repeal; and on 4 April it presented a long and enthusiastic account of the meeting of the "independent inhabitants of Westminster, in the interest of Mr. Fox and Lord John Townshend," which had taken place at the Crown and Anchor on the previous day. It was also diverted by its numerous *"elegancies,"* some relating to music, some to poetry, some to French fashions, some to boxing, and on 4 April a half-column discussion of Swedenborgian theology; and from 8 April on it was further diverted by the trouble at Jack's Coffeehouse in Bristol.

On 11 April the spurious *Star* again digressed, this time to help the *Morning Post* or, more specifically, the third of the Stuart brothers, Daniel, who, since his name appeared in the colophon of that newspaper, would be held legally responsible for its content:

> The wretched and mean attempts to turn the loyal rejoicings of the Royal Household [over the King's recovery] into ridicule, originate with a *contemptible being* who owes his all to the mistaken patronage of the HEIR APPARENT. This fellow, who dares thus to insult Majesty, and interfere in the politics of the nation, is an *alien,* recently raised from abject indigence, and has made a property of a *public print,* for the dangerous purpose of converting the liberty of the press into the most abandoned licentiousness. A conduct like this should not be overlooked—the object is of magnitude, and calls for the attention of the magistracy. The most bitter enemy to the people of this country, and the glorious Constitution under which they live, and by which they are protected, could not devise a measure more prejudicial to both, than the publication of libels, which must render the press obnoxious. If the person alluded to cannot totally give up his *literary pursuits;* if he must continue a *man of letters,* let him advert to his *original profession,* the *baking of gingerbread alphabets.*

The *Morning Post* had evidently published some paragraphs which, it had reason to fear, the Government might regard as libels on the King; and the purpose of the spurious *Star's* remarks was to remind William Pitt, who was already well acquainted with the fact, that the

Prince of Wales's maître d'hôtel, Louis Weltje, was responsible by contract for the literary department of that newspaper and that a prosecution would therefore involve "the HEIR APPARENT," to the great embarrassment and displeasure of the King. The fact that this paragraph was itself embarrassing to everyone concerned and especially to the Prince of Wales, to whose "cause" the spurious *Star* was supposedly dedicated, did not trouble the Stuarts in the least.

The spurious *Star* had nevertheless been keeping a watchful eye on the political barometer, for, in planning for any election, the Opposition always had the disadvantage of not knowing when the election would be held. All it could learn about the date had to be conjectured from Pitt's conduct and the conduct of newspapers under his control. At the beginning of April, the *World* began to interest itself in the case of Philip Withers, who was being sued for libel by Mrs. Fitzherbert, and the spurious *Star* evidently interpreted this interest to mean that the time for the elections was approaching. For it promptly notified its readers of an impending dismissal of Parliament, and on 4 April it informed "THE PUBLIC" that "[an] excellent and commodious House is nearly finished in an elegible situation, to which the Printing and Publishing of STUART'S STAR, will be removed as soon as possible." The *World's* interest in Withers continued, and on 11 April the spurious *Star* made a coarse and altogether personal attack on Topham and Este, whereupon the *World* turned its attention to other matters. The spurious *Star* was evidently puzzled. On 13 April it implied that there might not be an election after all. The King, it said, was still ignorant of what had been going on, for, having not recovered "his former strength and spirits," he had "not yet taken a full review of the measures adopted [by the Government] during his illness." He might, therefore, allow Parliament to adjourn on its own motion, and, as soon as it adjourned, he might go to Germany for the summer, in which case, the paper admonished, "the PRINCE of WALES ought undoubtedly to be REGENT, subject only to his ROYAL FATHER'S commands." This admonition was backed by elaborate praise of the Prince's filial virtues and monarchical qualifications and almost equally elaborate praise of the character of John Williams' friend, Lord Barrymore.

On 14 April the spurious *Star* directed some further abuse at Topham and Este, and, since the *World* was still silent regarding Withers, it turned its attention to the "SPORTING INTELLIGENCE at

NEWMARKET," which, along with the "IRISH INTELLIGENCE," would, it promised its readers (15 Apr.), appear in *Stuart's Star* one day earlier than in other newspapers. But on 17 April it carried another announcement of its new address. This one was more specific:

### TO THE PUBLIC.

An excellent and commodious NEW HOUSE, No. 6, NEWCASTLE-STREET, STRAND, will be opened on MONDAY NEXT, for the reception of the FRIENDS of STUART'S STAR, to which the Printing and Publishing of THIS PAPER will be removed.

It is earnestly requested, that all LETTERS, ADVERTISEMENTS, and other ARTICLES, designed for PUBLICATION in this PAPER, may be addressed to "STUART'S STAR, *No. 6, Newcastle-street, Strand."*

FUTURE ARRANGEMENTS will be mentioned in a day or two, by which it will be evident to the PUBLIC, that STUART'S STAR is at present superior to every effort of caprice and malignity.

This announcement was repeated on 17 April. The last sentence referred to the paper's difficulties in Bristol and its more recent difficulties in Bath. On 20 April the announcement was revised to read that the "NEW HOUSE" was "now opened," and elsewhere the paper observed that "Opposition never stood more high in the public opinion than at present. Their becoming loyalty on HIS MAJESTY's recovery, has endeared them to all the impartial." The revised announcement was reprinted daily through 25 April, when it was dropped, although, according to the colophon, the "NEW HOUSE" was not actually occupied until 4 May.

Since the announcement of "FUTURE ARRANGEMENTS" was part of the surprise which the spurious *Star* had in store for the Government, it was, of course, delayed until the Opposition was quite certain that the elections were imminent. Again it seems to have taken its clue from the *World,* for on 24 April the *World* suddenly resumed its interest in the case of Philip Withers, and on Saturday, 25 April, the spurious *Star,* which had heretofore been promising its announcement "in a day or two," promised it for the following Monday. The announcement did appear on 27 April in the first number of the *Morning Star* and was reprinted on 28 and 29 April:

### TO THE PUBLIC.

Notwithstanding the malignant opposition which has been exerted, the uncommon success of STUART'S STAR demands the warmest acknowledgments.

Hence the Printer is convinced, there remains but one opinion of his conduct
—that, in acting with laudable spirit, he supported a proper dignity and independence of character.

The Printer has frequently received urgent letters from his Friends, complaining of the inconvenient time of publication. Those in the country have
often expressed their regret, that their newspapers were not transmitted
regularly by the post; while the Subscribers in town represented, that the intelligence was rendered of little use to them by being delivered at an hour
when more important business engrossed general attention, and when people
had already perused the MORNING PAPERS.

To obviate these objections and to render THIS PAPER of more importance
both to the ADVERTISER and to the mere READER, an alteration of the time of
publication has been deemed necessary. In London few people ever think of
any other than a MORNING PRINT, it being served at a regular and convenient
time for perusal; and in the Country, similar sentiments are prevalent, the
MORNING PRINTS possessing a greater circulation and influence. It must be confessed, that whenever the present publication was sufficiently known, it was
designed to alter the time of its appearance, by transforming the Evening
Paper called

STUART'S STAR

INTO

THE MORNING STAR.

Therefore, the friends of THIS PAPER are respectfully informed, that in
future the NEWS-MEN will serve them with THE MORNING STAR at the same
early and convenient time of delivery appropriated for the other MORNING
PAPERS; and that although the Printer continues in the joint management
and direction of what has obtained considerable reputation, more extensive
ARRANGEMENTS have been formed, by the kind assistance of Gentlemen conversant in every topic of LITERARY NOVELTY and ATTRACTION.

To talk of a competition with the former feeble opponents of THIS PAPER
[the proprietors of the genuine *Star*], would be absurd and ridiculous. We
shall not war with the *dead*, but aim at more noble exploits, and endeavour to
hold a competition with the INDUSTRIOUS and INTELLIGENT CONDUCTORS of the
MORNING PRINTS.

This announcement seems to have been framed with several objects in view. The first, of course, was to attract subscribers and advertisers. By this time the spurious *Star* was as ill-prepared "to hold a
competition with . . . the MORNING PRINTS" as a newspaper could be.
Despite the expenditure of the "SEVERAL THOUSAND
POUNDS," the quality of the paper had considerably worsened.
The leading article had disappeared, the information was much less

impressive than it had been before, and the "entertainment," although original, was often in the coarsest possible taste. The advertising, which for a few weeks had included some notices from Bristol and Bath, was again reduced to theatrical listings, occasional Government announcements, and a half-dozen statements regarding perfumes and patent medicines, totaling in all about three-fourths of a page. Notices of the Whig Club had been dropped for reasons of caution. The sale had probably sunk to approximately 200 a day, for the paper was now being effectively boycotted in Bristol, where it had had its largest sale; and, although on 27 April it "informed" its "numerous READERS in BATH . . . , that THIS PAPER may be had any night, about TEN or ELEVEN o'clock at No. 15, on the NEW BRIDGE, and that our SUBSCRIBERS shall be served with it on the very same evening," it was equally unwelcome in Bath. It was also evidently having trouble in London, for on 17 April it had apologized to Richard Wilson for having "mistakenly" said that he was "*beaten* in the Piazza Coffeehouse by the celebrated GEORGE BRERETON" "some years since"; and during the Easter term an action for "Trespass" had been brought against Charles Stuart by one Margaret Maxwell, the case being heard in the Court of King's Bench and Miss Maxwell awarded £20 damages plus 62*s*. costs.[36]

The second object was to persuade the Government that the change in time of publication was only an accommodation to the readers and had nothing to do with the elections. Not only did the spurious *Star* seem to have no interest in the elections, but, as it indicated in a separate paragraph, it was under the impression that the elections had been indefinitely postponed: "From the best authority, we hear that the resolution of DISSOLVING PARLIAMENT, is given up for the present." The possibility that it might have some connection with the Whigs was further denied in a succession of paragraphs, in which the spurious *Star* informed George Rose, in the kind of language which Rose understood, that it had been employed by the Prince of Wales to demand a new Regency Bill and to support his interests with respect to it. "A message is to be sent from HIS MAJESTY in a few days, signifying his intention of visiting his GERMAN DOMINIONS, and desiring the LORDS and COMMONS to provide for the safety of the kingdom in that event," the paper proclaimed on 27 April. This proclamation was followed by a somewhat irrelevant comment on Pitt's consumption of red port ("He is a *six-bottle* man. . . . The MINISTER will yield the

Bacchanalian palm to none but DUNDAS."), after which the paper returned to the matter at hand: "In the new REGENCY BILL, there is one
of the *blood-royal* reported as intended to preside, which will astonish
the empire. It is his HIGHNESS of GLOUCESTER!/ If there be any other
PRESIDENT than the accomplished and amiable HEIR APPARENT, it is
not difficult to foretell that much mischief must befal the country!
Divide, and govern, seems to be the plan of the minister." The
paper concluded its present remarks with the observation that
"CARLETON-HOUSE [*sic*] will be the most elegant of any town-residence,
when finished. This is not at all wonderful, when it is considered that
the PRINCE has the finest taste of any man in Britain." But on 28 April
it came back to the matter of that "new REGENCY BILL," informing its
readers, with every indication of alarm, that "ADMINISTRATION by no
means wish the KING to go abroad. They have been doing every thing
to prevent him, as they are afraid that such a Regency as they will
adopt, shall by no means meet the approbation of the country."

The announcement was also intended to persuade the Government
that the vicious attacks on the personnel of the *World,* which occupied
most of the space in the newspaper, were equally innocent. The spurious *Star* had previously "[held] competition" with the other daily
evening newspaper: it was now "[aiming] at more noble exploits, and
[endeavouring] to hold a competition with . . . the MORNING
PRINTS," of which the *World* happened to be the first. That it had
been selected in preference to one of the other newspapers was only
because it seemed to the spurious *Star* to be opposing the Prince's
interests with respect to the "new REGENCY BILL"; of its campaigning
activities the spurious *Star* seemed to be totally unaware. On 27 April
the paper presented some doggerel, signed "BOW-WOW" and entitled *"An* EPISTLE *from a* CERTAIN PERSONAGE *in* DUBLIN,
*to his* FRIEND *in* LONDON"; but, although the doggerel was an
attack on "Simkin," who was currently assailing Burke in the *World,*
it was concerned only with the Prince's friends in Ireland. On 28 April
the paper ventured as its own opinion that, "although not faultless,
and too full of flights of imagination," Burke was nevertheless "a
scholar and a man of great genius"; but even this statement was a
defense of Burke as an "Irish gentleman," not a prosecutor of Warren
Hastings.

The final object of the announcement was to protect Peter Stuart
in case an action should be brought against the newspaper, for the

notice of a "joint management and direction" was only a declaration that "P. STUART" was no longer responsible for the whole content of the paper. There had, of course, been a "joint management and direction" from the beginning, but, whereas "P. STUART" had previously been in little danger, no one could predict the Government's reaction to Charles's confessions. The "more extensive AR-RANGEMENTS," which had been "formed, by the kind assistance of Gentlemen conversant in every topic of LITERARY NOVELTY and AT-TRACTION," seem in the main to have been "formed" some time earlier; for, except for William Jackson's communications from the Continent, which began on 11 May, there is no indication of any new "ATTRACTION." It may be significant, however, that on 1 May, 1789, Daniel Stuart resigned as publisher of the *Morning Post,* for, although, according to his daughter,[37] he thereafter wrote for the *Post* and the *Argus,* a radical newspaper begun by Sampson Perry on 7 March, 1789, one does not actually catch sight of him again until 30 November, when he was a partner in a new enterprise, the Peterborough Press; [38] and it would seem more likely that he had spent part of the interim writing for the spurious *Star,* especially since Sheridan made a similar shift at approximately the same time.

## THE CONFESSIONS OF CHARLES STUART

WHEN Louis Weltje bought into the *Morning Post,* the *Post* became Sheridan's newspaper and hence the organ of all his intra-Party intrigues. The spurious *Star* was a Whig newspaper, and, although Sheridan had negotiated for Charles's confessions and planned the mode of their presentation, the confused and clumsy management of the paper thereafter is sufficient evidence that he had been only occasionally concerned in it. But from 27 April on the spurious *Star* was in the hands of an expert. The new manager was someone with imagination, with long experience, and with a thoroughgoing knowledge of the character of his opponent, the wily George Rose. The pretended alliance with Carlton House, for example, might have been invented by a Charles Stuart, but only Sheridan would have made it seem plausible by devising an issue, namely the "new REGENCY BILL," which, however fantastic, was still the sort of thing which, as Rose knew, might appeal to the ambitious and unrealistic Prince of Wales. The war with the *World,* too, was not in itself a tour de force. With two of Topham's personal enemies, Colman and Bell, associated with the spurious *Star,* some hostility was inevitable, and much of it would have been personal. Since Sheridan also had a grudge against Topham, one might even have predicted that there would be a war. But without Sheridan's acumen the war would finally have been waged along the same general lines as the war with the original *Star,* which had itself been patterned on the war between the two *Posts.* Sheridan saw to it that this particular war was conducted on a strictly and coarsely personal basis.

Sheridan made only one mistake, and even this one turned out to be trifling. On 27 April the spurious *Star* mentioned that "Letter I. of AN INJURED MAN, to the ELECTORS of GREAT-BRITAIN, but more especially to those of WESTMINSTER, is received, and shall be inserted on Wednesday [29 Apr.]." On 28 April it promised "Letter I. of AN INJURED MAN to-morrow." The effect of these announcements was to activate George Rose, who, according to Charles Stuart (spurious *Star,* 29 Apr.) , sent around "a SOLICITOR for the STAMP-OFFICE," John Frost, for the purpose of making a settlement. Charles was in a quandary. If he accepted payment, he was no longer "AN INJURED MAN," and he had already been paid (and had spent) ''SEVERAL THOUSAND POUNDS'' on account of his injury; yet he had no excuse for refusing it. But by 29 April he had thought of an excuse, or Sheridan had thought of one for him, the excuse being that, although Frost had "[*acknowledged*] the DEBT, [he had offered,] at the same time, such terms of accommodation as no man of honour could accept." By 6 May (spurious *Star*) this charge had been softened to read that Rose must have at least *"obliquely* ordered" Frost "to *compromise,"* for "he certainly ATTEMPTED" to compromise. Rose, of course, had given no such order, and Frost had made no such attempt. Under the circumstances the bill would have been settled in full, and Charles would probably have been offered a bonus in addition.

The first letter from "AN INJURED MAN" accordingly appeared on Wednesday, 29 April. It was addressed *"To the* ELECTORS *of* GREAT BRITAIN, *but* ESPECIALLY *to those of* WESTMINSTER" and labeled "CORRUPT INFLUENCE by a PERSON VERY HIGH IN ADMINISTRATION, CLEARLY PROVED!" The writer identified himself as a man who had been "ARRESTED" because of money owed him by a certain person, having been *"employed* by the PER-

SON alluded to, in the WESTMINSTER ELECTION [of 1788]."
"Still, however," the letter went on,

has the injured party never given up the *name* of this MAN HIGH IN OF-
FICE, but has undergone the ignominy of supposed embezzlement, merely to
save that OFFICIAL MAN's *character*. For a minute disclosure of the whole
transaction must not only hurt him in the public estimation, but *sully* the
CHARACTER, too, of the HIGHEST in the government, from this peculiar
circumstance, that the FIRST SUM *advanced* could *not* be given, until the
*principal came in from riding,* which was actually the case.

A *candid* statement of the whole shall be given in this Paper, which shall
. . . throw an *indelible stain* on SOME *characters,* hitherto high in esteem for
their supposed virtue. . . .

. . . The GREAT MAN was the SOLE EMPLOYER, and not the agent,
in the debt alluded to.

Proofs, the most unequivocal, shall be produced. . . .

It may be of more consequence to the WESTMINSTER ELECTION,
than *thousands* of *bad votes.* It may be of much consequence, likewise, in *opening* the *eyes* of the PEOPLE, to perceive clearly, that MALIGNITY and
INJUSTICE exist in the *bosoms* of *those* who are *deemed* PURE and IM-
MACULATE!

AN INJURED MAN.

*The name of the injured man is left with the Printer.*

\* As a proof of [the] justice [of the debt, the official] gave 50*l.* of it in *part
payment,* by a draught on his Banker.

LETTER II. *containing more unequivocal particulars, on Saturday.*

Although Rose and Pitt could hardly have been more clearly identified, on 30 April the spurious *Star* published a letter to "AN IN-
JURED MAN," which read: "SIR,/ Your letter is a riddle.—Why not
declare the parties?—Should your assertions be proved, you will be
supported by every/ INDEPENDENT ELECTOR."

On 1 May the spurious *Star* bewailed the fact that Pitt was drag-
ging out the session with no concern for the health of the King, which,
it declared, demanded an immediate change of climate, and it went
on to condemn his treatment of Prince William, who had just returned from the West Indies. On 2 May it filled its pages with paragraphs of praise of the Prince for his exquisite taste and unstinting
devotion to his father, with a comment or two on the Duke of Gloucester, who, "if nominated in the Regency Bill," will "easily be swerved

by our subtle minister," and with the second "LETTER FROM AN INJURED MAN." This one, addressed to "GEORGE ROSE, *Esq.*, *One of the* SECRETARIES TO THE TREASURY," identified the "GENTLEMAN" who was the actual employer, but was *"out a-riding"* at the time of the original interview as "MR. PITT." Having detailed the circumstances of that interview, which took place at Pitt's "house, at DOWNING-STREET," it referred provocatively to a later meeting which the author had had with Rose "by [Rose's] desire, at the Archbishop of CANTERBURY's, in *Lambeth,*" but decided to "wave [*sic*] that for the present." On 4 and 5 May the spurious *Star* was puzzled that the King had not expressed his disapproval of the Minister's conduct, especially since, as it said on 6 May, "Mr. PITT's arrogance and duplicity have been fully ascertained since the unfortunate malady of our beloved Sovereign." The paper had a good deal more to say on this subject in the days which followed.

The third letter from "AN INJURED MAN" appeared on 6 May. It was a chronicle of promises made and broken by George Rose, which concluded by asking: "Do you imagine that you are a *Secretary* of FRANCE—instead of being a *Secretary* of ENGLAND?/ Do you think that ENGLISHMEN can *bear* the BASTILE, even in their *minds,* without HORROR?" On 7 May the spurious *Star* discoursed at length on the subject of the "new REGENCY BILL." By this time the King had supposedly spoken out in favor of the Prince of Wales, but the result, said the spurious *Star,* was only a new series of Ministerial villainies:

The King is determined to visit HANOVER this summer, in order to remove himself from the fatigue of business, to which his PHYSICIANS have *advised him.*

All reports to the contrary, are as *absurd* as they are *untrue.*

HIS MAJESTY has been so much pleased with the PRINCE's conduct during his illness, that he has signified, within these few days, his ROYAL WILL to place him at the *head* of the REGENCY, while he is abroad. . . .

The real *truth* [respecting Pitt's failure to submit the last item on the agenda, the budget,] is said to be the *intention* of *delaying* the *prorogation* of PARLIAMENT, in order to *prevent* HIS MAJESTY from going to HANOVER.

It is certain that the IRISH nation will *not* consent to the appointment of ANY REGENCY, during the KING's ABSENCE, in which the PRINCE of WALES is *not* to have the *leading part.*

ADMINISTRATION CALCULATE, that they can *carry* a REGENCY BILL through the ENGLISH PARLIAMENT, to *exclude* the PRINCE; but, with *all* their EFFORTS, they *cannot* bring the PARLIAMENT of the SISTER KINGDOM to *join* in *disgracing* the HEIR APPARENT.

His Majesty *himself* has expressed *most certainly* a desire, that the PRINCE should be at the *head* of the REGENCY.

When it came to the game of politics, Sheridan had no second, and one can only be lost in admiration at the genius of these paragraphs. The real reason for Pitt's *"delaying* the *prorogation* of PARLIAMENT" was, of course, the letters from "AN INJURED MAN," for the Government was not going to risk elections until it silenced Charles Stuart. But the spurious *Star's* interpretation placed Pitt in a much worse light, for he seemed to be flaunting the King's wishes and deliberately sacrificing his health in order to preserve his own power. The spurious *Star* said so flatly on the following day.

The next set of paragraphs (8 May) was headed "REGENCY BILL." It was Pitt's present intention, the paragraphs began, to designate the Duke of Gloucester as principal regent, all the other regents to be appointed by "PARLIAMENT, *that is,* by Mr. Pitt": "He appoints not only the PRINCE of WALES as PRINCE REGENT, but likewise *all* the *other* LORDS of the REGENCY, *himself!"* Since the Duke of Gloucester was already a tool of Pitt, the whole bill, explained the spurious *Star,* was a cunning scheme to make Pitt the actual regent. The King was pleading that he wanted the Prince of Wales to be, not his *"creature,* but his REPRESENTATIVE" with all the powers of a monarch, but his pleadings were being ignored, and his health was suffering accordingly:

Had Mr. PITT's *Bill* been *approved* by the KING's *friends,* he would have gone for HANOVER about the *fifteenth* of *this* MONTH.

But as the ROYAL FAMILY, as well as his MAJESTY, by no means approve of it, the *rising* of PARLIAMENT is to be *procrastinated,* until the season is *too far advanced* for HIS MAJESTY to accomplish HIS JOURNEY.

The *resistance* to the KING's WISHES has occasioned a very *visible* DEJECTION of MIND; and it is with the utmost difficulty that he can be *roused* from this MELANCHOLY SITUATION, in order to go through the *forms* of BUSINESS. . . .

It is with *regret* that we [add] that *some* OTHER branches of the ROYAL FAMILY have *not* been proof against those TEMPTATIONS that work *peculiarly* on the *temper* of AGE. A *transaction* of a PECUNIARY NATURE has been for *some time* CARRYING on between the MINISTER and a certain DUKE [Gloucester, of course]. In consequence of which treaty, he has *promised* HIS SUPPORT to the MINISTER, and *deserted* the CAUSE of his NEPHEWS, to whom he so *recently* gave his WARM SUPPORT in the HOUSE of LORDS for maintaining the *honour* of the ROYAL FAMILY.

The spurious *Star* here denied an *"absurd* report which was begun to be propagated by the *retainers* of ADMINISTRATION, on Thursday last, of the PRINCE having *separated* from THE PARTY./ On Friday morning [the Prince] called on Mr. Fox, and walked with him, arm and arm, in St. James's-street, for upwards of an hour, in order to convince the public that the *implicit confidence* he has always had in that Gentleman is *entirely* UNDIMINISHED."

This denial was the first hint of trouble, for Sheridan's ruse depended for its success upon the Prince's endorsement or supposed endorsement of the Whigs. Since the Prince had himself nothing to gain from the letters of "AN INJURED MAN," Pitt and Rose had to believe that he had sanctioned their publication in his newspaper because of his *"implicit confidence"* in Fox. There was further indication of trouble on the following day (9 May), when the spurious *Star* published the first installment of the fourth letter from "AN INJURED MAN," for, although the letter was addressed to George Rose, it had almost nothing to add to what had already been said. Moreover, although the paper had previously made it very clear that the King's trouble was mental, it now made it equally clear that the trouble was physical. This column was headed "THE SOVEREIGN":

It is with the most *unfeigned affliction* that we are under the DISAGREEABLE NECESSITY of mentioning what must meet with the most SINCERE CONCERN from *all men.*

His MAJESTY's STATE of HEALTH renders him *incapable* of attending to PUBLIC BUSINESS. He is afflicted with an *extreme* LASSITUDE.

An *abscess* is forming in his GROIN, which gives considerable *apprehension* to his Physicians.

[But] we are happy to say, that his MIND is as *recollected* as at ANY TIME OF HIS LIFE! . . .

All the FAITHFUL FRIENDS of HIS MAJESTY, *regret* that he has been *called* into OFFICIAL EXERTIONS *before* his HEALTH *permitted it!*

These statements were themselves softened on Monday, 11 May, when the spurious *Star* reported that, "notwithstanding some late reports," the King was looking "very well." "His journey to HANOVER, within these few days, has been set aside for this season," it went on. "Sea-bathing will certainly be substituted. The place not yet determined."

"It is hoped that ADMINISTRATION will keep the KING's *mind* as *free* from BUSINESS as possible. This is the mode to be prescribed towards a perfect restoration of strength." These were the statements of a very frightened newspaper, and the reason for its fright is evident from a paragraph which the spurious *Star* had itself published on 12 March: "We are desired to mention by way of caution, that the Judges have declared it as their opinion to be TREASON to assert, either *orally* or *in print,* that the KING's mind is *deranged,* or that he is not in a capacity to act as SOVEREIGN of the BRITISH EMPIRE." There was apparently a rumor that the Government intended to prosecute the newspaper for publishing numerous libels on the King.

Meanwhile on 9 May the spurious *Star* had promised the second installment of the fourth letter from "AN INJURED MAN," this one to be addressed to William Pitt, for Tuesday, 12 May; but on Tuesday it was *"obliged to be deferred till Thursday, on account of an influx of temporary matter."* This *"temporary matter,"* which was only further attacks on the personnel of the *World,* crowded out, not only the letter to Pitt, but all mention of the King, the "new REGENCY BILL," and William Pitt. On 13 May the spurious *Star* mentioned that the Ministers' attempts to win over Prince William and the Dukes of York and Cumberland had failed, adding a paragraph in defense of Lord Malmesbury "because he proved his *Loyalty* to the PRINCE, when the KING was *incapable."* Otherwise the paper was again preoccupied with *"temporary matter."* On 14 May Pitt was assailed on another account:

### INFORMERS.

These maurauders on SOCIETY have multiplied very rapidly of late. Formerly we never heard of the avocation, unless in times of *public commotion,* or against SMUGGLERS, who certainly evaded the law WILFULLY.

But some late acts of Mr. PITT, have been injurious to many industrious families, who never meant to defraud the revenue.

They have been *undone* by a sett of villains, who live in the parish of ST. MARTIN, in an elegant stile, by plundering the unwary, on account of a STAMP *error,* which either proceeds on their side from *intentional* HURRY, or on the DEFENDANT's *side,* from the IGNORANCE of a *servant* or *child.*

These acts are chiefly the SLAVE *tax*—the PERFUMERY *tax*—and the HAT *tax.* Poor industrious people have been forced to sell even the beds from under them to pay the fine, which has almost invariably been extorted by these infamous informers, without the worthy tradesman even intending to hurt the Revenue.

The reason of these pests of the poor citizens being encouraged, is owing to some HIGHER POWERS, who share in the produce of their LEGAL ROBBERY.

A more particular account of their ART and PERSONS shall soon appear in this paper, whose only basis is PUBLIC FREEDOM, and in protecting the *humbly honest* from the *machinations* of the VILLAIN of a *higher sphere!*

This article may have been submitted by the perfumers, who were still advertising in the newspaper. It may have been submitted by Peter Stuart, who had an old score to settle with Mr. W. J'Anson, J'Anson having in 1787 sued the *Morning Post* and hence Peter as printer of the newspaper for naming him as ringleader of a group of "divers swindlers and common informers" who made an avocation of preying on innocent people.[39] It may also have been submitted by Charles Stuart for reasons known only to himself, although Charles's authorship would be somewhat ironic, since from 1794 to 1797 he was one of the "sett of villains" himself (*Telegraph, Oracle, Star,* 3 Febr., 1797; *Morning Chronicle, True Briton, The Times,* 4 Febr., 1797). But it was certainly published without the knowledge of Sheridan, for the declaration that the paper's "only basis" was "PUBLIC FREEDOM" contradicted all the previous declarations that its "only basis" was "the *cause* of the HOUSE of HANOVER, in the person of HIS ROYAL HIGHNESS," the Prince of Wales. As one might have anticipated, the "more particular account" did not appear.

The same number of the spurious *Star* (14 May) carried the second installment of Charles's fourth letter. Although the letter was, in fact, addressed to William Pitt, it was not what the readers had been led to expect. For, whereas the first two letters in the series had stated positively that the "GREAT MAN was the SOLE EMPLOYER" and had promised "Proofs, the most unequivocal," this letter effectively absolved him from any "participation" in Rose's "conduct." "Sir," the letter began:

Whether or not it was proper in your Secretary, Mr. ROSE, to interfere in the WESTMINSTER Election, by disseminating *his* most low and violent abuse of Opposition, is not now the question. But ought he not to have honourably discharged all those debts which were contracted in promulgating *his* ribaldry?

In extenuation of his conduct, it must be confessed, indeed, that the *official* man who could thus *descend* to interfere by publishing scurrility, might afterwards endeavour to forget to pay for it. . . .

I cannot, it is true, charge you with participating in his conduct. . . .

To prove . . . the justice of my demand on your confidential man, in my next letter I shall publish the PARTICULAR INCIDENTS on the account. This, I presume, will even be more entertaining than Major SCOTT's *Morning Herald* BILL. It will likely promote, too, considerable laughter at your table, as some of the company may recollect their own abortions in the perusal of these *items.*

I shall afterwards *republish* some of the most singular of *these* BALLADS, &c. . . .

When I have stated the whole, with suitable remarks, I shall then *sue* Mr. ROSE for the debt.

I wish much that you may soon advise a *parliamentary dissolution,* as then I could *repay* your SECRETARY a debt of *durance,* which I most certainly owe him. If he did not choose to discharge *his debt* to *me,* I should, in that case, most punctually discharge MY DEBT TO HIM.

AN INJURED MAN.

On 15 May the spurious *Star* returned to the matter of the "new REGENCY BILL" and William Pitt with a series of paragraphs, which began:

Prince WILLIAM HENRY will certainly be soon created a British Peer, *not* by the *Minister,* but by MAJESTY.

Mr. PITT, when he *framed* the *heterogeneous* REGENCY BILL, left a *niche* for Prince WILLIAM, as the *only* PEER which his *amiable* BROTHER could CREATE.

It was done, however, with this idea, that MINISTRY were *sure* of the PRINCE *joining them.*

Report says, that he had been offered a *seat* at the ADMIRALTY *Board,* if he would fight under the *banners* of PITT.

But the spurious *Star* was happy to say that the Prince had refused to be a party to Pitt's scheme of *"sowing* DISCORD in the *House* of BRUNSWICK."* The paragraphs were continued on 16 May with the announcements:

The present Administration are losing ground every day, owing to the *disrespect* they have all along endeavoured to instil into the minds of the *people,* respecting the *younger* branches of the ROYAL FAMILY.

PRINCE WILLIAM, however, has *checked* the PARAGRAPHIC FIRE which was attempted against him, by certain characters. It was not more by the threats of an ACTION, than by the threats of PRINCELY *coercion.*

Captain TOPHAM will write no more against his Royal Highness.

These were the last editorial attacks on Pitt until 23 May.

By this time the spurious *Star* was in more serious trouble. The first indication of new difficulties was a notice which appeared on 15 May:

## TO THE PUBLIC.

Several COMPLAINTS having been lately made of the IRREGULAR DELIVERY of THIS PAPER, we have only to request, that if our friendly complainants do not immediately meet with *redress* from their REGULAR NEWSMEN, they will be so kind as to transmit immediately their *intention* to *the* PRINTER, and it shall be *instantly obeyed*. It is particularly requested, that the FRIENDS of the MORNING STAR will give their orders, either to the PRINTER, or to the NEWS-MEN of the GREEN DRAGON, *Fleet-street,* who will particularly attend to their instructions.

The notice was reprinted on 16 May and then dropped. This was not a piece of propaganda, but a statement of fact: someone, whose identity *"the* PRINTER" did not know or was afraid to expose, was blocking delivery of the newspaper.

Meanwhile the fifth letter from "AN INJURED MAN," "addressed to GEORGE ROSE, Esq. and containing the CURIOUS INCIDENTS of an ACCOUNT due by HIM," was on 15 May promised, "if possible to-morrow." On Saturday, 16 May, it was "deferred till Monday." On Monday it was promised *"positively to-morrow—when the* delay *shall be properly accounted for."* It did appear on Tuesday, 19 May, but there was no explanation of the "delay," nor were there any "CURIOUS INCIDENTS." "Although I pledged myself to the public, that I would THIS DAY bring forward my reason of *delay,* I shall, on THURSDAY, adduce *sufficient reasons* to them that I am at present not FULLY PRE-PARED," the letter began. "However, not to disappoint their EXPECTA-TIONS and *your* FEARS, I have published, underneath, the *duplicate* of *one* of MY BILLS to you./ BREAKFAST *afterwards* with what *appetite* YOU MAY!" The bill was followed with the comment: "The above is only the *bare record* of a CLERK. I shall afterwards . . . *expand, explain* and *confirm."* The sixth letter was first mentioned on Thursday, 21 May, when it was promised for Saturday, and on Saturday "AN INJURED MAN" finally "adduced" his "reason of *delay."*

## EVASIONS, EXTENUATIONS, AND SILENCE

THE WAR with the *World* continued to be prosecuted with vigor. But there were now long periods during which the spurious *Star* was afraid to speak of politics and was therefore free to turn its attention to other matters. One of them was extortion, for the "SEVERAL THOUSAND POUNDS" were exhausted, and the paper was incurring debts, for which Charles Stuart would finally be responsible. On 15 May the spurious *Star* took advantage of the suicide (13 May) of "the *Hon.* WILLIAM JOHN TOWNSHEND" to attempt to extort money from his relations. "A young gentleman of the first rank, put a period to his existence on Wednesday," it observed. "He was the *son* of a PEERESS in her own right. He was the *nephew* of a MARQUIS, and the *brother* of a DUKE./ Various causes are assigned for this rash act. Some say it was owing to INSANITY. Others, owing to the *harshness* of the PARENT./ We *know* the CAUSE; but, out of *delicacy* to the FRIENDS of the *deceased,* it shall be *waved* [*sic*] for THE PRESENT." The clause, "it shall be *waved* for THE PRESENT" (cf. the second letter from "AN INJURED MAN") , pretty well marks Charles Stuart as the author of these observations. On 16 May the spurious *Star* named "the *deceased*" and added enough details of the suicide to persuade the relations that it knew what it was talking about:

### JACK TOWNSHEND!

PALL MALL was the fatal spot!—In the house of a friend, nearly opposite to the STAR and GARTER.

He drank three bottles of champaigne [*sic*], before he voluntarily became an . . . exile from this world of joy and sorrow.

He snatched the momentary opportunity of his amiable friend and host's absence, to commit a deed, which made this friend the more shocked on his entrance, as it was *not* effected by a PISTOL, although the weapon was STEEL.

Mr. T. has been for some time past observed to be in a *desponding* state. By *some* it has been construed into INSANITY.

But surely an INSANE MAN would not *fortify* himself with three bottles of wine, in order to perpetrate his death?

Like HESSE, it is said that his *fortune,* and not his MIND was *deranged.*

He has left a very disconsolate sister—besides his other relations.

The worthy MARQUIS and his whole family are in tears!

The paper had more to say on 19 May:

### *Hon.* WILLIAM JOHN TOWNSHEND.

Many have been the causes assigned for his committing the act of suicide; the best founded seems to be, derangement of his affairs, and disappointment of pecuniary assistance from a quarter where he had *some reason* to expect it.

From the first, there was not the smallest hope of affording him relief,— yet he survived twelve hours in the most excruciating pain!

Mr. TOWNSHEND was the only surviving son of the late Right Hon. CHARLES TOWNSHEND by Lady GREENWICH; he was half-brother to the Duke of BUCCLEUGH and nephew to the Marquis TOWNSHEND. He was in a peculiar degree the favourite of his noble uncle, who is overwhelmed with grief at his unhappy fate.

Lady GREENWICH has been very unfortunate in her children by her *second* marriage. Her Ladyship was daughter to the great John Duke of Argyle and Greenwich. She married first the Earl of Dalkeith, son to the Duke of Buccleugh, to whom she bore, among other children, his present Grace of that title. She next married the Right Hon. Charles Townshend, younger brother to the present Marquis Townshend.

. . . . [Though] she brought Mr. Townshend TWO SONS—one of them was *found dead* in his tent in one of our homecamps, where he was on duty during the late war. The other has been taken off by his own hands.

There remains now to this aged Lady only a daughter *Ann,* married to the late Wilson, who lately destroyed the peace of a noble veteran of the navy, by carrying off his daughter.

The family seems to have responded, for on 20 May the spurious *Star* brought the matter to an end with the announcement: "W. J. TOWNSHEND was insane for the six weeks before he put an end to his existence."

The spurious *Star* continued its harassments of the dead, but it was also mindful of the living. On 22 May, for example, it retracted some statements which were "considered to reflect on the character" of the Earl of Moira and his son, Lord Rawdon, whom it now represented as two of the finest gentlemen in the country. In other instances its harassments were less successful. On 25 and 28 May it made a final and desperate effort to extort money from the residents of Bristol with, it appears, no results whatever. By this time it was desperately in need of money; for, according to the records of the Court of King's Bench, Trinity Term, 1789,[40] an action for debt had been brought against Peter Stuart by one Anthony Grove for the recovery of £20, to which the Court added 62s. costs. Peter was evidently unable to pay this amount, for Theophilus Swift's verses, "On IMPRISONMENT FOR DEBT," which were published on 3 June, seem to have been written with him in mind.

The spurious *Star* also busied itself with the matter of personal grudges, of which there were many. The most space-consuming of the group was a grudge held by George Colman, the first evidence of which was a letter, published by the spurious *Star* on 16 May. It was addressed "To a Covent Garden Performer" and signed only "Momus," and it consisted of the warning: "Sir,/ If you do not *reinstate* an amiable woman, who has had *many* Children to you, the public will call you to account on the stage./ Mrs. Inchbald, to her honour, befriends your wife./ But if you *continue* to substitute a *prostitute* in the place of a worthy woman, the Town may laugh at your *public* Mimicry, and very soon execrate your *private* Acting." On 19 May the spurious *Star* added its own warning:

> The *Covent Garden* Performer who has turned into the streets a *worthy* woman and *several children*, has taken a *wretch* to his bed, whose *former* Keeper was among the first that *danced* off the new drop!
>
> There have been such a series of *cruelties* practiced upon the *wife* and *children*, that for the honour of the Profession, and indeed for *human nature*, we hope he is not in his *perfect mind*—therefore we treat him at present with lenity.
>
> If, however, it appears that he is *otherwise*, he shall *immediately* be taught to know, that no *mummery* shall gloss over *inhumanity*.

The "Performer" to whom these paragraphs alluded was John Edwin, who was to be assailed by the spurious *Star* for the next several weeks. Edwin's sin was not a sin against *"human nature,"* but against the Haymarket, which he had deserted for Covent Garden, and the "lenity" of the treatment did not depend on his sanity, but on his return.

The period of "lenity" lasted exactly three days. On 22 May the spurious *Star* identified the principals in the drama:

> The *insane*, or *cruel* Performer's name is Edwin. He has not only turned his *wife adrift*, and *six children*, but has adopted another *Mrs. Edwin*, whose *maiden* name has been *long* lost.
>
> Her first keeper, Burke, danced off the *New Drop*. Besides being Mrs. Burke, she has been *alias* Mrs. Slack, *alias* Mrs. Shaw, *alias* Mrs. Wilson, and now, *alias* Mrs. Edwin.
>
> Because Mr. Colman has engaged his *wife*, and his *eldest* son, the *unnatural parent*, and the *horrid husband* vows, that he will not play at his theatre, until he *discharges them!*
>
> The Town *must* and *will* interfere.
>
> The *private* Tragedian is the most shocking of all characters. What signify *comic* powers, when their *encouragement* only tend to embitter the *feelings of kindred*.

The *"New Drop,"* which was a trap-door contrivance installed in the Newgate gallows in 1783 as a substitute for the cart, had figured more heavily in the amours of *"alias* Mrs. EDWIN" than the spurious *Star* first supposed, for on 23 May the paper reported: "The newly *adopted* Mrs. EDWIN, has *lost* two husbands already at the *new drop*. The first was BURKE; the second was WILSON, the pawn-broker./ Her maiden name is *Hubbard*. Her father is a soldier of fortune—in the *Guards.*"

The spurious *Star* of 23 May also carried a letter from "A FE-MALE," demanding that "the Play-going folks" take action against Edwin, who had, she said, *"kicked* one of his BOYS out of his house to-day, because the child, who is now an apprentice, came to ask him for *relief!"* A "Mr. and Mrs. CROSBIE" had already taken action by turning Miss Hubbard out: "She now lives, I believe, in Howland-street." This story deeply stirred "THE MAN OF FEELING," who responded by addressing two long letters to the newspaper. The first, which did little more than eulogize Colman, was published on 26 May; and on 27 May the spurious *Star* wholeheartedly agreed that "Mr. COLMAN has behaved with the most praiseworthy liberality to Young EDWIN and MOTHER." "COLMAN, this season, has succeeded wonderfully, without a London company," it added parenthetically. "This was always his aim." On 28 May there was a "PROLOGUE/ *To* UT PICTURA POESIS; *or,/ The* ENRAGED MUSICIAN./ WRIT-TEN BY G. COLMAN./ SPOKEN BY MR. EDWIN, JUN.," and on 29 May there was the second letter from "THE MAN OF FEELING."

This letter, dated *"Haymarket Green-room"* and addressed "TO THE PUBLIC," reviewed the circumstances of Edwin's previous marriage. Edwin had been "some years ago a *very low* comedian in BATH, at a salary of *fifteen shillings* a week," it said, when he happened to meet "SARAH WALMSLEY, a woman of some means, currently a milliner." At his insistence, she subsequently sold "her stock of milli-nery" and turned over the money, which amounted "to near *one thou-sand pounds sterling,"* to him, and he "applied it to what purposes his whim or caprice dictated." "Between TWENTY and THIRTY YEARS have now elapsed," said "THE MAN OF FEELING," during which period Sarah Walmsley "has *always* been acknowledged by Mr. EDWIN and FRIENDS as HIS WIFE; and, under that description, the CHILDREN . . . came into the world." "The PRINTER" appended to this chronicle the information that Edwin and "Mr. [Thomas] RYDER," another per-former at Covent Garden, had called at the spurious *Star* office during his absence and "used the language of MENACE and TERROR!" He also added the usual praise of Colman. On the following day he was compelled to apologize to "Mr. RYDER," whose name had been added because of the "blunder *of a servant,"* Edwin having actually been alone; but on 1 June he had a new grievance: *"The impudent Letter sent to the Printer of this Paper by the abandoned female associate of* EDWIN, *the* mad mummer *of Covent Garden Theatre, has been received. The Printer considers the* TERRIFIC THREATS *of* EDWIN *and his* BILLINGSGATE BELLE *with the most sovereign contempt. From the injuries and outrages committed against a worthy* WIFE *and* CHILDREN, *may* GOD *send the* SUFFERERS *a speedy deliverance."* With this prayer the paper concluded its attacks on Edwin, except for periodic reports of the hisses and boos which greeted each of his appearances on the Covent Garden stage, and on 13 June, 1790, Edwin married Mary Hubbard. He died in October.

On Friday, 22 May, the spurious *Star* promised that the sixth letter from "AN INJURED MAN, *with Mr.* ROSE's Flash Song," would appear *"to-morrow."* It also promised that, *"[the] paper of* LETTER V. *containing Mr.* ROSE's *account having been all sold, and urgent demands being made at the office for that very curious letter, it shall be reprinted on* MONDAY." This last promise was repeated on Saturday, 23 May, and on that day the sixth letter did actually appear. It was addressed to George Rose, and it began with a long-overdue explanation:

Sir,

My reason of DELAY, was in order to sift a malicious report to the bottom, which some of your adherents had circulated, respecting the OPPOSITION exciting me on to a publication of these letters.

I am sorry that I cannot trace it yet up to the *high source* from whence I suppose it originated. But in order to prove the fallacy of such a paltry rumour, I deemed it proper, yesterday, to go to GUILDHALL, and make the following

AFFIDAVIT,
Before Mr. ALDERMAN SWAIN.

I, —, the author of the *Letters* inserted in the MORNING STAR, under the signature of *An Injured Man,* solemnly swear, that I have written them of my *own accord,* in order to *expose* Mr. ROSE, for not paying *all* my ELECTION BILLS.

I further swear, that I am not *impelled* to the writing of THESE LETTERS

by any *individual* or *individuals* of the OPPOSITION, as has been *falsely reported;* and that they know nothing of the business, through me, directly or indirectly, excepting what they may read in this paper. For though I have been always a *faithful* AGENT, I scorn to be the *mean* TOOL of any set of men whatever.
*Sworn at the Guildhall,*
*London,*
*May* 22, 1789. . . .
    *The Original is left with the clerk of* THE MORNING STAR OFFICE, *for inspection.*

The remainder of the letter consisted of the text of "A FLASH SONG," which the "INJURED MAN" had "received . . . from [*Rose's*] *hands,* at Mr. PITT's," and a promise that "[in his] next, [he would] bring forward some more of those *elegant* productions."

Since to swear to a false affidavit was to consign one's soul to the Devil,[41] there were very few false affidavits in the eighteenth century. But a consideration of this concomitant pact would not have given Charles Stuart eight days' pause. What did give him pause was obviously that "malicious report," which had to be "[sifted] to the bottom" and its *"source"* ascertained before he could go down to Guildhall and commit his act of perjury. It is easy enough to surmise the nature of this "report," for all the trouble had started with the "*absurd* report which was begun to be propagated by the retainers of AD-MINISTRATION . . . of the PRINCE having *separated* from THE PARTY." As matters stood, everything depended upon the Prince of Wales. If he said that he was not connected with the spurious *Star,* the Government would immediately prosecute the newspaper for publishing libels on the King; if he said nothing and meanwhile indicated a continuing fondness for the Whigs, the newspaper was safe. But, in fact, there was the beginning of a rift between Carlton House and the Whigs, and the Whigs could not therefore know whether the "malicious reports" they were hearing were invented by the Government or whether they actually did originate with the Prince. The task of "[sifting them] to the bottom" and ascertaining their *"source"* would, however, have been Sheridan's, not Charles Stuart's, and it is notable that Sheridan had been absent from the newspaper since at least 16 May. He had probably spent almost the whole of the intervening period at Carlton House.

Sheridan seems to have come away with the feeling that everything was settled, for on 23 May the spurious *Star* resumed its attacks on the Government with every evidence of relief. "In the *Injured Man's* Bill to Mr. ROSE, there is a sum due, it appears, for *one thousand* OUT-RAGES, committed by the *Blue* and *Buff,* and their *crew,*" it observed. "—Query, therefore,—Who committed those outrages? Was it not Mr. ROSE's *crew?*—This ought to be explained." This query was followed by a letter, supposedly written by Topham, directing Este to continue his abuse of the Duke of Clarence until the Duke returned to Germany. There was also a great deal of editorial commentary:

> We are extremely sorry to hear, that a GREAT PERSONAGE continues in a very lethargic state.
> The distemper in his legs is by no means removed, and he is still very weak, and averse to business.
> Administration are so afraid of the influence of the PRINCE of WALES, and of the firm attachment of his BROTHERS to the *cause* of his Royal Highness, which is indeed the cause of the House of BRUNSWICK and the CONSTITUTION, that they are now endeavouring, at WINDSOR, to obtain the SOVEREIGN's command, for the spirited DUKE of YORK's return to Germany.
> They are likewise endeavouring to *re-imbark* the ROYAL SAILOR [the Duke of Clarence], with all expedition, as they cannot, by all their machinations, make CLARENCE follow the footsteps of his UNCLE [the Duke of Gloucester].
> If they can divide, by absence, the PRINCE from his BROTHERS, they think that it will much weaken his power.
> In this, however, they are much mistaken, as the influence of the PRINCE of WALES is every day increasing in all parts of the country.
> His MAJESTY ought certainly to be advised to keep his *Birth-day* at ST. JAMES's, as usual. If this does not take place, it will afford much scope to the tongue of *truth* as well as *calumny.*

Again, something seems to have gone wrong, for this was the last political commentary until 29 May. Moreover, the reprinting of the fifth letter from "AN INJURED MAN," promised (23 May) because of *"urgent demands"* for 25 May, was *"by an accident postponed"* until 26 May, a *"Petition of Lord* HOOD's *voters for* SUBSISTENCE," promised on 25 May for *"to-morrow,"* was omitted altogether, and the seventh letter from "AN INJURED MAN," promised on 27 May for *"to-morrow,"* was withheld until 29 May. By 29 May the spurious *Star* was also having further trouble with its distributors, for on that day it addressed another notice:

### TO THE PUBLIC

*Many of our* READERS *having complained that they do not receive* THIS PAPER *till a late hour, we beg them to* CHANGE *the* NEWSMEN *who neglect them. The* MORNING STAR *being published as early as any other Morning Paper, unless detained by the* PARLIAMENTARY DEBATES.

*By accident, or ill design,* THIS PAPER *has not been properly circulated about the* ROYAL EXCHANGE *these two days past. The blame lies not at* THIS OFFICE, *but shall be remedied.*

*Our* ADVERTISING FRIENDS *are requested to observe, that no other Office is appointed for receiving their favours than that at No.* 6, NEWCASTLE-STREET, STRAND. *This notice is given, as many* ADVERTISEMENTS, *intended for* THIS PAPER, *have, by mistake, been carried to an obscure Evening Print* [the original *Star*].

On 29 May the spurious *Star* nevertheless published the seventh letter from "AN INJURED MAN," which, like most of the others, was addressed to "GEORGE ROSE, *Esq., One of the* TREASURY SECRETARIES." Most of the letter was a repetition of material already "advanced," and the £200, which Pitt had given to Rose, was now represented as a personal loan:

Having a total disregard for the dignity of your office, . . . you first voluntarily *send* for a person to become your AGENT in the Westminster election, and afterwards you honourably endeavour to *trick* him out of the debt which he contracted on your account!

Is this, Mr. ROSE, just? How must your immaculate master, the MINISTER, feel on this disagreeable business, as you remember that you were then so *poor*, that you could not advance the first sum until, as I hinted before, Mr. PITT came in from riding. . . .

It has been reported to me, that you have abused Mr. FROST for not liquidating the remainder of your bill. I shall not touch upon that at present, as I mean to make it the subject of a FUTURE LETTER.

But what can THE PEOPLE think of *you*, Sir, a Treasury Secretary, and indeed the very *Mungo* of MINISTRY, to issue out the most *low abuse* against Lord HOOD's *opponent*, and all the OPPOSITION, by *misrepresentation, fallacy,* and *slander*, while you are now, with the most bare-faced *mock patriotism*, endeavouring to *invalidate* HIS ELECTION!

There was a typographical error in this letter, which was corrected on 30 May, when the conductors took the opportunity to mention that the "many enquiries at the Office concerning the authenticity of what is advanced by [AN INJURED MAN], convince us what strong effects the production has had."

On 5 June the spurious *Star* concluded an account of the Queen's reception in celebration of her husband's birthday (4 June) with the statement: "BY THE ABSENCE OF HIS MAJESTY THERE WAS A GENERAL AND MELANCHOLY GLOOM OVER ALL THE PROCEEDINGS OF THE DAY!" This was the only subsequent reference to the King's health; and, since the paper was frightened into silence on that subject, it was *ipso facto* frightened into silence on the subject of the "new REGENCY BILL." But meanwhile Charles Lennox, a nephew of the Duke of Richmond and a colonel in the Duke of York's Coldstream Foot-guards, had provided another ambush by challenging the Duke of York to a duel because of some remarks the Duke had made about him. The duel was fought on 26 May, the Colonel grazing the Duke's temple, the Duke holding his fire, and on 29 May the spurious *Star* broke a five-day political silence to speak of it. The implication of its remarks was that Colonel Lennox has been suborned by Pitt and the Duke of Richmond and that the two were now trying to incite similar acts of violence against the Prince of Wales:

> It is now clear that there are TWO PARTIES in the kingdom: *one* composed of the FRIENDS of the KING and the ROYAL FAMILY, at the head of which the LORD CHANCELLOR [Lord Thurlow] has now stood boldly forward; the other party is that of Mr. PITT, and the Duke of RICHMOND, countenanced by a certain PERSONAGE [the Duke of Gloucester], whom we do not wish to name.
>
> Some infamous insinuations have been lately made in the *Ministerial Prints,* respecting the PRINCE of WALES, tending to stir up *personal attacks* on his Highness, whose goodness of heart, as well as high rank, renders it impossible for him to do any thing that can hurt the feelings of the meanest individual.
>
> It is to be noticed, that any attack upon the life of the PRINCE of WALES, if such an attack can be proved, is HIGH TREASON.

By 30 May the spurious *Star* could "assure the public" upon "uncontroverted authority" that "his MAJESTY has notified to the DUKE of RICHMOND his royal censure of the conduct of his nephew." However, it added, "It is rather a matter of astonishment, that a very high PERSONAGE [the Queen], who possesses so much sensibility as to *melt into tears* on every interesting occasion that calls for such exertions, should receive, without any emotion, the accounts of the danger of her beloved son." The attack on the Queen was not explained, and the remainder of the paper was devoted to praise of the Duke of York for his magnificent "courage" and "generosity."

In the days which followed, the spurious *Star* struck at Pitt on various accounts, but always in defense of the royal brothers, whom Pitt was supposedly persecuting. On 1 June it denounced his intimacy with Colonel Lennox:

> Mr. PITT's *unbecoming* conduct, in walking at *Ranelagh, arm in arm,* with the man, who a few hours before *aimed* at the LIFE of the PRESUMPTIVE HEIR to the THRONE, has shocked the feelings of some of his warmest partizans.
>
> [No] one dare justify the *indecency* of the MINISTER, not to give it a harsher term, in *walking* and *supping* in public, with the very person who *shot* that day at the SECOND SON of his ROYAL MASTER!
>
> Every one of the BLOOD-ROYAL of EUROPE, will *detest* such an unnatural act of the PREMIER.

The denunciation was continued for almost a column. On 2 June it returned to Pitt's bribing of the Duke of Gloucester:

> Respecting the DUKE of GLOUCESTER, what we foretold in the most *delicate* manner, *six* weeks ago, now begins to be apparent to every one of HIGH RANK, who pretends to be conversant with POLITICAL INTRIGUE.
>
> The MINISTER, after vainly endeavouring to take YORK HOUSE, or CUMBERLAND HOUSE, by *sop,* found a very ready way to become possessed of GLOUCESTER LODGE.
>
> The price was an *annuity* of FOUR THOUSAND POUNDS, payable out of the IRISH TREASURY, and a COMMANDERSHIP in *reversion.*
>
> His Highness having THREE THOUSAND *per annum* out of that country, the people there begin to grumble much at this *ministerial extortion.*

On 3 June the spurious *Star* concluded some additional remarks on Pitt's intimacy with Colonel Lennox with the declaration that a "SERIES of INSULTS has been for some time past *studiously* aimed at the ROYAL FAMILY, with a rancour and malignity that have not been paralleled, and tending to deprive them of that deference and respect to which their rank and amiable qualities so highly entitle them"; and it called on the public at large to unite "in asserting their rights, and aiding these GALLANT BROTHERS in OPPOSING the ENEMIES of their COUNTRY." On 5 June the paper told its readers why the Duke of Clarence had not taken his seat in the House of Lords. The truth was, it said, that the Duke had asked to be introduced by his two brothers, but Pitt had ruled that he would be introduced by the Dukes of

Richmond and Chandos. The Duke had then suggested his two uncles, but in this instance Pitt had refused to accept even the Duke of Gloucester, for "every branch of the House of BRUNSWICK is alike systematically obnoxious to the *Advisors of his Majesty*." The Duke had then "begged leave to decline the ceremony altogether." But the spurious *Star* was "happy to learn that a sort of compromise has at length taken place, and that the DUKE of MONTAGU is substituted for the DUKE of RICHMOND." By this time the readers would have supposed that the fate of the House of Brunswick was balanced perilously on the next elections.

It was now beginning to look as if the end of the present session of Parliament was finally in sight, and, in anticipation of the impending elections, John Bell had already (1 June) begun his own newspaper. The spurious *Star* was meanwhile mustering whatever courage remained for its own final assault on William Pitt. On 4 June it accordingly published the eighth letter from "AN INJURED MAN." The letter was addressed to *"the Right Hon.* WILLIAM PITT," and, although it avoided specific charges, it was far more vituperative than any of its predecessors:

Your *confidential* and *efficient* SECRETARY, Mr. ROSE, is charged in these letters, with the meanest acts that ever disgraced any one, in his official situation.

A *Secretary to the Treasury,* and a *Member of the House of Commons,* stands now convicted of not only *interfering* in the late WESTMINSTER ELECTION, by *writing* and *publishing* the most *rancorous, false,* and *low abuse* against the *leaders* of OPPOSITION, but endeavours to *defraud* the very *Agent* he employed, out of the *expence*s attending such publication!

By choosing such a man, Sir, let us examine a little into your own actions. In the madness of the moment the credulous people of England stiled you, the *immaculate* MINISTER.

But as *immaculate* sometimes signifies *improper* [not according to the *Oxford English Dictionary*], as well as *pure,* the epithet is by no means inapplicable. The latter undoubtedly alludes to your *chastity,* while the former must be solely confined to your *policy.*

Indeed, upon an impartial retrospect of your political life, we find every thing but *patriotism* and *consistency.*

The letter proceeded to examine Pitt's political life, showing that his motive had been personal ambition and his method expedience; and it concluded with the statement that, when one surveyed a "political conduct, wherein nothing can be traced, but patriotic professions, and contradictory actions, whose policy is cunning, and whose wisdom is to temporize and prevaricate," he realized that "no one was so fit to second [such] operations as Mr. ROSE." The spurious *Star* responded (5 June) to this letter with an endorsement of Fox: "CHARLES FOX is a true ENGLISHMAN, and as hearty a fellow as ever lived. He has no *Airs of* IMPORTANCE—no silent and contemptuous *Self-sufficiency;* but the open manliness of his character adds a charm to the superiority of his talents, and renders him irresistible. HE IS THE MAN this Country should look up to with confidence and gratitude."

On 5 June the spurious *Star* promised for *"to-morrow"* "LETTER IX. *of* AN INJURED MAN, *containing Mr.* ROSE's Election Ode, *superior to* [Thomas] WARTON [the Poet Laureate]," and also "Mr. VENTURE's *Letter against Mr.* PITT." But, although both letters appeared on schedule, neither of them had any force. The first one was little more than a transcription of the "Ode" ("Choice Spirits at the Shakespeare"), which Charles had received from Rose on the occasion of their first interview; and it concluded with the announcement: "Now, [Mr. Rose,] I shall, for the present, take my leave, with the promise, that I shall occasionally continue to *divert* you, by your *own publications,* and those of *your friends,* in order to *jog* your MEMORY, and put you in mind of your SCURRILOUS TALENTS against the *ensuing* GENERAL ELECTION." "LETTER I." from "THOMAS VENTURE, *No.* 27, *Buckingham-street,"* was even more disappointing, for it was a some-what mild indictment of certain gentlemen in the War Department, and its only criticism of Pitt was that he had failed to answer the author's letter of "Wednesday, 27 [May]." But the indignation which was lacking in Venture's account was supplied by the spurious *Star* in the form of a headnote:

*The following* LETTER *of* REMONSTRANCE *against the conduct of Mr.* PITT, *contains so much good sense and truth in every particular, as to demand the serious attention of every individual, who trusts to the honour and justice of Administration. The* GENTLEMEN *in the* ARMY *are essentially interested in the fate of the* AUTHOR, *who has frequently preferred his claims to* GOVERN-MENT, *with a patience, modesty and forbearance unparalleled in the annals of the art military. If those at the head of the* WAR DEPARTMENT *feel no shame in the recital of Mr.* VENTURE's *injuries, and [do not] grant him im-mediately that redress to which his rights and grievances entitle him, the*

GENTLEMEN *in the* ARMY *have but slender and trifling assurances in the preservation of their rights, when a long series of hard service may render them subject to all the disagreeable concomitants of infirmity and old age.*

The last efforts of the spurious *Star* were devoted mainly to praising George Colman and Mrs. Goodall, abusing Charles Este and Major Topham, and drawing "heart-felt pictures" of "THE THREE ROYAL BROTHERS," who were depicted (15 June) as being bound to each other by the "strongest fraternal affection" and yet separated from each other by individuality of talents, the Prince of Wales being by nature "a ruler," the Duke of York by nature "a military leader," and the Duke of Clarence by nature "a naval conductor." But the paper also had a great deal to say about William Pitt. On 10 June, for example, it observed that the "number of *appellations* given to Mr. PITT must surely cause just surprize to foreigners. Previous to his being called *Pope* Pitt, *Emperor* Pitt, *Prince* Pitt, or Premier, he was styled the *immaculate* boy, the *miraculous* Minister, the *pattern of virtue,* the *picture of chastity,* and the *Minister of the Crown.*—It is a wonder that he has not yet been called, the *Grand Turk;* but there is one title which he can never attain, and that is, the *Minister of the People.*"

Pitt's budget, which was finally submitted to Parliament on 10 June, included to everyone's surprise an increase in the newspaper tax from 1½d. to 2d., and it also asked for a loan to make up a deficit in the Secret Service funds. The spurious *Star* responded (12 June) with the promise of a tenth letter from "AN INJURED MAN" for *"tomorrow,"* this one to be addressed to George Rose and to deal with *"the* MINISTER's *encroachment . . . on the* LIBERTY *of the* PRESS," and with the declaration that the "only real SECRET SERVICE-MONEY of last year, was [spent] on account of the WESTMINSTER ELECTION, as Mr. ROSE well knows. This should be investigated." On 13 June it added the observation that the "expences attending the WESTMINSTER ELECTION, and the petition now pending before the HOUSE of COMMONS, must be enormous. Lord HOOD's party say, his Lordship's cause is supported by *subscription,* but carefully conceal the names of the *Subscribers.* There are those, however, who assert that these expences make a part of '*the extraordinary demands* on the public money,' which have thrown the Minister into so '*unexpected a situation,*' that he is obliged to '*require a loan.*' "

On the same day (13 June) "AN INJURED MAN" spoke out on the subject of the proposed increase in the newspaper tax:

Sir,

It is well known to many, besides yourself, that the present Administration have been hitherto supported in their places, not by the rectitude of their measures, but by the *newspaper puffs* of their numerous retainers. . . .

Rightly calculating that you have by no means now the command of the MORNING PRINTS, in the last year's proportion of *seven* to *three,* and craftily foreseeing that the impolicy of your measures may soon withdraw others from supporting you, there is no step so effectual to secure you from obloquy, as *gagging* . . . the free and bold press of England. . . .

But if, Sir, in your resentment for the late conduct of THIS PRESS, so justly exerted against you, instead of endeavouring to cramp all the newspaper presses in Britain, for the boldness of THE MORNING STAR, you should have confined yourself to it alone [*sic,* sentence].

Or, if you meant to have only checked the *licentiousness* of the press, why not put a *two-penny* stamp upon every *posting-bill, hand-bill,* and *ballad,* during *election-time.*

Had you taken this step last year, you know we are both certain that by your *own publications,* in the late WESTMINSTER ELECTIONS you yourself would have *paid* a REVENUE of *some thousands* into Government, instead of having *expended one.*

To these opinions the spurious *Star* added its own opinion that the real purpose of the tax was "to diminish the number of NEWSPAPERS, and thereby withhold . . . information from the people," and on 15 June it expanded this comment into an article, entitled "PITT's LIBERTY OF THE PRESS." Pitt, it said, had no need for additional income, but he did have a need for fewer newspapers, and "Mr. ROSE"

knows the value of every newspaper too well, not to be chagrined at losing some, and the prospect of losing more, from the late violence of their proceedings.

If, therefore, Mr. ROSE calculates that they could extinguish every paper, but *their own,* by next year, they would not grudge another tontine million, to pay all future newspaper stamp-duty deficiency.

Mr. PITT has a plan in view, which he means next year, to bring forward, that all *authors, printers,* and *booksellers,* shall take out a *license* . . . as they are a great nuisance to *himself* and his *creatures,* by exposing the infamy of their conduct.

This was the penultimate number of the spurious *Star,* the ultimate number appearing on 16 June. The paper expired suddenly, for on Monday, 15 June, it promised its *"Correspondents"*: "NATIONAL IM-PROVEMENTS *positively to-morrow.*/ HAMLET *to the* QUEEN, *on*

*Wednesday./ Another* LETTER *from Mr.* VENTURE *to Mr.* PITT, *to-morrow, or Thursday./ More acknowledgements to-morrow."* It was only fitting that it should conclude its existence with what amounted to a declaration of war on its political fellow traveler, the *Gazetteer,* which it accused (15 June) of pilfering all its material and having "nothing in its favour to support it, but the *charitable donations* of Mr. ALDERMAN SKINNER, and the *offals* of two or three more *Auctioneers."* Someone on the staff of the spurious *Star* evidently had a new grudge against someone on the staff of the *Gazetteer.*

On 5 August, 1789, Peter Stuart wrote to Burns, and it is evident from the reply,[42] dated late August or early September, that Burns was under the impression that, although Peter had resigned, the spurious *Star* was still in existence:

That you have done well in quitting your laborious concern . . . I do not doubt; . . . [for] your health is a matter of the last importance, but whether the remaining proprietors of the paper have also done well [in permitting you to quit?], is what I much doubt. . . . I can hardly conceive it possible to continue a daily paper in the same degree of excellence: but if there was a man who had abilities equal to that task, that man's assistance the proprietors have lost. . . .

Adieu, my dear Sir! So soon as your present views and schemes are concentred in an aim, I shall be glad to hear from you. . . .

But there is no record of the spurious *Star* after 16 June, and it would seem unlikely in every respect that it was continued even until the end of the month. Before the first of July, the proprietary would have been lacking Colman, who was compelled by illness to quit newspapers altogether, turning over all his activities, even the management of the Haymarket, to his son.[43] It would also have been in desperate financial straits. All newspapers suffered a slump in sales during the summers, and this particular summer they faced an increase in the newspaper tax as well, the increase to become effective in August. Since the spurious *Star* was already heavily in debt, Charles could not himself have supported it beyond the adjournment of Parliament, and the Whigs would not have supported it. For by 15 June they knew that the elections had been postponed until 1790, and the paper was therefore useless to them until Parliament reconvened. It was somewhat useless anyway, inasmuch as "AN INJURED MAN" had long since said everything he was willing to say and for that matter everything the Whigs were at present willing for him to say.

Sheridan's brilliant strategy of hiding the spurious *Star* behind a "new REGENCY BILL" had failed to allow for the possibility of a rift between Fox and the Prince of Wales. Fortunately the rift was "not so deep as a well," or the spurious *Star* would have been prosecuted, but it was enough to drain the lifeblood from the newspaper. Yet in one respect the strategy failed by succeeding too well, for, by destroying the *World,* upon which the Government had relied to see it through the elections, by exposing some of the machinations of George Rose, and by representing Pitt as an implacable enemy of the House of Brunswick, the spurious *Star* had been singly responsible for the post-ponement of those elections. It had probably also been responsible for the increase in the newspaper tax, for newspapers like the spurious *Star* would henceforth cost the Whigs much more than "SEVERAL THOUSAND POUNDS," and the Whigs had no national Treasury behind them. All in all, one cannot think of another newspaper which achieved so much in so short a period as this one.

# CHAPTER VII

# The Daily Press (1789–1792):
# Pitt and the Pendulum

## ROSE'S MANAGEMENT OF THE DAILY PRESS: 1788–JUNE, 1789

DURING the elections of 1788, the Treasury had controlled seven morning daily newspapers: the *Daily Advertiser*, the *Morning Chronicle*, the *Morning Post*, the *Public Advertiser*, the *Public Ledger*, *The Times*, and the *World*. Three had been controlled by the Opposition: the *Gazetteer*, the *General Advertiser*, and the *Morning Herald*. By the beginning of 1789, the Treasury had lost one of its seven papers, the *Morning Post*, which was so disreputable that the loss could almost be counted a gain, and it was in the process of losing another, the *Morning Chronicle*. But in mid-February it added to the list of its adherents the *Star, and Evening Advertiser*, and on 30 March it also acquired the *Diary, or Woodfall's Register*, a new newspaper, begun by William Woodfall in the Government's interest. By the end of March, 1789, therefore, the Treasury controlled seven newspapers, the same number it had controlled during the elections of 1788. But by this time the Opposition also controlled seven, and, whereas the Opposition press had previously been torn to pieces by intrigues, it was now solidly united against Pitt and behind Fox.

In addition to the *Gazetteer*, the *General Advertiser*, and the *Morning Herald*, the Opposition now controlled the *Morning Post*, the *Morning Chronicle*, the spurious *Star*, and the *Argus*. The *Morning Chronicle* was conducted by James Perry, who was also the nominal conductor of the *Gazetteer*, the *Morning Herald* by the proprietor, the Rev. Henry Bate Dudley, the *General Advertiser* by the proprietor, John Almon, the spurious *Star* by Charles and Peter Stuart and their brother-in-law, James Mackintosh, the *Morning Post* by John Taylor, under the supervision of Sheridan, and the *Argus* by Sampson Perry. The *Argus* is supposed to have been anomalous. This paper, which on 11 April, 1789, was "Printed and published by W. Justins, No. 35,

317

Shoemaker-row, Blackfriars, near Ludgate Hill" and "Published also at the ARGUS office, No. 80, St. James's Street," was begun by Sampson Perry on 7 March, 1789, at a cost of "four thousand pounds." [1] Perry, who was always one of the proprietors and, by at least 1792, the sole proprietor, is said to have devoted the paper from the outset to "the most revolutionary doctrines" [2] and even to have instituted it as a service to Talleyrand.[3] But, if one judges from the issue of 11 April, 1789, no other issues being available until 1791, the *Argus* was only another blackmailing sheet, which took its political stand with the Whigs. Although all of these newspapers were probably subsidized by the Whigs, as all the Ministeral newspapers were, in fact, subsidized by the Treasury, the amounts of the subsidies are known in only a few instances. It is known that the *General Advertiser* received £200 annually through 1789, with the promise of another £100 later, the money being supplied by Lord Robert Spencer; [4] and, according to Charles Edmonds,[5] whose own authority was Sir Robert Adair, James Perry received £300 annually for the *Morning Chronicle* from 1789 on, the donors in this instance being "a few of the influential Whigs." By at least 24 March the Whigs, or, more specifically perhaps, the Duke of Norfolk, had "deposited" "SEVERAL THOUSAND POUNDS" "at a Banker's" for the spurious *Star.*

With respect to the management of newspapers, every advantage was on the side of the Government, for, whereas the Whigs had to finance their newspapers themselves, the Government had at its disposal the Secret Service Funds, for which, since the "Funds" were "Secret," it was obliged to make no accounting. In addition, the Government had at least four means of intimidating or punishing recalcitrants, none of which was available to the Opposition. It could, for example, starve a newspaper into submission by blocking its channels of information, as it was inclined to do if one of its own newspapers got out of line. It could increase the newspaper tax, thereby creating a crisis in the Opposition press, which was always precariously financed anyway. It could devise "trouble at the Stamp Office" and thereby acquire a newspaper at almost no cost. Or it could prosecute ex officio.

The advantage of an ex officio prosecution was that the Government controlled the prosecution at every step. As soon as one of the Houses moved that a prosecution should be ordered, the Attorney General issued a formal indictment, but what happened from this point on depended entirely upon the pleasure of the Government, which in turn depended upon the conduct of the indictee. If he was willing to come to terms, the Attorney General forgot to bring him to trial; or, if he was willing to come to terms after the trial, the Attorney General forgot to bring him in for sentencing. If, of course, he ever defected on his defection, he incurred the wrath of the Court and could therefore count on the pillory as well as prison. In the case of a real trouble-maker, the Government employed another device. After the man was convicted and before he was sentenced, the Government sent around one of the Crown lawyers, who, purportedly speaking on his own authority and for the man's own good, urgently advised him to abscond. If he did abscond, he was outlawed, and the Government was rid of him for good; or, at least, if he ever did return, the Government could imprison him for two offenses rather than one. There was, of course, nothing to prevent the Opposition from asking for the prosecution of a Ministerial newspaper, but, since the Government controlled the vote in both Houses, it could block the prosecution at its source, and it could also block it at every subsequent step. In short, the Government completely controlled ex officio prosecutions, so that everything which happened as a result of them happened with the blessing of the Government.

Until 10 March, 1789, the political issue was the Regency Bill; after 10 March it was the general elections, supposedly scheduled for May or June. Of the seven daily Ministerial newspapers, the most influential were now *The Times* and the *World,* both of which had been newly purchased. But the Government had always had trouble with *The Times.* In 1787 it had appointed its proprietor and conductor, John Walter, Printer to the Customs; and, at the beginning of 1789, Thomas Steele, one of the Secretaries of the Treasury, had added a £300 annual subsidy.[6] Walter had been encouraged by these favors to begin a second newspaper, the triweekly *Evening Mail,* the first number evidently appearing in February, 1789, since the issue of 28–30 September of that year is numbered 92; and for it he had been granted an additional £200. But the trouble had continued; and by February, Steele had sent over a new writer, John Heriot, whom he had "engaged [at the beginning of 1789] to answer, by pamphlets and in the newspapers, some of the arguments [against the Government],"[7] to assist Walter with the paper's political department. Since Heriot's contribution was some vehement abuse of the Prince of Wales and the Dukes of York and Clarence, the snag in the relationship between Walter and the Treasury seems to have involved Carlton House. There was no snag in the relationship between Edward Topham and the Treasury, for, in return for his £600 annuity, Topham had placed the powerful *World* at the complete disposal of the second Secretary of the Treasury, George Rose. Since the Government could rely upon this newspaper to see it through the elections almost singlehandedly, it intended to concentrate its campaign in the *World;* and the issues which it had selected were the marriage of the Prince of Wales and the trial of Warren Hastings, the first to be handled by a supposed defense of Philip Withers against Mrs. Fitzherbert, the second by general abuse of Burke, all of which could be charged to Warren Hastings's agent and the Government's friend, Major John Scott.

Of the seven Opposition newspapers, the most influential were the *Morning Herald,* the *Gazetteer,* and the *General Advertiser,* but two of these newspapers were in trouble. The *General Advertiser* was damaged beyond repair. By this time the proprietor and conductor of that newspaper, John Almon, had been convicted of publishing (18 Nov., 1788) a libel on the King and had reacted with such panic that the Government was postponing judgment in the expectation that it could persuade him to flee. The *Morning Herald* was also having difficulties, although of a less serious nature. On 20 May, 1786, James Barr had been replaced as printer by William Perryman, and on 8 February, 1788, Perryman had been indicted for a libel on the Commons in its inquisitorial capacity, the occasion being a paragraph condemning Sir Elijah Impey, printed by the *Herald* on 6 February. Since the paragraph had been copied by the *Gazetteer* (7 Febr.) , Mary Say, the printer of that newspaper, had also been indicted. Neither case had been "brought to an issue," probably because the Government was not certain it could get a conviction, Impey having been exonerated and that matter therefore closed. There was also the fact that, in its dealings with both newspapers, the Government was compelled to settle for the printers, the conductors' names not appearing in the colophons.

In the case of the *Morning Herald,* this presented a real problem, for the Government supposed that the Whigs would concentrate their own campaign in this newspaper and, although it knew very well that the paper was owned and conducted by the Rev. Henry Bate Dudley, it could not produce the proof. Since it was unable to strike at him through the newspaper, it seems to have tried another tactic. For on 8 December, 1788, one Edward Dodwell had brought Dudley into the Court of King's Bench to answer to a charge of "criminal conversation with his wife," for which offense he asked £3,000 damages (*Morning Herald*, 9 Dec., 1788). But, if the Government had, in fact, instigated this action, it was again frustrated, Dudley being acquitted for lack of evidence; and, very shortly thereafter, Perryman was again indicted, this time for publishing a libel on the King, the Prince of Wales, and the Cabinet. Although the precise date of Perryman's trial is not known,[8] it may have been his experience which moved the spurious *Star* to "mention [12 Mar., 1789,] by way of caution, that the Judges have declared it as their opinion to be TREASON to assert, either *orally* or *in print* that the KING's mind is *deranged,* or that he is not in a capacity to act as SOVEREIGN of the BRITISH EMPIRE." That what the Government actually wanted from Perryman was only a statement implicating Dudley is evident from the events which succeeded.

The Government's supposition that the Opposition would concentrate its campaign in the *Herald* proved to be mistaken, for the Opposition selected for the purpose the obscure evening newspaper the spurious *Star*, the conductor of which, Charles Stuart, had been an agent of the Treasury during the elections of 1788 and, having not been paid, was willing to sell his confessions to the Whigs. In preparation for the role which it was to play, the spurious *Star* augmented its staff with a number of scurrilous writers, among them James Boaden, Theophilus Swift, John Williams ("Anthony Pasquin"), Andrew MacDonald, the Rev. William Jackson, who seems to have acted as foreign correspondent, and perhaps Daniel Stuart; and on 27 April, 1789, the elections then being supposed only a few weeks away, suddenly appeared as a morning newspaper and, on the pretext that it was supporting a "new REGENCY BILL." in behalf of the Prince of Wales, released its exposés of George Rose and at the same time commenced a series of coarse and vicious attacks on the personnel of the *World*, including Major John Scott, all of whom, it insisted, were hostile to the Prince and his friends. Sheridan, who had planned and effected the strategy, had assumed that it would have the approval and tacit blessing of the Prince of Wales, which would have insured the newspaper against prosecutions. But by this time the Whigs could no longer count on the Prince's connivance, and the persistent rumors of impending prosecutions frightened the newspaper into long periods of silence, and on 16 June, 1789, silenced it altogether. Meanwhile, however, the spurious *Star* had completely destroyed the prestige of the *World* and had so damaged the reputations of Pitt and George Rose that the Government felt obliged to postpone the elections one year in order to recover.

It was characteristic of the Opposition that, having gone to so much trouble to assemble precisely the right staff for its purposes, it made no attempt to hold it together and, in fact, gave no further thought to the elections until the following year. Fortunately most of the staff remained or tried to remain loyal. Charles Stuart, who was left with *"Star* debts of near twelve hundred pounds,"[9] subsequently wrote for various Opposition newspapers, notably the *Morning Post;* and Daniel Stuart seems also to have returned to the *Post,* if, of course, he had ever left it, taking with him perhaps Andrew MacDonald. Along with them, too, went Dr. John Wolcot, who had previously supplied not only the verse, but some "whimsical articles" for that newspaper. There had been a few changes in the *Post* during the preceding months, but no change of grave consequence, for the "literary department" was still leased to Louis Weltje, who also owned two shares of the property as agent of the Prince of Wales, and, since the Prince had no interest in newspapers and Weltje was only a good-natured "German cook," whose principal accomplishments were his "broken English and familiarity,"[10] the actual management was still in the hands of Sheridan. The *Post's* real problem was Richard Tattersall, who constantly forgot that his authority was limited to "money concerns" and interfered in "literary" matters, to the exasperation of the editor, John Taylor, and to the utter destruction of everyone's peace of mind. Since Tattersall particularly disliked Dr. Wolcot, whom he refused to put on a regular salary, and Taylor, who in his opinion "had not devil enough for the conduct of a public journal," there were constant quarrels.[11] The printer of the newspaper was now William Williams, and since 1 May, 1789, the proprietors had published the paper themselves. Williams, who was later (1796) an active proprietor of the *Gazetteer*[12] and author of several pamphlets,[13] was probably also a regular contributor, although his only signed contribution was "The Hervarer Saga, a Gothic Ode," published on 24 December, 1791.

James Mackintosh seems to have moved from the spurious *Star* to the *Morning Chronicle,* thence to the *Oracle,* and thence to the *Morning Post.* Although all biographers are vague about his activities during this period, it is generally agreed [14] that, in the autumn of 1789, he and his wife, née Catherine Stuart, toured the Low Countries, that they returned "towards the end of the year," and that he subsequently undertook the "superintendence" of the "foreign news" for the *Oracle*, the "engagement" with Bell having been made "by a mutual friend." The "mutual friend" was, of course, his brother-in-law Peter Stuart, who was by this time working for Bell himself. This particular "engagement" seems to have lasted until the summer of 1790, although the dates are not specified. The inevitable question of how Mackintosh financed the tour is answered by certain contributions to the *Morning Chronicle*, which, according to one biographer,[15] included some "letters with the signature of 'the ghost of Vandeput,' and a character of Mirabeau." Since only a few numbers of the *Chronicle* are available for this period, the contributions have not been found, but they were probably mailed from the Continent and Mackintosh was probably making his tour as correspondent for that newspaper.

The remainder of the staff transferred its services to the *Oracle*, and some members of the staff seem to have begun the transfer while the spurious *Star* was still in existence. Theophilus Swift, for example, wrote for both newspapers, for the verse epistles, signed "BOW-WOW," "BROTHER BILLY," "WINIFRED," and so forth, of which he was apparently the author, appeared in both the *Oracle* and the spurious *Star* from 1 to 16 June, 1789, as so did the abuse of Colonel Lennox. Swift evidently reissued this abuse in the form of a pamphlet, and it was evidently because of the pamphlet rather than the newspaper paragraphs that, at the end of June, 1789, the Colonel challenged Swift. In this duel the Colonel fired directly into Swift's body, Swift's pistol going off without effect.[16] Since there were several pamphlets on the subject,[17] all unsigned, one does not know which one was Swift's, and it is, of course, possible that he wrote them all. The Rev. William Jackson seems also to have worked for both newspapers, continuing as foreign correspondent for the *Oracle* until 1794, when he returned to England, to be replaced by John Bell himself. John Williams, who first shifted his scurrility to the *Oracle* and later to the *Morning Post*, at least atoned for his participation in the attacks on John Edwin by publishing (1791) the sympathetic biography, *The Eccentricities of John Edwin, Comedian: Arranged and Digested by Anthony Pasquin, Esq.*

Peter Stuart may not have been released from prison until after the spurious *Star* was defunct and therefore may have had no connection with that newspaper from the end of May, 1789, on. By 5 August [18] he was out of prison, but he was also unemployed. Since on 27 August, 1795, the *Oracle* stated that he and James Boaden had then been associated with its literary department "for nearly SIX YEARS," they evidently did not join the staff until the end of 1789 or the beginning of 1790. There is no clue to Boaden's interim activities, but, during the last part of 1789, Peter may have worked for the Opposition. For on 26 December, 1790, he submitted a "claim of £50 for the Excise business." "On the whole of this business," he said,[19] "I feel myself so equivocally treated (although one and all acknowledge I did all) that it is not much for the credit or even policy of the party, that I should be so ill used." "Be so kind as to ask Mr. Bell's opinion of my exertions," he added in a postscript. "I know he is hurt at the shabby treatment I have experienced. Whatever the funds may be, it appears to me, that what ought to be appropriated, for actual services, are bestowed upon favourites as idle sinecures. This, perhaps, might do when in place [i.e., if the Whigs were in office], at least in a degree—but in no degree will it do out of place, where you . . . have to *level* the very ALPS of *prejudice* and *power!*" Although this letter is endorsed only "Stewart—the writer," there can be no doubt of the identity of the author, for Bell would have known nothing of the "exertions" of Charles or Daniel. There is, however, some doubt as to the period of the employment. The "Excise business" began on 16 June, 1789, when Pitt submitted a plan for transferring the duties on tobacco from the Customs to the Excise, his argument being that tobacco was the principal article of contraband, whereas it should be a lucrative source of revenue. The plan occasioned great alarm among the manufacturers of tobacco, for, in cases of Excise violations, the offender had no right to a trial by jury; and it occasioned equal alarm among the Opposition. Since the issue was not actually resolved for years, Peter may have been involved in the "business" at any time from June, 1789, on.

## PREPARATIONS FOR THE ELECTIONS OF 1790
## AND THE PROBLEM OF EDMUND BURKE

WHILE the Opposition was thus dawdling, the Government was hard at work. Its final act before Parliament adjourned in June, 1789, was to increase the newspaper tax, the increase to become effective in August, and by 16 June it was rid of the spurious *Star,* the demise of which reduced the number of Opposition newspapers to six. Meanwhile it had persuaded John Almon of the *General Advertiser* to flee and had outlawed him; and, at approximately the same time, it seems to have sent William Perryman to prison for publishing the libel on the King, the Prince of Wales, and the Cabinet, for on 15 June, 1789, Perryman was replaced as printer of the *Morning Herald* by J. Luxford. It was also readying its own newspapers.

In May or June, 1789, the Opposition had moved that *The* Ministerial *Times* be prosecuted for three libels on the Royal Family: the first, published on 21 February, having censured the conduct of the Duke of York, the second, published on 26 February, having stated that the Prince of Wales had incurred the "just censure" of his father (*Public Advertiser,* 5 Febr., 1790), and the third, published on 5 May, having accused the Duke of Clarence of returning to England without the permission of the Commissioners of the Admiralty. But, since *The Times* was much easier to handle with John Walter in prison, the Government not only made no protest, but saw to it that the Attorney General acted. On 11 July, 1789, Walter was accordingly tried in the Court of King's Bench before Lord Kenyon and a special jury for having published the libel on the Duke of York. Erskine had been retained as counsel for the Crown, Walter being represented by Bearcroft and Dallas. He was convicted and, after one deferment (21 Nov., 1789), was sentenced on 23 November, 1789, to twelve months in Newgate Prison and one hour in the pillory, fined £50, and ordered to find securities for good behavior for seven years in the amount of £500. Rather than stand the expenses of two additional trials, Walter allowed those judgments to go by default.

Since the paragraphs in question were the work of the Treasury writer, John Heriot, Walter was understandably indignant. He expressed his indignation to various members of the Administration, none of whom responded, and on 1 February, 1790, he wrote to James Bland Burges, Under-Secretary of State for Foreign Affairs: [20]

> Little did I ever expect ever to be an inhabitant of this vile receptacle, or that any political sin would doom me to so severe a sentence. . . . Even Almon, convicted before my trial for a most atrocious paragraph against the whole family on the throne, escapes without being brought to judgment.
>
> I am ordered up again on Wednesday to receive sentence on the infor-

mations on the Prince of Wales and the Duke of Clarence, that the measure of my sufferings may be full. Had I not listened to Mr. Bearcroft's advice but made a defence on trial with the Duke of York [i.e., stated that John Heriot was author of the libels], and not permitted judgment to go by default on the others, I should doubtless have been this moment at liberty. . . .

Walter went on to complain of Newgate, which was, in fact, regarded as "the most detestable gaol in London," as opposed to King's Bench, which was considered "the least abhorrent," [21] but these complaints also achieved nothing. For on 3 February, 1790, John Walter, "late an Insurance Broker" (*Public Advertiser*, 5 Febr., 1790), was brought back to the Court of King's Bench for further sentencing; and, since the Government was getting along very nicely without him, he was committed to Newgate for another year and fined another £100 for the libel on the Prince of Wales. For the libel on the Duke of Clarence, he was fined £100. There was no prison sentence in the last case because the libel was later retracted and Walter proved that it had been inserted without his knowledge. On 21 February, 1790, Thomas Erskine mentioned to Burges [22] that Walter had appealed to the Prince of Wales through his daughter, Mrs. Knox, and that the Prince was favorable to the appeal, but was unwilling to appear "officious." This must have been welcome news to the Government, for, since the Prince's affairs were to play a major role in the elections, it could not afford to have Walter freed until the elections were over.

One might suppose that the Treasury's principal problem would have been the *World*, which was now a shambles, owing to the on-slaughts of the spurious *Star*. But Rose seems to have had no doubt that the paper could and would recover, and hence his only concern was to keep alive the issues of the Prince of Wales's marriage and Warren Hastings' trial until mid-1790. This required some ingenuity, for the *World* had dealt with the Prince's marriage by purporting to defend Philip Withers against the supposed persecution of Mrs. Fitz-herbert, and, once Withers was sentenced, as he was on 21 November, 1789, this matter seemed to be concluded. The *World*'s effort to main-tain interest in the case notwithstanding received another setback in December, when Withers stated in effect that the correspondence between himself and Horne Tooke which had been appearing in the *World* was a forgery. The trial of Warren Hastings required even more ingenuity. All of the Ministerial newspapers had been ridiculing the trial, and, although Edmund Burke was especially sensitive to such ridicule, the trial was, in fact, so unpopular that even the Opposition newspapers had declined to speak up in its defense. But the *World*'s incessant taunts that the trial had alienated Burke from his party finally compelled the Whigs to demand a prosecution of the newspaper or alienate Burke altogether. On 16 June, 1789, therefore, the Whigs had moved that the printer, Robert Bostock, be indicted ex officio for having published a libel on the Commons as an investigative body, and, the Government having offered no protest, the motion passed. Bostock was not, of course, tried, and the abuse was not discontinued.

But on 8 December, 1789, the Attorney General brought William Perryman, former printer of the *Morning Herald,* back to court to be tried for having published the libel on Sir Elijah Impey almost two years earlier. The reason was that Perryman's twelve-month sentence for having libeled the King, the Prince of Wales, and the Ministers would expire at approximately the time the next elections began, and the Government wanted no further trouble with him. Perryman was not only convicted, but he was evidently given a particularly severe sentence, for on 16 March, 1792, he applied to the Whigs [23] collectively and individually for "further assistance either annually or by a specific compensation" in consideration of "hardships" he had "experienced for upwards of three years" as a result of his service to the Party. By this time he finally had the Government's promise that he could set himself up as a printer without being further molested, provided his "conduct should not prove hostile to administration." Mary Say, the printer of the *Gazetteer,* may have been tried and sentenced at the same time as Perryman.

One can say almost positively that the real issue between Burke and the Whigs was not the French Revolution, but the trial of Warren Hastings, for, so strongly did Burke feel about that trial, that he was going to be kindly disposed toward anyone who purported to feel as he did. Moreover, Burke was not a politician, and he was playing the political game with some masters. The first crack in his relationship with the Whigs, which was already present in early 1789, could have been mended if only the Whigs had insisted upon the prosecution of Bostock; or it could have been widened into a complete break if the Government had prosecuted Bostock itself. The difficulty was that, although both parties wanted Burke, neither of them wanted him enough to pay the price. But the Government at least pretended that it did. Since Burke had had very little experience with the promises of Rose and Pitt and a great deal of experience with the promises of Sheridan and Fox, he was already half a convert to the right by the end of 1789. On 9 December, 1789, the Government even went so far as to try John Stockdale for an old (14 Febr., 1788) libel on the Commons respecting the trial of Hastings, and, although Stockdale was acquitted, Burke had the satisfaction of knowing that the Government had acted. At the beginning of 1790, George Rose gave Burke an additional push to the right by seeing to it that abuse of himself and the trial of Hastings was discontinued by every one of his newspapers except the *World,* the *World* being represented as somehow unmanageable because of Major Scott's association with it; and he followed the push with a hard shove, which settled the matter of Burke's political allegiance for the remainder of his life.

On 21 January, 1790, a Lieutenant John Frith hurled a stone at the King's carriage as the King was on his way to Parliament. Although the Opposition newspapers tried to dismiss the incident as the act of a "maniac," as, in fact, it was,[24] the Treasury newspapers made it an occasion for general alarm, denouncing Frith as a would-be regicide in the pay of the French Government and representing the country as teeming with French agents. The result was that the Government finally had an answer to those demands for reforms which had plagued Pitt ever since he became First Minister; and the answer was so effective that, from this point on, the Government was able, not only to ward off reforms, but to tighten the existing laws with new acts of oppression, by the simple expedient of inventing another alarm. The result, too, was that the Government, which understood Burke much better than Burke understood himself or it, acquired a convert of such zeal that whatever was lacking in its scheme it could count on him to supply. What was principally lacking was the evidence that there was an alarm, and, since it was lacking, Pitt would not himself have been so foolish as to present the matter to Parliament. But Burke believed what he read in the Treasury newspapers, and the Treasury newspapers were telling him that the country was on the eve of a revolution and were defending the Test and Corporation Acts as if they were the last bulwarks against an English reign of terror. The result was that Burke transmitted the alarm to Parliament in lieu of Pitt, and, because he was still regarded as a member of the Opposition and because no one could doubt his sincerity, terror became a substitute for fact.

On 9 February, 1790, Burke quarreled with Fox and broke with Sheridan over the issue of the French Revolution, but, although the *World* was the principal alarmist newspaper and was therefore bound to side with Burke, it, in fact, sided with Sheridan, and by 23 February it was ridiculing Burke's "Pamphlet *'on the affairs of France,'* " then in the making. Since he could get no satisfaction from either the Opposition or the Government, Burke appealed to his friend, General Burgoyne, who on 21 May moved that the Attorney General prosecute Major Scott and the *World* for a libel, contained in a letter which had appeared in that newspaper over Scott's signature. Both parties were thrown into a panic. Debate on the motion was postponed for six days, and, by the time it was resumed (27 May, 1790), Bostock had been tried and convicted. Scott was thereupon reprimanded and the motion for a new prosecution of the *World* withdrawn. At the conclusion of the debate, Fox assured Burke publicly that he had himself always defended the trial of Hastings, the implication being that some other members of the Opposition Party had not. Since Rose made his explanation in private, one does not know what he said, but on 9 June, 1790, Bostock's counsel moved for a new trial, and the Attorney General did not protest; but the new trial never occurred, and so Bostock was never sentenced.

Rose may, however, have made a settlement with Burke, for it appears from a letter of Topham's [25] that no information was sent to the *World* from any Government office after 10 June, 1790, and that the newspaper was thereafter dependent upon Major Scott for whatever it knew, having not even been notified of the prorogation of Parliament. At this time the *World* was in an anomalous position. Since anything it said about Burke could be charged to Topham's friend, Major Scott, and since it was in every respect completely subservient to the Treasury, it was the most useful of all the Ministerial newspapers, and it was therefore secure against ex officio prosecutions. But it was also in a state of rapid decline, and it was therefore bound to become the scapegoat for Rose's various intrigues. In this instance Rose may have persuaded Burke that the best way of dealing with this supposedly unmanageable newspaper was to starve it out of existence by blocking all channels of information. How he explained the blockage to Topham one does not know, for Topham said later [26] only that he had been "certainly ill-used."

At the beginning of 1790, the Treasury contracted for an eighth newspaper, the *Oracle, or Bell's New World,* printed by Buchanan

Millan and owned and conducted by John Bell. Bell had begun the newspaper on 1 June, 1789, and, in the expectation that the elections would be held that year, had immediately offered the political control to the highest bidder. But, despite the fact that it had inherited most of its staff from the spurious *Star*, the Opposition indicated no interest, and even the Treasury offered only £200 a year. By January, 1790, it was being edited by Peter Stuart, James Boaden, and James Mackintosh, who was " 'superintending the foreign news,' with great industry," [27] and, in addition to other refugees from the spurious *Star*, it had added to its staff the "able writer," Dr. Thomas Campbell.[28] John Heriot had also been moved to the *Oracle*, where he remained until at least late 1790 and perhaps until mid-1791. Heriot's recollection [29] that he was at this time receiving "a handsome annual salary" from the Treasury is not supported by the records, which list only two payments made to him during 1790, each amounting to £50,[30] but he would, of course, have received another salary from Bell. By the time the elections began, the Treasury had also acquired the *Morning Herald*, the circulation of which was estimated at "between 4 and 5,000 a day." [31]

According to the *Gazetteer* (18 Oct., 1790), Pitt acquired the *Herald* through "*treachery* of the worst kind." What happened, of course, is that someone on the staff of the *Herald* had agreed to testify to Dudley's connection with the newspaper, and Dudley had chosen to deliver the paper to the Treasury rather than spend another year in prison. The traitor may have been the printer, J. Luxford. On 10 May, 1790, the *Herald* had questioned the accuracy of the *Gazette*'s statements regarding Nootka Sound, and Luxford had promptly been indicted for publishing a libel on the Government, to which he had pleaded guilty. At this point there is a six-month gap in the *Herald* files, and by 11 November, 1790, the paper was being printed by Nicholas Byrne, and it had long since shifted its allegiance to the Government. Although Dudley did not accept the first Treasury check until 11 June,[32] the *Herald* was evidently performing Treasury services on 1 June, for on 3 June the *Oracle* reported that the "*fighting* EVANGELIST of a Morning Print is said to be so affected in his *left side*, that all *opposition* is fruitless to prevent him from TURNING to the RIGHT—to the imminent peril of his *existence*." The Treasury paid £600 a year for the *Herald*, the same amount it was paying for the *World;* and, since Dudley refused to continue as conductor, the conduct was assigned to Thomas Y. Hurlstone.[33] But, although someone had obviously implicated Dudley, it was not necessarily Luxford; or, more probably, it was Luxford, but Luxford later changed his mind. For, having forgotten the matter for over six months, the Government suddenly on 27 November, 1790, called him into the Court of King's Bench to be judged for publication of the libel, and, although this summons was evidently only a warning, judgment being deferred, it called him again on 25 January, 1791, when he was sentenced to spend one hour in the pillory and twelve months in King's Bench Prison, plus whatever additional time was required for him to furnish £100 security himself and to find two friends capable of furnishing £50 each. Since Dudley was capable of some rather awful vengeance, as Robert Haswell had learned many years earlier, Luxford may have decided to settle after all for the vengeance of the Government.

## SOME ELECTION AND
## POST-ELECTION MANIPULATIONS

BY THE time the elections of 1790 began, therefore, the Treasury controlled nine daily newspapers: the *Daily Advertiser,* the *Diary,* the *Morning Herald,* the *Oracle,* the *Public Advertiser,* the *Public Ledger,* the *Star, The Times,* and the *World.* The Opposition controlled five: the *Argus,* the *Gazetteer,* the *General Advertiser,* the *Morning Chronicle,* and the *Morning Post.* According to Trusler,[34] there was a fifteenth daily newspaper in existence at this time, the *Patriot,* published near St. Dunstan's Church, Fleet Street; but of this one nothing is known. The pivotal newspaper for the Government was the *World,* which was now conducted by Topham with the assistance of Robert Merry, Este having quit the paper in February in order to escape an action for libel; and the issues were Mrs. Fitzherbert's persecution of Philip Withers (and hence by implication her marriage to the Prince of Wales) and the trial of Warren Hastings, to which was added the seditious state of the country. The pivotal newspaper for the Opposition was the *Morning Post,* but the *Post* is lacking for almost the whole of the year.

Horne Tooke later estimated[35] that, during the two preceding elections, the Government and the Opposition had spent £100,000 apiece on Westminster alone, Lord Hood's petition following the election of 1788 having itself cost the Government over £14,000. Since neither side could afford to continue this kind of expenditure, he said, it was decided in advance to compromise the next Westminster election, for which reason the parties had combined to pass the *"frivolous and vexatious act,"* making it "impossible for a non-factional candidate, representing merely the people, to run, for, if he fails, he must pay the whole costs for the three." The act actually enabled the Commons to tax any petition which was deemed "frivolous and vexatious," the tax to be paid by the petitioner to the injured party. But, although the Westminster election of 1790 was less violent than the election of 1788, there was no indication of economy on anyone's part. Although the records of Treasury payments to newspapers are highly incomplete, one does know that during 1790 Thomas Harris collected £400 for the *Diary,* £400 for the *Morning Herald,* and £100 for the *Public Ledger;* that Topham collected £600 for the *World;* that Walter collected £500 for *The Times* and the *Evening Mail;* and that on 16 October John Bell, who described himself on the receipt as "Conductor, Proprietor, & Printer of The Oracle," collected £200 "for the Oracle & various Services in the Papers." [36] One knows also that James Perry was still collecting £300 a year for the *Morning Chronicle* from "a few of the influential Whigs." In addition, the Treasury employed a host of agents as before, and on 9 March, 1791, it paid Lord Hood, the Ministerial candidate, £1,500 "for the former Westminster Election in part of an Arrear." [37] Meanwhile Charles Stuart realized enough from the Opposition during this election to "[settle] upwards of a thousand [pounds]" of the debts he had incurred in connection with the spurious *Star.*[38]

Parliament was prorogued on 10 June, 1790, and the elections began on 16 June. The Ministerial candidate for Westminster was Lord Hood, the Opposition candidate Fox, and there was a third candidate, Horne Tooke. None of the newspapers understood Tooke. In 1787 he was thought to be in the service of Mrs. Fitzherbert; during the election of 1788, he had helped the Ministerial cause with some insulting "Portraits" of Fox and his friends, published in the *Morning Post* and the *World;* in 1789 he had at least not protested the *World's* publication of some forged correspondence between himself and Withers; and no one knew what he had in mind at the moment. But, since he insisted in his campaign speeches that he was running "as a candidate of the people in order to save the people from Fox," the newspapers assumed that his candidacy was some kind of Treasury trick, and he was therefore supported by the Ministerial press and assailed by the Opposition press. In addition, he was given every assistance by James Mackintosh, who, according to "one of his friends," [39] "was parading the streets with Horne Tooke's colours in his hat" when he should have been "attending to his business [with the *Oracle*]." But by this time Mackintosh was evidently quite prosperous, for, although he had been unable to train for the Scotch bar because he had no money and his father's fortune "was thought too small for [him] to venture on so uncertain a pursuit," [40] less than two years' work for the London newspapers had enabled him to train for the English bar; and he had accordingly been admitted to Lincoln's Inn on 28 April, 1790. Tooke fared better than he or anyone else anticipated. Having expected only "one vote," he got, according to his own calculation,[41] "almost 1700 votes." According to the final tabulation in the newspapers, he got 1,679 votes, Lord Hood 3,217 votes, and Fox 3,516 votes, the election being compromised.

Tooke's involvement was never satisfactorily explained. On 9 July, 1790, the Ministerial *Public Advertiser* declared angrily: "The Opposition Writers who are *determined* to make Ministry account for every thing in their *veracious* statement of Mr. Horne Tooke's expenditure at the late Westminster Election, (which they state at *five thousand pounds*) insinuate very strongly that he *was supported by Ministry,* as the *Ex*-Minister of Brentford, they say, could not be . . . capable of spending so much money." Insinuations of this kind, the *Public Advertiser* felt, should be regarded as libels and dealt with accordingly. But, if the Government had financed his campaign, it soon had reason to regret its action, for, as soon as Parliament reconvened (25 Nov., 1790), Tooke submitted a petition to the Commons, demanding an investigation of the Westminster election on the ground that it had been unfair. Although most of his charges had to do with the fact that, on "the one day in which he polled more than his adversaries, his audience was attacked by thugs, one man being killed," [42] some of them had to do with the injustices of a system which prevented a majority of the citizens from voting. The petition was presented on 9 December, 1790, and it seems to have taken everyone aback. But, in consideration of the fact that Tooke had diverted Fox's vote, not Lord Hood's, the Opposition moved that the petition be regarded as "frivolous and vexatious." Pitt was bewildered. After some hesitation he agreed that the petition might be so regarded, but it was his opinion that the judgment should not be hasty. The petition was thereupon referred to a committee, which on 7 February, 1791, voted to treat it with "silent contempt."

On 12 February, 1791, Walpole mentioned to one of his correspondents: [43] "Horne Tooke before Christmas presented a saucy libel to the House of Commons as a petition on his election. The House contemptuously voted it only frivolous and vexatious, and disappointed him of a ray of martyrdom; but his fees &c., will cost him three or four hundred pounds, which never go into a mob's calculation of the ingredients of martyrdom." The newspapers put this somewhat differently. By at least 19 January, 1791 (see, e.g., Gazetteer), they were contending that he had been motivated by a desire for publicity. Tooke himself declared [44] that his sole motive throughout had been to test "the frivolous and vexatious act." But, although he complained of the restriction of suffrage only because he happened to be a victim of it, the complaint classified him as a reformer; and Tooke may therefore have been right in charging [45] that Pitt had directed the committee "in advance" to find the petition "frivolous and vexatious" and had indicated that he would not be unhappy if the committee found it "libellous and scandalous" as well.

An inevitable effect of the first alarm had been to activate the reformers; hence, as soon as the elections were over, the Government prepared for its real battle, compared with which the elections had been only a minor skirmish. By July, 1790, it had lost two of its nine newspapers, the Daily Advertiser, which was almost non-political, and the Star, which was very mildly political, reverting to a neutral or moderately liberal position. Payments to the other seven newspapers during the years 1791 and 1792 remained approximately what they had been before, the Morning Herald and the World receiving £600 a year, the Diary £400, The Times £300, the Oracle £250 (an increase of £50), and the Public Ledger £100.[46] There is no record for the Public Advertiser, but, since it was one of the most vigorous supporters of the Ministry, it was, of course, being subsidized as well. Not all of these newspapers were worth what the Government was paying for them, the most notable examples being the Morning Herald and the World. As the Gazetteer observed on 12 August, 1790, the Herald began to deteriorate as soon as the Treasury acquired it:

A DIALOGUE between Mr. ROSE and Parson DUDLEY,
on the late Revolution in the Politics of the

## HERALD.

"WHERE's all your wit and spirit flown,
Which once we thought to make our own,
When we the golden touch applied?"
ROSE to the venal PARSON cried;
"No sooner is the bargain bought,
Than all at once 'tis good for nought."
"Lord!" quoth the PARSON, "do not vapour,
We have your gold—you have our Paper;
But wit—that's quite a different thing,
For who could e'er contrive to bring
The pliant genius of his wit
Such measures, Sir, as your's to fit?"

The *Gazetteer* had not yet learned that the *Herald* was being conducted by Hurlstone, not Dudley, and that it had been acquired by "*treachery* of the worst kind." Under Hurlstone's management the circulation of the *Herald* dropped from "between 4 and 5,000" in mid-1790 to "not . . . more than 800 a day" by the end of 1793.[47] The *World* was much worse off than the *Herald*, for, not only was it having serious troubles with its staff, but by September, 1790, the last shreds of its prestige were being destroyed by Este's assaults on Topham in the *Gazetteer*.

On 16 October, 1790, the Government reduced the number of Opposition newspapers to four by silencing forever the "independent voice" of the *General Advertiser* (*Gazetteer*, 18 Oct., 1790). Although it was now ready for the *Argus*, it delayed its attack on that newspaper until Burke's *Reflections on the Revolution in France* had come through the press. Publication of Burke's *Reflections* was announced by all Treasury newspapers on 1 November, and on 2 November they proclaimed it the greatest political work of all time and a complete vindication of their contention that the country was in grave danger. Most enthusiastic were the *Public Advertiser* and the *World*, which, for the next ten days, were given over to lengthy excerpts from the work, punctuated with exclamations of rapture and followed by ecstatic commentaries and hints of new plots against Church and State. As the *World* noticed on 17 November, the Opposition press was silent. "It is curious to observe with what *narrow*, and *determined* prejudices in favour of Party—some Opposition Prints act," it mused, "not only in *omitting* to give any Extracts from Mr. BURKE's late

Pamphlet on the French Revolution, but in abusing the author by the sidewinds of detraction and ridicule. . . . But the reason is here— Messrs. Fox and SHERIDAN, *have openly espoused the French Revolution.* . . ." In the midst of all this hysteria, which had the effect of a second alarm, several papers mentioned that on 5 November "an information [was] filed ex officio by the Attorney-General, against Mr. Sampson Perry, as proprietor of the newspaper called the Argus, for publishing on the 5th of November . . . a scandalous libel, charging Administration, and particularly Mr. Pitt, with falshood, corruption, and fraud, in the account published in the London Gazette, dated November 4, respecting the arrival of Mr. Dressings, the Messenger, with news of the ratification of the late Convention with Spain." By this time the *Argus* had moved to No. 5, Catherine Street, where it was first printed by H. Roaf and later printed by J. Powell, Roaf having perhaps quit to print the *Morning Herald,* which he at least was printing by 2 March, 1792. But no printer was mentioned in the indictment.

The *Gazetteer* and the *Morning Chronicle* were not molested, but the Whigs were evidently afraid that one or both newspapers might defect. Since late March, 1789, Fox's friend James Perry had been responsible for both of them, functioning as active conductor of the *Chronicle* and nominal conductor of the *Gazetteer;* and, although the Whigs were certain of Perry, they were not certain of the proprietors. In September, 1790, there was apparently some danger that a thirty-second share of the *Gazetteer,* then for sale, might fall into the wrong hands, for at that time Perry proposed himself as a purchaser.[48] But, before this purchase could be effected, there was apparently greater danger with respect to the *Chronicle,* for, by the end of the year, Perry and James Gray, "sometime an under teacher at the Charter House," [49] were negotiating for the purchase of that newspaper instead. Although the *Chronicle* then had a sale "so small, that it only just paid its expenses, and that with the utmost economy," [50] Perry could count on the £300 annuity from "a few of the influential Whigs," and it was Redding's understanding [51] that, in addition, the "Duke of Norfolk, in private friendship, . . . gave [Perry] the house in the Strand." The "house in the Strand" was the first home of the *Chronicle,* which until late February, 1791, moved about with its printer. By 14 December, 1790, the paper had moved from No. 79, Fleet Street, to No. 201, Strand, where it was being printed and published by R. Westley; on

7 or 8 February, 1791, it moved to No. 1, Great Shire Lane, Temple Bar, where it was printed by J. Lambert; and on 26 February, 1791, it announced that its new and permanent office was located at No. 474, Strand, but that it was printed by J. Lambert in Great Shire Lane and published by R. Westley at No. 201, Strand. Having resigned his connection with the *Gazetteer,* Perry had by December, 1790, concentrated his efforts on building up the *Chronicle,* sending to Scotland for "two friends . . . , of the name of [William and Robert] Spankie" to "aid him in his new undertaking." [52] The result was that by 1793 the *Chronicle* was selling several thousand copies a day and reputedly "[clearing] £6,000 a year." [53] The *Gazetteer,* which, from January, 1791, to January, 1793, was conducted by William Radcliffe, was in a state of decline.

Before Sampson Perry could be brought to trial, the affairs of the *Argus* had become intertwined with the affairs of *The Times.* While the Ministerial newspapers were shouting the praises of Edmund Burke and William Pitt, now represented as the heroic defender of the Constitution, John Walter, the conductor of *The Times,* was still in Newgate Prison, where he was sentenced to remain until 23 September, 1791, for publishing libels on the Prince of Wales and the royal Dukes. He had also been sentenced to pay fines totaling £250 and, sometime before 23 September, 1790, to stand in the pillory for one hour. But Walter did not stand in the pillory, as the *Morning Post* had discovered by 5 February, 1791. "The Libeller of the King's Sons has escaped the ignominious part of the punishment awarded to his offence," it informed its readers. "Mr. PITT has it now in his power to shew, how much more grave and enormous is the offence of a supposed Libel on his Majesty's Ministers.—The Public will of course look with some attention to the difference of the proceedings in the case of *Walter* and *Luxford.*" Although Pitt did not intercede in behalf of Luxford, the Prince of Wales had, in fact, interceded in behalf of Walter, as the Whigs would have known by late September, 1790; and, as they would also have known, he would undoubtedly extend the scope of his intercession to ask for Walter's release. Since the Whigs had gone to considerable trouble to put Walter in Newgate, they were evidently willing to go to a little more trouble to keep him there, for in early October, 1790, the *Argus* prepared the ground for an action to be brought against *The Times* by John King.

What the *Argus* had to say was that John Walter and his son,

William Walter (always referred to by the newspapers as "Old Log"
and "Young Log" because of the Logographic Press, upon which *The
Times* was printed), along with their editor, "The Irish Monster"
(James Finey), had made a practice of composing letters reflecting
on the morals of individuals, of pretending that the letters had been
sent to *The Times* with large sums of money for their insertion, and of
accordingly demanding large sums of money for their suppression.
The charge was many times repeated, and during November and
December the *Argus* even cited some examples of the practice, one
victim being identified as "a Gentleman in Leicester-fields," who was
willing to come forward if need be. Nothing was said of John King,
but on 9 December, 1790, the *Diary* reported that a "true Bill of Indictment was found by the Grand Inquest, on the last day of the
Term, against John Walter, the printer and publisher of the Times,
for a Libel on Mr. King, of Duke-street, Westminster." King was
maintaining that *The Times* had accused him of swindling Mr. Price,
a jeweler, out of large amounts of money and that, although Walter
had privately admitted that *The Times* was in error, he had refused
to publish a retraction unless he was "handsomely paid" for it. The
date of these events was not specified, but the libel was obviously published before Walter was sentenced and hence before 23 September,
1789. John King, known to his contemporaries as "Jew King," was,
according to Taylor,[54] "the chief agent in his time for money-lend-
ers," a man of numerous virtues and abilities, and "an able writer on
political subjects." He was also a zealous adherent of Sheridan and at
least a subeditor of the *Argus*. Hence in late January, 1791, John and
William Walter commenced a retaliatory action against the *Argus*,
based upon paragraphs published by that newspaper on 8 October
and 30 December, 1790, and on 7 January, 1791.

Now that the elections were over and the Prince of Wales's marriage was no longer an issue, the Government had no objection to
John Walter's release, but it made no attempt to procure the release
until after the Walters had filed their action against the *Argus*.
Whether the Government had planned that action or not, it clearly
regarded it as a service, for on 1 or 2 February, 1791, James Bland
Burges, still Under-Secretary of State for Foreign Affairs, wrote to
Thomas Erskine, Attorney General to the Prince of Wales,[55] requesting, in effect, that Walter be released:

I have just received the enclosed letter from the son of Walter the printer at present confined in Newgate for a libel on His Royal Highness the Prince of Wales. . . . There can be no doubt that the insolence of the paragraph on which he was convicted was inexcusable, or that he deserved a very marked punishment for having presumed to insert in his paper anything reflecting on so exalted a character. Should it, however, be true that His Royal Highness no longer considers this person as deserving of correction, and that he does not object to his being released from confinement, there will not, I presume, be any difficulty in obtaining a dispensation for the remainder of a punishment from which, I am convinced, nothing ought to relieve him but the operation of His Royal Highness's clemency. This is a matter with which I have no official concern; nor should I have presumed to take any part in it had not the enclosed application come to my hands.

Erskine not only arranged for the release, but agreed to defend Walter against the action being brought by King, despite the fact that he had already been engaged by the Whigs to defend Sampson Perry against the action being brought by the Government. As one might have anticipated, the Government saw to it that both cases were tried in the same court on the same day.

On 23 February, 1791, therefore, John Walter was tried in the Court of King's Bench for the libel on John King, and on the same date Sampson Perry was tried in the same court for the libel on the "Administration, and particularly Mr. Pitt," both defendants being represented by Erskine. Walter and Perry were convicted. Two weeks later, specifically on 10 March, 1791, the *Star* noticed that "[yesterday] morning, Mr. WALTER was liberated from his confinement in Newgate, in consequence of . . . his MAJESTY's . . . pardon, at the instance of . . . the PRINCE of WALES, after an imprisonment of near sixteen months." Moreover, on 1 June, 1791, the Treasury awarded "M$^r$ Walter as a Gift" the sum of £250,[56] evidently to cover his fines, and sometime later, it appears,[57] another £700, probably for legal expenses and imprisonment; and the Government also succeeded in quashing the action brought by King. How this was achieved is not clear, but Walter was certainly never sentenced. The Government was obviously grateful, and so evidently was Walter, for *The Times* was thereafter regarded as Pitt's newspaper, just as the *World* was regarded as Rose's. Or, as the *Post* put it on 9 August, 1791: "Mr. PITT, unlike his predecessors, does not use the polished weapons of satire and ridicule, to parry . . . assaults. . . . His common weapon of defence is—a LOG!"

Sampson Perry, of course, had no such luck. On 15 June, 1791, he was tried for the libel on the Walters and was again convicted; and on 9 July he was brought back to the Court of King's Bench on three separate accounts. The first was the libel on the Walters. In this instance Erskine stated in behalf of the plaintiffs that the offense would be forgiven if Perry made a public apology. Perry refused on the ground that everything the *Argus* had said was true, and he was promptly sentenced to six months in King's Bench Prison. The second was a new action, being brought by Lady Fitzgibbon, wife of the Lord Chancellor of Ireland, who was himself a friend of Pitt. To her charges Perry pleaded guilty. The third was the libel on the Government. Perry seems to have dismissed Erskine as soon as he discovered that Erskine was representing the Walters, and he was now acting as his own counsel, for Lord Kenyon postponed judgment, advising Perry to "get some good legal assistance." On 12 July, 1791, Perry was sentenced to another six months in King's Bench Prison and fined £200 for the libel on Lady Fitzgibbon. Although he asked to be sentenced for the libel on the Government at the same time, Lord Kenyon refused: he could do nothing, he said, until the Attorney General moved for judgment, and no such motion had been made. Since Perry was incarcerated until 9 July, 1792, anyway, the Government was now in a position to bargain with respect to its own case, and it must have been given to understand that the *Argus* would mend its ways. For on 26 November, 1791, the *Morning Post* reported that on the previous day the Attorney General had moved for judgment in the case of Sampson Perry, convicted of publishing a libel on the Government, and that the judgment had consisted of only a fine of £100. The paper may actually have modified its position for a while, but the next available number, dated 29 February, 1792, indicates no modification whatever. Although it had been renamed the *Argus of the Constitution*, it was still outspokenly liberal and still being printed by J. Powell. Hence, one day after he was released from prison, specifically on 10 July, 1792, Perry was indicted for another libel.

## "CONSTITUTIONALISTS" VS. REFORMERS: THE ISSUE OF GEORGE ROSE

WITH the appearance of the *Reflections,* the battleground of the Constitutionalists, or denouncers of the French Revolution, versus the reformers, or condoners of the French Revolution, was extended to include pamphlets. On 14 January, 1791, the *Post* remarked that "eight pamphlets have now appeared in answer to Mr. BURKE"; and, it added on 9 February, "we speak from authority, when we say that the Pamphlet [*A Vindication of the Right Honourable Edmund Burke's Reflections on the Revolution in France, in Answer to All His Opponents*] comes from the ingenious pen of Mr. *James* Boswell!" Boswell's first name was italicized in mock respect, since the newspapers usually called him "Jemmie." [58] On 24 February the *Morning Chronicle* announced that Thomas Paine's *Rights of Man*, originally scheduled for "to-day," would not be available; and on 7 March it added the information that "Mr. PAYNE . . . has returned to town. His Answer to Mr. BURKE, which, on account of local knowledge, authentic information, and historical and scientific research, is much in request, will once more make its appearance about the latter end of this week." Although the *Rights of Man* was selling so fast that it could hardly be kept in print, it was of less interest to the leaders of the Opposition than another pamphlet, which was being "finished in a great hurry, . . . the first part having been . . . committed to the press before the last was written." This pamphlet was the *Vindiciae Gallicae: A Defense of the French Revolution and Its English Admirers, against the Accusations of the Right Hon. Edmund Burke,* by James Mackintosh. Mackintosh had followed his campaigning in behalf of Horne Tooke with a trip to the Highlands and had then retired to "a small house in the village of Little Ealing, in Middlesex" to prepare his own answer to the *Reflections,*[59] perhaps at the suggestion of Thomas Christie, whose *Letters on the Revolution in France* appeared at approximately the same time as the *Vindiciae*. Christie and Mackintosh were now inseparable.[60] The pamphlets were well timed, for on 6 May, 1791, Fox broke with Burke over the issue of the French Revolution, and the two defenses of that Revolution were available a few days earlier. Fox said nothing of Christie's work, but on 26 May he mentioned in a letter: [61] "There is a pamphlet by one Mackintosh, which I hear a great character of, though it is said to go too far in some respects, but I have not yet had time to read it." He had found time to read it by June, when Mackintosh was introduced to him at "his house in South Street." [62]

Political parties selected one or, at the most, two newspapers as spearheads for their operations, the other newspapers providing background support of various kinds and degrees. Since Rose and Sheridan handled the press for their respective parties, the selection of the spearhead was theirs, and Rose had long since chosen the *World*. With the collapse of the spurious *Star*, Sheridan had moved back to the *Morning Post*, which therefore saw the Opposition through the elections of 1790, and he had thereafter moved to the *Argus*. But the Government's assaults on that newspaper necessitated another move, and this time he had very little choice. In addition to the *Argus*, the Opposition now controlled only the *Gazetteer*, the *Morning Chronicle*, and the *Morning Post*, the evening *Star* being too tepid to be counted. But the *Gazetteer* represented the point of view of the Constitutional Society, which was becoming increasingly radical, and the *Morning Chronicle* represented the point of view of Fox, which was far too conservative for Sheridan's taste. Sheridan was left, therefore, with the *Morning Post*, which was the weakest and the only disreputable one of the three. The *Post* did, however, have certain advantages, the most notable being its connection with Carlton House, which was good insurance against an ex officio action and which at the same time gave him complete control over the newspaper, even though he had no legal right to any control whatever. For, now that the Government was establishing a camaraderie with the Prince of Wales, it would have been even less inclined to sue a newspaper which was leased to the Prince's maître d'hôtel, and the Prince's only concern throughout had been to divorce himself from the paper as completely as possible. His evident desire to forget the whole transaction had already alarmed John Benjafield. For, although Benjafield had collected his £350 annuity for 1789 and 1790, he had no assurance that he could collect it in the future, the "real security" which was to have been provided by mid-February, 1789, having not been provided. In December, 1790, Benjafield had accordingly threatened to file a suit in Chancery to compel "the performance of [Louis Weltje's] agreement"; and, in order to "prevent" this action, Tattersall "[had come] forward on the part of Weltje," and on 21 December, 1790, he and Benjafield had "executed an agreement, by which *Mr. Tattersal* [sic] engaged, from that period, to pay the annuity: and also, that on or before the 1ˢᵗ of January, 1793 [the date on which the lease expired], the same should be secured on his real estates, in the counties of *Cambridge* or *Lincoln*, or one of them." [63] Tattersall did pay the annuity until 1 January, 1795, but he did not provide the securities, probably because the Prince of Wales neglected to pay for them.

Since the *Morning Post* was to spearhead the reform movement, Sheridan's first concern was to engage a suitable staff. The paper was still being printed by William Williams and edited by John Taylor, with the occasional assistance of Dr. Wolcot, and, by the end of 1790, it had also acquired Robert Merry. Everyone was retained except Taylor. Taylor himself said [64] that he was dismissed by Tattersall, who wanted less politics and more "antidotes"; for, "not understanding the meaning of the word," said Taylor, "it is not wonderful he should have forgotten the sound." Although, as Taylor pointed out, Tattersall had no "authority" to dismiss him, his "authority" being limited to "the money concerns," he nevertheless "signified [his] readiness to relinquish the management" and at once went to work for the Treasury at a salary of £3 3s. a week. On 17 May, 1791, he collected £100 as "Advance" to Michaelmas for "[writing] in the Papers"; [65] and by March, 1793, he was being paid £160 a year in quarterly installments.[66] The truth was that no one had the "authority" to dismiss Taylor except Louis Weltje, who was far removed from the scene; but, with the backing of Sheridan, Tattersall was evidently willing to attempt it, although the reason he gave for the dismissal was hardly straightforward. Taylor's successors were "two young Irishmen"; and, Taylor went on,[67] "[knowing] the dashing spirit of the Irish character, I advised the printer, who received a weekly sum to be responsible for the contents of the paper, to be careful what he inserted. He assured me with thanks that he would be cautious; but the result was, that soon after he was confined to Newgate during twelve months for the insertion of a libel. . . ." One of the "two Irishmen" was D. E. MacDonnel, who on 21 April, 1791, was "struck such a blow" by a Captain Essex Bowen "as to divide a branch of the temporal Artery and to cover him in a few seconds with blood!" (*Morning Post, World,* 23 Apr., 1791; *Morning Chronicle,* 25 Apr., 1791). MacDonnel's offense had been to interest the *Post* in the Gunning scandal. No other editor is mentioned by the newspapers, but there is merit in Hindle's suggestion [68] that the other Irishman was Dennis O'Bryen, for O'Bryen was an intimate of Sheridan, in whose behalf he had lately tried to mediate the quarrel with Burke.[69] In addition to MacDonnel and O'Bryen, who was undoubtedly associated with the newspaper, whether he was an editor or not, the *Post* engaged James Mackintosh, who joined the staff in May. Although Mackintosh's contributions were chiefly prose, they included at least two poems: "Ode to Liberty," which was published by the *Post* on 3 October, 1791, and "Lines by J. M.," copied from the *Post* by the *Star* on 6 December, 1791. There were also many other poets, some of whom may have been poets of consequence. "A Sonnet to the Lark," signed "W. W." and published on 19 October, may conceivably, for example, have been submitted by Wordsworth, and the long poem, "Netley Abbey: An Ode," printed by the *Post* on 14 November and reprinted by the *Star* on 16 November, was the work of William Sotheby. Under Sheridan's management, the *Post* was slowly regaining some of its lost prestige.

On 12 May, 1791, the *Morning Chronicle* informed its readers that Edmund Burke had committed political suicide: "The great and firm body of the Whigs of England, true to their principles, have decided on the dispute between Mr. Fox and Mr. Burke," it said; "and the former is declared to have maintained the pure doctrines by which they are bound together, and upon which they have invariably acted. The consequence is, that Mr. Burke retires from Parliament." The *Chronicle* was greatly mistaken, for the Whigs were held together partly by expedience, partly by family connections, and partly by loyalty to Fox, and they had no "doctrines" "upon which they invariably acted," especially not in the matter of reform. Hence Burke's *Reflections* would not in any event have fallen upon deaf ears, but the work would not have had the strong and lasting effect it did had it not been for William Pitt, who, by seeing to it that the country seemed to be in peril, constantly supplied the evidence upon which Burke's arguments depended. There were no major alarms during 1791, but the Treasury newspapers referred darkly to certain seditious activities which they could not at this time specify, and Pitt, who seemed also to have some ominous information which could not be revealed, asked only that the Commons have "confidence" in him. So successful was this technique that by late June, 1791, the *Morning Post* was reporting that people were burying their treasures, and attestations of loyalty to King and Constitution were beginning to appear in Treasury newspapers.

Since there was no evidence and hence nothing which could be proved or disproved, the Opposition newspapers turned their attention to the reformers. A great deal of publicity was given to a new society, called Friends of the Liberty of the Press, organized by Mackintosh, Merry, and other friends of Sheridan on 3 June, 1791, and at least as much to the celebrations of 14 July, commemorating the second anniversary of the French Revolution. Although the celebrations were held in taverns throughout London and the provinces, the one which received most attention was that at the Crown and Anchor, for which Merry provided the "ode," Mackintosh functioned as master of ceremonies, and at which Paine was expected, although he did not appear. There were also some bewildered reports of the Birmingham riots against dissenters, which had begun on the same day, but not a great deal was said of them, for a day or two later the Opposition discovered or thought it had discovered the means of getting rid of George Rose.

A Mr. George Smith, proprietor of the Star and Garter Public House in Westminster, had filed suit against George Rose in the Court of King's Bench to recover £110 5s. for "work and labour, diligence and attention of the Plaintiff, from the 21*st of September,* 1789, to the 17*th of April,* following; which . . . makes up the space of *Thirty Weeks,* at *Ten shillings and Sixpence per day,* in discovering and collecting proofs of a multitude of bad votes that were polled for Lord John Townshend, at a late contested Election [the election of 1788] for the City of Westminster." Involved in the negotiations had been John Frost, "Solicitor and Agent to Lord Hood"; but, according to a witness, George Clubb, who identified himself as *"a Messenger of the Treasury,"* the final arrangements with Smith had been made by Rose himself in the presence of Thomas Steele, then the other Secretary of the Treasury, and William Pitt. The Whigs evidently learned of this action only a few days before it came to trial, for on 19 July, 1791, they suddenly settled a long-overdue account with Charles Stuart and returned him to the *Morning Post*. The trial occurred on 21 July.

On 22 November, 1790, Charles Stuart had addressed a letter to the financial secretary of the Whigs, William Adam,[70] to whom he had probably been referred by Sheridan:

My situation at present is very embarrassing indeed. My only dependance is on an engagement I have from the *Morning Post,* and the gentlemen concerned have told me that unless I come to town during the sitting of Parliament, they cannot continue me.

Now, sir, I cannot properly appear until I make a settlement. Out of *Star* debts of near twelve hundred pounds, I have settled upwards of a thousand of it, and could I have £50 or £60 I could make a complete settlement of the remainder.

Be so kind as to take my case into immediate consideration. Here I am sequestered for debts owing to my zeal in the cause of the party. . . .

If you condescend to write me, my address is "at the Ten-mile Stone, Hounslow, Middlesex."

You generously and humanely stepped forward last winter to gain me a temporary relief—and if you will again repeat it now, you will restore an active and faithful retainer of your party to the world, to be proving his zeal and gratitude on every political occasion, many of which will happen during the ensuing sessions.

The "£50 or £60," for which Charles was applying, were part of 143 guineas owed him for writing the weekly column, "Abridgment of Politics," for the *Morning Herald* for "nearly three years under the engagement of Mr. Sheridan." In November, 1790, however, the Whigs had had no need for the services of "AN INJURED MAN," for at that time their target was John Walter, not George Rose, and their paper was the *Argus,* not the *Morning Post;* and so Charles remained "sequestered" for another eight months. But the action being brought by George Smith reopened the whole matter of the Westminster election of 1788, and, whereas the exposés of Rose in the spurious *Star* had only purported to be sanctioned by Carlton House, anything which appeared in the *Morning Post* inevitably carried the stamp of the Prince of Wales. On 19 July, 1791, therefore, the Whigs settled Charles's account in full,[71] and Charles was back in London in time to attend the trial.

Burke's *Reflections* had appeared at a very propitious time; his *Appeal from the Old to the New Whigs* appeared at the worst possible time. The Treasury newspapers announced its publication on 6 August, 1791, and followed the announcement with long commentaries, the gist of which was that the "New Whigs" were traitors. But by this time public attention was focused upon George Rose, and the readers were not greatly interested in Burke. Rose was tried on 21 July, the jury awarding Smith the whole amount of his claim, and for the next month the *Morning Post* talked of little except the trial. On 23 July it summarized the proceedings and transcribed Smith's testimony, and on 1 August it transcribed all the testimony involving Pitt. It then settled down to its own commentaries, so that, while the Treasury papers were commenting on Burke's *Appeal,* the *Morning Post* was commenting on the conduct of George Rose and William Pitt and speculating as to what some of the testimony meant. Meanwhile the Whigs had had another bit of luck, for John Frost had filed suit against Lord Hood, from whom he was demanding £12,168 for services during the Westminster election of 1788 and the "scrutiny" which followed. In this case the Court of King's Bench had referred judgment to "three Gentlemen," who on 6 August, 1791, ordered Lord Hood to pay £9,238 10s. 11d.

Although the Government took no action against the *Morning Post*, it did move to block Charles Stuart's activities in another sphere. Now that he was back in London, Charles had been taking advantage of the Gunning scandal to attempt to blackmail one of the principals. With, one suspects, the connivance of the younger Colman, he had been writing a farce, entitled *She Would Be a Duchess*, and the farce was announced as a future production in the Haymarket advertisements of 8 and 9 August. But on 10 August the Lord Chamberlain (Lord Salisbury) interfered in behalf of General Gunning, "at [whose] instance," said the *Morning Post* (15 Aug., 1791), the farce was re-titled *The Irishman in Spain* and subjected to such drastic "curtailments" that, when it was finally produced (13 Aug.), "it appeared so destitute of plot; and all the characters, excepting the Irishman, were so much enfeebled, that [one] cannot pardon the Manager for allowing it to come forward in its imperfect state." The work, now reduced to one act, was published by Ridgway later in the year, along with an indignant preface, in which Charles swore that the farce, "in its original state, shall be published in the course of the Winter." But he was much too canny to publish it, and he wrote nothing further for the stage.

The *Morning Post* had never said anything about the Prince of Wales, but, while these events were in progress, the paper suddenly turned on Louis Weltje, whom it ridiculed on various accounts during the last half of August and throughout September. The ridicule began on 13 August, 1791, with the paragraph, "WELTJIE [*sic*] has written a German SONNET on the beauties of his flame, *Madame Schwellenbergen*, which has been set to music by HAYDN!" Subsequent paragraphs appeared at the rate of about three a week, ripening into derision as the weeks progressed. On 27 September the *Post* announced that "WELTJIE has not yet been knighted, though much interest has been made for him by Madame Schwellenbergen. His pretensions are, that he is descended in a right line from a German Prince, and has conferred a singular honour on the Royal Family, by giving his aid in the *Royal Kitchen!*" The last of the series, which appeared on 29 September, reported that "WELTJIE is become quite a *lobby-lounger—*

those who have seen the *corpulent wag* in the crowd at the King's Theatre, conceive him to be *perfumer* to the House!" The reason for this ridicule was not indicated by the *Post,* but it was certainly not diversionary. The best guess is that Rose was entreating Weltje to interfere in the conduct of the *Post* in his behalf, and the *Post* was demonstrating to Rose that Weltje was afraid to interfere even in his own behalf.

On 19 November, 1791, Frost brought Lord Hood back to court to complain that he had still not been paid, but this case was dismissed since Lord Hood assured the Court that he had given the money to his present solicitor, who would settle the account immediately. Meanwhile the *Post* continued to belabor Rose, and in late February, 1792, its efforts were underscored by a pamphlet entitled *The Trial of George Rose, Esq. Secretary to the Treasury, &c. for Employing Mr. Smith a Publican in Westminster, upon a Late Election, and Not Paying Him; on Which He Was, on Thursday the 21st of July, 1791, Cast [sic] in the Court of King's Bench, by a Special Jury, in the Sum of One Hundred and Ten Pounds Five Shillings!* The pamphlet was published by J. S. Jordan, No. 166, Fleet Street, the printer's name being withheld, and it was dedicated to Lord John Russell by "THE EDITOR," who in his preliminary remarks stressed the fact that "[the King's] *virtuous, immaculate, and heaven-born Minister,* was privy to [the disgraceful] transactions." Following the transcript of the testimony were some "Reflections addressed to George Rose, Esq.," which were compounded of several of the letters from "AN INJURED MAN."

The Opposition, which had evidently been waiting for this pamphlet with some impatience, acted at once. On 1 March, 1792, Thomas Thompson, one of the Whig leaders, gave notice that, having just seen a shocking publication, entitled *The Trial of George Rose, Esq.,* he intended to bring forward a motion on the subject "this day sennight." This notice was apparently followed by some threats on the Government's part, for on 9 March, Thompson postponed his motion to 13 March, despite Rose's insistence that he introduce it at once. On Tuesday, 13 March, the Treasury newspapers announced the publication "this day" of a pamphlet, entitled *A Refutation of Factious Calumnies on the Character of George Rose, Esq., Secretary to the Treasury;* but the Whigs had recovered their courage, and Thompson therefore rose to move "That this House will, upon Friday next, resolve itself into a committee of the whole House, to inquire into all Abuses committed, by persons in office, at the election of a member to serve in parliament for the city of Westminster in July 1788, as far as the same relate to penalties incurred under the excise laws, or lottery act." He pointed out, in support of his motion, that George Smith had, sometime previous to his meeting with Rose, been fined £50 for a violation of the excise laws and that, in consequence of his labors, "part of the fine was remitted to him." Lambton, who seconded the motion, cited another case, in which a Mr. John Hoskins, who had been unable to pay a £700 fine, incurred for violations of the Lottery Act, was released from prison under very strange circumstances when he sent word to Rose that he could deliver sixty votes to Lord Hood. The motion was rejected by a vote of 221 to 84, and a few days later Rose filed a private suit against the *Morning Post*. Charles Stuart escaped reprisal by immediately offering his services to the Home Department, which was now readying its army of spies and informers.

The *Morning Post* for 1792 is almost completely lacking, but it appears from the indictment that the paragraph which Rose cited as libelous was paraphrased from Thompson's speech, the *Post* having said that Rose was "making the revenue laws an engine for subverting the rights of free elections." It was the opinion of the Opposition newspapers that, in failing to handle this matter ex officio, the Government was admitting Rose's guilt, but the *World* felt otherwise. "If Mr. Rose *be* guilty," it said on 19 March, 1792, "he is the most imprudent man alive, for he means to have the business of the *Excise Fine* sifted to the very bottom in a Court of Justice, by a prosecution against the PROPRIETORS and EDITOR of a Morning Paper, for a Libel against him upon that very subject." The indictment actually named only Tattersall as conductor and Williams as printer. This indictment was immediately followed by a second indictment, the exact date of which is not mentioned by the newspapers. In this instance the action was brought by Lady Elizabeth Lambert against Tattersall as conductor. Lady Lambert was accusing the *Post* of having published numerous libels over a period of several months, charging her with incontinence and more specifically with improper relations with her footman. But, in fact, she might have sued any one of a number of newspapers, for, according to the *Morning Herald* (30 Apr., 1792) , "Lady E. LAMBERT, from the superior elegance of her manners, in addition to her personal charms, is become an object of pretty general envy in the female circles:—she is therefore daily disposed of in *matrimony* according to the wishes of her own sex:—this will account for other absurd, but ill natured reports, which have been foisted into several of the public prints, respecting this accomplished young Lady." The fact that Lady Lambert chose to sue the *Post* and that she directed her suit against Tattersall rather than Williams indicates that she may have had some advice from one of Rose's friends.

By this time the Government was also in the process of punishing one of its own newspapers. The *Oracle* was not a newspaper of which the Treasury had any reason to be proud. As the title, the *Oracle, or Bell's New World* (by 3 June, 1791, shortened to the *Oracle, or Bell's World*), indicated, the paper was conceived as an imitation of Topham's *World,* with special emphasis on scurrility and Della Cruscan poetry. But the *Oracle* had no poet comparable with "Della Crusca," and, although readers were still interested in poetry, their interest in Della Cruscan poetry had somewhat declined by the time the *Oracle* was begun. William Gifford liked to think [72] that his ridicule of Bell's poets in the *Baviad* (1791) initiated the decline, but at most it only accelerated a process which was already underway. Also Bell was a bookseller, not a newspaperman, and he was therefore incapable of adhering to the first principle of newspaper ethics: loyalty to the subsidizer. But, although the *Oracle* was neither a credit to the London press nor a credit to the Government, the money which the Treasury invested in the newspaper was not a complete loss, for, since Bell's present friends happened to be sympathetic with the Opposition and his enemies with the Government, the *Oracle* might otherwise have become another *Argus.* As it was, it had been a hodgepodge, Treasury rantings against the reformers being intermixed with notices of the reform societies and eulogies of Pitt and Burke with eulogies of Sheridan, Erskine, Lord Lauderdale, and every other Opposition leader except Fox. In particular, the *Oracle* could not resist putting in a good word on occasion for Peter Stuart's brother-in-law, James Mackintosh. "The Second Edition of Mr. MACKINTOSH's *Vindiciae Gallicae* is in the Press, and there are now printing an impression of the same work in *Dublin,* and a Translation of it at *Paris,*" the *Oracle* observed proudly, for example, on 25 June, 1791. "Considering the price of the Book, the lateness of its appearance, and the want of previous Celebrity in the Author's name, its success has been unexampled." Similar paragraphs acclaimed the appearance of subsequent editions, despite the fact that the *Vindiciae* was an answer to Burke's *Reflections*, which the *Oracle* was being paid to defend.

Because of Mackintosh's connection with the *Morning Post*, the *Oracle* had always been somewhat sympathetic with that newspaper, and, when Charles Stuart also joined the staff, it was inclined to side with the *Post* against George Rose. By 7 January, 1792, the Government had lost patience, and Bell was accordingly indicted ex officio for having published two libels on the Guards. The first, which appeared on 5 January, 1792, consisted of the paragraph: "Certain Scoundrels, wearing the Uniform of that most execrable of all nuisances, the Guards, with the butt-ends of their firelocks, beat several persons about the head so effectually, as to fell them to the ground. The Majesty of the people suffered all this; but after they bear to be driven into their own highways by the wretches they supply with daily bread, what will they bear?" The second paragraph, which appeared on 7 January, was evidently similar. But, instead of behaving itself, the *Oracle* reacted with a defense of Sheridan, which began on 12 January with the protest, "Though, God knows, far enough removed from any connection with the [Whig] PARTY, yet we should blush to be thought for an instant combined with Men who assail the *private* Character of this Gentleman," and which was continued throughout the remainder of January and well into February. On 7 February Bell was indicted again.

In December, 1791, James Evans had published *A Commiserating Epistle to James Lowther, Earl of Lonsdale and Lowther, by Peter Pindar,* and on 17 December the *Oracle* had said, by way of comment on the pamphlet: "The Painters are much perplexed about the *Likeness* of the *Devil*. To obviate this difficulty concerning his *Infernal Majesty,* the humorous PETER PINDAR has recommended to his friend [John] OPIE the countenance of Lord Lonsdale." Lord Lonsdale took no notice of the remark until 7 February, 1792, when Mingay suddenly appeared in the Court of King's Bench and in Lonsdale's behalf filed informations for libel against James Evans, bookseller, and John Bell, proprietor. Bell at once named Peter Stuart as author of the paragraph and on 10 February entered a plea that Stuart's name be substituted for his. Dr. Wolcot had meanwhile asked that his name be substituted for Evans'. Neither request was granted, but on 13 February Lord Lonsdale filed additional informations against Stuart and Wolcot. It was immediately evident that this time the Government had got the right man, for, although the Whigs had indicated no uneasiness about the indictments of Bell, they were greatly disturbed about the indictment of Stuart. Erskine, who represented Stuart at this hearing, said that, since the paragraph was obviously not a libel, Lord Lonsdale was suing for extra-personal reasons; and, he added, "the noble Earl . . . had acted imprudently, in discovering so much impatience to-day against the author of this paragraph, and that of his eagerness to bring this person to trial he would hereafter have reason to repent." But Lord Lonsdale and the Court remained firm, and the four hearings were scheduled for the next session.

Although Lord Lonsdale, familiarly known as "The Bad Earl," was a friend of the Government, he was not beloved by any newspaper, and hence his actions received a good deal of unsympathetic comment even from some of the Treasury prints. On 15 February, 1792, for example, the *Morning Chronicle* published some verses, entitled "ON A PROS-ECUTION FOR A LIBEL":

> A Lord like the Devil was painted by Bell,
> For which he was threaten'd with Law and with Hell:
> 'Tis hard to conjecture how th' affair will be ended,
> For the Lord and the Devil are both much offended.

On 20 February the *Public Advertiser* noticed: "From a prosecution just now commenced, it appears, that *comparisons are odious*. The equity of the Court will be put to the test, as they will be required to give *the Devil* his due." And on 3 March the *Chronicle* protested: "A prosecution against a printer, for saying *a man might sit for a picture of the Devil,* is a new thing. If the figures the Artists now attempt for a portrait of Satan were inspected, we should find an attempt at uniting the *Hercules* and *Antinous,* and surely comparing a Noble Lord to a figure built upon such models, is rather compliment than satire. When the character of his infernal Highness was in much lower estimation, Swift compared an Irish Peer to the Devil, and was not prosecuted."

Meanwhile the rejection of Thompson's motion and the subse-quent actions against the *Morning Post* had by no means discouraged the Whigs, who called a meeting of all Westminster electors for 20 March. At this meeting it was resolved to continue the fight against Rose by petition, and on 21 March the *Morning Chronicle* spoke up in support of the resolution. "The very serious nature of the charges against Mr. Rose, for undue interference in the Westminster Election, may be collected from the pains taken in the Treasury Papers, to calumniate every gentleman, directly or indirectly concerned in promoting an enquiry into his conduct," it said. As the time for the presentation of the petition approached, the Treasury newspapers became increasingly interested in the case, and there was a storm of comment on 3 and 4 April, the laurel going to the *Public Advertiser,* which on 3 April stated as a matter of fact: "Notwithstanding the many insidious attempts that have been made, and are now making to *pluck the Rose,* he still defies the malice of his enemies, and holds up his head with additional lustre, the more he is touched by polluted hands, like a *true Rose,* the emblem of Innocence, after refreshed by gentle dews, he expands his leaves, and establishes his never-fading colour." Since any reply to this paragraph would have seemed to outrage the very soul of poetry, the *Morning Chronicle* contented itself with the wry observation (4 Apr., 1792) : "The friends of Mr. ROSE are rather premature in their expressions of congratulations on the Honourable Secretary's escape from enquiry. They forget, that a Petition, already signed by several thousands of the Electors of Westminster, must bring his *attention* to his friend SMITH, and his great *knowledge of the Excise Laws,* again before the House of Commons." Fox presented the petition on 4 April, 1792, giving notice that he intended to make a motion on the subject later. But, by the time he made the motion, the political climate had taken another turn for the worse.

## "CONSTITUTIONALISTS" VS. REFORMERS:
## CONSOLIDATION OF FORCES

IN SEVERAL respects the Opposition had played directly into Pitt's hands. However much popular interest there was in the action against George Rose, the action was still a diversion, for, even if it had succeeded, nothing would have been gained for the cause of freedom. The real Achilles heel of the Administration had been the fact that there was no evidence to support Burke's hysteria or Pitt's broodings except the act of one single "Maniac," and there was a limit to how long the hysteria and broodings could continue under such circumstances. Since all Pitt could hope was that the tactics would drive some of the reformers to untenable extremes before the alarmist bubble burst, the Opposition should have concentrated its efforts on seeing that this did not happen. It should have denounced radicalism in every form, have controlled and moderated the activities of reform societies, and, most important, have seen to it that there was no suggestion of a link with France. But it did nothing of the sort. Not only did Opposition newspapers approve of reformers indiscriminately, but they gave their activities an inordinate amount of publicity, so that anyone reading an Opposition newspaper would have supposed that the country was, in fact, teeming with sedition.

On 16 January, 1792, for example, all the Opposition newspapers noticed the appearance of Part II of Paine's *Rights of Man,* and the work was evidently acclaimed by the *Argus* and the *Morning Post.* On 25 January, Thomas Hardy, who had migrated to London from Scotland eighteen years earlier and was now a shoemaker with a shop in Piccadilly, was encouraged by the various replies to Burke's *Reflections* to begin the Corresponding Society.[73] The Corresponding Society was intended for workingmen. The dues were fixed at a penny a week, the penny to be spent on correspondence with other societies and on circulation of literature, especially the *Rights of Man;* and, since membership was open to everyone, the nine who attended the first meeting were soon joined by a host of "mechanics, labourers, porters, coalheavers, and persons of that class" to perhaps the number of 3,000. The Corresponding Society was mischievous in many respects. Its goals, which were universal suffrage and annual parliaments, were too drastic for the times, and, although it expected, it said, to reach these goals through gradual reforms, there was a real danger that it would become impatient. Moreover, no one knew the size of its membership, which was always deliberately exaggerated, being sometimes estimated in the "scores of thousands," and neither did anyone know what link, if any, it had with France. Under all these circumstances the Opposition press should have been cautious. Yet the opening Address to the Nation, which was written by the Frenchman Maurice Margarot, was printed in full by the *Argus,* as so were, it appears, all subsequent addresses, and notices of the society were carried by all Opposition newspapers and by the *Oracle.* The principal member of the society, Horne Tooke, who had redeemed himself in the eyes of the Opposition by publishing (10 June, 1791) *A Review of the Constitutions of England,* fared even better, so far as publicity was concerned, than the society itself.

The middle-class Constitutional Society was also mischievous. For some time it had been moving in the direction of radicalism, and, by the beginning of 1792, its goals were identical with those of the Corresponding Society, both societies recognizing Thomas Paine as their patron saint. But the *Gazetteer* was almost the official organ of the Constitutional Society, and the society's activities were lauded by the Opposition press generally. The Opposition newspapers greatly simplified the work of the Government by seeing to it that everyone knew that the two societies existed, that they were prosperous and active, and that they were menacing in their objectives. For, owing to their labors, the Treasury newspapers had only to link an individual with one of the societies to establish the fact that he was "seditious." Here they received no assistance from the Opposition press, which at least took care to separate the activities of the Whig leaders and its own writers from those of the societies. Mackintosh, for example, was identified only with the Friends of the Liberty of the Press, and readers were given to understand that he had long since resigned from the Constitutional Society. Hence the news that he had accepted an honorary membership in that society was suppressed by all Opposition newspapers and was evidently supposed to be suppressed by the society itself. For on 28 March, 1792, *The Times* reported that "JAMES MACKINTOSH and JOEL BARLOW, Esqrs. who have been elected Honorary Members of a certain seditious Society, perhaps may not be so well pleased at the PUBLIC information from the Secretary."

While the petition from the Westminster electors was still awaiting Fox's motion, the Whigs finally took a step they should have taken a year earlier. On 11 April, 1792, they organized the Society of Friends of the People, Associated for the Purpose of Obtaining a Parliamentary Reform. As the name implied, the Friends of the People was conceived as an augmentation of the very respectable Friends of the Liberty of the Press, which nevertheless continued to exist as an independent unit, and it was equally conservative. It had, in fact, no specific objects other than to modify and control the activities of the Corresponding and Constitutional Societies and to convert the reform movement generally into a slow and deliberative process. Among the original 149 members, were not only most of the leaders of the Opposition but several journalists, notably James Perry from the *Morning Chronicle* and Robert Merry, Dennis O'Bryen, D. E. MacDonnel, and James Mackintosh from the *Morning Post*. The fact that it was already too late for such an organization was indicated by the absence of the names of Fox and the other more cautious Whigs from the roster, and it was further indicated by every event which succeeded.

On 11 April, 1792, the *Oracle* had announced that "The Society for Constitutional Information has made TOM PAINE one of the Stewards of its Anniversary Dinner," and notices of the dinner had been appearing in all the Opposition newspapers for several days. By 16 April there were references to it in every newspaper. For, while the toasts to Paine, Horne Tooke, Joel Barlow, and the "other Stewards" were being drunk, Paine was suddenly taken into custody and whisked away to prison. Two of the guests, "Joseph Johnson and George Wilkie, booksellers," followed the officers to learn why Paine was being arrested and, after receiving a number of evasive answers, were finally told that he was arrested "on suit of Mark Gregory and others," to whom he owed £200. They thereupon provided the £200, and after some further delay Paine was released. Although this was perhaps not the outcome Pitt had planned, the incident was sufficiently ominous to give even the *Gazetteer* pause.

Of the Friends of the People itself, nothing was said, and the society proceeded with its plans. On 27 April it adopted a "Declaration," on the basis of which Grey was to move for reform, and, in accordance with its resolution, sent copies to all newspapers for publication. The "Declaration" was published on 30 April by all the Opposition newspapers, the *Oracle,* and the *Diary.* It was not published by the *World* and probably not by the other Treasury newspapers. The *Morning Herald* not only returned its copy to Lambton with an outraged note, but devoted a third of a column to a denunciation of the society's "Commander in Chief," "Field Marshall [*sic*] Sheridan"; to its "Lieutenant Generals," the Earl of Lauderdale, Charles Grey, Samuel Whitbread, Thomas Maitland, William Baker, William Lambton, John Wharton, and William Smith; to its "Brigadiers," George Rous, William Cunningham, John Godfrey, and James Mackintosh; and to its "Joint Aids-du-Camp [*sic*]," Philip Francis and John Scott. There would be daily reports on the seditious activities of this group henceforth, the *Herald* promised. On the same day (30 Apr., 1792) Grey gave notice that he intended to submit his motion "in the course of the next session" and was given cautious support by Fox, who pointed out that the objects which the Friends of the People had in mind were far different from those expressed in the *Rights of Man*. Burke took violent exception. Under the circumstances, he said, any reform was an invitation to a revolution, and he could therefore see no difference between the Friends of the People and Thomas Paine.

From this point on, events moved rapidly. On 7 May the *Public Advertiser* declared that the "new Association, who style themselves '*The Friends of the People,*' are disaffected and dangerous innovators." The *World* and the *Morning Herald* strongly concurred, and the *Morning Chronicle* called on Pitt to prove at this crucial moment that he was not the "apostate" that he appeared to be. On 8 May the petition from the Westminster electors was read in the House of Commons, but Fox's motion to refer it to a committee was defeated 81 to 34. By 16 May, according to the *Gazetteer,* the "publisher of Mr. PAINE's work, on the Rights of Man, [J. S. Jordan, had] received a notice of prosecution from the Attorney General," and by 17 May, according to the *Morning Herald,* "Mr. THOMAS PAINE" had left London. On 19 May the *Gazetteer,* which had been making some inquiries about the debt for which Paine was arrested, reported that there had been such a debt, but that payment had never been demanded. On 21 May Whitbread presented a petition from some of the victims of the Birmingham riots, on the basis of which he moved that all information respecting those riots and the subsequent trials of the rioters be placed before the House, although there was no possibility that the motion would pass, in view of Burke's declaration of 11 May that Unitarians were *ipso facto* Jacobins. And, on the same day (not on 25 May, as stated in the *Parliamentary History*), Henry Dundas read to Parliament the King's Proclamation against Seditious Writings. Dundas had been Secretary of State for the Home Department since June, 1791.

The reading was followed by a paroxysm of loyalty "addresses," published by the newspapers as advertisements, and by announcements of defections, the old followers of Lord North and even the Duke of Portland having by this time deserted to the Government. Among the defectors was the Prince of Wales, who on 31 May journeyed to the House of Lords to speak in support of the Proclamation. This was his first speech in Parliament, and certainly no one had better reason to wish for some curbing of the press than he, who had probably been more abused in newspapers and pamphlets than any man in England. Even as he spoke, his audience was probably thinking less of what he was saying than of his turf transactions, an exposé of which had been published on 27 February, 1792, under the title, *Jockey Club; or A Sketch of the Manners of the Age,* the author supposedly being

Charles Pigott. But a few of his auditors may also have remembered that he was himself associated with one of the most flagrant examples of "Seditious Writings," the *Morning Post*.

On 24 May the *Morning Herald* spoke out for the first time on the subject of the Constitutional Society. "*The* ADVERTISEMENT *and* RESOLUTIONS *from the* SOCIETY *for* CONSTITUTIONAL INFORMATION *we reject,*" it thundered, "*as hostile to the present orderly Government of this realm.—A* DARING ASSOCIATION *which publicly boasts of its alliance with the levelling* CLUB *of* JACOBINS *at Paris, shall not broach their baneful doctrines through the channel of this Paper.*" On 8 June the *Public Advertiser* spoke out on the subject of Robert Merry: "Mr. Merry's chief motive for his visit to France, is for the purpose of presenting his last Ode on the French Revolution to the National Assembly. Mr. Merry, in politics, as in poetry, is an *enthusiast.*" Merry had returned to England by August, but he did not return for the celebrations of 15 June. On 11 June, 1792, Fox's Libel Act, which empowered juries to decide the whole issue in cases of libel, finally passed the House of Lords, having passed the Commons a year earlier. Its passage was regarded by the Opposition as a triumph; and on 13 June the Opposition newspapers and the *Oracle* published advertisements, inviting the public to a celebration dinner on 15 June, sponsored by the Friends of the Liberty of the Press, reservations to be made with one of the "Stewards"—the Earl of Lauderdale, Thomas Maitland, Samuel Whitbread, the Rev. Samuel Parr, James Martin, Charles Pigott, George Rous, James West, Lord Kinnaird, Philip Francis, Sheridan, Sir J. Throckmorton, Thomas Rogers, John Hurford Stone, William Lambton, and James Mackintosh. On 16 June the same newspapers carried accounts of the dinner: "Mr. Serjeant Bond took the Chair, and Mr. Rouse [*sic*] moved the Resolutions. . . . They bore the stamp of the nervous pen of Dr. Mackintosh." The Society of the Friends of the Liberty of the Press was still active at the end of the year, its most prominent members being Mackintosh, Dennis O'Bryen, Erskine, Sheridan, and Tierney, but it had nothing further to celebrate.

The passage of the Libel Act was itself no cause for celebration, for the very fact that the Government had permitted the bill to pass and had even supported it indicated that it no longer regarded juries as a threat. The reason was the Proclamation against Seditious Writings. Not only was this proclamation bound to have an effect upon juries, but it had provided the Government with an excuse for setting up two societies of its own. The first was the Association for Protecting Liberty and Property against Republicans and Levellers, which might better have been called the Society of the Enemies of the Press. This organization, referred to by the newspapers as "The Crown and Anchor Association" or merely "The Association," was subsidized by the Treasury and managed by a long-time friend of William Pitt, John Reeves, and its principal purpose was to publish and distribute reactionary literature. Although the newspapers had followed Reeves's career with interest, there had been no mention of it since 4 July, 1791, when the *Star* stated that "Mr. REEVES is not appointed Judge Advocate of Newfoundland, there being no such Court there; but he is appointed Chief Justice in the Court of Civil Jurisdiction, instituted in consequence of an act passed last Session of Parliament, for determining causes during the fishing season only."

The second organization was lacking a name, but it was much more vicious than the first. This one consisted of a group of agents, who penetrated the reform societies, attended public lectures, and frequented taverns, partly for the purpose of informing, partly for the purpose of agitating. Some of them were paid for their informations by the piece; others, such as John Taylor, William Augustus Miles, and Charles Stuart, were on salaries. Their activities were sponsored by the Home Department and hence were supervised by the Secretary of State for the Home Department, Henry Dundas, and the Under-Secretary, Evan Nepean, who correlated their work with that of the Treasury. Some of the agents seem, in fact, to have worked for both departments. At first the Opposition did not take this organization seriously, chiefly because no one had ever taken Dundas seriously. His linguistic awkwardness, his boastfulness, especially about his popularity in Scotland, and his genial lack of principle had made him the target for a good deal of newspaper fun, dating back to at least 5 February, 1784, when the *Morning Post* had commented: "Mr. DUNDAS's speech on Monday last, [abounded] with that innate modesty, for which the learned gentleman has long been noticed." Mackintosh put it rather well when he said in his *Letter to . . . Pitt:* [74] "The frank and good-natured prostitution of DUNDAS, which assumes no sort of disguise, and affects no principle, almost disarms censure, and relaxes us into a sort of contemptuous indulgence for one whom we can neither hate nor respect." The Tories had long been puzzled by Pitt's attachment to such a man: "Pitt . . . stands a willing sponsor for [Dundas'] transgressions," Lord Bulkeley had said in 1788,[75] and "supports him through thick and thin. Dundas sticks to Pitt as a barnacle to an oyster-shell, so that if he chose it he cannot shake him off, and everybody believes he . . . likes him, and really wants him in the House of Commons; besides, there is no man who eats Pitt's toads with such zeal, attention, and appetite, as Dundas, and we all know the effect of those qualities." But Dundas managed his string of spies better than anyone anticipated.

On 4 July, 1792, the Opposition newspapers and the *Oracle* announced publication "this day" of *A Letter to the Right Honourable William Pitt, on His Apostacy from the Cause of Parliamentary Reform.* The author was James Mackintosh, and the *Letter* took a very sober look at the present situation. It is unhappily true, the *Letter* began, that "all ferments of the mind" tend to "divide men into extreme camps," but, by "creating a panic" and "shouting that the Constitution is in danger," Pitt had exaggerated the extremes to such a degree that war with France now seemed almost inevitable. Yet this was a war which could only end in defeat, for, if England won, "radical Toryism" would engulf the whole of Europe, and, if France won, no nation could stand out against "Republicanism." Because of this fact, the Friends of the People had attempted to "reconcile these extremes, to mitigate Toryism and Republicanism through liberality and moderation," and the attempt had been blasted by a proclamation which condemned any political change "as the wildest kind of subversion." Yet the author still ventured to hope that Pitt would undo the damage he had done before it was too late.[76] The strength of the hope was indicated by the fact that the *Letter* was signed only "AN HONEST MAN," although Mackintosh had not hesitated to attach his name to the far-more-outspoken *Vindiciae* one year earlier. On 16 August the *Oracle* mentioned that "MACKINTOSH (the *Vindiciae Gallicae*) is at *Boulogne,* not however vindicating the present MOBOCRACY of France," and on 25 September it added the information that "MACKINTOSH rejected the proposal of being elected as a Member of the *French* NATIONAL CONVENTION." The last bit of information seems to have corrected a paragraph in one of the Treasury newspapers.

## ORDEALS OF THE OPPOSITION PRESS

As SOON as the country was in a proper state of panic, the Government set out to complete some of its unfinished business with the newspapers, and the first newspaper to be dealt with was the *Oracle*. Although Dr. Wolcot was involved in some of the proceedings against the newspaper, he was himself still connected with the *Morning Post*. In February the Government's quarrel with the *Oracle* had been directed primarily at Peter Stuart, but it was now directed primarily at John Bell, for the reason that Bell was in the process of turning the whole newspaper over to the Whigs. The transactions which were going on behind the scenes can be conjectured from the progress of the litigations. On 27 April, according to the *Star* (28 Apr., 1792),

in the Court of King's Bench, Mr. Erskine shewed cause against a rule moved for last Term, for an information against Dr. WALCOT [*sic*], for a libel against Lord LONSDALE.

The Court were of opinion that the publication was not only a Libel upon Lord LONSDALE, but upon the whole LOWTHER family, through the space of five hundred years, and directed the Rule to be made absolute.

Mr. MINGAY then enlarged the Rule to next term, against Bell and Evans, and understood that Mr. Stuart had made his peace with the Earl of LONSDALE; if so, nothing more would be said about it.

Bell had evidently made some promises which the Government did not entirely credit and which, as it turned out, Bell apparently did not fulfil. For on 25 June, again according to the *Star* (26 June, 1792), "There were Rules calling on Mr. EVANS and Mr. BELL to shew cause why criminal informations should not issue against them for printing and publishing certain alledged libels on Lord Lonsdale./ Mr. Mingay, on the part of the prosecution, said he wished these Rules to be enlarged, as he understood the business was not settled. They were enlarged accordingly." The *Oracle* carried a similar report. Although the newspapers make no further reference to this "business," the Government had certainly not solved its problem with Bell, for on 9 July, 1792, it brought him back to court to be tried for the libels on the Guards. Although it was urged in Bell's behalf that this was his first "criminal indictment" during the twenty years he had been connected with London newspapers and that the libels were inserted without his knowledge and to his profound regret, he was convicted.

In the case of the *Morning Post*, the Government was extremely cautious. Both actions pending against that newspaper were civil, and both of them were directed against Tattersall as "conductor," although, as the Government knew, Tattersall could produce documents to prove that he was not the conductor, the conductor being, according to the terms of the lease, Louis Weltje. The question was whether Tattersall would produce these documents or not. He did not. On 9 July, 1792, he was tried in the Court of King's Bench for having published numerous libels on Lady Elizabeth Lambert, and on the same day he and William Williams were tried in the same court for having published a libel on George Rose. Both trials resulted in convictions. In the first case, Lady Lambert was awarded £4,000 damages; in the second case, Rose was awarded £100 damages from each of the defendants.

On 13 July the *World* declared with some exasperation: "The manner in which Mr. ROSE brought action, was perfectly fair and constitutional. By bringing it *civilly* for DAMAGES, he gave the [Whig] Party an opportunity of JUSTIFICATION, and *no Justification was attempted.* Of course, the JURY brought in the Defendant subject to DAMAGES, which all the PARTY-*wit* of Mr. ERSKINE could not do away. —Lord KENYON's charge amply testified this." But the case had been intended as a test, not of the Whigs' knowledge of Treasury practices, but of Tattersall's loyalty to the Prince of Wales. With respect to the libels on Lady Lambert, Tattersall did say that he "had very little to do" with the paper's "arrangement or its management. As soon as he discovered that those calumnies were thus dispersed, he used every effort in his power to discover the Authors of them; and he was still in hopes that those efforts would not be ineffectual"; but he did not say who was responsible for the "arrangement" and "management." In return for his silence respecting Weltje, Carlton House had obligated itself to pay half the expenses of all litigations brought against the *Post.* As it turned out, it had not fulfilled its obligation with respect to this particular litigation by 1795, when Tattersall died; and the executors of his estate were evidently also unable to collect, for in February, 1796, the case was taken to court. But all that is known of the action is contained in a paragraph published by the *Morning Chronicle* on 1 March, 1796: "A moiety of the Damages and expences of defending the action brought by Lady ELIZABETH LAMBERT against a Morning Paper, amounting to £5000 form a part of Mr. TATTERSALL's claims on the PRINCE's Commissioners, which they have refused to admit: they are therefore to become a question before Lord KENYON and a Special Jury, the sittings after next term."

The two civil actions against Tattersall were tried on 9 July, 1792, and on 10 July Tattersall was brought back to court to be indicted ex officio for having published "an atrocious libel" on the King. The newspapers report that this time he chose to plead guilty and throw himself on the mercy of the Court, and there is no further reference to the case. The probability is that Tattersall, who had accepted the fines since a "moiety" was to be paid by Carlton House, was unwilling to remain silent when a prison sentence was involved, so that, in order to avoid embarrassments, his name was erased from the indictment and the name of William Williams substituted. It is at least true that Tattersall was not sentenced, whereas, according to Taylor,[77] Williams was "confined in Newgate during twelve months for the insertion of a libel." The confinement evidently began sometime during the course of 1792, for, although the *Morning Post* is lacking for most of the year, Williams was still printing the paper on 5 January and by 6 December he had been replaced by J. Norris. Except for Williams, who was probably in prison, and Charles Stuart, who was working for Henry Dundas, the staff of the *Post* seems to have remained intact until early 1793. The character of the newspaper also remained unchanged, although on 17 December, 1792, the *Morning Post, and Daily Advertiser* dropped its subtitle, to be known henceforth as only the *Morning Post.* The Weltje-Tattersall lease expired on 1 January, 1793.

Meanwhile on 10 July, 1792, the Government had commenced a new action against the *Argus.* Although Sampson Perry left an account of his experiences as conductor of that newspaper,[78] the account is of limited value, partly because Perry had forgotten what happened and partly because he never knew. It was his recollection, for example, that he had served a one-year term in King's Bench Prison for "questioning the qualifications of the ministers, and the accuracy of the royal Gazette, on the Nootka Sound affair," but, in fact, his punishment for that offense had consisted of only a £100 fine. He had been sentenced to prison for having published libels on the Walters and Lady Fitzgibbon. As to his subsequent actions, Perry went on, he, of course, resumed the conduct of the *Argus,* "which for some time had been my own property," dedicating the paper to "liberty." But, before his term of imprisonment had even expired, he said, he had been "served with the copy of an information filed by the attorney-general, in the name, as it were, of the house of commons, for inserting in the *Argus* in the month of May preceding," a paragraph stating that, since the Commons was not composed of the people's representatives, the people were to be commended for their "docility" in submitting to its laws. He was also warned that he was to be arrested, held without bail, and denied writing materials. To avoid this fate, he fled to France in the fall of 1792; and, a few days after he left, the *Gazette* offered a £100 reward for his apprehension, the offer being signed by "Wm. Chamberlayne, Solicitor to the Treasury." He was tried *in absentia*, convicted, and outlawed.

From this point on, Perry's account is a tangle of accusations. In one context Perry said that, although he was a victim of Ministerial persecution, "a wretch—a hypocrite, accredited as a patriot of the first class, [assisted] at the door of this . . . cabinet, with the view, no doubt, of making his way to ministerial favour and preferment, by an *amende deshonorable* for his former refractory conduct. Perhaps the under secretary of state's [James Bland Burges'] *budget* may hereafter be *opened* to public view; it will turn out a very surprising entertainment." Again Perry said that he was "obliged to leave [the *Argus*] to the vicarious superintendance of *promising,* but *deceiving* friends." For, having been warned that the Government intended to arrest him and hold him without bail, he consulted an "acquaintance, distinguished since, if not by *apostacy,* at least by an *unpardonable indifference* to the cause." The "acquaintance" said that, "from his professional connection with certain *great personages,* and *characters,*" he would advise flight and that "I might fully rely on *his* attention, as *one* of my friends, for . . . preserving . . . the *Argus.*" In still another context Perry said that, shortly after he left England, he received a letter, informing him that, inasmuch as he had opposed both political parties, the parties had been equally hostile toward the paper and hence "the trouble at the Stamp Office"; that "———— was an enemy, in the disguise of a friend; [and] that, in concert with the D————r, whom he has so often made the subject of his censure, he planned the scheme of destroying the *Argus,* that nothing might stand in the way of his own particular sinister views." The author of the letter had got his information from "————."

The Mr. "————" whom Perry consulted would have been Sheridan, whose ardor for democracy had, in fact, cooled by the time Perry was writing (1796). "The D————r" whom he "so often made the subject of his censure" and with whom he was supposedly allied in "the scheme of destroying the *Argus*" could have been only Dr. James Mackintosh. And the Mr. "————" who supplied the information that Sheridan deliberately subverted the *Argus* in order to "[make] his way to ministerial favour and preferment" was most likely James Bland Burges, the "under secretary of state," himself, although he may also have been John Heriot. But the information was entirely false, for the situation was much more complex than Perry realized.

Sampson Perry was released from prison on 9 July, 1792, and, according to the newspapers, he was not indicted for the libel on the Commons until the following day. The libel had been published on 8 May. Prior to Perry's release, the *Argus* had supported the Corresponding Society and Thomas Paine, and, although the paper is not extant for the last half of 1792, it is clear from the occasional references to it that it thereafter became militantly democratic. But the Government, which was so eager to indict Perry, indicated no eagerness to bring him to trial. Instead of concerning itself further with him, it turned its attention to its old friend, John Frost, whom it indicted for the use of "seditious language," and to its most vigorous assailant, Thomas Paine, both of whom it persuaded to abscond. The first notice of their departure appeared in the *Diary* of 14 September, which stated only that on 10 September Paine had fled to Paris "with a large party of English." This statement was later (22 Sept., 1792) corrected by the *Public Advertiser,* which published a letter from Paine to Dundas, dated 15 September and saying that Paine had not left London until 13 September. The reason for his leaving, according to the letter, was that "Mr. Audibert" had brought him news of his election to the National Convention, and, in order to accept the honor, he was obliged to accompany "Mr. Audibert" back to Paris, Frost having decided to go along. But Paine was lying, said the *Public Advertiser,* for, by authority of the Royal Proclamation against Seditious Writings, the Customs House officers at Dover had seized his papers and found them to include a notice from the Attorney General that an action was being brought against him as author of *The Rights of Man.* This statement was in turn later corrected by the *World,* which on 23 October, 1792, announced that "TOM PAINE is in the high road to be outlawed, for, as he will not appear to the summons that will be issued against him, and has fled for various debts, the law will take its course." The purpose of this correction was perhaps to explain why the Customs House officers had permitted Frost and Paine to leave the country, when they knew that both men were under indictment.

Sampson Perry did not leave with Paine, for on 24 September,

1792, William Augustus Miles addressed the following letter [79] to Charles Long:

> I do not know that the inclosed will be printed in either of the two papers to which I have addressed it, as I have observed that by a kind of etiquette established between the conductors of our public prints they are never to arraign each other's conduct, so that these gentry . . . are . . . rendered invulnerable. But I have had several hints at different times from Frenchmen in constant relation and intimacy with M. de Chauvelin [the French Minister Plenipotentiary] and his family, that the editors of the "Morning Chronicle" and of the "Argus" have received considerable sums of money, and that they have each of them a large monthly allowance. I have no doubt of the fact, and wish it could be proved in Westminster Hall, and the purpose for which the money is paid. This I know, that the personal attendance of the parties in Portman Square [the French Embassy] is constant.

One of the "public prints" to which Miles had "addressed" his information, most likely *The Times* (see *The Times*, 10 Nov., 1796), evidently published it, but withheld the names of the newspapers, for on 25 September, 1792, the *Chronicle* responded with the paragraph: "A morning paper says, that there are two daily Journals of London actually bribed by the Jacobins of France, to spread sedition in England—and that one of them, in particular, has 10,000 livres per month for its treason. It would have been a faithful service to their country to have named the particular Journals, so infamously corrupted by foreign gold . . . that the Crown officers may bring the abandoned writers to legal punishment."

By this time the *Chronicle* had made some additions to its staff, much of its material being signed "J. T. R.," and it had also made some arrangements with the *Star*. For, although the *Chronicle* was conducted by James Perry, printed by J. Lambert at No. 1, Great Shire Lane, and housed at No. 474, Strand, and the *Star* was printed and conducted by John Mayne, Temple Bar, the two newspapers were regarding themselves as a morning and evening edition of the same newspaper.[80] The fact that the *Chronicle* did respond to the charge is rather good evidence that James Perry had been visiting Portman Square, but anyone who glanced at his newspaper would have known that it was not in the pay of the French. The paper carried occasional poems in praise of the French Revolution, one of them, "Song for the Anniversary of the Revolution" (12 Nov., 1792), being supplied by George Dyer, but even these poems made it clear that England already had her freedom, and the *Chronicle* was meanwhile vehemently opposed to the importation of French ideas into England. The *Argus* was quite another matter. One can well believe that Sampson Perry was receiving "a large monthly allowance" from the French Government. But, since there was no statute forbidding foreign subsidies of English newspapers, there was no investigation.

The Treasury's two principal writers during this period were William Augustus Miles and John Heriot. Miles's financial affairs are complicated. During 1792 the Treasury paid him a "salary" of £500 [81] and on 18 November, 1792, an additional £40 "for the publication of pamphlets." [82] But on 13 September, 1796, the *Morning Post* charged that he was then "[continuing] to enjoy two Pensions from the Treasury," one supposedly through a Secretary of the Treasury, the other through the Secretary of State for the Home Department; and on 10 April, 1798, it added the information that Miles had, to its knowledge, been receiving a £300 "pension" from the Treasury since 1792. The pamphlets for which he was paid have not been identified. The only pamphlets which he is known to have written prior to 1793 are *A Letter to John Fielding, . . . Occasioned by His Extraordinary Request to Mr. Garrick for the Suppression of the Beggar's Opera* (1773), *Remarks on an Act of Parliament . . . Intituled "An Act for the Encouragement of the Fisheries"* (1779), *The Artifice, a Comic Opera* (1780), *Letters of Neptune and Gracchus Addressed to the P[rince] of W[ales] and other Distinguished Characters; Now First Collected from Their Original Publication in the Morning Post* (1784), and *An Answer to Mr. De Lolme's Observations on the Late National Embarrassment, by Neptune* (1789). Miles's activities, so far as the Treasury was concerned, were sponsored by Charles Long, who had succeeded Thomas Steele as the second Secretary of the Treasury in the spring of 1791; Heriot's activities were sponsored by George Rose.

In 1791 Heriot's salary was £200, payable in quarterly installments, and it seems to have remained the same in 1792, except that, from the middle of the year on, it was paid semiannually. [83] In return for this salary, Heriot, like Miles, furnished propaganda for the various Treasury newspapers; but, unlike Miles, who had no other employment, Heriot was also on the staff of the *World*, which paid him an additional "2gs. a week" as "reporter." [84] Since Topham placed no particular value on Heriot's services, which had to do chiefly with the drama department, he may have employed him as a favor to Rose. This supposition would at least help to explain his indignation when Heriot suddenly quit the *World* to begin the *Sun.*

The most complete and certainly the most provocative account of the origin of the *Sun* is one which purports to be Heriot's: [85]

About this period [that is, 1790–92] the celebrated Edmund Burke . . . went repeatedly to the Treasury, urging the propriety and necessity of Government having a newspaper, the principles of which the members of the Government could depend upon, and, in a great measure, direct. Those in authority concurred with him. . . . Mr. Heriot had so recommended himself to one of the Secretaries of the Treasury [George Rose], that he became his personal friend. That gentleman . . . broached the subject to him, and proposed his undertaking the establishment of a daily paper. . . . Funds were supplied to him by two individuals connected with the Government, but wholly out of their own pockets. Mr. Heriot set briskly to work; a prospectus was issued in a few days, and on the 1st of October, 1792, "The Sun" appeared, and soon obtained an extensive, and, at that time, unparalleled circulation.

At the time Burke was making his "repeated" calls on the Treasury, the Government could already "depend upon, and, in a great measure, direct" the "principles" of six newspapers, and it controlled two of these newspapers, the *Morning Herald* and the *World,* absolutely. Although the other four may have been disinclined "to arraign" the "conduct" of the Opposition prints with as much violence as the Treasury could have wished, these two had no scruples. But, as long as there was a trial of Warren Hastings, there would never be a perfect union between Edmund Burke and William Pitt; and, since Rose could not tell Burke the truth, namely, that the ridicule of the trial, which was still appearing in the *World* and by early 1792 was appearing in other Ministerial newspapers as well, was published with the blessing of the Treasury, he had obviously shifted the blame to the conductors. Burke's "urgings" that the Government should then begin a newspaper of its own must have created a problem. For the Treasury was unwilling to alienate the newspapers it was subsidizing by putting its own newspaper into competition with them, and it was even less willing to alienate the most useful friend it would ever have, Edmund Burke. The problem, so far as the other newspapers were concerned, was solved by bringing out the *Sun* as an evening newspaper, so that it was in competition only with the Opposition *Star,* and by advertising it as Heriot's; the problem, so far as Burke was concerned, was solved by assigning the financing and therefore the control to "two individuals," who, being themselves "connected with the Government," would see to it that the paper adhered to those "principles" respecting the trial of Warren Hastings which, Burke was given to understand, were as dear to the Ministry as they were to himself. The "two individuals" were James Bland Burges, Under Secretary of State for Foreign Affairs, and Charles Long, the other Secretary of the Treasury.

The first plan was probably to seize a newspaper already in existence rather than to begin a new one. A newspaper with some financial difficulties and with a single proprietor who was threatened with the pillory and a long prison term for the publication of an "atrocious" libel was usually easy prey for the Government, which, by the simple expedients of persuading the proprietor to abscond and then devising some "trouble at the Stamp Office," could acquire the newspaper at a nominal cost. The Government had acquired the *General Advertiser* by just such methods two years earlier, and it was to acquire the *Argus* by the same methods two months later. But in September, 1792, the *Argus* was not ripe, Sampson Perry having not yet been tried for his libel on the Commons, and so the only newspaper which fulfilled all necessary conditions was the *Oracle*. But this time the Whigs were alert. What precisely happened is, of course, a mystery; but on 24 September there was a marked change in the *Oracle*. The paper dropped its subtitle, its appearance improved considerably, and Buchanan Millan's name disappeared from the colophon, to reappear on 1 October in the colophon of the *Sun*. The new printer of the *Oracle* was James Bell, who, according to Morison,[86] was possibly John Bell's grandnephew. He was certainly the same James Bell who was an original member of the Friends of the People and by 1793 an active member of the Friends of the Liberty of the Press (*Morning Chronicle,* 4 Mar., 1793). There was no statement of a change in management or policy, but on 16 October, 1792, the *World* remarked: "A Morning Paper, remarkable for its Billingsgate abuse and infamous sedition, has got a *new Head*—that of the Conductor too requires changing, for it is obviously *turn'd.*" It had probably already been changed, Bell being replaced by Peter Stuart. The result was that Burges and Long had to find a new house and purchase new equipment.

According to the colophon, the *Sun* was printed by Buchanan Millan at No. 112, Strand; and it could hardly avoid being an immediate success, inasmuch as the morning newspapers had to look to it for a good deal of their information, and the Treasury purchased hundreds, if not thousands, of copies of it for free distribution throughout the country. For his part in the enterprise, Heriot was probably given a share in the newspaper, and his salary was continued through at least mid-1793.[87] In addition, on 28 December, 1792, he collected £58 10s. 6d. "for Advertisements in different Papers" and on 1 March, 1793, £172 16s. 3d. "for Printing Pamphlets and advertising in different Papers." [88] There was a good deal of speculation as to the actual conductors of the *Sun,* and it was not until 19 July, 1793, that the *Morning Chronicle* finally identified one of them as "Under-Secretary *Placid,*" "Placid" being, of course, Bland Burges. On 26 July the *Chronicle* added the information that "a Secretary to the Treasury and an Under-Secretary of State are the principal Proprietors and Directors, . . . the most *placid* and *reasonable* people imaginable." Since Rose was usually described as "fragrant," the "reasonable" Secretary of the Treasury was probably Long.

The Treasury newspapers knew as little about the *Sun* as the Opposition newspapers, and they resented it a great deal more. On 15 October, 1792, Burges wrote a somewhat amused letter to his fellow proprietor, Long: [89]

> I have just had a visit from young [William] Walter, who is furious about the success of the *Sun* and came to me as an impartial person, to complain of the partiality shown by the Government, and especially by Mr. Rose, to that paper, which he said was very unjust. . . . He told me it was well known that Rose recommended the *Sun,* and patronised its publisher and he threw out sundry strong hints of Mr. [George] Aust [the Under-Secretary of State for Foreign Affairs] giving early accounts of Foreign Transactions. . . . He said he knew the people who wrote for this paper; and assured me I might depend upon it, that Coombe wrote "Alfred," "Tacitus," and the "Jacobin Emissaries." [These were written by Burges himself, who republished them in pamphlet form.] . . . How he procured his intelligence about Rose having recommended the paper, I do not know; but, from what he said relative to this office, I am perfectly satisfied he must have had it from some of the people employed here, who have given him a tolerably correct report of what Mr. A[ust] has said on the subject. . . . From the whole tenor of his conversation, however, it was evident that he had not the slightest idea of either of us having anything to do with it; and he was much too angry not to have mentioned such a circumstance if he had suspected it.

Topham was even angrier than the Walters, for, in return for its utter dedication to the Treasury, the *World* was supposedly under the special protection of Rose, and yet Rose had not only betrayed it, but had employed for the purpose a member of its own staff. But, although Topham regarded the *Sun* as a particular outrage, the truth was that it represented only one of a series of betrayals, for Rose had always made the *World* the whipping boy in his dealings with Burke. In mid-1793 he sacrificed it altogether.

While the other Treasury newspapers continued to ridicule the trial of Hastings, the *Sun* treated it with respect and evident sympathy, so that Burke finally had what he wanted: a newspaper which represented what he thought were the Government's true "principles" respecting that trial. But, although the *World* was now no more abusive than the other Treasury newspapers and was of considerably less consequence, Burke could evidently not forget his experiences with it in the past, for the Whigs' motion of 12 June can only be regarded as an Opposition prank. On 27 May, 1793, all the Treasury newspapers except the *Sun* had quoted a statement by the Archbishop of York to the effect "that it was impossible for him to sit silent, to listen to the illiberal conduct of the managers [of the proceedings against Hastings], that they examine a witness as if he was not a witness, but a pickpocket; and that if Marat or Robespierre were there, they could not conduct the impeachment in a more scandalous manner." Two weeks later, specifically on 12 June, 1793, Whitbread rose to move "That the said paragraphs contain matter of a scandalous and libellous nature" and that the *World* be prosecuted accordingly. Francis seconded the motion, and the Opposition withdrew to await developments. As anyone could have anticipated, the motion was at once passionately supported by Burke, and, since his speech was a plea that this time the Commons would deal with Robert Bostock himself rather than turn him over to the courts, he had obviously been told that the Government deplored Bostock's previous escapes as much as he and that the fault lay with the Attorney General. As anyone could also have anticipated, however, the Government was silent, and the House adjourned without a division. But on 20 June, 1793, the Government made amends by discontinuing its payments to the *World*, so that Burke was placated, and no one actually suffered except Major Topham. The Treasury did not suffer, for by this time Rose had wrung the *World* dry, and since June, 1792, he had been gradually transferring his activities to the *Morning Herald* and the *Public Advertiser*. At the beginning of 1793, he transferred them to the *True Briton*.

## AN END AND A BEGINNING

" 'THE SUN' was no sooner established," said Heriot,[90] "than [I] formed the plan of a daily morning paper, making the former a pedestal for the latter; and on the 1st of January, 1793, appeared 'The True Briton.' The undertaking was a bold one. . . ." But "the plan" was actually "formed" by George Rose, and in context the "undertaking" could hardly be described as "bold." The year entered its final explosive stage on 1 December, 1792, when the *Diary* reported that "The Attorney General, on Wednesday [28 Nov.] preferred seven bills of indictment for libel against publishers and printers, all of which were found true bills by the Grand Jury." On the same day a dozen men ran through the streets shouting that The Thames had been poisoned, several thousand Londoners barricaded themselves in their houses, the Duke of Richmond threw himself into the Tower, and the King called out the militia to put down an uprising of which no one saw the least evidence and the nature of which Pitt could not disclose for, as he said, security reasons. But the Treasury newspapers made it clear that there had been numerous "acts of riot and insurrection" and that they were the direct result of Paine's *Rights of Man*. While everyone was in a state of panic, Sampson Perry was tried (8 Dec., 1792) in the Court of King's Bench for the libel on the Commons, and, since it was proved that he had been the proprietor of the *Argus* at the time the libel was inserted, the jury overlooked the fact that he had been in prison at the time and brought in a verdict of guilty. A few days later he fled to France to join Frost and Paine, probably at the urging of one of the Crown lawyers; and, according to a later (26 Mar., 1795) number of the *Oracle*, "an advertisement . . . appeared in the London Gazette, December 15th, 1792, offering a reward for his apprehension."

On 13 December the King asked Parliament for legislation to restore peace and order, and by 18 December the newspapers were flooded with loyalty "Addresses" and with notices of fresh arrests. On 18 December, too, Thomas Paine, whose *Rights of Man* had supposedly incited the supposed "acts of riot and insurrection," was tried *in absentia* in Guildhall before Lord Kenyon and a special jury, which returned a verdict of guilty without leaving the room and without even waiting for the summing-up of the Attorney General. Reports of the trial appeared in all the newspapers, and the *Morning Post* devoted an entire issue (20 Dec., 1792) to it and to Paine's counsel, Erskine, whom it represented as the hero of the day. But the hero was, in fact, William Pitt, and Erskine's defense of Paine had only damaged the cause of the Opposition further. The country was now prepared to accept repressive legislation and even to welcome a war with France.[91] Everything had gone so well for the Government that on 25 December, 1792, it hurled an initial bolt at the *Morning Chronicle*, indicting James Perry, Gray, and Lambert for the publication that day of an advertisement tending to incite further "acts of riot and insurrection." According to Farington,[92] the advertisement consisted of "a seditious letter written by Dr. [Erasmus] Darwin"; according to the newspapers, it consisted of an address from a political society at Derby. At approximately the same time, the Government foreclosed on the *Argus,* the occasion for the foreclosure being the usual "trouble at the Stamp Office." The *Argus* was immediately converted into the *True Briton,* which appeared on 1 January, 1793, carrying in its masthead the motto, "NOLUMUS LEGES ANGLIAE MUTARI," and being printed by A. Wilson at the *Argus*'s address, No. 5, Catherine Street, Strand. Since priority of information continued to go to the evening *Sun,* the *True Briton* was largely ignored by the other newspapers; but it proved valuable to Rose as a replacement for the *World.* Rose's precise connection with the newspaper was not discovered until 12 November, 1796, when the *Morning Post* announced that "GEORGE ROSE [had] furnished the money necessary to give [the *True Briton*] existence"; but by that time no one actually cared, and the announcement was hardly noticed.

On 5 January, 1793, *The Times* reported that "The *Argus* newspaper was intended to be re-printed in Paris on the 1st of January. The Conductor may there give unlimited scope to his treasonable abuse of our Government." But by 1 January the *Argus* had become the *True Briton,* and so the Government had no worries that it would be "reprinted" anywhere. In any event its sole concern was to get its critics out of the country, and its sole fear was that one of them might come back. In this instance two of the trio of Paine, Frost, and Perry did.

The first was John Frost, who on 9 February, 1793, returned to England to face trial for the use of "seditious language." He was convicted on 27 May, and on 19 June his name was stricken from the list of attorneys, and he was sentenced to six months in Newgate Prison and one hour in the pillory. The *Morning Post,* which regarded this as an extremely severe sentence, was certain the King would mitigate it. For, if, it mused (21 June, 1793), His Majesty should be "informed that Mr. FROST was the Agent of Lord HOOD at the Westminster Election in 1788, which was so warmly supported by the Court, why should we wonder if he should become the object of Royal Clemency." But the *Morning Post* had forgotten that Frost had later sued Lord Hood, and it was also overlooking the fact that Frost was being made an example to discourage other Englishmen who might want to return from France, among them Sampson Perry. Frost was greeted by a large crowd when he appeared in the pillory and by a larger crowd when he was released. He was escorted home in triumph, looking, according to the newspapers, "very ill," and nothing further was said of him for several years. But on 10 June, 1797, he was suing Lord Hood again, this time to recover an additional £354, which, he said, he had promised to pay a Mr. Bradshaw in Lord Hood's behalf for services during the same election and "scrutiny." The case was again referred to "three gentlemen" (*Star,* 13 June, 1797).

By 1795 Sampson Perry was also back in England, having just spent 401 days in French prisons as an enemy alien. Although he had tried to enter the country secretly, he had hardly arrived when, according to his account,[93] a woman reported his presence in order to collect the reward offered by the Treasury, and he was therefore arrested and "committed to the most detestable gaol in London," Newgate, "because Mr. J. WHITE, solicitor of the treasury, and Mr. JONES, marshal of the *King's Bench Prison,* [would] have it so." His arrest was announced on 28 March, 1795, by the Opposition *Morning Post* and the Ministerial *Oracle.* The *Post* said only: "Thursday [26 Mar.] Captain PERRY, formerly Proprietor of a Paper called the ARGUS, was taken into custody by CARPMEAL, one of the Bow-street runners. This Gentleman was driven from this Country during the rage of prosecutions for what were deemed Libels. He has been since that time, it is supposed, in France. He was taken at Camden Town, and is to undergo an examination before the Privy Council." The *Oracle* imparted the information in the form of a lecture:

## SAMPSON PERRY

Has lately returned to town. He was formerly Proprietor of the *Argus,* and a violent reviler of Government, for which he suffered imprisonment in the King's Bench; but that by no means abated his acrimony against the blessings of the English Constitution, and in consequence he thought fit to go in search of an happier clime.

The *Jacobinical* system of France seduced him from his native country, and, in the miseries of the Revolution, he revelled for some time until he became obnoxious, *suspected* as an Englishman of being a friend of religion and Royalty.

It was then he felt the scourge which his own folly had invited. He was thrown into prison, and experienced all the horrors which massacres and perpetual dread and alarm occasioned. It was now high time to cast a longing eye to his native land. His ingenuity and enterprise gained him a passage on board a neutral ship; and he arrived in London twelve days ago, inviting the abode of Newgate as an *asylum,* rather than dwell in the land of *discordant* and *merciless freedom.*

He therefore subjected himself to be apprehended on Wednesday evening last [25 Mar.], at No. 3, Frederick's Place, Tottenham-Court Road, by those active officers of the police *Carpmeal* and *Miller,* who acted under the direction of an advertisement which appeared in the London Gazette, December 15th, 1792, offering a reward for his apprehension.

He was yesterday taken into the custody of the Sheriffs of Middlesex, on a Writ of Outlawry, and conveyed to Mr. *Wright's,* in Carey-street, where he will remain for the future directions of his prosecutors.

The conduct of this violent person, and his present situation, may serve as an useful lesson to all discontented or speculative persons in this country, who are actuated by party paroxysms rather than from prudent principles.

On 3 April, 1795, George Rose's *True Briton* added the caution: "As Captain PERRY is taken into custody, it will become a certain *poetical* Politician to *mend his pen,* lest he should chance not to be quite so *festive* as his *name* imports." The caution was directed at Sheridan, "festively" nicknamed "Sherry."

On 22 April, 1795, the *True Briton* mentioned that "Captain PERRY, who lately returned from Paris, is to be brought up from Newgate to the Court of King's Bench this day, to plead to an Outlawry issued against him in his absence." The outcome of this hearing was not reported. On 24 October, 1795, the *Morning Chronicle* advertised the first number of a fortnightly journal, published that day, entitled the *Argus; or, General Observer of the Moral, Political, and Commercial World.* The author was "Sampson Perry, editor and proprietor of the late newspaper, the *Argus*." Of this journal nothing further was said, and nothing further was said of Perry for over a year. The last bit of information comes from the *Morning Post* of 23 December, 1796: "Captain Perry, late Editor of the Argus, now lies dangerously ill in Newgate of an epidemical distemper, which at present rages with much violence in that prison, whereof many of the women have died, and many more are not expected to recover." No one knows when Perry was finally released from prison and if or when he was sentenced. He may still have been in prison in 1797. Yet during this period he wrote and somehow published *Oppression: Appeal of Captain Perry to the People of England* (1795), twenty-four numbers of the *Argus, or General Observer* (29 Oct., 1795, to 18 May, 1796), *An Historical Sketch of the French Revolution* (1796), and possibly the *Origin of Government* (1797).

Sampson Perry was completely mistaken about Sheridan, who certainly did not subvert the *Argus*. But Sheridan's efforts to save the Opposition newspapers were frustrated by the events of December, 1792, which broke the morale of the Whigs. Since the Whigs were too discouraged to spend further money on newspapers, the Opposition lost, not only the *Argus,* but the *Oracle,* which, at the beginning of 1793, reverted to the side of the Government and was more solidly Ministerial than it had ever been before. On 5 February, 1793, John Bell, who had evidently resumed the conduct of the newspaper, was finally summoned to receive the judgment of the Court of King's Bench for having published the two libels on the Guards. He did not appear, and, according to *The Times* (6 Febr., 1793), the "process of the court was taken out against him." But, now that he had made his peace with George Rose, the Court was ready to make its peace with him, and so the matter was peacefully adjusted. The nature of the adjustment was revealed by the *English Chronicle* of 7–9 March, 1793: "A public apology from Mr. John Bell, Proprietor of the *Oracle,* for a Libel which appeared in that Paper against the three regiments of the Guards, and for which he had been convicted in the Court of King's Bench, was, on Tuesday morning [5 Mar.], read on the Parade in St. James's Park. This apology had been previously accepted by his Royal Highness the Duke of York and the Officers; the prosecution of course subsides." Bell was now free to begin his long and desperate struggle to retain possession of the newspaper.

At the beginning of 1793, therefore, the Treasury controlled nine daily newspapers: the *Diary,* the *Morning Herald,* the *Oracle,* the *Public Advertiser,* the *Public Ledger,* the *Sun, The Times,* the *True Briton,* and the *World.* Of the seven newspapers which the Opposition had controlled in early 1789, it had lost all but three, the *Gazetteer,* the *Morning Chronicle,* and the *Morning Post,* and had added only one, the tepid *Star,* now the evening edition of the *Chronicle.* The *Daily Advertiser* had withdrawn from politics altogether. One of the Opposition newspapers, the *Morning Chronicle,* was already under indictment for libel, and another, the *Morning Post,* was facing an uncertain future, now that the Weltje-Tattersall lease was no longer in effect. All of them would have serious financial problems, for there would be little money to be got from the Whigs, and all of them could expect further trouble with the Government. Since eighteenth-century newspapermen were not generally remarkable for stupidity or integrity or bravery, the Opposition press might well have ceased to exist at this point. But, in fact, it survived and even prospered. Partly perhaps because of personal loyalties, partly, no doubt, because of the sheer animal excitement of playing such a desperate game at such desperate odds, the *Gazetteer,* the *Morning Chronicle,* and the *Morning Post* remained firm in their convictions, and other newspapers arose or tried to arise to take the places of those which had disappeared.

Even at the beginning of 1793, the Opposition press was better off than it appeared to be. Of the Treasury newspapers, the only two which were at all formidable were *The Times,* which was now selling almost 3,000 copies a day,[94] and the *Sun,* the circulation of the once-powerful *Morning Herald* having declined to perhaps 1,500 a day. The *Public Ledger,* now edited by Alexander Chalmers, the *Public Advertiser,* still conducted by Henry Sampson Woodfall, and the *World,* now managed by Isaac Swan, were kept alive only by Treasury subsidies, and the *Oracle* was in financial straits. The *Diary* was presenting another kind of problem, for the contrived panic of 1 December, 1792, had frightened William Woodfall in a way Pitt had not intended. Although the *Diary* continued to denounce the radical reformers, it was thereafter somewhat sympathetic with the cause of moderate reform, so that its position was tending to converge with that of the *Morning Chronicle.* Meanwhile, although the *Gazetteer* was losing ground, the *Morning Post* was making a small recovery, and the *Chronicle* was growing apace. There was also very little the Government could do about the *Chronicle,* for the paper was still receiving financial assistance from the Whigs, and it was too cautious to get into trouble. Although the Government had secured an indictment against James Perry, Gray, and Lambert, its case against them was so weak that it did not bring them to trial until 9 December, 1793, when they were acquitted.

One of the newspapers which attempted to join the Opposition daily press was the *Observer; or Sunday Advertiser,* which was content to remain a weekly until the *Sun* began "to garble the debates of Parliament and to send them into the world in such a state as to bias the minds of the unwary in favour of whatever measure the ministry may think proper to adopt, and against whatever may derive from real independence." Since it seemed to the proprietor of the *Observer,*[95] then William S. Bourne, "that a real opposition should be given to this paper" and since no other newspaper was providing the "opposition," he wrote to William Adam on 13 November, 1792, suggesting that he convert his "weekly publication to an every day one," dedicated to "detecting misrepresentation and correcting error." "In consequence of a situation I hold in the Post Office I shall [also] be enabled to counteract in a great degree the exertions which are making to extend the circulation of the Sun throughout this kingdom," he added. Adam evidently gave him no encouragement.

The *Courier* was another matter. This newspaper had a predecessor in the *Cabinet,* a morning newspaper, which was begun on 2 January, 1792, the printer being C. Macrae, Charing Cross. But the *Cabinet* was discontinued after a few numbers, and on 22 September it was replaced by the evening *Courier,* which was printed by R. Harris, No. 38, Charing Cross. "The Literary *Cabinet-makers* who failed some months ago, have again opened their shop in the West end of the town, as *Curriers,*" the *Oracle* observed sarcastically on 25 September. The reason for the *Oracle*'s sarcasm was that the conductor of the *Courier* was its own former editor, the Rev. Charles Este. The *Courier* had evidently been financed by John Parry, but Este was probably also a proprietor. For, since he still possessed his "valuable MS. so materially necessary to the due *controul* of [such a] concern, and which . . . would make the fortune of a Paper" and since he certainly had a free hand to manage this paper as he pleased, one may suppose that he had exacted the same terms from Parry as he had previously exacted from Topham. One of Este's assistants was Thomas George Street, heretofore known only as author of the pamphlet *Aura; or,*

*The Slave, a Poem* (London, 1788) ; but one can credit Street's statement (*Courier,* 11 Jan., 1811) that he had nothing to do with the early policy of the *Courier,* being "a mere servant on a salary, under the controul of the Proprietors."

Since Este intended to support the *Courier* by extortion, the paper was not dependent upon either political party for financial support, but he was also unwilling to forego any possible advantage; and, since he was *persona non grata* with the Government, he offered the *Courier* to the Whigs. The nature of the offer is evident from the following letter,[96] written by Robert Adair, addressed to William Adam, and dated 12 October, 1792:

> A few days before I left town I had the offer of a new evening paper made with a request that I would communicate the proposal. It is called the *Courier,* and as yet has taken no decided line. The proprietors intend next February establishing a daily morning paper of the same name and so to run them both upon the plan of the *Morning Chronicle* and the *Star.*
>
> The person who made the proposal is Mr. Este the clergyman. He asks no money either now or hereafter, but a living *when we come in;* and for this I think he will take my assurance . . . verbally given.
>
> . . . . Certainly we have no party paper at present, and the objections to commencing one are in some degree obviated by finding this already set up and in some decent degree of circulation. I own I am for it, as it is become absolutely necessary to curb the insolence of [James] Perry. Perhaps some such vigorous measure on our parts would reclaim that insufferable coxcomb.

Adam did not hesitate. For, although Este was not the ideal conductor of a "party paper," he did have one quality which the Whigs were beginning to value above all others: the ability to keep a newspaper alive by his wits. Hence, by the beginning of 1793, the *Courier* had joined the *Gazetteer,* the *Post,* and the *Chronicle-Star* as the fourth Opposition newspaper. Three of them had already played a valiant role in the struggle for freedom, peace, and human sanity: the four were to play an even more valiant role in the years which immediately followed.

# APPENDIX I

# From the *Oracle*, 1 June, 1789

### JOHN BELL
### TO
### THE WORLD

PUBLIC *and positive Accusations require ample Refutation: Truth and Character ought to be supported:—even the most insignificant individual has a claim on public opinion; if his actions are generous and just, he has a right to public protection. It is on this principle I wish to build my Fame. I am now at issue on the question, immediately with* EDWARD TOPHAM, *Esq. and collaterally with* MILES PETER ANDREWS, *Esq. and Mr.* CHA. EDW. WILSONN. *It is with reluctance, however, that I sacrifice so much of my first paper to explanations respecting myself; but in order that my positions may be clearly maintained, it is necessary that I should descend to Particulars.*

---

J. BELL's *Hand-Bill was distributed on Sunday,*      7
*May* 10, *and the contents appeared also in*
*the Public Papers on Monday, May* 11, *viz.*

---

#### A NEW NEWSPAPER
will be published on the First of June 1789.
The Title will be announced shortly.

THE ARRANGEMENTS *are now preparing on a* LARGE *and*
LIBERAL SCALE.

J. BELL, of the BRITISH LIBRARY, *Strand*, respectfully informs the Public, that he is no longer interested, directly or indirectly, in the Newspaper, which he originally instituted and established, under the Title of THE WORLD, as even the printing thereof has been rashly and unhandsomely withdrawn from him by CAPTAIN TOPHAM.—J. BELL, at present a free, and he hopes an irreproachable agent, therefore means to submit a NEW DAILY PAPER to the Patronage of the Public.

His PLAN will be novel, interesting, and useful. If long experience—extensive literary connexions—the most immediate and unbounded sources of intelligence, and a proper stile of communication, can warrant a hope of attraction—all these qualifications the Publisher has to offer in his favour. Every exertion shall be made to gratify Public Taste, and completely to answer the best purposes of a Daily Print—

"Tis not for mortals to command success,
"But we'll do more, Sempronius, WE'LL DESERVE IT."

*Extract from* THE WORLD *of* May 11.
## TO THE PUBLIC.

The great increase of the commercial Business of this Paper, has of late made it inconvenient to have the Advertising Office and the Printing and Publishing Offices detached: On these accounts, for the accommodation of the Public, the following arrangements have taken place:

The Great White House, No. 335, opposite Somerset House in the Strand, is now The World Office.

Till Monday next, Advertisements will be received at the Old Office, the Corner of Exeter Change; and all Orders and Letters may be sent there till that day.

After that day, the Great New House before mentioned, which will then be the only Office, will alone receive Advertisements, etc.

The WORLD of this day, is printed, as its Readers will see, on an entire New Letter. The beauty of it has to boast Mr. Caslon as its Founder. It has been some months preparing with the utmost care.

*From* THE WORLD *of* May 14.

An Hand-Bill having been distributed through the Town, with the name of J. BELL at the bottom of it, in which were these words—"That the Printing of this Paper had been unhandsomely withdrawn from him by Captain TOPHAM;"—we can from our own knowledge say, that the express conditions of the legal agreement were complied with, by which Captain TOPHAM had a right to order the Printing of his Paper to be where he chose, and to be taken when he chose, away.

That such was the agreement, signed by each Party, when Captain TOPHAM paid the said J. BELL the sum of Four Thousand Pounds, for the share given by him in the first instance to the above J. BELL, in the origin of the Paper.

And we for ourselves say, that on the part of Captain TOPHAM, we made, as the legal agreement specified, a tender of purchasing the Letter, Presses, and Materials formerly used in the Printing of this Paper, with which offer Mr. BELL declared he was satisfied, but declined accepting it.

We have further to add, that we have not, nor never had, any interest or concern whatever in this Paper.

MILES PETER ANDREWS.
CHARLES EDW. WILSONN.

*London, May* 13, 1789.

The PROPRIETOR of THIS PAPER would have held the above in his own mind perfectly needless; but as some people, from want of due information,

might judge wrong, it was held proper to publish it. In removing his
PROPERTY to his own premises, he intended to take care of it: if he has been
mistaken, he alone is to blame.

---

### J. BELL's STATEMENT *of* PREVIOUS FACTS.

---

### ORIGIN *of the* WORLD.

In the year 1786, having sold my Shares of the *Morning Post,* and reserving to myself a perfect freedom and irreproachable liberty to act as I pleased
with respect to any new undertaking whatever—about the month of June,
Captain TOPHAM being casually at my House, I communicated to him my
plan and resolution of publishing a NEW PAPER on the first of January following; with the observation, that I had declared such resolution previous to
my having parted with my property in the *Morning Post.* Captain TOPHAM
then approved of my resolution, and proposed himself as a Partner in the
undertaking. My terms were concise: to this effect, and nearly in the same
words—"Sir, I will not risque one shilling of my own property to my proposed
undertaking: I consider my experience, my judgment, the time and fatigue
which I must necessarily devote to the establishment, as equal to any sum of
money that can be required: I therefore propose to reserve *one fourth share*
of the property, whatever it may be, and to admit *Partners* for the rest, who
will advance to the extent of two thousand pounds, if required, to be appropriated, *at my discretion,* but solely to the establishment of the paper: if
the property should not succeed at the end of twelve months, or if the two
thousand pounds should be sooner expended, then every party should be at
liberty to relinquish any further concern in the property.—After a few days
consideration, Captain TOPHAM agreed to my terms, and reserved *three
fourth* parts to himself. A few weeks afterwards, I perceived that the *fatigue*
of the establishment would principally rest on myself; I thought *one fourth*
part of any *possible* success, would be very inadequate to my deserts, considering that the money to be advanced would be merely a loan, if the property succeeded, as it was to be returned out of the first profits. I therefore
proposed to make my share one *third* of the *whole,* by taking an additional
twelfth, subject to a proportionable pecuniary risque. Captain TOPHAM
acquiesced. The agreement was concluded. The plan, as suggested and conducted by myself, was carried into execution. It was continued under our
joint direction until the 31st of December last, when I sold my property
therein.

### THE SALE

Was agreed on between us; Captain TOPHAM chusing to become a purchaser on my terms, rather than a seller at the price I offered him—*My terms
were expressed as follows:*

I will receive four thousand pounds for my one third share of the News-paper.

I will continue to print the Paper on terms which any Printer of reputa-tion will print it.—I enforced the Printing of it, as being materially necessary to my own pursuits in business, and therefore a consideration with me not to be departed from. To all this Captain TOPHAM readily acceded. On the Conveyance being considered, Mr. CHARLES EDWARD WILSONN was present—an idea was stated, that the Printer of a Newspaper might have it in his power to injure the property of his employer; but in order to obviate those appre-hensions with respect to myself, I proposed to bind myself in a penalty of one thousand pounds, not to cause, or suffer any injury whatever to his property, that could be in the power of any Printer to prevent:—at the same time declaring, that I would not bind Captain TOPHAM to continue the Printing longer with me than he should find it his interest to do so; farther, that if required, he should take any Printing Materials at a fair valuation, if ever he should determine to remove the Printing: *observing also emphatically, as I had always declared before, that understanding I was about to sell my Shares, I would not part with them without its being clearly understood, and fully agreed, that I should retain the privilege of Printing a New Paper, or of being concerned in any old one, at any time whatever.*

These declarations were answered by Captain TOPHAM and Mr. WILSONN, that notwithstanding I was then about to sell my property to him (Captain TOPHAM) *he considered me at liberty the next moment to be concerned in, or to set up, one or one-and-twenty Papers, if I chose. He observed, it never could, nor ought to be, a matter of objection in his mind; and therefore, I was then, and always should be free, in his opinion, to do as I liked about Papers, notwithstanding I had sold my Shares to him.*—This being under-stood, we parted friendly. The bargain was confirmed, with declarations from Captain TOPHAM, that he hoped we should be better friends than ever:—he should never think of removing the Paper so long as I would undertake to print it:—that I might still retain the privilege of writing what I chose in it; and he should endeavour to answer the purposes of my business in the Paper, as much as if I was still a Proprietor.

The mutual professions and declarations at this meeting, as above stated, were seemingly considered by the parties present, as friendly and sincere, and perfectly consonant to the wishes of each other—but mark

## THE SEQUEL.

I was with a friendly party near CHELMSFORD *three days after the preced-ing transactions;* and was sent for by Captain TOPHAM to the *Black Boy Inn,* where he had stopped, accompanied by an intimate friend of his, on their way to COWSLIP HALL.

## INTRODUCTION.

Captain TOPHAM—"Ah, Mr. BELL, I am very glad to see you: very cold weather:—come sit down.—Well, Mr. BELL, I have been considering about this business: you know we are very good friends; and I wish to continue good friends:—I hope we shall be better friends than ever.—I think printing a Newspaper is no object to you; your concerns are of so much more consequence; and therefore, it had better be taken from you: you know I wish to serve you; besides, *this Paper,* you know, is of such consequence, and you may still do as you like in it. Pray how long will you be casting a new Type? you know that it is a great object: I shall always have my Types of you; and that, you know, will be of great advantage; besides, *this Paper,* I think it had better be printed altogether, as the *Herald* is[;] besides, the *thing,* you know, is in the agreement. I have a legal right to remove the Paper when I please, you know; and therefore the *thing* is settled. I shall stay in the country a few weeks; and of course *the thing* can be done and ready. You and I, I am sure shall be always good friends. You know *this Paper* is of great consequence, and you shall do as you like: you can say what you please in it, and have your advertisements displayed as you like; and therefore, Mr. BELL, *the thing* had better be done." After having attended to a repetition of this jargon uninterruptedly for near half an hour, I begged leave to remark as follows:

*Sir, Printing the Paper is an object to me; it was the second and material condition of our agreement, although I voluntarily declaimed [sic] binding you to any penalty, after having proposed one from myself in your favour, supposing that your promise would be equal to my written obligation.*

*However, I am happy, Sir, to meet you on this occasion in the presence of your own friend. I shall make but few remarks, and I beg they may be strongly impressed on his mind, and fully answered by yourself, in order that we may not be misunderstood, nor misrepresented in future, without having the advantage of an appeal.*

*Q.* by J. BELL.—Have you given directions already for removing the Paper, and are you resolved on it?

*A.* Capt. TOPHAM.—I have given directions for a house to be found and taken for the purpose.

*Q.* J. BELL.—Have you any cause whatever to complain, either in reference to myself, or to the conduct of my Printers, or on any other account whatever, to justify so sudden a change?

*A.* Capt. TOPHAM.—No cause of complaint whatever. It is in the written agreement, and I wish to have the Offices together.

*Q.* J. BELL.—And now, Sir, it was also understood by all parties, on signing the agreement, that you can have no cause of complaint whatever, nor right of censure hereafter, should I now, or at any time hereafter set up a

NEW DAILY PAPER. Is it so understood by you, and do you retain the same opinion?

*A.* Capt. TOPHAM.—You are at liberty to set up twenty Papers if you please, at any time; and are as perfectly at liberty on that account, as if we were entire strangers to each other.

J. BELL.—Permit me now to observe, this resolution of your's is extraordinary, and surprises me much; but, nevertheless, you have my free consent to act as you please. I will not only release you from the obligations of taking my Printing Materials, but I will Print your Paper as long as you please, until you can get properly accommodated; and if possible, I will be more watchful and diligent to preserve and serve your property, than I was in the time of our partnership. I will assist you in completing your arrangements, if you determine to remove;—but on the day of your removal, I will announce my resolution of starting a *New Daily Paper,* which shall be published as soon afterwards as possible. I do not mention this as a threat to alter your purpose, but merely to advise you of the consequences. I am very happy to hear you acknowledge it was understood, and still remains your opinion, that I have not only a right, but your free permission, to Print and Publish another Paper whenever I please.

Captain TOPHAM, after some pause and confused conversation, observed, that as he found from my manner and explanation, that Printing the Paper was an object to me, and that I considered it of serious consequences in reference to my general business, he should from that time relinquish all ideas of removing it; and therefore desired I would think no more of what had passed.

It is not necessary at present to refer to dates; but I believe Captain TOPHAM remained at COWSLIP-HALL more than a month.—In the mean time, the Rev. Mr. ESTE did me the honour of a visit, for the first or second time in his life. The purpose was to inform me, that he had received a letter from Captain Topham, wherein he desired me to be assured, that the *Paper should remain with me, and that I might set my heart at rest.* I explained to Mr. ESTE the conversation which had passed, and the *history of my own life* [a reference to Este's *My Own Life* (London, 1787)], so far as respected the Origin and Printing of THE WORLD. He was pleased to acknowledge, that I had acted perfectly right; that my manner was candid, and evidently sincere. He said that the Printing *ought to remain,* and *should remain with me.*

I thought but little more of the subject, and heard still less, until Captain TOPHAM's return to Town. On the first interview, he shook me by the hand, and said he had desired Mr. ESTE to call and assure me that he should never think of removing the paper.—In answer, I said it was very well; I was then in a hurry, and had not time to talk with him on the subject, nor was it material.

From that day until the *ninth of May last,* which was the day of the PAPER BEING REMOVED, I never had the least knowledge, directly nor indirectly, of any such intention. At my breakfast hour, I was informed that the Paper was to be removed in the afternoon. In the meantime, two friends of my own accidentally came into my shop on business, and were in conversation with me on the arrival of MILES PETER ANDREWS, Esq. and Mr. CHARLES EDWARD WILSONN.—After desiring the *Ambassadors* to be unreserved, for they might consider the Gentlemen present as common friends, Mr. WILSONN opened his *Credentials* by saying, they came from Captain TOPHAM, to acquaint me with his resolution to remove the Paper in the afternoon, and that he was ready to take my Printing Materials at a fair valuation, according to the *Bond* of Obligation; observing farther, they were not material to Capt. TOPHAM's use or convenience, as he was completely prepared to Print his Paper, at the *Great White House,* on the next day.

## CONVERSATION.

J. BELL.—Gentlemen, this business requires farther explanation. I have questions to ask, which in my opinion can only be answered to my satisfaction and your conviction by Captain TOPHAM, and therefore I will send for him.

Mr. ANDREWS and Mr. WILSONN.—It is unnecessary to send for Captain TOPHAM; he will not come.—and we can take upon us to answer any questions you can propose respecting this business.

J. BELL.—I shall not be satisfied without Captain TOPHAM's presence. I *will* therefore send for him, and if he will not come hither, I beg that we may all wait on him.

Accordingly a message was sent off to that purport to Captain TOPHAM, who returned for answer, that he was engaged with a particular friend, and therefore could neither come to my house, nor see the party at his own.

I then addressed myself to Mr. ANDREWS and Mr. WILSONN, in the presence of my own friends, to this effect:—Gentlemen, finding that Captain TOPHAM will not give me the meeting, it is necessary for me to ask whether you are fully in possession of Captain TOPHAM's sentiments and resolutions: Whether you are competent to answer my questions with as much decision as Captain TOPHAM; and whether you will pledge yourself for Captain TOPHAM's acquiescence with your answers?

*Answered* by Mr. WILSONN and Mr. ANDREWS.—We are competent to answer any questions respecting this business:—We know Capt. TOPHAM's motives and sentiments, and we will pledge ourselves that Captain TOPHAM will acquiesce in our answers and observations.

Q. J. BELL.—Has Captain TOPHAM any cause whatever, directly or indirectly, to complain of the management or printing the Paper, or otherwise in reference to myself, or to any person concerned under my direction in the Paper?

A. by Mr. WILSONN.—None in the world: no cause of complaint whatever. —Captain TOPHAM's only reason for removing is, that the business of the

Paper is increased; he finds it inconvenient to have the Printing-Office and other Offices separate; he wishes to have them all together; and that is his only motive. He has it in his power by the articles of agreement to take the Printing away whenever he pleases, and we are now come to say that Capt. TOPHAM is ready to take your Printing Materials at a fair valuation. They are not, however, necessary to his purpose; he is prepared completely to Print his next Paper.

This observation and declaration were confirmed, and repeated nearly in the same words by Mr. ANDREWS.

Q. by J. BELL.—Mr. WILSONN, you were present at most of my agreements with Capt. TOPHAM, and therefore must remember, that I am at perfect liberty to set up any other Newspaper. Can you and Mr. ANDREWS now answer for Capt. TOPHAM, that he is sensible of that privilege; and do you, as the friends of Capt. TOPHAM, answer for him, and for yourselves, that there will be in your minds and his, no right of censure, should I set up another Paper immediately?

A. by Mr. ANDREWS and Mr. WILSONN.—You, Mr. BELL, have as much right to set up a New Paper, or as many Papers, as you please, and when you please, as any one of us; Capt. TOPHAM understands it so; he can have no objections; he has none:—you are as much at liberty as the greatest stranger to him.

Observation by J. BELL.—Now, Gentlemen, I am satisfied. You have pledged yourselves, from a perfect knowledge of Captain TOPHAM's sentiments, that he has no cause whatever of complaint against me, or dissatisfaction with one or any part of my conduct:—he still considers me at perfect liberty to act as I please with respect to Newspapers. I now tell you, as Captain TOPHAM is provided with Printing Materials, he will not have occasion for mine; I will therefore relieve him from the expence of purchasing them, and keep them myself; and I further declare, that I will immediately announce my resolution of starting another paper as soon as I possibly can; but I beg you will present my Compliments to Captain TOPHAM, and assure him that I will not take any advantage of his illiberal and unhandsome treatment: I know it is not in his power to print his paper on Monday without great difficulty and much risque—I therefore request you to inform him, that he may continue to print it in my house till his arrangements are complete and perfectly convenient to himself; or if he has any objections to continue the printing in my house for a few days, I desire he will accommodate himself with any conveniences that I have; send to my office for any articles that will be useful to him; and I will render him any personal services, if needed, until his arrangements are complete—but tell him also, I am at this moment decided and determined to start a NEW PAPER.

Mr. ANDREWS and Mr. WILSONN took their leave by observing, that my conduct was explicit, liberal, and candid throughout. This was on Sunday morning the 10th instant, from which moment I have strictly adhered to my declarations and intentions.

On Saturday afternoon [16 May], I found that Captain TOPHAM, and Mr. WILSONN, who has acted as the *cunning* Agent throughout all the business, had *outwitted* themselves—they had provided Printing Materials, but they had not provided any workmen to use them; they had, I am persuaded very unintentionally, laid themselves at the feet of my mercy; they had depended on SEDUCING all my men from my service at a moment's notice, without even the common civility of asking my permission.—Captain TOPHAM provided a dinner on the same day [10 May], to entertain them, and for the first time, invited them into his service, although his Paper was to be printed the next day, without having any other Printers to depend on. It is the rule of law in the Trade, that no Printer shall leave his employer without giving a fortnight's notice, and therefore it was absolutely impossible for Captain TOPHAM to have printed his Paper for many days afterwards, without my concurrence.—Instead of acting by Captain TOPHAM at that crisis, as I am persuaded Captain TOPHAM would have acted by me, in exchanged situations, I suffered my men to serve him, and actually assisted him by the loan of many articles, without which he could not have printed his Paper on Monday at the necessary hour —for which, indeed, I have never had even his Thanks, nor any other return from him than ILLIBERAL INSINUATIONS.

In drawing up this state of facts, I have obtruded, I fear, on the patience of my Friends and my Patrons, the public—they had a right to an explanation from me: I have given it with truth, though in tedious terms; however, sufficiently explicit, I hope, to warrant my former assertions.

*In reference to the Advertisements of* J. BELL *and Capt.* TOPHAM, *which are inserted in the preceding part of this account, I will presume to draw the following*

### CONCLUSIONS.

First, I hope it will not be considered in the opinions of any one, as too *severe* an epithet to say, that Captain TOPHAM *unhandsomely* withdrew the Printing of the old WORLD from me; which, with the addition of *rash*, was the only charge I made against him in my first Advertisement. The rashness of the measure, I apprehend, is *self-evident, even to himself* at present.

*In reference to* MILES PETER ANDREWS, *and* CHAS. EDW. WILSONN:

It will appear that they have subscribed an assertion, to the truth of which they were entire strangers—or, knowing the circumstances, they have asserted as a fact, what they at the time of subscribing knew to be an UTTER FALSEHOOD; for, if there was any *giving* of Shares of the old WORLD, in the first instance, in the origin of the Paper, *I was the giver,* and *not* the person *given to.*—I invited Captain TOPHAM to the enterprize; I dictated the terms; I suggested the plan; carried it into execution; was principally instrumental in establishing and supporting it:—my services were more than equal to the stipulated loan, the extent of which however, was only 600*l.* and which was refunded to him, according to agreement, out of the profits of the Property;—and therefore *if any gift was in the question, I was the generous donor.* Those who know Captain TOP-HAM, *will not even suspect him,* I believe, *of giving,* or being *liberal,* where an advantage can be *taken.*

I acknowledge my declaration of *being satisfied,* when the tender was made by Messrs. ANDREWS and WILSONN for the purchasing my *letter, presses,* and *materials:* but *that* satisfaction, as already expressed by myself, went only to the answers they had given to my questions, and *not to the conduct* of Captain TOPHAM, as they would willingly and *fallaciously* have implied in their Advertisement.

Captain TOPHAM certainly had a legal right to remove his own property to *his own premises,* where he may take care of it—if it should suffer, *he alone is to blame;*—but I believe any other person would have taken it away in a much more open, more *manly,* and in a *handsomer* manner: for it can be proved that he and Mr. WILSONN have been *plotting* and *planning their cunning measures* ever since the 31st of January last, although they have been acting ever since with the *duplicity* of apparent friendly confidence and professions of esteem, to the most obedient Servant of the Public,

J. BELL.

# APPENDIX II

## From the (Spurious)
## *Star, and Evening Advertiser,*
## 13 February, 1789

### P. STUART'S REASONS
### FOR ABANDONING
### THE EXETER-STREET STAR

Although it be an irksome task for an humble individual to obtrude himself upon the public attention, yet when my professional character and rectitude of conduct are attacked and abused, I have too great confidence in the
liberality of an unbiassed people, to hesitate in appealing to that justice and
impartiality. Conscious that by the decision of my fellow-citizens I shall stand
or fall, a plain statement of unquestionable facts is best calculated for a refutation of my insidious enemies. I shall therefore be as brief as is consonant with
perspicuity. Should I happen, by a misconception of opinion, to deviate from
truth, my infallible opponents possess a sufficiency of politeness to check my
digression.

About a twelvemonth ago, I left the MORNING POST. I formed then an idea
of establishing an EVERY EVENING NEWSPAPER. Being in the habits of friendship,
or at least intimacy, with a certain BOOKSELLER [the elder John Murray], I
communicated to him my plan. He approved of it. Besides, with all the apparent warmth of a friend, he requested me to add his name to the list of
proprietors.

I cannot help owning, that I was so partial to his professions of regard, that
although several pointed out the ROCK, my unsuspecting nature drove me on
it, as the BEACON of my HOPES.

It is natural for youth [Peter was twenty-eight or thirty] to place a confidence in age; especially when such age seduce by trivial attentions, well-timed
and consequently properly applied. Notwithstanding, therefore all the strong
hints from a late celebrated Historian of an unfortunate Queen [Gilbert Stu-
art]—notwithstanding living Historians fully confirmed his declarations—
Still was I so much infatuated by the blandishments of this man, that my ears
were shut against all advice and reproof.

No sooner, however, was the undertaking begun, than I was convinced
partly of my error; but the person alluded to, finding that I would not sacrifice

the interest of a general concern to his particular views, and that his attempts at overbearing were treated by others, as well as myself, with contempt, he absented himself for several months from all meetings, which caused harmony to become fixed, and THE STAR rose subsequently by that happy event, and strong exertions, to its present pre-eminence as the *first* EVENING PRINT.

It is common to court a fortunate man, or a successful undertaking. Thus it proved with my friend. A few weeks since, he returned—knowing the STAR to be THEN in the *city phrase* A GOOD THING, to the meetings;—and appeared so contrite, that I could not help commiserating his former error, flattering myself that it was only the effect of a hasty temper, when the senses were intoxicated, and the heart at rest wrapped up in its own integrity.

But soon I was undeceived. Whenever this man found that he had lulled me, as he thought, he then set about forming in return for my kindness, a phalanx against me, or at least, to render my situation so disagreeable, that no gentleman could hold it any longer, under such trammels, who pretended to the least spirit or manly sentiment.

He duped another of his own profession [William Lane], to lead by EPICUREAN INTRIGUE, the rest of the PROPRIETORS into his own INTERESTED views. The BAIT took. If *conviviality* sometimes overcomes the understanding of the SKILFUL, it is no wonder that the unsuspected [*sic*] heart, unhackneyed in the ways of men, should be MISLED.

In the present lamentable situation of national affairs,

## POLITICS,

Should be tenderly and impartially treated, by the great engine the PRESS, which is our MODERN MAGNA CHARTA of BRITISH LIBERTY.

It is the duty, therefore, of the CONDUCTOR of a paper, to keep it as free from the rancorous bias of PARTY, as patriot frailty will admit. I am conscious that I have been actuated by this principle.

The above BOOKSELLER [Murray], and his *duped* colleagues wrote me a letter, that "I must support Mr. PITT, *through* THICK *and* THIN." These were their elegant expressions. And in order to do this completely, they sent me a number of paragraphs, some of which were even *wretchedly spelt,* against His ROYAL HIGHNESS the PRINCE of WALES!

My nature revolted at these *literary scavengers,* when they endeavoured to make me the *assassin* of *my* PRINCE.

As to Mr. PITT, several parts of his conduct I respect, and I am conscious that my feeble aid has been occasionally exercised in his service. But then it has been with the freedom of a MAN—not by compulsion—but by conviction.

Besides, must the PRINCE of WALE's [*sic*] *reputation* be wounded, in order to support the Minister "through thick and thin?" I am sure that if Mr. Pitt did not spurn this base act of such *hostile* flatterers, he ought to forfeit all claim to the support of society.

But to be brief—These men carried it by a majority, that I was to act according to their dictates—that is, to *stab* through the medium of *my name,* every person whom their dastardly minds chose to assail.

How did I act? as there is no honour to be held with the vile, I apparently acquiesced, that I might, at a future period, be prepared to do myself justice. It is here necessary to observe, that the LITERARY GENTLEMEN connected with me, joined to my own exertions, raised THE STAR from nothing to ABOVE TWO THOUSAND daily. When it was thus raised, as we deemed it a most dishonourable act to fetter our will, at the same time expecting our exertions, we prepared for the worst. Still, however, we hoped that the rest of the Proprietors would open their eyes to the arts of these men. But unfortunately they thought otherwise. For last night—as an act of gratitude for my indefatigable labour to accelerate the interests of their property—they generously DISMISSED ME AT A MOMENT'S WARNING.

I have now only to add, that THE STAR, which I now print and conduct, shall never be pledged to any man or set of men, to *assassinate* for them "through thick and thin," but if possible it shall increase in IMPARTIALITY, in CANDOUR, and in TRUTH.

On these grounds only I hope for the continued patronage of the PUBLIC, for whenever THIS PAPER deviates from IMPARTIALITY, I am sure that it will soon dwindle into its original obscurity.

Notwithstanding all my laudable exertions, my conduct has been arraigned. For what? Because I have raised the consequence of THE STAR to the eminence which the most sanguine proprietor never could believe it would have arrived to—because I have been actuated by principles of impartiality —and because I have censured and praised Mr. Fox and Mr. PITT for particular measures, and supported as far as my feeble talents could effect, the PRINCE of WALES, and every friend to the BRITISH CONSTITUTION. This is the full extent of my offence, for which I am obliged at this time to appeal to my best friends the Public, not doubting but that they will protect the injured, and preserve me from the machinations of oppressors and rapacity.

As Printer and Conductor, I thought I always possessed a discretionary power to act for the general benefit of the Proprietors. I therefore adopted those measures which I found necessary for their interest. When the Paper increased daily in sale, I apprehend that there was no reason for complaint.

I shall not be the first to mention the names of any individual proprietors; but if they think proper to sport them as a sanction for their proceedings, every transaction shall be sifted to the bottom, and those who are connected shall be again called upon to condemn the malefactors.

To prove to the PUBLIC the purity of my intentions, I declare, that should ALL MY FRIENDS wish for a reconciliation, I shall be very happy to re-unite with them on amicable terms; and whoever shall express himself to that effect before TOMORROW EVENING, shall be accepted with every testimony of cordiality.—But I can never consent to relinquish the power and controul to TWO VERY HONOURABLE MEN [Murray and Lane], whose measures, I am well informed, have within these few days sunk the sale of the Paper between *two and three hundred a day*.

I am the PUBLIC's most obedient,
Very humble servant,
P[ETER] STUART.

No. 9, Feather's-court,
Drury Lane.

# APPENDIX III

# From the (Spurious)
## *Star, and Evening Advertiser,*
# 16 February, 1789

## TO THE PUBLIC

It is with much regret I was compelled to enter into a newspaper altercation with two *honourable men,* who attempted to make me instrumental in
*assassinating* the character of the PRINCE of WALES and HIS FRIENDS. In vindication of my conduct, I solicit, for a few moments, the attention of the community, while I state the STUBBORN and UNQUESTIONABLE FACTS that must
completely refute the malignant and scurrilous invectives which the *Proprietors* of the *Exeter-street Dog Star* have thought proper to publish.

If low ribbaldry and unfounded assertions be admitted as solid argument,
the Addresses in the glimmering *Dog Star* have every claim to the approbation of an enlightened people. Mr. Murray and Mr. Lane—two very respectable Booksellers—are pleased to say, that the LATE PUBLICATION of *The
Star,* and the complaints concerning the irregular delivery of the paper, proceeded from my mismanagement. To this charge I plead *not guilty.* The late
publication, and all the disagreeable consequences of it, resulted from the
wretched parsimony and avarice of *certain* ACTING PROPRIETORS, who, very
often, when every operation of the day was completed for the press, WOULD
NOT ADVANCE ONE FARTHING FOR STAMP-PAPER, TO SAVE THE PROPERTY FROM
DESTRUCTION! By these unfortunate circumstances, the existence of the concern was for sometime in a very doubtful state, the Printer not receiving *one
sheet* of stamped paper, *till nearly the hour appointed for publication.* About
two months ago, it was with the utmost difficulty *The Star* made its appearance. The principal Clerk applied to the ACTING PROPRIETORS for cash to
purchase the necessary number of stamps for the Day. His earnest solicitations
were treated with contempt, and these CONFIDENTIAL GENTLEMEN peremptorily *refused to give the least pecuniary assistance* for the SALVATION of the
PROPERTY, although he represented to each, the very dangerous state of the
concern; and had not a very worthy friend granted a loan for IMMEDIATE RE-
LIEF, the existence of the Paper must have that day terminated. That amiable
and spiritual gentleman has made several applications to be refunded the sum
lent, but has not yet been able to obtain his money. The testimonies of *sixteen*

or *eighteen* persons now employed about *The Star,* will corroborate my assertions.—So much for the LATE PUBLICATION!

Ought these men, then, to be entrusted with the direction and controul of a valuable concern, when it must be evident, that by the spleen and caprice of the moment, they might totally destroy the trust reposed in them.

AS TO THE NEWSMEN—it is an incontrovertible truth, that the ACTING PROPRIETORS invited them to a FEAST, and, after supper, when the President had complimented them with all the oratorical flowers of *Leadenhall Market,* those very ACTING PROPRIETORS, thinking themselves in their Star-Chamber Committee, *abused, assaulted,* and *wounded* many respectable NEWSMEN, their WIVES, and CHILDREN!—This was verifying the old adage—*inviting them to a feast, and sticking the visitants with the spit!*

The Proprietors of the *Dog-Star* seem to lay much emphasis on my acting in the sole capacity of their SERVANT, but their treacherous memory deserves reprobation, when they forget to mention, that I WAS THE ORIGINAL and PRINCIPAL PROPRIETOR, and made them PARTNERS in the PROFITS of an INVENTION ENTIRELY MY OWN, and whose property—*united, indeed, with my own*—I had, by my faithful and unwearied exertions, improved to a degree beyond their most sanguine expectations. In return for these benefits which I have conferred upon them, Mr. Murray and Mr. Lane—two very honourable men— seduced my Brother Proprietors to combine against me, and, like a GROUP OF INGRATES, to *force* from me MY RIGHT of CONTROUL and SUPERINTENDENCE in the insertion of what articles I thought most advantageous for the *good of the Proprietors at large.* But this was not all—*"your orders are, that you must* SUPPORT *Mr.* PITT THROUGH THICK AND THIN—*reprobate and condemn Mr.* FOX *and Mr.* SHERIDAN, *as enemies to their country—and asperse and vilify the* PRINCE *of* WALES *and a certain amiable Lady* [Mrs. Fitzherbert], *as foes to Mr.* PITT *and* HIS ADMINISTRATION!*" If any person entertains the most distant shadow of a doubt with regard to these bitter truths, my instructions, with PARAGRAPHS and LETTERS in the HANDWRITING of these MISERABLE SCRIBBLERS, are in my custody, for the inspection of the curious. I have it in contemplation to print the articles alluded to—gibbet forth their calumny to posterity with their own respective signatures—which, to use their own gentleman-like language, in the *Dog-Star,* "will blast their names for ever!"

These worthy men have the impudence to call my RIGHT of PRINTING ANOTHER STAR in question! I despise the greatest efforts of their malignity. Dare they deny that I WAS THE PROPRIETOR AND ORIGINAL INVENTOR OF THE STAR, and received them into a partnership of whatever profits should accrue from the undertaking? But the two Papers are perfectly distinct properties—The *Dog Star* has nothing to recommend it but by a wretched imitation of my original plan—and STUART's STAR is supported by ALL THE LITERARY TALENTS and CONNECTIONS which the *Dog Star* Proprietors *inadvertently* declare "have hitherto distinguished him [*sic*] beyond his contemporaries."

With regard to the question of RIGHT—Supposing *A* is the original inventor and proprietor of any particular species of manufacture—Not having a sufficiency of money to carry his plans into effect, he admits into PARTNERSHIP with him *B* and *C*.—*A* advances one thousand pounds as a proportion for his share—*B* and *C* advance also one thousand pounds each, as their proportions. *A* ONLY being capable of managing for the general interest, is entrusted with the *unlimited controul* and direction of the whole.—By *A*'s activity, knowledge, and indefatigable perseverance, the property becomes important and lucrative. *B* and *C* acknowledge *A*'s talents, integrity, and success; but, say *B* and *C*—*who are notoriously ignorant of the business in which they have embarked*—although we acknowledge your uncommon success with the PUBLIC, yet, because we, (*B* and *C*) have received *certain considerations* for an experiment, WE,—AS THE MAJORITY—instantaneously deprive you of the CONTROUL and DIRECTION of that property which we cannot deny YOU ONLY have established, and insist, that you form your manufacture in a different manner from that which has hitherto distinguished your endeavours—*A* remonstrates firmly and decisively on the folly of the measure, and foretells that the adoption of it will be immediate ruin—*B* and *C* reply, "WE ARE the MAJORITY—know better than you how to conduct the business—therefore notwithstanding YOU WERE the ORIGINAL INVENTOR and PROPRIETOR, and still continue to be a PROPRIETOR and the CONDUCTOR, we immediately—*at a moment's warning,* and without any pecuniary consideration for your faithful service—dismiss you from the management and direction of that property which your talents and industry have raised, because you will not act *cordially* for the destruction of it—*A* finding himself dismissed ON ACCOUNT OF ESTABLISHING THE PROPERTY, and DISCHARGING THE TRUST REPOSED IN HIM WITH FIDELITY—has recourse to that mode of defence which the LAW of NATURE has afforded, declares his resolution of commencing BUSINESS FOR HIMSELF, rather than have his share involved in ruin, and puts the evil machinations of his illiberal partners to defiance. This is a statement correctly analogous to the subject of dispute.

To that property, which owed its existence and establishment to me, and in which I WAS A PRINCIPAL PARTNER, I could not be considered in the mere capacity of a servant. I never had abandoned MY RIGHT OF CONTROUL. All the allurements and plausibility of my BROTHER PROPRIETORS could never force me to commit a suicide on my reputation, by tamely publishing the scandalous and miserably-written libels which were sent to me against the PRINCE of WALES, whose character is an honour to humanity, and whom every good subject of HIS MAJESTY looks to with respect and admiration.

To support Mr. PITT or any other MINISTER, through THICK and THIN, would be an infamous prostitution of that confidence which the Public has given me. I shall never be dragged into the degrading trammels of a party, and tamely become the despicable tool of the unprincipled attempts of its most abandoned and dastardly retainers. Through the medium of my name, they wished to stab the most distinguished and respectable characters in the kingdom; and trembling at the expectation of their own outrages against the Laws of society, they sheltered themselves under the mask of MERCANTILE HONOUR and INTEGRITY!

I am the PUBLIC's most obedient,

Very humble servant,
P[ETER] STUART.

No. 9, Feather's-court,
Drury Lane,
February 16.

# APPENDIX IV

# From the *Star, and Evening Advertiser,* 16 February, 1789 (Reprinted from the *Star* of 14 February, 1789)

## PROPRIETORS' ADDRESS TO THE PUBLIC

The Proprietors, from the Conduct of their Servant the late Printer, had reason, for some time past, to believe that he had, for *certain considerations,* upon his own authority, agreed to change the Line of their Paper and carry the Influence of the STAR to support a Faction inimical to the Interests and Prosperity of this Country. The Complexion of the Paper from day to day just-tified their Suspicions, and they came to various Resolutions, to which the Printer himself acceded, to prevent his design, and to preserve Public Virtue and Consistence of Character. Still, however, there appeared a tendency in their Conductor to counteract their Views. And what was worse, it was at last reported, that in order to insure success to this virtuous scheme, he had con-ceived a Design hostile to the whole concern, by a New Print: to the destruc-tion of the present Property of his friends, who had embarked in it with a view purely to give him employment. A Design so treacherous and unprincipled, it was imagined could not be harboured in the breast of a man, who had been recommended, countenanced, and employed, chiefly from the opinion enter-tained of his integrity. And the Proprietors were pleased to find, that when openly called upon, he totally and unequivocally, disclaimed, all such profli-gate intentions. And in testimony of his abhorrence of the design imputed to him, the execution of which would render his name infamous, he agreed to, and signed the following Resolutions with twelve other Proprietors.

5th *Feb.* 1789

RESOLVED,

"That the line of the STAR shall in future be kept in favour of Mr. PITT and his Administration, and all the Minutes upon this subject are approved and confirmed.

And further, the Printer being conversed with upon this point, declares he will keep the line of the Paper PALPABLY in favour of Administration, and in future draw cordially with the majority of Proprietors.

And further, the Printer has declared that he has at present given up every idea of an interest in any other Newspaper, and never will be concerned in any adventure of that kind, the execution of which will impeach his character for dishonour with the present Proprietors."

    (Signed)        P. STUART.

After the settlement of these minutes, the Proprietors met again on the 12th, when Mr. Stuart once more disclaimed all engagements with any other Paper. Now, Reader, mark the Sequel.

On the 13th, Mr. Stuart . . . PRINTED a new Paper in EXACT IMITATION OF THIS; which from undoubted proofs had been long in preparation; in order to usurp, or to grasp the whole property for the emolument of himself, and a few desperate associates.

It is true that Mr. Stuart, after long forbearance and lenity, had been discharged on the 12th as Printer of the Star, for repeated acts of Disobedience, Contumacy, and Breach of Promise. And he will no doubt adduce this necessary step of the Proprietors, as an apology, or in extenuation of his guilt. . . .

It would be folly in the extreme, to waste time in loading a man of this Complexion with the epithets he deserves. He excites greater pity in the breasts of the Proprietors than indignation; they lament the sudden and total corruption of a heart they once placed confidence in; and . . . they take leave of the friendship and services of Mr. Peter Stuart for ever.

# APPENDIX V

# Letters from "An Injured Man"

FROM THE (SPURIOUS) *MORNING STAR*, 29 APRIL, 1789

*To the* ELECTORS *of* GREAT BRITAIN, *but* ESPECIALLY *to those of*
WESTMINSTER. CORRUPT INFLUENCE by a PERSON VERY HIGH in
ADMINISTRATION, CLEARLY PROVED!

[The Writer] Being *employed* by the PERSON alluded to, in the WEST-
MINSTER ELECTION, there is a CONSIDERABLE BALANCE *owing* him,
for which, as being *responsible* to *others,* he was by them ARRESTED!

Immediately on this, he sent a very polite letter to the person, *informing*
him of his SITUATION, and requesting that *debt* and *costs* should be immediately discharged. To this, however, he has as yet received no answer, although
EIGHT WEEKS have elapsed! unless, indeed, of late, when a SOLICITOR
for the STAMP-OFFICE [John Frost] *came* to him, *acknowledging* the
DEBT, but offering, at the same time, such terms of accommodation as no
man of honour could accept.

Still, however, has the injured party never given up the *name* of this
MAN HIGH IN OFFICE, but has undergone the ignominy of supposed embezzlement, merely to save that OFFICIAL MAN's *character.* For a minute
disclosure of the whole transaction must not only hurt him in the public estimation, but *sully* the CHARACTER, too, of the HIGHEST in the government, from this peculiar circumstance, that the FIRST SUM *advanced* could
*not* be given, until the *principal came in from riding,* which was actually the
case.

A *candid* statement of the whole shall be given in this Paper, which shall
. . . throw an *indelible stain* on SOME *characters,* hitherto high in esteem for
their supposed virtue. . . .

The . . . writer . . . has not taken this step until *nine weeks* after the
arrest.

. . . . [It] would surely be madness . . . to allow the CONSEQUENCE
of the arrest to *continue,* merely to preserve A NAME longer *secret,* that
evades the payment of a just debt*, and throws it on an agent, who refused
payment at one time, while he has lately offered to compromise it. The
GREAT MAN was the SOLE EMPLOYER, and not the agent, in the debt
alluded to.

Proofs, the most unequivocal, shall be produced. . . .

It may be of more consequence to the WESTMINSTER ELECTION,

than *thousands* of *bad votes*. It may be of much consequence, likewise, in *opening* the *eyes* of the PEOPLE, to perceive clearly, that MALIGNITY and IN-JUSTICE exist in the *bosoms* of *those* who are *deemed* PURE and IMMACU-LATE!

AN INJURED MAN.

*The name of the injured man is left with the Printer.*

* As a proof of its justice, he gave 50*l*. of it in *part payment*, by a draught on his Banker.

FROM THE (SPURIOUS) *MORNING STAR*, 2 MAY, 1789

LETTER II. *From* "AN INJURED MAN" *to* GEORGE ROSE, *Esq., One of the* SECRETARIES TO THE TREASURY.

Sir,

The GENTLEMAN, to whom I alluded, as being *out a-riding*, was MR. PITT.

Did *you* not tell *me*, in his house, at DOWNING-STREET, that you *could* NOT ADVANCE the *money* to *carry* on the ELECTION-*business* until HE *came in?*

Did I not wait there, by your desire, for an hour and a half, until Mr. PITT came in, by the *garden-stairs*, into the ROOM where *I was;* and did you not, in *two* MINUTES, come out to me *with the* MONEY?

Did I ever say to you, that this was *public* MONEY? . . .

As to calling upon you, by desire, at the Archbishop of CANTERBURY's, in *Lambeth*, I shall wave [*sic*] that for the present.

AN INJURED MAN.

FROM THE (SPURIOUS) *MORNING STAR*, 6 MAY, 1789

LETTER III. *From* "AN INJURED MAN" to GEORGE ROSE, *Esq., One of the* SECRETARIES TO THE TREASURY.

Sir,

As a proof that you have *acknowledged* the DEBT,

Did you not give me, in *part payment*, a *draught* on COUTT's, Bankers in the Strand, for *fifty pounds?*

Let their BOOKS be examined, if *your* name and *mine* do not appear together in the draught.

Did you not, at your house *near* LYNDHURST, *New Forest*, HAMP-SHIRE, declare to me, that you had given orders to Mr. FROST, through Mr. ESTCOURT, to merge *your* account in the *general business?*

Did you not, before the CHRISTMAS Holidays, promise, upon your *word of honour,* that you would give me ALL, or PART?

Did you not go out of town, in VIOLATION of your word of honour, without giving me all, or part?

. . . . Did you not order Mr. STEELE [Thomas Steele, the other Secretary of the Treasury] to send me an *apology* for your *breach* of PROMISE?

Did he not, in consequence, send Mr. [William] CHENNERY to me, your *private* SECRETARY, with an assurance of my bill being discharged, or the greatest part of it, when you came to town?

Were those repeated promises ever performed?

Did I, notwithstanding, remind you, even *once,* of your *neglect,* until I was ARRESTED for *your* DEBT?

Did you take any notice of MY APPLICATION, until seven or eight weeks thereafter, when you *obliquely* ordered Mr. FROST to *compromise* with me, which he certainly ATTEMPTED[?]. . . .

Do you imagine that you are a *Secretary* of FRANCE—instead of being a *Secretary* of ENGLAND?

Do you think that ENGLISHMEN can *bear* the BASTILE, even in their *minds,* without HORROR? . . .

AN INJURED MAN.

## FROM THE (SPURIOUS) *MORNING STAR,* 14 MAY, 1789
### LETTER IV. *From* "AN INJURED MAN" *to the Right Honourable* WILLIAM PITT.

Sir,

Whether or not it was proper in your Secretary, Mr. ROSE, to interfere in the WESTMINSTER Election, by disseminating *his* most low and violent abuse of Opposition, is not now the question. But ought he not to have honourably discharged all those debts which were contracted in promulgating *his* ribaldry?

In extenuation of his conduct, it must be confessed, indeed, that the *official* man who could thus *descend* to interfere by publishing scurrility, might afterwards endeavour to forget to pay for it. . . .

I cannot, it is true, charge you with participating in his conduct. . . .

To prove . . . the justice of my demand on your confidential man, in my next letter I shall publish the PARTICULAR INCIDENTS on the account. This, I presume, will even be more entertaining than Major [John] SCOTT's *Morning Herald* BILL. It will likely promote, too, considerable laughter at your table, as some of the company may recollect their own abortions in the perusal of these *items.*

I shall afterwards *republish* some of the most singular of *these* BALLADS,

&c. when I . . . shall convince the world . . . that Mr. ROSE and his friends, are not only good *poets,* but are perhaps unrivalled in the more refined *classical* compositions of HAND-*bills,* HAT-*bills,* as well as POSTING-*bills.*

When I have stated the whole, with suitable remarks, I shall then *sue* Mr. ROSE for the debt.

I wish much that you may soon advise a *parliamentary dissolution,* as then I could *repay* your SECRETARY a debt of *durance,* which I most certainly owe him. If he did not choose to discharge *his debt* to *me,* I should, in that case, most punctually discharge MY DEBT TO HIM.

AN INJURED MAN.

### FROM THE (SPURIOUS) *MORNING STAR,* 19 MAY, 1789

LETTER V. *From* "AN INJURED MAN" *to* GEORGE ROSE, *Esq., One of the* SECRETARIES TO THE TREASURY.

Sir,

Although I pledged myself to the public, that I would THIS DAY bring forward my reason of *delay,* I shall, on THURSDAY adduce *sufficient reasons* to them that I am at present not FULLY PREPARED.

However, not to disappoint their EXPECTATIONS and *your* FEARS, I have published, underneath, the *duplicate* of *one* of MY BILLS to you.

BREAKFAST *afterwards* with what *appetite* YOU MAY!

G. ROSE, Esq; DEBTOR.

Duplicate of a Bill delivered, of 1471. 8s. 6d. Part of which Mr. ROSE has paid. The Particulars are as follows:

| 1788 | | £. | s. | d. |
|---|---|---|---|---|
| July 20 | To 250 WORDS *in point,* a large posting bill | 1 | 7 | 6 |
| | To 200 ditto, on writing-paper in 4$^{to}$ | 2 | 5 | 0 |
| | To 2000 HOOD and TOWNSHEND | 2 | 5 | 0 |
| July 21 | To 3000 *Roast Beefs!* | 3 | 18 | 0 |
| | To 1000 *Vicar of Brays* | 1 | 15 | 0 |
| | To 1000 *Contests* | 1 | 5 | 0 |
| | To 1000 *Deaths and Liberty!* | 1 | 6 | 0 |
| July 22 | To 500 *Courts* at the *Shakespeare,* a posting bill | 1 | 11 | 6 |
| | To 1000 *England's Glory!* | 1 | 6 | 0 |
| | To 1000 *Dingy Jacks* | 1 | 6 | 0 |
| | To 1000 *Hoods for ever!* | 1 | 6 | 0 |
| | To 1000 *Inscriptions for Covent-Garden Church-yard!* | 1 | 15 | 0 |
| | To 4000 *Jack Townshend's* HONOUR | 6 | 0 | 0 |
| July 24 | To 3000 *Political Conversations* respecting *Dingy Jack* | 3 | 7 | 6 |

|  | £. | s. | d. |
|---|---|---|---|
| To 2000 *Hoods and Glory!* | 2 | 12 | 0 |
| To 2000 *more Dingy Jacks* | 2 | 12 | 0 |
| To 2000 *more Hoods for Ever!* | 2 | 12 | 0 |
| To 3000 *Westminster Election abuse,* posting-bill | 4 | 10 | 0 |
| To 2000 *more Townshend's* HONOUR | 3 | 0 | 0 |
| July 25  To 1000 *Flash Songs* | 1 | 6 | 0 |
| To 1000 *more Courts at the Shakespeare,* posting-bill | 3 | 3 | 0 |
| To 3000 *more Vicar of Brays* | 3 | 18 | 0 |
| To 3000 *more* of *Dingy Jack's political Conversations* | 3 | 7 | 6 |
| July 26  To 750 *more Flash Songs*—and 750 *more Hoods for Ever!* | 1 | 19 | 0 |
| To *twenty-two thousand* HAT *cards,* of No Fox!—No TOWNSHEND!—No *White-boys!* | 33 | 0 | 0 |
| To 1000 JACK TOWNSHEND's *Bottle of Wine,* and **Butter** | 1 | 15 | 0 |
| July 27  To 1000 more *Bottles of Wine* and *Butter* | 1 | 15 | 0 |
| To 500 *Electors* for *Westminster* | 0 | 15 | 0 |
| To 100 *more Electors* for *Westminster* | 0 | 3 | 0 |
| To 500 *Serious Addresses* against DINGY JACK | 0 | 15 | 0 |
| To a *thousand* OUTRAGES, by *Dingy* Jack, and his Crew | 1 | 5 | 0 |
| July 28  To 1000 *more Bottles* of WINE and BUTTER | 1 | 6 | 0 |
| To 1000 more *Vicar of Brays* | 1 | 15 | 0 |
| To 750 more *Flash* Songs, and 750 more *Hoods* for **ever!** | 1 | 19 | 0 |
| To 500 more *Electors* for *Westminster,* ballad paper | 0 | 12 | 6 |
| To 500 more HOODS and TOWNSHENDS, *ballad paper* | 0 | 12 | 6 |
| July 29  To 1000 more *Flash Songs* | 1 | 6 | 0 |
| To 1000 more Hoods for ever! | 1 | 6 | 0 |
| To 500 *Dingy Jack* Townshends, ballad paper | 0 | 12 | 6 |
| To 4000 more *Flash Songs* | 5 | 4 | 0 |
| To 4000 more *Hoods for Ever* | 5 | 4 | 0 |
| To 1500 Letters on Covent Garden Inscriptions | 2 | 12 | 6 |
| July 30  To 1500 *Choice Spirits,* posting bill | 2 | 12 | 6 |
| To 1500 *Cockers* and *Bates* | 2 | 12 | 6 |
| To 1500 Rotation Reids | 2 | 12 | 6 |
| To 1000 more *Bottles* and *Butters* | 1 | 6 | 0 |
| To 2000 more *Choice Spirits* | 3 | 10 | 0 |
| To 2000 more *Flash Songs* | 2 | 12 | 0 |
| To 2000 more *Hoods for Ever!* | 2 | 12 | 0 |
| July 31  To 2000 more *Choice Spirits* | 3 | 10 | 0 |
| To 1000 *Ways and Means of Blues and* **Buffs** | 1 | 6 | 0 |

|                                      | £.   | s.  | d. |
|--------------------------------------|------|-----|----|
| Aug  1  To 1000 more *Choice Spirits* | 1    | 15  | 0  |
| To 1000 more *Flash* Songs           | 1    | 6   | 0  |
|                                      | £147 | 8   | 6  |

The above is only the *bare record* of a CLERK. I shall afterwards . . . *expand, explain* and *confirm*.

AN INJURED MAN.

FROM THE (SPURIOUS) MORNING STAR, 23 MAY, 1789

LETTER VI. *From* "AN INJURED MAN" *to* GEORGE ROSE, *Esq., One of the* SECRETARIES TO THE TREASURY.

Sir,

My reason of DELAY, was in order to sift a malicious report to the bottom, which some of your adherents had circulated, respecting the OPPOSITION exciting me on to a publication of these letters.

I am sorry that I cannot trace it yet up to the *high source* from whence I suppose it originated. But in order to prove the fallacy of such a paltry rumour, I deemed it proper, yesterday, to go to GUILDHALL, and make the following

AFFIDAVIT,<br>Before Mr. ALDERMAN SWAIN.

I, ——, the author of the *Letters* inserted in the MORNING STAR, under the signature of *An Injured Man*, solemnly swear, that I have written them of my *own accord*, in order to *expose* Mr. ROSE, for not paying *all* my ELECTION BILLS.

I further swear, that I am not *impelled* to the writing of THESE LETTERS by any *individual* or *individuals* of the OPPOSITION, as has been *falsely reported;* and that they know nothing of the business, through me, directly or indirectly, excepting what they may read in this paper. For though I have been always a *faithful* AGENT, I scorn to be the *mean* TOOL of any set of men whatever.

*Sworn at the Guildhall,*

*London,*

*May 22, 1789. . . .*

*The Original is left with the clerk of* THE MORNING STAR OFFICE, *for inspection.*

 . . . . [I have only] to add . . . that I received the following FLASH SONG, from *your hands,* at Mr. PITT's, in order to be published.

It has since undergone, you know, some alterations; and is sung at the CONSTITUTIONAL CLUB, the very first at every meeting.

A FLASH SONG,

*Sung at the* SHAKESPEARE *by a* MEMBER *of the* WHIG CLUB.

I am a sturdy Beggar, a Patriot, and a Whig;
I go to Clubs, and know the rubbs, I'm up to all the rig.
   *And a begging we will go, we'll go, we'll go;*
   *And a begging we will go.*

..............................................................................

In my next, I shall endeavour to bring forward some more of those *elegant* productions I received from you.

AN INJURED MAN.


FROM THE (SPURIOUS) *MORNING STAR*, 29 MAY, 1789

LETTER VII. *From* "AN INJURED MAN" *to* GEORGE ROSE, *Esq., One of the* TREASURY SECRETARIES.

Sir,

Before I republish any more of your ELECTIONARY ABUSE, it is necessary to pause a little upon what I have advanced; besides touching lightly on ANOTHER BILL, and but lightly, as indeed, you liquidated it *daily*.

Having a total disregard for the dignity of your office, . . . you first voluntarily *send* for a person to become your AGENT in the Westminster election, and afterwards you honourably endeavour to *trick* him out of the debt which he contracted on your account!

Is this, Mr. ROSE, just? How must your immaculate master, the MINISTER, feel on this disagreeable business, as you remember that you were then so *poor*, that you could not advance the first sum until, as I hinted before, Mr. PITT came in from riding. . . .

It has been reported to me, that you have abused Mr. FROST for not liquidating the remainder of your bill. I shall not touch upon that at present, as I mean to make it the subject of a FUTURE LETTER.

But what can THE PEOPLE think of *you*, Sir, a Treasury Secretary, and indeed the very *Mungo* of MINISTRY, to issue out the most *low abuse* against Lord HOOD's *opponent*, and all the OPPOSITION, by *misrepresentation, fallacy,* and *slander*, while you are now, with the most bare-faced *mock patriotism*, endeavouring to *invalidate* HIS ELECTION!

Had you behaved as honourable [*sic*] in discharging the bill of 1471. as you was in discharging your BALLAD-SINGERS, &c. bill of about 6001. your actions might have still escaped censure, owing to that secrecy to which every agent feels himself bound, when his employer endeavours not to defraud him.

But my candour can easily frame an excuse for you. The BALLAD-SINGERS, *cum multis aliis*, could not, or would not, go on without *daily* pay. Even some of your own PRINTS, as you termed them, (for you boasted that you had all but the HERALD and GAZETTEER) would not obey the *gratis nod* of your PRIVATE SIGNATURE, but insisted on *double price,* as it was ELECTION TIME.

Now, from this it is easy to perceive, that you liquidated the *large* bill *daily,* from POLITICAL NECESSITY.

While having the *small* bill upon *credit,* you have *honourably* evaded payment from PRIVATE *principle.*

May 28.                                                AN INJURED MAN.

## FROM THE (SPURIOUS) *MORNING STAR,*
### 13 JUNE, 1789

LETTER X. *From* "AN INJURED MAN" *to* GEORGE ROSE, *Esq., One of the* SECRETARIES TO THE TREASURY.

Sir,

It is well known to many, besides yourself, that the present Administration have been hitherto supported in their places, not by the rectitude of their measures, but by the *newspaper puffs* of their numerous retainers. You confessed to me, last summer, that you commanded every MORNING PAPER except the *Herald* and the *Gazetteer.* As I doubt that you included the GENERAL ADVERTISER, by mistake, this was exactly *seven* to *three....*

Rightly calculating that you have by no means now the command of the MORNING PRINTS, in the last year's proportion of *seven* to *three,* and craftily foreseeing that the impolicy of your measures may soon withdraw others from supporting you, there is no step so effectual to secure you from obloquy, as *gagging* . . . the free and bold press of England [by means of a new tax]. . . .

But if, Sir, in your resentment for the late conduct of THIS PRESS, so justly exerted against you, instead of endeavouring to cramp all the newspaper presses in Britain, for the boldness of THE MORNING STAR, you should have confined yourself to it alone [*sic* sentence].

Or, if you meant to have only checked the *licentiousness* of the press, why not put a *two-penny* stamp upon every *posting-bill, hand-bill,* and *ballad,* during *election-time.*

Had you taken this step last year, you know we are both certain that by your *own publications,* in the *late* WESTMINSTER ELECTIONS you *yourself* would have *paid* a REVENUE of *some thousands* into Government, instead of having *expended one.*

AN INJURED MAN.

# APPENDIX VI

# Chronological Table

**1772**

21 October        Samuel Taylor Coleridge is born at Ottery St. Mary.

2 November       The Rev. Henry Bate (Dudley), the Rev. John Trusler, John Bell, and others begin the *Morning Post*. The paper is conducted by Bate and supports the Government. Daily newspapers already in existence are the *Daily Advertiser* (est. 1730), conducted by J. Jenour; the *Gazetteer* (est. 1735), conducted by Charles Say, probably edited by Edward Benson; the *Public Advertiser* (est. 1752), conducted by Henry Sampson Woodfall; the *Public Ledger* (est. 1760), edited by the Rev. William Jackson; the *Morning Chronicle* (est. 1769), conducted by William Woodfall. All newspapers support the Wilkes faction. The newspaper tax is 1*d.*, advertisement duty 2*s.*, and newspapers are priced at 2½*d.* Lord North, a Tory, is First Minister, the Earl of Sandwich being First Lord of the Admiralty, Lord Thurlow Attorney General, Sir Fletcher Norton Speaker of the Commons, and Fox having a subordinate position in the Treasury.

**1773**

*c.* 1 January     William Faden leases the *Public Ledger* for three years, Jackson continuing as editor.

15 March         Goldsmith's *She Stoops to Conquer* is produced at the Haymarket.

10 June          Parliament passes the Regulating Act for the administration of East Indian affairs, the first Governor General being Warren Hastings and the first Chief Justice being Sir Elijah Impey.

16 December      The Bostonians dump three cargoes of tea into the harbor.

**1774**

11 February       The Commons orders Henry Woodfall to appear at the bar in connection with a letter printed in the *Public Advertiser*, signed "STRIKE—but HEAR" and containing a libel on the Speaker. Woodfall appears on 14 February and identifies the person who submitted the letter as John Horne (Tooke). Woodfall and Horne are arrested,

|  | but not tried, Horne being released on 18 February, Woodfall on 24 February. |
|---|---|
| 16 February | Fox moves that William and Henry Woodfall be indicted ex officio for having published in the *Morning Chronicle* and the *Public Advertiser,* respectively, a libel on the Constitution, contained in a letter signed "A South Briton"; the motion is approved. |
| 24 February | Fox quarrels with the Tories, is dismissed from office, and allies himself with the Rockingham Whigs. |
| c. 27 February | Fox sues John Williams, publisher of the Ministerial *Morning Post,* for libel. |
| 7 March | The King sends a message to Parliament regarding "the outrageous Proceedings at Boston"; the harbor is subsequently declared closed. |
| 4 April | Oliver Goldsmith dies in London. |
| 9 July | Williams, publisher of the *Morning Post,* is convicted of having published a libel on Fox. |
| 11 July | William and Henry Woodfall are convicted in King's Bench of having published libels on the Constitution in the Opposition *Morning Chronicle* and *Public Advertiser* and are later sentenced to three months in King's Bench Prison and fined 200 marks each. |
| 12 August | Robert Southey is born at Bristol. |
| 21 November | John Williams is sentenced to one month in King's Bench and fined £100 for having published a libel on Fox. |

*1775*

| 17 January | Sheridan's *The Rivals* is performed at Covent Garden. |
|---|---|
| 30 January | Walter Savage Landor is born at Warwick. |
| 10 February | Charles Lamb is born in London. |
| Late winter | Dr. Samuel Johnson publishes his *Journey to the Western Islands of Scotland.* |
| 19 April | Beginning of war with the American colonies. John Almon collects American "intelligence" for sale to London newspapers. |
| July | Charles Say dies, his possible successor as conductor of the *Gazetteer* being John Huddleston Wynn. |
| 10 November | Lord George Sackville-Germaine becomes Secretary of State for the Colonies. |
| 16 December | Jane Austen is born at Steventon, Hampshire. |

*1776*

| 1 January | H. Randall becomes conductor of the *Public Ledger,* Jackson continuing as editor. |
|---|---|

| | |
|---|---|
| Late winter | Edward Gibbon issues the first volume of his *Decline and Fall of the Roman Empire,* the final volume being issued in 1788. |
| 4 July | The American colonies declare their independence. |
| 6 July | The newspaper tax is increased to 1½*d.*, the price of newspapers to 3*d.* |
| November | William Cooke begins the *General Advertiser,* which supports the Wilkes faction. |
| 4 November | News-vendors and other ex-employees of the *Morning Post* begin the spurious *Morning Post,* which is conducted by George Corral and Edward Cox. |
| 14 December | The spurious *Morning Post* ceases publication. |
| *c.* 17 December | Randall, printer of the Opposition *Public Ledger,* is convicted of having printed libels on the Government respecting the American war and is later (Febr., 1777) fined £100. The *Gazetteer* had also been indicted, but the prosecution was dropped because of Say's death. |

*1777*

| | |
|---|---|
| | James Perry joins the staff of the *General Advertiser* as paragraph writer, but is soon advanced to conductor. |
| 16 January | Sheridan's *School for Scandal* is produced at Drury Lane. |
| *c.* 21 October | The Rev. William Jackson quits the *Public Ledger.* |

*1778*

| | |
|---|---|
| 10 April | William Hazlitt is born at Maidstone. |
| 16 June | Lord Loughborough replaces Lord Thurlow as Attorney General, Lord Thurlow becoming Lord Chancellor. |
| July | Mary Say, printer of the Opposition *Gazetteer,* is indicted ex officio for having printed a libel on the Constitution. She pleads guilty. |

*1779*

| | |
|---|---|
| Spring | Dr. Johnson issues the first four volumes of his *Prefaces Biographical and Critical to the Works of the Most Eminent English Poets,* the final six volumes being issued in 1781. |
| 19 April | Fox demands the removal of the Earl of Sandwich. |
| 23 April | Lord Bristol demands the removal of the Earl of Sandwich. |
| 25 April | Mary Say, printer of the *Gazetteer,* is fined £50 for having printed a libel on the Constitution. |
| 25 November | John Almon begins the *London Courant* in the interests of the old Wilkes faction, the editor being Hugh Boyd. |

*1780*

| | |
|---|---|
| 6 April | The Commons passes the Dunning Resolution, committing itself to reducing the power of the Crown. |
| c. 11 April | Middle-class liberals organize the Society for Promoting Constitutional Information, otherwise called the Constitutional Society. |
| 24 April | The Duke of Richmond files suit for libel against the printer of the Ministerial *Morning Post,* Robert Haswell; the action is later dropped. |
| 29 April | The Duke of Richmond files suit for libel against the conductor of the *Morning Post,* the Rev. Henry Bate. |
| 1 June | The advertisement duty is increased to 2*s.* 6*d.* |
| 2 June | The Gordon riots against the Papists begin. |
| 22 June | The Rev. Henry Bate is convicted in the Court of King's Bench of having published a libel on the Duke of Richmond. |
| 11 July | James Wallace replaces Lord Loughborough as Attorney General. |
| 19 September | The Rev. Henry Bate quits the *Morning Post,* his successor as conductor being J. Jackman and his successor as principal shareholder John Bell. |
| 1 November | Sheridan enters Parliament as Member for Stafford and immediately assumes management of the press for the Rockingham Whigs. |
| 1 November | The Rev. Henry Bate begins the *Morning Herald* in the interests of the Rockingham Whigs, Bate being conductor and Dennis O'Bryen probable editor. |
| Autumn | John Henley Wall becomes editor of the *Gazetteer.* |
| c. December | The King arranges an annual subsidy for the *Morning Post,* which still supports the North Government. |

*1781*

| | |
|---|---|
| 1 January | The King leases the *Morning Herald,* which shifts to the side of the North Government. The probable editor through 1783 is Alexander Chalmers. |
| 20 January | The *Noon Gazette,* conducted by Vincent Trehearn, Jr., is in existence by at least this date. |
| June | George Crabbe publishes *The Library.* |
| June | John Almon quits the *London Courant* and politics in order to avoid a prosecution for libel involving the Russian ambassador. Hugh Boyd also quits, the *Courant* being turned over to John Stockdale. |
| 25 June | The Rev. Henry Bate, quondam conductor of the *Morning Post* and present proprietor of the *Morning Herald,* |

|                  |                                                                                                                                                                                                                                                                                                                                                                                                                                                                                                                                                                          |
| ---------------- | ------------------------------------------------------------------------------------------------------------------------------------------------------------------------------------------------------------------------------------------------------------------------------------------------------------------------------------------------------------------------------------------------------------------------------------------------------------------------------------------------------------------------------------------------------------------ |
|                  | is sentenced to twelve months in King's Bench Prison for having published a libel on the Duke of Richmond. |
| 4–5 July         | Numerous printers are sentenced for having accused Ivan Simolin, the Russian ambassador, of stock-jobbing: among them Joseph Cooper, printer of the *London Courant,* who for originating the libel is sentenced to twelve months in King's Bench and one hour in the pillory and fined £100; Vincent Trehearn, printer of the *Noon Gazette,* who, for attempting to justify the libel later, is sentenced to eighteen months in prison and fined £100; James Barr, printer of the *Morning Herald,* who is sentenced to twelve months and fined £100; and Mary Say, printer of the *Gazetteer,* who is sentenced to six months and fined £50. |
| Mid-August       | The *General Advertiser* is sold to William Parker and is henceforth subsidized by the Rockingham Whigs. The new conductor is Parker, the editor Dennis O'Bryen, James Perry being dismissed. |
| *c.* 18 September | John Almon secretly resumes conduct of the *London Courant,* now in the pay of the Rockingham Whigs. The new editor is John Miller. |
| 18 September     | John Miller, editor of the *London Courant,* is arrested for having published a libel on the Russian ambassador when he was printing the *London Evening Post.* |
| 19 October       | The American war ends with the surrender of Lord Cornwallis at Yorktown. |
| 28 November      | John Miller, editor of the *London Courant,* is sentenced to twelve months in prison for having published a libel on the Russian ambassador, having been denied counsel and trial by jury. |
| Late December    | *Morning Post* and *Morning Herald* shift their support from Lord North to Lord Shelburne. Major John Scott commences his journalistic activities in the *Morning Herald,* which therefore abuses Burke and glorifies Warren Hastings. |
| *1782*           |                                                                                                                                                                                                                                                                                                                                                                                                                                                                                                                                                                          |
| 21 January       | The *London Courant* absorbs the *Noon Gazette.* |
| 20 March         | The North Government resigns. The King now controls only the *Morning Herald,* the *Morning Post* having joined the other daily newspapers in supporting the Rockingham Whigs. |
| 27 March         | The Rockingham Government takes office, Lord Rockingham being First Minister, Fox Foreign Secretary, Lord |

Shelburne Home Secretary, Lord Thurlow Lord Chancellor.

20 April                    Lloyd Kenyon succeeds James Wallace as Attorney General.

27 May                      The Commons resolves to recall Hastings, Governor General of India, William Hornsby, President of the Council, and Sir Elijah Impey, Chief Justice.

June                        Fox quarrels with Lord Shelburne. The King recovers the *Morning Post,* now edited by a "friend" of Lord Shelburne.

1 July                      The Rockingham Government ends with the death of Lord Rockingham.

9 July                      The Shelburne Government takes office, Lord Grantham being Foreign Secretary, Lord Thurlow Lord Chancellor, George Rose Secretary of the Treasury, and William Pitt Chancellor of the Exchequer.

30 November                 Great Britain signs a provisional treaty with America at Paris.

*1783*

                            William Blake publishes his *Poetical Sketches.*

20 January                  Great Britain signs preliminary articles of peace with France and Spain at Versailles.

21 February                 The Tories and the Rockingham Whigs combine to censure the Shelburne Government for the terms of the peace.

24 February                 The Shelburne Government resigns.

8 April                     The Coalition Government takes office, the Duke of Portland being First Minister, Fox Foreign Secretary, Lord North Home Secretary, and Sheridan one of the Secretaries of the Treasury.

*c.* 10 April               The *London Courant* ceases publication, possibly as the result of a stock-jobbing venture.

May                         George Crabbe publishes *The Village.*

6 May                       James Wallace succeeds Lloyd Kenyon as Attorney General.

*c.* 1 July                 Carl F. Badini succeeds Lord Shelburne's "friend" as editor of the *Morning Post,* which thereafter becomes non-political.

18 July                     Statement of new editorial policy indicates that James Perry has assumed the conduct of the *Gazetteer,* which thereafter represents the point of view of the Constitutional Society.

2 September                 Great Britain signs a preliminary treaty of peace with Holland at Paris.

| | |
|---|---|
| 3 September | Great Britain signs a definitive treaty with America at Paris and definitive treaties with France and Spain at Versailles. |
| November | Badini is replaced as editor of the *Morning Post* by Captain John Williamson, and the paper thereafter supports the Coalition. |
| 11 November | The Prince of Wales is introduced into the House of Lords; he supports the Rockingham Whigs. |
| 18 November | John Lee succeeds James Wallace as Attorney General. |
| 26 November | Lloyd Kenyon replaces John Lee as Attorney General. |
| 17 December | Fox's East India Bill is defeated in the Lords as a result of "secret influence" by the King. |
| 18 December | The Portland (Coalition) Government is dismissed. |
| 19 December | The Pitt Government takes office, William Pitt being First Minister, Lord Thurlow Lord Chancellor, and George Rose and Thomas Steele Secretaries of the Treasury. |
| c. 19 December | The *Morning Herald,* last of the Shelburne papers, defects to the Coalition as the Rev. Henry Bate resumes control. The possible editor is John Williams ("Anthony Pasquin"). All newspapers now support the Coalition. |
| c. 30 December | The Treasury buys two shares in the *Morning Post* through the agency of John Benjafield. Major John Scott transfers his pro-Hastings anti-Burke activities from the *Herald* to the *Post.* |

*1784*

| | |
|---|---|
| 23 January | Pitt's East India Bill is defeated in the Commons. |
| 23 January | Fox obtains leave to bring in a new East India Bill. |
| 24 March | Parliament is prorogued for the general elections. The *Morning Post,* now strongly Ministerial, is edited by the Rev. William Jackson with the assistance of W. A. Miles and probably John Almon. |
| 30 March | Richard Pepper Arden replaces Lloyd Kenyon as Attorney General. |
| 1 April | The general elections begin. The candidates for Westminster are Fox and the King's friends Lord Hood and Sir Cecil Wray. All newspapers support Fox except the *Morning Post.* |
| Mid-May | William Parker, proprietor and conductor of the *General Advertiser,* dies. |
| 17 May | The general elections conclude with an overwhelming victory for the Government. The Westminster seats go to Lord Hood and Fox. Sir Cecil Wray demands a "scrutiny." |

| | |
|---|---|
| 7 July | Burke asks Pitt to make himself responsible for the investigation of Impey's conduct. |
| 26 July | The Westminster Scrutiny begins. The *Public Advertiser* shifts to the side of the Government. |
| 30 July | Burke moves for papers relating to Hastings's affairs; a lively quarrel ensues between Burke and Major Scott. |
| 9 August | Pitt's East India Bill is passed. |
| September | John Almon acquires the *General Advertiser* by marrying the widow of William Parker. The paper supports both parties, although still in the pay of the Rockingham Whigs. |
| 13 December | Dr. Samuel Johnson dies in London. |

*1785*

| | |
|---|---|
| 1 January | John Walter begins the *Universal Daily Advertiser*, later (1 Jan., 1788) retitled *The Times*, in the interests of the Pitt Government. |
| 1 January | The Opposition cancels its subsidy of the *General Advertiser*, which continues to vacillate. |
| Late January | W. A. Miles quits the *Morning Post*. |
| 16 February | Philip Francis and Fox move for additional papers relating to affairs of Hastings and the East India Company. |
| 3 March | The Westminster Scrutiny ends with the seating (4 Mar.) of Fox and Lord Hood. |
| July | William Cowper publishes *The Task*. |
| 15 August | Thomas De Quincey is born in Manchester. |
| Late October | Pitt files an action for libel against the printers of the *General Advertiser* and the Opposition *Morning Herald* (John Almon and James Barr), the two papers having accused him of stock-jobbing. He asks £150,000 damages from each. |
| *c.* 15 December | John Bell is appointed bookseller to the Prince of Wales. |
| 21 December | The Prince of Wales marries the Roman Catholic Mrs. Fitzherbert. |
| 1785 or 1786 | John Williams ("Anthony Pasquin") quits the *Morning Herald*. |

*1786*

| | |
|---|---|
| 1 January | John Benjafield and Richard Tattersall lease the *Morning Post* for a period of seven years. John Bell quits the newspaper, probably selling his shares to Tattersall, who is henceforth the principal proprietor. |
| 13 January | The *Public Ledger* is now printed and conducted by Francis Blythe. |

| | |
|---|---|
| 17 February | Burke charges Hastings with the commission of high crimes and misdemeanors. |
| 20 February | John Almon, printer of the *General Advertiser,* is convicted in Westminster Hall of having printed a libel on Pitt, but jury reduces amount of damages from £150,-000 to £150. The Opposition renews its subsidy of the *General Advertiser,* which thereafter supports Fox. |
| *c.* 20 February | James Barr, printer of the *Morning Herald,* is convicted of having printed a libel on Pitt, but jury reduces amount of damages from £150,000 to £250. |
| Spring | The Rev. William Jackson is dismissed as editor of the *Morning Post;* the new editor is Peter Stuart. |
| *c.* April | Burke sues the Ministerial *Public Advertiser* for libel, asking £5,000 damages. The jury subsequently awards him £100. |
| 26 April | Hastings requests a hearing; the Commons accedes. |
| 4 July | Benjafield and Tattersall agree that the literary department of the *Morning Post* will be handled by Benjafield, the business by Tattersall. |
| 31 July | The first (Kilmarnock) edition of Burns's *Poems Chiefly in the Scottish Dialect* appears. |
| 13 September | Boswell's *Journal of a Tour to the Hebrides with Samuel Johnson* is published in London. |
| *1787*<br>1 January | Major Edward Topham and John Bell begin the *World,* Topham being conductor and the political department being managed by Sheridan. |
| 1 January | John Crowder inherits the *Public Ledger.* |
| 24 April | Sir Gilbert Elliot (Lord Minto) gives notice that he will move for the impeachment of Impey, but the motion is withdrawn because of the press of other business. |
| 27 April | Alderman Newnham signifies his intention of applying for payment of the debts of the Prince of Wales; Rolle threatens to demand an investigation of the Prince's marriage. |
| 30 April | Fox denies that the Prince is married. |
| Early May | Horne Tooke publishes his *Letter to a Friend,* which acknowledges the Prince's marriage on the evident authority of Mrs. Fitzherbert. |
| 10 May | The Commons votes to impeach Hastings. |
| 15 May | Peter Stuart, printer of the Ministerial *Morning Post,* is convicted of having published a libel on W. J'Anson. The sentence is unknown. |

21 May          On Burke's motion, Hastings is taken into custody, the
                Lords being informed of the action. Having heard the
                articles of impeachment, Hastings is then released on
                bail so that he can prepare an answer.

24 May          Parliament votes to pay the Prince's debts and to allow
                payment for part of the work on Carlton House.

October         The Rev. Charles Este assumes the editorship of the
                *World*.

5 December      Hastings submits his defense, and a special committee
                is appointed to examine it.

7 December      Burke notifies the Lords that the Commons finds Has-
                tings's defense unsatisfactory.

12 December     Elliot moves for charges of impeachment against Impey;
                the motion passes.

*1788*

1 January       Este becomes a proprietor of the *World*.

22 January      George Gordon Lord Byron is born in London.

4 February      Daniel Stuart replaces Peter Stuart as editor of the
                *Morning Post*.

4 February      The Commons considers articles of impeachment against
                Sir Elijah Impey, Impey appearing in his own defense.

8 February      On complaint of Impey, the Commons votes to prosecute
                the printers of the Opposition *Morning Herald* and the
                Opposition *Gazetteer* (William Perryman and Mary Say)
                for libel, the libels being published on 6 and 7 February,
                respectively.

13 February     Warren Hastings goes on trial before the Lords. Among
                the managers of the trial are Burke, Sheridan, Fox,
                Windham, and Sir Gilbert Elliot.

14 February     On complaint of Fox, John Stockdale is indicted ex of-
                ficio for having published a libel on the Commons re-
                specting the trial of Hastings, the libel being contained
                in a pamphlet, entitled *A Review of the Principal
                Charges against Warren Hastings*.

3 May           Peter Stuart begins the *Star and Evening Advertiser*,
                which carries the insignia of the Prince of Wales.

9 May           The Commons drops its charges against Impey.

28 June         Sir Archibald Macdonald replaces Arden as Attorney
                General.

11 July         Parliament is prorogued for the general elections.

18 July         The general elections begin. The Ministerial candidate
                for Westminster is Lord Hood; the Opposition candi-
                dates are Fox and Lord John Townshend. The Treasury

|  | now controls seven daily newspapers to the Opposition's three (*Morning Herald, Gazetteer,* and *General Advertiser*). The election is characterized by unprecedented violence and corruption. Lord Hood is defeated. |
|---|---|
| 6 August | Lord Hood forms the Constitutional Club for the purpose of protesting the results of the Westminster election. A petition is prepared, and the first signatures are obtained. |
| c. 7 September | The Prince of Wales responds to a libel on Mrs. Fitzherbert by offering Topham £4,000 and a lifetime annuity of £400 for the *World*. Topham refuses, and a subsidy is arranged instead. |
| c. 15 September | The *World* represents Mrs. Fitzherbert's faction, which calls itself the "New Whigs" and includes among its members Sheridan, Burke, Windham, Lord Loughborough, and the Duke of Norfolk. The faction demands that Fox resign as Party leader in favor of Sheridan. |
| 10 November | All newspapers publish accounts of the King's illness. |
| c. 20 November | John Almon, conductor of the Opposition *General Advertiser,* is indicted ex officio for having published a libel on the King. |
| 25 December | Topham buys Este's shares in the *World* for a lifetime annuity of £400, Este to continue as conductor. |
| 25 December | The Treasury contracts for political control of the *World*. Major Scott moves to the *World* from the *Morning Post*. |
| 31 December | Topham buys Bell's shares in the *World*, Bell remaining with the *World* as printer. |

*1789*

|  | William Blake publishes his *Songs of Innocence* and *Book of Thel*. |
|---|---|
| 2 January | Benjafield sells his interests in the *Morning Post* to Louis Weltje, agent of the Prince of Wales. The paper is managed by Sheridan in the interests of the "New Whigs" and edited by John Taylor. |
| 5 February | Pitt introduces the Regency Bill. |
| 12 February | The Regency Bill passes the Commons. |
| 13 February | Peter and Charles Stuart and James Mackintosh quit the original *Star* to begin the spurious *Star* in the interests of the Prince of Wales. The original *Star*, thereafter conducted by John Mayne, supports the Government. |
| 13 February | The Regency Bill passes the first reading in the Lords. |
| 16 February | The Regency Bill passes the second reading in the Lords. |

| | |
|---|---|
| 19 February | The Lords adjourn on the Regency Bill until 24 February. |
| c. 20 February | Mrs. Fitzherbert sues Philip Withers for a libel, contained in *Nemesis*. |
| c. 22 February | John Walter, conductor of *The* Ministerial *Times*, is indicted ex officio for having published a libel on the Duke of York. |
| 24 February | The Lords postpone further action on the Regency Bill until 2 March. |
| 26 February | The Irish Parliament invites the Prince of Wales to assume the government of Ireland independently. |
| c. 27 February | John Walter, conductor of *The* Ministerial *Times*, is indicted ex officio for having published a libel on the Prince of Wales. Walter pleads guilty. |
| 2 March | The Lords adjourn on the Regency Bill until 5 March. |
| 5 March | The King notifies Parliament that he will indicate his pleasure on 10 March. |
| 7 March | Sampson Perry begins the Opposition *Argus*. |
| 10 March | The King's recovery is officially announced. The Regency Bill is shelved, and the "New Whigs" cease activity. |
| c. 10 March | John Almon, conductor of the Opposition *General Advertiser*, is convicted of having published a libel on the King. |
| c. 10 March | William Perryman, printer of the Opposition *Morning Herald*, is convicted of having published a libel on the King, the Prince of Wales, and the Ministers. |
| 28 March | William Woodfall quits the *Morning Chronicle* after a political quarrel with the proprietors. His successor as conductor of the *Chronicle* is probably James Perry, who meanwhile continues as nominal conductor of the *Gazetteer*. The *Chronicle* shifts its support to the Opposition. |
| 30 March | William Woodfall begins the *Diary* as a service to the Government. |
| 2 April | Parliament repeals the shop tax. |
| 3 April | Lord Hood's petition relating to the Westminster election of 1788 is referred to a committee of the Commons. |
| 27 April | The spurious *Star*, still posing as a Carlton House newspaper, but actually in the pay of the Whigs, appears as a morning newspaper. It immediately releases exposés of George Rose and commences a series of vicious attacks on |

|  | the Ministerial *World*, the next general elections being expected in June. |
|---|---|
| *c.* 6 May | John Walter of *The* Ministerial *Times* is indicted ex officio for having published a libel on the Duke of Clarence. Walter pleads guilty. |
| 25 May | John Bell is dismissed as printer and publisher of the *World*. |
| 1 June | John Bell begins the *Oracle*, offering the political department to the highest bidder. |
| *c.* June | William Perryman, printer of the Opposition *Morning Herald*, is sentenced to twelve months in prison for having published a libel on the King, the Prince of Wales, and the Ministers. |
| 15 June | Philip Withers is convicted of having published a libel on Mrs. Fitzherbert. |
| 16 June | The spurious *Star* ceases publication, having reduced the *World* to a shambles and so discredited Rose and Pitt that the elections are postponed until 1790. |
| 16 June | Robert Bostock, printer of the Ministerial *World*, is indicted ex officio for having published a libel on the Commons regarding the trial of Hastings. |
| 18 June | The committee examining Lord Hood's petition discovers that it cannot finish its work before Parliament adjourns. |
| 6 July | Lord Hood withdraws his petition. |
| 11 July | John Walter of *The* Ministerial *Times* is convicted of having published a libel on the Duke of York. |
| 14 July | The storming of the Bastile introduces a wave of insurrections in France. |
| August | The newspaper tax is increased to 2*d.* and the advertisement duty to 3*s.*, the price of most newspapers being advanced to 4*d.* |
| 21 November | Philip Withers is sentenced to twelve months in Newgate for having published a libel on Mrs. Fitzherbert. |
| 23 November | John Walter of *The Times* is sentenced to twelve months in Newgate and one hour in the pillory and fined £50 for having published a libel on the Duke of York. |
| 8 December | William Perryman, former printer of the Opposition *Morning Herald,* is convicted of having published a libel on Sir Elijah Impey. He was later sentenced to twelve or eighteen months in prison. |
| 9 December | John Stockdale is acquitted of the charge of having |

libeled the Commons in the pamphlet *A Review of the Principal Charges against Warren Hastings.*

**Late 1789**　　John Almon, conductor of the Opposition *General Advertiser,* fails to appear for judgment respecting his libel on the King and is outlawed, the newspaper being sold.

*1790*

Blake publishes his *Marriage of Heaven and Hell.*

**1 January**　　The Treasury acquires the *Oracle,* currently edited by Peter Stuart and James Boaden, James Mackintosh handling the foreign intelligence and John Bell acting as conductor.

**21 January**　　Lt. John Frith, later proved to be insane, attacks the King's carriage. The Treasury press represents the attack as a French plot and Frith as a French agent.

**3 February**　　John Walter, conductor of *The Times,* is sentenced to twelve months in Newgate and fined £100 for having published a libel on the Prince of Wales; he is fined an additional £100 for having published a libel on the Duke of Clarence.

**9 February**　　Burke breaks with Sheridan over the issue of the French Revolution.

**c. 18 February**　　The heirs of the third Earl Cowper sue Major Topham, Charles Este, and Robert Bostock, proprietor, conductor, and printer of the *World,* for libels on his memory. Este flees, and Bostock pleads guilty. Topham resumes conduct of paper, which is edited by Robert Merry.

**23 February**　　The Ministerial *World* jeeringly announces Burke's *Reflections.*

**2 March**　　Fox moves for repeal of the Test and Corporation Acts.

**4 March**　　Henry Flood moves for leave to bring in motion for Parliamentary reform.

**5 May**　　The King notifies Parliament of the seizure of British ships in Nootka Sound and asks for augmentation of forces.

**10 May**　　J. Luxford, printer of the Opposition *Morning Herald,* is indicted ex officio for having questioned the *Gazette's* statements regarding Nootka Sound. He pleads guilty.

**21 May**　　General Burgoyne moves for the prosecution of Major Scott and the Ministerial *World.* Debate on the motion is postponed until 27 May.

**26 May**　　Robert Bostock, printer of the Ministerial *World,* is convicted of having published a libel on the Commons re-

|              | specting the trial of Hastings, having been indicted on 16 June, 1789. |
| --- | --- |
| 27 May | The Commons reprimands Major Scott, the action against the *World* being dropped. |
| *c.* 1 June | The Government leases the *Morning Herald,* installing Thomas Y. Hurlstone as editor. Dudley retires. |
| 9 June | Bostock's counsel moves for a retrial. The action against him and the Ministerial *World* is quietly dropped. |
| 10 June | Parliament is prorogued for the general elections. |
| 16 June | The elections begin. Although the parties had agreed to compromise the Westminster election, the candidates being only Lord Hood and Fox, Horne Tooke enters the contest as an "independent." All newspapers regard Tooke's candidacy as a Government trick. The Treasury controls nine daily newspapers, the Opposition five. Fox and Lord Hood are elected. Merry quits the *World.* |
| 1 July | Major Topham, proprietor of the Ministerial *World,* is convicted of having published libels on the memory of Earl Cowper. |
| 14 July | Louis XVI accepts the first draft of the new French constitution. |
| 10 September | Este advertises his intention of selling his interests in the *World* (£400 a year or a fourth of the profits). |
| 16 October | The Opposition *General Advertiser* ceases publication, having been purchased by a Treasury printer a few days earlier. |
| 28 October | The British Convention with Spain is signed at Madrid. |
| 1 November | All Treasury newspapers extol Burke's *Reflections on the Revolution in France.* |
| 5 November | Sampson Perry, conductor of the Opposition *Argus,* is indicted ex officio for having charged the Ministers with fraud concerning the Convention with Spain. |
| 27 November | J. Luxford, quondam printer of the *Morning Herald,* is summoned for judgment regarding the libel respecting Nootka Sound, but judgment is deferred. |
| 3 December | J. Beauchamp replaces James Perry as conductor of the *Gazetteer,* which continues to represent the Constitutional Society. |
| *c.* 8 December | John King, editor of the *Argus,* files a suit for libel against John Walter of *The Times.* |
| 9 December | Horne Tooke's petition regarding irregularities in the Westminster election is read in the Commons. |

| Late December | James Perry and James Gray purchase the *Morning Chronicle*, which continues to be supported by the Whigs. |
|---|---|
| *1791* | |
| January | William Radcliffe replaces J. Beauchamp as managing editor of the Opposition *Gazetteer*. |
| 25 January | J. Luxford, quondam printer of the *Morning Herald*, is sentenced to twelve months in prison and one hour in the pillory and fined £100 for having libeled the Ministers regarding Nootka Sound. |
| 29 January | The suit for libel against Topham, proprietor of the Ministerial *World*, brought by the relations of Earl Cowper, is dismissed on the ground that the laws of libel are not applicable to the dead. Este returns to London as editor of the *Oracle*. |
| Late January | John and William Walter, conductors of *The* Ministerial *Times*, file an action for libel against the Opposition *Argus*. |
| 7 February | A committee of the Commons votes to treat Tooke's petition regarding irregularities in the Westminster election of 1790 with "silent contempt." |
| 23 February | John Walter, conductor of *The* Ministerial *Times*, is convicted of having published a libel on John King, editor of the Opposition *Argus*. Walter was never sentenced. |
| 23 February | Sampson Perry, conductor of the Opposition *Argus*, is convicted of having published a libel on the Ministers respecting the Convention with Spain. |
| 24 February | Part I of Thomas Paine's *Rights of Man* is announced. |
| 9 March | John Walter, conductor of *The* Ministerial *Times*, is released from prison with a full pardon on petition of the Prince of Wales. |
| Early Spring | John Taylor is replaced as editor of the Opposition *Morning Post* by D. E. MacDonnel and Dennis O'Bryen. |
| Spring | Charles Long replaces Thomas Steele as the second Secretary of the Treasury. |
| *c.* 1 May | Mackintosh publishes his *Vindiciae Gallicae*. |
| 6 May | Burke breaks with Fox. |
| 16 May | Boswell's *Life of Johnson* appears in two volumes quarto. |
| June | Henry Dundas becomes Secretary of State for the Home Department, one of his principal tasks being to organize an army of spies and informers for Government. |

| | |
|---|---|
| 3 June | Mackintosh, Merry, Sheridan, and others organize the Friends of the Liberty of the Press. |
| 15 June | Sampson Perry, conductor of the Opposition *Argus*, is convicted of having published libels on John and William Walter of *The* Ministerial *Times*. |
| 20 June | Louis XVI attempts to flee, but is stopped at Varennes and returned to Paris. |
| 9 July | Refusing to make a public apology, Sampson Perry, conductor of the Opposition *Argus*, is sentenced to six months in prison for having libeled the Walters. |
| 9 July | Lady Fitzgibbon, wife of the Lord Chancellor of Ireland, files an action for libel against Sampson Perry, conductor of the Opposition *Argus*, who pleads guilty. |
| 12 July | Sampson Perry, conductor of the Opposition *Argus*, is sentenced to six months in prison and fined £200 for having published a libel on Lady Fitzgibbon. |
| 14 July | The Birmingham riots against the dissenters begin. |
| 21 July | George Smith, an innkeeper, recovers £110 5s. owed him by George Rose for "work and labour" relating to the Westminster election of 1788. |
| 6 August | The Ministerial newspapers eulogize Burke's *Appeal from the Old to the New Whigs.* |
| *c.* 1 September | Este, quondam conductor of the *World,* sues Topham for collection of his annuity; the case was still unsettled on 16 January, 1793. |
| 14 September | Louis XVI accepts the final version of the French Constitution. |
| 23 November | The Duke of York's marriage to Princess Fredericka of Prussia is celebrated in London, having been celebrated in Berlin on 29 September. |
| 25 November | Sampson Perry, conductor of the Opposition *Argus*, is fined £100 for having published a libel on the Ministers respecting the Convention with Spain. |
| *1792* | |
| 2 January | The Rev. Charles Este and John Parry begin the *Cabinet*, which survives only a few days. |
| 7 January | John Bell, conductor of the vacillating *Oracle*, is indicted ex officio for having published two libels on the Guards. |
| 16 January | The Opposition newspapers announce publication of Paine's *Rights of Man*, Part II. |
| 25 January | Thomas Hardy organizes the London Corresponding Society. |

| 7 February | Lord Lonsdale files an action for libel against John Bell, conductor of the *Oracle*. |
| 13 February | Lord Lonsdale files an action for libel against Peter Stuart, editor of the *Oracle*. |
| 23 February | Sir Joshua Reynolds dies. |
| March | John Almon, quondam conductor of the *General Advertiser*, surrenders and is imprisoned. |
| 1 March | Thomas Thompson notifies the Commons of his intention to move for an investigation of the Ministers' management of the Westminster election of 1788. |
| 13 March | Thompson moves for an investigation of the Ministers' interference in the Westminster election of 1788; the motion is negatived. |
| 15 March | George Rose files an action for libel against Richard Tattersall, conductor, and William Williams, printer, of the Opposition *Morning Post*. |
| 20 March | The Westminster electors meet with Opposition leaders to petition for an investigation of Rose's interference in the election of 1788. |
| c. April | Lady Elizabeth Lambert files an action for libel against Richard Tattersall, conductor of the Opposition *Morning Post*. |
| 4 April | Fox presents the petition of the Westminster electors, indicating his intention of making a motion on the subject later. |
| 11 April | The Sheridan wing of the Opposition organizes the Society of the Friends of the People. |
| 20 April | France declares war on Prussia and Austria. |
| 27 April | Lord Lonsdale drops his action against Peter Stuart, editor of the *Oracle*. He later also dropped his action against John Bell. |
| 30 April | Grey gives notice of his intention to submit a bill for Parliamentary reform. |
| 8 May | The petition from the Westminster electors is read and rejected without a debate. |
| 21 May | Dundas reads the King's Proclamation against Seditious Writings. |
| c. June | Isaac Swan succeeds Topham as conductor of the Ministerial *World*. |
| 11 June | Fox Libel Act is passed by the Commons, having already been passed by the Lords. |
| 4 July | Mackintosh publishes his *Letter to . . . Pitt, on His Apostacy from the Cause of Parliamentary Reform*. |

| | |
|---|---|
| 9 July | John Bell, conductor of the *Oracle,* is convicted of having published libels on the Guards. |
| 9 July | Richard Tattersall, conductor of the Opposition *Morning Post,* is ordered to pay Lady Lambert £4,000 damages for libel. Tattersall's heirs later filed a claim against the Prince of Wales to recover half the damages and the cost of defense. |
| 9 July | Richard Tattersall and William Williams, conductor and printer of the *Morning Post,* are ordered to pay George Rose £100 damages apiece for having published a libel on him. |
| 10 July | Richard Tattersall, conductor of the Opposition *Morning Post,* is indicted ex officio for having published a libel on the King. He pleads guilty. But no action was taken, and the charge was later transferred to the printer, William Williams, who was sentenced to twelve months in prison. |
| 10 July | Sampson Perry, conductor of the Opposition *Argus,* is indicted ex officio for having published a libel on the Commons. |
| 25 July | The Duke of Brunswick, commander of the Austro-Prussian army, issues his proclamation against the French Revolution. |
| 4 August | Percy Bysshe Shelley is born in Sussex. |
| 10 August | Massacres begin in Paris. |
| 21 September | The French National Convention abolishes the monarchy, declaring France a republic. |
| 22 September | The Rev. Charles Este and John Parry begin the evening *Courier,* which supports the Opposition in return for a promise of later rewards. |
| 1 October | At the instance of Burke, the Government begins its own newspaper, the evening *Sun,* which is edited by John Heriot and subsidized by James Bland Burges, Under Secretary of State for Foreign Affairs, and Charles Long, a Secretary of the Treasury. |
| 6 November | John Reeves, an agent of the Treasury, begins the Association for Protecting Liberty and Property against Republicans and Levellers, otherwise known as the Crown and Anchor Society. |
| 1 December | The King calls out the militia to put down a supposed insurrection in London. |
| 8 December | Sampson Perry, conductor of the Opposition *Argus,* is convicted of having published a libel on the Commons. |

| | |
|---|---|
| 13 December | The King asks Parliament for legislation to restore peace and order. |
| 15 December | Sampson Perry, conductor of the Opposition *Argus,* fails to appear for sentencing and is outlawed. |
| 18 December | Thomas Paine is convicted *in absentia* for publishing Part II of the *Rights of Man.* |
| 25 December | James Perry and James Gray, conductors of the Opposition *Morning Chronicle,* along with John Lambert, the printer, are indicted ex officio for having published seditious material. |
| *c.* 29 December | The Treasury seizes the Opposition *Argus* after some "trouble at the Stamp Office." The paper is reissued (1 Jan., 1793) as the Ministerial *True Briton.* |
| *1793* | |
| 1 January | The Weltje-Tattersall lease on the *Morning Post* expires; the *Oracle* takes a firm stand on the side of the Government; John Heriot begins the *True Briton,* which is subsidized by George Rose. The Treasury now controls nine newspapers (the *Diary,* conducted by William Woodfall; the *Morning Herald,* conducted by Thomas Y. Hurlstone; the *Oracle,* conducted by John Bell and edited by Peter Stuart and James Boaden; the *Public Advertiser,* conducted by Henry Sampson Woodfall; the *Public Ledger,* conducted by John Crowder and edited by Alexander Chalmers; the *Sun,* conducted by John Heriot; *The Times,* conducted by John Walter; the *True Briton,* conducted by John Heriot; and the *World,* conducted by Isaac Swan) . The Opposition controls five (the *Courier,* conducted by the Rev. Charles Este; the *Gazetteer,* conducted by William Radcliffe; the *Morning Chronicle,* conducted by James Perry and James Gray; the *Morning Post,* conducted by Richard Tattersall and probably still edited by D. E. MacDonnel and Dennis O'Bryen; and the *Star,* conducted by John Mayne) . The *Daily Advertiser,* still conducted by J. Jenour, is politically neutral. |
| 16 January | Frederick Bourne replaces William Radcliffe as editor of the *Gazetteer.* |
| *c.* 2 February | D. E. MacDonnel quits the Opposition *Morning Post* to become editor of the Opposition *Gazetteer.* |
| 5 February | John Bell, conductor of the Ministerial *Oracle,* fails to appear for judgment for having published libels on the Guards. |

| | |
|---|---|
| 13 February | Sir John Scott succeeds Sir Archibald Macdonald as Attorney General. |
| 5 March | John Bell, conductor of the Ministerial *Oracle*, makes a public apology for having libeled the Guards, and the action against him is dropped. |
| 26 April | Outlawry proceedings against John Almon, quondam conductor of the Opposition *General Advertiser*, are reversed. |
| 8 May | John Almon, quondam conductor of the Opposition *General Advertiser*, is released from prison; sentencing for the publication of a libel on the King is postponed indefinitely. |
| 12 June | The Opposition moves for a prosecution of the *World* for libel, relating to the proceedings against Warren Hastings. Burke supports the motion, but the House adjourns without a division. |
| 20 June | The Treasury discontinues its subsidy of the *World*, which thereafter prints propaganda for both parties. |
| 30 August | The *Diary* discontinues publication. |
| 9 December | James Perry, James Gray, and John Lambert, conductors and printer of the Opposition *Morning Chronicle*, are tried for the publication of seditious material; the jury acquits. |

# NOTES

## CHAPTER I

1. For an account of Wheble's involvement, see *Annual Register . . . for the Year 1771*, I, 60–63, 183–85; *Select Statutes Cases and Documents to Illustrate English Constitutional History*, ed. Charles Grant Robertson (London, 1935), p. 479; Robert L. Haig, *The Gazetteer 1735–1797* (Carbondale, 1960); pp. 102–12.

2. See Arthur Aspinall, "Statistical Accounts of the London Newspapers in the Eighteenth Century," *English Historical Review*, LXIII (1948), 201–32, for the Audit Office accounts during this period. According to the records (*EHR*, LXIII, 227, 228), the publisher of the *Middlesex Journal* during the years 1769–1772 was "Thomas Wheble," but the records are frequently in error regarding first names. They are also in error in numerous other and more important respects. The *Middlesex Journal*, founded (1769) in the interests of John Wilkes by several of his friends, had played a prominent role in the battle between Parliament and the City of London.

3. *EHR*, LXIII, 228.

4. Haig, p. 125.

5. *EHR*, LXIII, 228.

6. Wheble was again publishing the *English Chronicle* in 1786 (*EHR*, LXIII, 231). Meanwhile in 1784 he and a Mr. "Justins" undertook the publishing of the (Suffolk) *County Chronicle, and Weekly Advertiser*, which paper Wheble was still printing and publishing in 1812. See *EHR*, LXIII, 231, 232; John Benjafield, *Statement of Facts* (Bury St. Edmunds, 1813), pp. 4–5. In 1793 Wheble was also publishing the *Sporting Magazine* at No. 18, Warwick Square (*Star*, 23 Jan., 1793).

7. *Annual Register . . . for the Year 1764*, I, 76, 108; *Annual Register . . . for the Year 1765*, I, 65.

8. *The Autobiography of Arthur Young*, ed. M. Betham-Edwards (London, 1898), p. 63.

9. Wilfrid Hindle, *The Morning Post 1772–1937: Portrait of a Newspaper* (London, 1937), p. 43.

10. For characters of Bate, see Hindle, p. 15; James Boaden, *Memoirs of the Life of John Philip Kemble, Esq.* (London, 1925), II, 38; John Taylor, *Records of My Life* (London, 1832), I, 102–6.

11. *Annual Register . . . for the Year 1774*, I, 135, 163.

12. *EHR*, LXIII, 229.

13. *EHR*, LXIII, 228.

14. H. R. Fox Bourne, *English Newspapers: Chapters in the History of Journalism* (London, 1887), I, 206, note.

15. Hindle, p. 43.

16. *Journals of the House of Lords*, XXXI, 65.

17. Allardyce Nicoll, *A History of English Drama 1660–1900* (Cambridge, 1955), III, 235, 237.

18. The Cox-Bigg partnership seems to have been dissolved on 2 March, 1776, when the office at No. 405, Strand, was destroyed by fire. See Plomer Bushnell Dix, *Dictionary of Booksellers and Printers 1721–1775* (Oxford, 1932).

19. Haig, pp. 158–60.

20. The *New Post* is thought to have survived until February, 1777. See, for example, Stanley Morison, *John Bell, 1745–1831* (Cambridge, 1930), p. 3. But the only evidence that this is the case is the *Post*'s announcement of 27 February.

21. *EHR*, LXIII, 229.

22. *EHR*, LXIII, 230, 231. In 1790 the *Courier de l'Europe* was published by Swinton (*EHR*, LXIII, 232).

23. *The Letters of Horace Walpole Earl of Orford*, ed. Peter Cunningham (London, 1831), VI, 391–92.

24. *EHR*, LXIII, 230.

25. Benjafield, pp. iv–v; Arthur Aspinall, *Politics and the Press c. 1780–1850* (London, 1949), pp. 278–79, note.

26. Taylor, I, 103, note.

27. BM Add. MSS. 20733.

28. Bourne, I, 222. But Bourne is mistaken regarding Stoney's first name, which he gives as George.

29. Walpole's *Letters*, VII, 374.

30. There are various spellings of O'Bryen's name. For an account of his life, see David Erskine Baker, Isaac Reed, and Stephen Jones, *Biographia Dramatica; or, A Companion to the Playhouse* (London, 1812), I, 544–45. A pamphleteer and playwright, O'Bryen was active in the later history of many newspapers, including the *Morning Post*. See Hindle, p. 63; *The Farington Diary by Joseph Farington, R.A.*, ed. James Grieg (London, 1922–28), II, 250.

31. Taylor, I, 103, note; II, 165.

32. Sylvester Douglas, Baron of Glenbervie, and William Frere, *Reports of Cases Argued and Determined in the Court of King's Bench, in the Nineteenth [to the Twenty-Sixth] Year of the Reign of George III.* (London, 1813–31), I, 391.

33. See James Grant, *The Newspaper Press: Its Origin, Progress, and Present Position* (London, 1871), I, 316.

34. "The Memoir of James Perry, Esq.," *European Magazine*, LXXIV (1818), 88–89.

35. Percy Fitzgerald, *The Life of George the Fourth* (London, 1881), I, 66.

36. Taylor, II, 270.

37. *EHR*, LXIII, 230.

38. Hindle, p. 43.

39. Quoted by Haig, p. 200.

## CHAPTER II

1. John Taylor, *Records of My Life* (London, 1832), II, 165.

2. See the obituary of Daniel Stuart, *Gentleman's Magazine*, n.s., XXVIII (1847), 322–24.

3. "The Prisoners of the '45," ed. Sir Bruce Gordon Seton and Jean Gordon Arnot, *Publications of the Scottish History Society*, 3rd ser., XIII (1927), 107–8; XV (1929), 218–19, 221.

4. *Letters from the Lake Poets to Daniel Stuart*, ed. Mary Stuart (London, 1889), pp. ix–x.

5. Daniel Stuart, "The Late Mr. Coleridge, the Poet," *Gentleman's Magazine*, n.s., X (1838), 24.

6. *The Letters of Robert Burns*, ed. J. De Lancey Ferguson (Oxford, 1931), II, 372.

7. *Lake Poets*, p. ix.

8. *Lake Poets*, p. ix.

9. "Editors and Newspaper Writers of the Last Generation, by an Old Apprentice

of the Law," *Fraser's Magazine*, LXV (1862), 174. See also William Jerdan, *Autobiography* (London, 1852–53), I, 92.

10. James Amphlett, *The Newspaper Press, in Part of the Last Century, and Up to the Present Period of 1860* (London, 1860), p. 10.

11. *Lake Poets*, p. ix.

12. *GM*, n.s., XXVIII, 322–24.

13. Allardyce Nicoll, *A History of English Drama 1660–1900* (Cambridge, 1955), III, 310.

14. Nicoll, III, 310.

15. Wally Chamberlain Oulton, *The History of the Theatres of London . . . from the Year 1771–1795* (London, 1796), II, 162.

16. Oulton, I, 104.

17. Robert L. Haig, *The Gazetteer 1735–1797* (Carbondale, 1960), p. 179.

18. Haig, pp. 187, 305.

19. Arthur Aspinall, *Politics and the Press c. 1780–1850* (London, 1949), p. 452.

20. See, for example, *Autobiography of Leigh Hunt*, ed. J. E. Morpugo (London, 1949), p. 153.

21. Chatham Papers PRO 30/ GD 8/ 289, 308.

22. See the Catalogue of the British Museum.

23. John Genest, *Some Account of the English Stage, from the Restoration in 1660 to 1830* (Bath, 1832), VI, 296.

24. Although it is Haig's opinion (see Haig, pp. 187–88) that Perry assumed the conduct of the *Gazetteer* in January, 1784, the announcement of a revised editorial policy did not appear until 18 July.

25. [Mary Wells,] *Memoirs of the Life of Mrs. Sumbel, Late Wells* (London, 1811), I, 66.

26. See Wilfrid Hindle, *The Morning Post 1772–1937: Portrait of a Newspaper* (London, 1937), p. 43.

27. John Benjafield, *Statement of Facts* (Bury St. Edmunds, 1813), p. iv.

28. Hindle, p. 43.

29. Benjafield, p. iv.

30. Aspinall, p. 72.

31. Benjafield, p. iv.

32. Taylor, II, 326.

33. See Lucyle Werkmeister, "Notes for a Revised Life of William Jackson," *Notes and Queries*, n.s., VIII (1961), 44.

34. *N&Q*, n.s., VIII, 44–45.

35. *Reports of Cases Argued and Determined in the Court of King's Bench*, ed. Sylvester Douglas (London, 1790), I, 283.

36. See, for example, *Memoirs of the Colman Family*, ed. Richard Brinsley Peake (London, 1841), II, 217–18.

37. Benjafield, p. 4.

38. *The Correspondence of William Augustus Miles on the French Revolution 1789–1817*, ed. Rev. Charles Popham Miles (London, 1850), II, 271–72.

39. *A Biographical Dictionary of the Living Authors of Great Britain and Ireland* (London, 1816).

40. Benjafield, pp. iv–v, notes.

41. Benjafield, p. v.

42. Hindle, p. 44.

43. Benjafield, p. 23, note.

44. Benjafield, p. 23, note.

45. See Arthur Aspinall, "Statistical Accounts of the London Newspapers in the

Eighteenth Century," *English Historical Review*, LXIII (1948), 231, 232; Benjafield, pp. 4–5.

46. Aspinall, p. 452.

47. James Boaden, *Memoirs of the Life of John Philip Kemble, Esq.* (London, 1825), I, 344–46.

48. *EHR*, LXIII, 231.

49. *EHR*, LXIII, 231, 232.

50. Taylor, II, 269–70.

51. See *N&Q*, n.s., VIII, 45–46.

52. Taylor, II, 267.

53. *Reports of Cases Argued and Determined in the Court of King's Bench*, ed. Charles Durnford and Edward Hyde East (London, 1787), I, 748–54.

54. *Biographical Dictionary*.

55. *Wells*, I, 66, 67.

56. Percy Fitzgerald, *The Life of George the Fourth* (London, 1881), I, 235; but Fitzgerald quotes from the *Diary of Sir Philip Francis*.

57. Tooke, pp. 46–47.

58. The Duke of Buckingham and Chandos, *Memoirs of the Court and Cabinets of George the Third* (London, 1853–55), I, 363. See also Fitzgerald, I, 111–12.

59. *The History of The Times 1785–1841* (London, 1935), p. 33.

60. *Boswell's Life of Johnson, together with Boswell's Journal of a Tour to the Hebrides and Johnson's Diary of a Journey into North Wales*, ed. George Birkbeck Hill and L. F. Powell (Oxford, 1934), III, 92, note 2.

61. Chatham Papers PRO 30/ GD 8/ 144–45, 274.

62. Fitzgerald, I, 94.

63. Aspinall, pp. 72–73, 272.

64. George Bernard, *Retrospections of the Stage* (London, 1830), II, 114.

65. Taylor, I, 92.

66. Taylor, II, 265–67.

67. Benjafield, pp. xxxix–xliii.

68. Benjafield, pp. v–ix, 4–5.

69. *History of The Times*, p. 51.

70. Aspinall, p. 272.

71. Aspinall, p. 272.

72. Benjafield, pp. v–vii, note.

73. *The Life and Times of Frederick Reynolds, Written by Himself* (London, 1827), II, 122.

74. Hindle, p. 43.

75. Taylor, I, 23.

CHAPTER III

1. *Memoirs of John Almon, Bookseller of Piccadilly* (London, 1790), pp. 14–17; Robert L. Haig, *The Gazetteer 1735–1797* (Carbondale, 1960), pp. 50–56; Robert R. Rea, "Bookseller as Historian," *Indiana Quarterly for Bookmen*, V (1949), 75–78.

2. *IQB*, V, 78–80.

3. See Haig, p. 55.

4. Arthur Aspinall, "Statistical Accounts of the London Newspapers in the Eighteenth Century," *English Historical Review*, LXIII (1948), 226.

5. *A Complete Collection of State Trials*, ed. T. B. Howell (London, 1814), XX, 803–53, 870–96.

6. See *Annual Register . . . for the Year 1771*, I, 60–70, 183–88; *Select Statutes Cases and Documents to Illustrate English Constitutional History*, ed. Charles Grant Robertson (London, 1935), pp. 479–80.

7. Almon's *Memoirs*, p. 119.

8. Stanley Morison, *The English Newspaper: Some Account of the Physical Development of Journals Printed in London between 1622 & the Present Day* (Cambridge, 1932), p. 173.

9. *EHR*, LXIII, 226.

10. See Haig, pp. 129–33.

11. [John Almon,] *Biographical, Literary, and Political Anecdotes of Several of the Most Eminent Persons of the Present Age* (London, 1797), I, 287–321.

12. *Annual Register . . . for the Year 1774*, I, 102.

13. *EHR*, LXIII, 229.

14. Alexander Andrews, *The History of British Journalism, from the Foundation of the Newspaper Press in England, to the Repeal of the Stamp Act in 1855* (London, 1859), I, 213–18.

15. *The Letters of Horace Walpole Earl of Orford*, ed. Peter Cunningham (London, 1861), VI, 46.

16. BM Add. MSS. 20733.

17. See BM Add. MSS. 20733.

18. "The Memoir of James Perry, Esq.," *European Magazine*, LXXIV (1818), 188–89.

19. BM Add. MSS. 20733.

20. Haig, pp. 148, 215.

21. H. R. Fox Bourne, *English Newspapers: Chapters in the History of Journalism* (London, 1887), I, 206, note.

22. See Haig, p. 112; Fox Bourne, I, 172; Robert R. Rea, "The Earl of Chatham and the London Press, 1775," *Journalism Quarterly*, XXXI (1954), 186–92; Robert R. Rea, "Anglo-American Parliamentary Reporting: A Case Study in Historical Bibliography," *Papers of the Bibliographical Society of America*, XLI (1955), 212–29.

23. See *JQ*, XXXI, 186–92; *PBSA*, XLI, 212–29.

24. *Proceedings of the Massachusetts Historical Society, 1869–1870* (Boston, 1871), pp. 7–9.

25. See also Andrews, I, 225.

26. Almon's *Memoirs*, pp. 121–26.

27. *EHR*, LXIII, 229–30.

28. *EHR*, LXIII, 230.

29. HO 42/32.

30. BM Add. MSS. 20733.

31. *EHR*, LXIII, 230. Fleming was later (1785) the first printer of *The Times;* Thirlwind was publishing *The Times* in 1792.

32. According to the transcription of the Audit-Office Records (*EHR*, LXIII, 230), Miller printed the *London Mercury* through 1783; but either the transcription or the records are frequently in error. For example, Miller is also listed as an occasional printer of the *London Courant* during the periods 1784–1787 and 1790–1791 (*EHR*, LXIII, 231, 232); but the *Courant* expired in 1783.

33. *EHR*, LXIII, 232; but this record is mistakenly dated 1790–1791.

34. Arthur Aspinall, *Politics and the Press c. 1780–1850* (London, 1949), p. 153.

35. HO 42/32.

36. HO 42/32.

37. Since the newspapers do not mention the trial, I rely upon Almon's *Memoirs*, pp. 126–27, 236–49.

38. HO 42/32.
39. By Morison. See *English Newspapers,* pp. 232–33.
40. Almon's *Memoirs,* pp. 136–43.
41. BM Add. MSS. 20733.
42. *EHR,* LXIII, 232.
43. *A Biographical Dictionary of the Living Authors* (London, 1816).
44. [Mary Wells,] *Memoirs of the Life of Mrs. Sumbel, Late Wells* (London, 1811), I, 77.
45. BM Add. MSS. 20733.
46. BM Add. MSS. 20733.
47. BM Add. MSS. 20733.
48. Quoted by Rea. See *IQB,* V, 86.
49. HO 42/32.

## CHAPTER IV

1. For the text of Bell's address, cited frequently throughout this chapter, see Appendix I.
2. *The Life and Times of Frederick Reynolds, Written by Himself* (London, 1827), II, 45–46.
3. *Reynolds,* II, 38–39.
4. See *Public Characters of 1805,* pub. Richard Phillips (London, 1805), p. 205.
5. [Mary Wells,] *Memoirs of the Life of Mrs. Sumbel, Late Wells* (London, 1811), I, 57–59.
6. George Bernard, *Retrospections of the Stage* (London, 1830), II, 244–46.
7. *Public Characters of 1805,* p. 205.
8. *Wells,* III, 116.
9. *Gifford's Baviad and Maeviad . . . to Which Is Prefixed the Author's Memoir of His Own Life* (London, 1827), p. 4.
10. James Boaden, *Memoirs of the Life of John Philip Kemble, Esq., including a History of the Stage* (London, 1825), I, 384.
11. *Wells,* I, 82.
12. *Wells,* II, 220.
13. *Wells,* I, 69.
14. *Public Characters of 1805,* p. 205. For characters of Andrews, see *Reynolds,* II, 25; John Taylor, *Records of My Life* (London, 1832), II, 296; *Memoirs of the Colman Family,* ed. Richard Brinsley Peake (London, 1841), II, 217.
15. *Wells,* I, 99–100.
16. *Wells,* I, 66.
17. *Reynolds,* II, 45, 185–87.
18. For a list of the prominent members, see Bernard, II, 140–41, 165–66.
19. *Wells,* I, 69.
20. Boaden, I, 385–86.
21. James L. Clifford, *Hester Lynch Piozzi* (Oxford, 1941), p. 249.
22. *Gifford,* pp. 3, 40–41, notes.
23. *Gifford,* p. 6.
24. *Wells,* I, 66, 67.
25. Taylor, II, 289–90, 292, 300–301.
26. *My Own Life, by C. Este, Clerk* (London, 1787), pp. 26–27.

27. *Wells,* I, 71.

28. *Reynolds,* II, 210–11.

29. *Wells,* I, 69.

30. *Wells,* I, 65, 68, 70.

31. *Reynolds,* II, 31.

32. See Arthur Aspinall, *Politics and the Press c. 1780–1850* (London, 1949), pp. 72–73, 272.

33. See Chatham Papers PRO 30/ GD 8/ 148, 237, 243, 245–46, 289, 317–18, 333–34.

34. *Reynolds,* II, 159, 160.

35. *Reynolds,* II, 119–22.

36. *Reynolds,* II, 25.

37. *The Letters of Horace Walpole Earl of Orford,* ed. Peter Cunningham (London, 1861), IX, 165.

38. Philip Withers, *Alfred's Apology, Second Part, . . . with a Summary of the Trial of the Editor of Nemesis, on the Prosecution of Mrs. Fitzherbert, for a Libel* (London, 1789), p. 111.

39. Philip Withers, *Alfred, or a Narrative of the Daring and Illegal Measures to Suppress a Pamphlet Intituled, Strictures in the Declaration of Horne Tooke, Esq.* (London, 1789), pp. 4, note; 33–40.

40. See Walter Sichel, *Sheridan* (London, 1909), II, 422, 426.

41. [Philip Withers,] *History of the Royal Malady* (London, 1789), pp. 10–11, 41–42.

42. *Alfred,* pp. 4, note; 9, note; 33.

43. [Philip Withers,] *Alfred to the Bishop of London* (London, 1789), p. 52.

44. *Alfred to the Bishop of London,* pp. 7, 47.

45. [Philip Withers,] *Alfred's Appeal, Containing His Address to the Court of King's Bench, on the Subject of the Marriage of Mary Anne Fitzherbert, and Her Intrigue with Count Bellois* (London, 1789), pp. 48–50.

46. Clifford, pp. 338–39.

47. Boaden, I, 385.

48. *Reynolds,* II, 187–88.

49. *Memoirs of the Late Mrs. Robinson* (New York, 1802), II, 96–97. But Mrs. Robinson's biographer is mistaken in saying that she wrote nothing for the newspapers until "the winter of 1790."

50. Allardyce Nicoll, *A History of English Drama 1660–1900* (Cambridge, 1955), III, 204, 233.

51. Colmans' *Memoirs,* II, 217.

52. *Reynolds,* II, 321.

53. *Reynolds,* II, 36, 45–46.

54. *A Complete Collection of State Trials,* ed. T. B. Howell (London, 1814), XX, 1318–68.

55. *Alfred's Appeal,* pp. 49–50.

56. *Alfred's Appeal,* p. 41.

57. *Alfred's Appeal,* p. 22.

58. For the entire text of this letter, see *Wells,* III, 219–23.

59. *Wells,* III, 129.

60. Taylor, II, 295.

61. *Wells,* I, 84.

62. *Wells,* I, 84–86.

63. Bernard, II, 242.

64. See David V. Erdman, Lucyle Werkmeister, and R. S. Woof, "Unrecorded

Coleridge Variants: Additions and Corrections," *Studies in Bibliography*, XIV (1961) , 236, 238.

65. *The Speeches of the Right Honourable Charles James Fox in the House of Commons*, ed. J. Wright (London, 1815) , IV, 90–91, 94–95.

66. *Wells*, I, 100; III, 149, 156–59.

67. William Jerdan, *Autobiography* (London, 1852–53) , I, 91; Cyrus Redding, *Fifty Years' Recollections, Literary and Personal* (London, 1858) , I, 72.

68. *Wells*, I, 78.

69. Robert L. Haig, *The Gazetteer 1735–1797* (Carbondale, 1960) , pp. 231–32.

70. *Wells*, I, 76–77.

71. Haig, p. 224.

72. Aspinall, p. 451.

73. *Wells*, III, 128.

74. I shall deal with the Gunning scandal separately.

75. *Wells*, I, 80.

76. *Wells*, I, 76–77.

77. *Wells*, I, 73.

78. *The Annual Biography and Obituary for the Years 1817–1836* (London, 1817–37) , XVIII, 48.

79. *Wells*, I, 75, 80.

80. See Aspinall, p. 73.

81. *Wells*, I, 75, 80.

82. Bernard, II, 246–47.

83. *Wells*, I, 121–32; *Reynolds*, II, 135–51, 153.

84. *Wells*, I, 74.

85. *Wells*, III, 128–29.

86. *Wells*, I, 77–78.

87. Taylor, II, 293–94.

88. *Wells*, I, 71–72.

89. Isaac Espinasse, *Reports of Cases Argued and Ruled at Nisi Prius, in the Courts of King's Bench and Common Pleas, from Easter Term 33 George III. 1793, to Hilary Term 39 George III. 1799* (London, 1803) , no page number.

90. *The Professional Life of Mr. Dibdin, Written by Himself, together with the Words of Six Hundred Songs Selected from His Works* (London, 1803) , III, 219–24.

CHAPTER V

1. For the whole text of Peter Stuart's statement in the spurious *Star* of 13 February, 1789, cited frequently in this chapter, see Appendix II.

2. John Taylor, *Records of My Life* (London, 1832) , II, 267.

3. For the whole text of Peter Stuart's statement in the spurious *Star* of 16 February, 1789, cited frequently in this chapter, see Appendix III.

4. For the whole text of the proprietors' statement in the *Star* of 16 February, 1789, see Appendix IV. The statement probably first appeared in the *Star* of 14 February.

5. Daniel Stuart, "The Late Mr. Coleridge, the Poet," *Gentleman's Magazine*, n.s., X (1838) , 26.

6. *GM*, n.s., X, 24–25.

7. H. R. Fox Bourne, *English Newspapers: Chapters in the History of Journalism* (London, 1887) , I, 206, note.

8. Samuel Smiles, *A Publisher and His Friends: Memoirs and Correspondence of the Late John Murray* (London, 1891) , I, 24.

9. Stanley Morison, *The English Newspaper: Some Account of the Physical Development of Journals Printed in London between 1622 & the Present Day* (Cambridge, 1932) , pp. 189–90, 229.

10. *Letters from the Lake Poets to Daniel Stuart,* ed. Mary Stuart (London, 1889) , p. ix.

11. See *Lake Poets,* pp. ix–x; *Public Characters of 1806,* pub. Richard Phillips (London, 1806) , p. 224.

12. Arthur Aspinall, *Politics and the Press c. 1780–1850* (London, 1949) , pp. 446, 448.

13. *The Life and Times of Frederick Reynolds, Written by Himself* (London, 1827) , I, 282–83. For the text of the address, see Walley Chamberlain Oulton, *The History of the Theatres of London . . . from the Year 1771–1795* (London, 1796) , I, 136–37. There is some confusion as to who was retiring and who recited the address. According to Genest, Mrs. Yates was retiring, and, although Mrs. Bellamy was supposed to recite the address, she was so frightened that Miss Farren recited it for her. See John Genest, *Some Account of the English Stage* (Bath, 1832) , VI, 342. According to Oulton, the address was recited by Mrs. Bellamy and Miss Farren together. But, according to Reynolds, Mrs. Yates had retired some years earlier, Mrs. Bellamy was currently retiring, and the address was written for and recited by Miss Farren. Since Reynolds witnessed the performance, was greatly moved by it, and left a stirring account of it, I have preferred to trust him.

14. Allardyce Nicoll, *A History of English Drama 1660–1900* (Cambridge, 1955) , III, 310. According to Genest (VI, 436) , it was performed on 11 May, but Genest is mistaken.

15. Nicoll, III, 310.

16. Genest, VI, 481.

17. Boswell saw the performance of 3 May. See *Private Papers of James Boswell from Malahide Castle,* ed. Geoffrey Scott and Frederick Pottle (Mount Vernon, 1928–34) , XVII, 27.

18. On 5 September, 1792, the *Morning Chronicle* advertised what may have been a planned fourth edition.

19. Quoted from the second edition, pp. v–viii.

20. Chatham Papers PRO 30/ GD 8/ 186.

21. *Memoirs of the Life of the Right Honourable Sir James Mackintosh,* ed. Robert James Mackintosh (Boston, 1853) , I, 20–21, 32, 41, 44; *Lake Poets,* p. x.

22. Mackintosh's *Memoirs,* I, 51–52.

23. *Public Characters of 1806,* p. 224.

24. *Public Characters of 1806,* p. 220.

25. Mackintosh's *Memoirs,* I, 52, note.

26. *Public Characters of 1806,* p. 224.

27. Mackintosh's *Memoirs,* I, 50.

28. *Public Characters of 1806,* p. 224.

29. *Public Characters of 1806,* p. 224.

30. *Public Characters of 1806,* p. 224.

31. *Lake Poets,* pp. ix–x.

32. Mackintosh's *Memoirs,* I, 54–55, 56.

33. James Boaden, *Memoirs of the Life of John Philip Kemble, Esq.* (London, 1825) , I, 428.

34. Lucyle Werkmeister, "Some Account of Robert Burns and the London News-

papers with Special Reference to the Spurious *Star* (1789) ," *Bulletin of the New York Public Library,* LXV (1961) , 498–500.

35. Lucyle Werkmeister, "Notes for a Revised Life of William Jackson: A Postscript," *Notes and Queries,* n.s., VIII (1961) , 266–67.

## CHAPTER VI

1. See Arthur Aspinall, *Politics and the Press c. 1780–1850* (London, 1949) , pp. 446, 448.

2. For significant passages from Charles Stuart's letters in the spurious *Star* of 29 April—13 June, 1789, see Appendix V.

3. See Chatham Papers PRO 30/ GD 8/ 187. This account and the two which immediately follow are printed by Aspinall (see Aspinall, pp. 420–21) with, in the main, minor variations.

4. See Chatham Papers PRO 30/ GD 8/ 245–46. Aspinall reads the name as *Hewardine,* but I am inclined toward the reading *Stewardine.*

5. Chatham Papers PRO 30/ GD 8/ 144–45, 189.

6. Chatham Papers PRO 30/ GD 8/ 185.

7. Chatham Papers PRO 30/ GD 8/ 144–45, 194. In the tabulation the payment is dated 29 July, but Charles's receipt is dated 28 July.

8. Chatham Papers PRO 30/ GD 8/ 190.

9. See also Chatham Papers PRO 30/ GD 8/ 144–45, 193.

10. Chatham Papers PRO 30/ GD 8/ 144–45, 188.

11. Daniel Stuart, "The Newspaper Writings of the Poet Coleridge," *Gentleman's Magazine,* n.s., IX (1838) , 578.

12. Chatham Papers PRO 30/ GD 8/ 144–45, 300.

13. Chatham Papers PRO 30/ GD 8/ 145, 303, 304.

14. Aspinall, pp. 446, 448.

15. *Memoirs of the Colman Family,* ed. Richard Brinsley Peak (London, 1841) , II, 195–96, 215–16.

16. Lucyle Werkmeister, "Notes for a Revised Life of William Jackson: A Postscript," *Notes and Queries,* n.s., VIII (1961) , 266–67.

17. *A Biographical Dictionary of the Living Authors of Great Britain and Ireland* (London, 1816) .

18. *Epistle,* p. 19.

19. Advertisement for *Shrove Tuesday* in *The Children of Thespis* (London, 1792) . For Peter Stuart's "Distich," see *ibid.,* p. viii.

20. *The Life of the Late Earl of Barrymore, Including a History of the Wargrave Theatricals and Original Anecdotes of Eminent Persons, by Anthony Pasquin, Esq.* (London, 1793) . Barrymore had died on 6 March, 1793.

21. Daniel Stuart, "The Late Mr. Coleridge, the Poet," *Gentleman's Magazine,* n.s., X (1838) , 25.

22. The ensuing account of Burns's connection with the spurious *Star* is cursory, since I have treated the subject at length elsewhere. See "Some Account of Robert Burns and the London Newspapers with Special Reference to the Spurious *Star* (1789) ," *Bulletin of the New York Public Library,* LXV (1961) , 483–504.

23. The nominal conductor was James Perry, but Beauchamp succeeded Perry as conductor on 27 November, 1790. See Robert L. Haig, *The Gazetteer 1735–1797* (Carbondale, 1960) , p. 217. Beauchamp may already have been the editor.

24. See Lucyle Werkmeister, "Two Early Versions of Cowper's 'The Negro's Complaint,' " *Notes and Queries,* n.s., IX (1962) , 26–27.

25. See Colmans' *Memoirs,* II, 198–200.

26. See *Biographical Dictionary.*

27. H. R. Fox Bourne, *English Newspapers: Chapters in the History of Journalism* (London, 1887) , I, 206, note.

28. Stanley Morison, *The English Newspaper: Some Account of the Physical Development of Journals Printed in London between 1622 & the Present Day* (Cambridge, 1932) , p. 173.

29. *Public Ledger,* "Bicentenary Supplement" (1960) , p. 3.

30. Aspinall, pp. 396–97.

31. *Private Papers of James Boswell from Malahide Castle,* ed. Geoffrey Scott and Frederick Pottle (Mount Vernon, 1928–34) , XVIII, 185.

32. Boswell's *Papers,* XVIII, 215.

33. Haig, pp. 216–17.

34. John Payne Collier, *An Old Man's Diary, Forty Years Ago* (London, 1871–72) , II, 43.

35. Chatham Papers PRO 30/ GD 8/ 245–46, 289, 292–93, 295–96, 298, 317–18, 334.

36. PRO 6271.

37. *Letters from the Lake Poets to Daniel Stuart,* ed. Mary Stuart (London, 1889) , p. x.

38. See the Prospectus in the British Museum.

39. *Reports of Cases Argued and Determined in the Court of King's Bench,* ed. Charles Durnford and Edward Hyde East (London, 1787) , I, 748–54.

40. PRO 6271.

41. See, for example, *The Letters of Horace Walpole Earl of Orford,* ed. Peter Cunningham (London, 1861) , IX, 289.

42. *The Letters of Robert Burns,* ed. J. De Lancey Ferguson (Oxford, 1931) , I, 358.

43. Colmans' *Memoirs,* II, 195, 215–16.

## CHAPTER VII

1. Sampson Perry, *An Historical Sketch of the French Revolution, Commencing with Its Predisposing Causes, and Carried on to the Acceptation of the Constitution in 1795* (London, 1796) , I, 4.

2. See, for example, Alexander Andrews, *The History of British Journalism, from the Foundation of the Newspaper Press in England, to the Repeal of the Stamp Act in 1855* (London, 1859) , I, 233.

3. *Anti-Jacobin Review,* XV (1803) , 516.

4. HO 42/32.

5. *Poetry of the Anti-Jacobin,* ed. Charles Edmonds (London, 1854) , p. 245.

6. *The History of The Times 1785–1841* (London, 1935) , pp. 51–52; Arthur Aspinall, *Politics and the Press c. 1780–1850* (London, 1949) , p. 74.

7. *The Annual Biography and Obituary for the Years 1817–1836* (London, 1817–37) , XVIII, 44–45.

8. My authority is F. Knight Hunt, *The Fourth Estate: Contributions towards a History of Newspapers, and of the Liberty of the Press* (London, 1850) , II, 65.

9. Aspinall, p. 447.

10. Percy Fitzgerald, *The Life of George the Fourth* (London, 1881) , II, 111.

11. John Taylor, *Records of My Life* (London, 1832), II, 268, 270–71.

12. Robert L. Haig, *The Gazetteer 1735–1797* (Carbondale, 1960), p. 245.

13. *Rights of the People; or, Reasons for a Regicide Peace*, which was written in anticipation of Burke's *Regicide Peace; A Reply to Burke's Two Letters;* and a sacred poem, entitled *Redemption*. All three pamphlets were published in London in 1796.

14. See *Memoirs of the Life of the Right Honourable Sir James Mackintosh*, ed. Robert James Mackintosh (Boston, 1853), I, 53, 54, note; *Public Characters of 1806*, pub. Richard Phillips (London, 1806), pp. 221–22.

15. See Mackintosh's *Memoirs*, I, 54, note.

16. See *Annual Register . . . for the Year 1789*, I, 215–16.

17. See *A Letter to Sir W. A. Brown, Bart., on a Late Affair of Honour with Colonel Lenox* (London, 1789); *Letter to the King, in Which the Conduct of Mr. Lenox, and the Minister, in the Affair with . . . the Duke of York, Is Fully Considered* (London, 1789); *A Letter to Colonel Lenox, on His Conduct towards the Duke of York, by an Officer in the Army* (London, 1789). The last pamphlet, published by George Kearsley, was probably the work of Swift, since an announcement of its appearance was carried by the *Oracle* (1 June, 1789).

18. See *The Letters of Robert Burns*, ed. J. De Lancey Ferguson (Oxford, 1931), I, 358.

19. Aspinall, pp. 447–48.

20. *Selections from the Letters and Correspondence of Sir James Bland Burges, Bart., Sometime Under-Secretary of State for Foreign Affairs*, ed. Dr. James Hutton (London, 1885), pp. 157–58.

21. *Historical Sketch*, I, 22.

22. Burges' *Letters*, p. 159. Burges had himself been writing for the *Diary*. In 1790 George Kearsley published a collection of his contributions, entitled *Letters Lately Published in The Diary, on the Subject of the Present Dispute with Spain, under the Signature of Verus.*

23. See Aspinall, pp. 488–89.

24. Frith was confined in Newgate Prison on a charge of high treason for over twenty-two months. On 11 December, 1791, he was acknowledged to be insane and was released on condition that he be placed in an asylum or cared for by a responsible person. His lawyer was William Garrow.

25. [Mary Wells,] *Memoirs of the Life of Mrs. Sumbel, Late Wells* (London, 1811), I, 76–77.

26. See Aspinall, p. 73.

27. Mackintosh's *Memoirs*, I, 53.

28. *Private Papers of James Boswell from Malahide Castle*, ed. Geoffrey Scott and Frederick Pottle (Mount Vernon, 1928–34), XVIII, 26.

29. *Annual Biography*, XVIII, 45–46.

30. Chatham Papers PRO 30/ GD 8/ 213, 245–46, 269, 289.

31. *The Farington Diary by Joseph Farington, R.A.*, ed. James Greig (London, 1922–28), I, 28.

32. Chatham Papers PRO 30/ GD 8/ 245–46, 291.

33. *Wells*, I, 77.

34. John Trusler, *The London Advertiser and Guide* (London, 1790), p. 135.

35. John Horne Tooke, *Proceedings in an Action for Debt, between the Right Honourable Charles James Fox, Plaintiff, and John Horne Tooke, Esq., Defendant* (London, 1792), pp. 8–9, 16–19.

36. Chatham Papers PRO 30/ GD 8/ 207–9, 237, 241, 243, 245–46, 289, 291, 295, 296, 298.

37. Chatham Papers PRO 30/ GD 8/ 272–73.

38. Aspinall, p. 447.

39. Mackintosh's *Memoirs*, I, 52.

40. Mackintosh's *Memoirs*, I, 20.

41. Tooke's *Proceedings*, p. 35.

42. Tooke's *Proceedings*, p. 35.

43. *The Letters of Horace Walpole Earl of Orford*, ed. Peter Cunningham (London, 1861), IX, 283.

44. Tooke's *Proceedings*, p. 35.

45. Tooke's *Proceedings*, pp. 63–64.

46. Chatham Papers PRO 30/ GD 8/ 289, 293, 295, 317–18, 328, 333–34. The records are, of course, incomplete.

47. *Farington Diary*, I, 28.

48. Haig, p. 217.

49. *Farington Diary*, I, 28. On 28 August, 1790, Perry and Gray said, or Boswell understood them to say, that they were then the editors of the *Gazetteer* (Boswell's *Papers*, XVIII, 91–92); on 10 February, 1791, Perry told him that he had the "whole" of the *Chronicle*. See *Letters of James Boswell*, ed. Chauncery Brewster Tinker (Oxford, 1924), II, 422.

50. John Payne Collier, *An Old Man's Diary, Forty Years Ago* (London, 1871–72), II, 43–44.

51. Cyrus Redding, *Fifty Years' Recollections, Literary and Personal* (London, 1858), I, 96.

52. Collier, II, 44.

53. *Farington Diary*, I, 28.

54. Taylor, II, 341–43.

55. Burges' *Letters*, p. 156.

56. Chatham Papers PRO 30/ GD 8/ 317–18.

57. See Aspinall, p. 75.

58. See Werkmeister, "Jemmie Boswell and the London Daily Press (1785–1795)," *Bulletin of the New York Public Library*, LXVII (1963).

59. Mackintosh's *Memoirs*, I, 54–55, 58.

60. *Public Characters of 1806*, p. 225.

61. *Memorials and Correspondence of Charles James Fox*, ed. Lord John Russell (London, 1853–57), II, 363.

62. Mackintosh's *Memoirs*, I, 322.

63. John Benjafield, *Statement of Facts* (Bury St. Edmunds, 1813), pp. ix–x.

64. Taylor, II, 270.

65. Chatham Papers PRO 30/ GD 8/ 317–18, 328.

66. Chatham Papers PRO 30/ GD 8/ 333–34.

67. Taylor, II, 268.

68. Wilfrid Hindle, *The Morning Post 1772–1937: Portrait of a Newspaper* (London, 1937), p. 63.

69. Walter Sichel, *Sheridan* (London, 1909), II, 209.

70. Quoted by Aspinall, p. 447.

71. Aspinall, p. 448.

72. See introduction to the *Maeviad*.

73. For accounts of the Corresponding Society, see *Memoir of Thomas Hardy, Founder of, and Secretary to, the London Corresponding Society, for Diffusing Useful Political Knowledge among the People of Great Britain and Ireland, and for Promoting Parliamentary Reform, from Its Establishment in Jan. 1792 until His Arrest, on a False Charge of High Treason, on the 12ᵗʰ of May, 1794, Written by Him-*

*self* (London, 1832) ; see also Daniel Stuart, "The Late Mr. Coleridge, the Poet," *Gentleman's Magazine*, n.s., X (1838) , 125.

74. *A Letter to the Right Honourable William Pitt, on His Apostacy from the Cause of Parliamentary Reform* (London, 1792) , p. 18.

75. Duke of Buckingham and Chandos, *Memoirs of the Courts and Cabinets of George the Third* (London, 1853) , I, 364.

76. *Letter to Pitt,* pp. 32–43.

77. Taylor, II, 268.

78. For Perry's statements, cited in the passage which follows, see *Historical Sketch*, I, 3–10.

79. *The Correspondence of William Augustus Miles on the French Revolution 1789–1817*, ed. Charles Popham Miles (London, 1850) , I, 333–34.

80. See Aspinall, p. 449.

81. Chatham Papers PRO 30/ GD 8/ 158, 163, 333–34.

82. Chatham Papers PRO 30/ GD 8/ 159.

83. Chatham Papers PRO 30/ GD 8/ 206, 221, 271, 289, 317–18, 328, 333–34.

84. *Farington Diary*, I, 228.

85. *Annual Biography*, XVIII, 48–49.

86. Stanley Morison, *John Bell, 1745–1831* (Cambridge, 1930) , pp. 42–43.

87. Chatham Papers PRO 30/ GD 8/ 270, 333–34.

88. Chatham Papers PRO 30/ GD 8/ 302, 314, 333–34.

89. Burges' *Letters*, pp. 226–27.

90. *Annual Biography*, XVIII, 49.

91. Of the several excellent studies of this period, one of the best is Philip Anthony Brown, *The French Revolution in English Literature* (London, 1923) .

92. *Farington Diary*, I, 27–28.

93. *Historical Sketch*, I, 19–22.

94. *History of The Times*, pp. 34–35.

95. See Aspinall, p. 451.

96. See Aspinall, pp. 449–50.

# BIBLIOGRAPHICAL NOTE

DESPITE the multitude of books on the subject, scholars still know remarkably little about eighteenth-century newspapers. The principal reason is that historians have been misled by the journalists themselves into accepting as the truth, the whole truth, and nothing but the truth what is actually evasion, extenuation, rumor, and falsehood. The trouble began in the late eighteenth century, when the first journalists felt called upon to publish their apologies, for, since other journalists followed suit, there was soon a spate of such publications: *Memoirs of John Almon, Bookseller of Piccadilly* (London, 1790); memoirs of Sampson Perry, affixed to *An Historical Sketch of the French Revolution Commencing with Its Predisposing Causes, and Carried on to the Acceptation of the Constitution in 1795* (London, 1796), 2 vols.; John Benjafield, *Statement of Facts* (Bury St. Edmunds, 1813); "Memoir of James Perry, Esq.," *European Magazine and London Review*, LXXIV (1818), 187–90; John Taylor, *Records of My Life* (London, 1832), 2 vols.; "John Heriot" in *The Annual Biography and Obituary for the Years 1817–1836*, XVIII (1834), 44–49; Daniel Stuart's various apologies and accusations in the *Gentleman's Magazine*, n.s. IX (1838), 485–92, 577–90, and X (1838), 22–27, 124–28, and George Lane's reply in the *Gentleman's Magazine*, n.s. X (1838), 274–76; William Jerdan, *Autobiography* (London, 1852–53), 4 vols.; Cyrus Redding, *Fifty Years' Recollections, Literary and Personal, with Observations on Men and Things* (London, 1858), 3 vols.; James Amphlett, *The Newspaper Press, in Part of the Last Century, and up to the Present Period of 1860: The Recollections of [the Author]* (London, 1860); "Editors and Newspaper Writers of the Last Generation, by an Old Apprentice of the Law," *Fraser's Magazine*, LXV (1862), 169–83; and John Payne Collier, *An Old Man's Diary, Forty Years Ago* (London, 1871–72), 4 Pts. To these were added other biographies and collections of anecdotes, based primarily upon hearsay and yet also purporting to be factual: *Public Characters of 1801–1806*, publ. Richard Phillips (London, 1801–6); John Nichols, *Literary Anecdotes of the Eighteenth Century* (London, 1812–16), 9 vols.; *A Biographical Dictionary of the Living Authors* (London, 1816); and C. H. Timperley, *A Dictionary of Printers and Printing* (London, 1839), reissued in 1842 as *An Encyclopaedia of Literary and Typographical Anecdote*.

In 1850 this material became the basis for the first general survey of the press, and today there are many such surveys, the most important being F. Knight Hunt, *The Fourth Estate: Contributions towards a History of Newspapers, and of the Liberty of the Press* (London, 1850), 2 vols.; Alexander Andrews, *The History of British Journalism, from the Foundation of the Newspaper Press in England, to the Repeal of the Stamp Act in 1855* (London, 1859), 2 vols.; James Grant, *The Newspaper Press: Its Origin—Progress —and Present Position* (London, 1871), 3 vols.; Henry Richard Fox Bourne, *English Newspapers: Chapters in the History of Journalism* (London, 1887), 2 vols.; and Harold Herd, *The March of Journalism: The Story of the British Press from 1622 to the Present Day* (London, 1952). However impressive these works appear, they have done the cause of scholarship little good. Not only have they discouraged caution with respect to the memoirs and anecdotes, but they have introduced new material with the same reckless disregard for source. In almost any other field, works so slightly documented as these would have had no stature whatever, but in this particular field they have been and still are regarded as standard for the simple reason that there has been no alternative. Moreover, they do have a value of sorts, for, however vague and erroneous they are in detail, they are sometimes correct in substance, and hence they occasionally supply a clue which might otherwise be forever lacking. This is particularly true with respect to the earlier histories, namely, those of Hunt, Andrews, and Grant. All one can do, therefore, is to attempt to discover the source of the material and, when such discovery is impossible, to apply the yardstick of plausibility. But one must be wary; for the source of a great deal of the material was the journalists themselves, and no self-respecting eighteenth-century writer boasted of his connection with the newspapers. He admitted the connection only when it was already common knowledge, and he wrote or talked only for the sake of glossing over his own crimes and the crimes of his various employers and associates. From such a man writing and talking for such a purpose, we cannot expect the whole truth.

Although there has been no real attempt to correct or even evaluate the memoirs, anecdotes, and histories, there has been some valuable supplementation. John Trusler, *The London Advertiser and Guide* (London, 1790) and James Savage, *An Account of the London Daily Newspapers, and the Manner in Which They Are Conducted* (London, 1811) seem to be sound; and *Catalogue of an Exhibition Illustrating the History of the English Newspaper. . . . from the Library of The Press Club, London* (London, 1932) and Stanley Morison, *The English Newspaper: Some Account of the Physical Development of Journals Printed in London between 1622 & the Present Day* (Cambridge, 1932) are at least noteworthy, although they lean too heavily upon Bourne to be altogether reliable. Far more reliable are three accounts of individual newspapers: Wilfrid Hindle, *The Morning Post 1772–1937: Portrait of a Newspaper* (London, 1937); *History of "The Times,"* Vol. I (London, 1935); and Robert L. Haig, *The Gazetteer, 1735–1797: A Study in the Eighteenth-Century English Newspaper* (Carbondale, 1960). All three of these accounts are based upon primary sources, including, in the last two cases, examinations of the newspapers. But the most significant of the supplementary works is, of course, Arthur Aspinall, *Politics and the Press c. 1780–1850* (London, 1949), which ended (or should have ended) once and for all any naive thinking with respect to the late eighteenth- and early nineteenth-century press.

It is too much to expect that any study of late eighteenth-century newspapers will be entirely adequate or completely accurate, for the field is new, and the subject is enormously complex: the best any scholar can hope is that his work will make some kind of contribution. Contributions are usually assessed in terms of bibliography, but in this instance I am inclined to think that bibliography is less important than methodology. How, in short, does one study the newspapers? It is my opinion that he should begin by reading them, not one of them, but all of them together, and that he should supplement this reading with a reading of pamphlets, Parliamentary debates, Court records, and plays. For the newspaper press was primarily an arena for the waging of political wars, and the same wars were being fought in the pages of pamphlets, on the floor of Parliament and the various Courts, and on the stages of theaters. Having put the newspapers into context, one is in a position to begin the search for evidence. Here his problems are manifold, for the evidence is scant, it is widely distributed, and very little of it can be taken at face value.

In the main this evidence will come from four sources: letters and diaries, litigations and semi-litigious actions, financial records, and the memoirs, anecdotes, and early histories, to which reference has already been made. The first source is almost inexhaustible, for, since newspapers were themselves news, almost everyone had something to say about them, the only questions being how much the sayer was likely to know and how much he was likely to reveal. This source is perhaps also the most important, for diarists and letter-writers are notoriously less discreet than keepers of formal documents. Considerable research has already been done in this field, a number of letters relating to the journalistic involvements of the Whigs, the Prince of Wales, the Home Department, and the Treasury being included in the *History of "The Times,"* *Politics and the Press,* and Aspinall's three-volume edition of *The Letters of King George IV, 1812–1830* (Cambridge, 1938) ; but there is still considerable research to do. The second source is disappointing, for, even when the testimony and the various affidavits are available, they add little to what one might already have learned from the newspapers, which is itself little. In the case of most ex officio actions, the printers were paid to be scapegoats, and they stood their trials without unduly embarrassing anyone. Even in the case of private actions, everyone was circumspect: there were certainly no exposés of politicians or the press generally. The fact remains that some of the intra-newspaper litigations, especially those reported by Haig, provide concrete information about the business of running a newspaper, which is not only significant in itself, but significant also, I suspect, in political context.

The third source is in most respects also disappointing. What one would most like to find is a straightforward account of the financial transactions of a newspaper, but this he will probably never find, for the reason that it probably never existed. What he may find and what Hindle and Haig have, in fact, found are newspaper ledgers and minutes of meetings, which identify personnel, list salaries, and record the legitimate operations of the paper. But, for an account of those extra-legitimate operations upon which every newspaper depended for much of its income, he must look elsewhere, and he will often look in vain. The ledgers of Buckingham House, Carlton House, the Home Department, the Whig Party, and the reform societies are, so far as anyone knows, lacking, so that what remains are some fragmentary Treasury records, dealing with the disbursement of Secret Service funds. These records, discovered by Aspinall and first printed in *Politics and the Press,* are therefore the only financial records presently available, but they are enormously helpful, especially when they are combined with the information derived from diaries, letters, and the newspapers themselves. In fact, by this time one knows enough about the political workings of the press to examine the final source, the memoirs, anecdotes, and early histories, judiciously. He may not, of course, be able to prove or disprove all the statements, but at least he can deal with them on the basis of probabilities.

All of this has entailed a great deal of labor, and it is only the beginning, for it has concerned itself with only the political aspect of the problem. There are numerous other aspects, for, although newspapers derived most of their extra-legitimate income from politicians, they derived some from the theaters, some from societies of various sorts, some from individuals, some from businesses, and some, even before 1792, from stock-jobbers. Since there has been no investigation of any one of these aspects, a great deal of work remains to be done before anyone can write a definitive history of the press. I should myself doubt that a really definitive history will ever be written.

# INDEX

Acton, J., 129

Adair, Sir Robert, 318, 379

Adam, William, 148, 206, 345, 378, 379

*Advertisers:* age of, 2, 4, 5; political activities, 8, 9, 11; influenced by *Morning Post*, 5–7

Agg, John, 278

Aitken, James, 182, 183, 184, 187, 196, 197

Albany, Countess of, 252

"Alfred." *See* Philip Withers

Almon, Charles, 142, 145

Almon, John: connection with *Gazetteer*, 110, 111, 112; association with Earl Temple, 110–11; association with Wilkes, 111–12, 114; as Whig pamphleteer, 110–12; begins *Political Register*, 11, 112; prosecuted for printing Junius' letter, 112–13; possible connection with *British Monitor*, 112; possible founder of *London Packet*, 113, 281; begins *London Museum*, 112; connection with *London Evening Post*, 112, 118; answers own pamphlets, 114–15; sells American news, 115–16, 117–18; early connection with *General Advertiser*, 118; begins *London Courant*, 118–20; retires to escape prosecution, 121–23, 125, 131; resumes conduct of the *Courant*, 123–24; demands from Fox Commissionership in Stamp Office, 124, 128, 135, 145; stock-jobbing, 66, 129; services for Rockingham Whigs, 126–27; duplicities, 131; loses *Courant* and bookselling business, 129–31; employed by Treasury, 132, 133; connection with *Morning Post*, 133; asks Pitt for Commissionership in Stamp Office, 136, 137; marries Mrs. Parker, 122, 132; duplicities regarding *General Advertiser*, 136–37; opens printing shop, 137; loses Whig subsidy, 137; sued by Pitt, 138; regains Whig subsidy, 139; conducts *General Advertiser* for Whigs, 139, 317; begins *Sunday Chronicle*, 139–40; prosecuted for libel on the King, 140–42, 320; sells *General Advertiser* and printing shop, 143, 145; supposed flight to France and outlawry, 144–45, 325; attempts to placate Pitt, 144, 145, 148; *Memoirs*, 121, 122, 144, 145–46; surrender and imprisonment, 146–48

American Colonies, 115, 117, 121

American war: opposed by old Advertisers, 8; news concerning, 115–16, 117; stock-jobbing on, 67–68; mentioned, 32, 126, 128

Andrews, Miles Peter, 107, 155, 156, 157, 158, 172, 184, 185, 188, 189, 191, 192, 194, 201, 203, 218

"Anna Matilda." *See* Mrs. Hannah Cowley

"Anthony Pasquin." *See* John Williams

*Argus:* beginning of, 291, 317–18; titles, 340; addresses, 317–18, 336, 373; proprietors, 318; conductors and editors, 291, 317, 338, 342; printers and publishers, 317, 336, 340, 373; other personnel, 291; character, 318; political position, 317, 331, 342, 346, 354, 365, 366, 367; prosecuted for libel on Government, 336, 340, 363; prosecuted for libel on Commons, 363–64, 365, 369, 372; sued by the Walters, 338, 340, 363; sued by Lady Fitzgibbon, 340, 363; alleged subversion by Sheridan, 364–65, 376; transformed into *True Briton*, 373; mentioned, 335, 374, 375, 376

*Argus; or, General Observer*, 375–76

Argyle, John Campbell, fifth Duke of, 206

"Arley." *See* Miles Peter Andrews

Armstrong, John, 125

Arnold, Dr. Samuel, 71, 72, 240

Audibert, Mr., 365

Aust, George, 370

*Ayre's Sunday London Gazette*, 92

Badini, Carl Francis, 70, 72, 76–77, 78

Baker, William, 356

Barker, James, 119, 120, 124, 129

Barlow, Joel, 355, 356

Barr, James S., 33, 36, 42, 49, 91, 92, 139, 320

Barrymore, Richard, second Earl of, 174, 183, 273, 286

Bate, the Rev. Henry. *See* Dudley, the Rev. Henry Bate

Bath, citizens of, 242–43, 256, 259, 261–62, 270, 287, 289

Bearcroft, Edward, 37, 48, 50, 138, 139, 325, 326

Beauchamp, J., 276, 439, n.32

"Beef-steak Club," 98, 156–57, 158

Beckford, William, 143

Bell, James, 369

Bell, John: original proprietor of *Morning Post*, 20, 28, 33, 40; assailed by

449